本书由中国和平发展基金会、德国阿登纳基金会共同资助

金砖在失色？

"金砖国家治理体系和治理能力现代化建设国际研讨会"论文集

【中英对照】

周余云 栾建章 主编

BRICS: Not Glittering?

Papers from "The International Seminar on the Modernization of Governance Systems and Capacity of the BRICS Countries"

中央编译出版社
Central Compilation & Translation Press

图书在版编目（CIP）数据

金砖在失色？："金砖国家治理体系和治理能力现代化建设国际研讨会"论文集／周余云，栾建章主编．—北京：中央编译出版社，2016.9
ISBN 978－7－5117－3091－6

Ⅰ．①金…
Ⅱ．①周…②栾…
Ⅲ．①世界经济－经济发展－国际会议－文集
Ⅳ．①F113.4－53

中国版本图书馆 CIP 数据核字（2016）第 204728 号

金砖在失色？

出 版 人：	葛海彦
出版统筹：	贾宇琰
责任编辑：	王　琳
责任印制：	尹　珺
出版发行：	中央编译出版社
地　　址：	北京西城区车公庄大街乙 5 号鸿儒大厦 B 座（100044）
电　　话：	（010）52612345（总编室）　　（010）52612341（编辑室）
	（010）52612316（发行部）　　（010）52612317（网络销售）
	（010）52612346（馆配部）　　（010）55626985（读者服务部）
传　　真：	（010）66515838
经　　销：	全国新华书店
印　　刷：	北京印刷一厂
开　　本：	787 毫米×1092 毫米　1/16
字　　数：	700 千字
印　　张：	40.25
版　　次：	2016 年 9 月第 1 版第 1 次印刷
定　　价：	180.00 元

网　　址：	www.cctphome.com　　邮　箱：cctp@cctphome.com
新浪微博：	@中央编译出版社　　　　微　信：中央编译出版社（ID: cctphome）
淘宝店铺：	中央编译出版社直销店（http://shop108367160.taobao.com）　（010）52612349

本社常年法律顾问：北京嘉润律师事务所律师　李敬伟　问小牛
凡有印装质量问题，本社负责调换，电话：（010）55626985

序 言

"志合者，不以山海为远"。数年前，天各一方的五国，为增加新兴国家在全球经济治理中的代表性和话语权，维护自身发展利益而走到一起。近年来，在外部特别是西方国家的一片"质疑"甚至"唱衰"声中，金砖国家开展合作的意愿愈发强烈，推动合作的决心愈发坚定，合作的深度和广度得以不断突破。如今，金砖国家合作"实心化"车轮不断向前。在金砖国家内部，对"金砖国家"这一身份的认同度在不断提高。在其外部，无论是"傲慢与偏见"，还是"客观与公正"，金砖国家已然成为不能被忽视的政治存在。愈来愈多的有识之士站在金砖国家整体的立场上，为实现共同发展积极地贡献着自己的智慧。与此同时，国际社会亦愈来愈积极地看待金砖国家的发展，更加理性地听取金砖国家的声音。

"问渠哪得清如许，为有源头活水来"。在全球化不断深入的时代，"国内问题国际化，国际问题国内化"的特征日益明显。面对复杂险峻的内外形势，只有不断获取新的智识，才能超越认识的局限，摆脱思想的束缚，才能在探索国家治理的道路上保持清醒的认识，获得不竭的前进动力。毫无疑问，处在相似的发展阶段，面临相似发展问题的金砖国家，不仅有必要加强交流互鉴，推动智力资源在金砖国家内部自由流动，而且更有必要秉持一种包容开放的精神，兼收并蓄，博采众家之长。这种包容开放的交流探索之路亦为外界观察、理解金砖国家，发展同金砖国家的交流合作提供了机会。

中共中央对外联络部作为金砖国家智库理事会的中方牵头单位，一直致力于推动金砖国家在研究领域的交流合作，希望通过金砖国家各方的共同努力，为金砖国家合作之路探寻方向，提供指引。正是基于上述考虑，中联部研究室偕同中国和平发展基金会和德国阿登纳基金会，于2014年11月19—20日在北京联合举办了主题为"金砖国家治理体系和治理能力现代化建设"的国际研讨会。在两天的会议中，来自金砖五国和欧美国家的八十余名知名智库代表或独立学者，从不同角度、不同层面无私分享了所在国家的治理经验，坦诚交流了对金砖国家发展的看法。虽然我们不一定完全认同他们的观点和看法，但是对处于起步阶段的金砖国家研究而言，它们的参考和借鉴价值不言而喻。因此，我们特将他们的会议发言以及为会议撰写的论文编辑成册以飨读者，希望能为推动金砖国家研究，增进外部对金砖国家的了解做出一点贡献。

由于工作繁冗，加之中英文审校十分耗时，本书出版时间较长，很多作者为此打来电话或发邮件询问，在此向作者和读者表示歉意。我还要借此机会再次感谢与会的各位学者朋友，他们的努力和专业保障了会议的成功。我相信，他们的智慧和坦诚也将使广大读者朋友受益。最后，我还要再次感谢中国和平发展基金会、德国阿登纳基金会、中央编译出版社，会议的成功举办和本书的顺利出版离不开他们的大力支持。

栾建章

2016 年 3 月 17 日

目　录

建设法治社会　深化金砖合作 ················· 郭业洲 / 3
金砖国家间加强合作以对全球治理施加影响 ··· ［巴西］里纳托·鲍曼 / 7
全球治理视角下的金砖国家合作 ··············· 刘劲松 / 14
缓慢的经济增长模式下的创新和治理挑战
　　 ······················· ［巴西］安娜·雅瓜里比 / 18
国家能力与创新政策：来自金砖四国的启示
　　及对其建议 ················ ［巴西］安娜·卡斯特罗 / 26
金砖国家在保护世界和平与安全中的作用
　　 ······················ ［俄］格奥尔吉·托洛拉亚 / 35
金砖国家携手共同促进全球治理的有效性
　　和世界秩序的平等性 ········· ［俄］维多利亚·帕诺娃 / 43
国家安全和国家可持续发展 ········ ［俄］阿列克谢·恰格林 / 52
乌克兰危机后的俄罗斯和金砖五国 ··· ［俄］亚历山大·卢金 / 55
针对国际金融和货币体系改革形成金砖五国
　　的共同立场 ············ ［俄］米哈伊尔·戈洛夫宁 / 59
全球治理中的金砖国家务实合作 ··· ［印度］哈里哈拉·维斯瓦纳坦 / 62
金砖国家在全球能源治理中的合作 ····· ［印度］阿努纳巴·戈什 / 69
金砖国家国际金融危机及治理的挑战 ····· ［印度］班迪·普拉萨德 / 75
电子政务：印度领先一步 ··········· ［印度］拉吉尼什·阿胡伽 / 93
中国国家治理中的司法现代化改革 ··················· 郭　锋 / 99
"城市发展陷阱"——金砖国家地方治理的重大难题 ······· 袁宝成 / 103
务实推进金砖银行合作 ························· 邹力行 / 108
全球经济治理中的金砖国家 ··············· 赵忠秀　孙靓莹 / 115
金砖国家治理能力现代化评析——国家构建的视角
　　 ································· 褚松燕　贾路南 / 131
国家治理现代化中的党的领导与依法治国 ············· 郑长忠 / 144

中国的治理现代化：优势、问题与措施……………………鲍传健 / 148
新世纪巴西加强国家治理能力建设的做法及启示……………陈晓玲 / 157
从南非大选看非国大执政挑战………………………………舒　畅 / 163
金砖国家在全球改革中的作用：我们的愿景是什么？
　　………………………………………[南非] 纳尔尼亚·尔博赫勒 / 169
金融流动性和资本流动对南非的影响 …[南非] 赛拉吉·莫哈迈德 / 179
促进南非治理现代化的响应和创新能力
　　………………………………………[南非] 丹尼尔·普拉提杰斯 / 193
欧盟和金砖国家……………………………[英] 弗雷泽·卡梅隆 / 200
金砖国家现代化过程中的危机管理与风险预防
　　——以对印度的观察为例………………[德] 克劳斯·沃尔 / 208
种族隔离结束后南非的治理…………[德] 阿诺德·威姆霍纳尔 / 212
关于金砖国家对全球治理所做贡献的评估：一个局外人
　　的看法 …[法] 爱丽丝·埃克曼　[法] 弗朗索瓦兹·尼古拉 / 218
从长远角度看大趋势、新兴技术以及治理面临的挑战
　　…………………………………………[美] 班宁·加雷特 / 228
金砖国家间的合作对全球治理意味着什么？
　　………………………………………………[美] 拉尔夫·科萨 / 245
德国经验与金砖国家治理 ……………………[德] 卡斯腾·科伯尔 / 262

Contents

Deepening BRICS Cooperation with the Society Governed by Law
·· Guo Yezhou / 269
Cooperation among BRICS in Order to Influence Global Governance
·· Renato Baumann / 275
BRICS Cooperation from the Global Governance Perspective
·· Liu Jinsong / 285
Challenges for Innovation and Governance in a Slow Growth
  Economy ·· Anna Jaguaribe / 291
State Capacities and Innovation Policies: Lessons from and for the
  BRICS ·· Ana Célia Castro / 303
BRICS Role in Safeguarding Global Peace and Security
·· Georgy Toloraya / 315
BRICS Cooperation to Promote Effective Global Governance
  and Fair World Order ·· Victoria V. Panova / 326
National Security and Sustainable Development of the State
·· Aleksei Chagrin / 340
Russia and BRICS after the Ukrainian Crisis ·· Alexander Lukin / 344
Forming of BRICS Joint Position on International Financial
  and Monetary Systems Reform ·· Mikhail Golovnin / 350
Concrete Cooperation among BRICS Countries in Global
  Governance ·· H. H. S. Viswanathan / 354
BRICS Cooperation in the Global Governance of Energy
·· Arunabha Ghosh / 363
BRICS International Finance Crisis and the Challenges of
  Governance ·· Bandi Prasad / 371
India Moves Ahead: Courtesy E-Governance ·· Rajnish Ahuja / 398

Judicial Modernization Reform in China's State Governance
·· Guo Feng / 406
"Urban Development Trap" — A Major Problem Concerning
　Local Governance in BRICS Countries ············· Yuan Baocheng / 412
Promoting BRICS Bank Cooperation in a Pragmatic Way ······ Zou Lixing / 421
BRICS in the Global Economic Governance
·· Zhao Zhongxiu　Sun Jingying / 432
Analysis on Modernization of State Governing Capacity of BRICS
　— From the Perspective of State-building ··· Chu Songyan　Jia Lunan / 452
Leadership of CPC and Rule of Law in State Governance
　Modernization ·· Zheng Changzhong / 472
China's Modernization of Governance Capabilities: Advantages,
　Problems and Measures ······································ Bao Chuanjian / 478
Brazil's Approaches to Strengthen the Building of Its National Governance
　Capacity in the New Century and the Inspirations ······ Chen Xiaoling / 489
ANC's Challenges in Governance — Reflected in the 2014
　Election ·· Shu Chang / 499
The Role of BRICS in Global Reform: What Is Our Vision?
·· Narnia Bohler - Muller / 507
The Impact of Financial Liquidity and Capital Flows on South
　Africa ·· Seeraj Mohamed / 520
Responsive and Innovative Capacity to Promote Governance
　Modernization in South Africa ···························· Daniel Plaatjies / 539
The EU and the BRICS ·· Fraser Cameron / 548
Crisis Management and Risk Prevention in BRICS Countries'
　Modernization Process — Observations about India ········· Klaus Voll / 558
Governance in South Africa after Apartheid ······ Arnold Wehmhoerner / 564
Assessing BRICS's Contribution to Global Governance: An Outsider's
　Perspective ······························· Alice Ekman　Françoise Nicolas / 572
Taking the Long View: Megatrends, Emerging Technologies, and
　Challenges to Governance ································ Banning Garrett / 585
Cooperation among BRICS: What Implications for Global Governance?
·· Ralph A. Cossa / 608
German Experience and Governance in BRICS ········· Carsten Körber / 630

金砖在失色？
"金砖国家治理体系和治理能力现代化建设国际研讨会"论文集

BRICS: Not Glittering?
Papers from "The International Seminar on the Modernization of Governance Systems and Capacity of the BRICS Countries"

建设法治社会 深化金砖合作

郭业洲*

女士们、先生们、朋友们：

首先，我谨代表中联部以及中国当代世界研究中心，对"金砖国家治理体系和治理能力现代化建设国际研讨会"的顺利开幕表示热烈祝贺，对来自金砖国家以及美国、欧洲等其他国家和地区的朋友们表示热烈欢迎。在此，我还要感谢为本次会议成功举办而付出辛苦努力的中方、外方有关单位和人士。其中，我想特别提及德国阿登纳基金会。他们虽然不是金砖国家合作机制成员，但仍希望通过努力让金砖国家的朋友们一起开展对话，探讨共同感兴趣的问题，我也借此机会向德国阿登纳基金会表示感谢。

"金砖"一词几乎是和新世纪同时诞生的。2001年，美国高盛公司经济师奥尼尔（O'Neill）首次提到"金砖"这一概念，在过去13年多的时间里，金砖国家不仅在经济发展速度上位居世界前列，而且在社会发展、消除贫困等方面均取得了重大进展，为落实联合国千年发展目标做出了突出贡献。在2008年全球金融危机爆发之后，金砖国家的表现更是不俗，对全球经济和贸易增长的贡献十分显著，成为世界经济发展的一道靓丽的风景线。当然，我们也注意到，近两年来，金砖国家发展速度面临着很大的下行压力，金砖国家的社会治理面临着许多挑战，国际社会也出现了"金砖在失去光泽""金砖在失色"的声音。对此种观点，我们可以从两个角度来理解。一方面，我们不排除有一些人希望通过这样的论调唱衰金砖国家，因为同经济一样，50%的政治同心理学相关。另一方面，这些论调提醒了我们一个事实，那就是在构建国家治理体系和培育国家治理能力方面，包括中国在内的金砖国家确实面临着许多挑战，同时也面临新的机

---

* 郭业洲，中共中央对外联络部副部长。

遇。为此，中国共产党在 2013 年召开的十八届三中全会上做出了全面深化改革的决定，在 2014 年召开的十八届四中全会上做出了全面推进依法治国的决定。这两个决定共同服务于一个目标，就是要推动中国国家治理体系和治理能力现代化，实现"两个一百年"的目标，实现中华民族伟大复兴的"中国梦"。在此，我想集中向各位与会朋友简要介绍中国共产党十八届四中全会的有关内容。

外国朋友们经常向我提及两大问题：一是依法治国能不能以及如何与中国现行政治制度，特别是政党制度对接和兼容；二是中国推进依法治国的进程如何同自身传统文化和文明对接。对于第一个问题，我的答案是我们能，我们也必须要能。因为，依法治国的这条道路既是许多国家在实现现代化进程中正反两方面经验教训所证明的唯一正确的道路，也是为中国过去 60 多年发展经验教训所证明的正确道路。中国要推进国家治理体系和治理能力现代化必须要走依法治国的道路。关于如何与自身传统文化、政治制度等对接和兼容，十八届四中全会已给出了如下具体答案：

一是要实现依宪治国。中国的宪法是根本大法，是一切法律活动的基础。在中国，讲依法治国，首先讲的是依宪治国；讲依法执政，首先讲的是依宪执政。为此，十八届四中全会提出了很多具体措施。比如，为提高全社会、全民对宪法的了解和遵守宪法的意识，我们把每年的 12 月 4 日定为宪法日，今后全国各级人大及其常委会任命的官员都要向宪法宣誓。

二是要实现法治政府。政府一切行为必须有法律作为依据。政府应该有一个明确的权力和责任清单，同司法之间的边界应十分清晰。我们正在制定这两个清单，清单中将明确规定政府应该做什么以及怎么做。

三是要实现司法公正和司法独立。单从文本上看，中国现有的法律体系是比较完备和健全的。当然，我们还会根据改革和发展的需要及时把一些政策和经验上升为法律，同时也会根据需要不断调整、修订现行法律。但是，更重要的问题是如何更公正、更透明地执行好现有的法律。为此，十八届四中全会提出了许多具体措施。比如，加大对法官和律师队伍的培育；通过各种机制保证各级法院在人、财、物上的独立，确保司法过程不受地方政府利益的影响；记录并公开任何官员或者党的干部干预司法的行为，对导致严重后果的干预行为进行终生追责；让法官对他们的判决实行终身负责制，等等。

四是要建设法治社会。要让更多的人掌握法律知识，提高守法、护法、执法的意识。农耕文明曾长期在中国占据主导地位，我们对法律的理解同其他国家并不相同。我父亲告诉我，在他成长的村子里，大部分人认为法律主要指刑法，刑法之外的法如交通法、税法、环保法等还不算法律。一个触犯了刑法的人会感到羞耻，不愿意被谈及，但一个违反了交通法的人却常不以为耻，有时反而在自己的朋友圈里炫耀。建设法治社会，就是想让尽可能多的中国公民拥有法治精神，产生自觉守法、主动维护法律尊严的意识。同培养法官和制定几部法律相比，培育法治社会的任务将更为艰巨。

五是要把依法治国和以德治国紧密结合。大家都知道依法治国的好处。但是，中国如此之大，多样性如此之明显，我们不可能把社会生活各个角落都法治化，那样做意味着过高的社会治理成本。中国是拥有5000年文明的国度。在5000年发展的历程中形成了许多虽不成文却印刻在人们心头、制约着人们行为的道德规范，是我们管理这个社会的基本参照和依据。我们想在推进建设法治国家的进程中让它们发挥更大的作用。"以德治国"虽听起来是典型的中国说法，其实在许多国家的管理实践中也有这种做法。我曾同家人探讨过什么是以德治国，我父亲给了我一个简单的答案。他说，当你根据交通法在绿灯亮起之时前行，就是依法行驶，但当你发现道路中间有人，即便绿灯已亮也会停车，这就是德性的表现。我想在这一点上各国概莫如是，但中国大而多样的特征使以德治国对中国而言显得尤为重要。因此，必须在中国未来的治理过程中发挥5000年文明所积淀的道德准则的作用。

十八届四中全会提出的改革举措多达185项，在此不能逐一介绍，但我希望大家能多了解有关文件和材料内容。看过之后，就能基本把握中国未来发展的方向和轮廓，这是我们增进相互了解的基本参考。相互了解是相互理解的基础，相互理解则是相互合作的前提。

金砖国家之间开展机制化合作已经历一段时间，金砖国家本着开放、包容、合作、共赢的金砖精神，相互合作取得了很大的进展。**首先，合作内容不断深化。**我们从一般的经济和贸易问题入手，2014年在巴西福塔莱萨金砖国家领导人峰会上宣布建立金砖国家开发银行和应急储备机制，金砖国家合作取得了重大进步。**其次，合作领域不断拓宽。**我们不仅在2010年吸收南非加入金砖国家合作机制，而且具体合作领域已从经济、贸易拓展至政治、安全、环保、人权等，经贸以外的内容占据了《福塔莱萨宣言》的三分之一篇幅，就是很好的证明。**第三，多边机构和多边场合的相互支持和相互协调在不断加强。**在二十国集团和联合国框架内，金砖国家都在积极共同发声。我还清晰记得，2014年3月在荷兰举行的核安全峰会上，五国外长就有关国际问题共同表达了一致看法。这些都展现了金砖国家开展机制化合作所取得的积极成果，以及这些合作所表现出的令人喜悦的发展势头。

金砖国家智库在金砖国家合作进程中发挥着十分重要的作用。智库被人们称为"思想的工厂"和"政策的基地"。金砖国家智库已成立自己的理事会，一直为金砖国家开展机制化合作献计献策。其中许多主意和想法在经过智库层面的讨论后，已经进入到金砖国家机制化合作的最高决策层。我们对此感到特别高兴。今天，我们举办"金砖国家治理体系和治理能力现代化国际研讨会"是金砖国家智库开展合作的又一重要事件。我希望大家在研讨过程中能够坦诚交换意见，做到知无不言，言无不尽。大家在这里讨论的一切都可能不同程度地通过不同形式反映到各国治理实践当中。我也希望通过两天的讨论能够为实现金砖国家治理体系和治理能力现代化、推动金砖国家在更大程度上共同参与全球治理做出重大贡献。

最后，预祝会议圆满成功，谢谢大家！

金砖国家间加强合作以对全球治理施加影响

[巴西] 里纳托·鲍曼*

一、令人忧心的趋势：偏离中心

2009年，有关国家在俄罗斯叶卡捷琳堡召开峰会，"金砖四国"机制正式形成。会后的声明包含16项条款，重点阐述的观点是：（当时的）四个经济体已经足够强大，应该在全球治理中享有更大的发言权。声明确立了国家首脑、外交和财政部长及安全和农业合作领域的定期会议机制，还确定了通过商业论坛和智库年会让社会团体积极参与的机制。

他们期望影响全球治理的目标立场是新兴经济体国家表现出的比工业化国家高出许多的GDP增长速度的反映：2005年至2009年（即第一次"金砖四国"峰会召开的那一年），四国GDP年均增长率分别为：巴西：3.6%；俄罗斯：4.1%；印度：8.1%；中国：11.4%。同期，高收入国家的年平均增长率为0.9%，而世界平均值为2.1%。

金砖国家第六次峰会2014年在巴西福塔莱萨举行。会后发布的宣言至少包含72项条款（随后又发布了一个包含23个项目的行动计划以及另外五个"可以考虑的新合作领域"的清单）。毫无疑问，这些条款所涉及的主题是相当多样的。

大多数关于福塔莱萨峰会的分析倾向于几乎完全聚焦于金砖国家开发银行的正式成立和金砖国家应急储备安排的达成，而忽略了其他那些同样重要的决定。

例如，《福塔莱萨宣言》明确提及联合国的"2015年后发展议程"，其中包括采用共同的方法衡量社会指标、五国出口信贷机构间的合作、五

---

* 里纳托·鲍曼（Renato Baumann），巴西应用经济研究所国际部主任，巴西利亚大学经济系教授，巴西外交学院教授。

国保险和再保险提供机构间合作的可能性、要求世行修订配额、遵守外层空间活动的行为规范以及在打击网络犯罪和反腐败方面进行合作。

另外还有两个方面值得强调。首先，从德班峰会开始，宣言就提到过金砖国家对于非本集团国家的一些担心。《德班宣言》明确提到七个国家，而《福塔莱萨宣言》提到至少 12 个①国家。这显然是该集团面对国际形势采取的一个新的、前所未有的立场。

第二个重要的方面是，德班峰会后，金砖国家的首脑们会见了一些来自非洲的国家首脑。人们普遍认为，南非正式加入金砖国家组织与其说是因为其经济潜能，不如说因为其在该地区的事务中有相对高的重要性。但一些分析家们吃惊地获悉，福塔莱萨峰会后，金砖国家的首脑们会见了一些拉丁美洲的国家首脑。这给该集团注入了迄今为止一直缺乏的一个地区元素，可能会有重要的意义。

这些信息可以做两种解读。首先，六次峰会宣言中条款数量的变化显示金砖国家需要应对的问题在迅速增加。第二，与上面一条有直接联系的是，该集团的形成是谨慎地基于有关各国的相似性，即因为四个创始国对它们在影响全球治理方面起到的作用感到不满。随着时间的推移，原来仅基于经济因素的考量，现在加入了新的因素，发展到了全新的领域。

对于这种议程的多元化官方辩护是，因为这些国家之间的互相了解非常有限，以至于发现合作行动余地的机会越高，存在共同利益的领域就越多。

不言而喻，对于该集团来说，这种战略隐含的危险是偏离那个维持它们的凝聚力和一致立场的中心。

二、优势互补，令人欣慰

关于金砖国家的辩论往往集中在四点。

首先，众所周知，"金砖国家"这个名称是一位来自金融市场的经济学家创造的，他当时想找到一个称呼来指代那少数几个具有良好商业机会的经济体。

其次，经常有人对该集团未来前景表示怀疑，因为这五个国家有非常不同的历史轨迹、明显不同的利益和生产结构。

第三，强调导致该集团形成的基本原因特征。它们与一系列指标有关。比如，巴西、俄罗斯、印度和中国（以及美国）是为数不多的同时显

---

① 如果"阿拉伯—以色列"冲突也包含在该统计中的话。

示出三大特征的国家：(1) 地理规模巨大（超过200万平方公里）；(2) 名义上GDP超过6000亿美元；(3) 人口规模巨大，超过1亿居民。另外，这些国家集中了全球一半的贫困人口。金砖国家构成了世界总人口的42%、全球GDP的14%和外汇储备总量的大约四分之三。①

所有金砖国家都是目前全球治理方面最重要的论坛——二十国集团金融峰会的成员。这些会议的部分参加者称，二十国峰会以前，金砖国家之间就进行了系统的协商，远比任何一个金砖国家与其邻国的协商要密集。这似乎说明，这五国对于他们之间的共同立场的重视超过了对成为特定地区的代表的重视。

贸易可能是一个有助于五国之间巩固凝聚力的因素。但对于不同的金砖国家来说，双边贸易的实际重要性是不尽相同的。对于金砖国家的依赖，巴西比五国中任何其他国家都严重。另外，五国的贸易密集度也各不相同：对于巴西而言，其贸易密集度超过了20%，而中国还不到8%。这就使有关国家间必须在其他方面寻找共同利益。

相比之下，这五国的财政问题都比较少，它们都是美国的债权人，购买了大量美国国债。因为它们向多边金融机构贡献了超过800亿美元，可以预期，随着时间的推移，金砖国家将不断敦促这些机构对决策过程进行改革。

另外，所有金砖国家现在都被分类为"投资级"，短期内，这种身份将维持不变，即使个别国家，如巴西和俄罗斯，会因过分依赖商品出口，容易受到价格波动的影响。

金砖国家（尤其是中国）经常被预测为将很快在经济上超过美国。这使得这五个国家不仅是经济大国，还难以避免地在定义全球政策的过程中扮演活性剂的作用。

另一种较少有人研究的怀疑观点，强调五个国家都有不同的与邻国发生冲突的历史记录。最近发生的是俄罗斯和乌克兰公开的武装冲突，以及中国海那里的潜在问题。印度与其邻国也经常出现问题。

这可能给金砖国家带来外交上的挑战。该集团创建的大部分原因就是联合起来对全球治理施加更明确的影响。这个隐含的意思对当前的现状提出了质疑。并不是说金砖国家喜欢反西方的言论，但显然它的决定意在寻求另一种国际秩序。影响现有秩序的能力与金砖国家间凝聚力的强弱有关。各国能否联合行动，向一个方向前进是一个基本的条件。

---

① 仅中国就占金砖国家价值4万亿美元外汇总储备量的几乎四分之三，显示出在依循程序帮助流动短缺的经济体方面遇到的困难。

导致西方经济采取制裁，这就带来了一个微妙的局面，因为必要的集团凝聚力会号召其他金砖国家提供支持。如果其他金砖国家在每个具体冲突上采取更亲西方的立场，那么这一点是很难做到的。

总之，既有支持金砖国家的极度乐观的预测，也有质疑这种可能性的争论。

三、对全球治理施加影响

第一次金砖国家峰会以来发生了哪些重要的变化？

正如前面所说，一个明显的变化就是议程变得越来越广泛。这拓展了潜在的共同利益和相互间的了解，同时也在定义集团的真正目标方面带来失去重心的危险。

另一个差异是新兴经济体和富裕国家之间在年度 GDP 增速差距方面的收窄。增长率差距的缩小弱化了前者在"谈判"中的硬气度，因为他们比以前需要更多的时间来追赶了。这一急迫的现实，使快速改变全球治理变得合理，这已不仅是一种调整的愿望。

一个经常被人津津乐道的金砖国家取得的胜利是正式批准国际货币基金组织（IMF）配额方面的改变。然而来自美国国会（和来自欧洲国家）的阻力，使这件事仍处于没有结果的状态，迄今为止没有任何改变。

原计划在世界贸易组织（WTO）那里本该能促使多哈回合多边谈判的起飞，却被金砖国家内部的一个意见分歧所扼杀。这个分歧导致印度抵制相关的农业政策。

以上几点应结合两个基本特征一起看：（1）金砖国家内部贸易仍然存在多重障碍，而且看不到能克服这些障碍的迹象：如果一个金砖国家花精力找到了有比较优势的产品，却被另一个金砖国家强行设置障碍，这个国家必须向福塔莱萨的贸易部长提交投诉，但往往不会有人采取任何具体的措施；（2）双边投资的流动仍基本上是针对资源。

近几年 WTO 的作用相对减弱使一种与之平行的谈判活动开始出现，涉及双边和多边优惠协定。有些谈判①在最大的经济体之间进行，包含远远超过 WTO 框架内的谈判涉及的科目。这对某些金砖国家构成了挑战，因为它们并不参与任何有关计划。相关谈判涉及的规模和谈判议程的野心

---

① 其中最重要的几个谈判成果包括：《跨大西洋贸易伙伴关系》（TTP）,《美国—欧盟自贸协定》（TTIP）,《亚洲国家间区域性经济合作伙伴关系》（RCEP）,《国际服务贸易协定》（TISA）。

程度很容易让人担心可能会对大多数贸易流量产生重大的影响。

综合来看，这些情况出现后，有必要对金砖国家对全球治理影响的潜力进行谨慎的评估。叶卡捷琳堡峰会以来很多事情已经发生了变化。这并不是要贬低金砖国家对全球治理影响的潜力。也许能从这个组织获得的益处不会像原来期望的那么多，但对这五个国家来说它们手中仍握有相当可观的谈判资本。

金砖国家必须牢记的一个方面就是它们不是一个新的"布雷顿森林体系"。也就是说，所有谈判的进行必须遵循现有的规则，并在现有的制度结构内进行。

就拿金砖国家开发银行举例。持怀疑观点的人会强调其最初批准的资本规模太小，比如比世界银行小得多，更不要说与金砖国家各自国内的开发银行相比，如中国和巴西的开发银行比较了。这个观点忽视了以下事实：(1) 银行从较小规模开始发展，在金融市场中积累信心是明智之举；(2) 一旦正式创建，该机构就可以不断扩展其资本规模，并使其业务活动多样化。

鉴于这些新的情况，对于金砖国家来说，可以利用哪些可能的方式来影响全球治理呢？也许你会为相关行动提一些建议。

一个重要的也是难以避免的起点是，要认识到金砖国家间的凝聚力程度越高，它们影响国际形势的能力就越强。

所以，第一套计划必须与提升五个经济体的趋同性有关。这些计划包括：(1) 通过减少金砖国家间的贸易壁垒加强合作；(2) 通过技术交流加强合作；(3) 食品和能源领域的合作；(4) 增加基础设施投资；(5) 反腐败和反逃税方面的合作；(6) 听取企业和智库机构的建议，以发现新的行动领域和/或新的方法。

第二，从福塔莱萨峰会开始，金砖国家就有了它们自己的可以支配的、具有相当潜力的政策工具。金砖国家开发银行是布雷顿森林体系之后的第一个非地区性国际机构，由来自不同地区的合作伙伴组成。它必须遵循金融市场中好的实践方法，但同时可以让其具有独立性，区别于其他的多边机构。该银行如果能高效运行，可以成为重要的经济和政治工具。

从金砖国家开发银行正式成立的那一刻起，如果各成员国增加其资本，它就可以成为更好的工具。对于这家银行的研究分析，不能忘记其最重要的方面就是其作为一种机制的存在，而这个机制是可以改进的。

第三，金砖国家可以也必须尝试对总体贸易形势施加影响。俄罗斯是WTO最新的成员。但所有其他成员随着时间的推移表现出了不一致，发展中国家已经从谈判中获利，富国执行的政策对于欠富裕国家的经济有负面影响，例如出口补贴及各种各样的非关税贸易壁垒。

恢复 WTO 的职能，除了发挥其约束作用，举行多边谈判，也是必需的。但这必须根据新的贸易特点进行。金砖国家应携起手来，对那些对它们有害的或在不远的将来将损害其利益的标准的采用实行施加影响。

对于贸易，至少有两个方面需要注意。

金砖国家应共同努力开展协调一致的行动以应对目前正在谈判中的超级协定可能带来的影响。有几个金砖国家没有参加这些谈判，但所有国家都会受这些正在谈判的新事物所带来的后果的影响。

另一个问题越来越令人关注。需要采取一致行动培养技术合作和互相协调的标准，以应对所谓的"自有标准"。一些富裕的进口国为某些产品制定最低标准，一旦不符合他们的标准就拒绝进口。因为这不是政府行为，无法对其进行正式投诉。但其可能会对发展中国家的出口带来很大的伤害。

第四，金融领域还有一整套活动可以执行。金砖国家应加强在二十国集团内的协调行动，确认共同的利益，并采取一致的行动。二十国集团是为重大决策制定举办的论坛，金砖国家不应该放弃利用它推动自己的目标。

金砖国家一直，而且应继续给国际货币基金组织施加压力，使其履行其正式承诺，对配额进行实质性的调整。在二十国集团内曾经有过倡议，要求实施所需调整，但迄今为止并没有实现。这仍应是大家共同关注的问题。

出于同样的原因，依据《福塔莱萨宣言》，也应该采取行动，推动世界银行治理的改变。这些改变的一部分就是必须打破永远是由欧洲公民担任国际货币基金组织的总裁、而由美国公民担任世界银行总裁的传统。当然，这不仅仅是国籍上的变化那么简单。能够提名来自新兴经济体国家的人担任领导人，应该意味着被提名者将致力于推动一个适合发展中国家情况的议程。

最后同样重要的一点是，我们已经看到的许多（但仍然是有限的）20世纪 90 年代中期以来数次危机发生后强加于金融市场的、已被国际普遍采用的规则都是在一些显然很少有，或者根本没有发展中国家参加的论坛上决定的。这就解释了，为什么当一些国家试图修改自己国内的金融法规以与比如《巴塞尔协议Ⅲ》对接时，一些困难就被强加到了自己头上。因此建议金砖国家在这些论坛里更加积极地发声。这就需要大量接受过良好训练的专门人员以及前文已强调过的充分的程序和必要的调整。

四、结束语

金砖国家集团仍然还是一个发展中的组织。它已经取得了举世瞩目的成就,但仍然需要确立一个更加明确的形象。其初衷是希望成为一个重新塑造全球治理的工具,现在却演化成了一系列善良愿望的载体。

本文中强调的观点是这个集团不应该忘掉其最初的目的。金砖国家应采取共同举措加深双边关系,牢记根本,即我们实际上是在巩固一个重要的、能够影响全球治理的工具,不论是通过多边组织运行的新标准,还是通过影响贸易准则,甚至是通过操作基础设施项目资金的替代来源。

本文试图说明金砖国家还有很多行动的余地。要实现这一点,各成员国必须思考怎样才能在国际政策上加强合作。

全球治理视角下的金砖国家合作

刘劲松*

尊敬的郭业洲副部长、同事们、女士们、先生们：

很高兴参加今天的研讨会。我谨代表外交部国际经济司，向"金砖国家治理体系与治理能力现代化建设国际研讨会"的召开表示热烈祝贺！

治理，在英文中主要是自上而下的管治的涵义，中文涵义却很丰富，大约2300年前，荀子首次提出"治理"这个词，意思是明确各人的职责，区别事情的轻重缓急，让大家都觉得公道。我感觉这样去理解"治理"，更有时代意义。

就在几天前的11月15日，金砖国家领导人在澳大利亚布里斯班举行非正式会晤，这个会议很成功，因为它反映了一种新的全球治理结构和理念。各方重申，金砖国家奉行开放、包容、合作、共赢的精神，进一步加强全方位合作，推进开发银行和应急储备安排筹建进程，敦促落实国际货币基金组织（IMF）改革的承诺，加强在二十国集团重要议题上的协调，支持国际社会合作应对埃博拉疫情。我注意到，金砖五国领导人有这样一些突出的共识：一是金砖合作机制要政治和经济双轮驱动，既做世界经济增长的引擎，也做国际和平之盾；二是金砖国家要加快推进合作项目，特别是推进金融合作领域取得更大进展，金砖开发银行和应急储备安排要落实到位，加快国内审批进程；三是主张积极推动经济治理，敦促发达国家采取负责任的货币政策，防止负面外溢效应。加大投资，特别是基建投资，寻找可持续增长的动力。

当前，新兴市场国家和发展中国家群众性兴起，国际地位不断上升，在国际事务中的作用不断提高，成为21世纪国际关系的突出特点。正是在

---

* 刘劲松，中华人民共和国外交部国际经济司副司长。

这个大的时代背景下，金砖国家合作快速发展，成长为促进世界经济复苏、影响国际关系演变和大国关系互动、完善全球治理的重要力量。从2009年金砖国家领导人第一次会晤开始，金砖国家合作大发展的这几年，正是国际金融危机之后全球治理机制改革方兴未艾、逐步深入的几年。今天的会议以金砖国家治理体系和治理能力现代化为主题，应当说抓住了国际关系民主化、全球治理多元化的历史潮流，具有积极的现实意义。下面，我简单谈谈对金砖国家合作的看法。

一、金砖国家是全球治理不可或缺的重要参与方

金砖国家幅员辽阔，人口众多，市场广阔。根据2013年的统计数据，金砖国家人口占世界的42.6%，国土面积占29.3%，GDP占21.3%，贸易总额占16.4%，社会经济发展成就令世界瞩目。尽管国际舆论对金砖国家前景有各种疑问和唱衰的论调，当前金砖国家的经济确实也面临一些波动和困难，但事实上，金砖国家的经济金融形势肯定要比一些发达国家好，仍然是世界经济增长的引擎。金砖国家整体债务率要远低于发达国家的平均水平，经济政策空间还比较广阔，手段充裕，劳动力、创新发展和内需市场的潜力远未完全释放。金砖国家是联合国、世界银行、国际货币基金组织、二十国集团、金融稳定理事会等主要国际组织和机制的重要成员，正不断向世界舞台中心迈进。世界和平与安全、经济、金融、贸易、发展等重要议程都离不开金砖国家的参与。

二、金砖国家有共同的全球治理目标

2014年7月的福塔莱萨会晤是金砖国家领导人第二轮会晤的首场，面临承前启后、继往开来的重要使命。会晤首次提出了"开放、包容、合作、共赢"的金砖国家精神，这既是金砖国家合作历程的宝贵经验，又体现了金砖国家对全球治理的共同愿景。《福塔莱萨宣言》明确提出，"基于以往国际力量格局形成的全球治理架构逐渐失去其合法性与有效性"，"金砖国家是对现行机制进行渐进式变革的重要力量，有助于实现更具代表性和更公平的全球治理、促进更具包容性的全球增长，建设和平、稳定、繁荣的世界"。

在我看来，这种渐进式的、非对抗性的改革包含三个目标，一是推动国际关系民主化，有事大家一起商量着办，推动国际体系朝着更加公正合理的方向前进。二是改革世界银行、国际货币基金组织等国际金融机构，提高新兴市场国家和发展中国家的代表性和发言权。三是提高在气候变化

问题、能源问题等全球性问题上的影响力，提供更多公共产品，这也是金砖国家参与全球治理的共同目标。

三、金砖国家设置全球治理议程的能力不断增强

近年来，金砖国家合作机制不断完善，已形成以领导人会晤为引领，以安全事务高级代表会议、外长会晤、常驻多边使节磋商、各领域务实合作为支撑的多层次合作架构。合作领域不断拓展，已形成政治和经济"双轮驱动"的模式，涵盖外交、经贸、智库、金融、科技、农业、统计、卫生、税务、海关等二十多个领域。金砖国家的利益汇合点不断扩大，共同立场和主张越来越多，在国际事务中发出金砖国家声音、提出金砖国家方案、贡献金砖国家智慧已经成为当今全球治理的现实。此外，金砖国家更加重视同各地区发展中国家的交流合作，2013年在德班首次举行金砖国家同非洲国家领导人对话会，今年在巴西利亚举行金砖国家同拉美国家领导人对话会。这些新型的对话关系有助于从更广范围反映新兴市场国家和发展中国家的共同诉求，进一步壮大在国际事务中的力量。

女士们，先生们，中国一直是金砖国家合作的坚定支持者和建设性参与者、推动者。加强同金砖国家的合作是中国外交的重要方向。中国一贯认为，金砖国家的合作符合多边主义和国际关系民主化的历史潮流，在加强自身伙伴关系的同时，也能成为沟通南北对话和南南合作的重要桥梁。我们支持金砖国家以兼济天下的情怀和气魄，使金砖国家合作造福于各国人民。我们希望金砖国家朝着建设一体化大市场、金融大流通、基础设施互联互通和人文大交流的方向迈进，不断深化各领域务实合作，特别是加快落实开发银行和应急储备安排等重大项目，实现金砖国家参与全球治理能力的新飞跃。

当然，不能否认，金砖国家还处于起步阶段，并不完美，国际上也不乏质疑金砖国家能走多远的声音。但金砖国家潜力巨大，前景光明，未来广阔。中国古人讲，君子"不诱于誉，不恐于诽"。习近平主席讲，金砖国家要扎扎实实把自己的事情办好，把金砖国家合作伙伴关系发展好，把金砖国家合作机制建设好。只要我们坚持对金砖国家发展道路的自信、对金砖国家合作的自信，不为任何风险所惧，不为任何干扰所惑，金砖国家的事业一定能兴旺发达。

女士们，先生们，智库合作是金砖国家合作的重要组成部分，是目前金砖国家合作中开展时间最长、积累合作经验最丰富的领域之一，特别是在为金砖国家合作出谋划策、提供智力支持方面发挥了独特作用。智库理事会就像一支勘探队，为金砖国家未来合作探寻新资源，发扬新动力。

金砖国家治理体系和治理能力现代化，最关键是要加强规划，把全球治理和国内议程的关系理顺，实现政治、经济、社会的全面协调发展。在这方面，金砖国家领导人对智库合作寄予厚望。我注意到，2014年3月在巴西举行的金砖国家智库理事会会议决定，金砖国家智库将联合编制《金砖国家长期合作战略》文件，并将"推动经济增长与发展合作，和平与安全，社会公平、可持续发展与生活质量，政治和经济治理，通过共享知识与创新获得进步"作为这份文件中的五大支柱。金砖国家分工合作，分别牵头起草一个支柱。这是一项很有意义的工作。

金砖国家领导人在15日的非正式会议上认为，金砖国家除了共同推动布里斯班峰会制定的以结构改革为核心的全面增长战略以外，还有必要加强自身的改革，推进经济合作路线图，在基建、应对气候变化、贸易投资便利化等方面发挥引领作用。

可以告诉大家的是，我们在金砖国家协调人渠道也正在商讨制定《金砖国家经济伙伴战略》。这份文件中有不少内容与智库理事会的文件不谋而合。这充分说明金砖国家的政府间合作和智库等非政府间合作正朝着一致的目标前进。事实上，为了打造金砖国家官、产、学联动的合作机制，我们迫切需要智库广泛参与到金砖国家合作的各个层面和领域中。希望各位专家学者为金砖国家合作积极建言献策，共谋金砖国家发展，共商金砖国家合作大计。

最后，还是回到"治理"一词，它在中文里也是一个医学用词，就是不仅要查准病因，还要对症下药；不仅需要开膛破腹，还要帮助缝针，帮助患者调整直至康复。今天我们推进国际治理改革，以及应对热点问题，不能仅仅像外科医生把病人肚子打开，不管缝合治愈，这样是不行的，这样糟糕的情况已经太多。恐怕得有全科大夫的手段，坚守"希波克拉底誓言"，也就是永远将人类的公益放在第一位。

衷心希望各位专家学者通过充分讨论交流，推动《金砖国家长期合作战略》文件取得更多进展，为金砖国家勾画美好的明天。预祝研讨会圆满成功，祝各位在北京工作、生活愉快！谢谢大家。

缓慢的经济增长模式下的创新和治理挑战

[巴西] 安娜·雅瓜里比*

一、概论

本文概述了金砖国家在当前缓慢增长的全球经济中所面临的挑战，回顾了一些金砖国家在全球经济中发挥的潜在作用，以及它们如何应对当前缓慢增长的全球经济和不断加深的附加值竞争的一些主要假设。有人会认为，过去十年进一步推进经济和社会成就的国际环境已经发生了改变，我们需要重新认识经济发展和增长模式。与鼓励创新有关的政策以及新政策制定能力已占据中心舞台。当前情况下所需的思维定势、体制框架和能力与以前的现代化和赶超任务不同。

金砖国家在为可持续发展模式的全球性挑战合作开发创新解决方案和替代方案方面具备独特的机遇优势。各个机构应将制定科学和技术政策合作框架作为重中之重，并应为之付出努力。

二、引言

金砖国家的崛起与20世纪90年代的全球化格局有关。贸易和投资的扩大、全球制造链的崛起和前沿行业的划分，如电子行业，这些都有助于为全球经济创造新的增长机遇。

中国的爆炸式增长速度及其成功转型为全球电子制造业中心的事实就足以证明这些发展趋势。90年代全球化浪潮引发了制成品和商品贸易的变革。不断增长的对商品以及低价格的需求，都有助于驳回生产和商品间不平等贸易条款的长期经济假设。

金砖国家已经成为这一增长情况下的受益者。投资增加和商品需求表明新兴经济体的经济潜力已经从大西洋转至太平洋，并从旧工业化国家转

---

* 安娜·雅瓜里比（Anna Jaguaribe），巴西—中国研究所主任。

至新工业化国家。

金砖国家目前占全球创造价值的25%。世界上几乎一半的人口居住在金砖国家，未来在金砖国家会出现更多大型城市。

金砖国家的经济活力使其成功渡过2008年的信贷危机，这表明经济发展已经过渡到了一个转折点。新兴经济体，特别是金砖国家，凭借其内部市场的扩大，成功探寻全球市场机遇，并因此实现了自给自足的发展模式。有助于金砖国家实现这种增长模式的主要因素包括：内部市场的性质和比重、内部压抑和不断增长的需求、仍需改革的经济欠发达的服务行业，以及基于各国内部特征而出现的新生产和服务需求。

此外，创新生产和沟通的大规模扩散缓解了生产力瓶颈，加快了将低收入群体纳入市场的沟通转变。

正是基于这些经济事实，金砖国家才能得到全球的肯定。同样，金砖国家通过推进能够保证可持续发展的全球治理政治议程来获取凝聚力。

尽管金砖国家成功渡过了经济危机，但很明显，面对目前缓慢增长的全球经济，金砖国家现在面临着许多国家和全球性的挑战，包括一个危机和两个过渡。一个危机是指金融危机对维持过去十年经济成果的影响，两个过渡是指向非对称多极化的新地缘政治和放缓的经济周期的过渡。

缓慢的国际化发展、不断减少的贸易和生产性投资对国民经济造成了额外压力，以致其难以实现再分配政策。这也限制了金砖国家的改革能力，扩大了大型新兴中产阶级所要求的社会服务。在全球经济中获得优势地位的同时赶超新技术前沿也变得越来越难。下图表明了金砖国家目前所面临的部分挑战。

协商集团而不是谈判集团	● 短期：制定治理议程 ● 转向制度建设 ● 推动变革到主动改变的转变
就广泛贸易扩张性全球经济而言，商品价格高，投资、全球价值链和电子行业分裂	● 转向新型缓慢增长的经济 ● 竞争加剧 ● 新创新驱动者 ● 地缘政治上的挑战

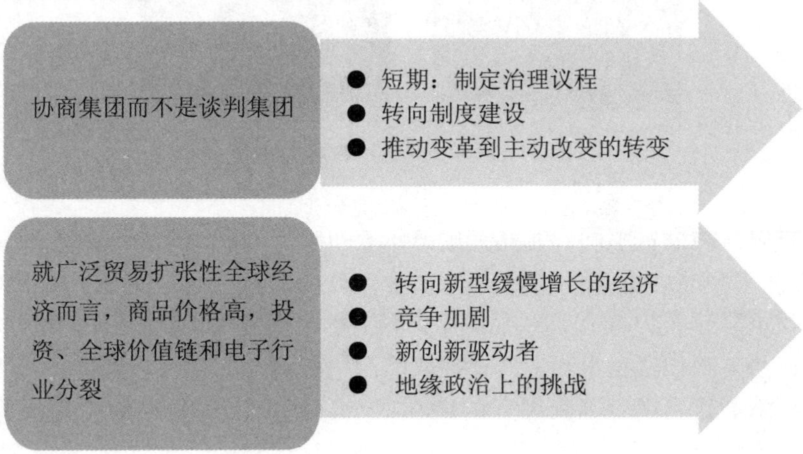

图1　金砖国家目前所面临的部分挑战

对全球化的分析师来讲，经济增长缓慢并不单纯是为应对和适应2008年的危机，而是希望通过一种全球模式实现从制造领域到服务领域，最终到创新型经济的转型。这种趋势往往会加大各经济体之间的现有竞争差距。在复杂的市场中，与大型创新有关的成本和风险正在逐渐增加，通过渐进式产品创新来获得股份和优势的竞争也在不断加剧。正如丹·布莱兹尼茨（Dan Breznitz）所说的，渐进式创新就像《爱丽丝梦游仙境》中的红女王，为了要在这一竞技场中占据一席之位，她甘愿为之付出不懈努力。

经济增速放缓往往会造成商品价格降低、新生产性投资减少和制造业需求的减少，这些都是过去十年经济发展的特点。对于金砖国家来说，国际经济发展放缓和附加值竞争的加剧彰显了中等收入——或更确切地说是中等技术——陷阱。

这也就是指实现中等收入水平的可能性。大多数国家都尚未掌握大步迈向创新型经济的发展条件。金砖国家仍须为实现赶超任务和国家机构改革付出大量的努力。

此外，经济增速放缓是由于技术不确定性造成的。而发展模式的改变依赖于非可再生能源，这是显而易见的。这种新技术推动发展的模式转变尚未实现。

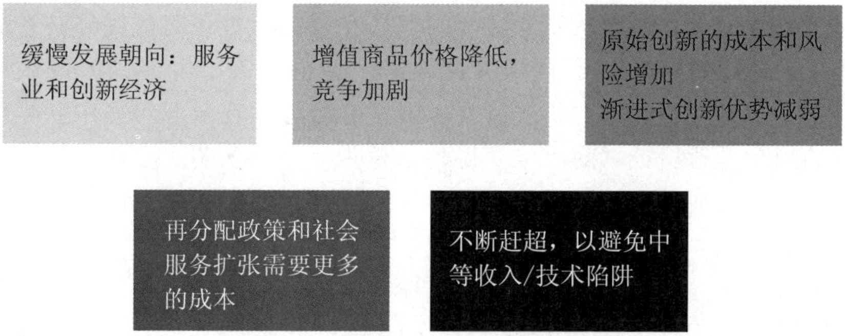

缓慢发展朝向：服务业和创新经济	增值商品价格降低，竞争加剧	原始创新的成本和风险增加 渐进式创新优势减弱
	再分配政策和社会服务扩张需要更多的成本	不断赶超，以避免中等收入/技术陷阱

图2　过去十年经济发展的特点

与以前的危机不同，尤其是皮奥尔（Piori）和萨贝尔（Sabel）所称的20世纪70年代工业生产上的大分水岭，目前的危机似乎并未凸显出技术策略的重要性。70年代那些强调生产模式替代选择①的技术仍在不断发展，未来那些支配长期技术和生产选择的能源挑战将会引发很多后果。

技术创新表现为不断展开的潜在改革，而不仅仅是一种明确的选择，

---

① 这是大鸿沟的本质。

这一事实引发了一场争论，即创新在经济增长中发挥的作用及公共政策的性质在支持创新驱动模式方面发挥的作用。

三、缓慢的增长与创新

面对缓慢增长的全球经济，附加值竞争日益激烈，创新在未来的辩论中起着至关重要的作用。有许多迹象表明，20世纪90年代开始的伟大的全球扩张已经圆满完成。

当达到一定发展水平时，产业转型的推动力和赶超任务就会逐渐减少。服务业向更优质的技术驱动型服务业迈进的脚步会逐渐放缓，强度也会日益减弱。

金砖国家面临着严重失衡的社会和经济发展局面，为维持目前的经济增长格局，金砖国家需要不断投资才能弥补这一缺口。从这一方面来讲，赶超是指增加国家潜力以寻求附加值的一个连续的过程。

当前关于创新前沿的学术讨论直指信息和通信技术的不断变革能力，以及新知识平台对生物学、力学和物理学的潜在破坏性。为应对这种趋势，就需要提出一种可持续发展的新增长模式。同时，我们还需要对能量矩阵的变化进行探究，其中还包括食品生产、水的使用和可持续发展城市的组织。

可持续发展并不是一个明确的经济或技术等式。

齐斯曼（Zysman）指出，信息革命很快就会发生，因为半导体行业已经发展成为一个新工业部门。美国政府曾针对这一行业进行了大量的研究和开发。此外，反托拉斯法案中禁止某些活动的内容也促成了诸如思科、英特尔等大型公司的新产品。

如今，能源矩阵已经确定并已开始运作，这往往会涉及陈腐措施的重新利用。系统性变化不会因市场压力、卓越的技术或合理的成本而实现。这通常要求有一种清晰的愿景，以及政策思维定势和长期规划的改变。同时，这也需要国家发挥系统性变革推动者的作用，而不是作为市场失灵的制衡力量。

四、全球变化和国家治理挑战

在增长放缓和竞争加剧的国际背景下，我们更加需要一种有效的治理体系，各个机构应能制定和实施变革政策。罗德里克（Rodrick）和豪斯曼（Haussman）曾指出，任何一种伟大的模式或正确的路线都不能确保国家经济成功或良好地融入全球经济中。制定政策的时机和历史机遇有时要比一些先天性的因素更为重要。各国如何发动内部改革和融入全球经济将取决于他们的制度背景。

20世纪90年代的全球化正如一部世界史,每个金砖国家都有其不同的发展故事。然而,尽管有着显著的差异,金砖国家间仍存在一些重要的共同点。

对大多数金砖国家而言,经济发展凸显了社会阶级化,提供了许多可以改变未来预期的经济和教育机会。这种由经济机遇和农村生活引发的社会流动模式使储蓄与消费转型国家的市场和社会发生了深刻变革。此外,人们对社会机遇的需求和生产力差距的压力依然存在,当前的治理体系已难以应对教育、基础设施和卫生体系不足带来的压力。

在应对复杂的国内和国际需求方面,金砖国家经济体面临着极大的挑战。他们需要满足广大公民不断提出的对机遇的需求,在全球市场中争取附加值,促进有利于创新型经济国家政策和机构的发展。增速放缓的全球经济制约了这一系列任务的完成,而且还对国家政策创新提出了特殊要求。

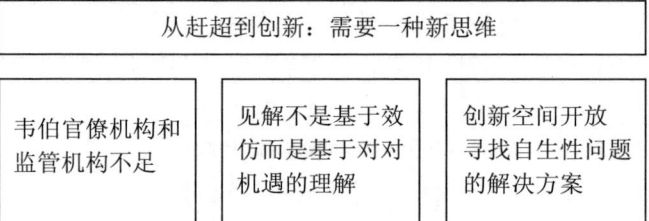

图3　全球变化和国家治理挑战

在过去十年中,大多数金砖国家已为国家创新体系的更新和改革做出了特别的努力,希望能有效地实现知识型经济发展模式。

金砖国家的国家创新体系有着显著差异。除了支出、性质和研发范围的差异外,金砖国家在机构形象、教育禀赋、文化和科学成就史上也存在显著差异。

教育差异尤为明显。巴西、印度、南非的小学和中学的教育体制的质量不同,就连中国和俄罗斯的教育体制也存在不同。在金砖国家中,从工程学校毕业的学生数量很多,质量很好,其中以中国为首。

还有一个有趣的不同点是资金来源和研发地点。巴西和中国一直在稳步增加其在研发方面的投资,在巴西,大部分资金是公共的,也只能用于基础研究,而在中国,由于强调渐进式创新,研发成为企业的发展重点。

因为经济因素和过程融入特定的经济、社会和政治环境中，政策都是针对特定国家而制定的。由此可见，理论和政策建议具有很强的个性化和普遍性，因此应慎重开展能力建设和机构改革。

然而，很明显，金砖国家依然存在一些共同的挑战。事实证明，具备相关性和确定性的策略往往能取得更有利的结果。经济合作与发展组织创新调查一致指出，稳定不变的宏观经济政策以及宏观经济、商业和产业政策之间的融合有利于创新型驱动模式的发展。事实证明，科技方面的长期投资已经成为信息技术发展的基本资产。为引导商业企业进行创新，我们急需为技术方案的反复试验提供一个试验场地，开发全球知识，有效利用外国直接投资，以及刺激国家市场上的竞争。这些方案为我们实现二次创新提供了一条成功路径。中国和韩国在这方面的成功经验就是一个值得效仿的例子。

所有这些政策战略已经融入可以促进或延缓既定目标的实现的制度安排中。创新型经济体需要制定一种灵活的体制和稳定不变的国家政策。"韦伯式的官僚机构"和监管机构是最基本的需求，但并不足以应对治理挑战。

科学和技术的发展需要一些看似矛盾的政策：不仅需要担保长期投资和体制连续性来保证研究的开展，而且还需要灵活的政策机制和快速的应对能力来刺激实验融入商业活动中。

在一个有关金砖国家治理的研究中，贝塔斯曼研究所提出了一种将能力与问责制联系起来的管理指标。下图对贝塔斯曼研究所提出的与能力有关的变量进行了重新分组，你可以从中看出政策目标与政策实施之间的相互作用。

在图4中，所有变量都是相互关联的。但很明显，指导和战略能力、制度学习、适应能力和组织改革能力都需要有效的结果，并直接影响到政策的执行。同样，制度学习依赖于政策的实施，知识来源于失败，改革能力受协商、交流和证据型工具的影响。

显而易见的是，各种不同的能力之间存在一种系统性关系。协调和指导能力不只是特定官僚机构的一种特点和（或）品质，而是由稳定不变的制度学习和适应能力造成的。

由于有效的制度体系是高度相关的，当必须面对发展和技术挑战时，我们就要将制度体系放在首位。

这就是实现创新型经济的过程。它需要对公共政策产生一种新思维，并对公共和私人生产领域之间的关系提出一种新战略。它不仅需要一个有效的和任人唯才的制度框架，而且还需要一种没有效仿的长远目标。对机

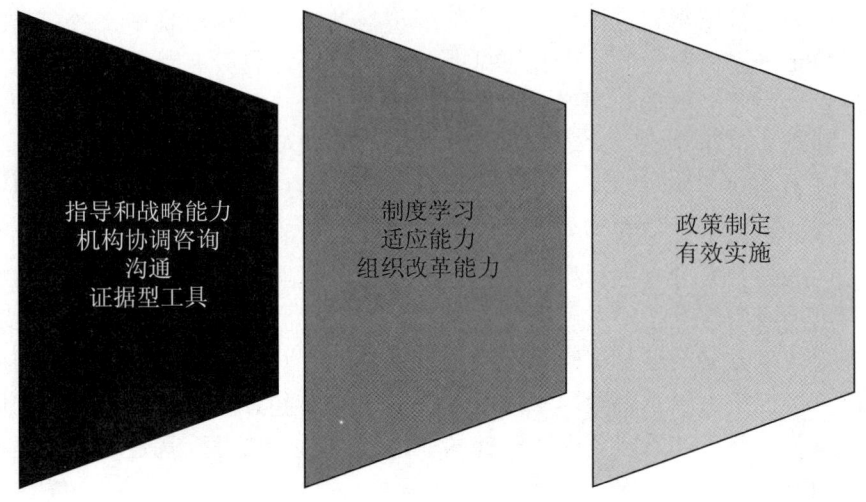

图 4　贝塔斯曼研究所提出的与能力有关的变量

遇的深刻了解使我们能为创新提供一个开放的发展空间，从而解决本土问题。

五、合作机遇

金砖国家不是一个谈判论坛，而是一个磋商论坛。在短时间内，他们就已经针对当前的全球治理体系需要改革这一问题达成了共识，并着手开展制度建设。因此，他们成功摆脱了推动变革或发起改革的窘境。

金砖国家如今所面临的经济和社会挑战与他们实现可持续增长模式及进行创新和与之相关的技术挑战的方式直接相关。

金砖国家在国家创新体系和发展挑战方面有许多共同之处。他们极有可能在制定全球共同发展挑战方案上进行合作，并积极参与共同挑战研究问题的设计和编制。①

与 20 世纪 80 年代相比，如今的科学与科学研究更为广泛，科学协议基本能实现共享，但质量中心仍集中于金砖国家之外的中心和大学。虽然国家创新系统越来越开放，相关性越来越大，研发中心也越来越全球化，但金砖国家的研发工作主要还是在国内开展。

在接下来的几十年中，我们所面临的创新挑战将是如何将科学突破与解决社会和经济问题的颠覆性技术相关联。在很大程度上来说，这些挑战

---

① 详见英国皇家学会 2011 年最终报告《知识、网络与国家》。

就是要处理与全球和社会"公域"有关的问题，而受针对社会"公域"做出的正确决策影响最大的还是金砖国家的人口。

金砖国家已经准备好在生物和制药、替代能源、粮食生产和流动性，以及可持续发展城市的设计方面展开创新合作。在未来十年中，所有新的大型和特大型城市将由新兴经济体产生。为适应更加可持续的增长模式和更具包容性的城市生活和文化要求，我们不得不重新思考这些新城市的城市化模式。

金砖国家目前应针对这些新的创新挑战制定一个行动框架。事实上，金砖国家的政治资本和新型机构的目标、任务和范围不应局限于目前的治理挑战，或弥补全球性机构的不足，这不仅是一种包容性需求，而且还涉及未来所面对的共同挑战。

金砖国家要建立一个合作框架，以及一个工作议程和方案，以交换和评估科技试验，应对创新挑战和做出制度安排，从而促进国家中心和公共实验室在具体项目中展开合作。

参考文献

［1］ Bertelsmann Stifung（ed.），"Change Ahead Sustainable Governance in the BRICS"，2013.

［2］ Dan Breznitz，*The Run of the Red Queen*，Yale University Press，2011.

［3］ J. Cassiolato，*Brics and Development Alternatives*，Anthem Press，2011.

［4］ Carl Dahlman，"Innovation Strategies China, India and Brazil"，Oxford Papers，SLPMD number 023.

［5］ "China Innovation Survey"，OECD，2007.

［6］ Piori and Sabel，"The Second Industrial Divide"，*Basic Books*，1984.

［7］ D. Rodrick and R. Haussman，*Economic Development as Self Discovery*，Harvard University Press，2003.

［8］ J. Zysman，"Brie Policy Papers"，2007.

［9］ "Royal Society Knowledge Networks and Nations Report"，2011.

国家能力与创新政策：
来自金砖四国的启示及对其建议

[巴西] 安娜·卡斯特罗*

塞丽娜·索萨（Celina Souza）说："简而言之，国家能力的定义就是国家用于设立目标，将其转化为政策并予以执行的一套工具和制度。"或者，按照彼得·埃文斯（Peter Evans）的说法，国家能力是关乎国家**执行力**的能力。[1]由于这个概念含义深刻，对其各组成部分认真剖析将有助于指导其在现实中的应用。国家能力所蕴含的政治含义为"游戏规则"，即调整政治、社会及经济行为的规则。由此，分析那些决定政党制度、立法与执法关系的正式或非正式体制是十分有益的，这些体制还关系到利益调节和冲突解决的渠道。

国家能力中的**公共政策**因素涉及影响政策**形成**、制定和执行的**体制和战略**。从这个角度而言，公共政策因素包含：（1）确定管辖具体政策的体制特点；（2）分析具体政策从形成至实施的运行轨迹；（3）**制定政府内部协调机制或政策实施协调机制**；（4）打造行政管理能力，以及调查政策制定及执行时所展现出的专业能力；（5）税收制度，政府税收与支出，国家将征税用于政策支出、提供公共产品及在不同社会群体中进行收入再分配的能力。[2]

以下定义有助于理解国家能力，尤其是政策能力，换言之，也就是政策实施的能力。

政策能力源于彼此联系的三个政策选择：技术进步与创新的性质及来源；**促进**经济增长的方式，尤其是促进技术进步的方式；公共管理是否成熟，能否提供上述两种政策选择，并加以实施。政策能力并非连续统一的能力，而是制定政策的**诸多方法**。[3]

---

* 安娜·卡斯特罗（Ana Célia Castro），巴西里约热内卢联邦大学法律与经济科学中心教授。

国家形成、管理及实施科技政策和创新政策的能力为本项目研究目标,旨在以巴西、中国和阿根廷的国家创新体系为基础,对国家能力和政策能力进行比较,进一步阐明上述内容,即体制与战略、协调机制、融资及创新政策实施。正如彼得·埃文斯在《创新国家》[4]中指出的那样,"在此进行比较有益于发现创新在现实生活中的组织形式,以及**如何以更好的形式组织创新**"(着重号为笔者所加)。

最近,大多数关于科技创新及公共政策安排的文章均强调企业型政府的角色及其在中等收入国家(及诸如美国的发达国家)中对发展政策所做出的根本贡献。这些观点一致认同创新在赶超发达国家和跃进式发展中的作用。[5][6][7]本文通过有力的分析进一步认可了创新在赶超发达国家和跃进式发展中的作用。但创新很可能落入技术陷阱,这是生产转型快速发展的国家所面临的共同问题。人们认为产业政策(与创新政策)对克服所谓的"发展门槛"起到至关重要的作用。

> 在非西方国家中,成为发达国家的为数不到十国,这样说其实也扩大了"非西方""发达"和"国家"的概念,因为在这不足"十国"的清单中包括了日本、俄罗斯、中国台湾、韩国、中国香港、新加坡和以色列这类国家和地区。数量如此之少表明"二战"后出现的大量"发展产业"很难称为是成功的。这些非西方国家取得成功的案例存在两个共同点:首先,具有能够侵略并占有其领土的外部敌对国家;其次,它们**更加积极活跃、擅长管理**,而不是实行广泛采纳的新古典发展策略。[8](中国香港并非完全与第二点所述一致。)

在成为发达国家的进程中,创新,作为提倡发展的政府产业政策的一部分,似乎是成功的关键,或许也是步入发展型国家还是发展中国家的关键所在。跨过发展门槛的国家便可到达其最重要经济领域的技术前沿,而且大多数情况下这些国家是在高效地引领这些领域的发展。

科里亚(Coriat)和沃勒斯坦(Wenstein)从另一角度证明了本文所做分析,并呼吁人们关注其所谓的"技术范式"(这一范式以科学为基础)正在变得愈发重要。[9]在这些似乎是科技前沿之所在领域中,如生物技术和信息技术,有两点不可或缺:资金(资本市场)和知识产权(相关专利及知识产权体系)。这两点是相辅相成的,并蕴含于这一新的科学范式之中。

同样，"二次创新"这一概念亦是如此①。[10]二次创新的核心是能力建设。关于中等收入国家所面临的技术陷阱，至少有三点需要考虑：首先，作为供应商（分包商）的产业和公司在全球价值链中所处的位置。[11]在此，技术陷阱源于难以实现技术能力创新，甚或源于其在价值链中所处位置给其造成的障碍。即使仅以赶上发达国家为主要目标，这一目标似乎也难以实现。不过，对此类国家有利的是，许多发展道路已众所周知，并且业已由众多走在前列的国家所尝试。与此相反，有些产业或公司有能力赶超已经走在技术前沿的国家。过去有几个国家做到如此，它们已经能克服技术发展上的门槛，还有几个国家与此目标相差不远。除了这两种各处一端的情况外，还存在发展位于中间状态的国家，如巴西和中国，它们有些产业已走在世界前沿（如低污染的热带农业和深海石油勘探，此外，巴西在中小型飞机制造业中也处于领先地位），但是有些产业竞争能力相对落后。在此情况下便出现了"二次创新"并存的现象。

吴晓波等指出，如果技术发展并非完全处于同一领域，各国可通过不同途径或其他路径进行发展，但在此过程中很可能遇到与其技术能力相关的限制因素。这是发展进程中典型的危机情况。这些限制因素一旦克服，就会形成其自己的国家发展道路，这一道路考虑到本国的具体因素，使该国具有继续发展的竞争优势。创新以及创新借以实现的国家创新体制可谓一个国家到达其在某些领域科技前沿的杀手锏，在这些领域中，该国在体制方面具有比较优势。这也是对巴西、中国和阿根廷的情况进行比较分析时所要突出强调的一点。

如果在企业型政府②应激励和改善哪些领域、时下的科技前沿是什么以及这些国家能否达到科技前沿或引领创新步伐等方面形成的**结构性共识**是合情合理的，上述杀手锏才有可能发挥作用。[12]形成结构性共识有赖于：是否有足够的科研机构可从事前瞻性（和回顾性）研究，能否将这些研究有效运用于决策过程；能否经常做出调整以实现持续创新或持续的技术创新；预见利益冲突的能力，以及在打造结构性共识时平衡各方利益冲突的

---

① 在此补充以下内容：如果某个国家在历经二次创新后跨越了技术前沿或正位于科技前沿；如果这一过程是与某一特殊、成功的道路相结合的；如果这一道路可以展现其自身所能给予的资源或赋予的能力，那么该国很有可能引领这个领域的技术前沿和社会技术前沿。"社会技术"的概念可参见 R. Nelson and B. Sampat, "What Enables Rapid Economic Progress: What Are the Needed Institutions?" *Research Policy*, 37 (2008), pp. 1-11.

② 对哪些产业应予以优先发展并获得创新政策的支持形成结构性共识并非唯一可行的战略，但对于中等收入国家而言似乎却是必要的，或是更加有效的。对诸如美国这样的国家而言，正如布洛克（Block）所言：共识便是对那些位于科技前沿的国家提供支援。

能力；最后，还要有一个成熟高效的金融创新体系。按照凯特尔（Kattel）的说法，问题的核心并非能力或专业知识多多益善（"能力的连续统"），而是在制定、实施技术政策时，要有一套关于这方面长远战略和协调运作的决策程序。

在指出这些案例研究的主要指标前，有必要强调，对巴西、中国和阿根廷的比较研究是在中等收入国家的框架内展开的。对案例的分析结果可进行"移花接木"，换言之，由分析得出的观点不仅对制定战略性决策有重大意义，对创新政策方面的知识管理[13]也具有同等重要的意义。对于案例，不仅要借鉴①，更需了解分析的重点是案例研究在何等程度上强调了不同体制所面临的挑战或陷入的僵局，以便在制定和实施创新政策时可更好地借鉴巴西的制度优势。[14]

通过对上述三个国家科技体制、创新体制的制度结构进行比较，可以看出巴西整体的制度框架比阿根廷更为严谨复杂；毫无疑问，在此方面比中国的制度框架也更为严谨复杂。可以说阿根廷的制度框架与巴西的体制相似，只是阿根廷在此方面还处于发展初期，但考虑到其近期的发展趋势，可以看出与巴西的发展方向相同。但就中国而言，其强调的是制度设计或结构无需反映决策能力，更不用说反映其在采纳创新战略前达成**结构性共识**的过程了，这一点参见下文。

巴西创新体制结构所追求的是将教学、研究和创新融资体系合为一体，这主要是通过巴西国家发展银行（BNDES）、巴西创新署（FINEP）和产业基金会来实现的。但中国的创新融资却不是国家创新体系组织图上的一部分，而是直接通过银行体系实现的。银行机构与各级企业（无论是国家级、产业级还是区域级企业，尤其是当地企业）均合作密切，这就保证了企业融资不受资本结构的影响。但是，国有企业更受青睐，其对中国技术和产业发展所做出的积极贡献受到高度赞誉。因此，此方面也是需要强调的差异。相比之下，创新融资则是阿根廷体制的弱点。

巴西早在1950年便开始构建其法律体系，经过长期实践形成了如今坚实的法律框架。其科技融资体制建设亦是如此，而且现在还将创新这一概念融入其中。巴西历任政府的首要工作便是开发可利用资源、完善融资体制和融资工具。然而，巴西在服务企业方面缺乏必要的灵活性，在提供和保护创新资金方面所发挥的作用更是不足，这都是其体制特点所决定的。这一体制设有诸多规定、法律框架和各种监管，尤其是来自审计部分

---

① 这一基本概念与各种不同的可能性、对不同路径的依赖性及不同的资本结构是有矛盾的。制定单一的体制显然是错误的，通常都会产生不良后果。

（Tribunal de Contas）的监管，因此很少有新的企业想利用该体制，而且它们也无法兑现所承诺的创新。

在中国，科学技术部通过中国科学技术发展战略研究院和中国社会科学院这样的智库发挥其协调作用，于悄然之间将技术前瞻活动融于同一长远战略规划之中，该战略规划将最终决定为哪些产业和技术融资。达成共识或结构性共识，与技术前瞻活动和战略选择的统一是密不可分的。安刚将这一过程命名为"集体管理"[15]。

在巴西，类似上述中国智库的政府机构，如巴西科技部战略研究中心（CGEE）和巴西工业发展局（ABDI），主要是通过对目前和过去巴西创新体制的特点和所面临的挑战进行系统的回顾性研究来发挥其作用的。但是，即使分析上层，却似乎未见将分析结果、形成结构性共识以及对哪些领域做出战略性选择这些方面做出整合。①

概言之，本文所得出的结论似乎表明中国具有以下制度性比较优势，这些优势同时也是警示，但可以为巴西和阿根廷所借鉴。

1. 中国的创新体制改变了，或者更加确切地说是推翻了巴西和阿根廷体制特有的运行模式。**源于现实经济体系的技术创新是创新体制的灵魂，不是无足轻重的。**无论是个人还是公共部门所从事的研究都是创新的起点，而非终点。

2. 创新体制的第二层是战略决策顾问机构。战略决策由研究机构、智库、大学等机构制定。

3. 技术前瞻须持久展开、定期审核。该问题在形成选择哪些领域制定长期战略这一结构性共识时要从根本上认真考虑。

4. 创新融资涵盖范围似乎甚广，并非仅对某些领域或根据资本结构划分的某类企业提供融资，而且也未设置诸多管控。银行系统是实施创新融资的机构。最后这一点并非根植于创新体制的制度安排，因此不应将其视为制度性比较优势，而应视为中国体制独有的特点。

5. 似乎是在达成共识或集体形成这一结构性共识的过程中产生了战略选择。在中国体制中看不到利益联盟的诉求，而这是西方代议民主制的特点，并且也存在于巴西和阿根廷的决策过程之中。

对巴西案例的研究似乎表明其具有以下制度性比较优势，且不应忘记中国所面对的警示、挑战及可能的障碍。

1. 巴西创新体制历经几十年的发展，结构严密，体制成熟，能为决策

---

① 由于这些采访都是在去中国实地考察前做出的，当时这一假设正在形成阶段，因此在此方面无法对阿根廷做出评价。

提供充分的依据，并考虑到不同的利益主体，在国家科技和创新体制（SNCTI）的多个制度框架中均有所体现。

2. 虽然无法直接参与决策制定，但巴西的大学和研究机构，与创新机构关系最为密切的那些组织，均对提高科学技术和创新水平做出了贡献，这从巴西的科学产出便可窥见一斑。①

3. 巴西体制所需的融资方式根植于其自身的体制结构，从理论上说应能够完全满足其体制运行。但是，对融资方式的过度监管消除了巴西创新融资体制的制度优势。因此，时常可以听到巴西国家发展银行和巴西创新署抱怨前来寻求技术改造融资的创新型企业数目寥寥。

4. 各种评价表明巴西的法律结构完全可以满足其创新体制之所需。但法律的各种规定和实际应用仍旧令人们产生质疑，望而却步。这使原本具有竞争力的制度优势在人们看来却并非如此。

5. 创新体制的管理已注意到在创新过程中要考虑和代表不同的利益团体。但此般考虑似乎仅局限在一定范围内，未能真正考虑到那些迫在眉睫且应当关注的利益关系。

根据中国的经验似乎可以看出巴西最严重的制度弊端为：

1. 尽管巴西创新体制历史悠久，复杂严谨，并且最重要的是以其科学产出获得公认的赞誉，但该体制的"第二层，战略决策顾问机构这一层，如研究机构、智库、大学等"，在发展巴西创新政策时，并未完全加入到制定战略选择的过程中来。

2. 巴西偶尔也会开展技术前瞻活动，但中国是系统地进行此类活动。因此，这也是构建合作平台时要重点推荐的一条建议。

3. 创新政策中哪些是需要优先解决的问题，如选择、支持，甚至保护哪些领域，形成有关这些方面的结构性共识的过程可谓巴西科技和创新政策最薄弱环节之所在。②那些已经克服发展门槛的国家，研究其过往实践经验可以发现达成共识与战略选择对发展创新政策是至关重要的。

---

① 巴西不仅科技文章产出多，使其位于突出位置，而且其历次召开的国家创新大会，如2010年召开的第四次创新大会，均表明巴西在诸多知识领域均处于领先地位。"巴西由于其目前所处的历史时期、区域和文化的多样性，其人口数量以及所达到的科技水平，均赋予巴西打造可持续发展模式的独有机会，这一模式是尊重自然和人权的。这一模式必须使所有巴西人民接受发达的科技知识和教育。"（路易斯·多维奇，巴西科技部战略研究中心，《第四次可持续发展科技和创新大会蓝皮书》，www.cgee.org.br/publicacoes/livroazul.php）

② 对阿根廷的分析由于没有充分的研究材料，非但未能得出类似上述的结论，反倒形成与这一结论相反的观点。

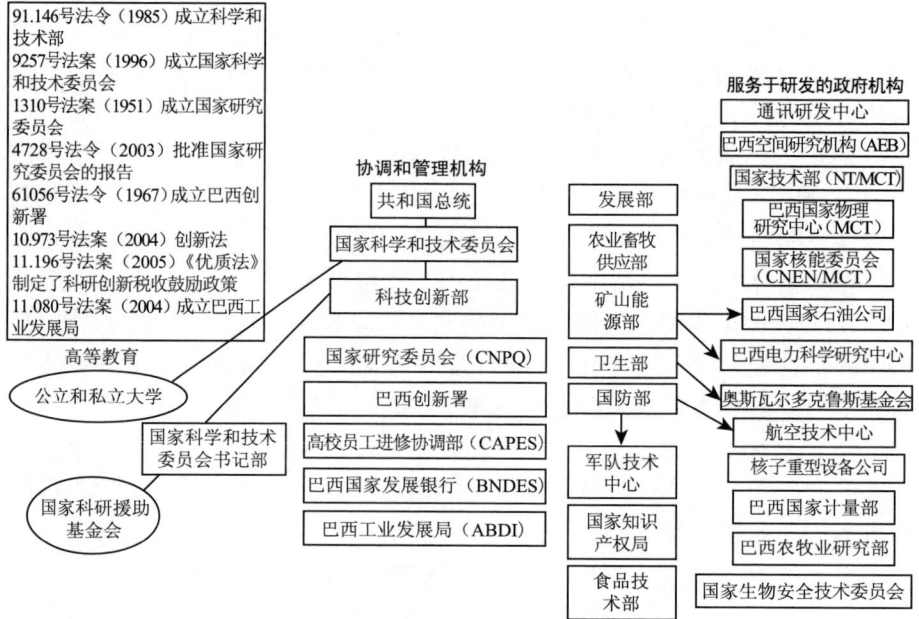

图 1 巴西科技和创新体制

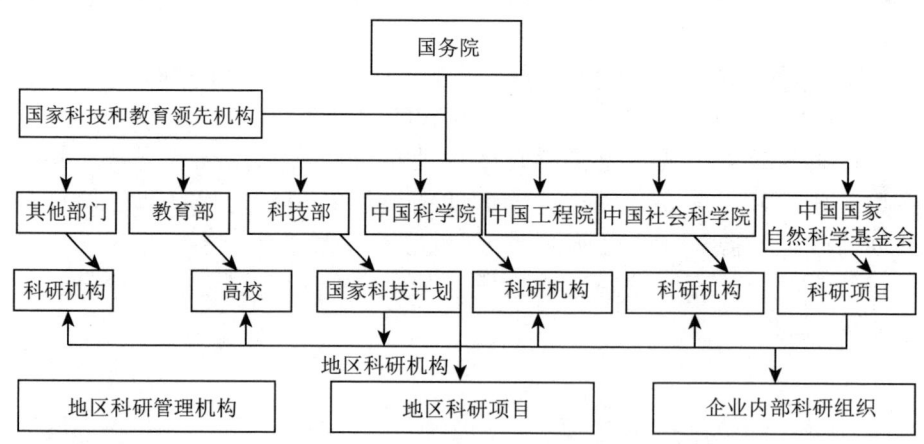

图 2 中国科技体制管理结构

资料来源：Rong Ping Mu, "Development of Science and Technology Policy in china", 2004, http://www.nistep.go.jp/IC/ic040913/pdf/30-04ftx.pdf。

参考文献

[1] Peter B. Evans, "O Estado como problema e solução", *Lua Nova Revista de Cultura e Política*, n. 28/29, 1993, pp. 107 – 156.

[2] Celina Souza, "Comparative State Capacitiy", research report to IPEA (Institute of Economics and Applied Research), emphasis added, text for discussion, 2015.

[3] E. Karo and R. Kattel, "Public Management, Policy Capacity, Innovation and Development", *Brazilian Journal of Political Economy*, Vol. 34, No. 1 (134), January-March, 2014, pp. 80 – 102.

[4] F. Block and M. R. Keller, "State of Innovation", *The U. S. Government's Role in Technology Development*, Paradigm Publisher, Boulder, London, 2011.

[5] L. Weiss, *America Inc. ? Innovation and Enterprise in the National Security State*, Cornell University Press, Ithaca and London, 2014.

[6] M. Mazzucato, "The Entrepreneurial State: Debunking Public vs. Private Sector Myths", Anthem Press, London, UK, 2013.

[7] F. Block and M. R. Keller, ob. Cit., A. Primi, "Promoting Innovation in Latin America — What Countries Have Learned (and What they have not)", in *Designing and Implementing Innovation and Intellectual Property Policies*, University of Maastricht, 2014.

[8] R. Wade, "Doing Industrial Policy Better, Not Less", unpublished manuscript, August 2014. 感谢罗伯特·韦德（Robert Wade）教授允许我引用这段话。另，阿布拉莫维斯（A. Abramovith）以前就曾指出外敌和特殊的政治条件对准备赶超发达国家的发展中国家是十分重要的，参见 A. Abramovith, "Catching-up, Forging Ahead and Falling behind", *The Journal of Economic History*, 46（2）, pp. 385 – 406。

[9] B. Coriat and O. Wenstein, "Science-based Innovation Regimes and Institutional Arrangements: from Science-based '1' to Science-based '2' Regimes", *Towards a New Science-based Regime? Industrial and Innovation.* 另一篇独具开创性的文章是 K. Pavitt, "The Innovation Process", in J. Fagerberg, D. Mowery, and R. Nelson (eds.), *The Oxford Handbook of Innovation*, Oxford University Press, Oxford, 2005。包容与可持续发展，增加了当今两大重要的层面。

[10] Wu, X., Ma, R., and Chu, G., "Secondary Innovation: The Experience of Chinese Enterprises in Learning, Innovation and Capability Building", *National System for Innovation Management*, in D. Teece, *Dynamic Capabilities & Strategic Management*, Oxford, 2009, Chapter 1.

[11] R. WADE, "States, Firms and Regional Production Hierarchies in East and Southeast Asia: Converging towards the Anglo-American Free Market Model, or Caught in a Medium Technology Trap?" in *International Seminar — Institutions and Economic Development: A Comparative Perspective on State Reforms*, Rio de Janeiro, Anais, Rio de Janeiro: UFRRJ, 1997.

[12] F. Block and M. R. Keller, "State of Innovation", *The U. S. Government's Role in Technology Development*, Paradigm Publisher, Boulder, London, 2011.

[13] L. Burlamaqui, A. C. Castro, and R. Kattel, *Knowledge Governance: Reasserting the Public Interest*, Anthem Other Canon, 2012.

[14] Peter B. Evans, "O Estado como problema e solução", *Lua Nova Revista de Cultura e Política*, n. 28/29, 1993, pp. 107 – 156.

[15] H. Angang, "Collective Presidency in China", Institute for Contemporary China Studies, Tsinghua University, June 2003.

金砖国家在保护世界和平与安全中的作用

[俄] 格奥尔吉·托洛拉亚*

当今世界已开始走向无序化,正如亨利·基辛格(Henri Kissenger)所说,"现在没有世界公认的规则"。西方国家、伊斯兰世界、中国和俄罗斯……都各持己见。①

一方面,世界经济全球化趋势渐趋明朗,跨国合作的影响不断增加,后工业国家(主要是指美国、西欧各国与日本)之间的相互依赖性越来越强,这一切使得通过武力方式解决国际冲突无利可图。另一方面,世界两极格局的瓦解和全球治理的缺失导致世界影响力出现新的分化。各地区和国家之间的社会、经济与技术差距不断扩大,与此同时,区域"力量中心"之间的对抗不断加剧。

如此一来,全球安全将彻底崩溃,部分问题通过国际法进行控制,另外的问题则通过纯粹的强权政治处理。某些行为试图寻找对国际行为体组成的独立团体有利的解决方案,而忽视了基于国际法建立起来的国际机制,"意愿联盟"是一个显著的例子。解决相似问题(科索沃—克里米亚)时采用双重标准已成为一种"规范",同时新型政治策略(以人权为借口,通过从外部支持"颜色革命"的方式破坏敌对国家)和"信息战争"被用于对抗敌对或不友好国家。

与此同时,通过运用新型武器技术试图打破现有战略平衡的结果是,让传统的"硬"战正在逐渐成为一种非唯一手段。尽管国际社会做出了巨大努力,但尚未成功详细制定出一套合适的策略来应对后两极时代的地方和区域威胁,尤其是那些跨界的种族与政治冲突(阿富汗、伊拉克、利比亚和叙利亚)。全球经济也因独立经济组织和自由贸易区的创建(通常出于政治目的)而变得四分五裂。

---

* 格奥尔吉·托洛拉亚(Georgy Toloraya),俄罗斯金砖国家研究委员会执行主任。

① http://www.spiegel.de/international/world/interview-with-henry-kissinger-on-state-of-global-politics-a-1002073.html。

金砖国家最初是被划分到一起的一组经济体。但它们很快发现，要维护金砖国家的首要经济利益，就必须改变全球治理的基本规则，金砖国家存在的首要原因就是成为当前金融和经济结构的"改革者联盟"。然而，这些结构一直以来都在西方大国的主导下，由"二战"后现有的政治、军事体系维护。没有人希望通过第三次世界大战来彻底改变现状（虽然具有讽刺意味的是，我们已经比25年前更加接近第三次世界大战）。因此，在大国之间地理政治矛盾、文化碰撞、地方冲突不断增多的这个动荡时代，金砖国家会谈的议程必须越来越多地关注国际安全问题。

我们应当牢记**金砖国家正面临着多重军事威胁**：外部威胁、内部威胁和跨境威胁（后者大多与恐怖主义相关）。"颜色革命"也可能导致跨境威胁，因为内部的不稳定可能导致外国势力介入，引发武装冲突。

而与此同时，针对金砖国家的直接军事威胁程度则相对较低。然而，金砖国家的部分成员国周边充斥着大规模武装冲突。例如，正如亚洲安全专家指出的，"尽管就在十年之前，世界大国之间的直接军事冲突似乎离现实还很遥远，但偶然的冲突和升级风险正在上升，尤其是东北亚地区"[1]。因此，虽然我们都应该努力仅通过政治和外交途径来确保金砖国家的安全，但是如果金砖国家至关重要的共同利益受到了威胁，也应当备好其他措施，便于在万不得已时采用。

而且，金砖国家在全球武器市场中具有举足轻重的地位，这将为各成员国之间进行政策协调创建一个组织网络，还可能进入武器开发、生产和销售的直接合作层面。

通常情况下，金砖国家承诺通过促进发展中国家与发达国家之间的平等合作的和平外交与多边主义来**维护稳定、安全和公平的世界秩序**。这一世界秩序的特点是，结构松散，多个不同能力的权力中心并存，权力分散，责任适当共担。这种体系更像一种世界范围内的民主制，或者叫"国际民主制"（nationacracy）：各个民族国家各得其所，权利平等，责任不同。这不是一种由美国与其单极世界（北约和美国—亚洲大国同盟共同负责维护世界安全）框架中的同盟国推崇的全球君主制，或充其量，贵族制。

金砖国家各成员国一致认同多边网络外交和基于规则的全球治理结构是实现稳定的最佳保证，这种结构在尊重各国主权的基础上为维护共同的价值观和利益提供了一种有效的框架。因此，金砖国家尊重**国际法**的首要地位，虽然它可能有所不足。

然而，显而易见的情况是，国际法今天的"崇高地位"已衰落至极点。与国家立法不同，国际法没有单一的制定者，没有共同的执行机制，取决于各国主权的平等性和他们使用国际法的意愿。大国倾向于按照自己的喜好曲解国际法，而且他们的动机经常取决于各自国家的法律观念和公众观念。

另外，现行的国际法体系还存在一些基本矛盾。最难解决的不仅包括领土完整原则与民族自决原则之间的矛盾（具体表现如科索沃、阿布哈兹、克里米亚——以及最近的苏格兰与加泰罗尼亚）[2]，还包括代表全体人民利益的国家利益与个人权利和自由之间的矛盾。西方对待这个问题的方法是"人权无国界"[3]，但这既不符合客观现实，也不符合其他文明法律体系代表的利益。

现行的法律规范与系统植根于特定的国家土壤之中，经常反映出不同国家的观念。因此，各方就问题是否存在达成的共识，不能保证它们在选择解决方案的方法和途径时形成一致意见。当一些国家为解决问题提供长期的法律方案而制定详细标准时，其他国家则试图从短期利益的角度看待这个问题，按照短期利益修改法律标准。因此，要优先促成表示尊重国际法的全球参与者之间的合作，这非常关键。金砖国家在此可发挥核心作用。

企图在境外使用国家法律的行为应该受到坚决抵制——这就像战时的冒险，一个国家的公民在其他国家境内遭遇绑架后在某个国家法院出庭。

植根于大陆法系的规范主义与基于先例的盎格鲁-撒克逊传统法律体系之间存在基本的矛盾之处。[4]在先例基础上运用国际法具有盎格鲁-撒克逊法律体系的特点，该体系主张不惜一切代价获得期望的结果，这导致了由一个强国代表的虚拟"法官"的产生，让国内法取代国际法，从而促成了单极世界体系的形成。美国的"先发制人"主义和"人道主义干涉"、单边修改战略稳定协议、多次破坏1961年《维也纳外交关系公约》，这些似乎都不被视作某种"例外情况"的结果，但华盛顿坚持努力把国际法转变为关于"先例基础"的法律。这样反而只能将国际关系中"使用武力的权利"的重要情况合法化，导致我们退回到19—20世纪，甚至更远的中世纪。

欧洲国家（大陆法系的传统依然存在）出于各种政治环境因素的影响而无法提供真正的替代法律来逐步瓦解国际法的规范内容和功能。然而，由世界五大文明（来自亨廷顿的八大文明）组成的金砖国家可以承担这一使命。金砖国家中的三国——巴西、俄罗斯和中国——遵从大陆法系的传统，而其他两国 —— 印度和南非 —— 继承了英美法系，但并未将其视为绝对。① 对金砖国家而言，共同或独立追求一种支持多边国际秩序、国际法规则并增强联合国在维护全球和平与安全方面的作用的政策十分重要。制度而非临时联盟的作用也非常关键且应得到加强。

金砖国家在关键情形下能够团结一致，例如，2014 年春天在联合国大会（UNGA）投票表决克里米亚问题时的表现：金砖国家中的其余四国拒绝执行由西方国家发起的谴责俄罗斯的决议。这样或那样使用国际法的原则不应受制于意识形态教条或政治时刻，而是应该根据每个具体案例对应的明确国际法规决定。

所有金砖国家的法律都以"规范"为原则，这有助于在解决上述问题时产生突破。

● 详细阐述恐怖主义在法律上一致的定义（对于如何对待一系列国内冲突的参与者，定义不明会妨碍详细法律途径的制定，如叙利亚或乌克兰事件）和在联合国框架下与恐怖主义斗争的全球公约；

● "民族认同"问题及其在国际法律体系中与之相关的基本价值观；

● 在未经联合国组织授权的情况下单方制裁的合法性问题；

● 由国际社会发起的经济制裁和其他制裁对人道主义的限制问题；

● 对包括宣传和信息通讯技术在内的"间接攻击"和敌对活动的明确定义问题。

除了国际法，金砖国家合作的另一个重要领域是，**加强联合国的作用**以及区域组织在维护和平与安全中的地位，同时增强组织机构的作用。金砖国家认同联合国是维护国际和平与安全的一个主要机构，部分国家呼吁按照地理政治的现实进行联合国改革，让他们在保护全球和平与秩序的过程中有更多话语权。

尽管联合国安理会（UNSC）的扩展问题在金砖国家内部引起了争议，但这很具话题性。② 这一问题在现实情况下毫无进展，无疑妨碍了联合国应对当下挑战的所有进一步措施，而这反过来却为那些支持"动用武力的权利"的个人或组织提供了便利。

金砖国家应当远离 G4 集团（巴西、印度、德国、日本）以争取成为联合国安理会永久会员，并将此努力纳入金砖国家框架内，这也许会产生重要意义。这将更有利于关于联合国安理会应该更加充分地代表最大的几个发展中地区的观点。同时，否决权问题可能成为进一步磋商的问题。有

---

① http://en.wikipedia.org/wiki/Tort_law_in_India。
② http://debatewise.org/debates/2757-un-security-council-expansion-of/。

一种观点可能在考虑范围内，即新加入的永久成员在未来15年内主动拒绝使用否决权。

为了阻止国际法丧失信誉，金砖国家还可使用网络途径，通过经济、政治、文明和文化建立起来的影响力依靠更多团体：欧亚经济共同体（EurAsEC）、上海合作组织（SCO）、南方共同市场（MERCOSUR）、拉美加勒比共同体（CELAC）、南亚区域合作联盟（SAARC）、南部非洲发展共同体（SADC）等。

金砖国家也应该向世界呈现一个凝聚性的**国家发展和国际生活理论模型**，旨在详细阐述金砖国家在世界经济、政治和法律领域的共同价值体系和首要任务。一种全新的理念应该以集体主义和道德价值观为基础，具备金砖国家大多数成员国文明价值体系的特点，杜绝极端个人主义和消费主义，专注于可持续发展。这种理论方案的最终目的是创建一个全新的社会经济发展模型，从而取代自由资本主义。这种理念也会宣传金砖国家在全球的倡议活动。

从实践层面出发，可采取以下步骤：

- 专门建立金砖国家国际法委员会，就大部分紧急的国际问题开展定期磋商。交流和普及金砖国家哲学家和法学家的理论与历史传统。
- 创建一个"智者俱乐部"，由金砖国家的众多著名社会学者和舆论引导者组成，围绕人类未来发展道路开展研究讨论。
- 为金砖国家的法学专家与政治科学家提供机构层面和个人层面的常规交流平台。
- 创立一家基金会，为金砖国家在相关委员会、其他联合国组织和其他国际性组织编写国际法的共同倡议的永久实践提供支持。

当前不断增加的地理政治对抗也迫切要求金砖国家以组织形式和成员国身份在**冲突预防和危机管理**方面发挥主动作用。在后两极时代，制约独立政府成员和非政府行为者之间相互竞赛的华约组织和北约组织的作用开始走向衰弱，这让企图利用民族和宗教因素激起民族冲突、侵略性民族主义和分裂主义，鼓吹各种对抗观点从而攫取权力和财富的极端势力分子有了自由活动的空间，使得那些像乌克兰一样曾经稳定的地区的局势急剧恶化。

对军事冲突主要趋势的分析显示，自20世纪90年代两极世界瓦解之后，世界上的冲突数量一直处于稳定增长状态，不稳定的地区也在扩大。冷战期间，这一地带几乎深入中东。现在，起于西撒哈拉，延伸至中心地带，直到东欧、外高加索、东南亚、中亚，甚至远至存在一些岛屿纠纷的中国东海。全球核武器和常规战争的威胁有所减少，但是地方军事冲突和混合战争的威胁已有显著增长。

通常来说，最尖锐的纠纷都与交战各方的基本国家利益有关。这些利益包括国家主权、领土完整、国际社会体系中的社会、政治和战略稳定、国家宪法秩序、自由进出重要经济与战略地带和信息等。

金砖国家必须逐步发展成一个适合制定情境交流的平台，并通过相互协商设计可行可靠的机制来应对地方、地区和国际政治与社会动荡，如在中东、北非、亚洲和乌克兰发生的事件。这些机制必须包括在冲突管理的所有阶段协调外交、政治、军事、信息和其他活动的结构并取得实施该行动的充分授权。

金砖国家可以宣布下列用于预防冲突的基本原则：

- 尊重国际法和联合国的作用。
- 中立——以防发生金砖国家之间的冲突事件。
- 金砖国家在面对地方冲突时政策一致（通过协商）。
- 非暴力形式和公正性。

金砖国家可通过以下实际步骤来建立冲突预防和管理体系（其中有些部分已开始施行）：

- 外交政策人员/安全行政人员的长效协商机制。
- 面对冲突，在国际组织中协调立场。
- 相同的民族认同和人权保护政策。
- 与区域组织和延伸国家开展网络安全合作。
- 建议制定新兴安全领域的全球条约（外太空非武器化、新式武器等）。
- 发布金砖国家地区和平共存的联合声明或条约。
- 建立共同的维和部队——未来是否有可能？

合作的另一个重要领域是威胁全球稳定的**新型攻击性武器**，这些武器通常没有被任何特定协定所涵盖，对现有权力平衡具有破坏作用，投入使用后可能引发冲突。率先使用创新型武器的一方会取得先发优势，因此新型武器可能引发军备竞赛。

例如，无人驾驶飞机（UAV）是当前应用极为广泛的一种军事装备。但是，20世纪90年代早期签订最后一轮军备控制协议时，无人驾驶飞机尚未出现，因此它并不受任何国际准则的管制。[5] 金砖国家应当共同解决这个问题，建立一种国际监管体系。

金砖国家传统的合作领域是**非扩散及裁军**。

虽然印度不是《不扩散核武器条约》的签约国，但金砖国家支持现有的不扩散体系，应当采取措施加强这种体系。

金砖国家应当成立一个**外太空**工作组，让成员国各自的太空部门参与进来。该工作组的任务是制定一份关于在外太空和平合作的共识文件。俄中《防止在外空放置武器、对外空物体使用或威胁使用武力条约》（草案）可以作为基础。[6]

金砖国家可以共同解决一系列非传统的威胁和挑战，包括：

- **打击国际恐怖行径**

可能的合作领域包括制定恐怖主义的详细定义，推动联合国《全面制止国际恐怖主义公约》的通过；就恐怖团体融资进行信息交流合作；在相关执法部门之间加强合作；签订协议，共同调查恐怖活动；共同举行反恐演习。

- **打击毒品走私和国际有组织犯罪**

潜在的合作领域包括金砖国家相关禁毒部门交流最佳实践；就改进国家立法给出建议；签订协议，在调查非法毒品走私方面提供相关信息和帮助；共同开展教育项目，在中小学、大学、社区中心推动无毒社会的形成，重点在于青少年；相关的健康、禁毒、青少年和其他部门应当共同开展社会包容项目和健康采购，防止毒品使用在全国进一步扩大。

- **信息安全和网络安全**

潜在的合作领域包括就新的全球互联网治理架构达成共识；反思政府大规模互联网监控的根源和原因；在网络安全领域制定建立信任的措施；创建共同的信息技术基础设施和互联网项目。

- **海上安全**

潜在的合作领域包括海上领域相关国家法律体系和国际刑法的现代化和改进；建立商业舰队，护航共同体系或往返系统；金砖国家海军共同演习，打击海盗威胁；签订协议，发生战争时保护金砖国家的海岸线和内海空间。

- **非法移民**

潜在的合作领域包括协同打击人口贩卖和非法移民；交流最佳实践。

从整体上看，安全议程的内容应该越来越多样化，且应越来越多地出现在金砖国家的框架内。

参考文献

[1] "Advancing Cooperative Security in Asia Pacific: Ingredients of a 21st Century Security Order", Prepared by Paul Evans and Chen Dongxiao, concept paper for the third meeting of the Canada – China project on "Cooperative Security 2.0" to be held in Shanghai, 6 – 7, December 2014.

[2] Edita Gzoyan and Lilit Bandurya, "Territorial Integrity and Self-determination: Contradiction or Equality?" Http: //www. noravank. am/upload/pdf/07. edita% 20gzoyan% 20lilit% 20banduryan_ 21_ century_ 02 – 2011. pdf.

[3] Salil Shetty, "Human Rights Know No Borders", http: //www. amnesty. org/en/annual-report/2013/essay.

[4] Thomas Fleiner, "Common Law and Continental Law: Two Legal Systems", http: //www. thomasfleiner. ch/files/documents/legalsystems_ fulltext_ final. pdf.

[5] Eugene Miasnikov, "Threat of Terrorism Using Unmanned Aerial Vehicles", http: //www. armscontrol. ru/UAV/UAV-report. pdf; http: //www. micropilot. com/pdf/uav-export-controls. pdf.

[6] Treaty on the Prevention of the Placement of Weapons in Outer Space, /PROPOSED PAROS TREATY/Inventory of International Nonproliferation Organizations and Regimes © Center for Nonproliferation Studies, http: //cns. miis. edu/inventory/pdfs/paros. pdf.

金砖国家携手共同促进全球治理的有效性和世界秩序的平等性

[俄] 维多利亚·帕诺娃*

一、金砖国家——变革的推动力

第一轮金砖国家会议已圆满收官,今年,于福塔莱萨举行的金砖国家峰会标志着新一轮金砖国家会议的成功开启。尽管金砖国家内部渴望继续合作,但有关金砖国家发展前景的议论也在不断升温。今年年初,有不少人声称金砖国家已"人到中年"。不过,此种说辞难免有夸张之嫌,客观人士会发现金砖国家仍有继续存在的客观和主观原因。以下是金砖国家会继续保持强有力发展的原因:

即便在共同问题及其理解上取得进展(贸易和投资、金融和发展、粮食安全、网络安全,等等),哪怕是最强的成员国(中国)也不能迫使"北方俱乐部"做出让步,以维护公平的世界秩序。的确,中国有扭转乾坤的实力,如果愿意,她甚至可以改变世界的局面,但同时也得承认只有五个国家联合起来才能产生广泛的影响,也只有在这种情况下,七国集团或美国才能意识到无论从理论还是实际上来讲,其已不再是世界的统治者。最生动的实例可能要数国际货币基金组织份额改革这一问题了。众所周知,由于美国国会拒绝批准份额改革方案,原定于2010年进行的改革不得不被推迟。近期,金砖国家声称将新借款安排延长三个月而不是六个月,并且称今年年底将考虑采取进一步行动,富人俱乐部表示,他们必须开始采取行动,否则事情将不可控制。

相对于同质化的西式世界秩序而言,呼吁多种文化和不同文明和平共处、互利互惠、共同繁荣是金砖国家特有的一种理念。这种理念反对西洋化,反对将世界各地所有国家与文明强加到只符合发达经济体的单一模式

---

* 维多利亚·帕诺娃(Victoria V. Panova),俄罗斯金砖国家研究委员会战略规划首席顾问。

之下。我们现在正在和金砖国家合作伙伴一起讨论每个国家和每个公民认同社会文化的权利，并提出合理建议。我们认为，这可能会改变全球化发展的整体局面。

金砖国家的经济互补性以及市场整合、工业和经济合作等领域具有广阔空间。近期，中俄签署了一份价值 4000 亿的天然气交易合同，这无疑肯定了金砖国家经济进一步一体化的巨大可能性。上届金砖国家智库理事会会议也见证了金砖国家"可能考虑进一步推进贸易和投资合作，促进经济可持续增长和发展"，并且这应以各自经济体的紧密市场整合为目标。为实现目标，双方一致认为智库理事会将建议进一步"调查制度、行政和社会文化障碍以及阻碍跨境商业投资和发展的问题"。

近期的发展局势，即乌克兰危机以及该背景下金砖国家对澳大利亚声明做出的联合反应，体现了金砖五国相互支持的热切心情，即使这些国家并未全面了解合作伙伴立场。这对俄罗斯来说更是弥足珍贵，因为俄罗斯明白，金砖国家大都面临着内部问题，这使得他们很难在当前形势下确定大力支持俄罗斯方面的立场。这就造成了这样一种结果：金砖国家的坚定立场曾迫使强硬的澳大利亚（二十国集团现任主席国）立场柔化，并正式宣布无效。

还需指出的是，俄罗斯（金砖国家聚会的发起者之一）从一开始就高度重视这种模式，同时似乎越来越多的人认为这是一种最佳模式，因为尽管不同国家可能对不同问题持不同意见，但与其他机构不同，金砖国家乐于倾听彼此的心声，似乎没有国家会认为它们的观点是终极真理。然而，七国集团却表现出截然相反的倾向。当它们看到金砖国家持续存在，且奋起保卫其正当国家利益时，七国集团开始几近野蛮地宣扬它们的世界观。在这里，以最近我参加的七国集团峰会前夕的会议为例。参加这种聚会的人通常不仅包括（实际上很少）学者，还有负责峰会事务的政治家和专家。该会议在埃格蒙宫举行，埃格蒙宫是外交部大楼，官方活动经常在这里举行。令人沮丧的是，会议最终没有通过共同努力达成任何积极成果，而是充斥着各种分歧，首先就是关于乌克兰危机这一问题。但更让我惊讶的是他们对中国的负面言论，这主要归咎于中国东海局势，其次是中国南海附近局势的发展，最后是与越南的对峙。许多演讲者或提问者都会谈到七国集团应如何应对其所谓的"俄罗斯和中国的野蛮行径"。同时，还有言论称欢迎俄罗斯在适当情况下回归。然而，自 20 世纪 90 年代以来发生了很多变化——俄罗斯不必再服从于七国集团，也不会为了成为"精英俱乐部"的成员而妥协。虽然，存在合作方面的重要问题，但人们坚定地认为，目前金砖国家才是"精英"，因为它是由新兴大国而不是老牌西方国家组成。

因此，与金砖国家采取的有关改良（而非革命）方法的行动形成鲜明对比的是，七国集团已经开始认真考虑如何维护其主导地位，以试图让金砖国家成为世界发展的局外人。这是极不明智的，特别是认为中国和印度是世界第二和第三大经济体（根据购买力评价），俄罗斯和巴西为世界第六和第七大经济体。与此同时，我们的发展前景不容乐观，在不久的将来，我们的经济甚至还会出现滑坡。此时此刻，我们应团结一致，坚决反对错误倾向，或者缓和不良后果。因此我们应继续做好两个层面的工作——在已有机构内施加压力并创立类似机构。金砖国家开发银行和储备池将是一个良好的开端。我们应考虑：国家支付系统（俄罗斯计划拥有属于自己的具有整合水平的或可与中国系统相互替换的支付系统+亚洲其他支付系统）、评级机构、网络大学（联盟），包括金砖国家内部合作范围内，我们社会的所有利益相关者，还包括发展中国家（非洲除外），为他们提供合作协议和我们各自地区的互利合作计划等。

二、金砖国家多边合作框架

总的来说，任一金砖国家（包括巴西）都不会把老牌西方国家施加的限制纳入国家议程和政策决定中，这决定了金砖五国中的大多数（巴西例外）都会抵制侵犯国家主权和自主权的行为。因此金砖国家在外界看来就是维护与西方干预和经济金融自由化政策相抗衡的**主权保护和不干涉内政**原则的"主权鹰派"，《联合国宪章》明确载有该原则。另外，俄罗斯也乐于与金砖国家分享"网络外交"的好处（可避免"大多数西方机构提出的典型限制要求所施加的国内政治约束"）。[1]

还应指出，与一般的西方政治科学派别不同，俄罗斯学者透过《联合国宪章》观察世界形态，他们视民主为全球治理方案中至关重要的一部分，民主就是说所有国家一律平等，均拥有发言权，而不是由现存西方国家承认的民主国家组成的世界社会。这在俄罗斯联邦所持国际机构职能和国家关系的官方立场中也有所体现。

金砖国家另一个共同立场是支持**多边世界**反对单边主义。正如以上声明所示，20世纪90年代中期，俄罗斯第一次明确提出多边世界的想法，促进了中印俄三角关系和多元外交。这在俄罗斯官方文件中也有记载。90年代前期，随着俄罗斯的外交政策开始在理论和实践上尝试与西方国家和

西方主导机构完全整合,从 1997 年总统在联邦议会中的讲话可以看出,多元化发生的巨大变化。外交政策最重要的目的是:

● 在避免交锋对抗的前提下,以在国际关系中促进稳定和加强合作为基础,保护俄罗斯国家利益。

● 以"**多极世界,不应该有中心力量的统治**"的事实为基础,形成国际关系体系,"21 世纪的世界应更多地依赖法律力量而不是军事力量来解决分歧"。[2]

专家称,1997 年俄罗斯时任外交部长叶夫根尼·普里马科夫(E. Primakov)对拉丁美洲国家的一系列访问以及期间与该大陆主要国家签署的一系列"战略伙伴关系"协议是俄罗斯支持多极世界的开端。①

后来,从 2000 年 6 月新任总统普京领导下施行的俄罗斯外交政策新理念可看出,俄罗斯将努力促进"国际关系多极体系的形成",这反映了不同国家自身利益存在差异的事实,该事实以"**集体决策机制**"、国际法律优先和"**国际关系民主化**"为基础。[3] 2008 年,在新一届外交政策理念指导下,俄罗斯进一步强调,由于世界市场自由化,"全球增长新中心更加关注发展资源的平均分配",这表明了经济潜力的增强。因此,这些国家和地区的经济实力必然会产生深远的政治影响(偏向于多中心世界秩序)。

同时,2008 年外交政策理念详细阐述了"**传统军事政治联盟不能完成化解跨国界的现代威胁和挑战的任务**"的事实,另外,有建议称把国家活动建立在"网络外交"和多边主义灵活形式的基础之上。

世界发展的官方愿景承认"**国际竞争有史以来,首次考虑到文明这一话题,这是以民主和市场经济原则通用框架内不同的价值观和发展模式之间的竞争为先决条件的**"。该文件中,俄罗斯还指责西方"通过垄断全球化过程应对可能发生的损失",包括"遏制俄罗斯"。文件显示"**单边行动战略扰乱国际形势、激发紧张局势和军备竞赛、加深国家间矛盾、挑起民族和宗教仇恨、威胁其他国家安全并加剧不同文明关系的紧张局势**"。纵观所有官方话语和文件,还可看出对**联合国核心作用**的明确陈述,这离不开所有金砖国家对多极化、主权和法治原则的明确支持。[4]

如前所述,在金砖国家成熟时期,俄罗斯政府的加入使金砖国家变得更为强大。其实,虽然这一想法是由普京总统在 2006 年提出的,但是在梅德韦杰夫总统担任领导期间,金砖国家已处于领导地位。如今,俄罗斯精

---

① 详情见 B. Martynov, Mnogopoliarny ili mnogotsivizationny mir? International Trends, http://www.intertrends.ru/twenty-first/014.htm。

英赋予金砖国家的重要性是不可低估的。

新任普京总统读到过这样一篇文章：俄罗斯"**将继续重视金砖四国合作伙伴的合作。这种创建于2006年的独特结构，最生动地象征着从单极世界到更公平世界秩序的转变**"[5]。而后，俄罗斯外交部长拉夫罗夫（Lavrov）称，实践证明金砖国家的成立是"新世纪以来，最重要的地缘政治事件之一"，这进一步强化了上述观点。[6]

这种机制被视为全球关系的新模式，克服了区分东西南北的旧障碍，从而必然会逐渐转变成"**有关广泛世界经济和政治问题的多边战略伙伴关系**"。俄罗斯对金砖国家的未来抱有很大期望，相信金砖国家可以架起南北之间的"桥梁"，若只在南方活跃，将从根本上限制其在国际舞台上的独立能力。[7]

本着这种想法，可以这样概述俄罗斯眼中金砖四国将发挥的主要作用：

- 国际经济合作，建立一个更加民主和公平的金融和经济体系；
- 完善多中心世界和网络外交方法，包括通过在其各自大陆建立互补性整合机制（这是俄罗斯提出和协调建立欧亚联盟的方法）；
- 加强与联合国及其安理会的合作，巩固联合国作为全球治理主要机构的作用；
- 促进金砖国家在全球和地区组织范围内的合作，以维护国际和平与安全；
- 协调有关全球和区域稳定以及地区安全、防扩散和地区冲突管理问题的立场；
- 巩固联合国打击恐怖主义和实施联合国全球反恐战略的核心作用；
- 共同努力协调打击联合国和相关区域机构的贩毒现象；
- 共同维护国际信息安全，共同打击网络恐怖主义和网络犯罪；
- 配合金砖国家合作伙伴打击海盗行为，共同制定国际法律审判机制和对海盗实施的惩罚措施；
- 创建和加强金砖国家与领先发展中国家（阿根廷、印度尼西亚、委内瑞拉等）和国际组织（联合国、上海合作组织、非盟、东盟、欧亚经济共同体、南美国家联盟等）的外部联系；
- 鉴于金砖国家地大物博，劳动力资源丰厚，内部市场庞大，拥有实现经济现代化和高技术水平、确保粮食和能源安全、改善居民生活质量的共同目标，在经济、科学和技术领域以平等、互补、互利为原则开展合作。

三、国际治理中的金砖国家合作

协调金砖国家在二十国集团中立场的必要性是组织金砖国家领导人会晤的初始意图，金砖国家领导人会晤的主要目的是应对全球金融和经济危机。正如前面所提到的，2008 年，首次金砖国家外长特别会晤在叶卡特琳堡举行，2009 年金砖国家领导人也在该地会晤。目前，由于金砖国家与二十国集团的合作，国际金融机构改革（主要谈判在金砖国家和七国集团之间进行）成果显著，但仍然存在许多问题，且金砖国家必须采取额外措施以扩大其视野。在 2009 年的匹兹堡二十国峰会上，国际金融组织份额（IFI）问题引起了热议，也就是在那次会议上，梅德韦杰夫总统与其他新兴国家领导人一起提议为新兴经济体增加 7% 的总配额额度，且由发达经济体支付相关费用，因此最终文件中声明"不低于 5%"。因此，这从很大程度上证实由于五国的联合地位，新兴国家和发展中国家在世界银行配额总数中所占比例从 43.97% 提高到 47.19%，占国际货币基金组织配额总数的比例也从 39.5% 增加到 42.29%，从而使四个金砖国家跻身国际货币基金组织十大股东之列[1]〔中国第三，印度、俄罗斯（轻微下滑，从 2.49% 下滑到 2.71%）和巴西分别位居第 8、第 9 和第 10〕，拥有基金否决权所需占的比例为 85%，这样一来加上他们所占比例已几乎接近 85%（14.18% + 南非 0.6%）。[2]

据推测，由于这一决定批准过程持续时间较长，金砖国家也提出了一系列决策——包括研究建立金砖国家银行（9 月召开的国际货币基金组织和世界银行金砖国家财长边缘会议将就此做出报告），且申报的额外资源储备将国际货币基金组织推向第二道防线。今年 6 月，二十国集团会议前夕，金砖国家领导人会议最终做出了这一决定：中国承担 430 亿美元，巴西、印度和俄罗斯均承担 100 亿美元，南非承担 20 亿美元，但前提是，只有在资金不足且金砖国家能够监控资金去向和用途时，才能动用这些财力。因此，即使延迟分配额外财力是为了促使欧洲和美洲国家批准国际货币基金组织改革方案（虽然没有人承认，然而，在所承诺的 4560 亿美元

---

[1] 值得注意的是，目前为止，只有 2008 年国际货币基金组织的决定生效，金砖国家在 2010 年推动的改革方案仍未通过足够多必要国家的批准（国家数量及其重要性），其中包括美国（美国总统选举导致此计划到 2012 年年底生效的可能性破灭）和许多欧洲国家。

[2] 斯梅斯洛夫（D. Smyslov）针对改革历程问题展开了深入研究，见 D. Smyslov, "Reformirovanie Mezhdunarodnogo valyutnogo fonda: problemy I resheniya", Finansy I upravleniye, *Informatsionno-analiticheskiye materialy*, Dengi I kredit, #1/2012, pp. 36 – 43, #2/2012, pp. 33 – 44。

中，日本出资 600 亿美元左右，德国 547 亿，法国 414 亿，相比之下，所有金砖国家出资则达 750 亿美元），这也似乎是行不通的，虽然预留了大量财力，但仍没取得实质性的突破。

金砖国家对俄罗斯的重要性在于相互间在如下方面开展更强的合作，以维护世界经济稳定：远程医疗和药品、纳米和生物物理学、农业等联合项目以及能源和航空、和平利用空间、提高医疗体系质量等领域。

金砖国家不仅在二十国集团，而且在其他国际组织中也起着阐述和推进想法的主力作用。2010 年莫斯科农业部长会议建立了信息库，可用来分析金砖国家的粮食安全状态。同年，二十国集团将全球粮食安全列为首尔峰会多年行动计划的九大主要内容之一。这反过来促使粮农组织和其他相关国际组织开展研究，以缓解 2011 年 11 月二十国集团戛纳峰会中提出的食品价格波动风险，建议之一就是建立农产品市场信息系统（二十国集团领导人已批准）。后来，2012 年 3 月在新德里金砖国家峰会上，五个国家提出发布《金砖国家农业合作 2012—2016 年行动计划》，该计划强调金砖国家农业信息交换系统（由中国协调）应与农产品信息市场联系起来，"以防重复"，尽管该计划详细描述了所有交换的各个方面，但强调"所有成员提交的信息须仅在金砖国家农业部门之间共享"。[8]同样，总体战略发展行动计划（由巴西协调）① 的第二段中有关于"在粮农组织中创建一个金砖国家集团，该集团也将在联合国世界粮食计划署中发挥作用，以协调行动计划，促进粮食安全、粮食和学校饭菜安全项目以及激励购买本地家庭农业食品的机制"[9]的言论。

联合国内部协调是另一颇具争议的问题。如此一来，2011 年联合国安理会上，所有五个国家的出场，加强了金砖国家成员对国际和平与安全的对话。之后依然如此。

列入政治议程是金砖国家开始谈判的唯一方式，这主要体现在利比亚和叙利亚问题上。与此同时，一些国家虽然有类似的宣言水准，实际却存在内在分歧，因此不能加入金砖国家。其中有些可能与安理会改革和核裁军有关。

金砖五国中两个国家都是联合国安理会常任理事国，而其他三个也在努力争取（其中印度和巴西为四方联盟的成员，另外两个成员是德国和日本）。虽然大家对改革本身的必要性已达成共识，但是最终目标不同，因此在金砖国家内部只允许最低标准。这也是为什么新德里金砖国家宣言中

---

① 俄罗斯负责金砖国家农业合作贸易和投资促进这一副主题。

类似"**需要对联合国包括安理会进行全面改革,使其更具效力、效率和代表性,以更成功地应对当今全球挑战。中国、俄罗斯重申重视巴西、印度和南非在国际事务中的地位,支持其希望在联合国发挥更大作用的愿望**"的肯定性内容较少。[10] 同时,这似乎并没有直接满足其他三个国家的改革事业,也不会对金砖国家造成威胁,因为联合国安理会改革的绊脚石并不受限于对中国或俄罗斯甚至其共同扩张的反对声。在其他更高效的目标中,俄罗斯在这一问题上所持的立场其更具代表性,因为他考虑到了已经变化的世界现实,而且还"及时、妥善地应对出现的危机和问题"。同时,应承认没有一个改革模式会受到所有人的无条件支持,莫斯科认为试图让这些全部获得通过,只会适得其反,因为这会"**不可避免地使联合国大会两极化**",而非继续"**在不对最后期限造假的情况下,努力缓解不同国家的关系**"。但是,对俄罗斯来说,谈判计划中未列明的是联合国安理会的特权,包括否决权利。[11]

当先任命国际货币基金组织领导,特别是然后确定世界银行组织图时,类似情况出现了。巴西、南非站出来支持候选人,却输得仅剩下单一立场,发表了一个空洞的声明:"欢迎通过公开和择优的原则选择来自发展中国的候选人。"[12] 就世贸组织而言,可以说新兴经济体是成功的,因为现在巴西的罗伯托·阿泽维多(R. Azevedu)领导着这一组织。

与安理会改革不同,核裁军问题是一个多元化的问题,不仅对"富人"和"穷人","官方核俱乐部成员"和"非法拥有者"进行了区分,还对具备毁灭潜能的人和能力有限的人等进行了区分。

由于现有防扩散制度颇受争议,且所有金砖国家相应的解决途径也各不相同,俄罗斯倾向于依靠金砖国家内部或双边关系解决小问题,但对于同样重要的问题,如利益趋同程度可能相当高的问题,则远非如此。这类问题不一而足,如金砖国家在核安全方面开展的合作、日内瓦会议上开始就禁止将裂变材料用以生产核武器和核炸药协约展开的会谈或禁止在太空中部署武器的中俄联合条约。[13] 为推动这一条约的施行,所有金砖国家在联合国范围内展开紧密合作,且在禁止使用武力解决太空问题上已达成统一的立场。[14]

而对于处理潜在违反不扩散制度问题的唯一方法(以伊朗为例),俄罗斯与其他金砖国家坚持采用外交方式予以解决。否则,现有矛盾将直指各个政府就"金砖国家"身份所赋予的高度价值展开的双边会谈上。

参考文献

[1] Cynthia Roberts, "Polity Forum: Challengers or Stakeholders? BRICs and the Liberal World Order", *Polity*, Vol. 42, No. 1, January 2010, p. 10.

[2] 叶利钦总统致辞联邦议会, "Poriadok vo vlasti – poriadok v strane", 1997 年 3 月 6 日, 网址: http://www.intelros.ru/2007/02/05/poslanie_prezidenta_rosii_borisa_elcina_federalnomu_sobraniju_rf_porjadok_vo_vlasti__porjadok_v_strane_1997_god.html。

[3] "Concept of the Foreign Policy of Russian Federation", Moscow, June 28, 2000, Nezavisimaya Gazeta, "http://www.ng.ru/world/2000 – 07 – 11/1_concept.html.

[4] "Concept of the Foreign Policy of Russian Federation", Moscow, July 15, 2008, http://kremlin.ru/acts/785.

[5] V. Putin, "Rossija i meniyuschiysia mir", *Moscow News*, February 27, 2012, http://mn.ru/politics/20120227/312306749.html.

[6] S. Lavrov, "BRICS: A New-generation Forum with a Global Reach", in *BRICS: The 2012 New Delhi Summit*, eds. by J. Kirton, M. Larionova, and Y. Alagh, Newsdesk Media, 2012.

[7] S. Lavrov, Ibid.

[8] *BRICS: Action Plan 2012 – 2016 for Agricultural Cooperation of BRICS Countries*, March 2012, http://www.bricsindia.in/actionPlan.html.

[9] *BRICS: Action Plan 2012 – 2016 for Agricultural Cooperation of BRICS Countries*, March 2012, http://www.bricsindia.in/actionPlan.html.

[10] *Fourth BRICS Summit — Delhi Declaration*, March 29, 2012, http://www.mea.gov.in/mystart.php?id=190019162.

[11] Opozitsii Rossii na 66 sessii Generalnoi Assamblei OON, Ministry of Foreign Affairs of Russia, 2011, http://www.mid.ru/bdomp/ns-dmo.nsf/66d11ad1c1bc0a7bc32576790039c04a/b1d0994f63c95f86c32578ce0039986b! Open Document.

[12] Fourth BRICS Summit — Delhi Declaration, March 29, 2012, http://www.mea.gov.in/mystart.php?id=190019162.

[13] M. Ulianov, "Dalneishee razoruzhenie vriad li vozmozhno v formate tolko Rossii i SSHA", February 9, 2012, http://www.interfax.ru/txt.asp?id=230110.

[14] D. Medvedev, "Strany BRIC: obschie tseli-obschie deistviya", April 13, 2010, http://kremlin.ru/news/7443.

国家安全和国家可持续发展

[俄] 阿列克谢·恰格林*

近年来,人们开始在广泛的对象和意义(个性、社会、国家和整个国际社会)范围内重新审视安全。这与人类文明在向可持续发展过渡中出现的问题和思想相关,并且具有一致性。特别是,俄罗斯联邦的新国家安全战略在一定程度上反映了这一观点,同时该观点还涉及通过发展加强安全。

遗憾的是,人们对军事安全概念的性质和内容已形成了模糊认识,并且诠释也多种多样。对这些概念的模糊认识源于在广义上思考"安全"现象时使用了不同的方法。值得注意的是,近年来,一种确保安全发展(特别是关系到国家安全)的新方法正在酝酿之中。通过棱镜问题,目前正考虑向可持续的国家发展过渡。

在形式方法的背景下,安全可定义为不遭受内部和外部威胁的利益(包括国家利益)安全。

用于定义国家安全的公共方法侧重于在国家遭受破坏性影响时保持国家(作为一个社会系统的国家及其社会)的完整性、可持续性、稳定性和正常运作。

总之,众多安全领域的科学家和专家的心中始终牢记通过遏制危险、与实际存在的威胁和危险做斗争、遵循安全模式从而理解并解决理论和实际的安全问题的这一方式。

安全模式的本质比较简单。这可以表述为这样的论点:"我很安全,因为我能及时检测和预防危险。"在此情况下,必不可少的前提条件是,通过威胁和危险的棱镜来定义安全威胁和对周围世界的感知。

对危害和威胁进行分析和评估以确定他们发生的可能性是非常必要的。建议根据风险理论评估国家安全面临的威胁和危险数量。

---

* 阿列克谢·恰格林(Aleksei Chagrin),俄罗斯联邦武装力量总参谋部军事学院科研中心主任。

俄罗斯有着巨大的可持续发展潜力。该国在可持续发展道路上实现经济和社会复兴的先决条件是：强大的智能；基础和应用科学；丰富的自然资源；制定市场体制的依据；工业和通信基础设施元素等等。现今的主要目标是，加快本国经济和社会复兴、实现生产结构现代化、使俄罗斯跻身于全球可持续发展进程中的积极参与国和主导国之列。

应将工作重点和资源放在以下具体的可持续发展首要任务上：

- 通过保障人身安全以及提高生活水平来改善俄罗斯公民的生活质量；
- 通过发展国家创新体系和人力资本投资实现经济增长；
- 通过强化国家的作用和改善公私合作伙伴关系，发展科学、技术、教育、医疗和文化；
- 通过均衡消费、发展先进技术和对国家自然资源潜力进行适度再生产，实现生活系统的生态平衡以及环境管理和维护；
- 在俄罗斯积极参与发展世界多极世界秩序模式的基础上，发展战略稳定性和公平的战略伙伴关系。

俄罗斯联邦认识到需要进行可持续发展，并可能逐步向可持续发展过渡，包括平衡解决社会经济挑战，以保持有利环境和自然资源潜力，从而满足当前和未来的需求。

建议分三个阶段完成向可持续发展的过渡。在第一阶段，需要解决严峻的社会和经济问题；在第二阶段，在经济和社会领域开展以环境为中心的结构转变；在第三阶段，实现俄罗斯和前苏联矿物学家和地球化学家弗拉基米尔·沃尔纳德斯基（V. I. Vernadsky）提出的自然与社会和谐化理念。终极目标是，确保适合人们生活的环境和生态可持续发展。

新的安全愿景反映了当前趋势，以及在没有任何大变动和大灾难情况下的安全问题和逐步发展。这并非是广泛的以经济为中心的竞争发展模式（该模式不能被视为是一种稳定模式），而是一种可持续的、创新和稳定的均衡发展模式。采用这样的发展方式可将量化参数最小化，将发展因素和来源最大化。它强调人类与自然以及在社会范围内一致的协同进化互动形式。这在广义上与沃尔纳德斯基提出的人文发展的人类圈概念是一致的。

在这种情况下，我们不妨探讨一下可持续发展理念，即"可持续安全"理念。这种方法可推动我们向一种新型的文明模式发展，在这种模式下，安全和可持续发展不仅相互关联，而且代表一个统一的综合系统。在像俄罗斯这样的国家中，向这种模式过渡被视为主要与确保国家安全有关。

在人类活动的主要领域遵循关于实施风险、破坏过程和现象的某些原则，是实施新型文明模式的重要条件，在这种模式下，安全和可持续发展代表一个统一系统（功能单元）。

　　在人类活动的多个领域内进行识别、分析和风险评估，根据不同背景对它们进行分类、排列和开展其他系统化工作，是一个单独的、比较困难的但又非常重要的目标 。

　　要实现这一困难目标，需要对国际社会，特别是俄罗斯，在向均衡创新和可持续发展的新文明模式过渡的道路上所遇到的挑战、危险和威胁进行定量评估。

乌克兰危机后的俄罗斯和金砖五国

［俄］亚历山大·卢金*

一、两极格局后的金砖五国

20世纪90年代初期苏联的解体导致长期以来以两级对抗为基础的国际关系体系发生了根本性的转变。尽管在苏联时期，一些学者已经注意到随着区域大国力量的增长，世界格局出现多极化趋势，但苏联的突然离场在某种意义上留下了一个真空带。虽然许多国家，甚至西方世界以外的一些国家，厌恶甚至批评苏联，但苏联的缺席使许多国家，尤其是一些较大的国家，开始担心特定的威胁。首先，这些威胁源于维持特定国际秩序的两极格局终结产生的国际关系不稳定性，其次，威胁还来自世界仅存的权力中心在其摆脱外部困扰和平衡后可能蚕食其他国家的利益。

因而，当美国庆祝冷战胜利，弗朗西斯·福山（Francis Fukuyama）宣布"历史终结"时，中国、印度和亚洲、非洲、南美洲的其他许多国家开始不安地审视事态进展。若美国表现出一定的克制，后续的事件发展可能略有不同，但比尔·克林顿执政时期直至乔治·沃克·布什执政时期相当长的一段时期内，华盛顿开始巩固其胜利并且为美国实现世界统治地位。欧洲不能或不愿追求独立自主的路线，一如既往地与华盛顿的政策保持一致。

通过共同的努力，西方国家愈发试图充当国际仲裁员的角色，取代其自身对于国际法的决策。一旦联合国安理会的裁定与其期望不符，西方国家则不顾安理会的决议，授权北约组织及其各个成员国在未经安理会批准的情况下干预国际冲突，由此可见一斑。西方国家在伊拉克、南斯拉夫——尤其是通过武力使科索沃脱离塞尔维亚——以及后续在利比亚的冲

---

* 亚历山大·卢金（Alexander Lukin），俄罗斯国家研究大学高等经济学院国际关系专业系主任，莫斯科国际关系学院东亚与上海合作组织研究中心主任。

突中开展军事行动，无疑践踏了联合国安理会授予其的各种权利，继而在利比亚，西方国家不通过国际制裁，支持推翻合法政府的军事行动，破坏区域的稳定性，不可避免地引起非西方国家的深切关注。

在这种情况下，这些心存怨恨的国家开始建立彼此之间的联系。这种合作最初并非针对西方国家，因为这一过程中的所有参与者均在很大程度上与西方体制捆绑在一起，并且非常珍视与西方国家的协作。但是，他们尝试通过各种途径调整他们在由西方国家支配的世界格局中的地位，显然他们并不适应。这种愿望创建或加强了西方国家并未参与的各种体系和团体：例如东南亚国家联盟以及各种形式的合作、上海合作组织、拉美和加勒比国家共同体，当然还有金砖五国。

在这些团体中，金砖五国并不属于正式的组织，但吸引了最广泛的关注。这是由多种原因产生的。首先，这个团体汇集了世界上最大、最具影响力的非西方国家。其次，其不属于区域性的，而是一个全球性的团体，主张代表整个"发展中国家"，或者更广泛地说，代表整个非西方世界。再次，金砖五国积极提出其自身的举措，作为西方计划的替代物，组织全球经济政治秩序。

很有趣的是，金砖五国（最初为金砖四国）的名称是由高盛投资公司分析师吉姆·奥尼尔（Jim O'Neill）首创的，但是其演化与该分析师的预想有天壤之别。结果，政治原因而非经济或经济发展水平的相似之处为该团体的成员国提供了联合的基础。金砖五国形成的方式可以证明这一点，通过逐渐的演变，来自各大洲的几个国家走到了一起，而他们在其自身所处的区域已是自然天成的领袖。其起源可以追溯至俄罗斯和中国基于共同的地缘政治利益建立的友善关系。没有这长达二十多年的友善关系，很可能金砖五国根本不会出现。（尽管俄罗斯、印度和中国属于不同的集团，但这些差异在金砖五国形成后实际上并不明显。）最后加入的是南非，由此将金砖四国更名为金砖五国。

金砖五国通过对世界进程发表其自身的看法，从而具备地缘政治意义。金砖五国需要解决的一个主要议题是世界经济改革。金砖五国的成员国强烈提出在国际金融机构中增加代表非西方国家的席位，但受到传统全球金融大国的激烈抵制。金砖五国在改革世界银行和国际货币组织的努力中所经历的失望，迫使其寻求更多的公平地位，使得该团体建立自己的开发银行和货币储备池。虽然这些机构可能不能替代现有国际金融机构，但有助于纠正亲西方的偏见，并且为非西方国家为其金融发展选择国际金融机构时以及在应对重大经济危机时提供了一个可选的途径。

俄罗斯外交部首席金砖五国专家瓦迪姆·卢卡夫（Vadim Lukov）坚信，全球金融体制改革是该集团四个战略利益中最重要的一环。他将另外三个战略利益视作强化联合国安理会在国际体制中的角色，充分利用成员国经济的互补性，加速经济发展和社会领域的现代化以及上述国家的经济周期。[1] 正如我们所见，这些目标中只有一部分属于纯粹的经济性质。

二、乌克兰危机和金砖五国

很难高估乌克兰危机对金砖五国以及全世界所产生的意义。总的来说，乌克兰危机表明，西方国家将继续——比以往更加坚定——建立单极世界模式，将更多的"卫星"送上其外交政策轨道，并且要求遵守其对外和对内政策，使其背上西方所谓的"国际"甚至"全球"标准。非西方世界中的许多国家将其视作新一轮殖民主义，虽然在意识形态上使用"民主"代替了"更先进的文化"这一口号，但仍通过相同的方法达到相同的目的。当然，这些情况只会增加非西方社会相互协作的愿望。

当然，金砖五国各成员国彼此之间存在巨大的差异，其与西方之间的分歧也有各种不同的历史和政治原因。作为南美洲左翼和社会主义倾向的代表，巴西趋向于反对西方世界，尤其是反对美国的社会政策。对于一个几乎所有政党都冠以"社会主义"一词的国家来说，美国的整个政治谱系均过于"右倾"，与之格格不入。此外，南美对发达国家的任何独裁态度以及任何与门罗主义相似的思维尤其敏感。这与南非的情形有些许相似，共产党作为统治联盟的组成部分，而亲西方政治精英则被控资助和煽动种族隔离制度。同时，在俄罗斯和印度，反西方的情绪不仅表现为地缘政治形式，同样表现出以价值观为基础的含义。在刚刚经历了宗教复兴的国家，人们主要反对的并非是西方的政策，而是其宣扬的道德价值。西方社会的政治体系尽管存在差异，但并未引起特别的反对。更加世俗的中国可能在道德观上更加接近于西方，但其政治体系与西方的标准格格不入。并非这些差异，而是现实中差异确实存在但强烈的抵制西方专制态度的愿望促成了合作的基础。

对于金砖国家而言，重要的是，最近发达国家将该集团内的一名成员推到了对立面。这强化了金砖五国的团结，它作为一个整体已经表达了对二十国集团个别西方成员国禁止俄罗斯参加 2014 年 11 月于布里斯班召开

---

[1] 俄罗斯新闻社对俄罗斯外交部特使 V. B. 卢卡夫（V. B. Lukova）的访谈，2014 年 4 月 14 日，http://www.mid.ru/brp_4.nsf/newsline/33A1D346558B4C3944257CBD0032BFDD。

的峰会的联合抗议。2014年3月,金砖五国外交部长宣布"二十国集团的管理由全体成员国共同承担,任何一国不得单方面决定拒绝另一成员国参加峰会"①。这种联合的姿态显示了金砖五国作为二十国集团中非西方世界代表的地位,金砖五国始终如一地提出各种倡议,作为发达国家方案的替代选择。这一策略的成功表现为西方国家在二十国集团中的地位正在弱化。

西方国家停止八国集团活动,以此作为对俄罗斯的制裁,这一决定进一步体现了二十国集团内的两级对抗。此前,俄罗斯作为八国集团和二十国集团的成员,可以在一定程度上缓和这种两极分化,但现在二十国集团内将存在两个尖锐对立的集团:既纯西方的七国集团和代表世界其他国家的金砖五国。

这样,乌克兰危机只会使金砖五国更加团结。显然,金砖国家正在沿着正确的道路前进,应加强努力,协调行动,为西方社会加强单极世界格局的努力提供真正意义的替代选择。金砖五国将为建立真正的多极世界格局付出长期的努力。

就其本身而言,俄罗斯更有兴趣参加金砖国家框架内的合作。这不仅是因为莫斯科正在为与西方的对立寻求支持,而是还有更深的原因,即与西方之间的相互信任已经彻底瓦解。西方的制裁和利用经济杠杆施加政治压力的企图,以及俄罗斯所做出的回应均促使俄罗斯转向非西方世界。这一趋势在当前的危机开始前既已现端倪。考虑到这些制裁在可预见的未来不太可能撤销,亚洲和南美国家将逐渐取代欧洲作为许多商品,尤其是食品和农产品的对俄出口国。俄罗斯的油气出口正在逐渐转向中国也亚太地区。俄罗斯的政治精英开始认识到,没有与亚洲邻国的合作,则不能实现其西伯利亚和远东地区的战略发展目标。总体而言,欧洲和美国开始被视为不切实际的合作伙伴,其随时可能为了施加政治压力而牺牲经济合作关系。因此,不仅意识形态,而且客观情况和经济利益均迫使俄罗斯将其注意力转向其他区域。此外,与这些地区的政治经济领袖之间,如金砖国家成员,建立更深层次的合作将成为俄罗斯对外政策的焦点。

---

① 2014年3月24日在荷兰海牙举行的金砖五国外交部长/国际关系部长会议上的媒体声明,http://www.brics.mid.ru/brics.nsf/WEBmitBric/63AFCD6DA75BDFA544257CA70052CA90。

针对国际金融和货币体系改革形成金砖五国的共同立场

[俄] 米哈伊尔·戈洛夫宁*

2007—2009 年的全球经济和金融危机是全球化时代的第一个全球性冲击，同时也证明有必要对金融业进行改革，因为正是金融业导致了这场危机蔓延至整个国家和整个世界的整体经济。在金融业参与者激励的所有系统性缺陷中，应指出的是过于宽松的监管、金融业的规模相对过大、新金融产品的开发和地区间的套利。金融危机通过国际溢出效应大肆传播，因此，也有必要对整个国际金融系统进行改革。

所有的金砖国家，同时也是新兴国家和发展中国家集团的一部分，均在 2007—2008 年受到了全球金融危机的冲击，而这也是他们寻求将未来的类似冲击最小化的原因所在。金砖国家可以在三个层面上参与国际金融改革：（1）通过自身国家层面的政策；（2）通过在全球论坛上（例如二十国集团）阐述共同立场；（3）通过在金融业采取联合行动。

金砖国家在全球经济中的作用已显著上升，特别是在过去的十年。按目前的美元汇率计算，他们在全球国内生产总值中所占的份额显著增加，从 2005 年的 10.9% 上升至 2013 年的 22.9%。但除了中国和南非的某些情况外，这些国家金融业的发展均低于全球水平。例如，2013 年金砖国家国内银行对私营部门的信贷占 GDP 的比例各不相同，印度和俄罗斯为 51%—52%，巴西和南非为 70%—71%，中国为 140%，而世界平均水平为 89.6%。[①] 国内现货市场成交金额占 GDP 的百分比也各不相同，俄罗斯、印度和巴西的比例位于 33%—37%，中国为 71%，南非为 81%，而世界平均水平为 70%。[②]

---

* 米哈伊尔·戈洛夫宁（Mikhail Golovnin），俄罗斯科学院经济研究所副所长，俄罗斯经济全球化问题研究中心主任。

① http://data.worldbank.org/indicator/FD.AST.PRVT.GD.ZS/。
② http://data.worldbank.org/indicator/CM.MKT.TRAD.GD.ZS。

金砖国家的 GDP 地位与它们的货币对全球外汇市场的作用之间的差距更为明显。虽然金砖国家在全球外汇储备中的作用（主要是中国的原因）非常显著，但在 2013 年，所有金砖国家的货币在全球外汇市场交易额中所占比例之和仅为 7%（某一交易涉及两种货币的以 200% 计算）。① 2014 年年中，金砖国家持有的外汇储备占全球总量的 43%。② 因此，国际货币体系的目前状态取决于各个金砖国家的货币和财政政策，即汇率制度和各种准备金积累。

通过以上数字，我们可以知道，金砖国家在国内采取的行动对全球范的影响可能非常有限。这些行动通常涉及国际金融改革议程的实施措施，虽然中国的"人民币国际化"等特殊举措也应该加以注意，但这些措施主要包括准备实施《巴塞尔协议Ⅲ》、解决金融机构的重要系统性问题、加强对"影子"银行系统的监管、监管场外衍生品市场等。

从我们的角度来看，在国际金融体系改革议程方面形成共同立场更为重要。在这一改革过程中，金砖国家可能代表的不仅仅是各国自身的立场，也是新兴市场和发展中经济体中更普遍的看法。

首先，应该确定改革的范围。对我们来说，错误的诊断可能意味着错误的治疗和持续不断的疾病。正如我们在前面所提到的，最近的全球经济和金融危机的深层次问题在于金融业。这些问题与目前的国际金融体系改革方向高度一致，但仍然有一些重要的问题还没有得到完全解决。从发达国家的角度来看，这是为无限发展的金融活动建立奖励机制的问题。从新兴市场和发展中经济体的角度来看，最重要的问题之一就是源自发达国家的各种冲击（主要是金融冲击）的传播，而这与国际资本流动的监管问题有关。

其次，要想取得整个配套改革的成功，"对改革者进行改革"非常重要。这意味着有必要对国际金融体系进行改革。其中最敏感的一个问题就是新兴市场和发展中经济体在国际金融机构的决策过程中代表性不足的问题。因此，金砖国家的注意力应集中在提高这些国家在国际货币基金组织和世界银行中的地位上，包括完成第 14 次国际货币基金组织份额审查和启动下一轮复审。这一目标的实现有点复杂，因为改革不仅需要体现金砖国家的国家利益，还需要体现新兴国家和发展中国家的整体利益。

第三，目前的国际金融改革框架并没有考虑到新兴国家和发展中国家

---

① "Global Foreign Exchange Market Turnover in 2013", *Triennial Central Bank Survey*, Bank for International Settlements, Monetary and Economic Department, February 2014.

② 所依据的计算，参见 http://elibrary-data.imf.org/。

的具体情况，例如，一方面，这些国家的金融市场发展不充分，另一方面，某些领域存在着金融泡沫上升的风险（通常与外资参与程度高有关）。这也是国际金融改革方案应考虑到新兴市场和发展中市场具体特点的原因所在。金砖国家可以作为改革方案框架重新设计的推动力量。因此，当新兴市场和发展中国家在国家利益与国际金融改革中的路径一致时，金砖国家应该把重点放在协助制定和推进改革议程上。

第四，金砖国家应考虑到改革的成本和收益，避免推动成本过高的改革。其中最突出的一个例子就是主张改变国际货币体系的现状。虽然这一体系不可避免地受到国际货币体系缺陷的影响，但这些缺陷并没有造成全球性的动荡。如果美元在全球经济中的地位出现急剧变化，可能会导致新的严重动荡，而这也不是新兴国家和发展中国家的兴趣所在。当然这也并不是说国际货币体系的目前状态应该保持不变，而是说需要以渐进的方式推动改变。其中一个可能的改变就是可以扩大金砖国家货币的使用范围，还有就是上文已经提到的对投机性国际资本流动的监管。例如，金砖国家的专家和官员可以讨论在全球范围内推出一种托宾税的问题。

在国际金融和货币改革的这些方向中，金砖国家可以作为全球经济体的重要参与者制定这些改革的各种措施。金砖国家已经提出了两个重要的措施，目前正处在实施阶段：建立新的开发银行和外汇储备池。新的开发银行可以缩小新兴国家和发展中国家的开发性金融需求和它们对少数发达国家政府债券的官方外汇资产投资之间的差距。外汇储备池的目的在于稳定金砖国家的汇率，因为汇率波动给新兴经济体造成的危害比发达国家高。接下来就是采取措施，促进金砖国家货币在各国间的经济交往中的使用和在国际金融市场上发行以金砖国家货币计价的新证券。

全球治理中的金砖国家务实合作

［印度］哈里哈拉·维斯瓦纳坦[*]

在当今全球化的世界中，各国之间的相互依存关系日益紧密和复杂，全球治理，或者全球治理不足，成为人类面临的一个严峻挑战。跨国问题严重影响着数十亿人的生活，与此相关的讨论包括贸易自由化或投资，流行病或贩毒，气候变化或环境，人权或保护责任。

随着商品、资本、病菌和环境影响的高速传输，世界开始变为一个无国界的领域，全球治理不足已然成为全球化所面临的一个最艰巨的挑战。

在这一背景下，金砖国家的出现可谓意义非凡。金砖国家完美地解决了全球治理这一问题。然而，也因此引发了各种问题。金砖国家有什么企图？金砖国家能否引发深远的变革？金砖国家能否向希望维持现状的国家证明变革有利于所有人？金砖国家和其他新兴大国在全球治理这一问题上能否达成共识？

尽管"全球治理"是一个比较新的概念，但就历史而言，这一概念已经出现很长时间了。无论两个或多个实体（我们称它们为社会、部落或群体）是否定期进行交流，我们必须制定一些基本规则。不一定要有一个执行机构，但所有人必须明白这些规则有利于所有人。我们今天所谈的全球治理就是从这一基本概念出发的。当然，几个世纪以来，情况已经发生了变化。17世纪威斯特伐利亚州的创立使不同实体之间的关系变得异常僵硬，以致他们不得不相互对抗。由于每个人都在为个人利益而抗争，这就促成了一些常见的基本规则，每个人都认可这些规则有利于所有人，或者更准确地说，只有重要的竞争者才这样认为。这些规则主要适用于贸易、航运和卫生等领域。据说，1885年柏林会议（导致非洲大陆被分割为许多殖民地）正是由于刚果河两岸敌对力量之间的冲突日益加剧而促成的。从历史角度来说，全球规则是强权国家出于自身利益而制定的，这是一个不

---

[*] 哈里哈拉·维斯瓦纳坦（H. H. S. Viswanathan），印度观察员研究基金会杰出研究员。

言而喻的真理。

第二次世界大战之后，全球治理规则主要由胜利者制定。即使20世纪下半叶，亚洲和非洲出现了许多独立国家，但他们对全球治理这一问题做出的贡献微乎其微。显然，不管是从政治上还是从经济上来讲，他们都没有强大到足以影响或改变全球治理规则的固定模式。

一、全球化如何改变基本事实

之后又发生了什么变化呢？"全球化"这一神奇的词汇出现了。全球化这一过程成功地将各个国家以一种过去根本无法想象的方式联系了起来。美国学者詹姆斯·罗西瑙（James Rosenau）将其称为"一种疯狂拼布式的现代相互依存关系"。全球化通过商品、资本、技术、疾病、犯罪、毒品和环境灾害的高速传输创造了一个几乎无国界的世界。如今，任何国家都不能说全球化对他们没有任何影响。正因为全球治理意义重大，因此全球治理不足已然成为人类所面临的最重要的挑战。

全球化的另一个重大成果是新兴经济体的出现。许多人认为，经济支点已从发达国家转向发展中国家。这是一个引人注目的转变，因为新兴经济体成功地利用发达国家制定的规则加入到全球化这一竞技场中，而且还取得了巨大的成功。然而，他们是否已经在全球治理方面获得了相应的影响力呢？答案是否定的。有些人甚至认为"新兴大国"这一术语并不能充分反映他们的地缘政治意义。

在20世纪90年代初，许多经济学家预测，随着全球经济一体化的成功，地缘经济将取代世界上的地缘政治。然而，随后的事态发展表明，这种情况并未发生。地缘政治仍然保持着强劲的发展势头，"二战"后的体系结构并未发生改变。

二、全球治理究竟是什么？

让我们试着去了解一下全球治理的真正内涵。关于全球治理，人们已经给出了许多定义，但没有一个能如实反映其真正内涵。詹姆斯·罗西瑙将全球治理定义为"各种人类活动的规则体系，包括家庭和国际组织"。这个定义几乎包括了所有规则。应当注意的是，在这种定义中，我们不能将治理与政府混为一谈。准确地讲，是因为如果没有全球政府，就没有必要进行全球治理。从某些方面来讲，这与威斯特伐利亚州的情况相反。在那里，政府机构并不是先于全球治理而形成的，而是完全与之相反，治理理念是先于政府机构而形成的。另一种定义是"在无主权权力的情况下，对超越国界的关系的一种管理"。此外，还有这样一种最简单、最实用的定义："通过自愿性国际合作来管理跨国问题"。这是一种无正式政府的管理问题，而且这种合作是自愿的。

谈到全球治理，就必须要明确三个具体方面：价值观、准则和规则。公平和公正的全球治理应重视这三个方面的发展顺序，并应至少让绝大多数国家达成共识。只有这样，才能实现有效和公正的全球治理，也就是治理的第四个方面——实施。

全球治理中的许多问题都是由于缺乏对这三方面的重视而造成的，即价值观、准则和规则，或由这三方面而引发的问题。我们只能通过与人权、防扩散、保护责任或国际刑事法院有关的争议来理解全球治理中这三个阶段的正确顺序的重要性。

历史还表明，全球治理总是滞后于技术、贸易、旅游、流行病和环境问题的发展。各国只有在遇到危机时，才会清醒地认识到这些问题。因此，全球治理应被视为一种需要持续监控和改进的动态概念。

另一个在当今时代比较流行的术语是"全球公域"，这个术语与全球治理有关。通常包括全球资产，如海洋、大气层和外层空间。虽然这并不是一个新概念。早在17世纪，荷兰法学家胡果·格劳秀斯（Hugo Grotius）就曾提出海洋是国际空间这一说法。在当今背景下，这一术语还应包括网络空间。随着各大经济体之间的相互依存关系越来越密切，全球公域的公平管理已经成为一个绝对必要的问题。

此外，还需注意的是，在当今世界，全球治理不仅与主权国家政府有关。一些重要的非国家力量也为全球治理做出了突出贡献。其中，有三个重要的非国家力量：企业部门、民间社会和非政府组织。如果没有这些利益相关者，当下任何有关全球治理的新举措都不可能取得成功。

三、全球规范如何更具吸引力呢？

我们可以从全球治理历史中汲取什么经验教训呢？在这方面取得成功的案例有很多，如电报通信协调、海事约定以及诸如携带或预防传染病等的健康问题。全球所有移动通信系统运营商通过协商将"112"确定为紧急呼叫号码，这就是私营部门之间实现全球协调的一个最佳案例。SWIFT（环球银行金融电信协会）和IBAN（国际银行账户号码）则是金融领域的成功案例。政府方面取得的最显著成就是国际警察组织，它每年能为其成员国逮捕5000多名罪犯和逃亡的违法之人。

上述例子表明，如果对这个问题的论述并不限于主观道德原则，那么就可以成功实现全球治理,但应鼓励所有国家相互合作,这才是更为实际的做法。只有当所有利益相关者均认为新举措对他们有益时,这些新举措才更可能获得成功。在这种方法中,金砖国家可以作为一个有效的对话者。它可以通过有关全球治理的谈话和辩论,使全球规范变得更具吸引力。

四、全球机构的问题

全球治理的一个核心方面是规则监督执行机构的问题。这已成为当今世界最关键的一个争议性问题,原因不言自明。全球性机构支持殖民国家和第二次世界大战的胜利者,这种偏爱似乎已经根深蒂固。自然而然,胜利者在制定和实施规则时考虑的都是自身利益,很少顾及对他人的不良影响。只要全球形势保持不变,这种模式就能行得通。然而,冷战的结束和全球化时代的到来暴露了全球治理的缺陷,是时候重新审视跨国问题了。

谈到全球性机构,不得不提及这三个落伍的机构:国际货币基金组织、世界银行和联合国安理会。国际货币基金组织和世界银行的配额分配和表决权与当今世界上现有的经济实力分配没有任何关系。再加上,根据不成文的规定,国际货币基金组织将始终以欧洲为首,而世界银行则以美国为首。这种规则早已落后于时代的发展,我们怎能指望这些机构能够有效运行,并能处理复杂问题呢?如今,在所有重要的国际机构中,二十国集团似乎是唯一一个能正确地反映出全球现实的机构——这 20 个国家占全球 GDP 的 85%。

在这方面,金砖国家的举措相当有效。正是迫于金砖国家和其他新兴经济体的压力,二十国集团才会在 2010 年峰会上决定重新分配布雷顿森林机构的表决权。这只是一个良好的开端,但美国国会却阻止了其进一步发展。金砖国家仍需继续为之抗争。

金砖国家取得的另一个主要成就是成立了新发展银行(NDB),并达成了应急储备安排(CRA)。这些新成立的机构并不会取代世界银行和国际货币基金组织的地位,但肯定会使这些机构意识到应该进行彻底的改革。有人甚至评论说,如果这些机构能够随着时代的变迁而改变,新发展银行和应急储备安排也就无用武之地了。

还有一个落伍的机构:联合国安理会。为保证有效运行,它必须能体现出当前的全球现实,而事实并非如此。大多数人都认为联合国安理会有必要进行扩张,但在过去的 20 年间,这一想法并未付诸任何实施。作为南半球的代表,金砖国家有责任去实现这一目标。金砖国家的批判者认为,未就这一问题达成共识是金砖集团的一个弱点。如果这五个国家能就这一问题达成共识，那么这一集团的声誉将大大提高。

多边主义是全球治理的基石，而这五个国家则是这种方式的坚定拥护者。他们希望看到这个世界围绕着积极的多边主义而运作。他们也反对在国际关系中使用武力或以武力相威胁。

在全球治理这一问题上，金砖国家的着眼点并不是评论中屡次提及的"贵宾席"。新兴大国应成为国际决策机构的成员，这并不是一个目的。"占领贵宾席"这一屡次被提及的问题，在某种程度上来说，反而使这一问题变得繁琐了。重要的是在贵宾席上争论的问题和做出的决策，而不是谁坐在贵宾席上。当受邀参加会议时，金砖国家非常清楚他们应该保持怎样的立场。

一些批评人士认为，新兴国家希望在全球治理中拥有更大的发言权仅仅是因为这些国家的精英希望得到一定程度的认可。这简直是无稽之谈。在当今全球化的世界中，有关国际组织在全球性问题上做出的决定足以影响数以百万计人的生活和发展。看看人们就这些话题进行讨论的激烈程度，如气候变化、多哈回合贸易自由化、粮食安全、水资源问题、保护责任和人权问题，再来看看价值观、规范和规则，新兴国家和发展中国家从一开始就对这些概念的提出有着切身利害关系。

金砖国家也明确表示，他们所希望的全球治理改革是一种包容性和非对抗性的改革。不幸的是，当金砖国家谈起全球治理改革时，就会被看作是对西方的攻击。整个问题就变成了"西方国家与其他国家的对决"。然而，如今的现实是，西方国家需要其他国家的支持。即使人们承认第二次世界大战之后建立的国际秩序有那个时代的一些逻辑，如今的世界已经发生了翻天覆地的变化，这是显而易见的。无论怎么调整落伍的体系也是于事无补；所有利益相关者均有责任提出一些有创意的想法。如果2008年的全球金融危机再爆发一次，那么就会鼓动二十国集团采取措施，将金砖国家和其他新兴大国纳入决策过程中，以实现一些有益的成果。在开始进行改革之前，这个世界是应该坐等类似的危机在其他领域爆发，还是应该联合所有国家对现有结构和方法进行审查呢？

五、金砖国家的选择

关于全球治理的现行规范，金砖国家有以下四种选择：

（1）顺从，即适应现有体系。除了某些特定的领域外，这种方法几乎是行不通的。

（2）改革。金砖国家可以尝试修改现行规范和制度，但不做出彻底的改变。

（3）忽视。如果金砖国家认为某些领域的制度体系完全不公平，他们可以忽略它，只要不违反公认的国际法原则。

（4）重新创建。金砖国家可以创建新的规范和制度。比如新发展银行和应急储备安排。以后可能会采取更多举措。值得注意的是，即使新发展银行和应急储备安排是两个经济机构，但是这里隐含着一个更有意义的政治信息：这是300年以来第一个没有发达西方国家参与的全球性机构。

按常理来讲，金砖国家可以视具体问题和情况来考虑选择上述任意一种方法。然而，正如前面所提到的，这种方法不能有违共同发展这一目标。金砖国家将不惜一切代价提出一种能引起绝大多数国家共鸣的举措，特别是发展中国家。

六、金砖国家应探索的新领域

随着金砖国家在全球治理中的作用变得越来越重要，金砖国家应进一步去探索新的领域。网络安全是当今世界面临的一个严重问题。到目前为止，还没有提出一种有效的全球机制来解决这一问题。金砖国家似乎对这个问题抱有类似的看法，因此可以通过合作提出金砖国家的建议。另外两个可以引发兴趣的领域是标准化和基准。这两个问题都属于非政府组织的全球治理领域。随着这五个国家经济和技术的发展，金砖国家是时候开始在这些领域崭露头角了。例如，印度，中国和巴西是三大药品生产国，他们必须制定自己的标准，这才符合公平之道。同样，金砖国家必须就其他各种活动制定自己的基准。在适当的时候，我们也可以成立金砖国家信用评级机构。

总而言之，在当今世界中，全球治理影响着数十亿人的生活。因此，它必须将所有人纳入其中。有效的治理必须是一种公平、公正的管理模式。既然以前的体系不符合这种原则，那么就要对其进行审查和改革。金砖国家等新兴大国将会针对此问题提出新奇并富有创意的想法。他们就是从发展中走过来的，了解全球化的优势，而且还实现了令人瞩目的成就。他们所面对的许多问题极其类似于其他发展中国家。因此，他们能够以正确的观点来看待这一问题，而且还能在全球治理中承担起更多的责任。

除了在各种领域展开内部合作以外，全球治理的改革工作一直是金砖国家从成立之初就极其重视的目标之一。新发展银行和应急储备安排的成立就足以体现这一点。然而，金砖国家还有更多的工作要做。这就是为什么金砖国家智库理事会（BTTC）将"全球政治和经济治理"确定为"金砖国家长期发展战略"中的五大支柱之一。这一文件为金砖国家政府的行动方案提供了一个路线图。

金砖国家在全球能源治理中的合作

[印度] 阿努纳巴·戈什*

一、引言

资源安全对于金砖国家和全球经济都非常重要。这一点表现在新的矿产资源消费国的不断涌现（南—南资源贸易的规模目前已超过南—北贸易），大规模矿业生产在一些经济体内日趋集中，与三十年前相比，价格波动大幅度提高，金砖国家投向资源丰富经济体的对外投资迅速增加，以及与矿产贸易有关的国际争端不断增多的趋势。在这一背景下，环境对于资源勘探、生产和消费的制约也促使人们大幅度提高资源使用的效率。

全球能源市场的特点也因技术进步、环境压力、日益增长的需求、定价策略、冲突及供给冲击而不断发生变化。2013年年底，美国国内的原油产量自1995年以来首次每天超过进量200万桶。同时，中国已经成为世界第一大石油进口国。这些发展对于全球安全有着深远的含义，因为它们引发了关于海上航线保护的问题、对石油储量丰富但政治上脆弱国家的干涉问题，以及市场作用与资源民族主义的关系的问题。

金砖国家面临的重要任务是保持经济的高速增长。它们目前已经占有全球石油需求的24%和全球天然气市场的20%。到2030年，它们的石油需求预计将至少升至全球需求的29%，天然气需求升至26%。截至2040年，它们预计将占全球能源使用增量中的一半。像中国和印度这样的能源进口国对能源安全深为关切（截至2035年，两国92%和84%的石油需求将依赖进口）。

对能源的渴求并不仅限于金砖国家。它们在确保资源安全战略方面是否成功部分取决于大宗商品市场的运作方式以及其他资源需求大国是否愿

---

* 阿努纳巴·戈什（Arunabha Ghosh），印度水资源、能源与环境理事会首席执行官。

意互相合作而不是采取资源民族主义的策略。全球能源和粮食价格近几年变得越来越不稳定，已经升至 20 世纪 70 年代初以来的最高水平。石油价格只是在近几个星期才显著下降，但地缘政治紧张在世界各地仍普遍存在，意味着随着全球经济增长的加速，能源需求也将增加，石油价格还可能再次上涨。另外，随着华北平原和印度西北部土地含水层的过度开发，水资源的紧张和稀缺对工业、农业和发电业正构成日益严重的威胁。气候变化仍然是最复杂和最棘手的全球性挑战。许多金砖国家与它们的邻国共同承受着气候和水资源方面的风险。

能源、粮食、水和气候之间的关系将使政策选择变得更加复杂而有限。需要有效的国内政策，而且国际性驱动因素——大宗商品市场正在发生的变化、关于水资源的争端，或极端气候事件——将决定新兴大国采取怎样的应对措施。金砖国家应怎样互相合作，塑造全球的能源治理格局，以便不仅满足各自的能源需求，也提升全球能源市场的信心？

二、能源治理中的三种紧张关系

能源进口国希望有可预测的和不间断的供应，而出口国则希望有稳定的需求。但除此之外还有其他一些问题，如经济竞争力问题以及是否能获得技术和原料，同时还要保证环境的可持续性。这一系列问题加上复杂的制度和法规环境，至少显示出三方面的紧张关系。

首先是**多极机构和现有机构**之间的紧张关系。随着能源需求的转移，一个日益多极的世界将不得不寻找一个合适的论坛以便在能源贸易和投资政策上进行合作和协调。在能源领域，多极化并不会自动导致多边治理安排的实现。例如世界贸易组织只是多种选择中的一个。地区性机构为合作提供了其他合理的选择：靠近能源的产地和需求地（《北美自由贸易协定》，NAFTA）；聚焦综合的解决方式，包括保障供给，保护投资，为能源输送提供便利（《能源宪章条约》，ECT）；更广泛的地区利益，如 "东南亚国家联盟"（ASEAN）和 "西非国家经济共同体"（ECOWAS）。

此外，能源供应国中存在的小型国家集团间也有多边协议，即 "石油输出国组织"（OPEC）。亚太地区的能源消费大国组成了 "亚太经济合作组织（APEC）能源工作组"。人们呼吁建立一个能源稳定委员会，把主要供应国和主要消费国聚集在一起，在紧急行动上协调一致，替新兴经济体发声。尽管小型国家集团在决策效率上有优势，但它们需要吸收新的成员以提高自己的权威性。尤其是如果现有的地区性或多边性机构不包括新兴能源大国，其有效性将会削弱。另外，各国选择哪些论坛解决矛盾和争端也并不明确。

第二方面的紧张关系存在于**市场和国家**之间。自20世纪70年代石油危机以来，能源市场的性质已经发生了变化。原油的可替代性已经增加。目前有大约50%的原油（约每天4000万桶）在公开交易。石油现在既是实物商品，也是金融资产。液化天然气的增长填补了天然气现货市场发展的空白。如此大规模的交易在提高了能源市场效率的同时，也使能源市场面临更大的波动性风险。能源安全已成为各国政府的最关心的问题。能源市场的分散化加上新兴经济体不断增长的需求迫使各国思考是依赖市场来保证能源供应安全，还是通过国家机构掌握更大的控制权。

第三方面的紧张关系存在于**能源和环境**之间。全球来讲，还有大约16亿人口用不上电。甚至在中国和印度，还有一半以上的人口仍然依赖传统的生物质能源来做饭。今天的富裕国家要为气候危机承担责任（2010年，平均每个美国人排放的二氧化碳比印度人平均排放量多十倍）。但在非经合组织国家中，从现在到2030年，金砖国家几乎将对所有增加的与能源有关的二氧化碳排放量负责。因此，一方面，这些经济体必须在保证能源供应这一首要关切与气候变化之间寻求平衡，另一方面要思考贸易规则怎样才能对富裕国家和新兴经济体对能源的补贴进行管理。

三、全球能源质量的必要性

一个在能源供给、能源需求和新兴经济体方面多极化的世界对于不同国际组织间的协调有着直接的影响。现有的能源治理安排不能充分反映日益多极化的现状。在能源领域和新兴经济体，现有的大国之间并没有多少合作的迹象。中国和印度都应邀参加了国际能源局2007年举办的"委员会周"的活动，但至今仍然保持着观察员的身份。

国际能源局仍然只是经合组织下属的一个机构，一个发达国家的俱乐部，使新兴经济体难以成为其正式的成员。同时，能源需求、气候变化和贸易壁垒等相互交织的问题在不同的论坛上，如国际能源局、联合国气候变化框架公约（UNFCCC），或在世界贸易组织进行讨论，形成了一个学者们所称的"复杂且部分重合，但层次上杂乱无序的管理体系"。如果这些矛盾持续得不到解决，那么新兴经济体将寻找新的平台来保证能源供给的安全。

对于保证可预见的能源供应的关注至少可以追溯到20世纪上半叶。现在，尽管许多人都在谈能源独立，但世界主要经济体还是处在一个复杂的、试图对它们进行控制的能源流动和能源体系当中。因此产生的多极化意味着现有的能源贸易安排和投资需求并不一定适应新兴大国的要求。同时，全球石油和天然气市场已经变得越来越分散化，意味着谁也难以完全控制能源的流动。然而，有一部分最大的能源公司是国有公司，这使人们对市场和政府的相对影响感到担心。

从单独国家的角度来看，任何能源"管理"的概念，都可能意味着对保证能源供应安全性的操作方面自由的限制。从能源贸易系统的角度来看，一个不受约束的能源市场可能会衍生出严重的问题。能源安全，换句话说，已经越来越不是一个国家能单独追求的概念，而是主权国家、私营企业、金融市场以及地区性和全球性机构互动才能实现的功能。如果这种互动进行良好，那么对能源的需求、环境可持续性的需求和保持自由贸易与投资的需求这些互相交织的需求就有可能协调起来。否则，则可能动摇国家间的双边关系，甚至带来地缘政治方面的后果。

四、金砖国家在能源治理上应如何进行合作？

上述分析表明，对金砖国家来说，当前最需要立即着手应对的首要的全球治理问题之一就与能源有关。新兴大国，尤其是金砖国家必须认识到自己越来越提高的"规则制定者"的身份，而不仅仅是"规则接受者"，这使它们有机会为维护资源安全设计强有力的国际机制。以下是几点建议：

1. 联合投标以压低采购成本。一系列能源和矿产资源需求对进口的依赖难以避免。金砖国家，尤其是中国和印度，会继续在资源上展开竞争。尽管如此，两国仍时有合作（例如在苏丹、叙利亚或缅甸问题上），而且声称在石油勘探、生产、炼制、营销、研发、保护和贸易方面进行合作，并在第三国投标时联手合作。金砖国家如果在资源竞争的同时探索合作的途径，那么将能共同获益。首先，通过集中资金和技术资源，大型国有石油和天然气企业能形成规模巨大的集团，以解决能源安全问题。其次，这种伙伴关系可以缓解对能源供应商和需求方相互间争斗而导致价格上涨的担忧。

2. 发展最佳的能源供应基础设施。海上安全和能源安全交织的地方往往是潜在的摩擦的重要根源。世界贸易中的大部分（包括能源）依赖海上航线。当务之急是建设能满足长期资源进口和运输需求的基础设施。金砖国家须共同努力，同时也与亚洲地区其他能源需求不断增长的国家联手，在能源供应基础设施方面采取合作行动。例如，印度石油天然气公司的海外勘探子公司（ONGC Videsh）在从缅甸通往中国西南部的天然气管道中持有股份。中国和印度于 2013 年 8 月在中亚举行的首次对话中讨论了实施土库曼斯坦—阿富汗—巴基斯坦—印度（TAPI）管道中将会遇到的挑战。在第三国的投资可以帮助两国的企业获得合作的经验，逐步建立互信。中印两国还可以设想建设一个可供分享和开发俄罗斯、中亚和西亚地区资源的管道网络。

3. 探索石油和天然气的互换安排。另一个想法是通过互换安排利用对方的石油和天然气的权益股份。一些评论家认为印度可以将在俄罗斯萨哈林岛气田生产的天然气供中国使用，以交换中国来自中东的能源供应，这样双方都可以降低能源运输成本。我们面临的挑战是这方面的公开信息很少，包括在印度监管机构工作的专家对于两国之间是否有这种交换的意图或是否已成功进行交换都知之甚少。

4. 促进分散式能源商业模式。有人强烈主张通过混合不同的可再生能源和智能微型电网推动分散式能源基础设施。这将有助于减轻主电网的负荷，向那些没有基本现代能源供应的人群提供能源解决方案，并为可再生能源的生产利用创造机会（例如用于小型农业经营和偏远地区的电信设施、学校和医院等）。此外，分散式能源供应，如果有强大的研发支持（这在其他主要经济体中很普遍），可以降低关键基础设施在电网遭到任何形式的攻击后发生瘫痪的风险。

印度已有至少 250 家企业提供分散式能源服务，每家都尝试不同的商业模式：销售灯笼等产品，安装家用系统（太阳能电池板、沼气池），或开发微型电网。同时，中国也有一些世界上最大规模的清洁炉灶计划。和巴西和南非的创新者和企业家一起，来自中国和印度的分散式能源企业可以为南非、东南亚、非洲和南美地区开发分散发电商业模式。

5. 为能源方面的协调行动创建一个对话论坛。金砖国家应推动建立一个跨地区对话论坛，针对在能源方面的协调行动展开对话。论坛的首要任务应该是通过对石油和天然气的采购、长期合同和现货市场价格信息的定期发布提高能源市场的透明度。其次，论坛应创造条件，就怎样利用各成员国的战略储备提升对能源市场的信心，缓解短期供给的冲击展开讨论。第三，通过提供一个开放的成员平台，论坛可以吸引其他二线的，但发展迅速的能源需求国的参加，就减少能源供应的额外费用集体施压。第四，可以就能源供应重点线路的保护进行讨论（经由陆地和海上的线路）。第五，在更加制度化的形式下，可以对与能源有关的争端进行仲裁并保护海外投资。

如果金砖国家能在资产收购、能源基础设施投资、互换安排、促进可再生能源（包括分散式能源）和发展讨论能源治理的开放型论坛方面联手合作，那么将能极大地缓解人们对资源民族主义的忧虑。这也将向能源市场发出信号，主要新兴经济体将更有兴趣通过市场机制行事，而非主要依靠对海外能源领域进行股权投资。同时，也将强调全球能源秩序应变得更具包容性，以满足新兴经济体的需求。

金砖国家国际金融危机及治理的挑战

[印度] 班迪·普拉萨德*

作为个体,金砖国家中一些国家的经济增长可能正在经历波动,但作为群体,这些国家正在快速发展,并不断扩大其对全球经济和金融、地区和世界经济政策,以及多边倡议的影响。在21世纪头10年发生的两大全球经济和金融危机中,金砖国家也毫不例外地受到影响,但通过积极行动及采取措施,这些国家得以快速发展,并将在应对全球发展和治理问题中处于令人瞩目的位置。

本文讨论了2008年国际金融危机发生以来,金砖国家经济和金融市场发展的趋势,以及这些国家如何应对一些依旧困扰全世界的问题和不确定因素。本文还讨论了金砖国家所采取的、可能会导致他们在不断变化的政策框架以及全球治理更高标准中发挥更大作用的倡议和措施。

随着2008年国际金融危机的发生,金砖国家出现了以下一些重要趋势:

(1) 经济增长不平衡、不稳定。尽管金砖国家的经济在危机过后立即复苏,但少数国家仍然担心经济增长问题。中国展示了最快的增长速度,印度经济仍在复苏。

(2) 金融市场增长强劲。除中国和俄罗斯以外,股市指数在其他国家涨幅明显。外国投资者对金砖国家依旧很感兴趣。

(3) 金砖国家建立了具有多种现货和衍生产品市场工具的多资产类别市场,在市场深度上已见强劲增长。金砖国家的金融体系包括银行,也包括股票、商品、货币等细分市场的交易,以及全球排行榜中的债券交易。

(4) 全球金融市场发展带来的冲击并未彻底消失。2013年5月美联储削减量化宽松规模公告仍旧给巴西、印度、南非等国家带来了负面影响。

(5) 金砖国家在全球经济政策、治理标准以及金融稳定方面一直在发

* 班迪·普拉萨德(Bandi Ram Prasad),印度市场成长咨询公司创始人和首席执行官。

挥更大、更重要的作用。

（6）新开发银行（金砖国家开发银行）将为金砖国家在制定金融政策和策略过程中发挥更大、更重要作用带来新的前景。

（7）金砖国家不断增长的货币国际化程度将进一步巩固其在世界经济和金融市场的地位。

（8）公司治理框架得到显著改善，虽然公司业绩中还存在着一些小问题。

（9）金砖国家与其他发展中国家在贸易、经济关系、发展融资等方面的参与程度显著增加。

（10）金砖国家应在内部，以及与其他发展中国家和发达国家逐步建立广泛的合作框架，在更广泛的领域内，保持经济和金融市场发展的步伐，并继续参与全球经济和治理。

一、国际金融危机和金砖国家

2001年，以重要投资机会出现的"金砖国家"概念，保持并进一步强化了其十年后的增长和发展势头。作为五个国家的集合体，金砖国家在全球经济和金融活动及治理中发挥了更大作用，承担了更多责任。

2008年的全球经济和金融危机是十年内发生的第二次经济危机，在21世纪的前几年，发达国家特别是美国出现了由于互联网泡沫以及企业活动和绩效不足等导致的严重经济衰退。2003年下半年，经济开始强劲复苏并持续五年，直到2008年全球遭受另一场经济危机。这次危机是由金融市场崩溃和接踵而来的世界经济放缓引起的。

在全球经济和金融的缓慢增长和倒退过程中有个有趣的现象，那就是尽管全球经济总体放缓，但金砖国家中的中国和印度显示了相对强劲的经济增长。而所有金砖国家都显示了更强劲、更快速的金融市场复苏。

2001—2004年，中国实际的GDP增长徘徊在7.5%至8.0%之间。2001年，印度GDP年度增长率为4.2%，2003年，小幅回升至5.6%，2004年，回升至5.9%，巴西将其年度经济增长率从2001年的1.4%拉升至2003年的1.5%，2004年的3%。俄罗斯从5%小幅上涨至6%。因此，大部分金砖国家的年度经济增长率都超过了2001年2.4%的世界年度经济增长率，世界经济增长率2003年达到3.2%，2004年达到4.1%。

股市的复苏则更加强劲快速。在25个主要新兴经济体中，有20个国家和地区的股票价格在2003年上涨25%以上，2003年下半年股市反弹后，多达8个国家增长达到75%以上。同时，20个国家的货币兑美元升值。特别值得一提的是亚洲的新兴经济体，在经历了由亚洲经济危机带来的6年结构性改革后，它们也出现增长，其中中国和印度处于领先地位。具体到金砖国家，从2002到2003年，这些国家的股票指数大涨。中国从-17.2%涨到10.5%，印度从4%涨到80.4%，巴西从-45%涨到140.9%，南非从24.3%涨到42%，俄罗斯从38%涨到58.7%。在最严重的世界经济危机中，新兴经济体，特别是金砖国家的股市在不到两年内取得这样的成绩真是令人欣喜。

2008年发生的全球经济和金融危机强度高，影响大。从2008年9月雷曼兄弟（Lehman Brothers）申请破产开始，次贷危机触发了经济危机，对华尔街造成严重影响，也给主要的金融机构带来巨大的抛售压力。到2009年3月，标准普尔500指数跌到了三位数，道琼斯指数等全球指数也暴跌。在金融市场危机最严重时，标准普尔500指数中低于10美元的股票交易上涨10倍，为防止大规模退市，纽约证券交易所也暂停了其1美元的最低股价要求。2009年见证了自第二次世界大战以来最大规模和最具有协调性的全球经济增长复苏活动。各国所启动的财政刺激和财政支持项目，总额达到了全球GDP的30%。其中，美国推出7000亿美元不良资产回收计划（TARP），欧元区和英国也宣布采取广泛措施来救助银行或对其进行国有化。当时的报告提到，各国政府发行了将近1万亿美元的政府担保银行债权来救助受困银行。

国际货币基金组织也向低收入受困国家推出了特别援助计划。政府不得不购买银行股份来恢复银行的生存能力。在此期间，美国政府在花旗银行所持股份上升到34%，英国政府在苏格兰皇家银行和英国莱斯银行的持股增加到70%。

发达国家和发展中国家都推出大规模的财政刺激和财政支持计划。在美国，财政刺激规模占到GDP的5.5%，日本4.7%，澳大利亚5.4%，中国6.2%，巴西5.6%，南非7.4%，俄罗斯5.4%，而印度为1.8%。这些国家也大幅降低利率。为了与发达国家保持一致，除中国以外，其他金砖国家也大幅降低利率，其中南非降低400个基点，巴西350个基点，印度175个基点，俄罗斯100个基点。从2008年9月30日到2009年，美国联邦基金利率从2.00%降至0.15%，欧洲央行利率从4.25%降低至1.00%，印度储备银行回购利率从9.00%降低至4.75%。

所有发达国家和发展中国家的增长都受到了影响，后续影响甚至继续到现在。而发达经济体的年度经济增长率从2008年的0.1%下降至2010年的-0.1%，在2010上升到2.0%，2014年，可能再次滑落至1.6%。

2009 年，美国和欧元区的年度经济增长率分别是 3.7% 和 2.6%，在 2010 年分别降到不足 1%，而在 2014 年，有可能看到 0.2% 的负增长。

在金砖国家内，中国继续保持增长势头，2008 年，年增长率为 9.6%，2009 年为 9.2%，2010 年为 10.4%，2014 可能降低到 7.4%。印度从 2008 到 2009 年，年均增长率保持在 8%—9%，2010 年进一步上升至 10.3%，但自此一直下滑，2014 年可能下滑到 5.6%。巴西年经济增长率尽管在 2008 年达到 5.2%，但 2009 年很不理想，2010 年又达到 7.5%，而 2014 年可能下滑至 0.3%。俄罗斯在 2009 年公布的年增长率为 5.2%，在 2009 年下降到负 7.8%，在 2010 年又迅速上升到 4.5%，但在 2014 年，增长率可能低至 0.2%。南非在 2014 的年度经济增长率预计为 1.4%，低于 2010 年的 3.1%。

另一方面，股市的复苏明确，快速。2009 年 3 月全球股市达到低点后，在接下来的六个月内快速回升，升幅超过 50%。德意志银行当时的报告显示，涨势在过去六个月内达到 0.5%，这样的转败为胜仅在 1932—1933 年出现过。从 2009 年 3 月 9 日到 9 月 30 日，道琼斯指数从 6547 上升到 9712，富时指数从 3542 上升到 5133，标准普尔 500 指数从 677 上升到 1057，印度 BSE Sensex 指数从 8160 上升到 17126，上海指数从 2118 上升到 2779，Bovespa 指数从 36741 上升到 61517，RTS 指数从 576 上升到 1254。大多数金砖国家的股价进一步上涨，BSE Sensex 基准指数上涨到 27000（2014 年 10 月 30 日），巴西为 52411，南非为 48202。在 2014 年 10 月底之前，中国和俄罗斯的指数没太大变化，中国为 2435，俄罗斯为 1047。

二、持续存在的问题

虽然金砖国家在经济和市场管理上有很强的应变能力，但除中国以外的其他国家在实体经济和金融市场上出现不同程度的波动还是司空见惯的。2008 年危机后新兴市场主要的不确定性因素包括美国和欧元区财政刺激的减少，逐渐减少的债券购买以及紧缩的利率政策，这成为一般新兴经济体特别是金砖国家内金融市场的主要问题，同时带来不稳定性。

美联储可能的债券购买减少计划，以及紧缩的利率政策对金砖国家造成的巨大压力在 2013 年下半年开始显现，其中股票和外汇市场经历了剧烈的动荡，并加剧了经济增长中存在的问题。2013 年，一些金砖国家国内经济赠长速度的减缓也带来了新的压力。

在经济增长下滑和担心外国资本流入国内市场的背景下，金砖国家货币在兑换美元和其他主要国际货币时贬值严重。2013年5月22日，美联储主席做了第一次"削减量化宽松规模"的演讲，到2013年8月21日，巴西雷亚尔下跌了14.9%，印度卢比下跌11.7%，南非兰特下跌5.8%，印尼盾下跌6.9%，土耳其里拉下跌5.3%。然而，大多数新兴经济体，包括金砖国家的货币，在2013年9月重新升值。2014年年初，大多数新兴市场，尤其是金砖国家已成功地消化了削减量化规模带来的影响。尽管美联储发表了几次关于削减规模的言论，并实际开始削减，但并没有带来太大的波动。危机过后，新兴市场的前景很不均衡。尽管国内经济增长一直摇摆不定，但金融市场一直比较稳健。另外，对美国削减量化规模影响的担忧被日本大规模的财政刺激计划抵消，在2014年10月的最后一个星期内，市场对其反应非常积极。

增长不均衡仍然影响着包括金砖国家在内的新兴市场的前景。国际货币基金组织在其年度世界经济展望（2014年10月）中总结了不同地区的增长前景。其中金砖国家所在的亚洲地区为"稳健增长"；拉丁美洲（巴西）为"增长速度依旧不够"，俄罗斯为"正在应对地缘政治的不确定性"；而撒哈拉以南非洲地区（南非）则为"保持速度"。

三、金砖国家金融市场概览：规模不断扩大，实力不断增强

尽管经济和市场出现波动，但一段时间以来，金砖国家建立起了相对广阔的金融架构，这突出了金砖国家在全球金融市场的领先地位。从下文一系列金融指标中可看出金砖国家不断建立的金融市场规模之大。

根据2014年9月公布的相关数据①，金砖四国的市值约为9万亿美元，约占全球市值的13%。中国、印度和巴西的市值突破万亿美元或更多。股票交易价值约8万亿美元，约占股票交易全球股票市值的19%。单单中国就有4.7万亿美元的市值和6.6万亿美元的股票交易值。目前，金砖国家在股票市场上市的公司数量接近9000之多，其中大部分来自印度。目前，金砖国家资产类别呈现多元化，现货和衍生品市场比较成熟。指数期货（中国）、指数期货和期权（印度、巴西、俄罗斯和南非）、单一股票期货和期权（印度、巴西、俄罗斯南非）、ETF期货（南非）、外汇期货（印度、巴西俄罗斯、南非）、利率期权（巴西）、利率期货（中国、印度、巴西、俄罗斯和南非）、商品期货（中国、印度）以及大宗商品期货和期权（巴西、俄罗斯和南非）不断吸引全球投资组合，在金砖国家掀起投资金

---

① 世界交易所联盟，伦敦。

融市场的狂潮，其在金砖国家发展已相当成熟。金砖国家多元资产类别（包括股票、大宗商品、货币和利率）交易所在市场活动和交易量方面处于领先地位，广受好评。世界排名前 30 的衍生品交易所，金砖国家占 12 家之多。

在新发行市场上，金砖国家也有很强的代表性。世界上有史以来发行规模最大的首次公开募股（IPO）公司有三个来自中国（中国银行，2006 年 111 亿美元；中国工商银行，2006 年 219.8 亿美元；中国农业银行，2010 年 221.1 亿美元），且新兴阿里巴巴电子商务门户网站以其 250 亿美元的发行量跻身世界最大 IPO 公司之一。

金砖国家在全球金融许多方面都占有重要地位。巴西（圣保罗股市）和中国（上海和香港）位列市值排名前十。中国（上海、深圳）位列交易股票价值排名前十。印度位列股票衍生品排名前五。在股票期权最高地位。俄罗斯和约翰内斯堡位列债券交易排名前五。巴西位列利率衍生品排名前五。印度领先货币期货（合同数量）排名。印度位列商品期货排名前三。中国（香港）/南非位列异国衍生品交易排名前五。美元—卢比合同数量最大，处于领先地位。前 20 大金属期货合同中，来自印度的有八个。2011 年金砖国家占全球交易所筹集新资金的近 50%。过去三年，中国占全球筹集新资金的近 40%。2002 年至 2011 年十年期间，金砖国家所占市值的比例从 3% 上升至 13%；占股票交易值的比例从 1% 增至 9%，所占新发行资本的比例从 9% 上升至 21%。2013 年，世界银行 1000 强中，金砖国家银行所占数量上涨至 216 家（其中中国 111 家、印度 40 家、俄罗斯 38 家、巴西 27 家）。2013 年，中国位居世界银行 1000 强榜首（由伦敦《银行家》杂志发布的年度排名榜），一级资本可谓是中国工商银行撇开常居榜首的美国银行和摩根大通跻身排行榜榜的功臣。2014 年，中国工商银行仍居世界银行 1000 强榜首。

在银行业，世界银行 100 强中，21 家来自金砖国家，其中中国 3 家银行位列世界银行 10 强。各个金砖国家在全球银行 100 强中都占有一席之地。

金砖国家在外汇交易市场取得巨大进步。三年期中央银行外汇市场交投总额调查（2014 年 2 月）显示，金砖五国平均每日外汇市场交投总额分别为：俄罗斯 740 亿美元、中国 550 亿美元、印度 530 亿美元、南非 240 亿美元和巴西 180 亿美元。

2013 年 4 月，外汇市场平均每日外汇市场交投总额为 5.3 万亿美元，高于 2010 年 4 月的 4 万亿美元和 2007 年 4 月的 3.3 万亿美元。2013 年 4

月，外汇掉期交易最活跃，每日交易量为2.2万亿美元，紧随其后的是现货交易，交易量为2万亿美元。美元仍是老大，在全球外汇交易中，人民币升值扮演着越来越重要的角色，这有助于人民币国际化。2013年，人民币流通量飙升至1200亿美元，位列最活跃交易货币第9名，占全球外汇交易量的2.2%，这主要因为离岸人民币交易出现显著增长。2001年至2013年期间，人民币流通量占全球平均每日货币流通量的比例从几乎为零上升至2.2%，卢布从0.3%提高到1.6%，巴西雷亚尔从0.2%提高到1.1%，印度卢比从0.2%提高到1%，赞比亚兰特从0.9%提高到1.1%。

金砖国家金融市场合作范围进一步扩大。各个金砖国家的指数期货（基于基准指数）也在交叉上市。利用本地货币解决双边贸易问题的合作力度进一步增强。目前香港证券交易所和上海证券交易所正开展联合工作，这有可能进一步扩大亚洲和金砖国家证券行业的合作空间。

一直以来，金砖国家不断积极寻求国际贸易商机，投资海外市场。2000年至2010年期间，中国对外直接投资从10亿美元上升至680亿美元，其中对俄罗斯直接投资从30亿美元上升至510亿美元，对巴西直接投资从20亿美元上升至110亿美元。在此期间，金砖五国的外国直接投资总额从70亿美元上升至1460亿美元，且对外直接投资总额达6880亿美元。

金砖国家与欠发达国家和低收入国家（LICs）在双边贸易和提供发展援助方面建立了良好的关系。低收入国家对金砖国家出口额从2000年的150亿美元增长至2009年的610亿美元。2010年，低收入国家向中国和印度出口的农产品和原材料占其出口总量的90%。低收入国家出口的制成品超过50%流向中国，其次是巴西（14%），俄罗斯、印度和南非各占10%。低收入国家出口的主要产品为农产品、矿物质和其他原材料，特别是燃料和金属。例如，非洲与金砖国家的贸易额增长速度远胜于世界其他地区，2012年贸易额为3400亿美元，自2007年以来翻了一番，2015年有望达到5000亿美元。

信用评级机构穆迪（Moodys）（2013年）对金砖国家信用评级也相对较高，其中巴西为Baa2（2011年6月），俄罗斯为Baa1（2013年3月），印度为Baa3（2011年12月，至2014年10月有所上升），中国为Aa3（2013年4月），南非为Baa1（2013年7月）。

金砖国家在当地货币国际化方面也取得显著的进步。目前，人民币可对九种货币进行直接交易，包括美元、欧元、日元、英镑、澳元、新西兰元、俄罗斯卢布、马来西亚林吉特和新加入的新加坡元。根据德意志银行估计，2014年，人民币跨境贸易结算额将达6万亿元（9880亿美元），增长 50%。该行称这大约相当于中国全球贸易总额的 20%，而这一比例在 2013 年约为 17%。人民币占全球贸易结算额的比例仅次于美元。独联体国家之间大量的贸易货币为俄罗斯卢布。印度也正着手在双边贸易结算中使用当地货币。

四、新开发银行

2014 年 7 月于巴西福塔莱萨举行的第六届年会上，金砖国家决定创立新开发银行，这是金砖国家近期为进一步扩大影响力而采取的行动。开发银行这一想法是在 2012 年的新德里峰会上提出的。从几年前的一个想法到现在的代表集体共识的重要干预手段，新开发银行将可能成为进一步巩固金砖国家在全球经济和金融领域领导地位的关键因素，因为开发银行是一个更强大和有效的融资发展工具。从长期以来接受援助和帮助的国家可看出（现在一些国家仍在接受援助和帮助，如印度），目前，该组织内部之间及面向其他欠发达经济体将展开融资。

新开发银行面临的重要挑战和机遇是如何管理发展融资。当前的发展融资模板已受到受助方的严重抗议和质疑，特别是附加条件和资格方面（环境和治理区域等）。同样的，新开发银行的出现将削弱发达国家在开发银行业务委托方面的主导地位。新开发银行将如何接这一招，我们拭目以待。

尽管有了新开发银行，发展援助方面的需求仍得不到满足。虽然有世界银行以及每个地区的开发银行——亚洲（亚洲开发银行）、非洲（非洲开发银行）、拉丁美洲（美洲开发银行）和加勒比海地区（加勒比开发银行）以及世界各国的大量专业国内发展类金融机构，仍有 40 亿人无电可用，9 亿人无法饮用清洁饮用水，26 亿人用不上卫生设施。金砖国家拟议的新开发银行可能有助于解决这些问题。

新开发银行与众不同的地方在于它的定位。新开发银行与之前银行模式不同，之前发达国家建立开发银行的目的是向发展中国家扩大资金规模，是发达国家企图更大范围控制世界和继续扩张其在制定全球经济政策中的势力范围的一种手段。对金砖国家而言，新开发银行可能是其与现有全球权力大国抗衡的总体战略中的一个重要工具。从长远来看，新开发银行可弥补其他重大举措（如 2013 年德班峰会宣布的 1000 亿美元应急储备基金）的不足，这有助于金砖国家在外汇管理方面互帮互助，金砖国家交易所联盟可能在金融市场和金融衍生品（五个国家基准股票衍生品指数的交叉清单）和能源方面（建立燃料储备银行和能源政策研究所）对西方国家构成威胁，这将对现行《华盛顿共识》对大多数全球事务的控制构成强有力的威胁与挑战。中国和印度也将积极参与亚洲基础设施银行计划（拟投 1000 亿美元资金）。

五、全球治理的挑战

通过欧盟（欧洲议会，2012 年的一项研究）[1]，我们可以发现，新兴主导国家巴西、俄罗斯、印度、中国和南非（金砖国家）在国际发展合作中发挥的作用正发生着翻天覆地的变化。在过去的十年中，金砖国家（特别是通过与低收入国家的南南合作）加大了经济和技术援助力度，建立了独特的经济合作方式和手段。金砖国家正在努力扩大其政治影响力，从而与欧盟等老牌西方对外援助国家相抗衡。在贸易、外国直接投资和发展融资方面，金砖国家对低收入国家的影响非常显著，而这些南南合作的努力在欧盟发展战略中应有所体现。

虽然金砖国家的重要性及其在全球治理方面发挥的作用与日俱增已成共识，但特定群体的批评声仍此起彼伏。近期的一份报告[2]发表了一段与金砖国家的公认形象明显相悖的言论，该报告称"金砖国家纯粹只是一个"GDP 俱乐部"而已。作为资源丰富的经济体，他们对天然资源（如化石、生物燃料和矿物等）密集开采来促进发展，这大大推动了他们的出口业务。他们一味地追求 GDP 增长，很少甚至没有关注过人类发展，从而使贫富差距不断扩大。目前制订的计划也寥寥无几，其中建立金砖国家开发银行的提议，重点仍是加强基础设施建设，以支持新型开采模式，在当今金融不稳定、高成本和潜在性灾难环境压力和不平等日益严重的国际背景下，这种发展经济的做法显得日益动荡，不可持续。2009 年哥本哈根谈判时，世界各国希望就气候变化问题达成一项具有约束力的协议，而巴西、中国、印度和南非却更多地考虑他们资源开采的发展，让这一希望成为了泡影。然而，一些人认为："如果国际社会未能正视其最严重的挑战——建立一个稳健的全球经济架构去应对气候变化，那么金砖国家将首当其冲受害"。

金砖国家的治理框架应能够彻底妥善地解决这两方面的问题，以便实现协调可持续发展。世界各国不断地意识到金砖国家在全球治理方面发挥的重要作用，但，与此同时，一些批评人士指出金砖国家是一个剥削组织，几乎不关注人类、自然和环境的协调发展，如何消除这些负面言论是金砖国家智囊团面临的一项重要挑战。

考虑到金砖国家所处的立场以及其对经济增长和全球生产份额增加

（与发达国家相比）的期望，前者和后者在一系列寻常问题上表现不同也是很自然的。金砖国家的范围和重要性都在不断提升，主要驱动力就是经济和贸易的快速增长，而发达国家市场则更关心维持缓慢增长过程中已经获得的成绩。这种多样性必然会就全球治理领域的广泛问题产生重大分歧，发达国家和发展中国家在贸易自由化、气候变化、能源效率和环境保护等几个问题上的巨大差异就证明了这一点。

在这种背景下，参与金砖国家合作事宜的智囊团应多多商议发展框架和战略，以实现发展中国家引以为傲的经济快速增长与发达国家所倡导的人类和环境发展完美融合。由于金砖国家政治和经济制度的多样性，设计一个共同议程是一个相当大的挑战，可不像建立互惠互利的业务那样简单。虽然任务艰巨，但金砖国家仍有机会设计出一个更适合发展中国家的治理框架，同时也可以缓解发达国家的担忧。目前，发展中国家在全球事务中拥有较大发言权，开发适合发展中国家各个方面的增长和治理的新模式和模板空间很大。发展中国家全球框架的设计会受其国内条件的限制，这一观点在一些方面仍受到争议。[3]

首先，金融发展的法律和文化障碍似乎没有像人们从近期文献中得出的结论那么严重。有意思的是，要想使金融市场充满活力，不一定非要像英国那样发展，因为不是每个国家都这么好运气。然而，该国内部的政治结构是我们确定的主要障碍，克服起来比任何其他的结构性障碍都要难得多。不过我们想要表达的第二点是，从国家可以达到的开放程度上看，这使国内企业延缓金融发展变得更有难度。

现在金砖国家在创新形式和框架的构思和设计管理方面发挥着前摄作用。来自金砖国家的代表在某些国际组织，如世界贸易组织（巴西的罗伯托·阿泽维多，Roberto Azevedo）、联合国工业开发组织（中国的李勇任总干事）、国际货币基金组织（中国的朱民任副总裁）中居于领导地位，为在众多全球性事务中的互动提供了大量的机会，并提出了很多有意义的选择。

值得思考在此背景下出现的一些问题，这有助于显著扩大金砖国家治理的范围，有助于形成能回应国内关注的共识，有助于与全球性样板保持一致。下面将对这些问题展开讨论。

1. 经济自由性和包容性

世界人民越来越迫切地渴望政治和经济自由，发展中国家人民则有过之而无不及，因为只有这样他们才能从快速发展的经济中得利，不至于成为发展的"局外人"。不能否认的是，许多新兴市场中，经济的增长和发展扩大了贫富差距，收入差距的持续增长可能成为许多国家的致命要害。因此领导层要制定适当的政策和包容手段来解决这一问题，消除收入不平等引发的仇恨心理。金融体系可以提供更好的信贷和其他经济机会，在减少不平等现象中具有重要作用。因此金融包容性成为了许多国家的一项重要政策议程。而日益扩大的收入不平等在巴西以外的金砖国家中则异常明显。

2. 公共市场的作用

金砖国家经济增长较快，金融资源可以在公共市场和私人市场间流动，这可弥补现代经济的发展筹资的不足。然而，发展公共资本市场以提高透明度和披露水平是很重要的，这对市场的有序进行来说很关键。同样重要的是扩大内部安全网足够的投资、交易、套期保值和风险管理的资产类别和手段，作为投资保障。在发展公共资本市场的规模方面，金砖国家取得了良好的进展。但扩大活动和产品基地领域的空间仍很大。公共市场和私人市场的组合应充分利用金砖国家和其他发展中国家的企业和企业家的潜力。在扩大公共资本市场影响力的同时，金砖国家可以努力使自己在贸易、投资和双边援助方面成为其他发展中国家和转型国家的榜样。

3. 公司治理

在所有被认为造成全球金融危机的因素中，公司治理是最重要和最关键的一个。联合国贸易和发展会议（UNCTAD）[4]所做的关于公司治理的一份报告显示："全球金融危机对世界经济的影响有助于强调大型国际企业的健康发展与普通百姓生活之间的联系。可以肯定的是，这场危机的原因复杂，已经提出的补救措施也是多方面的。而公司治理则是主导。"有意思的是，发达国家一直催促发展中国家和金砖国家采用更强大的公司治理体系，但在发达国家部分地区的公共市场和私人市场中发现了很多非常有害的缺陷，招致了巨额的罚款和惩罚性措施。从调整伦敦银行同业拆借利率到不正当地销售结构性产品，大量的市场不当行为逐渐曝光。美国各大银行自危机爆发后同意支付1270亿美元的罚款，以平息针对他们的监管诉讼，而美洲银行自身自2010年以来已支付了多达745.8亿美元。欧元区的一些国家在危机后随即也面临着违约风险，因为当时的财政管理状况没有按照有关欧盟国家报告标准的现存协议公布信息。

虽然金砖国家已经大力革新并完善了公司治理制度，但一些意外情况仍时有发生。一些中国公司在美国市场上市时所披露的信息出现问题［浑水研究（Muddy Waters Research）提出的报告］，一些上市后的印度公司出现缺陷（开发贷款基金），巴西一家石油公司卷入贿赂丑闻（选举前真相浮出水面）（Petrobas），俄罗斯某些公司的公司治理在2013年年底出现问题（TNK – BP, OAO Pharmstandard and OAO Uralkal），这些引发了不同层面的关于金砖国家公司治理不足的讨论。

联合国贸易和发展中心（UNCTAD）的一项研究分析了22个新兴市场中188家公司的治理实践，包括金砖国家五大类52项披露内容，这五大类是：财务透明度、董事会和管理层的结构和流程、所有权结构和控制权行使、企业责任，以及合规和审计。该研究发现了四个问题：（1）审计相关问题的披露与联合国贸易和发展中心的国际会计和报告标准（ISAR）这一类的基准披露项存在着较大的差距，监管机构和公司的披露事项中存在着大量的信息缺失。鉴于审计披露对评估公司治理质量的重要性，监管机构应该考虑与国际最佳实践一致的新的披露要求。（2）投资者通常乐于接受更多的披露信息，但避免过度披露也有不少争论：报告花费较高，而且不是所有的信息都是有用的。监管机构应侧重于一系列核心的强制性信息披露项目。（3）有时一些公司并未遵守强制性信息披露规则。在大多数国家，直接执行政府的披露规则是不切实际的，需要检查的个人信息披露点太多了。政策制定者应该重点考虑一部分小范围的领导企业，或者进行随机审查。定期检查和适度罚款可使监管机构严肃对待披露内容。（4）监管机构不可能事事兼顾，而投资者作为市场参与者，必须发挥积极作用，并就信息披露的差距与被投资公司沟通。政策制定者应鼓励投资者负责任的投资和积极的所有权。应鼓励投资者与企业开展对话，以确保它们符合监管要求并主动做到最好。许多国家面对的一项政策挑战是如何使披露信息符合监管工作。本报告的研究结果显示了三方面的做法：增加要求披露项的数量；加大信息披露规定的清晰度；并确保广大民众理解这些信息。

4. 监管改革

在金融危机之后，美国①推出了一系列改革措施，涉及以下五个关键领域：（1）加强对金融公司的监督和管理；（2）全面监督和管理金融市场；（3）保护消费者和投资者免受金融滥用的影响；（4）完善管理金融危

---

① 美国财政部于2009年6月17日公布了一份关于金融监管改革的白皮书，命名为"金融监管改革——重建金融监管的新基础"（美国财政部，2009年）。(1)金融服务监督理事会，职能是"确定新兴系统风险，提高跨部门合作"（类似于欧洲系统性风险委员会的功能，下文将做讨论）。(2)消费者金融保护局，负责保护消费者在信贷、储蓄和支付市场上的利益。(3)全国银行监管局，对联邦特许存款机构负责。

机的工具；以及（5）提高国际监管标准并加强国际合作。虽然金砖国家也采取了类似的改革，但继续强化和执行这些措施以使金融体系有效、可靠、对人民负责方面的改革范围有所局限。随着所有金砖国家的全球投资以及越来越多地参与全球经济和金融事务，监管改革和完善已成为重要的政策选择。尽管监管已经稳定了旧的管理问题，但新问题也不断暴露出来。2014年二十国集团将专注于四个关键领域：（1）建立弹性的金融机构；（2）结束大而不倒现象；（3）解决影子银行的风险（2014年10月的IMF全球金融稳定报告就专门单列一章描述这一问题）；以及（4）使衍生品市场更加安全。早在2009年举行的二十国集团匹兹堡峰会上，就发起了很多对金融市场监管的改革，其中包括（1）用杠杆比例或反周期资本缓冲的方法投入更多更好的优质资本；（2）更好的流动性和风险计量；（3）加强资产负债表外的信息披露；（4）监管信用评级机构；（5）更好地调节市场实践和承保标准；（6）利用集中清算和更多场外交易（OTC）衍生品交易所；（7）通过长期价值创造，优化补偿；（8）利用监管联席会、法律框架和应急计划来协调危机中的跨境问题；以及（9）改善决议手段和框架。

由于金砖国家在二十国集团议程的规划和实施中发挥了重要作用，成员国的国内金融市场政策应适当借鉴监管改革的最佳做法。

5. 新兴的货币霸主

金砖国家正在崛起，一些国家正逐渐成为全球经济增长的主要贡献者，另一些国家，如中国和俄罗斯则正在成为新兴的货币霸主。比较而言，后者比前者更为重要。一项关于新兴货币的国际货币基金组织报告[5]指出："具有国际化潜力的主要新兴货币有巴西里亚尔、中国人民币、印度卢比、俄罗斯卢布和南非兰特。所有这些经济体都具有显著的区域重要性和经济实力。尽管相关数据不足，但仍有证据表明在过去几年这些新兴货币在国际交易中的使用显著增多。例如，在外汇衍生品的使用中，里亚尔增长了50%，卢比和卢布增加了1倍，人民币增加了约12倍。新兴货币的离岸市场也在增长，近年来涨幅激烈，这反映了新兴市场的全球经济影响力不断提高。离岸市场的发展增加了货币利率，并促进了其在国际上的使用。"70多个国家的900多家金融机构已经在用人民币做业务了。国际结算银行（BIS）[6]最近的一份报告提出了人民币国际化的几个重要方面，其中包括：（1）中国人民银行与20家海外中央银行和货币当局建立了双边本币交换设施，资金多达1.6万亿；（2）香港人民币存款和定期存款从 2010 年年底的约 3220 亿元增长至 2013 年底的近 1 万亿元，离岸人民币未清偿债券从 2010 年的 1000 亿元增至近 5000 亿元。

最新的国际结算银行三年期调查显示，人民币市场平均每日成交额从 2004 年的 6 亿美元飙升至 2013 年的 200 亿美元。亚洲开发银行（ADB）[7]的一份报告描述了中国货币逐渐成为贸易结算、债券发行、交易、投资和储备货币重要工具的特征。

自 21 世纪头 10 年中期以来，俄罗斯一直都在努力加强卢布的地位，使之成为双边结算货币，同时也向国际货币发展。俄罗斯贸易占据了独联体国家（CIS）间贸易额的 44%。包括蒙古、芬兰和土耳其在内的独联体国家都非常倾向于对俄贸易。俄罗斯也集中与保加利亚、叙利亚和波兰等波罗的海国家交易。中国和俄罗斯之间以本国货币结算的边境贸易作为一个试点项目在 2003 年已经开始，目前占以卢布结算的所有交易的 99%。2003 年到 2008 年间，以本国货币结算的边境贸易在中俄商品总成交额中的比例从 0.5% 提高到了 7.3%。根据各国央行的数据，2008 年俄罗斯与欧亚经济共同体国家（EurAsEC）间交易的商品支付额超过了 509 亿美元，其中，一半以上都是用卢布支付，美元支付位居第二，而欧元所占份额仅为 13%。

印度正准备游说日本、伊拉克和委内瑞拉等主要贸易伙伴同意采用卢比来结算部分出口贸易，这是一系列稳定货币波动，使之在全球更受欢迎的举措之一。限制大额交易用卢比支付而不用外币，可以保护印度免受持续投机性的攻击，但也会限制卢比利息以及国外投资的流入。2013 年 8 月成立的研究货币互换的一个小组已经获得了财政部、商务部和央行的支持，暂定了约 10 个国家通过卢比进行交易，主要包括石油出口国和其他对印度有巨额贸易顺差的国家。为节省宝贵的外汇，并加强卢比的地位，商务部[8]于 2013 年 12 月拟定了一份名单，包含了 23 个以当地货币与印度进行贸易的国家，例如安哥拉、阿尔及利亚、尼日利亚、阿曼、伊朗、伊拉克、委内瑞拉、卡塔尔、也门和沙特阿拉伯等石油出口国，还有俄罗斯、日本、新加坡、澳大利亚、印度尼西亚、韩国、马来西亚、墨西哥、南非和泰国等其他国家。

采用本国货币作为国际货币能够带来诸多益处，例如可降低交易成本和汇率风险；可以用本国货币结算；整体竞争力与机构竞争力和业绩的提高可降低资金成本。这些发展将会在商业、市场深度和交易密度的强度方面给国内金融体系带来巨大利益。尽管作为国际货币，管理其相关风险也很重要，但是相对而言，在金融系统没有足够规模和深度的情况下,制定国内利率的自主权降低、波动性增加、金融稳定性压力等问题更为严峻。

为进一步追求国际化,各国应重视发展各种政策措施,包括稳定宏观经济,加强金融基础框架,改革资本账户,加强流动性,适当协调各项改革,包括顺序安排、能力加强和能力建设。

金砖国家将受益于相互间的协同合作,有助于加强各自货币在双边贸易结算中的使用。

除此之外,从强化管理的角度看,金砖国家需要在促进经济增长、商业诚信和职业道德,承担企业社会责任,采用清洁技术和高效能源管理流程,保护环境和劳工法,支持气候管理,加强区域合作等的同时,给予其他重要方面应有的关注,例如重视能够促进竞争和私营机构的公平法律,加强融资渠道,使人们具备技能和专业知识,确保性别平衡等。

虽然国内经济增长在金融部门改革后经历了不确定期和动荡期,但金砖国家金融市场的发展步伐仍然相当惊人。关于发展中国家新出现的需求和要求,金砖国家已经在全球论坛上有力地论证并阐明了自己的观点,而即将出现的新开发银行则是对其承诺的践行。金砖国家还扩大了在一些国际金融机构和决策机构中的参与度和影响力,这有利于为进一步发展制定强大而稳健的流程。

虽然金砖国家凭借着人口实力和人口红利,凭借资源成本较低、市场准入较易等方面的优势,成为了一个强大且充满活力的团体,为国内经济增长设立了的新标准,并对世界经济做出了贡献,但管理措施的范围、质量和程度才是进一步发挥影响力和成功的最为重要的因素。

表1 金砖国家的公司治理

编号	联合国贸易和发展会议国际会计和报告标准中披露项目列表	国家				
	所有权结构和控制权行使	巴西	印度	中国	俄罗斯	南非
1	所有权结构	9/10	10/10	8/10	8/10	10/10
2	年度大会召开过程	6/10	6/10	8/10	10/10	3/10
3	股权变更	7/10	8/10	7/10	6/10	7/10
4	控制权结构	9/10	8/10	7/10	8/10	6/10
5	控制权和相应股本	10/10	5/10	7/10	8/10	4/10
6	会议日程可用性与可获取性	8/10	9/10	7/10	8/10	9/10
7	控制权	7/10	6/10	8/10	10/10	6/10

续表

编号	联合国贸易和发展会议国际会计和报告标准中披露项目列表	国家				
8	金融市场公司控制权获取管理规则和程序	9/10	4/10	8/10	9/10	9/10
9	反并购措施	1/10	0/10	1/10	1/10	0/10
	财务透明度					
10	财务和经营成果	10/10	10/10	10/10	10/10	10/10
11	关键会计概算	8/10	9/10	9/10	9/10	8/10
12	关联方交易的性质、类型和因素	9/10	10/10	9/10	9/10	10/10
13	企业目标	10/10	10/10	10/10	10/10	10/10
14	可选会计决算的作用	5/10	5/10	7/10	8/10	9/10
15	批准关联方交易的决策过程	7/10	3/10	4/10	7/10	3/10
16	特殊交易管理规则和程序	4/10	6/10	5/10	9/10	5/10
17	董事会的财务沟通责任	10/10	9/10	9/10	8/10	9/10
	审计					
18	与内部审计员互动的过程	9/10	10/10	7/10	8/10	10/10
19	与外部审计员互动的过程	7/10	9/10	7/10	8/10	9/10
20	内部审计员预约过程	8/10	10/10	8/10	9/10	7/10
21	外部审计员预约过程/工作和责任范围	4/10	6/10	2/10	6/10	6/10
22	关于外部审计员独立性和完整性的董事会议	8/10	2/10	3/10	6/10	10/10
23	内部控制系统	10/10	9/10	10/10	8/10	7/10
24	当前审计员任期	3/10	9/10	5/10	3/10	1/10
25	审计合伙人轮换	2/10	0/10	0/10	0/10	2/10
26	审计人员的非审计工作和审计人员薪酬	3/10	9/10	7/10	4/10	4/10
	企业责任和符合性					
27	环境和社会责任政策和绩效	10/10	7/10	8/10	10/10	9/10
28	环境和社会责任政策对公司可持续发展的影响	7/10	7/10	5/10	5/10	6/10
29	董事会道德规范及道德规范豁免	4/10	10/10	2/10	2/10	2/10
30	全体公司员工道德规范	9/10	7/10	4/10	5/10	10/10
31	全体员工"举报信息"保护政策	6/10	8/10	2/10	1/10	6/10
32	其他商业利益相关者权利保护机制	10/10	9/10	5/10	7/10	9/10

续表

编号	联合国贸易和发展会议国际会计和报告标准中披露项目列表	国家				
33	企业管理中员工发挥的作用	8/10	7/10	4/10	3/10	3/10
	董事会及管理结构和过程					
34	管理结构，如为避免利益冲突而设立的委员会和其他机制	10/10	10/10	9/10	9/10	10/10
35	"制约和平衡"机制	10/10	8/10	9/10	6/10	9/10
36	董事会组成（执行官和非执行官）	10/10	10/10	10/10	10/10	10/10
37	管理委员会结构的作用和功能	10/10	10/10	9/10	8/10	10/10
38	董事会的作用和功能	9/10	9/10	10/10	10/10	9/10
39	风险管理目标、体系和活动	10/10	9/10	10/10	8/10	10/10
40	董事会成员的任职资格和个人简历	8/10	10/10	10/10	7/10	8/10
41	外部董事和高管职位的类型和职责	9/10	10/10	10/10	6/10	9/10
42	董事会和高管的重大利益	3/10	10/10	10/10	5/10	10/10
43	继任方案	4/10	6/10	7/10	1/10	9/10
44	董事合同的有效期限	10/10	10/10	10/10	9/10	7/10
45	因公司合并或收购而离职之高管的赔偿政策	0/10	0/10	1/10	1/10	0/10
46	董事薪酬决策与组成	3/10	10/10	10/10	7/10	10/10
47	董事会的独立性	7/10	10/10	10/10	6/10	10/10
48	董事持有之外部董事和高管职位的数量	9/10	10/10	10/10	6/10	10/10
49	董事会成员间利益冲突之解决程序	4/10	9/10	4/10	5/10	4/10
50	专业拓展和培训活动	3/10	6/10	2/10	4/10	7/10
51	报告期间顾问机构的应用与可用性	6/10	5/10	5/10	2/10	7/10
52	绩效考核过程	3/10	9/10	9/10	2/10	10/10

资料来源：新兴市场公司治理发现：法律要求与公司实践的数据分析，纽约和日内瓦，联合国贸易和发展会议，2011年。

注：每一行分子是满足每项标准的企业数量，分母是接受调查的企业数量。

参考文献

[1] "The Role of BRICS in the Developing World", Policy Department, *Directorate General for External Policies*, April, 2012.

[2] "On the BRICS of Collapse? Why Emerging Economies Need a Different Development Model", paper prepared by the Centre for the Study of Governance Innovation (GovInn) University of Pretoria (South Africa). The quote in the end of the paragraphs pertains to D. Rodrik, "What the World Needs from the BRICS", *Project Syndicate*, 10 April, 2013.

[3] A quote found in W. Bratton and J. McCahery, "Comparative Corporate Governance and the Theory of the Firm: The Case against Global Cross-Reference", *Columbia Journal of Transnational Law*, 38 (1999): 213-97.

[4] United Nations Conference on Trade and Development, "Corporate Governance in the Wake of the Financial Crisis: Selected International Views", New York and Geneva, United Nations, 2010.

[5] Samar Maziad, Pascal Farahmand, Shengzu Wang, Stephanie Segal, and Faisal Ahmed, directed by Udaibir Das and Isabelle Mateosy Lagoago, 2011, *Internationalization of Emerging Market Currencies: A Balance between Risks and Rewards*, SDN/11/17 Washington: International Monetary Fund, October 19, 2011.

[6] Chang Shu, Dong He, and Xiaoqiang Cheng, "One Currency, Two Markets: The Renminbi's Growing Influence in Asia-Pacific", BIS Working Papers, No 446, Monetary and Economic Department, Bank for International Settlement, April 2014.

[7] Il Houng Lee and Yung Chul Park, "Use of National Currencies for Trade Settlement in East Asia: A Proposal", *ADBI Working Paper Series*, No. 474, April 2014.

[8] *The Hindu Business Line*, December 24, 2013.

电子政务：印度领先一步

[印度] 拉吉尼什·阿胡伽*

全球化背景下，"金砖国家"的发展是非常重要的一部分。融合五个大国之力的"金砖国家"经济总量占全世界生产总值的近21%。当前，"金砖国家"面临如何保持良好发展势头和优化管理的双重挑战。最近几年，金砖国家的服务业占国内生产总值的比重不断提高。近年来，印度的服务业在国内生产总值中的比重持续保持增长，从2009年的54.5%提高到2013年的57%。这意味着印度的服务出口业经济持续增长。印度在信息技术和信息技术服务产业中的优势在全球得到广泛认可。

电子政务可以透明公开地监督政府服务、评估政务以及执行政务事项。将电子政务引进到现行经济的操作系统和程序中可以化解政务中的官僚主义瓶颈。我们可以通过一个发展指标来对此进行衡量。这个发展指标即联合国使用的用来评估全球电子化发展的指标——电子政务发展指标（EGDI）。电子政务发展指标由三个重要的部分组成：提供在线服务、保持电信接通、保证人员能力，该指标范围从0到1。印度和南非的电子政务发展指标处于中等发展组（从0.25到0.50），巴西、俄罗斯和中国的电子政务发展指标处于高等发展组（从0.50到0.75）。

印度政府于2006年5月18日实行"印度电子政务计划"（NeGP）①，在全国范围内实施了一整套实现电子政务的措施。实施该政务计划的目的是拉近政务服务与民众的距离，正如"印度电子政务计划"的宣言中所承诺：

> 让所有普通人，无论在什么地点，通过统一服务输出端口，都可以享受所有政务服务。并且务必要保证政务服务的高效性、透明性和可靠性，同时要保证这些服务的成本在可承受范围之内，以此实现普

---

* 拉吉尼什·阿胡伽（Rajnish Ahuja），印度帕弗勒（Pahle）基金会助理研究员。
① http://india.gov.in/e-governance/national-e-governance-plan。

通人基本的政务服务需求。

"印度电子政务计划"由31项任务模式工程（MMP）①组成，其中12项工程在中央实施，13项在国家层面实施，其他的部分进行综合实施。在中央层面实施的任务工程包括在银行、保险、收入所得税、养老金以及护照等方面的实施。

表1 "印度电子政务计划"任务模式工程

中央任务模式工程	国家任务模式工程	综合任务模式工程
收入所得税	各直辖政府	国家电子政务服务网页
中央消费税	教育	印度门户网站
电子政务	犯罪及罪犯追踪网络系统	电子贸易电子数据交换
保险	农业	电子法庭
移民、签证、外国人登记和追踪	公共分配系统	电子商务
企业事务部	卫生	普通服务中心
唯一身份认证工程	就业交换	
国家人口登记	电子村委会	
养老金	债券	
护照	商业税	
银行	电子区域	
邮政	道路交通	
	国有土地记录和现代化计划	

印度政府一直在朝着使治理范围最大化的方向努力。印度政府已经建立了一个印度政府发展网站（http：//www.indg.in/），登录该网站可以获取相关服务信息，网站主要为农村群众服务。网站上的服务包括农村贫困人口的就业信息注册、"村镇级企业家"注册。企业家可以通过网站向其他网民分享成功的经验及励志故事以及其他一切村民所需要知道的事情，比如每日农产品价格，还可以在网上出售农产品或教育服务。该网站也提供例如农村能源、农村卫生、社会福利等相关领域的信息。

---

① http：//india.gov.in/e-governance/mission-mode-projects。

为减少政府部门旷工的情况，印度政府 2014 年 10 月启动了一项监督检查新德里政府办公室工作情况的计划。网站（http://attendance.gov.in/）可以提供已在该网站注册的政府部门的数据以及政府工作人员的信息。

为降低执行成本，提高法律的透明度以及营造一个有利于工业发展的环境，印度劳动部于 2014 年 10 提出萨兰·苏威德门户（Shram Suvidha Portal）这项规定。该项规定保障劳工法的遵守执行，并且减轻了中小企业负担。工业长期以来期盼实现劳工监督透明化，该项规定包含了这些内容，萨兰·苏威德门户的四大主要特点如下：

- 每家单位都会获得独一无二的劳动识别编号（LIN）用于网上注册。
- 行业中建立自主认证以及在线回执。现在单位只需要建立一项统一在线回执，而不是以前的 16 个不同回执。
- 劳动部的监督人员 72 小时内必须上传监督报告。
- 通过该网站门户，可以及时调整不完善之处。

以下是印度各邦中实施电子政府比较成功的例子：

1. 古吉拉特邦

古吉拉特邦在实施电子政务领域的以下方面树立了杰出的榜样：

- 古吉拉特邦广域网（GSWAN）①——此广域网作为先进的通讯基础设施，位于不同区域的用户（即便是距离较远的用户）可以在该网站实现数据、声音、视频信息的交换。建立这个广域网的起因是为了促进政府外网通讯设施的现代化，从而提高政府办事的效率和效果，让民众更加信任和依赖"政府到政府"（G2G）的系统功能。该网络以 8 兆位/秒的网速连接 7 个地区，以 4 兆位/秒的网速连接 19 个地区，一个地区以 2 兆位/秒的网速通过租用线路连接行政中心甘地讷格尔。
- 应用技术关注全国范围内的投诉信息（SWAGAT）——这项举措通过先进的电子政务技术解决古吉拉特邦居民发起的投诉信息。每月的第四个星期四由首席部长主持会议。
- 古吉拉特邦政府建立并执行了综合工作流程和文件管理系统（IWDMS），以此提高政府在各个行政阶层的信赖度、透明度和效率。古吉拉特邦政府通过改变管理方式以及从上到下的策略来保证 IWDMS 项目的顺利实施。

---

① http://www.gswan.gov.in/。

• 古吉拉特邦的医学院/地区民用医院采用医院信息管理系统（HMIS），为群众提供高效和高质量的医疗卫生服务，提高了医疗服务的质量，尤其是为贫困人口带来了更好的医疗服务。HMIS 系统在医院为病人提供疗程服务时，为医生和其他医护人员及时提供病人信息，工作流程中减少纸张的出现，采用参数化的提醒信息，来帮助医务人员提高医疗服务质量。

• 古吉拉特邦获取土地模式——该模式由古吉拉特邦工业发展公司（GIDC）提出，已成功减少获取土地过程中遇到的各种复杂问题。如果一位企业家需要在古吉拉特邦购买土地，他可以选择购买私有土地、特区土地、工业园土地、古吉拉特邦工业发展公司所属土地或是政府所有的土地。土地购买流程必须保证公平对待土地所有者，以避免未来产生任何诉讼纠纷。因此，土地的价格由市场决定。GIDC 向土地所有者支付土地购买款以及 GIDC 收购土地价格的 10%（甚至更高）。GIDC 所有的土地属于非农业用地，所以不需要"无反对意见证书"。GIDC 承诺收购土地之后，为土地所有者家庭的一名成员提供就业机会。

收购土地之后，接下来需要发展道路、电力、供水等基础设施。如果是工业协会购买的土地，由 GIDC 公司依照公有私有合作模式（PPP）来进行基础设施建设。基础设施的升级由政府负责完成 60%，由 GIDC 负责完成 20%，剩下的 20% 由私有企业完成。土地发展完成后，最后一个步骤是土地的分配。土地信息在网上可以看到，其中也提及了该土地的基础设施状况。为了更好地进行土地管理，基于地理信息系统的应用会将现有土地信息发布到网站。这可以方便投资者对土地展开调查，为他们节省时间。为处理使用过程中遇到不满意的情况，GIDC 公司采用了米特拉（MITRA）系统，一个在线监测和处理不满意情况的系统。

• 古吉拉特邦引进了陀罗电子系统（E-Dhara）系统[①]，用于获得并维护乡村土地，这一系统将所有土地信息数字化，使得获取土地过程简单、透明、安全。陀罗·肯德拉电子系统（E-Dhara Kendras, e-DK）记录土地每天的状况，比如土地所在地市级机构的变迁，或者土地所有者权利。这可以帮助农村地区建立电子政务系统，农民和土地所有者可以通过缴纳象征性的费用获得土地所有者权利信息的电子版本。这种方式建立了新型的记录收入的方式，最大的益处是最大化降低了对土地信息篡改的情况，减轻了土地获取部门、土地分配部门的工作负担等。

---

① http://revenuedepartment.gujarat.gov.in/e-dhara-forms。

2. 马哈拉施特拉邦

马哈拉施特拉邦引进了马哈拉施特拉邦促进工业贸易和投资门户网站（MAITRI），这是一个政府到商业的系统，提供建立某工业所需条件的信息。该在线系统为投资者提供综合信息，包括如何对扩大现有规模进行投资，或者如何建立新的公司。通过网站的这些功能，在地区层面的流程以及授权的流程已经在该网站上建立办事框架。网上可以及时找到关于建立某行业所需要的所有支持文件的信息。MAITRI 为流程中相关部门的主要秘书、行业以及各节点的官员提供直接监督。该系统为价值达 1 亿印度卢比的工程提供服务。该系统将会提供多达 31 项建立行业所需要的通关和批准条件。

审批通关系统对投资者来说是很有帮助的，因为它在审批通过的全过程中可以让利益相关方看到整个流程的进展情况。投资政策、公民守则以及上至地区级别政府部门间协调情况和各种公告等内容在 MAITRI 上都能获得。该在线系统可以避免因多次造访政府相关部门而引发的冲突。由于信息采集渠道是单一的，所以该系统可以帮助删除冗余信息。

3. 拉贾斯坦邦

拉贾斯坦邦政府为投资者提供"单一通关窗口系统"，通过该系统可以在特定时间内发布许可证。拉贾斯坦邦政府规定，金额大于 1 千万印度卢比以上的工业投资必须由投资者通过该窗口系统进行申请。申请者在建立了必需的"企业家注册表格"之后，可以使用用户名和密码在该网站进行注册。这样做可以防止产生无效的用户 ID。对申请书状态的追踪有一套规范流程，不超越任何部门的权限。投资者可以收到提醒邮件，说明申请的进度，因此在整个流程中都可以保证公开、透明性。

4. 安得拉邦

在公有、私有部门合作提供服务方面，安得拉邦建立了塞瓦电子（e-Seva）中心/社区一站式商店，公民可以在这里交税、缴纳物业账单、开具出生证明和死亡证明、申请护照等。安德拉邦境内有 400 多家塞瓦电子中心。

以上列举的印度各邦为实现电子政务采取的先进措施，体现了印度在实现电子政务方面取得的发展。为减少官僚主义，确保政府职能最大化，印度政府计划举行"数字印度运动"。这一运动旨在以可负担的价格，让农村群众实现高速上网，其目的是为了增加宽带连接性，减少"数字文盲"。为增加宽带覆盖的范围，该项投资由公共行政和私有企业共同负担，利用已有的公共基础设施为私有市场提供宽带连接服务。目标包括：连接所有公共行政，向农村地区引进宽带建设投资，因为对现有的以市场驱动为主导的电信运营商来说，去农村地区建设宽带盈利空间不高，会拉大不同地区的数字鸿沟。

中国国家治理中的司法现代化改革

郭 锋[*]

当前，中国正在进行一场前所未有的司法现代化改革。上个月召开的中国共产党十八届四中全会专门研究和讨论如何在中国全面推进依法治国，并提出了建设中国特色社会主义法治体系、建设社会主义法治国家的法治建设目标。中国的司法现代化改革，就是为了进一步完善和发展中国特色社会主义制度，推进国家治理体系和治理能力现代化，实现美好中国梦。在此，我向金砖国家的各位朋友介绍三方面的内容。

一、中国为什么要进行司法现代化改革？

经过九十多年艰苦奋斗，中国共产党团结带领全国各族人民，把贫穷落后的旧中国变成日益走向繁荣富强的新中国，中华民族伟大复兴展现出光明前景。综合国力大幅提升，2011年国内生产总值达到47.3万亿元，载人航天、探月工程、超级计算机、高速铁路等实现重大突破。

但是，中国作为一个发展中的大国，还存在不少问题。主要表现为：发展中不平衡、不协调、不可持续问题突出；城乡区域发展差距和居民收入分配差距较大；社会矛盾增多，教育、就业、社会保障、医疗、住房、生态环境、食品药品安全、安全生产、社会治安、执法司法等关系群众切身利益的问题较多，部分群众生活比较困难；一些领域存在道德失范、诚信缺失现象；一些领域消极腐败现象多发，反腐败斗争形势严峻。

法治建设还不适应经济的高速成长，存在很大差距。主要表现为：有法不依、执法不严、违法不究现象比较严重，多头执法、选择性执法现象存在，执法司法不规范、不严格、不透明、不文明现象突出，群众对执法司法不公和腐败问题反映强烈；部分社会成员尊法信法守法用法、依法维权意识不强，一些国家工作人员、领导干部依法办事观念不强，知法犯

---

[*] 郭锋，中华人民共和国最高人民法院研究室副主任。

法、以言代法、以权压法、徇私枉法现象存在。

目前,中国官方和民间、学术界和实务界已经形成共识,这就是必须推行法治,把法治作为治国理政的基本方式,发挥法治在国家治理和社会管理中的重要作用。要坚持法律面前人人平等,保证有法必依、执法必严、违法必究。要进一步深化司法改革,完善司法制度,确保司法机关独立公正行使职权,强调中国共产党必须在宪法和法律范围内活动,任何组织或者个人都不得有超越宪法和法律的特权。

二、中国司法现代化改革的目标

1. 巩固中国特色社会主义制度。这就是坚持在中国共产党领导下,按照中国宪法建立的、符合中国国情的社会主义市场经济制度、社会主义民主政治制度、社会主义法律制度。这种制度的优越性是,可以促进人的全面发展,实现全体人民共同富裕,建设富强民主文明和谐的社会主义现代化国家。

2. 维护社会公平正义。我们强调,公平正义是中国特色社会主义的本质特征。要建立以权利公平、机会公平、规则公平为主要内容的社会公平保障体系,保证人民平等参与、平等发展权利。要通过司法的分配正义功能,使受到侵害的权利得到保护和救济,使违法犯罪行为受到制裁和惩罚。

3. 促进社会和谐。社会和谐是中国特色社会主义的本质属性。我们强调要保障和改善民生,创新社会管理,正确处理改革发展稳定关系,最大限度增加和谐因素,增强社会创造活力,确保人民安居乐业、社会安定有序、国家长治久安。

4. 形成公正高效权威的司法制度。司法机关应当在国家政治生活、国家权力运行中发挥重要作用,应当制约公权力。必须落实法院的宪法地位,法院代表国家行使审判权,审判权是不可挑战的终局性权力。

三、中国司法现代化改革的主要措施

1. 解决领导干部对司法的干预,维护司法权威。建立领导干部干预司法活动的记录、通报和责任追究制度。对干预司法的,给予纪律处分;造成冤假错案或者其他严重后果的,依法追究刑事责任。完善惩戒妨碍司法机关依法行使职权、拒不执行生效裁判和决定、藐视法庭权威等违法犯罪行为的法律规定。建立健全司法人员履行法定职责保护机制,非因法定事由,非经法定程序,不得将法官、检察官调离、辞退或者做出免职、降级等处分。

2. 解决地方保护主义对司法的干预，解决立案难问题。最高人民法院设立巡回法庭，审理跨行政区域重大行政和民商事案件。探索设立跨行政区划的人民法院，办理跨地区案件。切实解决行政诉讼立案难、审理难、执行难问题。改革法院案件受理制度，变立案审查制为立案登记制，对人民法院依法应该受理的案件，做到有案必立、有诉必理，保障当事人诉权。

3. 解决司法机关内部对司法的干预，落实办案责任制。明确司法机关内部各层级权限，健全内部监督制约机制。司法机关内部人员不得违反规定干预其他人员正在办理的案件，建立司法机关内部人员过问案件的记录制度和责任追究制度。完善主审法官、合议庭办案责任制，谁办案谁负责。

4. 推进以审判为中心的诉讼制度改革。在法庭上确保侦查、审查起诉的案件事实证据经得起法律的检验；全面贯彻证据裁判规则，严格依法收集、固定、保存、审查、运用证据，完善证人、鉴定人出庭制度，保证庭审在查明事实、认定证据、保护诉权、公正裁判中发挥决定性作用。

5. 推进法官制度改革。建立符合职业特点的司法人员管理制度，健全法官统一招录、有序交流、逐级遴选机制，完善司法人员分类管理制度，健全法官职业保障制度。目前，中国法官职业准入门槛太低，特别是最高法院、高级法院的法官准入资格与法院的权威地位不相称。根据《法官法》，年满23岁，本科毕业从事法律工作满两年就可担任基层法院、中级法院法官，从事法律工作满三年就可担任高级法院、最高法院法官。法官职业应向法律职业共同体开放，特别是向律师、法学院校教师、政府各部委开放，让具有丰富的法律法学从业经验、具有一定经济基础、具有一定社会声誉的法律人加入，从而迅速提升我国法官的整体素质。应该建立与法官职业、贡献、尊严相适应的激励机制。

6. 构建开放、动态、透明、便民的阳光司法机制。中国法院依托信息技术，大力推进"阳光司法"工程，全面开展和推进审判流程公开、裁判文书公开、执行信息公开三大平台建设，将司法权运行的各个环节置于当事人和社会公众监督之下。全国法院的信息化建设已基本形成硬件设备完善、网络覆盖法庭、数据即时生成、资源共享互通的管理模式。建立失信被执行人名单库，向全社会曝光失信被执行人。充分利用网站、手机短信、微博、微信等平台，向社会公布各类司法信息，提供在线诉讼服务。

7. 加强人权司法保障。落实罪刑法定、疑罪从无、非法证据排除等法律原则；完善对限制人身自由的司法措施和侦查手段的司法监督，加强对刑讯逼供和非法取证的源头预防，健全冤假错案有效防范、及时纠正机制。加快建立失信被执行人信用监督、威慑和惩戒法律制度。落实终审和诉讼终结制度，实行诉访分离。

8. 加强对司法活动的监督。规范司法人员与当事人、律师、特殊关系人、中介组织的接触、交往行为。严禁司法人员私下接触当事人及律师、泄露或者为其打探案情、接受吃请或者收受其财物、为律师介绍代理和辩护业务等违法违纪行为，坚决惩治司法掮客行为，防止利益输送。

"城市发展陷阱"
——金砖国家地方治理的重大难题

袁宝成[*]

尊敬的各位领导、各位嘉宾,女士们、先生们:

非常荣幸参加今天的研讨会。我来自中国南方广东省东莞市,一座有着"现代制造业名城"称号的城市。得益于改革开放带来的历史机遇,东莞在过去三十多年时间里,通过外向带动,实现了快速的工业化和城市化。全市2460平方公里土地上,集聚了超过60万市场主体,年生产总值达到5500亿元人民币,在中国大中城市中排第20位左右,进出口总额突破1500亿美元,在中国排第5位。与此同时,我们也与金砖国家的许多城市一样,面临着不少地方治理的难题。其中最突出的,就是今天想跟大家探讨的主题——"城市发展陷阱"。

"城市发展陷阱"是我根据"中等收入陷阱"引申出来的一个概念。"中等收入陷阱"由世界银行提出,指的是当一个国家或地区的人均生产总值达到4000美元左右,快速发展中积聚的矛盾容易集中爆发,如果不能有效转变发展方式,将导致经济停滞与社会动荡,最终无法进入高收入行列。东莞的人均生产总值早已超过了4000美元,接近10000美元,但仍然面临着经济转型与社会转型的双重压力。归根结底,一座城市发展到一定程度,原有的发展红利就会逐步消减甚至消失,面临着掉入陷阱的危险,城市发展有可能停滞甚至倒退。因此,我将"中等收入陷阱"引申为"城市发展陷阱"。接下来,我就和大家一起分享东莞的应对措施与体会。

一、东莞地方治理中遇到的"城市发展陷阱"难题及其应对

冰冻三尺非一日之寒。与金砖国家的一些城市一样,东莞面临的"城

---

[*] 袁宝成,广东省东莞市委副书记,市人民政府市长。

市发展陷阱"不是一天形成的，经济社会发展的同时，各类问题也在逐步积累，如果不及时化解，就可能产生比较严重的后果。

陷阱1——产业低端化与空心化

东莞应对措施——让转型升级成为发展的新常态。

金砖国家大多是发展中国家，许多金砖国家城市早期工业化基础薄弱，缺乏资金，缺乏技术，缺乏市场渠道，只能靠大量引入外资，借助国际资本实现快速的工业化。这毫无疑问会带来城市的快速繁荣，但也可能从一开始就埋下产业发展的一系列弊端：一方面，引进的企业大多处于产业链低端，产品附加值低；另一方面，当城市经济发展到一定程度，逐利而居的产业资本又会寻求搬迁到成本更低的地区，伴随梯度转移而来的产业空心化问题令人警惕。为此，东莞采取了有针对性的措施。**针对产业低端化问题**，主要是推动企业就地转型升级，从加工制造向技术研发、品牌销售等环节拓展，逐步占领产业链高端。东莞市政府设立了100亿元的科技专项资金，引导支持企业进行技术改造和研发。近三年每年的专利申请和授权量都超过了2万件，科技创新已成为全市发展的重要驱动力。同时，大力推动品牌建设，全市13%的加工贸易企业建立了自主品牌，其中收购国际知名品牌400多个。东莞有一家服装企业，通过改进生产工艺、打造高端品牌，最贵的一件毛衣能卖到12万元，其附加值远远超过一辆中档汽车的利润。此外，我市还通过产业链的整合提升，打造了电子信息、制鞋、服装等竞争力较强的产业集群。东莞的电脑整机配套率达95%，全球每10双运动鞋就有1双产自东莞，平均每5个人就拥有1件产自东莞的毛衣。**针对产业空心化问题**，主要是在扶持民营经济、增强内生发展动力的同时，坚持依法行政，优化政府服务，降低企业营商综合成本，以优越的法治化国际化营商环境留住优质企业，并不断以新的先进产业替换旧的落后产业，填补和增强产业梯度转移后的发展支撑，实现"腾笼换鸟""凤凰涅槃"。近三年来，全市为企业减免税费及相关成本超过80亿元。先后引进投资6亿元人民币或1亿美元以上的重大项目188个，总投资达3170亿元，全部投产后将释放产值超过1万亿元，相当于再造一个东莞经济。其中智能手机等新兴产业已经形成规模，大家熟悉的苹果、三星，以及中国的华为、酷派、OPPO等品牌都在东莞生产，手机出货量约占全球的八分之一。东莞用自身实践证明，转型升级只有进行时，没有完成时，只要坚持不懈地推进，产业低端化和空心化的陷阱是能够克服的。

陷阱 2——大量新移民的管理与服务难题

东莞应对措施——逐步推进基本公共服务均等化。

金砖国家快速的工业化，形成了大规模的集中生产。仅靠城市原住居民难以满足用工需求，必然要大量引进劳动力。就东莞来说，全市原住居民只有 180 多万，但整个城市的人口超过了 1000 万，是中国新移民最多的城市之一。这些劳动力与国际资本的结合，使得城市经济迸发出令人惊讶的活力，但也给城市服务与管理带来了巨大压力。一旦处理不好，就容易产生治安混乱、群体矛盾、贫民窟等问题。为此，东莞设立了专门的新移民服务管理机构，在加强社会管理、维护城市秩序的同时，积极推动基本公共服务均等化，努力为新移民提供市民化的待遇。比如在教育方面，采取积分制的方式，为新移民子女提供公办学位。加上民办学校创造的学位，全市共吸纳义务教育阶段就读的新移民子女 60.9 万人，占学生总数的 76.1%。又比如，在社保方面，尽可能将新移民全部纳入养老、医疗、工伤保险等保障体系。新移民每年只要缴纳几十元，就可以享受到住院医保年最高支付限额 20 万元的待遇，大病医保最高报销额可达 50 万元。当然，受政府财力等因素的限制，我们目前还不能为所有新移民提供市民待遇。但随着公共服务均等化力度的不断加大，新移民对东莞的归属感正在逐渐增强，庞大的人力资源正逐步转化为对城市发展更有利的人才资源。

陷阱 3——快速城市化带来的"城市病"

东莞应对措施——推动组团式的新型城镇化。

金砖国家快速的工业化，往往伴随着快速的城市化。在此过程中，不少城市都遇到了人口膨胀、交通拥堵、住房困难、环境恶化等"大城市病"。学术界有观点认为，城市化存在两种值得关注的模式：一种是大城市集中扩张模式，另一种是原传统行政区域就地城市化模式。东莞走的是类似后一种的新型城镇化道路。我们从市直接管辖镇的特殊行政架构出发，因势利导，形成了市区和 28 个镇"一中心、多支点"的组团式发展格局。这些组团之间保留了足够的生态隔离带，通过城乡一网全覆盖的路、电、水、气等基础设施来紧密连接，构筑了市内半小时交通圈，人流物流信息流高速通畅。这种组团式发展模式尊重了原来的乡村区域，能够有效避免单中心城市扩张带来的过度集聚弊病，使城市空间布局更加合理，生产流通更加有序，生态环境更加优良。东莞目前虽然人口超千万，但与一些同等规模的城市相比，并不显得很拥挤；全市有 160 万辆汽车，但平时较少堵车；房价也只是周边一些大城市的二分之一甚至三分之一。与其他城市相比，东莞市民的工作压力相对较轻，生活相对而言也比较舒适。

陷阱4——工业化对资源环境的消耗与破坏

东莞应对措施——大力推进污染整治和生态建设。

纵观全球发展历史，基本上老的工业城市都经历了一个"先污染后治理"的过程，不少金砖国家也不例外。东莞在高速发展的同时，同样面临着生态破坏、环境污染、资源瓶颈等一系列问题。近年来，我们深刻反思以牺牲资源环境为代价的粗放式发展道路，大力倡导生态文明理念，注重发展低碳环保经济，努力实现环境容量饱和基础上的绿色崛起。全市共投入了500多亿元，在整山治水、绿化美化、治理污染等方面做了大量工作，尽力弥补生态环境的历史欠账。其中，我们建立了覆盖市区与每一个镇的污水和垃圾处理系统，较好地促进了污染治理和生态修复。2013年东莞PM2.5指标均值在43左右，空气质量在中国城市中处于中上水平。此外，东莞拥有占全市近一半面积的生态保护区、16个森林公园、5个自然保护区。全市森林覆盖率36.7%，建成区绿化率44.3%，这在金砖国家的工业城市中是比较少见的。东莞被联合国环境署认定为国际花园城市，同时也是中国园林城市和环保模范城市。现在的东莞生态优美，山河湖溪与绿树鲜花交相辉映，就像一座美丽的大花园。东莞用自己的坚持和努力，逐步走出了一条制造业立市与生态发展相互融合、相得益彰的新路子。

二、应对"城市发展陷阱"的几点体会

第一，要处理好产业发展与城市发展的关系。 快速工业化和城市化是金砖国家的两大典型特征，应对"城市发展陷阱"的关键在于产城融合。英文单词"city"对应的汉语词汇是"城市"，这形象地说明对一座城市而言，既要有"城"，有硬件平台，也要有"市"，有产业基础。产业带动城市发展，城市服务产业升级。金砖国家既不能脱离产业去谈城市化，盲目"圈地造城"，这样的城市将变成建在沙丘上的城堡；也不能只顾发展产业而忽视城市的建设升级，这样会导致城市化水平滞后于工业化进程，无法承载高层次企业和人才的进驻，制约产业层次的提升。

第二，要处理好传统产业与新兴产业的关系。 产业的梯度转移和更新替代是正常的经济发展规律。但推进转型升级并不等于简单地淘汰传统产业，或者盲目地发展新兴产业。没有落后的产业，只有落后的技术；没有

夕阳的产业，只有夕阳的产品。传统产业生产的产品很多都是生活必需品，永远有需求，有市场，关键是如何转型升级，提高附加值。战略性新兴产业代表着未来经济的制高点，但不能盲目发展，与其他城市同质化竞争。必须立足当地产业基础，选择有比较优势的产业来重点发展，逐步形成新的产业特色。

第三，要处理好保护环境与促进发展的关系。中共中央总书记习近平曾说过："我们既要绿水青山，也要金山银山。宁要绿水青山，不要金山银山，而且绿水青山就是金山银山。"作为经济学意义上一种有"价格"、可交换的资源，生态环境既是自然财富，又是社会财富、经济财富，对一个地方的发展非常关键。金砖国家只有在坚持生态保护的前提下更好地推动发展，同时利用发展积累起来的财力、经验等，进一步建好生态、造好环境，才能实现经济与生态的有机统一，相互促进。

第四，要处理好政府引导与市场推动的关系。政府和市场是主导城市发展的两大力量。要有效应对"城市发展陷阱"，必须用好政府和市场"两只手"。一方面，政府要以对城市未来发展负责的态度，切实加强顶层设计，引导好产业发展和城市建设的方向。另一方面，应充分依靠市场力量来发挥配置资源的决定性作用，提高资金、技术、人才等各种要素的使用效率，从而激发经济社会发展的活力。

以上是东莞应对"城市发展陷阱"的一些做法和体会。在座各位都是金砖国家的杰出专家学者和政界商界精英。衷心欢迎大家到东莞参观考察，感受这座现代制造业名城的魅力，共同谋划金砖国家城市的未来发展。

谢谢大家。

务实推进金砖银行合作

邹力行[*]

2014年7月15日,金砖国家领导人第六次会晤签署的《福塔莱萨宣言和行动计划》正式宣布建立金砖国家开发银行(简称金砖银行),标志着金砖国家合作进入一个新的时期。金砖银行从宣布成立到实际运转,还有很多问题需要解决。其中,金砖银行的定位、与各方关系和运行机制,是特别需要关注的问题。妥善处理这些问题,务实推进金砖银行建设,对全球治理有重要影响。

一、合理选择金砖银行定位

金砖国家包括了当今主要的发展中大国,是21世纪"新兴力量"的主要代表。金砖国家五个成员国(按照国名英文字母顺序):巴西、中国、印度、俄罗斯和南非均为拉美、欧亚和非洲的主要大国,在世界政治中举足轻重。在过去20年,金砖五国都实现了经济持续高速增长,在世界经济中也变得举足轻重。但是,金砖国家在相当长的时期内建设任务仍然很繁重,与发达国家相比仍然有一定差距。由于内外各种因素的影响,尤其是内部的经济社会转型和外部的金融危机,金砖国家经济继续高速增长的有利因素在减少,不利因素在增加,金砖国家难以再现过去20多年那样的高速增长。21世纪,金砖国家是世界经济平衡发展的重要推动力量,但不可能完全改变全球现行治理格局。金砖银行既是发展中国家共同利益的建构者,也是全球治理改革中的参与者、补充者、合作者。

第一,金砖银行是国际金融结构调整的参与者。历史形成的国际金融结构存在严重不平衡问题,国际金融机构大多由发达国家主导,发展中国家话语权很有限,不利于全球善治和平衡发展。全球金融治理需要反映市场经济的变化和新型经济体发展的特点,成立金砖银行是全球金融体制改

---

[*] 邹力行,国家开发银行研究院副院长,中国社会经济体系分析研究会副会长。

革的重要内容。金砖银行顺应新兴国家和发展中国家的要求，积极参与国际金融改革，有助于促进全球平衡发展。

第二，金砖银行是国际金融机构的补充者。 金砖银行不可能取代世界银行，也没有必要取代世界银行。在多元化的国际市场，需要多元化的国际金融机构。世界银行对"二战"后全球经济复兴和发展做出了贡献，并将继续做出贡献。但是，仅依靠世界银行等现行国际金融机构难于满足金砖国家及广大发展中国家加快基础设施建设的需求。据初步研究，发展中国家基础设施投资每年有超过 1 万亿美元的资金需求，特别是巴西、南非、俄罗斯、印度的基础设施缺口很大，世界银行每年只能提供 1500 亿左右贷款，远不能满足发展中国家的需要。成立金砖开发银行是对现有国际金融机构的重要补充。

第三，金砖银行是国际金融体系的合作者。 当今世界各国、各地区内在一致性增强，金砖国家和全球社会互为市场，互为动力。金砖国家加强合作，共建金砖银行，既是不断强化自身增长动力的过程，也是催动经济全球化深入发展合作共赢得过程。金砖国家在深化自身改革的同时，积极参与全球治理，加强国际间宏观政策协调，推动国际金融体系改革，促进经济全球化朝着普惠共赢方向发展。

第四，金砖国家是发展中国家共同利益的建构者。 在全球治理格局中，发展中国家处于被动的角色和弱势的地位。如何在全球治理改革中反映弱者呼声，维护发展中国家的共同利益？首先，要认识到，发展中国家共同利益并不是放在那儿，等着我们去发现去维护，而是需要国际社会互动建构的。发展中国家共同的诉求和目标对国际政治经济的运行及国家本身的结构有着持久的重要影响。其次，在新的形势下，发展中国家需要树立自己的形象，采取新的战略，这是历史的经验和现实的选择。再次，金砖银行作为发展中国家代表机构，将是新的国际社会建构的实体，它将赋予特定的职能，并通过建立新的工作机制完成特定的任务，切实维护发展中国家的共同利益。最后，金砖国家在坚持创办有金砖特色现代银行的同时，坚持合作发展的思想，不论遇到什么困难，不论有什么样的障碍，始终高举合作的旗帜，体现合作的精神，坚持合作规划、合作建设，在合作中求同存异，共同发展。

总而言之，金砖银行作为一个新型的跨区域开发性金融机构，通过市场化运作，对现行国际金融体制进行参与、补充、合作、建构，支持金砖国家和其他发展中国家基础设施建设和可持续发展。合理选择金砖银行定位，有助于妥善处理金砖银行建设过程中各种复杂关系，减轻国际阻力。

二、妥善处理四大关系

1. 金砖银行成员国关系。金砖国家坚持"求同存异"原则,切实做好内部协调与合作,是推进金砖银行建设的基础。

一方面,抓住金砖国家内部的共同利益和共同诉求,寻找金砖国家之间有生命力的共同目标,增强金砖国家内部的认同感和互补性。金砖国家最大的共同点是都属于新兴市场国家,共同的诉求是经济发展,经济发展最容易达成共识的是基础设施建设。金砖国家都面临技术创新、产业升级、降低能耗、治理污染、保护生态、改善民生等任务。金砖银行通过融资融智服务,合理配置金砖国家生产要素,互通有无,优势互补,促进实现共同目标。

另一方面,应当承认金砖国家之间有差异,虽然金砖国家有着共同的利益诉求,但是并非绝对的利益共同体,开展业务时应充分考虑差异化问题。由于五国处于相近的发展阶段,在经贸领域存在一定的竞争关系;在政治制度、宗教文化、历史传统方面差异明显;在发展轨道上也有一定的分歧。因此,金砖各国应有宽容和理性的心态,多协调,多理解,悬置差异,求同存异,避免陷入零和陷阱,如此才能顺利推进金砖银行建设。

2. 金砖银行与其他发展中国家关系。金砖银行不仅属于金砖国家,也面向广大发展中国家;金砖银行是一家兼容并蓄、开放并举的跨区域开发银行,在某些方面虽然可以也应当侧重金砖国家利益,但是从更宏观的角度出发,如资金的来源和使用方向上,不局限于金砖五国范围,应当向更广阔的方向发展。这不仅有利于聚拢新兴经济体的向心力,也可为发展中国家合作提供一个新平台。

金砖银行与发展中国家还可在具有共识性的问题上开展制度性合作,建立捍卫发展中国家利益的"统一战线"。长期以来,世界经济的中心在发达国家,发展中国家一直处于边缘和外围地位,北强南弱是基本事实。发达国家在世界性金融机构中占据主导地位,对发展中国家的利益考虑不充分。金砖银行致力于体现和维护发展中国家理念和利益,为成员国和其他发展中国家的基础设施项目提供中长期低息贷款,避免采取强制性附加贷款条件,真正使发展中国家通过金砖银行实现"平等互利、共同发展"。

3. 金砖银行与国际金融机构的关系。金砖银行可能对现有国际金融秩序产生冲击,但是金砖银行与现有国际金融机构并非"零和博弈"的关系或替代关系,而是一种补充关系,是国际金融体系的有益补充。与世界银行和国际货币基金组织等世界性金融机构相比,金砖银行在发展问题上更强调对发展中国家基础设施的货款与投资，应急储备安排协议则主要用于帮助成员国应对短期流动性压力，加强全球金融安全网。金砖银行的成员国都是具有相似发展阶段的新兴国家，更了解发展中国家的实际和国情，能够通过优化机制使其所提供的服务适应发展中国家的经济发展需要。此外，在贷款审核时，金砖银行将只是审查借款国的财务情况，而不会干预其内部事务，这与现行国际金融机构的一些做法会有很大区别。

金砖银行与次区域开发银行，如亚洲开发银行、非洲开发银行、美洲开发银行，有着共同的利益诉求和相同的道义，服务于相似的主体，在地区目标上具有一致性，这是二者开展合作的基础。而与次区域开发银行不同的是，金砖银行是一个跨区域的洲际银行，在不同洲际之间调节配置，互通有无，优化资源配置，从而在一种宏观层面对次区域开发银行提供补充。因此，金砖银行与次区域开发银行之间也是一种合作和互补关系。这种合作和互补关系不仅体现在合作原则的一致性和合作精神的共鸣，还体现在金砖银行各成员国为推进所在区域发展和合作从各方面所做出的努力。

4. 金砖银行与联合国的关系。金砖银行是实现联合国千年发展目标、促进南南合作的新动力。金砖银行的出现，一定程度上说明新型经济体国家将拥有自身的投融资渠道，拥有相对独立的经济支持及组织架构，虽然金砖银行初期资金微薄，但这是新型经济体国家追求全球层面经济合理的一大步，也彰显金砖国家是全球经济治理改革的正能量。

金砖银行的设立以及金砖银行运作机制的设计，代表着南南合作的一种新范式。首先，这是一次民主的合作：初始认缴资本由各创始成员国均摊，银行总部设于上海，首位行长由印度推荐，首位理事会主席由俄罗斯推荐，首位董事会主席由巴西推荐。这样的制度安排体现了五个金砖国家的平等关系，没有任何一个国家独自得利。在应急储备基金的出资安排中，各国根据自身经济发展状况，决定储备金所承担的份额，同样体现了公平原则。其次，这是一次有实质内容的合作：成立金砖银行，意味着搭建了一个新的金融合作平台，使金砖国家的合作从抽象走向具体化，从名义合作走向实质合作，从经贸合作走向经济金融多方位合作。再次，这是一次有深度的合作：借助金融合作平台，有利于金砖五国进一步深化联系和沟通。

当今世界，经济增长潜能下降，投资支出低迷，贸易保护主义盛行，金砖国家面临新的挑战。特别是美国退出量化宽松政策后，部分新兴经济体出现资本外逃、货币贬值和经济减速等严峻问题。金砖银行的成立，有利于构筑金砖国家自己的金融安全网,减少对发达经济体的依赖以及国际货币政策调整带来的冲击,促进经济稳定、持续、健康发展。金砖银行还将成为南北沟通的重要桥梁,加强发达国家与发展中国家的对话合作,共同推进世界朝着更加均衡和普惠方向发展。

三、精心设计运行机制

1. 合理界定金砖银行职能。金砖银行的根本职能是融资融智,支持发展中国家基础设施建设和经济社会可持续发展。这是坚定不移的。但是从长远看,随着建设和发展观念、目的、手段的变化,金砖银行的职能有可能是动态的。在这方面,世界银行提供了可借鉴的经验。20世纪40年代末,世界银行全力推进欧洲重建,50年代到60年代初,世界银行注意力转到欠发达国家的经济问题,把支持贫穷国家国民生产总值的增长作为第一要务,现今世界银行的关注点拓展到收入分配、缓解贫困、环境保护、文化建设等方面。发展的手段同样发生变化,从关注资本积累、外汇、大工业项目比如交通和电站建设,向关注小农、再生产和提供城乡社会服务转变。这种转变体现了事物变化的规律,是顺应经济社会发展的需要。新成立的金砖银行也可能如此,应该要有这种战略意识和务实规划。

金砖银行职能中长期动态化并不影响近十年明确的任务。今后十年,新成立的金砖银行应有三大任务:

第一,咨询与规划。通过研究金砖国家和全球发展战略,编制金砖国家中长期投融资规划,组织人员交流培训,促进金砖国家协调健康可持续发展。

第二,贷款与投资。通过建立有效的投融资机制,为基础设施融资,支持金砖国家和其他发展中国家加快基础设施建设,改善经济社会发展条件;为农业、小企业和环保融资,支持金砖国家等发展中国家提升维护粮食安全的能力,支持中小企业发展和环境保护;为开发人力资源融资,增加基本卫生和教育服务,提升贫困人员的基本技能和就业能力;为改革融资,支持金砖国家和其他发展中国家治理能力建设,建设一个有利于长期稳定发展的政治环境和市场机制。

第三,担保与风控。通过担保和引导等方式,帮助金砖国家等发展中国家把自然资源转变为发展的动力,协助金砖国家提高生产力、生产水平,改善劳动条件;通过与其他国际机构贷款或担保进行协作,优先安排更迫切项目,促进国际贸易长期均衡增长;通过建立风险预警和风险防范机制,共同应对金融市场不稳定因素,维护金融安全和经济安全。

2. 积极探索金砖货币机制。借鉴国际货币基金组织特别提款权经验，创设金砖货币制度，作为金砖银行行使其职能的媒介。金砖货币可考虑三种选项。一是选择金砖五国货币作为一篮子货币；二是选择以金砖货币为基础适当拓展其他一些发展中国家货币，共同作为一篮子货币；三是以国际货币基金组织特别提款权一篮子货币为基础，增加包括人民币在内的金砖货币，建立新的一篮子货币。从渐进改革角度考虑，金砖银行初期可以采取双轨制，一方面继续使用美元作为媒介行使其职能，另一方面建立金砖国家货币货互换机制、加快创设金砖货币。金砖货币初期以第一种选项比较妥当，主要选择金砖五国的货币作为一篮子货币，设立与各国经济规模相等的比例，在金砖银行的各种金融活动和日常运行中行使货币职能。不管金砖银行做出哪种选择，都是对现行国际货币体系的补充和改善。

金砖货币制度除了金砖一篮子货币之外，还要建立记账单位，清算计算和储备制度。这些可以作为国际清算体系的一项新内容，也可以在条件成熟时考虑建立金砖清算机制。

金砖货币制度与国际货币基金组织特别提款权有本质差异。特别提款权是国际货币基金组织分配给成员国的一种使用资金的权利，金砖货币制度不是一种权力，而是金砖银行行使其重要职能的媒介制度，是促进使用金砖国家货币为基础的合作框架。

3. 大力创新金砖银行运行机制。机制比机构更重要，金砖银行的生命力在于机制创新。一是筹资机制创新，中国的经验表明，发展中国家不缺少资金，缺少的是一种筹措资金的机制，或者说缺少一种把各种资源转化为建设资金的机制。我们要想方设法设立一种有效的筹措资金的机制，把金砖国家和其他发展中国家的资源优势转变为筹资优势。二是银行治理创新，把先进理论科技和金砖国家实际情况相结合，设计合理的治理机构，体现公平与效率的结合，成为市场与政府活动的纽带。三是运行机制创新，坚持"战略互信、政策支持、专业管理、商业模式、风险分担、共同发展"的原则。以金砖国家战略互信为基础，各国制定和提供法律政策保障，集中资金支持跨区域基础设施建设和基础领域发展，发挥专业技术人员作用，构建合理的商业运作模式，建立风险控制体系和机制，确保金砖银行良性运行，促进金砖国家等发展中国家健康快速发展，为全球善治和平衡发展做出贡献。

中国国家开发银行在支持中国发展方面取得了引人瞩目的成绩。开发银行很愿意向金砖银行和其他国际金融机构学习，也愿意分享自身经验和技术，为金砖银行建设和全球经济可持续增长做出贡献。

参考文献

[1] Editors, H. H. S., "Viswanathan Nandan Unnikrishnan", in *Search of Stability, Security and Growth : BRICS and a New World Orders*, Observer Research Foundation, New Dalhi, 2012.

[2] 黄华光、周余云主编:《调整 创新 合作——2012年金砖国家智库论坛论文集》,北京:党建读物出版社2013年版。

[3] [美]玛莎·芬尼莫尔:《国际社会中的国家利益》,袁正清译,上海:上海世纪出版集团2012年版,第95—104页。

全球经济治理中的金砖国家

赵忠秀* 孙靓莹**

非正式政府间组织（IGO）的定义是：一组相互关联的、有明确共同期望的（而非签订正式条约的）、定期在一起开会的国家，但无独立的秘书处、总部或常设职工作人员。金砖国家允许其成员国寻求其在正式的政府间组织中扩大影响的目标。这种机制一直是有效的，部分因为这种安排允许它们在不同政治、经济和战略目标上保持灵活性。[1]金砖国家作为一个非正式政府间组织在全球经济治理中发挥着重要的作用。同时，改革已经在许多全球性治理机构中发生，以提高大型新兴经济体的代表性。

一、当前的全球经济治理

当前全球治理结构的建设是在美国主导下进行的。[2]1944 年在新罕布什尔建立的布雷顿森林体系被嵌入经济多边机制中，如国际货币基金组织（IMF）、世界银行和关税及贸易总协定（现称世界贸易组织，WTO）。这些机构确立了战后秩序，作为"游戏规则"确保全球的经济治理。尽管几乎没有新兴国家参与有关布雷顿森林体系的谈判，但如果不加入当前的经济体系当中，这些国家的经济崛起也无从谈起。因此，金砖国家还是希望维持当前体系的基本面。

然而，1945 年以来固定下来的全球经济治理方面的制度安排和国际协议，在新兴工业化经济体如金砖国家崛起的形势下正面临着新的挑战和机遇。[3]通向全球经济治理的合作关系新形式只会演化出更加合理的结构、目标和规范以反映一个多极化世界里新兴大国的选择。

根据金砖国家研究小组的数据，金砖五国合计占世界人口的 43%、地球陆地面积的 30% 和全球国内生产总值（GDP）的 25%。[4]世界经济增长

---

* 赵忠秀，对外经济贸易大学副校长。
** 孙靓莹，北京大学博士后研究员。

的近50%归功于金砖国家。随着金砖各国的增长率超过世界经济的年平均增长率,它们在世界经济中的份额还将继续提高。[5]

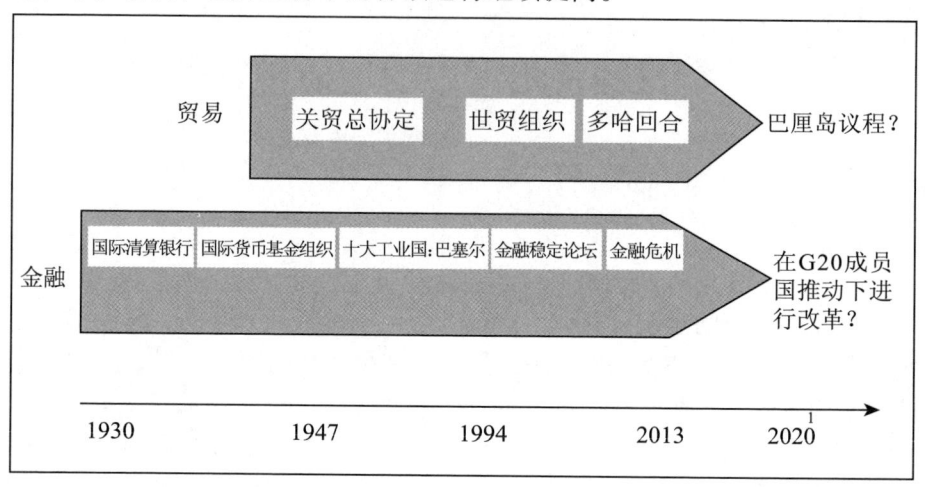

图1 全球经济治理有关谈判的进展

资料来源:Zhenbo Hou, Jodie Keane, and Dirk Willem te Velde, "Will the BRICS Provide the Global Public Goods the World Needs?" ODI Report, June 2014, http://www.odi.org/publications/8540-will-brics-provide-global-public-goods-world-needs. FSF (Financial Stability Forum), GFC (Global Finance Crisis)。

金砖国家占世界全部外汇储备的40%以上——总量达到约4.4万亿美元。①《经济学家》杂志上的一篇报道认为如果金砖国家拿出它们外汇储备中的六分之一,就可以创立一个类似国际货币基金组织规模的金融机构。另外,与西方的财政赤字和高企的债务形成对照的是,金砖国家的公共债务水平大都适度而平稳。[6]这五个国家之间的贸易额2011年达到了2300亿美元,年平均增长率为28%。预计到2015年,它们之间的贸易额将达到5000亿美元。②金砖国家在全球贸易中的份额在这段时间翻了一番,2008年时的份额估计为14%。③来自金砖国家的外国直接投资(FDI)从2002年的100亿美元骤增到了2010年的1460亿美元——尽管中国和俄罗斯代表了金砖国家对外直接投资总额的75%,而巴西和印度分别占据了10%左右。④

---

① http://www.bloomberg.com/news/2012-06-24/brics-biggest-currency-depreciation-since-1998-to-worsen.html.

② http://www.thehindubusinessline.com/industry-and-economy/article3254980.ece.

③ http://www.gfmag.com/archives/147-february-2012/11604-special-report-brics.html#axzz27VbP0CMR.

④ 联合国贸易和发展会议,2011年。

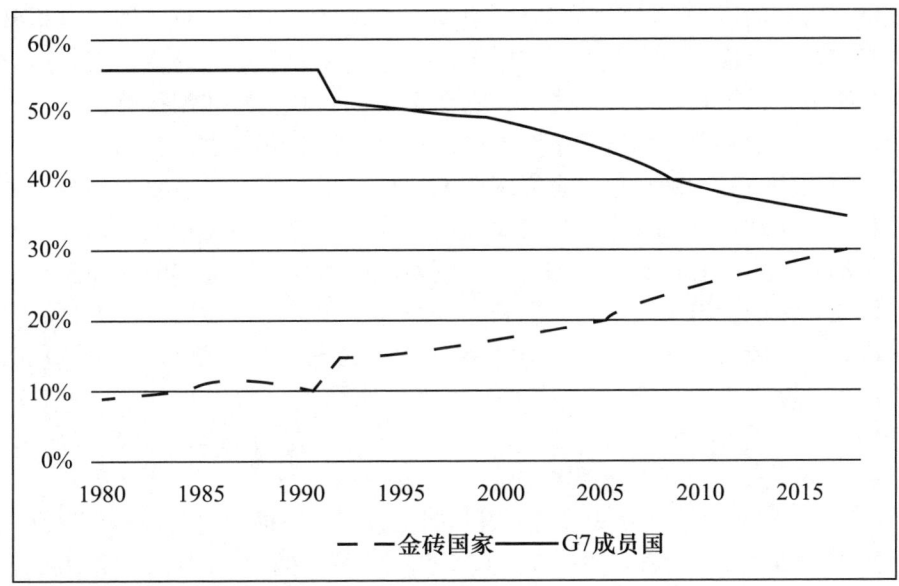

图 2　全球国内生产总值的份额（GDP）（PPP）

资料来源：国际货币基金组织，2013 年。

1. 国际货币基金组织/世界银行——配额份额和投票权

传统大国对国际货币基金组织和世界银行的主导是通过份额分配，即各国的出资额和与它们相关的投票权实现的。配额分配的基本模式早在 1944 年在布雷顿森林召开的会议上就确定了。配额的大小与创始成员国所控制的经济和其他权力资源大体成比例。截至 2008 年，在最近一轮配额谈判前，美国还持有世界银行 15% 和国际货币基金组织 17.41% 的配额。在上述两个机构中，重大决定须经绝大多数有投票权的成员同意（根据议题不同，比例从 70% 至 85% 不等），这意味着美国加上一两个盟友总是拥有有效的否决权。

作为基于成员资格的组织，国际货币基金组织和世界银行分别代表着 188 个国家，接近世界上所有国家的总数。最近通过的对国际货币基金组织和世界银行的治理改革对于提高新兴市场和发展中国家在这些机构中的声音和代表性是重要的一步。这将更加准确地反映出它们在世界经济中正在发生变化的重要性。

尽管国际货币基金组织的职能是监督国际货币系统及其成员国的经济和金融政策，但与一个国家持有一票的联合国大会不同，国际货币基金组织决策机制的设计反映的是每个成员国在全球经济中的地位。国际货币基金组织给每个成员国分配一个配额，这个配额决定其在国际货币基金组织中的财务承诺及投票权。同样的，它在贸易体制和贸易体制执行机制上没有制定规则的功能。与世贸组织不同，它的治理结构相对不那么民主。

世界银行和国际货币基金组织两家机构的根本问题是，它们的金融资产相对于全球资产总量来讲规模比较小。为了维持它们在塑造全球经济模式中的影响力，它们必须追加更多的资金。能增加认购资本的显而易见的来源是二十国金融集团中的大型新兴经济体，尤其是金砖国家。大型新兴大国，包括金砖国家很快就从2009年的金融危机中恢复过来。[7]金融危机发生前，新兴大国在全球金融中的重要性就已经得到了提高。例如，在2010年，世界前25家利润最高的银行当中，中国有五家，巴西有三家，俄罗斯有一家——其中前两名都是中国的银行。[8]

2010年11月，国际货币基金组织同意对其决策框架进行改革，以反映新兴市场和发展中国家日益提高的重要性。改革将把6%的配额转给生机勃勃的新兴市场和发展中国家。这个调整将赋予包括金砖国家在内的一批国家更多的发言权。要开始进行改革，须经国际货币基金组织理事会——国际货币基金组织的最高决策机构85%的多数投票权的同意，新协议才能生效。这项改革计划于2012开始实施。随后对配额和治理的改革也于2010年达成协议，但还没有生效。①

表1显示，金砖国家合计只占11.03%，少于美国的16.75%和七国集团的43.09%的份额。这反映出金砖国家在国际经济竞技场中还不是一个主导性力量。

表1　国际货币基金组织成员的配额和投票权（2012）

	配额		投票权	
	百万SDR	占总额%*	数量**	占总数%*
金砖国家	27 411.80	11.51	277 803	11.03
巴西	4 250.5	1.79	43 242	1.72
俄罗斯	5 945.4	2.50	60 191	2.39
印度	5 821.5	2.44	58 952	2.34
中国	9 525.9	4.00	95 996	3.81
南非	1 868.5	0.78	19 422	0.77
七国集团	108 044.90	45.37	1 085 608	43.09

① Http：//www.imf.org/external/np/sec/memdir/eds.aspx。

续表

	配额		投票权	
	百万 SDR	占总额%[*]	数量[**]	占总数%[*]
美国	42 122.4	17.69	421 961	16.75
英国	10 738.5	4.51	108 122	4.29
法国	10 738.5	4.51	108 122	4.29
德国	14 565.5	6.12	146 392	5.81
意大利	7 882.3	3.31	79 560	3.16
加拿大	6 369.2	2.67	64 429	2.56
日本	15 628.5	6.56	157 022	6.23

资料来源：国际货币基金组织网站，http://www.imf.org/external/np/sec/memdir/members.aspx#2。

[*] 目前，所有188个成员都是特别提款权（SDR）部门的成员。

[**] 根据综合部门对资金资源的使用，对于不同的事项，所需的投票权不尽相同。

尽管还没有达到在国际金融机构中取得更多投票权的目的，金砖国家已经向世人显示，它们是一支不容忽视的力量。2010年，作为世界上几个最大的发展中国家，金砖国家发表声明，宣称任命欧洲人为总裁的传统削弱了国际货币基金组织的合法性，呼吁该职位的任命必须以能力为基础。[9] 传统上，国际货币基金组织总裁一直由欧洲人担任，而世界银行总裁一直由该行最大的股东美国提名的美国公民担任。被提名人经执行理事会确认，任期为五年，可以续任。

关于世界银行和国际货币基金组织中的新一轮配额谈判开始于2008年下半年。[10] 配额的重新分配——俗称关于"几把交椅和多少股份"的辩论——是发展中国家长期坚持的主张。[11] 全球金融危机后，金砖国家一直寻求把国际金融机构的"改革"变成一个对自己有利的议题。金砖国家在把增加资本注入（认购资本）和配额改革联系起来这个广义的主题上达成了似乎很简单的一致意见：发展中和转型中的国家在世界银行和国际货币基金组织的运行中应有更大的发言权。

对于国际货币基金组织和世界银行的领导人选择程序，金砖国家显示出以一个声音行动的意愿。金砖国家的努力获得了积极的响应，取得了一致的结果。然而，与表1和表2显示的配额和投票权相比，新的领导人选择方式与整体全球经济治理上根本性的变革比起来只是一个多少具有象征性的尝试。

表2 主要全球经济治理机构及其各自的决策机制

		成员	决策体系
正式政府间组织	国际货币基金组织/世界银行	成员数量：188 巴西： 1946年1月14日 俄罗斯： 1992年1月16日 印度： 1945年12月27日 中国： 1945年12月27日 南非： 1945年12月27日	**国际货币基金组织** （1）理事会是其最高的决策机构，有权批准配额的增加，特别提款权（SDR）的分配、新会员的加入等。 （2）执行委员会（委员会）负责国际货币基金组织的日常运行。委员会由24个董事组成，这些董事由成员国或国家集团和常务董事任命或选举产生，常务董事为国际货币基金组织的总裁。 （3）总裁，目前是联席会议负责人，也是执行委员会的主席 **世界银行** 世界银行行长是整个世界银行集团的总裁。行长负责主持董事会的会议以及该行的总体管理。 董事会由世界银行集团总裁和25位执行董事构成。总裁是集团的首席官员，通常没有投票权，但在两边票数相同的情况下可投决定性的一票。执行董事作为个人除非受董事会的授权，不能行使任何权力或代表该行。 两个机构中，重大决定都要求有绝对多数票数的赞同（根据议题的不同，比例从70%到85%不等）
正式政府间组织	世贸组织	成员数：160 巴西： 1995年1月1日 俄国： 2012年8月22日 印度： 1995年1月1日 中国： 2001年12月11日 南非： 1995年1月1日	（1）通过成员的部长级会议或总理事会进行决策。在世贸组织基于规则的治理系统中，每个成员拥有一个投票权，所有新协议须经所有成员的同意。 （2）总干事在政策事务上的权力很小；该职位人员主要起顾问和管理作用。

续表

		成员	决策体系
非正式政府间组织	二十国集团/八国集团	加拿大、法国、德国、意大利、日本、俄罗斯、英国、美国、欧盟/阿根廷、澳大利亚、巴西、中国、印度、印尼、墨西哥、韩国、沙特阿拉伯、南非、土耳其	二十国集团没有常设秘书处或专职工作人员。该组织的主席职位每年由来自不同地区国家群体的成员国代表轮流担任。主席是由上届、本届和下一届主席国组成的，不断轮换的由三个成员构成管理集团的一部分，即所谓的"三驾马车"机制。 现任主席国在其任内建立一个临时秘书处，协调集团的工作，组织各种会议。"三驾马车"的作用是保证不同主办年份期间二十国集团工作和管理的连续性。

资料来源：国际货币基金组织、世界银行、世贸组织和二十国集团的官网。

(2) 世贸组织

世贸组织是一个基于规则的治理体系。在这个系统中，每个成员拥有一个投票权，所有新协定都必须获得所有成员的同意。所以这个体系在原则上是民主的，尽管在实际谈判中可能常常演变成为数不多的几个国家间的谈判，而且在立场上常常发生僵持的局面。这种情况越来越多地发生在美国和欧盟与新兴经济体之间。

关贸总协定和世贸组织之间的主要不同以及多哈回合的建立是因为发达国家和发展中国家的相互关系发生了冲突。关贸总协定转型为世贸组织时，经合组织国家间制成品的贸易几乎是没有障碍的。所以，此前的贸易议题谈判是围绕着经合组织国家与发展中国家之间、发展中国家贸易自由化与经合组织国家之间，以及发展中国家之间的贸易自由化开展的。[12]该议程的转变也是为了聚焦制造业以外的行业，如农业和服务业的市场自由化和市场自律。发展中国家，特别是新兴经济体，被要求在制造行业做出让步。同样人们也希望发达国家在它们的农业领域采取市场放开的措施。多哈回合中要克服的一个主要挑战是世贸组织成员力图将一系列不相干的议题放进一个一揽子方案中——即所有成员国都必须签字同意的"一揽子承诺"。[13]

(3) 二十国集团

二十国集团是其成员国关于国际经济合作和决策的主要论坛。其成员包括19个国家和欧盟。二十国集团的每届主席每年都会邀请数个国家成为客座成员。二十国集团已经成为一个解决金融合作问题的非正式国家间组织,由主要发达国家和部分新兴经济体的财政部长组成。目前,所有金砖国家都是二十国集团的成员。

表3 多哈回合中取得的进展和遇到的困难

进展	第九次部长级会议上达成的协定包括以下十个文件:巴厘岛贸易便利化一揽子协定、一般服务、出于粮食安全目的的公共储备、关于关税率配额管理的谅解、出口竞争、棉花、最不发达国家优惠性原产地规则、针对最不发达国家服务和服务提供商优惠待遇的豁免运作、针对最不发达国家的免税和免配额的市场准入、特殊和差别待遇的监督机制。
当前的问题	(1) 针对农业领域和粮食安全问题的市场放开。 (2) 农业出口补贴方面没有约束力的承诺。
立场上的分歧	没有明显的立场上的分歧。 (1) 有共同诉求的国家正在为达成一个国际服务贸易协定(即 TiSA)进行谈判。 (2) 对于应该怎样对待美国和欧盟的补贴和印度的保护性措施仍有不同的意见。 (3) 巴厘岛议程达成后进展迟缓。

资料来源:作者的分析。

发达经济体十国集团自 1962 年以来定期在巴塞尔开会讨论货币和金融事务。[14]与此对应,一个由 24 个国家组成的集团于 20 世纪 70 年代早期成立,是十国集团的南方国家副本,尽管这个组织在政策影响力上远远不及前者。相比之下,工业化国家组成的七国集团自 1975 年以来就定期开会。七国集团和十国集团国家于 1975 年成立了一个叫作巴塞尔银行监管委员会(BCBS)的工作小组,探索与全球金融有关的问题。这个小组于 1988 年拟定了《巴塞尔资本协议》,这是评估跨境银行资本状况的一个框架。1997年又确定了评估跨境银行资本状况的核心原则。1999 年,七国集团创立了"金融稳定论坛"(FSF),现在更名为"金融稳定委员会",旨在促进与商业金融机构监督和监测有关的信息交流和合作。但这三个工作组只是政府公务员级别的,而不是部长级别的。[15]

二十国集团是一个有益的组织,在增强互信方面将起到越来越大的作用(在诸如金融治理这样的领域)。重要的全球金融、财政和货币议题都在二十国集团中讨论。有了这个平台,二十国集团国家通过集体讨论,已经在财政和货币合作方面取得了许多进展,同时提供了一个可能比另起炉灶更好的环境。二十国集团也被用来推动世贸组织多哈回合的完成,却并不成功。另外,二十国集团还通过引入新的辩论议题,成功推进了全球的发展。

除此之外,二十国集团在不同的峰会上,对国际货币基金组织和世界银行的改革和议程也提出了建议。例如,二十国集团早期的收获之一是2009年达成的将国际货币基金组织的财力增加三倍的协议,将总规模增至7500美元,以支持2500亿美元的新的特别提款权,以及向贸易金融领域另外追加2500亿美元,外加1000亿美元支持向多边开发银行发放有条件的借款。二十国集团国家承诺推动国际货币基金组织中代表性超过其实力的国家把手中5%的配额移交到代表性过低的国家手中,并推动世界银行中发展中国家和转型中国家的投票权提高3%。然而,如何将他们的决议落实到有关机构的行动和执行中,人们心里有个大大的问号。

表4 2008年二十国集团呼吁改革后成员构成发生的变化

全球金融监察机构	先前的成员	先前的发展中国家成员	扩容发生的时间	扩容增加的成员
国际证监会组织(IOSCO)	澳大利亚、法国、德国、中国香港、意大利、日本、墨西哥、荷兰、加拿大、西班牙、瑞士、英国、美国	墨西哥	2009年2月	巴西、印度、中国
巴塞尔银行监管委员会(BCBS)	比利时、加拿大、法国、德国、意大利、日本、卢森堡、荷兰、西班牙、瑞士、瑞典、英国、美国	无	2009年3月	澳大利亚、巴西、中国、印度、韩国、墨西哥、俄国
金融稳定委员会(FSF/B)	澳大利亚、加拿大、法国、德国、中国香港、意大利、日本、荷兰、新加坡、瑞士、英国、美国	无	2009年3月	阿根廷、巴西、中国、印度、韩国、墨西哥、俄罗斯、沙特阿拉伯、土耳其、西班牙、欧共体

资料来源:根据 Griffith-Jones and Young(2009)and Griffith-Jones(2009)的资料改编。

二、金砖国家在当前全球经济治理中的作用

在全球层面上,金砖国家在经济和政治的重要性上可能不尽相同,但它们分别是自己所在地区的领跑者。金砖国家或多或少都超越当前主要的全球治理结构看待自己,并且在很多场合与传统列强的代表发生过对抗。金砖国家过去相同的经历在金砖国家间形成了概念上的共同基础。进一步推动金砖国家形成一个实体的是在多极原则基础上调整全球治理结构,反映全球政治和经济格局中新的发展。

金砖国家在全球经济中不断提高的重要性不会自动导致其在世贸组织或其他国家经济治理结构中有更多的发言权。更多的情况是,金砖国家在采取集体行动前,常常单独或通过更小规模的国家组织采取行动。

表5 金砖国家在当前全球经济治理中的立场

	贸易议题	金融议题
金砖国家	不同的观点;扩大发展中国家在有决定意义的"绿室会议"中的参与作用(贸易谈判阶段)	(1)巴西加入了印度、中国和南非已经加入的《巴塞尔协议Ⅲ》框架。俄国推迟到2014年1月才实施这个框架 (2)在国际货币基金组织或世界银行推动改革进程,提高新兴经济体和发展中国家在世界经济中的重要性,以便在2015年1月前实施2010年确定的改革。 (3)期待发起另一次世界银行份额审查,本届份额有效期将于2015年10月截止。
巴西	阻止了免税免配额(DFQF)协议	已落实《巴塞尔协议Ⅲ》
俄罗斯	主要关注消除伤害其国内生产者的贸易限制	俄罗斯将该框架的落实推迟至2014年1月
印度	支持关注最不发达国家议题的"小型一揽子方案"	已落实《巴塞尔协议Ⅲ》
中国	致力于世贸组织的多边化,但对诸边谈判也持开放态度	已落实《巴塞尔协议Ⅲ》
南非	支持发达国家给最不发达国家以优惠待遇的小型一揽子方案;支持海关经纪机构为推动贸易便利化分享信息	已落实《巴塞尔协议Ⅲ》

资料来源:作者的分析。

(1) 国际货币基金组织/世界银行的改革

2009年，金砖国家提议推动配额和选举权改革，推动国际货币基金组织和世界银行分别向新兴经济体和发展中国家转移7%和6%的配额和选举权份额，同时提出了一个新的配额改革计划。2014年6月，金砖国家领导人又一次敦促国际货币基金组织进行改革，以保证新兴经济体和发展中国家有足够的代表，同时，世界银行集团须在2015年10月前对新的份额百分比进行审查。[16]金砖国家对国际货币基金组织和世界银行改革的政策立场在金砖国家第六次峰会发表的《福塔莱萨宣言》中有明晰的反映。金砖国家"对2010年国际货币基金改革计划仍没有得到实施感到失望和严重关注"，希望加强"国际货币基金组织治理结构的现代化，以更好地反映新兴市场和发展中国家在世界经济中日益提高的重要性"。该基金必须保持以配额为基础的体制。金砖国家呼吁如果今年年底前2010年的改革计划还是不能生效，那么国际货币基金组织必须找到办法推进改革的进程。另外，金砖国家坚持改革最晚必须在"2015年1月完成"。①

金砖国家欢迎世界银行集团设定的帮助有关国家结束极端贫困、推动分享繁荣的目标。但是，金砖国家也呼吁"该机构及其成员向更加民主的治理结构有效推进"。金砖国家期待着尽快启动下一次世界银行持股份额的审查，以便在约定的截止时间——2015年10月前完成有关工作。

金砖国家在通过多边协作和金融合作计划改善国际金融架构方面一直十分积极。另外，金砖国家认为新开发银行是提高资源的多样性和可获得性、推动发展、保证全球经济稳定的一个补充措施。②

(2) 世贸组织

世贸组织中的20至25个主要贸易国并不都能经常被邀请坐上多边谈判的贵宾席或其他小集团会议。罗伯特·阿泽维多先生（Mr. Roberto Azevedo）被选为该机构的总干事，提升了巴西作为北方国家和南方国家调解人的作用。金砖国家在全球贸易系统中的重要性不断提升的一个标志就是世贸组织的决策过程在多大程度上为迎合它的需要进行了调整和改革。"老队伍"被新的群体代替，成为"新队伍"③，即所谓四国集团、六国集

---

① 第六次金砖国家峰会签署的《福塔莱萨宣言》，网址：http://www.chinadaily.com.cn/language_tips/trans/2014-07/17/content_17814819_2.htm。

② 第六次金砖国家峰会签署的《福塔莱萨宣言》，http://www.chinadaily.com.cn/language_tips/trans/2014-07/17/content_17814819_2.htm。

③ "新队伍"指的是世贸组织谈判中最重要的四个成员。它们是印度、巴西、美国和欧盟。

团、五大利益相关方、七国集团。这些组合代表着决策的贵宾席，通往共识的最早几步就从这里迈出，而巴西和印度（与欧盟和美国一起）被邀请参与所有相关的活动。在2008年的谈判中，这个组合扩大到七个成员，包括进了中国（以及欧盟、美国、巴西、印度、澳大利亚和日本）。这次把中国包括进来不仅仅是一种象征。因为2003年以来欧盟和美国反复使用否决权（自多哈发展议程在坎昆部长级会议上首次陷入重大僵局以来），巴西、印度和中国单独或联合地，再也不怕使用它们的否决权。

在贸易问题上，金砖国家重申了它们对一个开放的、包容的、非歧视性的、透明的和建立在规则基础上的多边贸易体系的支持，继续努力，"继2013年12月在印尼巴厘岛召开的第九次部长级会议（MC9）取得积极进展以后，促进世贸组织多哈回合的成功完成"①。

金砖国家还重申了"在已经取得的进展的基础上，今年年底前完成拟定后巴厘岛时代工作计划的承诺"。优先议题包括：出于粮食安全目的的公共储备和贸易便利化协定。金砖国家强烈支持作为多边贸易体系安全性和可预见性的基石的世贸组织的争议解决系统。除多边贸易体系之外，金砖国家还承认地区性贸易协定的重要性，同时努力保证它们的开放性、包容性和透明性，避免采用非包容的和歧视性的条款和标准。②

（3）二十国集团

二十国集团把发展中国家集结上了全球舞台以提高它们的代表性，金砖国家因此表明了它们对二十国集团所起作用的强烈支持，称二十国集团为"其成员国间国际经济协调与合作的第一论坛"，强调"二十国集团更广泛，更包容，更多样化，更具代表性和更有效"。人们认为，发展中国家在国际经济治理中代表性的提升，意味着歧视性贸易政策、制裁和胁迫将得到抑制。特别是，金砖国家经济体强调"发展中国家的可持续的发展模式和发展道路应得到充分的尊重，发展中国家必要的政策空间必须得到保证"③。

（4）金砖国家的新开发银行

金砖国家间的合作在新型全球经济治理的形成方面结出了不同硕果，

---

① 第六次金砖国家峰会签署的《福塔莱萨宣言》，网址：http://www.chinadaily.com.cn/language_tips/trans/2014-07/17/content_17814819_2.htm。

② 第六次金砖国家峰会签署的《福塔莱萨宣言》，网址：http://www.chinadaily.com.cn/language_tips/trans/2014-07/17/content_17814819_2.htm。

③ 巴西、俄罗斯、印度和中国在第二次金砖国家峰会上签署的联合声明，2010年。

不仅为其他发展中国家提供了潜在的范例,还为发达国家认识到目前全球经济治理中的缺陷提供了一个很好的榜样。

新开发银行(NDB)设有一位行长(首任由印度人担任,任期为六年)、一位理事会主席(俄罗斯人担任)、一位董事会主席(巴西人担任)、一个总部(在上海)和一个位于约翰内斯堡的地区中心。① 新开发银行的启动资金为 500 亿美元。与其他地区类似的项目一样,金砖国家开设的这一银行也采取同等份额、同等投票权的机制,五个签约国各出 100 亿美元。该基础资本初期将用于为金砖国家内的基础设施和"可持续发展"项目提供资金,但其他中低收入国家也将可以补购和申请资金。

金砖国家的新开发银行将为当前多边金融机构的不足部分提供补充。新开发银行是为更好和更有效地利用全球金融资源,是对当前和地区性金融机构的补充。另外,应急储备金安排(CRA)将在收支平衡困难时期向成员国额外提供 1000 亿美元的流动性保护。与新开发银行平均投入的资金池不同,应急储备金安排中,中国投入 41%,巴西、印度和俄罗斯分别投入 18%,南非投入 5%。在应急储备金安排中,中国对巴西、俄罗斯和印度的投票权之比分别为 2.2 倍,小于国际货币基金组织中美国(国际货币基金组织的最大股东,拥有 16.75% 的投票权)对日本(国际货币基金组织第二大股东,拥有 6.23% 的投票权)2.7 倍的差距。[17] 这项安排作为一项缓解短期流动性困难的重要机制性成果,将帮助成员国防止发生金融危机,促进新兴经济体间的货币合作,强化全球金融安全网络。

表6 金砖国家新开发银行

业务部门	资本安排	成员国义务	决策机制与投票权
银行资本	启动资金为 500 亿美元,以后将逐渐增至 1000 亿美元。	金砖国家初期各投入 100 亿美元,总额将达 500 亿美元。	其投票体系为一致同意机制。未经其他四个成员的一致同意,任何成员不得增加其资本份额。该银行将允许新成员的加入,但金砖国家的资本份额不得少于 55%。*

---

① Http://news.yahoo.com/cabinet-welcomes-brics-development-bank-115111670.html。

续表

业务部门	资本安排	成员国义务	决策机制与投票权
应急储备金安排	为1000亿美元。	中国投入41%；巴西、印度、俄罗斯各投入18%；南非投入5%。**	（1）管理委员会将在一致同意的基础上做决定，并对应急储备金安排重要的及战略性的决策负责； （2）常务委员将对应急储备金安排高官级别的和运营方面的决策负责，并由来自各成员国的一位董事和一位候补董事组成； （3）决策采取加权投票制，各方的权重根据以下原则获得：(i) 5%的总投票权将在各方平均分配；(ii) 余下部分将按各方承诺出资额相对规模分配。所以，金砖各国的投票权份额分别为：18.1%、18.1%、18.1%、39.95%和5.75%。***

* "BRICS Bank Ready for Launch-Russian Finance Minister", Russia and India Report, 10 July 2014, Retrieved 20 July, 2014, http：//in. rbth. com/economics/2014/07/10/brics_bank_ready_for_launch_-_russian_finance_minister_36599. html.

**《关于建立金砖国家应急储备安排的条约》。

*** 根据作者的计算。

三、金砖国家在全球经济治理中进一步巩固相互间关系的展望

金砖国家对全球治理的诉求，无论是单独的还是集体的，都推动了有关的改革和演进，而不是革命。金砖国家的基础植根于各成员国长期共同的经济利益，包括改革过时的全球金融和经济架构，强化国际法的原则和标准，支持各国经济中许多行业的互补性。金砖国家的参与使世界经济的增长更加多元化，成为国际经济关系更加民主化的推动力量。[18]

金砖国家之所以能走到一起，根源是全球经济危机带来的结果——以及各成员国希望在国际金融体系的管理中有更强大的声音的渴望。分析家指出，这些国家走到一起，为成员国提供了更加强韧的连接纽带。另外，金砖国家还能加入至少10个主要地区性组织。（见表7）如果能有效利用，它们将在一系列全球论坛中占据有利的战略优势。

表7　金砖国家和10个重要地区性组织

金砖国家	金砖国家参与的10个重要地区性组织
金砖国家	独联体（CIS） 集体安全条约组织（CSTO） 欧亚经济共同体（EurAsEc） 上海合作组织（SCO） 亚太经济合作（APEC）论坛 南美洲国家联盟（UNASUR） 南方共同市场（Mersosur） 非洲联盟（AU） 南部非洲发展共同体（SADC） 南亚区域合作联盟（SAARC）

资料来源：作者收集。

金砖国家的政策制定者们通过发现可以共同追求的目标，强化金砖国家全球影响力。金砖国家到目前为止主要的共同目标是进一步提升自己现有的全球影响力。因此把金砖国家定义为一个正在努力建设的过程中的组织更合理。金砖国家未来是否能够合作应对重要的全球性问题，如气候变化，并建设有效的、能供其他发展中国家效仿的国内体制，还有待观察。

为了与2014年峰会（福塔莱萨）的成果保持一致，各成员国已经采取步骤贯彻深化和扩大金砖国家间贸易合作的承诺。这些步骤主要是达成双边和地区性贸易协议，鼓励国内企业在金砖国家投资，创造新的机制推动贸易和投资合作，以及提议开发新的金融机构和工具。

参考文献

[1] "The BRICS and the Future of 'Informal' IGOs", February 5, 2014, http: //www. isn. ethz. ch/Digital-Library/Articles/Detail/? lng = en&id = 176226.

[2] Barry Eichengreen, *Globalizing Capital — A History of International Monetary System*, Princeton University Press, 1996.

[3] J. Keane and D. W. te Velde, *The New Landscape of Economic Governance: Strengthening the Role of Emerging Economies*, EDC2020 Working Paper, 2012, http: //www. edc2020. eu/121. 0. html.

[4] Ella Kokotsis, "Advancing Accountability in BRICS Governance", BRICS New

Delhi Summit, 2012.

[5] Mikhail Titarenko, "Potential to Boost Performance as an Engine of Global Growth", BRICS New Delhi Summit, 2012.

[6] Anon, "The Trillion-dollar Club", *The Economist*, 15 April, 2012.

[7] Carol Wise, Leslie Elliott Armijo and Saori Katada eds. , *Unexpected Outcomes: How Emerging Markets Survived the Global Financial Crisis*, book manuscript, under review.

[8] Philip Alexander, "Top 1000 Banks 2011", *The Banker*, 30 June, 2011.

[9] Robin Harding, "BRICS Say European IMF Claim 'Obsolete'", *Financial Times*, 24 May, 2011; Sebastian Mallaby, "Can the BRICs Take the IMF?", *Foreign Affairs*, 9 June, 2011.

[10] Martin A. Weiss, "Multilateral Development Banks: General Capital Increases", Washington, D. C. : Congressional Research Service, 27 January, 2012; Robert H. Wade, "Emerging World Order: From Multi-polarity to Multilateralism in the World Bank, IMF, and G20", *Politics & Society*, Vol. 39, No 3, 31 August, 2011.

[11] Kapur, "The Changing Anatomy of Governance", Edwin M. Truman ed. , *Reforming the IMF for the 21st Century*, Washington, D. C. : Peterson Institute of International Economics, April 2006.

[12] P. Collier, "Why the WTO Is Deadlocked: And What Can Be Done about It", Mimeo, 2005, Available at: http://users.ox.ac.uk/~econpco/research/pdfs/WTO-deadlock.pdf.

[13] J. Rollo, "Global Europe: Old Mercantilist Wine in New Bottles?" Special Issue on the *EU's New Trade Policy in Aussenwirtschaft*, Edited by Simon Evenett, 2007.

[14] J. A. Scholte, "Governing Global Finance", CSGR Working Paper, 2002, No. 88, /02, http://wrap.warwick.ac.uk/2030/1/WRAP_Scholte_wp8802.pdf.

[15] S. Griffith-Jones and K. Young, "Reforming Governance of International Financial Regulation: Have the G20 Done Enough?" IPD and Hewlett Policy Brief, 2009, http://policydialogue.org/files/publications/Griffith-Jones_Young_Policy_Brief.pdf; S. Griffith-Jones; "Perspectives on the Governance of Global Financial Regulation", paper prepared for the Commonwealth Finance Ministers Meeting, 2009, http://academiccommons.columbia.edu/catalog/ac:153941.

[16] Xu Xiujun, "BRICS and Global Economic Governance System Reform from the Emerging Economies Perspective", *Contemporary World*, August 2014.

[17] Jiang Xufeng, "The BRICS Change in Global Economic Governance Order", http://bank.hexun.com/2014-08-19/167661958.html.

[18] Zhang Yan, "BRICS Works for Shared Prosperity", *The Hindu*, 13 April, 2011.

金砖国家治理能力现代化评析
——国家构建的视角

褚松燕[*] 贾路南[**]

现代国家的构建是一个不断寻求国家与社会、市场关系合理化的持续性历史进程。但这个进程在不同的国家表现不尽相同。蒂里以欧洲为分析对象,将国家构建描述为"通过一个对特定群体实施垄断暴力的中央集权的独立国家来提供专业化的人事和控制领土完整性的永久性制度"[1]。欧洲通过家产制阶段(一直延续到1500年)、代理制阶段(1400年到1700年)、民族化阶段(1700年到1850年)和专门化阶段(从1850年起)四个阶段的发展,国家逐渐实现了对军事力量和税收的直接控制,建立军队、行政管理机关等专门机构,并通过这些机构,日益卷入了纠纷裁定、经济分配甚至生产活动当中,进而使国家的监控能力在深度和广度上都得到了扩大。摩尔(Moore)的《民主和专制的社会起源》对法国、俄国、中国、日本、印度、德国等进行了比较,指出这些国家中阶级关系或联盟关系的不同造成了暴力使用的对象和目标的差异,从而导致了民主政体、法西斯主义和共产主义的产生。[2] 斯克波尔(Skocpol)的《国家与社会革命》,在对18世纪末法国革命、20世纪初俄国革命和1911—1949年中国革命的分析中,指出了国家独立追求目标的能力是由其组织强制力量的能力以及它与国内外其他强大利益集团的关系决定的。她认为,虽然三个国家的内部结构和历史处境不同,但是革命的结果都产生了一个中央集权的、官僚制的、吸引民众的民族国家,自上而下的官僚制管理和自下而上的民众参与都加强了。[3] 上述学者们的研究无论是跨越了宏大的历史阶段,还是截取了在时间段上具有可比性的不同国家,都对国家能力在保持社会稳定和经济发展方面的作用予以高度的重视。但需要指出的是,不同的国家因发展时段和自身禀赋的差异,在国家构建路径上呈现出差异性。第二

---

[*] 褚松燕,国家行政学院教授、博士生导师。
[**] 贾路南,国家行政学院2014级博士生。

次世界大战之后新独立的国家，包括中华人民共和国在内，其国家构建的过程伴随着现代化进程，而这个过程也是国家能力强化的过程，是政治权力集中和对经济社会发展调控能力提高的过程。在这个过程中，包括中国在内的许多发展中国家都逐渐发现，西方中心的现代化理论抽离了西方的历史和经验则可能是布满鲜花的陷阱，现代化应当在充分考虑本国的历史传统、发展禀赋与全球角色基础上增强国家的实力。在对现代化认真反思与重塑的当下，金砖国家的兴起及其对现代化进程中的风险应对，开始展现出现代化与国家构建同步的阶段性实践经验。

一、国家治理能力：先行者与追赶者的经验

国家构建就是国家通过制度化建设调整国家与市场、国家与社会以及社会与市场之间这三重关系，使之有利于自己存在、维持和强大的过程。在这个过程中，国家既体现为理性的行为者，又是制度综合体。也正因为如此，国家与市场、社会之间的关系成为塑造和制约国家行为的外部要素，而国家内部的政党、官僚体系运作所体现出来的国家治理能力则反过来影响着市场和社会的发展情况。其中，国家行为的相对独立性不仅为经济和社会的发展提供秩序和制度保障，而且在国家、市场和社会之间的动态平衡中起着调节作用。从这个意义上说，一个国家的总体发展离不开国家治理行为的独立性和导向性。因此，国家构建不仅可以作为检视现代化进程的一个视角和基点，而且有助于动态地思考中国的政治发展。中共十八届三中全会专门将全面深化改革的总目标定为"完善和发展中国特色社会主义制度，推进国家治理体系和治理能力现代化"，其核心要义就是在新起点上凸显国家构建的重要意义。需要注意的是，中国语境中的"治理"与西方在20世纪80年代提出的"治理"概念事实上是有不同的。中国语境中的国家治理体系和治理能力现代化是从国家构建角度去谈的，更多强调的是国家层面的治国理政。而西方所提出的"少一些政府，多一些治理"更多的是在公共事务管理的操作层面。当前发达国家所面临的治理危机，以及中国所面临的国家复兴，其共同点反映在理论上就在于国家理论如何复兴，就是在当今的信息技术、后工业化以及人的流动性、跨界问题等复合风险环境中，如何去重新发现国家在其中的作用。这也是国家治理体系现代化超越工业化时代的现代化的关键所在。那么，国家治理能力主要包括哪些方面呢？

不同时期的不同研究者提出的答案也不尽相同。例如马克斯·韦伯（Max Weber）认为理性国家应当有自主能力、成本—收益的计算能力和制

度化能力。[4] 2010 年联合国发展研究所的报告《建设减少贫困的国家能力》中认为国家要有基本能力去保障五个方面，即帮助获取新技术、动员资源到生产性部门、执行标准和规制、建立社会公约、资助和监管社会服务项目提供。为此，国家必须能够有达成必要的同盟或政治解决方案的政治能力、为投资和社会发展提供资源的资源动员能力、向生产性部门和福利促进性部门分配资源的能力。[5] 无论研究者如何去界定国家构建进程中的国家能力，从总体上看，国家治理能力体现为两个基本方面：经济发展能力和矛盾调处能力。经济发展能力是国家构建的根本决定力量，而矛盾调处能力则是国家构建的成果得以巩固的检验性力量。这两个基本能力通过国家的制度化进程或法治进程体现出来，也都依赖于社会成员发展经济的积极性和和谐生活的合作性。因此，这个进程一方面要不断扩展社会成员主体地位的平等性，另一方面要不断使社会成员围绕着共同利益凝聚起来。中国已经深深卷入全球化当中，在国家构建和现代化进程中，不仅要看自己当下面临的现实以及未来的发展方向，而且还需要用国际视野去看中国的治理体系现代化问题。

1. 先行者的经验

欧美等发达国家作为已经完成现代化的国家，其国家治理能力所依赖的国家治理体系经由了漫长的制度化进程。英国 1640 年开始资产阶级革命，到 1688 年光荣革命似乎是结束，但不是这样的。1689 年的《权利法案》意味着立宪国家通过法律的形式规定了个人、社会与国家的基本关系，从制度上制约了国家权力的滥用，建立了国家法理合法性。尽管此后政党产生并形成了政党通过竞争产生政府的较为成熟的做法，但这仍然不是英国国家治理体系成熟的标志。国家治理能力依赖于国家治理的主体能力，直到 1928 年，英国女性享有普选权，才意味着英国治国理政的主体拓展到了全体成年公民。由此扩大了国家动员经济发展的能力，扩大了国家的税基，进而使国家调处矛盾的能力得到提升。美国从 1775 年独立战争到南北战争，再到 1964 年的《民权法案》，黑人才真正地享有了完整意义上的选举权。亨廷顿所总结的"现代性孕育着稳定，而现代化过程充满了动荡"[6]，实则是将西方发达国家现代性达成的过程中公民资格权利或公民身份抛却性别、种族差别的过程中的动荡置于一旁了。第二次世界大战后，西方发达国家在经济繁荣的同时普遍通过福利制度编织了几乎覆盖全民的社会保障安全网，将所有公民都连接在一起，这也使国家通过行政力量更有效地控制社会、个人和市场的能力得到强化。

这些发达国家的国家治理体系制度化和国家治理能力的增强，其经验路径主要表现在以下几个方面：首先，这些国家在治理现代化进程中都保持了国家主权的完整、独立；其次，这些国家权力来源的正当性得到了认同，而且这个认同已经推向了全世界，这就是基于人民主权的社会契约论；再次，国家治理体系通过向性别平等开放、族群平等开放、阶层在自由表达和选票的平等上的开放达到了政治吸纳的功效；最后，权力行使的可监督性和可视性通过相关的权力制衡设计和公民诸权利的扩张得以实现。

2. 追赶者的经验

相较而言，第二次世界大战后获得独立的国家，在现代化进程中国家治理能力的提升也首先通过政治体系的制度化来获得，但是，不少新独立的国家，如中国的近邻韩国、印尼、泰国，以及金砖国家中的巴西等，一开始都试图效仿西方的民主模式来获得国家治理能力的提升，但在政治体系全面开放和社会流动完全放开之后，收获的不是国家治理能力的提升，而是15年左右的社会混乱、发展停滞和矛盾冲突。[7]此后，军人干政形成了威权政体，国家治理体系高度浓缩，即政治权力高度集中且并不开放，将社会冲突压制到一定程度，但放开市场，由此获得了经济的高速发展。韩国、印尼等保持了30多年的经济增长，其结果是社会的利益结构和社会心理发生了变化，社会的开放程度也使人们的比较心理发挥出优势，形成社会的新整合，进而选择新的国家治理之道。这些国家的经验是：首先，移植西方制度后付出了代价，进而去寻找自己的发展道路；其次，不约而同地选择了威权政体，经济高速发展，在完成工业化的同时带来社会结构和价值观的变化，这样一来就促使了国家权力开放的进程与公民权利的进程相互协调，这样才能促进稳定的制度化。

1992年，邓小平在南方谈话中就曾经提到过，"恐怕再有三十年的时间，我们才会在各方面形成一整套更加成熟、更加定型的制度。在这个制度下的方针、政策，也将更加定型化"[8]。这是邓小平作为国家领导人，按照中国的经济社会发展状况从国家发展的战略层面做出的论断，而中国的实践也说明，到目前为止，中国也仍然是处于一种制度化的进程当中。西方民主理论学者在研究中国转型的时候，更多关注的是在西方的民主化、民主道路的导向之下中国怎么样实现政治转型，也做出过相关的时间点预测，但往往并不考虑中国国家构建或国家治理能力的状况。中国政治发展的长远目标是探索出一种超大规模的国家各个领域协调发展的社会主义民主政治。中国国家治理体系和治理能力的现代化事实上构成我们中国政治发展长远目标当中的一个阶段。按照邓小平的战略设想，到2022年左右，中国完成国家治理体系现代化，国家治理能力获得大幅度提升。这体现在两个方面，一个方面是提高执政党的执政能力，以顺应社会经济变化的要求，这主要是一个合法性的问题。另外一个方面就是提升政府的政治管理能力，动员和利用社会资源弥补社会统治的不足和缺陷。这两个方面综合起来，就是提高发展经济的能力和矛盾调处的能力。而这同时也意味着社会公众选择权的拓展以及执政党和政府对此所应做出的制度化回应。

二、金砖国家治理能力现代化进程中的主要风险与挑战

不少学者预测金砖国家在今后20年内对世纪经济的贡献将把美国远远抛在身后，甚至直接与七国集团等顶级国际组织旗鼓相当。然而，金砖国家都处于国家构建与现代化交织在一起的进程中。且这些国家的现代化进程基本上依赖于对国家自然资源或社会资源的大量消耗，巨量的财富积累并非造就了可持续发展的定型结构，现代化的前路充满变数，可以说挑战与机遇并存。面对新形势下现代化进程中出现的各种风险，金砖国家政府也在国家各方面体制的全面调整中寻找应对措施。

1. 金砖国家的经济增长方式面临不可持续的风险

巴西自独立以来所实行的现代化政策既促进了国家实现快速现代化的最初蓝图，又为现代化建设发展到一定阶段就会浮现危机埋下了伏笔。例如，巴西的经济增长很大程度上依赖通货膨胀式的经济策略，在一定程度上刺激了国内经济的繁荣，政府也利用"通货膨胀税"实现了资金较快积累，从保证投资额的角度上来说有积极意义。然而，长期通货膨胀导致的路径依赖使得这种不对称发展战略最终失去控制，虽然巴西政府在不遗余力地控制通胀的负面效应，但危机的根源依然难以移除，甚至存在爆发更大危机的风险。不对称的发展战略也造成巴西快速增长的工业产值与缓慢发展的农业经济间的矛盾，"巴西的工业化基本上是建立在出口农业的基础上的，内需农业相对萎缩，农村工业也未有适当发展，致使大量农村人口外流，形成严重的社会问题。这种工业化模式没有取得迅速缩小城乡差别的结果"。[9]另外，国家对资本经济的投入也远远高于社会事业，社会指数与经济指数不匹配，也是构成巴西现代化未来风险的重要因素。

俄罗斯在中央政府领导下实现经济转型方面长期面临困难。俄罗斯经济最大的阻碍在于，苏联时期的粗放型发展模式造成俄罗斯在新经济环境下缺乏核心竞争力，军事科技的优势也逐渐消失，苏联解体后过度依赖资源出口的经济模式实际上是粗放型经济模式的延续，在构建现代化经济增长模式中的消极作用越来越明显。因为这些风险主要是历史因素造成的，长期内不易化解。[10] 具体原因有：（1）俄罗斯的重要企业大多是资源型企业，且与政府部门的利益关联错综复杂，缺乏建立创新型经济的动力；（2）俄罗斯在进行资源型经济到创新型经济转型中面临旧经济体制所带来的巨大既得利益的诱惑，依靠资源提升本国综合国力也是俄罗斯在短期内的现实选择；（3）制造业水平相比发达经济体非常落后，实现从资源到产品的转化十分困难；（4）国家对创新型与高科技产业的投资不足，国际市场对俄罗斯经济发展的信心指数也不高；（5）高层政治集团对现代化与经济体制转型的兴趣不高，竭力保护既得利益的势力在决策集体内依然强大；（6）俄罗斯与西方国家的关系在总体上仍然被定义为相互利用大于合作共赢，所以俄罗斯的现代化借助发达经济体的力量存在诸多变数。

印度的软件和IT服务外包虽取得巨大成就，但过分偏重会导致因投资制造业过少而造成的整体现代化乏力，"做'世界后台办公室'就可以实现印度的现代化"只是当局的一厢情愿。理由有四：一是印度作为世界上人口最多的国家之一，对消费品的满足不可完全依赖国际市场。然而现状是印度国内服务制造业的基础设施落后，对技术创新的投入与扶持严重不足，造成国内没有形成接收软件研发成果的市场，只能徘徊在发达国家外围依赖技术换取产品。二是制造业的低迷造成现代化产业对农村劳动力的吸纳能力低下，城市化进展缓慢，农村地区也同样缺乏经济增长点，国家现代化成为无本之木。三是作为支柱产业的软件业对国际市场的过分依赖，只得根据国际需求走势随波逐流，难以形成稳定的宏观经济结构，而现代化的重要标准之一就是经济的稳定。四是软件行业所培育的社会团体均为精英集团，而且所占人口比重极小，占有社会收益的比重却极高，其他绝大部分人口处于无法获得利益的边缘部分。长期的结构性分配不平等容易导致国家经济社会发展畸形，即便实现了部分现代化也是被扭曲了的现代化，远远无法达到全面现代化的标准。

南非也同样依靠国内丰富的能源、贵金属与宝石矿藏为现代化提供了重要基础，同时在国际政治经济中占有举足轻重的地位。由于发达国家经济的持续回暖与发展中国家尤其是金砖国家经济增长重回正轨，南非的战略性资源在国际市场需求强劲。但是随着矿产资源储量日益减少,开采难度和成本逐年增加,采矿业在国民经济中的地位下滑趋势明显。过度依赖采矿业收入也为南非带来了长期积累的结构性困境,影响经济发展新空间的拓展。第一,南非家庭与企业的储蓄额过低,造成国内投资乏力,政府投资基础设施资金严重不足;第二,由于自身在财富积累过程中没有注意把握未来经济发展趋势,没有为高科技人才的成长提供合适的环境,导致低技术工人供应拥挤,高技术人才流失严重;第三,以物流、信息服务为新经济增长必备条件的基础设施提供效率低下,基础建设速度缓慢,遂成为提高经济核心竞争力的瓶颈。[11]

2. 金砖国家的国家治理体系未能与经济社会的发展进程相配合

巴西学者皮雷斯(Pires)认为巴西自20世纪30年代现代化伊始,就没有树立起彻底变革国家的政治经济体制,而是在外部世界的压力下做不触动利益分配格局、只反映经济诉求的"保守现代化",忽视了对经济社会全面发展的考量,因此时至今日巴西的现代化工程依然面临巨大的发展变数。国家对收入差距缺乏调控措施,基尼系数居高不下,不论在企业微观层面还是在国家宏观层面均出现了巨大的收入鸿沟。地区间发展不平衡显著,公共投入只关心让发达地区变得更好,而任由落后地区变得更差。城市外围严重缺乏管理和服务,成为城市现代化的阴暗面。[12]

俄罗斯的国家相较于市场来说,处于明显的强势地位,但是,政府的强势并不意味着国家治理能力就高。俄罗斯的经济结构远未摆脱苏联时期国家干预经济、控制一切经济社会计划模式的影响,国有经济占国民经济的比重过大。大型企业缺乏竞争与创新的动力,中小企业因进入市场成本过高而普遍发育不良,发展前景暗淡。为应对2008年金融危机,国家干预的力度与范围不减反增,与其他金砖国家相比,俄罗斯的经济市场化进程明显过缓。支撑现代化经济体制的各方面制度不完善,包括国家市场化程度低,效率差,政府行政管理和服务的能力差,俄罗斯多年来的市场化成果随着体制腐败程度的不断加深而几乎被消耗殆尽。严峻的形势迫使俄罗斯的领导集体开始思考政治体制的转型问题,梅德韦杰夫(Medvedev)就曾指出俄罗斯民主的目标应是国家的法制建设、综合国力建设、信息化建设与信用社会建设的统一。[13]

种姓传统以及政治生活中传统与现代之间未能很好地调和使得印度的国家治理体系陷入两难处境,一方面,政治精英集团努力维护自身的广泛权力,操纵政府和议会决策,轻视民主精神;另一方面又要极力为国家的民主制度之名进行辩护，浪费了大量可用于现代化建设的政治与社会资源，进而削弱了国家治理能力。

3. 社会问题随现代化变革的加深而愈发尖锐

巴西的社会问题表现在八个方面：（1）两极分化、贫困现象加剧。20世纪80年代经济改革后巴西出现了私有经济的蓬勃发展，但同时也伴随着大量国有资产被私人占有、贫富差距迅速拉大的现象。（2）失业和半失业人口不断增加。巴西在战后初期即开始的迅速工业化造成了农村经济相对萎缩，大量农村人口进入城市谋生，加之市场经济改革后国有部门吸纳劳动力的水平急剧下降和技术革命所带来的劳动者高技能化门槛，巴西社会的失业包袱短期内难以卸下。（3）城市犯罪率上升也是重经济发展轻社会建设的必然结果。（4）农村土地产权过度集中，大地主拥有巨量优质土地资源却不产出价值，而依靠种植为生的农民却因无地可耕长期生活贫困，极易引发分配不平等双方的暴力冲突。（5）歧视妇女的现象依然存在，加剧了社会不平等程度。（6）种族歧视问题长期得不到解决。从历史上看，巴西的发展很大程度上建立在殖民时期的农业经济基础上，得到解放的大批有色族裔人口却无法在社会分配制度中翻身，种族间各方面差异明显。（7）社会保障制度存在严重缺陷。随着巴西人口的急剧增加与老龄化社会的逐步形成，养老金制度面临严峻挑战，国家财政为支付高额养老金已形成巨大缺口，配合较高通胀率与收入分配不均，社会可持续前景堪忧。（8）教育滞后于经济发展。国家对基础教育投入不足，政策也未对国民教育事业进行必要的倾斜，导致社会投资按市场规律越来越聚集到高利润行业，与之相对应的是高辍学率与低识字率，无法为将来发展出高素质劳动者做储备。

印度存在着严重的人口素质低下和劳动力过剩问题，种姓制度基础上的社会分层现象加剧，城乡分配失衡无法得到有效控制，不稳定因素呈爆发式增长，这些都成为摆在印度的社会治理面前的难题。更加棘手的是，信息技术的突飞猛进有力推动了境内恐怖势力、宗教极端势力和分裂势力之间的联系。在网络时代，颠覆势力更加有效地联起手来制造事端，散布危险言论，使民众思维更加混乱，为社会现代化带来了巨大隐患。印度还面临严重的宗教风险，如锡克教、伊斯兰教、印度教等彼此之间互不相容，增加了社会分裂的风险。

中国的经济、政治和社会领域也都存在着不少问题，现在也面临着双重张力：一个是在外部，中国国力上升，国际空间的竞争加剧，冲突的可能性大增；一个在内部，一方面在工业化，一方面在后工业化，信息化升级，同时城镇化、老龄化等问题也出现，这些问题相叠加，使人们的参与欲望和权利主张的要求大大增加，而同时，国家治理体系是否现代化，就体现出是不是能够及时地用制度来对老百姓对权利的要求和参与欲望进行制度化，放开相关的通道，使老百姓有更多进行相关选择的权利，而目前，这个紧张关系越来越明显。

三、金砖国家国家治理能力的强化以及中国国家治理能力的重点

金砖国家都充分了解国家治理能力对政治秩序和经济—社会发展的重要性，因此也都采取了相关的改革措施来提升国家治理能力。中国也结合自身发展的实际提出了全面深化改革的主要举措。

1. 其他金砖国家强化国家治理能力的措施

巴西学者阿马多·塞尔沃（Amado Servo）指出，巴西的发展模式正在从单边主义，即对世界资本主义大国的完全依赖和埋头发展自身，转向多边主义路线，向由发展中国家组成的新兴市场和合作组织倾注更多精力。在经历了严重依赖出口型经济和自力更生开发国内市场这两个处于经济战略两端的发展模式之后，巴西提出的"相对自主战略"体现了国家在处理现代化路径选择问题上的成熟。一方面，巴西着重调整政府与社会公众之间的关系，如电子议员的实践就拉近了议会代表与选民之间的关系。另一方面，巴西重新调整政府间关系来平衡地区间发展差异，提高市级政府的管理能力，优化中央与市级政府的合作分工机制。地方政府积极引导公民社会与私人部门参与，为社会改革注入了新活力。对巴西地方政府推动的数据库创新计划的分析显示，60%的私人部门与公民社会或实体机构之间建立了某种伙伴关系，具体项目包括住房计划、社区建设、预算过程、发展规划、环境整治、公共服务外包、债务风险共担机制等。

俄罗斯则通过普京与梅德韦杰夫交替任职期间的努力，将国家存在的基础由统治集团对资源占有的强力转变为以人民为主体的支持度。立法放宽政党参与国家政策制定的限制和州长直接选举的决议扩大了政治领域的开放程度，政府与社会对话平台的建设与对反对派别的宽容政策也增加了执政党的可信度与支持度。在反对腐败方面，国家权力高层利用自上而下的改革措施推动官员财产透明化并建立包含总统在内的财产公示制度，还参照西方国家的政府改革经验，大规模裁撤多余机构，通过整合机构职能达到精简政府的目的，还通过与国际社会的合作遏制跨国腐败现象的上

升。谢列兹尼奥夫（Selezner）认为俄罗斯的国家治理体系发展必须明确几个基本原则。第一，俄罗斯应该把改革以最终实现现代化作为引领动力机制的总目标。第二，在保持中央集中领导为国家政治文化首要特征的前提下，激发社会组织参与政策体系建设的热情，使改革的动力实现双向运行。第三，在政治伦理方面重视公民对国家主义和平均主义的优先选择。第四，保证严格监督资金的划拨操作，与联邦和地区层次上的贪污腐败进行全面斗争。第五，调动起社会各方面力量，尤其是政府和企业两方面的努力，进一步完善法律制度，令改革事业的每一项举措都有法可依。[14]

印度在弥合社会分裂方面做出了巨大努力。首先，用法制保障少数民族的代表性。自1976年印度出台《公民权利保护法》，规定了不同种性和部族在联合政府中的席位比例，且经历了不断提高。至今在所有由中央政府和联邦政府运营的教育机构和各类组织中，列表种性和列表部族所占的比例已达到总席位的15%和7.5%，还为其他弱势阶层保留了27%的席位，配合专司地区发展的职能部门一同做好发展工作。其次，加强在北部地区招商引资的优惠力度，突出联邦财政转移支付的拉动作用。印度在国家建设2007—2012五年计划中，设立东北部地区管理委员会统领民族落后地区的发展规划与实施管理，综合运用"农村发展基金"和其他财政支持重点投入到基础设施建设、医疗卫生条件改善和农业技术推广上，努力缩小地区间发展差距。再次，为保护少数族群权益，印度政府每个五年计划中均规定，部落少数人群的教育经费要占到计划经费的一半左右。中央政府还对民族地区学生高等教育给予优待，保留其入学名额不少于5%。最后，通过民主议会制度合法地吸纳不同种族与种性的社会成员参与决策过程，在民族地区灌输民主政治观念，用现代化理念和全球化文明等"软权力"化解多种文化之间的隔阂，为社会冲突提供合理的碰撞机制和缓冲空间。

2. 中国国家治理能力的重点

2013年，中共十八届三中全会提出了全面深化改革的总目标，国家治理体系和治理能力现代化是其中的重要内容。中国走的国家治理体系和治理能力现代化道路，不同于发达国家曾经走过的路，也不同于第二次世界大战之后中国的近邻以及巴西、南非、俄罗斯等走过的路。总体上说，中国国家治理能力更多地需要在国家治理体系现代化的基础上予以增强，其核心是个制度化的问题，或者说是个法治问题。尤其对于当下的中国来说，发展经济的能力主要靠的是简政放权，只要政府行政审批改革继续进行,"法无明文规定不可为"成为限制政府权力的边界,政府在监管中加强执行,中国政府发展经济的能力就不会弱化。当前中国国家治理能力更多地需要着落在矛盾调处能力上,这需要着重在两个方面来加大力度。一个是政治整合,一个是政治参与。政治整合主要解决的是政治体系的弹性问题,政治参与主要解决的是包容性的问题。政治整合在于要凝聚共识,比如我们现在说反腐败,这是全社会的共识,但是有这个共识之后具体怎么做,共识基础之上如何做到利益妥协,这是一个政治参与的问题。

政治整合的情况,首先是政党整合,执政党的政治吸纳渠道是开放化的,从"三个代表"提出到十六大对党章的修改,实现了社会各阶层入党的无差别化。全能主义国家退出后,市场得以发展壮大,社会组织、社区组织的产生和蓬勃发展也是政府退出来后社会公共领域孕育的结果。值得注意的是,市场和社会发展壮大的同时,执政党的力量也深入其中,所以呈现出来社会建设中的政退党进的现象。比如在非公有制经济、社会组织中都要建立起党的基层组织,但是基层党组织怎么样发挥整合作用,目前来看各地探索情况不一样。具体怎么使党在基层、在社区、在社会组织和非公有制经济中发挥它的作用,目前还处于探索过程中。

对于政府整合来说,实行公务员制度之后,公务员的招募逢进必考已经得到了广泛承认。近些年来人大代表的城乡同比选举也已经开始实施,政协委员的精英网罗的作用也是发挥得比较明显。当前的反腐败运动在一定程度上也起到了政治整合的作用。

但是,政府的这种整合一方面受制于职业化水平不足的影响,另一方面依赖于政府对社会公众需求的回应情况。政治整合还受制于几个方面的问题。一个是国家治理体系当中精英共识联盟本身,以及精英共识联盟的沟通机制目前还正在形成过程中这一事实。为什么我们说知识精英的共识联盟呢?因为我们会看到政界、学界、商界、社会界,包括更广泛的演艺界等等,都需要有一个底线共识和智识流转来形成对更广泛的社会范围内共识的引领。各界精英人士目前来说相对缺乏信息共享和人力流转机制。最近这些年,学者到政府机关去挂职的现象开始出现,而且从2013年以来,在党政机关工作的公务员也可以到一些科研院所去做讲席,这是一个非常好的信号。而这种联盟有利于制度化进程的加速,去弥合精英集团内部分裂的可能。

另外一个就是利益实现的社会分流机制还没有形成。为什么这样讲?我们现在市场各种企业是一次分配,政府是二次分配,但是分配成功与否的评价机制相对来说还是比较单一,基本上是基于权和钱,其他方面都是去服从于权和钱,最终是服从于权。这样一来,社会评价机制的相对单一和集中化,不利于制度的执行和遵行,在这个时候更多是强调职业的多样化,比如说职业资格认证的社会化,而不是由政府来掌握职业资格的认证。如果社会分流的机制没有形成的话,政治整合的力度就会下降,反而不利于社会矛盾的解决。

还有一个方面就是政治参与。主要包括既有的政治参与渠道的畅通和激活,其中包括民意代表相关制度的完善、民意代表的选举。虽然是城乡同比选举了,但是这种民意代表候选人的产生与选区的划分等等,技术性的操作方面现在还比较粗糙。民意代表跟选民之间的联系机制,目前来说还没有普遍地建设起来。与选举的代表同时产生的就是非选举的民意代表意见的表达与采纳,很简单的说法就是意见领袖或者舆论的推手等等,他们在社会的很多议题的设置方面,影响力非常大,特别是在一些公共事务的议程设置方面。互联网带来的权力从政府向社会的流散,使得公共事务议程设置的协商化成为必要,这也是为什么我们现在很多的地方要提协商民主,但是协商首先就在于议程本身。

政治参与有序化还需要一个社会基础,而这个社会基础目前来看相对薄弱,包括社区和社会组织的自治化。社区方面,我们相关的调研显示,社区的党支部书记,再加上社区居委会的主任,往往不是社区的居民,所以这样就会形成"两张皮",无法使社区成为一个共同体。另外一方面就是社会组织,民政部民间组织管理局的数据显示,在民政部登记的社会组织刚超过50万,但人民团体在全国范围内的基层组织数量超过600万,这批存量没有发挥社会基础的作用,这方面怎么去发挥才能够使人们的参与通道完全打开?这也是中国国家治理能力提升迫切需要通过制度化、规范化、程序化去解决的问题。

参考文献

[1] Tilly, Charles, ed., *The Formation of National States in Western Europe*, Princeton NJ.: Princeton University Press, 1975.

[2] Barrington Moore, Jr., *Social Origins of Dictatorship and Democracy: Lord and Peasant in the Making of the Modern World*, Boston: Beacon Press, 1966.

[3] Skocpol, Theda, *States and Social Revolution*, Cambridge: Cambridge University Press, 1979.

[4] [德] 马克斯·韦伯:《经济与社会》,商务印书馆1998年版,英文版见 Max

Weber, *Economy and Society*, California: University of California Press, 1978。

[5] UNRISD, "Building State Capacity for Poverty Reduction", 2010.

[6] [美] 塞缪尔·亨廷顿:《变化生活中的政治秩序》,上海人民出版社2008年版,英文版见 Samuel Phillips Huntington, *Political Order in Changing Societies*, Yale Univeristy Press, 1968。

[7] 房宁等:《自由、威权、多元——东亚政治发展研究报告》,社会科学文献出版社2011年版。

[8]《邓小平文选》,第3卷,人民出版社1993年版。

[9] 张宝宇:《巴西经济发展与社会发展关系问题》,载《拉丁美洲研究》2005年第2期。

[10] 陆南泉:《俄罗斯经济二十年(1992—2011)》,社会科学文献出版社2013年版;王树春:《俄罗斯经济现代化前景探析》,载《现代国际关系》2011年第11期。

[11] 马燕坤:《南非软实力建设之理论实践》,载《河北北方学院学报》2012年第5期。

[12] [巴西] 马科斯·科尔代罗·皮雷斯:《经济增长、城市化和社会不平等:对保守现代化的思考》,载《国际社会科学杂志》2013年第4期。

[13] 陆南泉:《俄罗斯经济二十年(1992—2011)》,社会科学文献出版社2013年版。

[14] [俄] 谢列兹尼奥夫:《21世纪俄罗斯的改革选择》,载《求是学刊》2013年第1期。

国家治理现代化中的党的领导与依法治国

郑长忠[*]

在中国政治中,党的领导与依法治国关系处理,是人们十分关心的一个问题。而之所以受人重视,是因为这一问题关系到现代政治在中国的健康发展的重要内容。随着以依法治国为主题的党的十八届四中全会的召开,党的领导与依法治国关系的问题,再次成为人们关注的焦点之一。由于中国政治以及党的领导与依法治国的关系,都是基于处理现实公共事务即在国家治理过程中得以发展的,因此,我们认为可以从国家治理以及国家现代化角度来把握党的领导与依法治国的关系,以期在全面深化改革背景下,为正确处理这一关系提供一些理论思考与对策建议。

一、国家治理中的党的领导与依法治国

所谓国家治理,是指公共权力通过有效处理公共事务而形成有序的公共生活过程。实际上,它就是国家共同体范围内的政治别称,但在概念上,它与政治的区别在于,政治是以公共权力为轴心而定义的,而国家治理是以公共事务有效处理为轴心而定义的。在国家治理概念中,实践性与有效性倾向更为凸显。由此,所谓国家治理体系也就更多是从有效处理公共事务角度出发来考虑参与的权力主体的安排。

在现代条件下,政党、国家与社会是国家治理体系的三个主体要素,其中,国家是公共权力的主体代表,政党是联系社会并建构与运行公共权力的主要力量,社会是推动国家发展的决定力量。其中,根据马克思主义观点,社会要素又可以分为市场与狭义社会两部分。从国家治理的角度来看,只有上述三方面主体要素之间形成了良性合作关系,公共事务有效处理以及有序公共生活建构才能获得理想的效果。

由此,如何处理政党、国家和社会之间关系,就成为现代政治背景下

---

[*] 郑长忠,复旦大学政党建设和国家发展研究中心常务副主任。

国家治理体系建设中的一个关键问题。在现代政治背景下，国家要素的功能充分发挥的重要条件就是依法治国，同时，政党却具有领导功能，社会还具有决定作用。于是，政党、国家和社会之间的关系，就演变为党的领导、依法治国与人民当家做主之间的关系。

其中，党的领导，是指在政治结构空间之内的国家治理体系中政党处于领导地位，对公共权力建构与运行产生主导作用，以及对社会力量具有整合与引导功能。依法治国，是指在国家结构空间之内公共权力运行以及各项公共事务处理应该遵循宪法与法律规范。人民当家做主，是指不论是在政治结构空间内，还是在国家结构空间内，对于整个政治发展来说，以人民为基础的社会意志是具有决定性作用的。因此，三者之间，特别是党的领导与依法治国之间的关系，实际上，是针对不同逻辑空间内政治运行逻辑而言的，彼此是不存在矛盾关系的。正是基于此，中国共产党才提出应该推动"党的领导、人民当家做主与依法治国的有机统一"。

由于在现代政治发展逻辑与中国政治发展的历史逻辑共同演绎下，现代国家治理形态在中国的生成，是遵循党建国家路径来实现的。因此，党与国家的关系，就历史性地被提出来了，并成为了中国政治发展中的一个关键问题，于是，党的领导与依法治国关系的处理，就伴随着整个现代中国政治发展的全过程。

二、全面深化改革与国家治理现代化

为克服现代化建设对组织化的诉求与中国传统社会一盘散沙状态之间矛盾，建国之后，在宏观上，中国建立了以国家权力为主导的计划经济体制，微观上建立了以基层党组织为核心的单位社会体制，从而为现代化建设奠定了组织化基础。随着组织化逻辑演进，以党代政以及社会自主性萎缩等现象就开始出现。

为了使现代化建设获得可持续发展的内在动力，中国共产党做出了改革开放决定。经过一段时间的调整与改革，党的十四大决定建立社会主义市场经济体制，由此现代社会基因开始被植入。为了适应市场经济体制对国家法治建设的要求，党的十五大提出了依法治国，标志着现代国家建设进入了全面启动阶段。随着市场经济体制建立与依法治国提出，与之互动的政党自身建设也需要调整，于是党的十六大就提出了"三个代表"。市场经济深化与网络社会生成，一方面使社会多元特性开始出现，另一方面使大量社会组织开始生成，由此，党的十七大提出了和谐社会建设任务，标志着现代社会在中国生成。至此，作为现代国家治理体系的主体要素基本生成。

虽然主体要素基本生成，但是，我们也发现两个现象：一是各要素的功能尚未获得充分发展与发挥，二是各要素之间尚未基于现代国家治理体系整体要求形成内在有机化。为此党的十八届三中全会，提出了要基于顶层设计，全面深化改革，以推动国家治理体系与治理能力的现代化。

三、法治建设构建国家治理现代化基石

由上可知，全面深化改革以推动国家治理现代化，重点需要完成的任务有两方面：一是推动国家治理主体要素的功能得以充分发展与发挥；二是推动国家治理体系整体有机化。不论是从政治发展一般原理来分析，还是从中国现代国家治理体制生成路径来看，要实现上述两方面任务，都需要有政党与国家要素的推动以及自身发展。不过，政党与国家要素的作用与创新的内容存在着差异性。对于国家来说，强调的是依法治国，对于政党来说，强调的是领导和执政方式创新。

自从国家诞生以来，政治都是围绕着国家政权而展开，因此，国家要素在国家治理中总是处于根本地位。在现代政治条件下，国家行为是受宪法与法律所规范的，法治化是现代国家的重要标志之一。同时，全面深化改革中，需要解决的重点问题之一就是政府与市场的关系，而市场是由政府培育的，调整这一关系重点在于推动政府改革，而市场经济内在要求法治化，同时，从人类现代政治文明史来看，法治也是规范政府行为的重要手段。因此，不论是推动国家要素现代化，还是推动整个国家治理体系现代化，都需要将推动依法治国作为重点而展开。这就意味着在国家治理现代化进程中，法治将起到为现代国家建设与现代国家治理现代化构筑基石的作用。

基于上述分析，我们认为，应该在以下几方面，推进依法治国以实现国家治理现代化：一是强化宪法权威，以推动现代国家要素功能的有效性。二是强调法治在改革与建设中的作用，以推动依法治国的法治精神在改革中的体现。三是强化法治对政府的规范，使国家要素根据国家治理现代化要求实现自我调整。四是将全面深化改革成果转化并上升为法治建设内容，以推动国家治理现代化。

四、依法治国推进党的领导、执政方式创新

作为现代政党，中国共产党具有两种功能：一是领导功能，二是执政功能。领导功能是指党在政治结构空间内的作用而言，执政功能是指党在

国家结构空间内的作用而言。然而，不论是在哪个结构空间内，随着依法治国强化而导致国家要素的变化，都要求政党与其互动的具体实现方式进行创新与发展。

针对改革开放之前的党政不分和以党代政现象，改革开放之后，中国共产党开始推动以党政分开为主要内容的政治体制改革。经过多轮的改革，不论是在机构上，还是在职能上，都基本完成了政治体制改革的任务，从而标志着党的领导与执政方式，逐渐适应新的国家治理要求。

不过我们也看到，随着全面深化改革和国家治理现代化的提出，在强化依法治国的背景下，政治体制改革任务，也就由之前推动党政分开向规范党政关系转变。这也就意味着，强化依法治国和推动国家治理现代化背景下，政党与国家之间的关系构建已经进入了一个全新阶段，由此也意味着党的领导与执政方式创新，也进入了一个如何适应法治国家建设的阶段。

从具体内容来说，我们认为应该从创新领导方式与创新执政方式两方面而展开。党的领导方式创新目的有二：一是能够更好地领导社会以服务于党的有效执政。二是推动现代国家有效发展。党的执政方式创新的目的在于，能够遵循法治原则，规范党与国家机构之间的关系，同时，又能够有效地将党和人民意志转化为国家意志。

中国的治理现代化：优势、问题与措施

鲍传健*

一、引言

中共十八届三中全会提出，全面深化改革的总目标是完善和发展中国特色社会主义制度，推进国家治理体系和治理能力现代化。治理能力现代化一经提出便引发学术界的高度关注[1][2]，亦有学者称其为"四个现代化"（工业现代化、农业现代化、国防现代化、科学技术现代化）之后的第五个现代化[3]。本文认为现代化意味着一个不断完善的动态过程，对于"现代化"具体标准和总体措施的探讨非常重要，本文基于"治理"及"善治"概念在中国政策层面和学界的演化这一逻辑，梳理治理现代化的内涵与外延。

另一方面，四中全会专题讨论了依法治国问题。所谓法律是治国之重器，良法是善治之前提，中国特色社会主义法治体系的内涵、范式及构建是当前理论界探讨的热点。2012年党的十八大报告就提出全面推进依法治国，法治是治国理政的基本方式。其实，早在1996年，"九五"计划就将依法治国作为战略目标，认为依法治国是邓小平建设有中国特色社会主义理论的重要组成部分。[4]首先，法治（rule of law）与法制（rule by law）不同，一字之差反映了执政思想从依靠国家机器管制为主向社会主体共同治理为主的转变。[5]其次，法治更加不同于西方学者所称的授权统治（rule of mandates）[6]，后者从激励的角度探讨中国的官僚制度，有一定的合理性，但与社会主义法治体系的要求是不相容的。

治理思想在中国及西方都早已有之。在中国，著名的大禹治水和老子《道德经》中"治大国若烹小鲜"的说法，都蕴含了治理的思想。在西方，治理的概念最初可能来源于希腊词"kybernan"，意为引导、控制或指导，

---

* 鲍传健，中央编译局助理研究员。

后来拉丁语将这个词译为"guvernare"。[7]然而，系统地研究治理这一门学问，西方发达国家走在了前列。20 世纪 80 年代以前，治理在西方社会科学中仍然是零星的和边缘化的，治理在西方文献中的流行始于 Oliver E. Williamson 1979 年的文章《交易成本经济学：合同关系的治理》，而欧洲广泛讨论与研究治理则是从 90 年代开始的。此后，伴随着新制度主义学派的兴起，治理研究进入了西方社会学、政治学等研究的主流。[8]

中国学术界广泛接受并探讨治理思想是从 21 世纪初开始的。20 世纪，国内虽然有学者引介西方治理思想，但并不系统，学术界对汉语中如何翻译"governance"一词也还没有共识。直到 2000 年，"治理"——作为英文"governance"一词的对应语，才得到中国学术界广泛接受。[9]几乎是在同时，"善治"——作为"good governance"的对应语，亦开始在理论界引起广泛讨论。[10][11]需要补充的是，在中文语境"治理"经常被用作动词，因而，中文的"治理"有时应被视作"governancing"。而从西方来看，事实上许多国家的语言如欧洲各国语言、希伯来语中，仍然缺乏广泛接受的对"governance"一词的翻译。[12][13]

"多一些治理，少一些统治"是 21 世纪世界主要国家政治变革的重要特征。[2]治理和善治到底是什么？直到今天仍然有许多学者发出诸如此类的疑问。[12][14][15]世界银行定义的治理是指行使国家权力的各种传统和制度，包括三个方面，分别是选举监督和更替政府的过程、政府有效制定和实施明智政策的能力、市民和国家尊重管理经济和社会活动的制度。每一方面又可以由两个复合指标来衡量，共有六个维度。[16]

总结来看，治理在文献中至少有四种含义，分别表示一种结构、一种过程、一种机制或者是一种战略。[12]作为一种结构，治理表示正式和非正式组织的建筑架构；作为一种过程，治理意指漫长的政策制定过程中涉及的动态和调整作用；作为一种机制，治理指向决策、遵从和控制的制度程序；作为一种战略，治理表示利益相关者为了影响选择和偏好而规制操控制度设计和机制设计的工作。大多数治理文献聚焦于作为一种结构的治理，这可能反映了制度学派在社会科学中的突出地位。

关于善治的标准，世界银行发布的治理指数（Worldwide Governance Indicators，WGI）包括了六个维度，即话语和责任、政治稳定和消除暴力、政府有效性、管制质量、法治、遏制腐败。罗斯坦认为，消除腐败、代议制民主、政府规模、法治、行政效率等都不能算作善治的定义，善治应该是行使公共权力的公正（impartiality），即政府官员执行法律和政策时，不应考虑政策或法律事先没有明确规定的有关公民或案件的任何事务。[17]这一定义更加强调了制度的作用。本文认为，法治或者公正，都体现了制度对于发展和增进全民福祉的重要作用。

有发展经济学家认为，好的治理（善治）是经济和社会发展的重要推动力，而坏的治理（bad governance）可能带来国家增长的停滞。但在分析非洲国家的贫困时，也有学者认为治理对发展并没有显著的作用，因为非洲国家在其相对经济水平上已经有较好的治理[26]，但这一研究只是简单地将人均收入水平对复合治理指数做回归，其经验证据只是初步的。总体来看，激励公民储蓄、投资和创新的制度和政策体现了善治，发展和稳定需要善治作为保障。从现有的文献来看，我们可以认为，稳定是善治的一个维度，而善治对于维持稳定的作用，还有待进一步的理论和经验探讨。

从中国来看，持续三十多年的经济高速增长模式被称为"中国模式"，中国的发展经验被称为"北京共识"。然而，在几个流行的衡量治理水平的评价体系中（如世界银行的世界治理指数 WGI、透明国际的清廉指数 CPI 等），中国的得分并不高，甚至是很低。有学者认为这可以称之为中国悖论。[18]罗斯坦认为中国的干部组织不同于韦伯式的官僚体制，但对于中国的经济增长起到了重要作用。从国家官僚体制来解释国家治理的组织基础，有利于在理论上厘清政府权力、官僚体制与民众之间的关系。[19][20]

中国实现治理现代化有哪些独特优势？面临哪些可能的问题？治理现代化如何落到实处？下文将尝试做出分析。

二、中国实现治理现代化的优势

习近平同志指出："国家治理体系和治理能力是一个国家的制度和制度执行能力的集中体现，两者相辅相成。我们的国家治理体系和治理能力总体上是好的，是有独特优势的，是适应我国国情和发展要求的。"具体来说，中国实现治理现代化具备如下一些优势。

一是成功的社会转型。我国的渐进型转型克服了休克疗法等激进式转型的弊端，"摸着石头过河"的改革积累了丰富的成功经验。改革开放以来，在依法治国、公民参与、民主决策、社会治理、公共服务、政府问责、政治透明、行政效率、政府审批、地方分权和社会组织发展等方面，我们都可以看到巨大的变化。中国经济发展和社会转型的成功，或者说，中国能够在社会基本稳定的前提下保持经济的长期发展，首先得益于中国治理改革的成功。[2]

二是有效的顶层设计。国家性（statehood）创造了"科层阴影"（shadow of hierarchy），科层阴影为社会主体参与治理及治理现代化提供了组织激励。[21] 中国的政治体制为治理改革提供了一个强的科层阴影背景，确保了顶层设计具有高于有限国家性（limited statehood）的效率。无论是治理改革还是建构社会主义法治体系，党的正确领导确保了顶层设计的科学性，这包括适应我国社会主义初级阶段的国情。农村改革、国企改革、户籍改革、金融改革、财政分权、反垄断、反腐败、自由贸易区谈判、人民币国际化等一系列改革实践，都是从我国的国情出发，在顶层设计指引下的有效尝试。

三是自觉的制度创新。改革开放以来，在治理方面中国政府与各参与主体（公民社会）进行了有益而宝贵的探索，政府已经充分意识到制度红利的作用，通过各种方式鼓励制度创新，建立制度自信。国家治理体制改革创新的动力源自经济发展、政治进步、人民需要和全球化冲击，但其直接动力则是压力、激励和制度，其中制度是长久性的动力所在。[2] 制度创新也体现在治理思想的"西为中用"上。在建立社会主义法治体系的过程中，我们已经而且将继续学习国外的先进经验，听证制度、一站式服务、政府问责、律师制度、新闻发言人、参与式治理等，都是直接或间接地从西方发达国家引入的。资源禀赋、文化禀赋和技术变革都可以引致制度创新。[22]

三、中国治理现代化面临的问题

习近平同志指出："我们在国家治理体系和治理能力方面还有许多亟待改进的地方，在提高国家治理能力上需要下更大气力。只有以提高党的执政能力为重点，尽快把我们各级干部、各方面管理者的思想政治素质、科学文化素质、工作本领都提高起来，尽快把党和国家机关、企事业单位、人民团体、社会组织等的工作能力都提高起来，国家治理体系才能更加有效运转。"具体来说，在中国治理现代化过程中要重点关注以下问题。

一是社会不平等问题。当代中国深受社会不平等和社会不稳定的困扰。这两者都是民众失望情绪和骚动的原因，甚至有可能挑战党的执政能力。中国是世界上基尼系数最高的国家之一（0.47），中国的收入差距稳步提高，包括沿海与内陆的差距、省市内部的差距。富有的上层阶级越来越多地将资产转移到国外，在国外获得居留权，甚至移民。第十八届三中全会以来，统一了城乡养老保险，出台了医疗卫生改革的指导意见，积极应对了新疆和西藏的骚动。

二是官本位问题。就目前我国的实际情况而言，官本位观念和官本位现象是影响治理者素质的重要因素。官本位主义是长期支配我国传统社会的政治文化和政治体制，其实质是官员的权力本位，它与建立在公民权利本位之上的现代政治文明和现代国家治理是格格不入的，与社会主义政治文明是背道而驰的。当前"有权就有一切"的官本位主义流毒在现实中还大量存在，在一些领域和地方，官本位现象甚至有愈演愈烈的趋势。[2] 十八届三中全会《中共中央关于全面深化改革若干重大问题的决定》正式把"破除官本位观念"列为改革的重要任务，可谓切中要害。

三是腐败问题。当代中国腐败问题的范围更深更广，腐败问题导致中国损失数十亿元的生产率和税收收入，并会危及执政党的合法性。新一届政府启动了一场空前的反腐斗争，查处了一大批党政军高级干部。目前来看，这场"老虎苍蝇一起打"的反腐战役是令人鼓舞的，但是否能彻底治理好腐败问题还有待时间的检验。

四是环境污染问题。中国的环境可能是世界上最差的：日益减少且污染严重的水资源、威胁到日常生活的空气污染，还有沙漠化、滥伐森林、气候变化、能源浪费等。环境问题直接影响人们的健康、经济增长，导致全球变暖，也是一个潜在的政治不稳定因素。十八届三中全会以来政府发布了一系列新的应对污染措施。将干部考核与空气质量改善目标完成情况和大气污染防治重点任务完成情况挂钩，规定环境部门有"应当依法公开环境信息而未公开"等行为的，其主管人员和责任人将受到处分，将PM2.5浓度现状及改善纳入干部考核，对污染物大幅度提高排污收费标准等，都是令人鼓舞的重要措施，但关键还在于落实。

五是软实力与大国地位不匹配问题。作为一个新兴的全球性大国，中国的治理现代化不仅面向国内，还要面向世界。根据2013年皮尤全球态度调查（Pew Global Attitudes）的数据，中国的国际形象并没有特别正面或负面，各国对中国的偏好程度从2007年以来变化不大。比较而言，美国的全球形象较中国更加正面，只有中东地区国家对中国的正面评价高于美国。中国的"软实力赤字"在欧洲和北美最为明显，即便在拉美和非洲，中国的形象亦不如美国正面。

四、中国实现治理现代化的措施

国家治理体系现代化的关键在于制度的改革和创新，即制度的破与立。实现治理现代化是一个动态过程，要加强善治和优治（good enough governance），减少劣治和统治。这需要从政治、经济、文化和技术等多方面的制度创新入手。

一要推动依法治国，发挥协商民主。中国历史上的治理体系存在一种常规式治理与运动式治理并存的现象，尽管常规式治理建立了一套独特的体系逻辑，但运动式治理（或者称为国家运动）基本上是一种人治动员，"大跃进"和"文革"是近代史上人治运动的惨痛教训。[23][24]建立社会主义法治体系，由人治走向法治，是推动国家治理体系和治理能力现代化的重要抓手。这要求在全面深化改革过程中，要破除官本位思想，通过制度约束消除庇护主义和世袭主义，充分发挥中国特色协商民主的优势，"坚持破除各方面体制机制弊端"。要尊重宪法权威，充分发挥人民代表大会和政治协商制度的作用。正如习近平同志所指出："坚持依法治国首先要坚持依宪治国，坚持依法执政首先要坚持依宪执政。"

二要进一步创新治理逻辑，多层、多主体共同治理。中国的政治体制不同于"韦伯式国家"，有自己独特的组织和激励机制。现在的不少治理体制机制不尽合理，有些违背了政治学的公理，有些则严重损害了国家和公民的利益。现代治理的一个发展方向是多层治理（multi-governance），这要求充分发挥政府、非政府组织、公民社会的能动作用，在实践中落实制度创新，改善治理效果。要向市场和企业放权，向社会组织放权，向基层自治组织和地方政府放权，同时在党委、人大、政协、政府、司法机关之间实行决策权、执行权、监督权的相互分离和制约，倡行社会参与和监督，做强做大各类治理主体，激发经济社会发展活力。[1]

三要建设服务型政府，促进治理专业化。国家治理的现代化必然要求国家治理执行者具有胜任的专业知识技能，专业技能提升的关键是加强教育培训。中国目前一些领域的治理失效，与治理主体水平和国民素养水平不高有关。何增科建议培养职业的治理者，促进国家治理的专业化和职业化。[1]根据联合国的一项调查，我国是电子政府发展指数（E-Government Development Index，EGDI）较高的国家之一，但相比韩国、法国、日本和美国等国还有明显差距（United Nations Department of Economic and Social Affairs，2014）。我们可以借鉴国外实行电子政府的经验，改进政府提供公共服务的方式。

四要创新公共外交，提升国家软实力。作为一个负责任的大国，政府需要处理好公共外交与软实力的关系，前者主要来自于政府，后者主要来自于社会。国外社会和中国政府都认为中国的文化、思想和价值是特有的，而这正是中国软实力问题的根源所在。中国花费太多时间告诉世界什么是中国特色，而没有说清楚具有普遍吸引力的东西是什么。只有正确理解软实力的内涵及其与公共外交的区别，才能建立更正面的国际形象。[25]亚太经合组织峰会中美发表了《中美气候变化联合声明》，两国分别对二氧化碳排放做出了承诺，这一方面展现了中国应对气候变化的决心与信心，另一方面对能源领域的投资具有正向的引导作用，为中国赢得了广泛赞誉。

五要建立科学治理衡量指标，稳定激励预期。治理体系现代化不仅在宏观上应有明确目标，在微观上也应该是可度量的。治理的衡量目前是学术界研究的热点，并没有广泛接受的统一指标。[15] 流行的世界银行 WGI 和透明国际的 CPI 都是基于微观数据得到的复合指标，且没有完全公开其数据，因而引起了一些争议。从我国的治理实践来说，治理能力现代化应该伴随着治理衡量标准的科学化。目前我国缺少系统的治理衡量指标，要在经济治理、环境和气候治理、卫生和劳动治理、安全治理、公民社会等方面，逐步建立起完善的治理绩效指标，释放稳定的激励预期。

五、结论

习近平同志指出："一个国家选择什么样的治理体系，是由这个国家的历史传承、文化传统、经济社会发展水平决定的，是由这个国家的人民决定的。我国今天的国家治理体系，是在我国历史传承、文化传统、经济社会发展的基础上长期发展、渐进改进、内生性演化的结果。我国国家治理体系需要改进和完善，但怎么改、怎么完善，我们要有主张、有定力。"国家治理体系和治理能力现代化的提出，在理论上对中国如何维持高经济增长和建设社会主义法治国家做了回应。治理现代化借鉴了西方治理逻辑中善治（good governance）/优治思想，是执政党面对改革新形势借鉴西方理论与立足自身国情的理论创新。俞可平认为，国家治理现代化至少有五个衡量标准，即公共权力的制度化和规范化、民主化、法治、效率、协调。治理、善治与法治这三个概念层层包含，可以预见将在中国政治话语中发挥越来越重要的作用。推进国家治理能力现代化和依法治国，是对提高国家能力或政府能力以及党的执政能力的要求，是实现善治的具体步骤和重要依据。中国的治理现代化也将为其他发展中国家和转型国家提供治理改革的经验和借鉴。

参考文献

[1] 何增科：《理解国家治理及其现代化》，载《马克思主义与现实》，2014 年第 1 期，第 11—15 页。

［2］俞可平：《推进国家治理体系和治理能力现代化》，载《前线》，2014 年第 1 期，第 5—8 页。

［3］李景鹏：《关于推进国家治理体系和治理能力现代化——"四个现代化"之后的第五个"现代化"》，载《天津社会科学》，2014 年第 2 期，第 57—62 页。

［4］刘海年：《依法治国：中国社会主义法制建设新的里程碑》，载《法学研究》，1996 年第 3 期，第 50—56 页。

［5］Guillermo A. O'Donnell, "Why the rule of law matters", *Journal of Democracy*, 15 (4), 2004, pp. 32 – 46.

［6］Mayling Birney, "Decentralization and Veiled Corruption under China's 'Rule of Mandates'", *World Development*, 53, 2014, pp. 55 – 67.

［7］Volker Schneider and Dirk Hyner, "Security in Cyberspace: Governance by Transnational Policy Networks", in *New Modes of Governance in the Global System: Exploring Publicness, Delegation and Inclusiveness*, edited by Mathias Koenig-Archibugi and Michael Zurn, pp. 154 – 176. New York: Palgrave Macmillan, 2006.

［8］Claus Offe, "Governance: An 'Empty Signifier'?" *Constellations*, 16 (4), 2009, pp. 550 – 562.

［9］John P. Burns, "Western Models and Administrative Reform in China: Pragmatism and the Search for Modernity", in *Comparative Administrative Change and Reform: Lessons Learned*, edited by Jon Pierre and Patricia W. Ingraham, pp. 182 – 106, Montreal: McGill-Queen's University Press, 2010.

［10］何增科：《中国转型期的腐败、治理与善治》，载《中国社会科学季刊》（香港），2000 年秋季号。

［11］俞可平主编：《治理和善治》，北京：社会科学文献出版社 2000 年版。

［12］Laurence E. Lynn, Jr., "The Many Faces of Governance: Adaptation? Transformation? Both? Neither?" in *The Oxford Handbook of Governance*, edited by David Levi-Faur, pp. 49 – 64, New York: Oxford University Press, 2012.

［13］Jacob Torfing and Eva Sørensen, "The European Debate on Governance Networks: Towards a New and Viable Paradigm?" *Policy and Society*, forthcoming.

［14］Francis Fukuyama, "What is Governance?" *Governance*, 26 (3), 2013, pp. 347 – 368.

［15］Pippa Norris, "Measuring Governance", in *The SAGE Handbook of Governance*, edited by Mark Bevir, pp. 179 – 200, New Delhi: SAGE Publications India Pvt Ltd., 2011.

［16］Daniel Kaufmann, Aart Kraay and Massimo Mastruzzi, "The Worldwide Governance Indicators: Methodology and Analytical Issues", *Hague Journal on the Rule of Law*, 3 (02), 2011, pp. 220 – 246.

［17］Bo Rothstein, "Good Governance", in *The Oxford Handbook of Governance*, edited by David Levi-Faur, pp. 143 – 154, New York: Oxford University Press, 2012.

［18］Bo Rothstein, "The Chinese Paradox of High Growth and Low Quality of Government: The Cadre Organization Meets Max Weber", *Governance*, forthcoming.

［19］周雪光、练宏：《中国政府的治理模式：一个"控制权"理论》，载《社会学研究》，2012年第5期，第69—93页。

［20］周雪光：《国家治理逻辑与中国官僚体制：一个韦伯理论视角》，载《开放时代》，2013年第3期，第5—28页。

［21］Tanja A. Börzel and Thomas Risse, "Governance without a State: Can It Work?" *Regulation & Governance*, 4 (2), 2010, pp. 113 – 134.

［22］Vernon W. Ruttan, "Social Science Knowledge and Induced Institutional Innovation: An Institutional Design Perspective", *Journal of Institutional Economics*, 2 (03), 2006, pp. 249 – 272.

［23］冯仕政：《中国国家运动的形成与变异：基于政体的整体性解释》，载《开放时代》，2011年第1期，第73—97页。

［24］周雪光：《运动型治理机制：中国国家治理的制度逻辑再思考》，载《开放时代》，2012年第9期，第105—125页。

［25］Shambaugh David, "China at the Crossroads: Ten Reform Challenges", edited by Brookings, 2014, http://www.brookings.edu/~/media/research/files/papers/2014/10/01%20china%20crossroads%20reform%20challenges%20shambaugh%20b.pdf.

［26］Jeffrey Sachs, John W. McArthur, Guido Schmidt-Traub, Margaret Kruk, Chandrika Bahadur, Michael Faye and Gordon McCord, "Ending Africa's Poverty Trap", *Brookings Papers on Economic Activity*, 1, 2004, pp. 117 – 216.

新世纪巴西加强国家治理能力建设的做法及启示

陈晓玲[*]

一、加强治理能力建设的背景

1. 国家经济社会发展遭遇瓶颈

20世纪50—80年代，巴西从初级产品出口发展模式向进口替代工业化模式转型，工业化、城市化、现代化进程加快，国内生产总值以年均9%的速度增加，尤其1964—1973年增速高达11.3%，成为全球第八大经济体，步入中等收入国家行列，被称为"巴西经济奇迹"。但由于经济快速增长建立在依赖国际金融机构借贷之上，伴随着经济高速增长，外债急剧攀升。受70年代世界石油危机和国际信贷利率提高影响，巴西通货膨胀飙升，债台高筑，整个80年代陷入滞胀困境。90年代，巴西放弃进口替代工业化发展模式，推行新自由主义改革，实现了由内向发展模式向外向发展模式的转变、由国家主导型经济向市场经济的转变，虽然稳定了宏观经济，缓解了债务压力，但经济对外依赖性和脆弱性加大，1999年和2002年两次发生金融危机，经济低迷。同时，由于军政府及主张新自由主义的文人政府片面强调经济发展，忽视社会公正，经济社会发展失衡问题突出，社会分配严重不公，边缘化群体增多，各种社会矛盾呈激化趋势，几十年来基尼系数始终在0.6以上。

2. 陷入治理困境

1985年巴西结束威权体制，开启政治民主化进程。1988年制定宪法，确立多党制、总统制和联邦制政体，形成多党竞争、联合执政的格局。但

---

[*] 陈晓玲，中共中央对外联络部拉美局处长。

是传统政党执政表现不尽如人意，缺乏解决国家政治、经济和社会难题的能力和手段。首先是政府决策力和执行力因政党政治过分放大选举功能而弱化，无力推行深层次的制度性和体制性变革，缺乏有效化解政治矛盾的能力，难以推动经济社会持续协调发展；二是在应对利益多元化方面显得力不从心，缺乏社会整合的能力；三是一些党政领导人视法律为儿戏，有法不依，执法不严，贪污受贿泛滥，缺乏有效治理腐败的能力。民众对政党信任度下降，对政治失望情绪上升，代议制民主出现危机，国家治理陷入困境。

二、中左翼政府加强治理能力建设的主要做法

1. 加强民主协商，扩大民众权利，依法行政，推进国家治理民主化和法治化

一是团结最广泛的力量。组建政府之前，卢拉总统与竞选联盟各党派和社会各界加强对话和协商，主张抛弃党派歧见，组建由传统左翼政党、中右翼政党等组成的联合政府；执政后更是重视协调各党利益，甚至打破惯例，多次出席国会重要的活动并与反对党领袖接触，亲自做工作，争取各党议员支持。二是创建社会经济发展理事会，广开言路。理事会由来自政府、国会、企业、工会、宗教团体、教育界等82名代表组成，主要任务是反映民意，建言献策。三是协调联邦与地方政府的关系，争取地方的支持，提高行政效率。上任三个月内先后与全国所有州长和1900名市长直接对话。四是鼓励民众参政和建立基层组织。五是积极推动国家治理法治化。罗塞芙总统重视依法执政，明确责任体系和决策指导，提出打造"高效清廉政府"口号，果断处理政府内部腐败问题，执政头两年先后解除七位涉嫌贪腐的部长职务，推动修订反腐败法的有关条款。

2. 加强宏观调控，完善市场机制，推动经济稳定增长

卢拉上台后，注重发挥市场分配资源的积极作用，没有采取激进经济变革政策，坚持将初级财政盈余目标制、浮动汇率制和控制通胀作为主要经济政策。同时，全面加强政府宏观调控，批准实施公私合营计划，解决融资问题。增加政府对生产领域的投入，提高生产能力。加大公路、通讯等基础设施建设，加强经济发展的后勤保障，降低企业生产环节税赋，推动工业发展；增加外汇储备和重新安排外债，增强抵御金融风险的能力；鼓励企业提高科技创新能力，增加出口产品的附加值；为推动经济全面增

长和应对国际金融危机,分别于 2007 年和 2010 年两次推出"加速经济增长计划",通过抑制公共支出和增加基础设施投资等举措刺激经济增长。罗塞芙上台后,根据内外形势变化,果断调整宏观经济政策,确保经济稳定增长。实行灵活的货币政策和谨慎的财政政策。加强金融监管,提高金融交易税并扩大征收范围,遏制本币雷亚尔升值。扶持工业发展,出台"壮大巴西"、"中小企业优惠贷款"、"物流投资计划"等。强化贸易保护措施,保护本国工业和市场,稳步推进税制改革,统一各州商品流通服务税,扩大工业产品税和薪资税减免范围等。

3. 改善收入分配,扩大内需,缓和社会矛盾

2002 年卢拉在竞选总统时提出"社会公正、就业和福利"的口号,上台后制定了建设"所有人的巴西"的发展战略,将社会包容作为社会政策优先目标,将解决贫困问题和改善民生作为施政重点:一是新设"社会发展与反饥饿部",推行以全民扶贫和反饥饿为宗旨的"零饥饿运动"和"家庭救济金计划"。二是大幅增加对教育投入,推行"巴西扫盲计划",根据人口比例为印第安人和黑人学生提供奖学金,大规模兴建联邦技术学校、大学和大学城,实施"所有人上大学计划"和"高等教育助学金计划"。三是增加对农业的投入和技术支持,把家庭农业和资助金增长 8 倍,加大安置无地农民家庭力度。为家庭年收入低于 2000 雷亚尔的农民提供小额农业贷款,为遭受自然灾害的农民提供农业保险。罗塞芙总统上台后,继续将民生作为施政重点:推出巴西"无赤贫"计划,联邦政府每年拨款 200 亿雷亚尔(约合 100 亿美元),向赤贫人口发放救助金和提供生产技能培训等;推出"我的家,我的生活"安居工程,为中低收入家庭提供廉价经济适用房。通过"国家技术教育和就业""职业培训系统",为青少年提供能力素质培训课程,帮助其提高就业能力。通过"科学无疆界"项目,帮助巴西学生入读世界一流高等学府,预计到 2014 年将有 10 万人受益。

4. 加强生态保护,增强可持续发展能力

一是将生态保护纳入国家发展战略。巴西 2008 年出台《应对气候变化国家计划》,提出 2017 年实现森林砍伐率在 2006—2009 年平均水平基础上减少 49% 的目标。该计划于 2009 年重新审定后经议会批准成为法律,政府为此成立了专门管理委员会负责监督实施。二是出台自主、自愿减排计划。2009 年宣布温室气体自愿减排计划,提出通过治理森林砍伐,扩大生物燃料的使用,转变工业生产方式,推进电力供应清洁化,提高农牧业

生产效率等举措,到2020年将温室气体排放量在预期基础上减少36.1%—38.9%。三是加大对生态保护的投入,设立亚马逊基金、成立应对气候变化国家基金等。四是颁布有关建设和扩大国家森林公园和生态园地、加强对印第安人卫生健康保护的法令和行政措施。五是大力发展和利用生物能源,有效弥补传统能源供应不足。巴西在清洁能源,特别是生物能源的研究和利用方面一直居世界领先地位。2009年年底,卢拉政府颁布法令,规定市场上的柴油添加5%的生物柴油,汽油添加25%的乙醇。同时,加强生物能源对环境影响的评估和管控。2007年推出生物燃料"生态证书"机制,生产生物燃料的企业如有乱砍滥伐森林或对土地使用不当的劣迹,都无法获得生态证书和营业执照。

5. 推进大国外交战略,维护发展空间

卢拉政府在继续巩固与美欧传统关系的基础上,更加积极地发展同世界大国的关系和参与国际事务,以期在国际政治经济关系重构中发挥巴西作为地区大国的政治作用和影响,为经济增长营造良好的外部环境,争取更多外部资源,积累有利条件。一是致力于巩固与阿根廷的战略伙伴关系,加强南方共同市场建设,努力推进南美洲一体化。二是通过在国际事务的广泛参与,提高巴西的国际影响力。展开积极的外交攻势,推动联合国改革,争取成为安理会常任理事国;积极参与金砖国家、二十国集团等多边机制,争当全球贸易谈判主角。三是深化与发展中国家的多领域合作,加强与发展中大国之间的战略联盟,推动国际政治经济新秩序的建立。四是以务实的原则处理与发达国家的关系,坚决维护本国的国家利益及决策自主权,谋求同美欧建立"建设性和均衡性的密切关系"。罗塞芙上台后,外交上更注重巴西"大国"定位,在延续多元外交政策基础上,更加坚定地维护主权安全,打造"全球外交"战略。

三、加强治理能力建设取得的初步成效

1. 左翼执政地位不断巩固

一是劳工党连续三次赢得总统选举,顺利完成领导人新老接替,成为巴西自军政府还政于民以来执政时间最长的政党。二是执政联盟在国会的议席大幅增长,在参、众两院占比分别达到65%和68%,劳工党成为参议院第二大党和众议院第一大党,罗塞芙政府成为"再民主化"以来最强势的政府。三是中左联盟在全国州、市执政力量显著加强。2010年大选,赢

得了 27 个州中的 16 个州。2012 年市政选举取得全面胜利，劳工党赢得 635 个市长职位，比 2008 年市政选举增加了 14%。四是卢拉和罗塞芙总统的民众支持率达到历史高位，其中罗塞芙创下了 77% 的历史纪录。

2. 经济稳步增长

2003—2012 年，巴经济保持年均 4% 的增长率。进出口总额由 2002 年的 1069 亿美元增至 2012 年的 4657 亿美元。国家风险指数由 1460 点降至 180 点；公共债务占 GDP 比重由 60.6% 降至 40.3%。外汇储备由 378 亿美元增至 3790 亿美元。通胀率由 12.5% 降至 5.84%。失业率由 11.7% 降至 5.5%。经济总量全球排名由 2003 年的第 13 位上升至 2011 年的第 6 位。

3. 民生不断改善

2003—2011 年，巴西贫困人口减少 50.64%，赤贫人口减少 47%，提前完成联合国千年发展目标。创造了 2420 个就业岗位。新增中产阶级 4000 万人，中产阶级在全国总人口的占比达 52%。社会结构正逐渐由金字塔形转为橄榄形。基尼系数由 0.594 降到 0.519，为 1960 年以来最低值。

4. 生态环境持续有好转

2005 年以来，亚马逊热带雨林的砍伐面积逐年下降，2012 年达到砍伐最低值。2006—2010 年减少了大约 10 亿吨的碳排放量。同时，生物能源在能源消费结构中的比重提高到 24%，远远超过 13.6% 的国际水平。

5. 国际影响力上升

巴西"入常"的外交努力得到国际社会一定程度的认可，被视为"不再仅仅是西半球的参与者，已经成为实实在在的全球性的参与者"。在多哈回合谈判、国际金融体系改革谈判中，巴西已成为发展中国家的代言人。此外，巴西在世界减贫、能源和粮食危机问题、全球气候问题、联合国维和行动、人权问题等重要国际事务中发挥重要作用。由于其影响力上升，巴西成功申办 2014 年世界杯和 2016 年奥运会，极大地激发了巴西民众的民族自豪感。

四、几点启示

1. 以人为本是加强社会管理的方向

巴西在经济社会转型过程中，不平衡、不协调、不可持续问题突出，社会结构深刻调整，利益主体多元化，诉求差异加大，社会矛盾加剧。巴西中左翼政府关注民众所思、所想和所愿，关注社会人心向背，建立广泛、多层、制度化的协商民主机制，较好地把握了社会思潮，激发了社会创造活力，一定程度上促进了社会和谐。其经验说明，加强社会管理要坚持以人为本，服务为先的理念，建设服务型政府。

2. 处理好市场和政府的关系是加强经济治理的关键

巴西经历20年军事独裁之后推进新自由主义市场化改革，政府高度集权和放任市场自由发展两种治理模式的弊端充分显现。中左翼上台后在坚持市场配置资源的决定作用的同时积极发挥政府的调控作用，着力解决市场体系不完善、干预过多和监管不到位等问题，比较有效地保持宏观经济稳定，促进市场竞争，维护市场秩序，弥补市场失灵。其经验再次说明，市场经济的健康发展必须将市场自发调节同政府宏观调控相结合。

3. 最大限度体现公平和正义是加强治理能力的落脚点

巴西中左翼政府认为，分配不公是社会不安定的最大根源，故将社会政策置于优先地位，加大社会投入，努力使分配制度体现出社会公平和正义，使经济发展和财富增长的益处惠及广大人民群众，从而赢得民众支持和国际社会肯定，巩固了执政基础。其经验再次说明，加强治理能力要以促进社会公平正义、增进人民福祉为出发点和落脚点，在政治、经济、社会和文化领域促进机会公平、规则公平、权利公平和分配公平，着力保障和改善民生，努力让人民过上更好的生活。

从南非大选看非国大执政挑战

舒 畅[*]

2014年5月7日,南非举行了种族隔离制度结束以来的第五次全国大选。执政的非洲人国民大会(以下简称"非国大")以62.15%的得票率再次胜选,在400个议席中获249席;最大反对党民主联盟(以下简称"民盟")获22.23%选票,获89席,继续保持最大反对党地位;由非国大前青年联盟主席马莱马去年成立的"经济自由斗士"异军突起,获6.35%的选票,成为第三大党。在省级议会选举中,非国大继续保持除西开普省以外八省的执政地位,民盟则保持西开普省的执政权。

此次大选正值南非结束种族隔离制度和非国大连续执政20周年,是南非在后曼德拉时代迎来的第一次大选,也是新南非成立后出生的年轻一代首次进行投票,因此被认为对非国大及南非政治未来发展具有风向标意义,为外界广泛关注。

从大选结果来看,虽然最大反对党民盟实力稳步增长,新兴政党"经济自由斗士"异军突起,但非国大仍以62.15%的得票率保持明显优势,并在除西开普省之外各省均保持执政权,这显示非国大民众支持的基本盘仍较稳固。最大反对党民主联盟本次大选创纪录获得22.23%的选票,比上次全国大选16.66%的得票率有较大幅度上升,但与2011年南非地方选举22%的得票率基本持平,该党曾提出的30%得票率的目标并未实现。民盟支持基础仍主要是白人和有色人,其"白人政党"形象并无明显改观,未来上升空间有限。新兴政党经济自由斗士在本次大选中成为最大黑马,一跃成为南非第三大政党。在当前南非失业率居高不下、社会矛盾日益尖锐的背景下,该党提出的无偿分配土地、矿产和银行国有化等具有民粹主义色彩的激进政策主张对部分青年及底层民众具有一定号召力,但难以真正落到实处。此次该党分流了非国大部分选票,但主要是进一步挤压了其

---

[*] 舒畅,中共中央对外联络部非洲局干部。

他反对党的生存空间,且该党根基很浅,短期内难以对非国大构成实质威胁。其他反对党在南非政治格局中则被进一步边缘化。因此,虽然主要反对党在此次大选中的力量有所增强,但受种族划分、政策取向等因素影响,南非目前尚未出现可以跟非国大相抗衡的反对党,非国大一党主导的政党格局中短期内将继续保持。同时,在曼德拉逝世、执政联盟成员工会大会几近分裂、祖马总统私宅案丑闻升温和经济自由斗士强势崛起等严峻形势下,非国大此次也经历了20年来最艰难的考验,虽然获胜,但选情暴露出非国大未来仍面临不少困难和挑战。

一、选民对非国大政治热情呈下降趋势

民众参选率和对非国大的支持率均有所下降,青年选民政治参与热情不高。本届大选中,选民总体投票率有所下滑。据统计,今年共有约2539万合格选民进行登记,其中近1866万选民参加投票,投票率为73.47%,相比1999年的89.28%、2004年的76.73%和2009年的77.30%均有所下滑,反映出部分民众政治热情下降。尤其值得注意的是,首次获得投票权的青年选民投票热情不高。此次1994年新南非成立后出生的青年选民总人数达700万,约占合格选民的近三成,但登记率仅为33.3%,只占登记选民总数的2.5%。同时,非国大在本次大选中的得票率呈小幅下降趋势,从2004年的69.69%和2009年的65.90%下降为62.15%。特别是在东开普省、自由州、林波波省、姆普马兰加省、西北省等一些得票率原来接近甚至超过80%的传统票源地,非国大的得票率均有所下滑,其中东开普省、自由州和西北省得票率均已跌破70%关口,民主联盟的得票率则均有所上升。

当前南非官方公布的失业率高达25%,18—34岁青年人失业率更是高达70%;贫富悬殊巨大,基尼系数高达0.69。受2008年以来全球金融危机的影响,经济发展低迷不振,2013年GDP仅增长1.9%。85%的黑人仍属于社会低收入群体,自1994年以来只有6%的土地转到黑人手中,远未完成将30%土地重新分配给黑人的目标。南非社会长期存在的失业、贫困、不平等三大痼疾仍然突出。民众急于纠正历史不公、改善生活的强烈愿望得不到满足。在此形势下,民众更关心的是就业、生活,而不是政治、选举。部分非国大的传统支持者由于不满于政府不能解决其实际问题,选择不再支持非国大,甚至转而支持反对党。而新南非成立后出生的青年选民由于没有经历过种族隔离的痛苦,对非国大缺乏"感恩"心理。正如选前预测,对非国大来说,最大的敌人不是反对党,而是民众对其热

情的下降。非国大领导人民推翻种族隔离制度的辉煌历史已经逐渐淡去，未来只有真正解决民众特别是青年面临的贫困、失业等现实问题，切实提高民众的生活水平，才能提高民众的政治参与热情，扭转民众支持率下滑的趋势，巩固其执政地位。

二、非国大农村支持基础稳定，但城市支持基础不断萎缩

从大选结果来看，非国大在农村地区的支持率远高于在经济发达的城市地区，且在城市地区的支持率呈下降之势。非国大在经济发达程度相对较低的姆普马兰加和林波波省得票率接近80%，支持基础稳固。在经济最发达的豪登省和西开普省则支持率低于全国平均水平，甚至失去了西开普省的执政权。豪登省是南非最发达的省份，GDP占全国总量的33%，工业化和城市化程度也最高，该省还是非国大总部所在地，但非国大在该省的支持率一直呈下降趋势，由2004年的68.4%下降到2009年的64.04%。此次非国大在重新划分省际边界，将原西北省部分地区并入豪登省的基础上，在该省的得票率仍继续下降至54.92%，勉强保住过半多数。在最大城市约翰内斯堡和行政首都茨瓦内等主要城市，非国大与民盟支持率差距缩小到10个百分点以内。如不能及时妥善应对，非国大在2016年地方选举中可能丢掉上述两市执政权。西开普省是南非最大的白人聚居省，首府开普敦是南非经济最为发达的城市之一。非国大在2009年大选中失去该省执政权，本次大选获得34%的选票，与上次持平；民盟则获得57.26%的选票，进一步巩固并扩大了在该省的优势。

一般而言，农村地区选民受外界影响较小，对前民族解放运动的历史功绩更加认同，忠诚度更高，如林波波省是非国大武装斗争的发祥地，东开普省是曼德拉等多位反种族隔离领袖的家乡，非国大在这些地区拥有得天独厚的群众基础；而城市选民更加关注现实问题，思想更加多元，且受西方多党民主价值观念影响更深，更倾向于支持政党轮替。据统计，此次大选城市选民占43%，其中多数为黑人中产阶级。他们虽然是非国大政策的受益者，却因为经济地位变化和长期受西方民主价值观熏陶，与非国大离心离德。赞比亚、津巴布韦等国家的前民族解放运动组织力量下降都是从城市支持基础的萎缩开始，津巴布韦非洲民族联盟—爱国阵线曾几乎沦为"农村党"，2009年被迫与反对党组建联合政府。非国大目前的支持基础仍较稳固，但这一趋势值得高度警惕。

三、非国大自身建设存在不少问题，导致对选民吸引力下降

1994年上台执政以来，非国大的角色由民族解放运动领导者向执政党转换，工作重心转移到政府事务上。随着一大批资深领导干部进入各级政府部门，非国大一度对党的自身建设有所忽视，党员干部出现不少问题。**一是内部斗争持续不断。**长期以来，非国大及执政联盟内部左、右派力量围绕党的政策路线一直争执不断。2007年年底非国大五十二大时，祖马在非国大青年团及南非共等左派力量支持下上台，击败坚持新自由主义政策的姆贝基总统当选党主席。但迫于国内外资本力量的压力，祖马担任总统后仍基本沿袭了姆贝基在位时的政策路线，引起一些激进势力的不满，致使党内及执政联盟在政策路线问题上的分歧进一步加大。一些人认为非国大正逐渐背离其原有政治纲领，左翼色彩不断变淡，正滑向中间道路。党内斗争在非国大五十三大上再次激烈爆发，非国大内部分成"挺祖派"和"倒祖派"两个明显阵营。"挺祖派"以党内左翼力量为核心，全力支持祖马连任党主席，"倒祖派"极力反对祖马连任，一些人发起"ABZ"运动（Anyone But Zuma，除祖马以外任何人均可），并最终提名非国大副主席莫特兰蒂为党主席候选人。尽管祖马以约75%的得票率取得胜利，并将"倒祖派"主要人物挤出中央领导层。但此次选举被认为是非国大历史上竞争最激烈的一次选举，进一步凸显非国大内部斗争的严重程度。**二是党的组织建设跟不上。**目前，非国大党员人数已从2007年的60余万增加到125万，但随着党员数量的增加，党员质量问题日益突出。有些基层支部发展党员程序不规范，有的基层组织长期不开展活动，有的在党员数量上弄虚作假。据媒体报道，一些省级领导机构，如林波波省执委会内部拉帮结派，导致机构瘫痪，一些基层和地方组织甚至发生为争夺权力相互斗殴和雇凶杀人的事件。非国大迫切需要从"数量立党"向"质量建党"转型。**三是腐败问题严重。**执政后，部分党员理想信念日益淡薄，以权谋私、权钱交易等腐败现象日趋增多，甚至祖马总统及非国大高官也不时陷入各种腐败丑闻。去年南非司法部长拉迪贝曾表示，在过去的四年里，祖马总统在法庭诉讼上的花费共计880万兰特，这些费用主要用于军购弊案、"间谍录音带"和"古普塔门"案件等。特别是在临近大选之时，祖马又受困于"恩坎德拉私宅"丑闻。有关调查报告显示，祖马涉嫌以安全改造为名，用公款为其家乡私宅修建豪华游泳池、圆形剧场、牛栏等与安全毫无关系的休闲娱乐设施。该私宅装修成本在祖马担任总统后即直线上升，从2700万兰特预算飙升至最终实际花费2.46亿兰特，创下南非历任总统之

最，是前总统曼德拉两处私宅装修费用的八倍。此事在距离大选只有六周之时爆出，成为影响非国大选情的最大负面因素。反对党趁机煽动舆论持续炒作放大，加紧攻击抹黑祖马本人和非国大。部分南非民众认为非国大已经放弃了很多曼德拉代表的价值观，官员腐败是对南非解放事业的极大嘲讽。非国大必须在腐败问题上采取更强有力措施取信于民，增强其在后曼德拉时代的道义号召力。如果处理不好上述问题，有可能导致执政联盟分裂以及重要支持者流失，严重削弱其执政基础。

四、执政联盟"内忧外患"，"左右为难"

非国大长期与南非共产党和南非工会大会等左翼力量结盟。无论是废除种族隔离的斗争，还是新南非历次大选的胜利，非国大都离不开南非共产党和南非工会大会的有力支持。近年来，南非共产党和南非工会大会等联盟内部左派势力在国家发展道路上对非国大自由市场经济政策日益不满，特别是南非工会大会屡屡就南非高官腐败渎职、豪登省高速公路收费、劳工立法、青年就业津贴计划等问题向非国大公开发难，南非工会大会总书记瓦维等领导人公开批评祖马及非国大政府，并多次组织大规模罢工和游行示威活动。在此次大选前，工会大会分裂成激烈批评非国大和亲非国大的两派。工会大会下属最大的工会组织金属工人工会公开宣布拒绝在大选中支持非国大，并扬言要退出工会大会，组建新的工人运动或政党。金属工人工会成员超过30万，一旦其从工会大会出走，将对执政联盟带来不小打击。与此同时，一些新涌现的激进独立工会与主流工会分庭抗礼。2012年造成40多人死亡的马里卡纳暴力罢工事件即是由工会之间的冲突酿成。在马里卡纳矿区，隶属于南非工会大会的老牌工会——全国矿工工会经营已久，但其会员近年来受到新兴工会——矿业与建筑业工人联合会的蚕食，两个工会一直在为争夺该矿工人代表权明争暗斗。2012年8月，矿业与建筑业工人联合会在未经全国矿工工会同意的情况下在马里卡纳发起罢工，并冲击全国矿工工会在该矿的办公室，造成双方冲突暴力升级，9人丧生。南非警方在试图驱散罢工工人时开枪，造成34人死亡，78人受伤。这一事件被南非媒体称为"结束种族隔离制度以来南非最黑暗的时刻"，不仅严重影响了南非工会运动的团结，也在一定程度上动摇了矿业工人对非国大的无条件支持。此次大选中，非国大在矿业大省西北省支持率下滑趋势明显，由2004年的80.71%、2009年的72.89%下降到2014年的67.69%，而"经济自由斗士"首次参选即在该省获得了12.53%的选票。此外，执政联盟还受到来自外部的压力。在民众对非国大的期望与现实落差越来越大的情况下，一些极左政治势力开始赢得民众青睐，与执政联盟争夺空间。如此次大选中风头正健的"经济自由斗士"，该党领导人马莱马原为非国大青年团主席和祖马亲信，一度被祖马誉为非国大"未来的领导人"，后因反对祖马连任、破坏党内团结被开除出党。该党在大选前不到一年成立，但凭借其加快土改进程和矿业国有化等激进左派口号，加之马莱马本人的民粹主义形象和超凡煽动力，在当前南失业率居高不下、贫富差距不断扩大和社会矛盾日益尖锐的背景下得到不少青年和底层民众支持，在大选中成为第二大反对派力量。执政联盟在此次大选中首次面临民盟和"经济自由斗士"左右两翼的挑战。可以预见，非国大执政联盟还将在内外"左""右"逢源，"左""右"夹击的困境下艰难前行，能否处理好这一问题，是对非国大执政能力的重大考验。

金砖国家在全球改革中的作用：
我们的愿景是什么？

[南非] 纳尔尼亚·尔博赫勒*

一、引言

在短短一段时间内，金砖国家（BRICS，巴西、俄罗斯、印度、中国和南非）这一"新兴大国"就已经确立了其作为一个举足轻重的全球参与者的身份。[①] 从广义上讲，金砖国家是一个修正主义者，其工作重点就是如何重新平衡全球权力关系，以及开展经济和政治治理国际机构改革，这些结构包括联合国安理会（UNSC）、国际货币基金组织（IMF）、世界银行（WB）和世界贸易组织（WTO）。

在简要介绍完背景知识后，本文开始重点讨论金砖国家正在呼吁的各种改革。主要论述的问题是金砖国家在实现改革愿景方面是否已经取得了足够的进步。2013年，这五个成员国在南非创建了金砖国家智库理事会（BTTC），虽然他们清楚明了地表达了他们的共同愿景，但现有全球治理机构的改革工作一直进行得很缓慢。尽管如此，金砖国家仍继续利用其软实力来不断改善多边主义。通过不断扩大影响力，金砖国家很可能会加快未来的改革进程。

二、背景

《德里首脑会议宣言》和《德里行动计划》（2012）呼吁为金砖国家

---

* 纳尔尼亚·尔博赫勒（Narnia Bohler-Muller），南非人文科学研究理事会金砖国家智库秘书处成员。

[①] See in general Kornegay and Bohler-Muller, *Laying the BRICS of a New Global Order*: *From Yekaterinburg 2009 to eThekwini 2013*, AISA Press, 2013.

开展一般性学术评估并为未来发展制定长期愿景和战略。① 为筹备2013年峰会,南非授权人文科学研究理事会(HSRC)担任其智囊团,还邀请了原有的四大智囊团,他们是:

- 巴西应用经济研究所(IPEA);
- 俄罗斯金砖国家研究委员会(NRC/BRICS);
- 印度观察家研究基金会(ORF);
- 中国当代世界研究中心(CCCWS)。

2013年,这五大智囊团在南非举行的领导人峰会上会晤,围绕"金砖国家与非洲:致力于发展、一体化和工业化的伙伴关系"的主题进行了讨论。在人文科学研究理事会的领导下,他们签署了一份宣言,正式宣布了金砖国家智库理事会②的成立,并在2013年峰会上得到了金砖国家领导人的批准。会议的主要宗旨是:组织和协调金砖国家学术论坛的学术投入,提出政策建议并在年度峰会上为金砖国家领导人提供审议指导。金砖国家智库理事会的职责是针对与金砖国家相关的公共政策和发展规划动员、推动和促进研究工作,并就研究分析和建议进行交流。这些宗旨使金砖国家智库理事会发展成为一个二轨外交机构。金砖国家智库理事会的初始任务之一是为金砖国家制定一个长远的目标和策略,这符合上文所述的《德里行动计划》的规定。

在2014年举办的巴西福塔莱萨峰上,各国领导人采纳了金砖国家智库理事会的金砖国家长期愿景文件,其内容包括以下五个重点:

1. 促进经济增长和合作发展;
2. 维持和平与安全;
3. 提高社会公正、可持续发展和生活质量水平;
4. 改革全球政治经济治理架构;
5. 通过知识和创新共享,取得进步。

与本次北京研讨会的主题一致③,全球政治经济治理改革是一个重点主题,这是一个全局性的问题,包括和平与安全改革等诸多重要话题。正如自2009年叶卡捷琳堡金砖国家峰会举行以来,所有峰会宣言中提到的那样④,金砖国家成员国旨在利用多边外交来平衡和管控负责政治经济治理

---

① 关于第四次最高会议的宣言与行动计划,参见网址:http://www.brics5.co.za/about-brics/summit-declaration/fourth-summit/,登录时间:2015年1月7日。
② 如需了解金砖国家智库理事会的主要职责,请访问 http://www.hsrc.ac.za/en/departments/sabtt/bttc(于2015年1月7日登录)。
③ 金砖国家治理系统和能力建设国际论坛,2014年11月19—20日,北京。
④ 南非与2010年12月24日加入金砖国家,金砖国家正式成立。

的国际组织的重大改革和均衡代表性,这些国际组织包括:联合国安理会、国际货币基金组织、世界银行和世界贸易组织。

在多中心/多极化以及致力于多边主义的趋势中,金砖国家已经成为国际舞台上一个强有力的竞争者。金砖国家等组织的出现使得国际舞台更加公正、公平。

强调金砖国家差异以及形成共同立场的难度的观点跟不上外交演变的步伐,忽视了以下两点:

1. 金砖国家**已经**是一个既成的政治现实;
2. 在支持现有国际秩序规则和结构的改革中,金砖国家表现出了极大的政治团结性。[1]

在此背景下,金砖国家成员国承诺,伴随其日益增长的全球和地区经济政治的影响力,他们愿意在国际关系中发挥更加重要的作用。为了便于处理真正的变化,金砖国家有必要加强对共同利益的关注。对此,提出如下建议(不限于此):

● 分享治理和透明度经验;
● 商定联合国、世界银行和国际货币基金组织的全面改革,以便实现包容性、更好的效果、更高的效率;
● 促进改革,以鼓励生产性投资,抵制财政收益和无管制信贷推动下的投机行为。

本文其余章节将重点分析联合国安理会、世界银行和国际货币基金组织的改革。

三、联合国及其安理会的改革

尽管其他国家纷纷抱怨建立"另一种世界秩序"的观点,但金砖国家一直承诺认同联合国的核心地位,并尊重国际法规则。然而,自2009年以来,金砖国家一直呼吁对联合国进行改革,尤其是联合国安理会。改革主要集中在使安理会变得更民主,更具代表性,更有效,更高效,并能引起更大的反响。《福塔莱萨宣言》是这样描述这一承诺的(虽然很隐晦):

> 中国和俄罗斯重申了对巴西、印度和南非在国际事务中地位和作用的重视,并且支持三方希望在联合国发挥更大作用的愿景。(2014年《福塔莱萨宣言》)

---

[1] 见下文所述。

联合国将于 2015 年庆祝其成立 70 周年。自 1945 年由国际联盟过渡而来，联合国大会（UNGA）的成员已经从 51 位增加至 193 位（至 2013 年）。① 但由 15 个成员国（其中包括 10 个非常任理事国和 5 个常任理事国）组成的安理会决策机构基本维持不变。美国、中国、俄罗斯、法国和英国（5 个常任理事国）享有否决权，因此其在联合国维护世界和平与安全的策略上发挥着决定性的影响。

由于联合国安理会依旧代表着一种落伍的世界秩序（自 1945 年以来一直未改变），拒绝接受巴西、印度和（南）非洲等国家以及他们发表的言论，改革之声（包括金砖国家提出的改革）不断涌现。金砖国家的后期成员国都希望谋得联合国安理会常任理事国的席位，这已不再是什么秘密。举例来说，福塔莱萨首脑峰会之后，南非再次呼吁联合国安理会进行改革，要求非洲至少拥有两个常任理事国的席位。这与比勒陀利亚的"非洲议程"相一致，因为它们都坚决认为欧洲大陆是南非外交政策的核心。②

在 2013 年的第 68 届联合国大会上，南非总统祖马（Zuma）发表演说，并提议改革，要在 2015 年营造出一个更具包容性、民主性和代表性的安理会，届时正好也是安理会成立 70 周年。南非为使非洲获得在联合国安理会上的代表地位做出了很大的努力，这与《恩祖韦尼共识》中倡导的非洲大陆就联合国安理会改革问题所持的共同立场是一致的。③

《恩祖韦尼共识》旨在促使非洲联盟提名两个非洲国家成为联合国安理会拥有否决权的常任理事国，并欲争取五个非常任理事国的席位。虽然确实存在很大争议，但这也解释了为什么联合国安理会大多数决议与非洲有关。目前，南非和尼日利亚正在争夺常任理事国席位的提名④，但南非一直未被明确提出。通过对非洲常任理事国席位提出建议，巴西和印度（以及德国和日本，统称为 G4）已经向《恩祖韦尼共识》投了赞成票。俄罗斯和中国也呼吁联合国安理会进行改革，但希望继续拥有否决权，同时也不支持将否决权授予其他成员，即使是金砖国家中的合作伙伴也不行。举例来说，中国不支持印度加入联合国安理会并成为其中一个常任理事

---

① 如需了解联合国大会成员的详细信息，请访问 http://en.wikipedia.org/wiki/Member_states_of_the_United_Nations（于 2015 年 1 月 7 日登录）。

② 如需了解南非外交政策白皮书——《创造一个更美好的世界：乌班图外交》（国际关系与合作部）的详细信息，请访问 http://www.safpi.org/publications/white-paper-south-african-foreign-policy-building-better-world-diplomacy-ubuntu（于 2015 年 1 月 7 日登录）。

③ 如需了解非洲对联合国安理会改革的观点，请访问 http://www.safpi.org/news/article/2013/african-views-reform-unsc-ezulwini-consensus-and-sirte-declaration（于 2015 年 1 月 7 日登录）。

④ 同上。

国。虽然俄罗斯已经批准了联合国安理会的民主改革,但仍维持其原有立场,即最初十五年间,新成员不享有否决权。①

问题就在于拥有否决权和特权的俄罗斯和中国(联合国安理会五个常任理事国的成员)是否会公开赞同印度、巴西、南非三国对话论坛所持立场。② 竞任常任理事国席位,答案必须在当前形势中探寻,包括考虑到金砖国家的团结,这可以从 2014 年 7 月份新开发银行的发起和加拿大国税局的建立体现出来。随着越来越多的国家达成共识,有人指出,莫斯科和北京很快会认可南非等金砖国家合作伙伴竞任安理会常任理事国席位,但并不一定会放弃或授予否决权。因此,巴西、印度和南非将很可能不得不接受联合国安理会有限的改革,包括不修改或废除否决权。③

基于上述动态,我们得出金砖国家很有必要就联合国安理会改革的性质达成共识,因为如果没有共识,在可预见的时间里,改革是不可能发生的,即使是小范围的改革。

四、世界银行和国际货币基金组织的改革

改革议程的重中之重是:为确保有效的国际经济和金融治理,金砖国家成员国致力于在国际货币和金融体系改革方案的制定上,代表会员国、其他新兴市场和发展中国家(EMDC)发挥主导作用。这一任务的重点之一就是确保加强国际组织框架内的合作,以促进国际金融和贸易领域的共同利益。

改革工作取得了明显的进展。2014 年 7 月,金砖国家着手创办新开发银行(总部将设在上海),旨在为发展中国家的基础设施项目提供资金。新开发银行拥有 1000 亿美元的货币储备来帮助各国(包括成员国)解决短期资金流动性压力。(2014 年《福塔莱萨宣言》)该银行也向全球的南方国家提供帮助,例如无条件的贷款和援助,与布雷顿森林体系(国际货币基金组织和世界银行)实行的"一刀切"(也称为"饼干切块模型")形成鲜明的对比,后者给这些发展中国家造成了巨额债务。

为了说明金砖国家的修正主义议程,金砖国家不断对国际货币基金组

---

① 与俄罗斯外交官的私人谈话。
② Tshepho Mokwele, "South Africa's Call for UN Security Council Reform: An Explicit BRIC Countries' Backing Forthcoming?" 网址: http://thedailyjournalist.com/the-strategist/south-africas-call-for-un-security-council-reform-an-explicit-bric-countries-backing-forthcoming/ (于 2014 年 10 月 19 日登录)。
③ 同上。

织和世界银行施加改革压力,以使其变得更加民主、更具代表性和更有效。

金砖国家在《福塔莱萨宣言》(2014年)第18段中对国际货币基金组织未进行改革表示了非常强烈的批评:

> 我们对2010年国际货币基金组织改革方案无法落实表示失望和严重关切,这对国际货币基金组织的合法性、可信性和有效性带来了负面影响……我们呼吁国际货币基金组织成员寻找落实第14轮份额总检查的方式,避免进一步推迟。我们再次呼吁,如2010年改革方案在今年年底前无法生效,国际货币基金组织应研拟推动改革进程的方案以确保提高新兴市场和发展中国家的话语权和代表性,我们呼吁国际货币基金组织成员就新的份额共识和第15轮份额总检查达成最终协议,以免进一步危及已推迟至2015年1月的最晚期限。

第19段是这样阐述世界银行的改革方案的,但立场并不是很强烈:

> 我们欢迎世界银行集团制定帮助各国消除极端贫困和促进共同繁荣的目标。我们认识到这一新战略对支持国际社会实现雄心目标具有很大潜力。然而,实现这些潜力需要世界银行及其成员推动世界银行治理结构更加民主,进一步强化世界银行的融资能力,探索创新性方式加强发展融资和指示共享,以受援国为导向并**尊重各国发展需求**……(自我强调)

此外,很显然,金砖国家明确表示,新开发银行和应急储备安排不会取代世界银行和国际货币基金组织,但会与这些现有的国际金融机构并行运营。《福塔莱萨宣言》第19段对此做出了明确说明:

> 我们通过多边协调和金融合作行动,积极参与完善国际金融架构,以一种**补充的方式**增加发展资源的多样性和可及性,维护全球经济稳定。(自我强调)

1944年7月,各国代表在美国新罕布什尔州的布雷顿森林召开国际会议,创建了国际货币基金组织和世界银行(布雷顿森林体系)。这次会议的目标是建立一个经济合作与发展框架,以促进"二战"后全球经济的稳定和繁荣发展。① 虽然这是两个机构的核心任务，但随着经济面临的新发展和新挑战（如2008年的全球金融危机），它们的任务也在不断变化。

国际货币基金组织的任务是促进国际货币合作，并提供政策咨询和技术援助，从而帮助各国发展成为强大的经济体。② 该组织还提供贷款服务，并帮助各国设计政策方案，当各国不能长期提供充足的资金以满足国际收支净额的需求时，可以帮助它们解决支付平衡问题。按照国际货币基金组织的现行规范，基于各成员国在世界经济中的相对位置，为各成员国分配了一定的配额。成员国的配额大小决定了其在国际货币基金组织中的最大财政承担额及投票权，而且还会影响其获得国际货币基金组织融资的权利。

从另一方面来说，世界银行可以为各国提供技术和财政支持，促进长期经济发展和减少贫困，以帮助各国对特定部门进行改革或实施具体的项目和政策——例如，建设学校和医疗中心，供应水电，防治疾病，保护环境。③

就实现其愿景而言，金砖国家应在全球政治和经济治理中发挥领导作用，并为发展中国家，尤其是南方国家，寻求更公平的经济秩序，这是其义不容辞的责任。如前所述，金砖国家一直强调，布雷顿森林体系的改革是其核心任务，而且各成员国已通过全球平台（如二十国集团）和六次金砖国家首脑峰会表达了它们对**现状**的关注。

在世界银行和国际货币基金组织于2014年10月召开的会议上，金砖国家呼吁加快改革步伐。此外，国际货币基金组织的总裁克里斯汀·拉格底（Christine Lagarde）表示：

> 为了在21世纪有效地运营，我们（国际货币基金组织）需要足够的资源，并充分反映全球成员国的动态性……为此，我们绝大多数成员国已经通过了国际货币基金组织的治理措施：2010年配额改革。现在只等最大股东——美国的批准，对此我们都在翘首以待。（2014年10月）

---

① 如需了解布雷顿森林体系的发展史，请访问 http://www.brettonwoodsproject.org/2005/08/art-320747/（于2015年1月7日登录）。

② 如需了解国际货币基金组织和世界银行的任务，请访问 http://www.imf.org/external/np/exr/facts/imfwb.htm（于2015年1月7日登录）。

③ 同上。

美国迟迟未实施配额改革,该改革早由国际货币基金组织成员国于2010年商定,要求对改革方案中份额比重的排名做主要调整,使国际货币基金组织更好地反映全球现状。然而,尽管有奥巴马总统的支持,但美国国会尚未给予批准。国会的批准将会为新兴经济体获得更大的份额铺平道路。目前,美国拥有国际货币基金组织16.75%的投票权和17.69%的配额量。由于国际货币基金组织的重大决策需达到85%的支持率,因此没有美国的批准,这一改革是不可能实施的。①

虽然改革迟迟未实施,但我们在这方面已经取得了一些进展:金砖国家一致同意新兴市场和发展中国家增加份额,其在世界银行的总份额从43.97%上升至47.19%;在国际货币基金组织的总份额从39.5%上升至42.29%。金砖国家中的四个(南非除外)在国际货币基金组织的股东中位列前十。如果完成该配额制度改革,金砖四国的总投票权将从11%左右上升至14.68%。②

总而言之,就国际货币基金组织和世界银行的改革而言,金砖国家的目的是实现公平和公正的原则,这是金砖国家压倒一切的当务之急。有必要增加新兴经济体和发展中国家在布雷顿森林体系的投票权配额,这是这些机构达成的一个明确的共识。正如前面提到的,国际货币基金组织配额制度的改革拖延已久,但美国仍拒绝进行改革。然而,2011年,国际货币基金组织的常务董事斯特斯-卡汗(Strauss-Kahn)离任时,金砖国家没能公选出一个欧洲国家以外的候选人来任职,从而错失了证明他们已为亟须改革的事宜制定好了共同策略的机会。③

五、世界贸易组织的改革

1995年1月1日,世界贸易组织成立。这个"以规则为基础"的组织通过多边协定和贸易争端的解决为贸易自由化提供了一个谈判论坛。④ 截

---

① 如需了解国际货币基金组织的配额管理制度,请访问http://www.imf.org/external/np/exr/facts/quotas.htm(于2015年1月7日登录)。
② Victoria Panova, "BRICS's New Institutions and Their Impact on International Political Economy", 2014, 网址: http://www.e-ir.info/2014/09/27/bricss-new-institutions-and-their-impact-on-international-political-economy/(于2014年10月19日登录)。
③ Oliver Struenkel "Failure to Counter Lagarde's IMF Bid Shows that BRICS Are far from United", 2011, 网址: http://www.postwesternworld.com/2011/05/29/incapacity-to-counter-lagardes-imf-bid-shows-that-brics-are-far-from-united/(于2015年1月7日登录)。
④ 如需了解世界贸易组织的权限,请访问http://www.wto.org/english/thewto_e/coher_e/coher_e.htm(于2015年1月7日登录)。

至 2014 年 9 月，世界贸易组织的成员已由原来的 128 位发展为 160 位，此外，还有另外 24 个国家已申请加入世界贸易组织。俄罗斯于 2012 年加入世界贸易组织，是最后一个加入的金砖国家成员国。

在世界贸易组织过去几轮的谈判中，发达国家和发展中国家的谈判地位明显不对称。发达国家在世界贸易中占相当大的份额（仅美国和欧盟就占进口贸易的 38% 和出口贸易的 23%），这就赋予它们相当大的议价能力。① 除了具备相似的人均收入水平以外，这些国家在国际谈判中也经常表现出集体谈判的趋势。相比之下，新兴和发展中国家往往代表一种零散的、不协调的力量。金砖国家应团结新兴市场和发展中经济体，从而实现有效的集体谈判能力。如《福塔莱萨宣言》第 21 段所述：

> 我们认识到各国能力和发展水平不同，但在全球经济、金融和贸易事务中应当权利平等，参与平等。我们努力推动开放性世界经济，实现资源高效配置、商品自由流动、竞争公平有序，从而惠及各方。在重申支持开放、包容、非歧视、透明和基于规则的多边贸易体系的同时，我们将继续致力于成功结束世界贸易组织多哈回合谈判……我们强烈支持将世界贸易组织争端解决机制作为确保多边贸易体系安全性和可预见性的基石，加强在与之有关的实质性和务实性问题上的对话，包括正在进行的世界贸易组织争端解决机制改革……

六、结束语

很显然，金砖国家希望国际力量平衡变化，以此作为一种"新生力量"，以有利于自己以及发展中国家的方式去改变**现状**。

当前正在不断发展但又很重要的变化（如上文所述）有助于反映金砖国家以何种方式来"另辟蹊径"，正如维多利亚·帕内瓦（Victoria Panova，金砖国家智库理事会的成员之一）所说的那样：

> 采用决策的形式和方法，并提出新合作模式，没有独裁或强权，

---

① 如需了解世界贸易组织网站数据库查看全面的贸易概况，请访问 http://stat.wto.org/CountryProfile/WSDBCountryPFView.aspx? Language = E&Country = CO（于 2015 年 1 月 7 日登录）。

而是建立在相互尊重和支持的基础上。①

显而易见,所有成员国都认为有必要进行改革,而且这种事情宜早不宜迟。然而,要想改革,仍然必须面对很多问题和障碍。怎样改革?何时改革?这就需要金砖国家智库理事会发挥其重要作用,因为金砖国家的愿景和长期战略是建立在互相妥协的基础之上的。此外,通过不断加强软实力,金砖国家应通过国际和国内民间组织和非政府组织来声援各利益相关方关于加快布雷顿森林体系内部改革的呼声。显而易见,公众需要对改革进程进行监督。随着越来越多的国家开始参与全球改革,这种监督很可能有助于加快改革进程。

---

① Victoria Panova, "BRICS's New Institutions and Their Impact on International Political Economy", 2014, 网址: http://www.e-ir.info/2014/09/27/bricss-new-institutions-and-their-impact-on-international-political-economy/(于 2014 年 10 月 19 日登录)。

金融流动性和资本流动对南非的影响

[南非] 赛拉吉·莫哈迈德*

一、引言

本文重点讨论的是南非经济。这与此次论坛分议题"金砖国家在国际金融危机下所面临的治理挑战"和全球金融和资本流动的持续不良治理对南非经济的影响所论述的内容相关。本文将介绍南非的政策选择，以及它们在不合理的全球金融治理体系中是如何对政策结果产生影响的。

随着全球资本市场的逐渐一体化和资本流动的波动不定，后种族隔离政府的宏观经济和金融政策的相互作用对南非经济造成了一定的影响。在全球日益一体化和经济不稳定期间，经济政策的选择对南非经济产生了负面影响。在金融危机（包括亚洲金融危机和最近发生的全球金融危机）时期，经济对全球金融流动性极其敏感，并已受到深重的影响。笔者认为，在全球金融波动不定期间，放松管制的金融市场和流通对南非经济的重要影响已经波及南非的经济增长路径。在全球金融危机波及经济领域之前，资本存量的投资和增加受益于私人部门信贷的增长，而这反过来又导致债务驱动型消费和金融投机的增加。

本文认为，南非不仅仅是全球金融市场不良治理的受害者。自种族隔离结束后，金融业的巨幅增长、全球金融危机爆发前较高的经济增长率、经济增长路径表明，南非某些部门和社会领域短期内会受益于全球金融市场的波动性发展。然而，从整体上来说，南非并没有受益，后种族隔离政府解决高失业率、贫困和不平等的目标已经被该国的经济增长路径和经济政策选择所制约。

因此，南非不仅仅是全球金融市场不良治理的受害者，种族隔离结束

---

* 赛拉吉·莫哈迈德（Seeraj Mohamed），南非约翰内斯堡金山大学经济和商业科学院公司战略与产业发展研究项目主任。

后宏观经济和金融政策的选择也增加了与南非经济不良调控有关的波动性和危机的影响。减少波动、危机和控制危机蔓延的良好的全球金融治理将有利于南非经济的发展，但解决关键经济问题的能力将取决于经济政策及其在南非的执行力度。

二、全球治理的背景

金融动荡和危机是一个全球性的问题。自 20 世纪 70 年代布雷顿森林体系瓦解以来，金融市场出现了广泛的竞争性管制解除（Helleiner，1994年）。布雷顿森林体系的实施主要是为了维持第二次世界大战后全球金融体系的稳定，目的是让各国从战争中恢复过来，促进经济增长和发展，保持各国的充分就业和重建全球贸易体系。

大萧条时期（1928 年至 1933 年），布雷顿森林体系的创始人总结出来的一个教训是：保持全球金融的稳定性，并支持可能面临支付和财政平衡问题的国家。国家可以实行资本管制，以限制外国资本流入和流出对本国经济的潜在破坏性影响。布雷顿森林体系的瓦解为增加全球金融活动和避免资本管制创造了空间和机会。因此，欧洲货币市场的形成和其他离岸金融活动推动了许多国家金融活动的自由化。这些国家不再努力维持本国经济的稳定性，而是走上了通过放松管制的金融体系从其他国家获取外资的竞争之路。

金融市场的放松管制（其中包括跨国资本流动），实现了世界各地金融的一体化。同时跨境全球金融活动和投机性金融活动的数量也有所增加。很明显，早在 1982 年拉丁美洲出现全球债务危机以来，全球金融市场的放松管制和加速整合就带动了跨境资本流动的增长，这不仅为某个国家的宏观经济不稳定性创造了条件，而且还可能导致危机的蔓延，以致影响到其他许多国家。

这一问题不仅限于发展中国家。在 80 年代和 90 年代，小型发达经济体（如西班牙、瑞典、芬兰和挪威）也出现了银行危机。放松金融管制后，较大的金融中心也受到不断增加的流动性、经济泡沫和股市暴跌的影响，包括美国的情况（例如 1987 年的全球股市暴跌，也被称为黑色星期一，1989—1991 年的储蓄和贷款危机）和 1990 年日本的资产价格泡沫。据格拉贝尔所称（Grabel，2001），发展中经济体曾出现过 12 次金融危机，包括 1994 年的墨西哥危机以及 1997 年开始的亚洲金融危机。

80 年代和 90 年代期间，金融市场的普遍放松管制导致全球金融市场的巨幅增长和全球流动性的增加。例如，帕尔马（Palma，2009）表示，

"1980年至2007年间,全球金融资产股市的四个组成部分(股票、公共和私人债券、银行存款)实际上增加了9倍——从26.6万亿美元增加至241万亿美元。金融业的放松管制意味着金融机构可以通过提高杠杆率来增加流动性。衍生品和债务证券越来越普遍,新金融机构也出现了快速发展,如从事对冲基金和私募股权基金的机构。这些金融工具和金融机构的管制力度并不够。

据赫莱纳(Helleiner, 1994)所称,布雷顿森林体系时代的结束改变了全球组织和国家金融市场的治理。国家和国际机构的职责已经从防止金融危机变为危机后清理。这种变化也意味着国际货币基金组织和国际清算银行等机构将发挥更大的作用,因为它们实施的宏观经济政策改革有助于缓解各国的经济危机。然而,新的治理体系并没有实现全球金融体系的稳定。从某种意义上来讲,很多稳定全球金融体系的措施都是以一种不同于布雷顿森林体系的模式出现的。

联合国大会第63届会议主席米格尔·德斯科托·布罗克曼(Miguel d'Escoto Brockmann)在《联合国大会主席组专家委员会国际货币和金融体系改革报告》(2009年9月21日)的序言中称:

> 正如委员会不断强调的,目前的危机证明我们存在多方面的失败——理论、宗旨、政策和做法,以及一些潜在的失败,如道德和责任。本报告的主要观点是,这种多重危机并不是由失败的制度造成的。相反,制度本身,包括其组织和原则,以及其扭曲和缺陷体制,则是造成这些失败的主要原因。(United Nations, 2009, p. 8)

撰写这一报告的专家组成员来自世界各地,而委员会主席由诺贝尔经济学奖得主约瑟夫·斯蒂格利茨(Joseph Stiglitz)担任。他们很清楚,这个问题与倡导金融市场有限的国家参与这一自由市场经济观点有关,因为他们认为,金融市场的运作可以正确地反映出与金融交易相关的风险和成本的价值。按照这种观点,市场会对金融资产和危机的价值做出正确的估计,但这并不是由金融市场的内生性问题造成的,而是由政治干预和管制等外源性因素造成的。

在这一报告的序言中,德斯科托·布罗克曼还评论说:

> 2009年9月,美国爆发的金融危机是最近发生的最具影响力的一种危机,根据过去35年间在全球范围内落实的经济观点(往往是强

迫而为），同时爆发的粮食危机、水资源危机、能源危机和可持续发展危机与之密切相关。从这个角度来看，市场逻辑可以解决几乎所有社会、经济和政治问题。（同上）

他还对全球金融危机问责制和纠正措施的缺乏表示了失望，并指出了全球经济治理方面存在的一个问题。他说，危机的解决需要各国广泛的民主参与：

> 另一种补充性解释是，我们的全球经济治理体系中存在一个很大的缺陷。根据民主原则，那些深受相关政策影响的人最有发言权，而且应对大规模失败和伤害负责的人应承担起相应的责任。我们目前的全球经济治理体系不符合任何与民主治理有关的基本测试。（同上，第9页）

2009年，雷曼兄弟破产后，各国应对危机的一个重要反应是利用二十国集团这一更具包容性的论坛来建立一个金融监管和治理制度。本文不会对二十国集团的成败做出任何论述，只能说这是一个值得称道的举措，不会对大型经济体及其金融机构造成重大的影响。斯蒂格利茨（Stiglitz, 2009）曾公开批评二十国集团不去处理金融机构大而不能倒这一问题。我的看法是，他的批评指向了一个更大的问题，即美国等国家已对大型金融机构实施了救助，未来的经济活动大多与这些机构持续扮演的全球角色有关。因此，只要不对大型金融机构造成显著的负面影响，他们将会针对全球经济的监管和治理进行讨论。然而，这一观点并不是说二十国集团没有发挥任何作用，而是要表明，全球金融治理是一个应从不同角度理解并能产生不同的经济利益的艰巨任务。我们不应废除这种制度，而是要将其扩展到更多的国家。

本文的其余部分针对南非在金融活动中和机构监管不足的全球性金融体系下所面临着的困难进行了论述。正如引言中所述，本文所要论述的观点并不是南非是缺乏管制的全球金融环境的受害者。这表明，南非选择了这种导致全球金融市场监管不足的政策，因此它对全球动荡和危机更加敏感。本文还认为，全球金融动荡时期，这些政策选择对南非经济产生了负面影响。

三、南非和全球金融

20世纪80年代期间，受全球放松管制趋势的影响，种族隔离政府开始放开对南非金融体系的管制。下一标题将讨论南非银行体系的影响。其后将论述放松管制的跨境资本流动对南非的影响。

四、南非银行

南非现有银行体系结构的特点是高度集中化,由特定的殖民和种族隔离经济塑造而成。从20世纪80年代的种族隔离政府到2007年的金融危机,监管和自由化方法存在一种连续性。非银行金融机构(包括正式的和非正式的贷款人)已经具备其他机构投资者的职能,如对冲基金、风险投资基金和私募股权基金。按照金融服务委员会的定义,在后种族隔离时期,影子银行体系的规模出现了显著增长。1994年以后,外资银行开始在南非经济中扮演越来越重要的角色。

90年代期间,银行一直保留着它们的民族特性,直至采纳德科克(DeKock)委员会的建议。1985年的《金融机构法修正案》第106号文件就采纳了这一建议。银行放松管制的措施包括废除对银行活动的限制和住宅互助社团的股份化。这种放松管制,再加上80年代期间因政治原因造成的撤资,导致新银行集团的重组和整合,但市场仍然呈现出集中化的特征。放松管制后的南非银行业市场极其类似于1994年美国的多功能"超市银行"市场。

后种族隔离时期的改革符合巴塞尔(Basel)提出的充足性要求。全球金融危机爆发后,政策开始向"双峰"方案转变,这一政策转变使资本充足性和银行行为的监管与客户的监管发生了分离。双峰方案有助于解决南非监管环境的高度碎片化。但是,这种方案并不能解决历史不平等的现象和南非银行更直接的发展需求。因此,南非银行和其他金融机构的服务核心仍是同样的业务,主要是它们过去曾服务过的白人群体。与此同时,它们计划发挥金融化[①]在南非经济中起到的重要作用。银行在很大程度上仍将继续受储备银行的监管,而非银行贷款机构则须在国家信用监管机构注册。

因此,大型南非银行集团,并没有通过小型项目来增加针对以前无银

---

① 金融化是指金融在社会各行各业发挥越来越大的作用和影响。对非金融企业来说,金融化是指它们越来越多地参与金融业务,而且越来越多的利润和收入来源于金融附属公司和投机性金融资产。随着国家的撤出以及社会福利和基本服务的私有化,家庭也受到了金融化的影响。家庭将越来越多的资产用作金融资产和投资于消费型金融服务中,以积累养老基金和获取风险缓解和保险服务。总体而言,减少国家在经济中发挥的作用并放宽贸易和金融市场的新自由主义政策应负责为金融和金融化的发展创造条件。见爱泼斯坦(Epstein,2005),以了解金融化及其定义。

行账户的人提供的服务,它们的举止看上去极其类似于美国和英国的银行机构,它们逐渐放弃调解,开始实施证券化,外来金融工具的投资服务和交易以及金融化取得了较大的发展。

南非的银行也因此变得庞大且不能倒塌①,这不仅使南非国内经济变得集中化,而且进一步推动了南非经济活动的国际化。事实上,南非最大的银行现在不仅在积极向其他国家发展,而且已经成为大型全球银行集团(如英国巴克莱银行和中国工商银行)的一部分或与之建立了密切的关系。它们的业务变化、国际化和金融化使人们对南非银行以及它们在解决大批无银行账户的人方面所起的作用提出了很多质疑,尤其是它们是如何对南非经济发展做出贡献的。

据政府称,南非银行很安全,而且金融危机期间它们的适应能力也证明了这一说法。我认为他们是问错了问题。他们对安全的定义是建立在银行业务已经向风险越来越大的活动转移这一背景下的,他们不能对这些活动进行充分的监管,而且许多活动已经变得大而不能倒。南非银行可能已经度过了这场风暴,但它们变得更加危险,而且变得大而不能倒。它们之所以能经受住2008年的经济危机,是因为当时对剩余资本的管制使它们难以接触到美国的有毒债务。然而,80年代和90年代期间,金融和银行业的放松管制增加了金融系统性风险,南非银行开始不断变化其职能和行为,以与美国银行竞争。

五、全球资本流动

20世纪80年代期间,受全球放松管制趋势的影响,种族隔离政府开始放开对南非金融体系的管制。他们对资本流动的放松管制导致了银行危机的出现,种族隔离政府不得不于1985年宣布单方面暂停债务偿还。

后种族隔离政府继续实行金融自由化,并为资本的流入和流出提供了更多自由,在过去20多年间,非本地居民的资本流动相对不受管制,而本地居民的资本流出也相对更加自由。南非居民的跨境资本流动自由化发展得较慢,但从1994年起,南非的资本流出额定期会有所增加。

鉴于2004年南非的经济增长速度达到5%,2005年达到5%以上,

---

① 南非的银行大到不能倒的观点是由金融行业的分析者提出的。例如,彭博资讯发布一篇名为"渣打银行真的是大而不倒吗?"的文章(彭博资讯2010年8月13日,http://www.moneyweb.co.za/moneyweb-financial/standard-bank-is-too-big-to-fail),其中引用了英国著卫保险公司银行业分析师特雷西·布罗齐亚克(Tracy Brodziak)的一句话,他认为渣打银行"绝对是南非具有系统重要性的一家银行"。

2005—2007年间一直维持在这一水平,南非国家财政部对这一宏观经济的成功进行了庆祝。

然而,这些成功却受到了质疑。通货膨胀率之所以不断下降,是因为中国等国家进口量的增加,这也就意味着南非出现了进口通货紧缩。2004—2007年经济增长率较高,主要受益于债务驱动型消费的增长,这与美国和其他国家类似,而且房地产和股市泡沫导致了全球金融危机的爆发。高增长率是由债务驱动型消费以及房地产和金融市场的投机行为造成的。2003—2007年短期的高增长率对经济和社会造成了不利的影响。

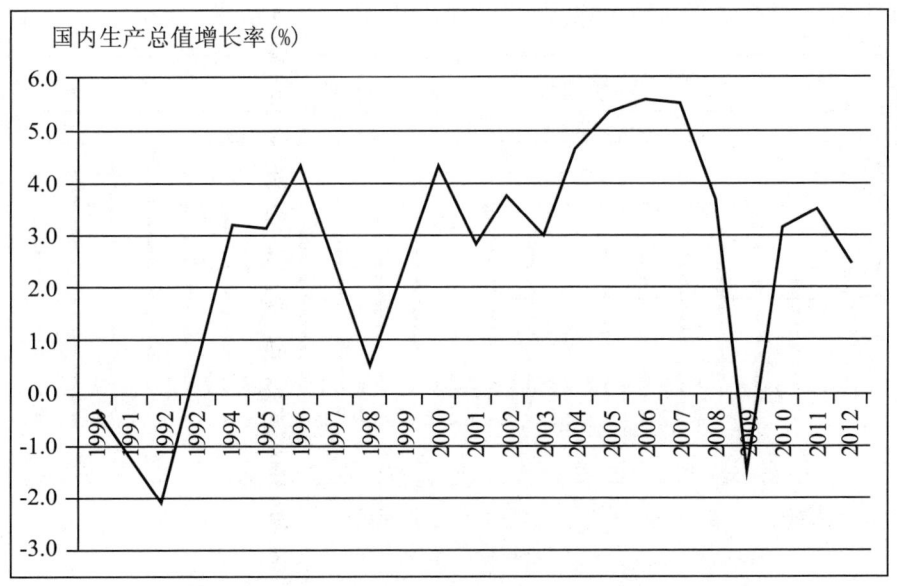

图1 南非国内生产总值增长率(以2005年价格为准)

资料来源:南非储备银行。

从1994年起,短期资本流入的增加对南非经济造成了极大的影响。正如上面提到的,短期投机性资本流动的出现使金融危机和危机的蔓延呈现出了宏观经济的脆弱性。短期证券投资净流入的波动性使汇率出现了大幅波动。投资者、进口商和出口商面临着更加严峻和不确定的商业环境。

加上由于进口增加和通胀目标而制定的低通胀制度,不受控制的资本流入为顺周期性的宏观经济政策创造了环境,而且还导致了与短期资本流入和流出有关的经济大起大落。一方面,短期资本流入与信贷的增加和兰特（南非货币）地位的增强有关，廉价进口和较低的通货膨胀率导致南非储备银行利率降低。低利率将进一步推动借贷债务驱动型消费和资产市场的投机行为。

另一方面，短期资本大量流出与兰特地位的弱化有关，进口的减少和通货膨胀的增加导致利率增加和信贷紧缩。2000年和2001年证券投资流入崩溃后，南非出现了货币危机，兰特较美元下跌了35%。为了应对通货膨胀和货币的贬值，南非储备银行在一年内将利率提升了四次。自全球金融危机期间证券投资流入崩溃后，南非储备银行愈加不愿意提高利息。然而，南非储备银行将通胀水平作为其主要关注点之一，南非的实际利率要比美国、大多数欧洲国家和其他贸易伙伴更高。

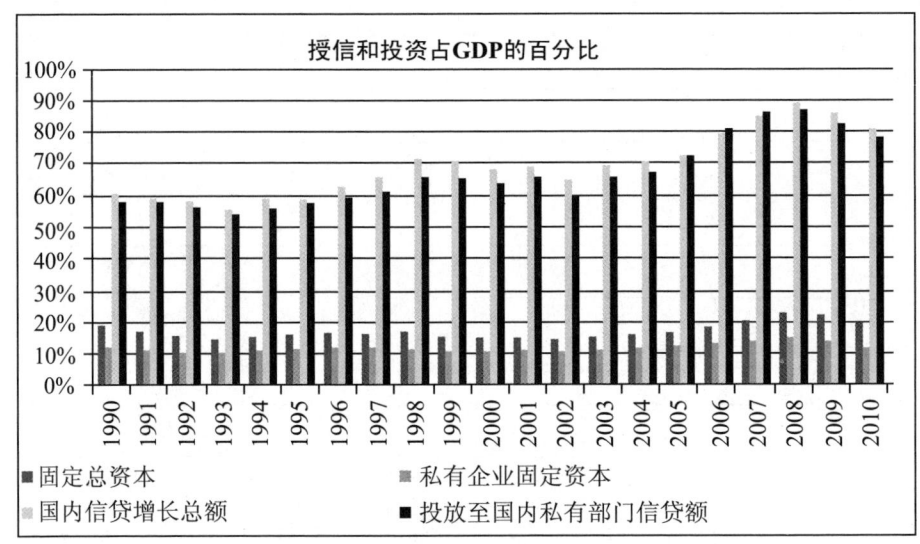

图2　授信和投资占GDP的百分比

资料来源：南非储备银行。

短期资本净流入的增加与国内金融市场流动性的增加有关。2000年至2008年期间，私营部门的授信增加了约23%，但民营企业投资仅增长了4%。与短期净资产组合流动激增相关的流动性增加并未用于生产性投资，而是为债务驱动型消费、房地产和金融投机的信贷分配不当创造了环境。

开放的资本市场是南非经济金融化的一个重要组成部分。机构投资者在整体经济中的作用已经完善，因为金融市场的自由化意味着私营部门在提供服务时发挥了越来越重要的作用。私营部门在分配退休金、保险和医疗援助计划，以及在提供教育和卫生保健方面发挥着更大的作用。

为富商和其他金融机构（如对冲基金和私募股权基金）提供服务的金融机构也有所发展。自2003年以来，衍生品和证券化债务市场也在加速发展（Mohamed，2010）。这些机构投资者和金融机构通过增加的信贷直接推动了房地产、股票价格和通过贷款来抬高资产价格的家庭的发展。通过对日益增长的家庭债务水平的支持，它们也间接引发了资产价格的上涨。它们使用衍生品和证券化债务来促使资本出现更大的流动性和提高债务水平。

图3显示了南非房价的增长趋势，图4则显示了股价指数的发展趋势。南非房价增长超过了世界上的其他任何国家。流动性的增加推动了人们对住宅和商业空间需求的增加，从而推高了房价，带动了新住房和商业地产的发展。房价的上涨使人们感觉社会财富在增加，驱使房价上涨，并刺激了房地产投机市场和投机性房地产开发的发展。股价也出现了攀升，房产泡沫直到全球金融危机开始后才开始破裂。结果导致资本错误地分配至投机性市场，以及投资水平的降低。

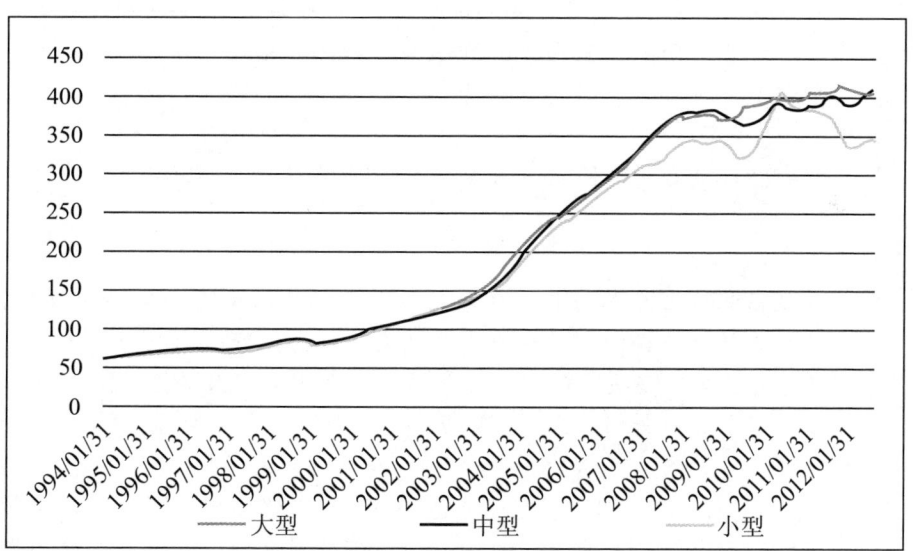

图3　南非联合银行集团房价指数

资料来源：Quantec。

南非非金融企业已金融化。20世纪90年代末，大量公司在海外上市，尤其是在伦敦和纽约，南非非金融企业金融化就是从那时拉开序幕的。这些公司被迫遵守90年代期间出现的股东价值运动的需求。

图4　约翰内斯堡证券交易所股票价格指数

资料来源：Quantec。

安永会计师事务所（Ernst and Young，2002）在审查2001年南非并购时称：

> 股东积极主义在南非兴起速度缓慢，但是像所有全球趋势那样，它很快就赶上了我们。在过去两三年里，发展良好的南非海外上市公司已领略全球市场要求的高透明度。定位于国内发展的南非公司正承受着效仿全球同行的压力。（第27页）

如上所述，21世纪初，股东价值运动对南非的影响已经开始加深。股东价值运动要求关注核心业务，简化公司结构和提高短期投资回报率。南非上市公司，甚至是英美资源集团公司（Anglo American Corporation）等巨头，也被迫重组、分解非核心业务并简化复杂公司结构。与其美国同行一样，这些大公司通过参与金融市场的金融活动和投机买卖来满足股东价值运动对更高回报的要求。

图5表明，至21世纪初期，南非非金融企业金融资产占固定资本存量的百分比已飞速增长至250%。与80年代相比，大约翻了一番，这一迅速增长与劳动力改革有关，因为劳动力改革加剧了政治动荡，加重了国际孤

立并且提高了采用新自由主义宏观经济政策后的利率。90年代产生的50%的增长可能与民主改革对商业造成的影响、劳动立法深层改革、贸易自由化以及非金融企业的金融化有关。

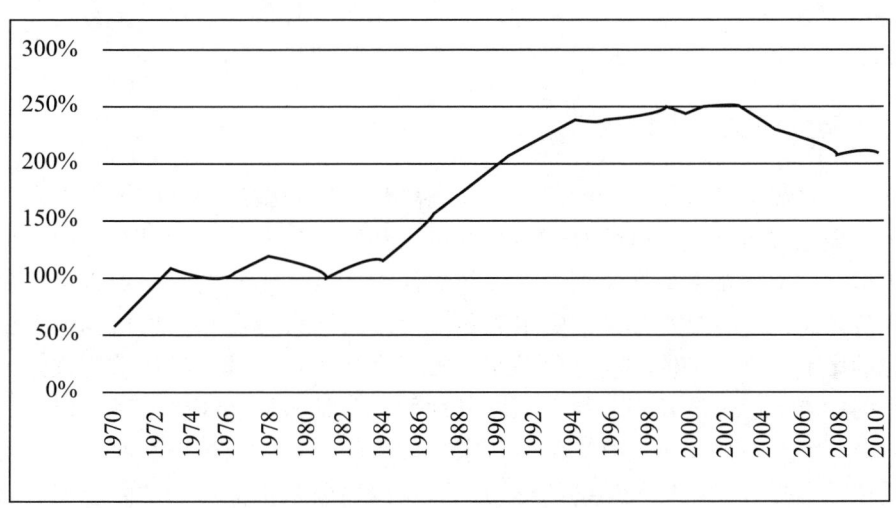

图5 南非非金融企业金融资产占固定资本存量的百分比：1970—2010年

资料来源：Ashman，Mohamed and Newman（2013）。

非金融企业的收入和利润对财政越来越高的依赖性和股东价值运动对其行为和结构的影响加深了这些公司的金融化程度。金融化带来的后果就是相对于80年代固定资产的增加来说，金融资产的迅猛增长不仅没有得到抑制反而势头更旺。这意味着，长期以来，南非非金融企业的留存利润和日益增长的债务已经从生产性投资转移到投机和短期投资。

80年代放松管制后，南非金融行业规模扩大。金融资产需求的增长和新型金融机构和金融工具的诞生致使金融机构规模扩大和职能增强。大型银行的业务已经从中介转向信用扩张和增加金融资产交易。后种族隔离政府的政策选择意味着政府不能引导当前和未来家庭与企业储蓄从金融活动转向生产活动。

金融业从国外吸引短期和投机性资本而非长期和生产性资本。短期资本流入不仅可以填补巨额经常账户赤字，还可能导致贸易赤字不断增长。短期资本流入与不断增长的资本账户相关，因为大型投资组合流入已导致过去十年里由经常账户转移的净生产要素收入平均金额超过国内生产总值的2%。短期资金流动可能有助于国际收支，但要以生产性投资和创造就业为代价。此外，政府通常会认为南非储蓄不足，低储蓄导致低水平的经济投资,这种观点必须被打破。储蓄总额的增加是受来源于其他国家的资本流入驱动的,因为南非的利率和资本市场回报率较高。如上所述,这些短期资本流入的剧增,增加了获取信贷的可能,也可能是国内储蓄总额自2002年以来一直停滞不前的原因。而且,值得一提的是,对大多数南非人来说,贫困和不平等才是国内储蓄低的罪魁祸首。

六、结论

主张民主的南非政府沿用了种族隔离政府所实施的新自由主义宏观经济和金融政策,包括解除对国内金融市场和跨国资本运动的限制。由于该项举措,南非金融市场受到了更多的关注,尤其是南非的银行业,然而该经济体越来越容易受到跨国资本流和发达国家金融企业和征信机构政策变化的影响。该经济体的金融化并非仅限于金融市场,其对经济政策逐渐增长的影响力已经波及南非社会的方方面面,包括服务和风险管理,以及针对家庭和企业的减负策略。南非几家超大型的公司已通过增强对资本市场的依赖、提升股东价值运动的作用,以及按照股东价值运动的意愿提升行政管理的一致性,实现了金融化。其结果是增加了对短期收益的关注,增强了对金融活动的依赖,为了达到利润预期增加了金融市场的投机活动。总之,对生产投资以及劳动力和技能的发展来说,这是一种较为短视的做法。

这一时期引发的金融危机反映了全球金融流动性的加剧以及海外投机资本的增加对该经济体的影响。该经济体虽然保持着良好的经济增长,但是投资停滞,失业率增加。资本流向了依赖债务推动型消费和金融投机增加来获利的领域。南非的经济增长途径受到了经济金融化以及金融作用强化所带来的影响。主要表现为该经济体未能成功地向提升工业化和增加就业的新型经济增长途径转变,反而失去了进一步工业化的资本存量和能力,并且更加依赖于采矿和采掘行业。此次金融危机表明这种经济增长模式是不可持续的。

由于政府的宏观经济和金融政策的影响,该经济体对外国资本流以及全球金融市场和征信机构主导者的决策更加敏感,并且更加依赖于短期资本流来平衡贸易赤字。由于全球金融市场持续存在管理问题,短期资金流的比重仍然较大,南非仍将遭受金融市场管制解除所带来的负面影响。

南非政府需要重新评估其宏观经济和金融政策。政策的转变会使很多发达国家的金融企业和征信机构普遍对南非经济政策的可信度表示担忧,并且会降低南非的信用等级,导致资金成本的上升。然而,金砖国家发展银行（BRICS Development Bank）的成立、应急储备的安排，以及与金砖国家合作者更加广泛的业务往来将会帮助南非向更为有效的宏观经济和金融政策框架过渡。金砖国家机构和合作伙伴关系将会降低南非经济政策过渡的成本，支持政府解决种族隔离遗留下来的经济问题。

如果南非政府选择保持其宏观经济和金融政策，金砖国家的应急储备安排和合作伙伴关系仍然会有力地帮助南非应对金融市场动荡加剧和由此产生的宏观经济风险，以及金融市场持续开放的脆弱性。然而，投资和创造就业的调整如果脱离了产业基础建设和深化过程中的消费和投机活动，将会降低调整的预期。包括南非银行和金融机构在内的大型企业已经实现了金融化，它们正在期待着依靠国内和国际金融市场的投机活动增加收益。

参考文献

[1] S. Ashman, S. Mohamed and S. Newman, "The financialization of the South African Economy and Its Impact on Economic Growth and Employment", a working paper produced for UNDESA, 2013.

[2] Bloomberg, "Is Standard Bank Too Big to Fail", by Tracy Broziak, August 13, 2010, http：//www.moneyweb.co.za/moneyweb-financial/standard-bank-is-too-big-to-fail (downloaded on August 15, 2010).

[3] Gerald Epstein, "Introduction：Financialization and the World Economy", in Gerald Epstein (ed.), *Financialization and the World Economy*, Edward Elgar, Cheltenham and Northampton, 2005.

[4] Ernst and Young, "Mergers and Acquisitions：A Review of Activity for the Year 2001", 2002, available online athttp：//www.ey.com/ZA/en/Home.

[5] I. Grabel, "Averting crisis? Assessing Measures to Manage Financial Integration in Emerging Economies", presented at the conference on "Financialization of the Global Economy" held by the Political Economy Research Institute (PERI) at the University of Massachusetts, Amherst, December 7 – 8, 2001.

[6] E. Helleiner, *States and the Resurgence of Global Finance：From Bretton Wooods to the 1990s*, Cornell University Press, 1994.

[7] Seeraj Mohamed, "The State of the South African Economy", in R. Southall, D. Pillay, P. Naidoo and J. Daniel (eds.), *New South African Review 1：Development or Decline*, Wits University Press, Johannesburg, 2010.

[8] G. Palma, "The Revenge of the Market on the Rentiers — Why Neo-liberal Reports

of the End of History Turned Out to Be Premature", *Cambridge Journal of Economics*, 33 (4), 2009, pp. 829.

[9] United Nations, "Report of the Commission of Experts of the President of the United Nations General Assembly on Reforms of the International Monetary and Financial System", UN Printers, New York, NY., 2009.

促进南非治理现代化的响应和创新能力

[南非] 丹尼尔·普拉提杰斯*

一、引言

形成于1994年的南非宪政民主国家体制不仅必须消除存在了几十年的经济、政治和社会上的隔阂和不平等，也要消除种族隔离制度因治理和政府结构与功能上的缺陷所导致的复杂的遗留问题。可以说，其宪法的合作治理性质也是建立在不同种族、民族和地区间在冲突结束后的政治和解基础上的。

本国的宪政国家体制和政府因此肩负着对不同省份（州政府和市政府）的结构和功能进行整合的义务，包括弥补经济结构上的缺陷。本文重点研究促使南非国内走上治理现代化有效途径的干预措施和机制。

这个宪政国家依据宪法法律和法规建立了自己的治理和政府体制，形成了一套监管和受规则约束的制度的基础。它是一个三权分立的政治体制，包括行政机构、议会和司法部门，各自承担着宪法赋予的权力。此外，它还根据宪法建立了一个多层次的宪政体制，包括国家（中央）、省级和地方政府。这些多层次的政府部门基本上是通过国家多层次宪法和立法行政部门构成的一个"政府间"合作治理体系发挥作用。

二、治理现代化的基本缘由

政府商业和资本利益，以及在政府和国家治理中的个人与社会组织，三者间形成了社会契约关系，对该契约关系做出制度性回应是一种义务。这种义务促使政府，尤其是中央政府找到有效的途径推动国民的社会和经济融合，提高凝聚力，以对抗结构性不平等和贫困。政府也意识到，要在这些方面更加有效，需关注能促进增长和发展的社会和经济基础设施，包

---

* 丹尼尔·普拉提杰斯（Daniel Plaatjies），南非人文科学研究理事会成员。

括为基础设施吸引更多的国内外直接投资。

种族隔离制度结束后的南非没有时间和条件允许其先建立一个治理体制，然后再寻找有效的途径对其进行现代化。两者必须齐头并进，以促进政治和社会的和谐和稳定，保证经济的连续性。因此，提高治理效率的更多原因和依据来自以下几个方面：

- 通过新的制度，通过新的组织框架、结构和系统，全面统一地应对妨碍可持续发展的结构性障碍。
- 通过各种机制改进政府和治理，促进公益，改善服务的提供。
- 创立新的机构，对种族隔离时期建立的机构进行调整，以适应新的宪政秩序和政治体制。
- 面对这个两极化的国家进一步提高认识，应对日益分化的经济和社会需求以及对国家资源的需求。
- 针对南非社会中经济精英和普通公民间存在的结构性问题，需要找到一种可持续的混合型解决方案。
- 鉴于该国过去的政府剥夺了大部分公民的参与权，现在要改进公民参与国家治理的制度和结构。
- 对外部因素对国内政府和治理的影响提高管理和控制能力，提升国家在国际和世界事务中发挥的作用。
- 加强和巩固受规则约束的机制和结构，因为这种机制在政策、法律、经济和治理方面有可预测的产出和结果（尤其在金融和财政管理方面），能改善问责机制。
- 为了保护国民的利益和国家主权，要提高对世界秩序日益多极化的认识。
- 主动拥抱新的知识和创新，提高政府和治理的整体表现。
- 包括能够对经济、政治和社会方面的表现与治理所带来的影响及有关特点进行管理。

三、中央政府的掌控能力

在过去的20年里，尽管一直由同一个政党执政，中央政府的掌控能力在不同政治行政管理部门和一系列政策改变（涉及"建设和发展规划""增长、就业和重新分配计划""南非加速和共享增长倡议""新增长道路"和近期出台的"国家发展规划"）的推动之下在教育、社会福利和保护及经济政策方面带来了一系列创新和改进。这些制度和组织安排上的变化反映了2009年以来日益强烈的为国家制定更长远经济、社会和政治愿景和计划的呼声。2009年上台的政府的掌控能力表现在对中央政府构成方面的一些改变，包括成立了一个由总统直接领导的国家计划委员会，这是从财政部脱离出来的一个经济发展部门（制订宏观和微观经济计划），也是一个执行监督和评估部门。

实际上，政府在计划和执行监督方面的战略管理改进和创新包括在中央政府内为有效治理、有效领导和有效管理创立的新制度。此外，政府还在以下方面取得了成绩：

- 通过一个以成果为导向的优先级（OBPs）系统制定新的、以实效为基础的政府计划。
- 12个OBPs覆盖了从社会服务到国家安全的所有部门——这是取代目标管理制度（MBOs）的一个创新之举。
- OBPs系统推动下的多层次计划和治理中与宏观经济框架相联系的新的政府战略计划形式。
- 附带了一个（几乎完全基于证据的）《诊断报告》的《2030年国家发展计划》，这个计划在很多方面对有关计划、规划和设计有重要的影响。
- 宏观经济框架包括一个横跨数年的中期战略框架（MTSF）、中期开支框架（MTEF）、OBPs和战略规划、中期预算政策说明（MTBPS）、国家预算回顾和政府间财政框架（收入部门）。
- 所有这些框架有助于政府和治理在工作中保持经济和社会政策上的稳定。
- 执行监督和评估系统主要建立在那12个OBPs之上。该系统为执行监督和评估部门（2014年改称"计划和执行监督部门"）进行监管成效评估提供了条件。

四、纵向和横向协调

在政府工作中，政策治理、领导和管理间的协调对于保持对政府的信任至关重要，也是对政府政策规划的一种投入，包括提高对不同政策和法律间相互影响的监控的能力。南非中央政府行政首脑（内阁）在执行政策、规划协调和管理治理事务中由一个内阁集群系统提供支持，这个系统涉及社会和经济、投资和就业、国际关系、和平和安全、司法和犯罪防范以及治理和行政管理。这些集群在国家层面开展工作，由相关国家行政机关（部委）组成。为了强化中央和省级政府之间在治理和执政方面的协调，成立了一个总统协调委员会。这个委员会由总统和九位地方政府（省级）首脑（省长）组成。各部长理事会的负责人也根据宪法关于中央和次级政府职能分配的规定,对总统协调委员会提供直接的政策协调支持。这些执行中央—省级政府职能分担的部长理事会由各部部长和省级政府行政委员会成员构成。中央政府各部门中的最高级行政长官以及省级政府的行政长官共同组成一个司局长论坛(Forum of South African Director Gentrals,简称FOSAD)。

五、更广泛的治理参与

政府成立了社会行动者经济和社会发展咨询论坛——国家经济发展和劳工委员会(NEDLAC)。也有开放的、地区性的和基础广泛的政府和公民间社区论坛/会议(imbizos),通常由中央政府高级官员召集。

六、财务治理和管理

南非通过议会的一个关于储备银行的法案,依据宪法建立了南非储备银行。该银行有权"为南非经济的可持续平衡发展对价格进行调控"。储备银行"在履行职责时有相当程度的自主权"。

由于立法和监管系统(受规则约束的系统)的推动,公共资金的财务和金融治理方面的创新和现代化能力日益提高。资金分配方案每年通过国家拨款法案和收入分配法案制定。金融和财政委员会在收入分配和政府间财政授权方面既有宪法赋予的影响,也有立法方面的影响。该委员会通过其对各省和地方政府的总体资金需求的估算等顾问功能发挥影响。

不同级别的政府,即中央、省级和地方政府管理部门涉及不同的财政立法。地方政府的立法包括城市房产利率法令(2004)、城市系统法令(2000)、城市建筑物法令(1998)和市政财务管理法令。

另一方面,中央和省级政府管理部门也根据宪法第10章第195节(公共服务的价值和原则)、公共服务法案(1996)、公共财政管理法案(1996)和政府间关系框架法案(2005)受到监管。

七、执行和行政治理中的完整性

依据宪法创立的制度的完整性对于有效促进和建立治理现代化机制至关重要。为了确保执行和管理的可靠性,政府对一部供高官使用的"部长手册"定期进行回顾检讨,以保证对政府高官的义务、福利和奖励措施等方面的治理及时有效,并受规则约束。这本部长手册加上"议员个人利益登记册"(议会成员)、"道德规范"和"执行与行政部门议会监督委员会"有助于实现善政廉政。宪法治理和政府的整体系统因维护宪政民主的国家制度如审计长、保民官和南非人权委员会等的支持而进一步得到加强。

八、基于效果的制度

为了在政府中建设和创立一个以结果为导向的机制，作为一项特殊的创新，南非于2009年引入了效果评价制度。监督和评估部（DPME）认为，创建这个制度的目的是"保证在政府中实施基于效果的（而不是简单的产出或活动）机制，把重点放在数量有限的关键性战略优先事项上，推动政府作为一个整体，协调一致，达到这些效果，而不是各自为政"（DPME，2013年1月）。

为了协助系统性思考，任何类型的效果模型在效果理论中都可以概念化为一个可视的效果结构，并呈现为一个垂直视觉层级结构。（见图1）层级结构的底部是参与者最低级别的活动（投入或干预），然后向上经过几个阶梯是能创造出产出的活动，这些活动与最终的效果有着因果联系，最后达到效果视觉模型（影响）的最高层。人们往往希望外界的一个程序或干预就能改善这些最高级别的效果。

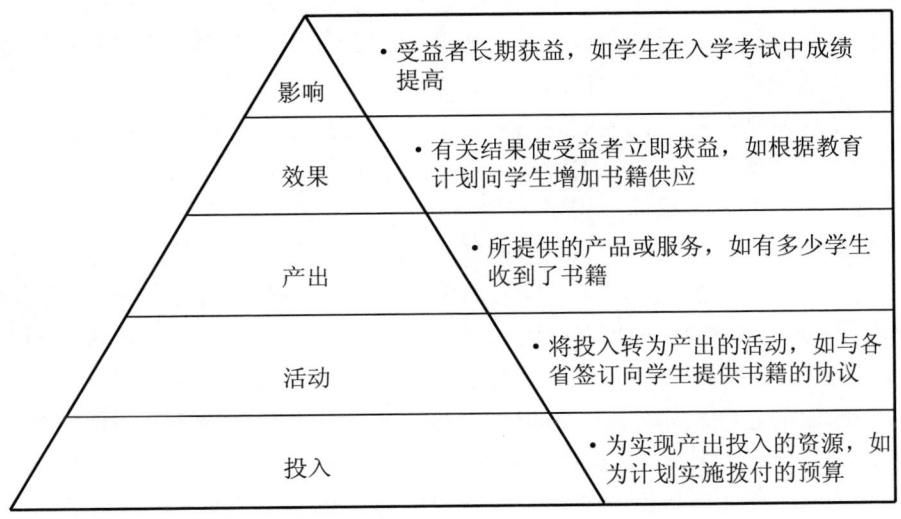

图1 成效指标和成果链层级结构图

资料来源：Based on DPME, "National Evaluation Policy Framework", *The Presidency*, November 23, 2001, Figure 2, p. 9。

上述成效指标层级结构图在 DPME 的《达到效果的方法指南》中曾清晰地阐述过（见该部门 2010 年 5 月出的第 27 版）。该书指出，效果计划要从想要达到的效果开始倒推着做。比如要改善人民的生活，就要找到达到这个效果的最佳方法，也就是要知道需要多少产出，以及要达到这些产出需要进行哪些活动，进行这些活动需要哪些资源。进行效果和影响计划还需要知道那些部门可以开展成果链上哪些特定的活动（出处同上）。

正如该文献阐述的那样，效果系统指的是试图对某种结果进行定义、安排优先项、辩护、衡量、指派和/或安排人员完成达到所希望的结果所需的任何活动，以及要达到这些效果需采取的步骤所构成的任何系统。不同的效果系统包括：结果管理系统、战略计划系统、绩效管理系统、绩效衡量系统、计划评估、循证实践系统、投资战略、性价比评估、标杆管理练习、效果承包系统、绩效薪酬系统等。因此，效果理论为把判断此类系统是否有效的原则概念化提供了空间，不论这些系统是否构建良好，为了在未来的设计中能对现有系统进行改进，允许做特别推荐。[1]

南非在开发效果系统时，其计划系统首先从问题分析着手，以保证对问题有清晰的认识（从计划受益人的需求和关注的角度），并且计划是有的放矢的和注重解决问题的根源的。接下来是在深刻了解前因后果的基础上发展一种"变革理论"，以便利用在对假设的关系的真实性进行测试所做的观察和评估中得到的证据，并积累可靠的知识，知道哪种方法在哪种条件下适用。效果系统的目的是为了便于计划管理，方便跟踪进展，测试产出是否是必要的，达到效果的条件是否充分。最后，计划系统确保在结果链条上的所有层次都有清晰的、可衡量的指标，有方便有效跟踪进展和评估结果的基线和目标（DPME，2010 年 12 月）。

也许，效果系统一个关键但常常被人忽略方面是，这是一个基于人权的（HRBA）发展计划。这个计划的中心是对 HRBA 的研究和分析。这些研究和分析能帮助人们理解行动的必要性，因此必须在省级、市级和地方政府进行。如果想要找到应对可持续发展所面临挑战的解决方案，就必须在国家层面进行。如果大家都积极参与，就能帮助社区提高既与他们自己相关，也与直接管理他们的地方政府的结构相关的能力。这将能帮助他们克服能力上的主要限制，使计划能有效实施。也将促使本地和国际发展伙伴支持政府在经济发展、社会动员和社区营造方面的基本战略，为寻求发展创建有效的伙伴关系。[2]

参考文献

[1] P. Duignan, "What Are Outcomes Systems?" *Outcomes Theory Knowledge Base*, Article No. 216, 2009, http://outcomestheory.wordpress.com/article/what-are-outcomes-systems-2m7zd68aaz774-15/.

[2] Urban Jonsson, "Human Rights Approach to Development Programming", UNICEF, 2009.

欧盟和金砖国家

[英] 弗雷泽·卡梅隆[*]

一、引言

近年来,金砖国家(BRICS)俨然发展为世界舞台上一个最奇特的集团。"BRICS"这一缩写是由高盛集团首席经济学家吉姆·奥尼尔(Jim O' Neill)于2001年创造的,该词指代世界四大发展中经济体——巴西、俄罗斯、印度和中国(南非于2010年加入金砖国家)。奥尼尔表明,金砖国家将在未来50年里重塑全球化,那时金砖国家将主导世界经济。他认为,到那时,我们再也不能简单地根据大型先进经济体来评估全球经济。全球政策问题,如货币、贸易失衡或气候变化,也不能继续由七国集团或八国集团——美国、日本、德国、英国、法国、意大利、加拿大(和俄罗斯)来定夺。

最初,奥尼尔选出的这四个国家对这一称谓产生了不同的反应。俄罗斯感到非常高兴,中国则困惑不已,巴西对此冷嘲热讽,而印度则抱以漠不关心的态度。南非通过大力游说成为非洲大陆的唯一代表。现在,各国都在利用这一概念来捏造一些暂时性的关联。有关金砖国家的年度峰会、部长级会议和小型发展行业不断见诸报端。

所有金砖国家都认为,美国或欧盟不应该主导世界经济。各国应该团结起来共同促进全球环境变化。他们反对西方国家在政治和安全事务上采取单方面行动——但当成员国强占邻国(俄罗斯/克里米亚)时却默不作声。他们致力于在国际货币基金组织和其他机构中产生更大的影响力。因此,金砖国家组建了这一集团来发展成员国之间的相关性,但在重大的政治、安全、经济和贸易问题上,金砖国家称不上一个具备凝聚力的集团。

欧盟与各金砖国家都建立了战略合作伙伴关系。迄今为止,欧盟并未

---

[*] 弗雷泽·卡梅隆(Fraser Cameron),布鲁塞尔欧盟—亚洲中心主任。

将金砖国家视为一个集团，也没有任何外界力量强制它这么做。布鲁塞尔认为金砖国家不具备在任何重大全球性问题上采取共同行动的能力。本文探讨了金砖国家的崛起，评估了金砖国家成员国之间的异同，尤其是在治理这一问题上，并分析了欧盟是如何对金砖国家做出单独和集体回应的。

二、金砖国家的崛起（和没落？）

金砖国家的崛起与他们近几年的迅速发展密切相关。金砖国家的世界产出份额在过去10年翻了一番，从7.5%增至15%。他们所占的全球人口比例（42%）和领土比例更高。中国和印度是目前世界上人口最多的两个国家，分别为13.9亿和12.7亿。与亚洲这两个人口大国相比，巴西人口为2.02亿，俄罗斯为1.42亿，南非为0.53亿。（欧盟为5亿，美国为3.22亿）

就经济方面而言，中国目前在金砖国家中占主导地位。按购买力平价计算，其全球输出份额从1980年的8%增至2013年的16.5%。2013年，中国在金砖国家中所占的输出份额约为53%，1990年仅为42%。而在过去20年间，巴西和俄罗斯的世界国内生产总值均未出现显著增长。就连印度的增幅也很小——从1990年的4%增至2009年的6%。金砖国家的崛起主要与这两个亚洲人口大国有关，尤其是中国。金砖国家这一概念确实抓住了将经济权力从旧的发达国家，尤其是西欧和日本，转向"新兴国家"这一事实。近期爆发的金融危机也加速了这种转变。

相比于欧盟和美国，中国和印度在金融危机中几乎毫发无损。在过去五年中，中国的经济年增长率为8.5%，印度为6.6%。然而，巴西、俄罗斯和南非的增幅很小。2014年，所有金砖国家仍继续维持缓慢增长的步伐。

金砖国家能否赋予世界发展活力？答案是不确定的。2013年，金砖国家的国内生产总值超过全球国内生产总值的30%，但主要归因于中国。金砖国家并未像其他国家那样发挥起"火车头"的作用，其发展主要以金砖国家内部为主。金砖国家对世界其他地区的净需求刺激主要依赖于其贸易盈余的减少或财政赤字的增加。

中国目前已经成为"世界工厂"——在制造业方面具备竞争优势地位的高投资、高增长的超级大国。中国的经济发展比印度更加开放：2013年，商品贸易额占中国国内生产总值的比例为67%，而印度仅为32%。但是，印度的技术密集型服务相对较强：服务贸易额占国内生产总值的比例为15%，而中国仅为7%。与中国和印度相比，巴西的经济发展相对封闭，

2013 年，其商品出口额仅占国内生产总值的 22%，服务出口额占国内生产总值的 5%。食品及原材料占其出口额的 50%。2013 年，俄罗斯制成品占出口额的比例不到 20%。俄罗斯是燃料和矿产品出口大国。

然而，这种趋势并不是一成不变的，治理方面产生的问题很可能意味着这种迅速发展的步伐不得不逐渐放缓。中国和俄罗斯目前所面临的问题可能要比世界其他地区更为严峻。就中国而言，经济增长放缓可能会导致一些更为严重的后果。而在俄罗斯，乌克兰冲突可能会导致该国经济下滑。西方国家的制裁以及投资者不断产生的焦虑感加剧了这种无论如何都不可避免的现象。今年，俄罗斯已损失了约 850 亿美元。

正如俄罗斯一样，巴西的商品出口在其 2000 年的经济成功中发挥了重要作用。俄罗斯出口商品主要以石油和天然气为主。巴西则以铁矿石和大豆、咖啡和糖等农产品为主。在近十年中，所有金砖国家的经济发展都出现了放缓的现象，其中巴西和俄罗斯的经济放缓步伐较慢。这两个国家的平均增长率一直低于中国和印度，而今年又出现了进一步的放缓。国际货币基金组织预计，在整个 2014 年中，巴西和俄罗斯的增幅很小——巴西为 0.3%，俄罗斯为 0.2%。

我们很有必要通过以下现象来研究一下上述数据的来龙去脉。举例来说，英国向比利时出口的产品要比金砖国家多。美国对比荷卢经济联盟的投资要比金砖国家多。欧盟向瑞士出口的产品要比金砖国家多。跨大西洋经济、贸易和投资关系仍然在世界上占据最重要的地位。

三、治理

金砖国家目前正在因腐败、管理不善和缺乏一致的监管规则而困扰不已。他们都面临着严峻的内部问题，尤其是不平等和贫困。一些金砖国家领导人，如习近平和莫迪，已经认识到了这些问题，而且已经将这些问题列入优先解决的政治事项中，但某些领导人，如普京、祖马、罗塞芙并不重视腐败问题。在 2013 年透明国际公布的全球清廉指数排行榜中，所有金砖国家的排名都非常靠前（南非 72/177，巴西 74，中国 80，印度 94，俄罗斯 127）。在最新公布的列格坦治理指数排行榜中，金砖国家也面临着同样严酷的情形（南非 54/150，印度 56，巴西 63，中国 66，俄罗斯 113）。

除了大规模的腐败外，金砖国家还面临着许多其他治理问题，例如，官僚机构的质量、基础设施的缺乏、法律的缺失、独立媒介、监管的疏忽、竞争、教育质量、技术工人等。这就是为什么金砖国家未能创建出谷歌、苹果、Facebook 之类的网站。金砖国家的经济基本上是由国家支配的，会对市场和环境造成不良后果。据世界银行估计，中国经济增长放缓，部分是由该国对环境的严重破坏造成的。

四、金砖国家的凝聚力如何？

世界重心可能会逐渐从美国和欧洲向亚洲倾斜，金融危机加剧了这一现象，但新的全球秩序不可能以金砖国家为中心。三个民主国家，一个有专制倾向的民主国家和一个极端专制的民主国家无法围绕这一集团所拥护的"共同价值观"而团结起来。

印度和中国不仅是战略盟友，而且还是战略竞争对手。印度因中国的军事崛起以及新德里民众所谓的北京有意通过战略港口包围印度的野心而惴惴不安。俄罗斯是一个资源出口大国，中国则是一个不知满足的进口大国。这两者可能是互补的。然而，当中国攫取非洲资源时，俄罗斯异常警惕，并小心翼翼地守护着它在中亚的影响力。巴西与其他三个国家间的竞争不太激烈。但是，它也站在世界的对立面。南非太小，尚不足以产生任何影响。

然而，这种冷嘲热讽的态度是不对的。其他集团之间也充满着矛盾和竞争。全球金融危机确实向由富国出于自身利益而主导的世界秩序发出了挑战。金砖国家有权要求在由欧洲国家主导的机构中拥有更大的发言权，如联合国和国际货币基金组织。面对全球对美元的过度依赖，他们考虑替代方案这种做法也是毋庸置疑的。

五、差异

除了规模和经济潜力外，金砖国家是否还存在其他共同点，这一问题有待商榷。这五大经济体的经济结构有很大不同，巴西专门从事农业出口，俄罗斯和南非注重商品贸易，印度专注于服务业，而中国则大力发展制造业。此外，他们对全球经济衰退的体会也有所不同。这是一个极其多元化的集团。其统一标准是高水平的经济增长、一定的经济落后水平和较大的规模。

在经济发展方面，俄罗斯要优于其他金砖国家。2013年，俄罗斯的人均国内生产总值为14612美元，是中国（6807美元）的两倍之多。高盛集团预测，到2050年，俄罗斯将成为唯一一个收入水平接近欧洲人均收入水平的金砖国家。在优越社会指标排行榜中，俄罗斯的高收入水平也是显而易见的。就大多数方面而言，俄罗斯较巴西更为发达，但与中国和印度齐平。最引人注目的是，俄罗斯达到大学年龄段的人口中三分之二的人都进了大学，而中国则不到五分之一。在教育方面，俄罗斯可以与西方国家匹敌。金砖国家的消费差异也很大。2013 年，俄罗斯人均汽车拥有量是中国的 7 倍（俄罗斯每 1000 人中拥有 233 辆，中国每 1000 人中拥有 34 辆）。

在乌克兰危机爆发之前，我们可以说，俄罗斯在许多方面已经达到西方国家的发展水平。在对联合国和气候变化的支持等问题上，俄罗斯的立场大多时候与欧盟而不是金砖国家保持一致。此外，该国大约一半的储备基金为欧元。

金砖国家也不会拥护和宣传单一的经济管理模式。事实上，巴西提倡的金融政策惯例支持的社会民主市场经济与俄罗斯日益专制的政治干预之间也存在越来越大的差异。在世贸组织多哈回合全球贸易谈判中，印度和巴西成为核心谈判小组中的成员，他们致力于维护全面的谈判立场。作为一个占据竞争优势地位的农产品出口国，巴西的利益与印度保护其小农户的愿望发生了冲突。

然而，除了要在国际货币基金组织中赋予发展中国家更多投票权这一长期争论不休的话题外，确实很难为无共同点的金砖国家确定一个具有共同利益的实质性话题。他们已经被迫放弃了汇率这一话题。印度和中国的工业差异以及邻国之间的文化差异几乎不可能进一步扩大了。中国一心一意专注于生产力和经济增长，在这方面，印度可能永远无法与之匹敌，而它的邻国也不太可能掌握印度的民主、民事和法律文化。

然而，金砖国家一直在隐瞒的集团内部的紧张关系，很可能会阻碍它们达成实质性的约定。这五个国家之间的贸易纠纷已经屡见不鲜。巴西与俄罗斯和中国之间长期存在市场准入的纠纷，而且其在多哈回合贸易谈判中提出的寻求全面开放的农产品贸易的战略有违印度保护本国稻农的立场。印度和中国觊觎俄罗斯的自然资源，特别是石油和天然气。作为莫斯科的老朋友，新德里在获取俄罗斯的能源储备方面也会受到限制，但中国具有更大的购买力。

政治不仅会让金砖国家团结起来，还会造成内部分裂。印度、中国和俄罗斯都在同一地区，而且都是核能大国，而巴西和南非既不是核能大国而且还位于其他大陆，这两个国家几乎与俄罗斯无任何贸易往来，与印度的贸易往来也很少。此外，中国和印度仍对两国之间的高度军事化的边境区域争论不休，双方已就这片领土展开了不少斗争。20 世纪 60 年代末，中国和俄罗斯经历了几场边境战争，几十年来两国相处一直不太融洽。

中国的学者、政策制定者以及广大市民都认为中国已经远远超过了这个国家集团的其他成员。高盛集团认为，在 2030 年前，中国很可能会发展成为世界上最大的经济体。到2032年，金砖国家经济体很可能会超越在全球经济管理中占据主导地位的七国集团。金砖国家的全球贸易份额已经超过了美国。2008年，中国已经发展成为世界上最大的商品出口国，再加上印度的软件和后台服务出口，俄罗斯的石油和天然气，以及由巴西拥有超级竞争力的农民支配的农产品市场。

那么，随着世界走出衰退，全球经济重心及其支配中心发生决定性转移的时刻到来了吗？这是像"二战"一样的紧要关头吗？在"二战"时期，充满自信、锐意革新的美国，把疲惫不堪、负债累累的欧洲经济体挤到了一边，重塑了全球金融架构。最迫在眉睫的是，目前金砖国家的消费者能够挑起替代贪得无厌的美国消费者、推动全球经济重归平衡的重担吗？

最有可能的答案是：为时尚早。金砖国家是由迥然不同的国家组成的集团，任何概括性的说法都存在问题。而作为占据压倒性主导地位的一员，中国似乎尚未摆脱依赖其他地区需求的经济模式。金砖国家的成员国更可能是因不同之处而非相同之处而选出来的。中国发展规模大，贸易更为开放，因此其经济影响力要比所有其他国家综合起来更强。印度虽然与中国的人口相当，但比中国贫穷且经济较为封闭，能引起投资者和贸易伙伴注意的是它的软件和商业服务。巴西除了拥有众多的制造商外，还是世界上最高效的农产品出口国之一；俄罗斯在多元化尝试无果而终后，只专注于石油和天然气销售。南非仍然存在诸多问题，如高失业率、不平等、犯罪、破坏投资和发展。

中国的增长模式倚重投资和出口，整个东亚地区拥有庞大的经常项目盈余，而美国则背负着与之相当的经常项目赤字。尽管中国在危机期间竭力维持经济增长，但有一点仍很不清楚：这个中央王国是否实现了朝着增加消费者需求方向的转变（那将为全球增长提供一个真正的引擎）？在经历了蓬勃发展后，中国在金融危机期间出台了一项重大的经济刺激方案，并放松了银行信贷。但其创造自主增长的能力令人怀疑。中国没有向消费者派发现金，刺激他们消费——这么做也会有助于鼓励进口，而是把大部分刺激资金投入一向受到青睐的固定投资。

虽然一些中国人拥有恣意挥霍的财力，但如果说十年来有什么不同的话，那么中国的消费型经济特征变得更弱，而不是更强了。这十年间总储蓄率有所上升。尽管这很大程度上源于企业储蓄率上升，但家庭储蓄率也同样出现了上升。而且，国民收入更多地流向了企业，而不是流入一线消费者之手。社会安全网的缺乏是中国的家庭储蓄的主要原因之一：教育需要、保障疾病和照顾父母。改变根深蒂固的结构性因素不会很快，也不会通过让人民币升值简单地实现。

至于金砖国家的另外三个成员，它们的趋势增长率低于中国，不太可能在近期内对全球需求产生显著影响。虽然巴西和印度在危机期间维持着良好的增长势头，但前者是个相对成熟的经济体，迅速增长的空间较小，而后者表现相对逊色，公共财政长期存在问题，家庭储蓄率甚至比中国还高。俄罗斯经济在全球经济衰退期间严重萎缩，目前仍要看油价的脸色。此外，南非经济虚弱，正在极力避免陷入经济衰退。

六、欧盟的态度

金砖国家要从美国和西欧手中夺下全球经济的指挥棒，仅仅凭借十年的快速增长是不够的。这一集团（或说其部分成员国）过去十年的发展或许令世界震惊，但它需要提升增长的质量，以及进一步的增长，来巩固这种权力的转移。

欧盟似乎无任何理由来插手金砖国家这一集团的事务，而且这种局面在短时间内是不太可能发生改变的。欧盟目前正在与俄罗斯、中国和印度这三个金砖国家商讨新的约定，与俄罗斯的谈判因乌克兰冲突而暂停。欧盟已与巴西和南非达成了约定。中国存在经济、贸易和政治方面的纠纷。中国是否已履行了其对世界贸易组织的承诺，如知识产权，欧洲投资者是否享有公平的竞争环境，关于这两个问题，还存在很多争议。新投资协议谈判将表明中国的态度。欧盟与印度的谈判在服务市场准入和环境与社会标准等贸易问题上陷入了僵局。

七、结论

金砖国家是一个松散的集团，它们喜欢联合起来向美国和欧洲展示新兴大国的崛起。目前，它们不断地通过召开会议来商讨政治安全和经济问题。然而，它们还存在许多差距和政策上的分歧，这就意味着，在政治、安全和经济问题上，金砖国家发展成为一个统一的机构的可能性微乎其微。值得关注的是，它们在新开发银行和应急储备安排上达成了一致。但这些成果现在还处于早期发展阶段，需要一定的时间才能评估其影响。

金砖国家并未同任何外部机构发展正式关系，鉴于上述差异，即使它们这样做也毫无意义。至于欧盟，它并不认为金砖国家可以参与任何有意义的政策问题。这一局面在短期内不太可能发生变化。同时，欧盟应该重视金砖国家，并应深化与金砖国家各成员的关系。当金砖国家的发展有损欧盟利益时，欧盟应确保每个金砖国家成员国都能将其视为一个重要的战略合作伙伴，这才是做出应对的最佳途径。

金砖国家现代化过程中的危机管理与风险预防
——以对印度的观察为例

[德] 克劳斯·沃尔*

我将在很大程度上对"印度案例研究"进行重点阐述,但也会提及印中双边关系。

我认为,清晰地理解金砖国家各自的权力体系和内在动态至关重要。希望在这次大会上能借助各国现有的知识在一定程度上完成这个任务并能为五个国家不同的形态制定一套理论方法。

这次大会的主办方谈到"现代化进程",但没有更详细地说明这个词究竟意味着什么。就我个人而言,我对玻利维亚政治学家菲利普·曼西利亚(H. C. Felipe Mansilla)提出的"现代化批判理论"的前提更感兴趣。一个国家的多个进化阶段只有通过历史和重建的方式才能充分地展现出来,而后才能对发展进程的不同情境进行评定。

对于经常不协调的现代化进程,要在 20 分钟内完成风险预防和危机管理分析自然是不可能的。谁是真正的参与者,谁按照相应的目标指挥这些进程?是不是只有国家在起作用?抑或个人经济参与者或民间社会团体也发挥了根本作用?

一、印度联邦多形态社会的相关数据

2014 年印度人口约 12.7 亿,而中国目前的人口为 13.7 亿。2028 年,印度人口将达到 14.5 亿,超过中国成为世界上人口最多的国家。预计到 2050 年,印度人口将达 16 亿,中国人口将达 13 亿。自 1947 年独立以来,印度人口在一百年内将增长 5 倍,同时给生态平衡带来巨大影响。

但是,在印度不可能从政治层面来控制人口。因此,考虑到大量的失

---

* 克劳斯·沃尔(Klaus Voll),布鲁塞尔欧洲进步研究基金会亚洲问题顾问。

业青年，人口优势可能会变成"人口诅咒"。

每年约有1200万人进入已存在大批失业人群的印度劳动市场。在失业人口普遍不断增长的条件下如何满足就业需求？

印度联邦内的分裂主义者和主张自治的派别分布在查谟和克什米尔邦以及印度东北部地区。他们采用武力和恐怖主义手段达到目的。

在印度国内众多地方，武装组织在印度共产党（毛泽东主义者）的领导下开展行动。

二、社会趋势

印度种姓制度的影响力日渐衰微（"沉默革命"），然而，我们可能观察到只占全国总人口17%—18%的传统上层种姓占据着主导地位。这些传统的种姓等级甚至可追溯至宗教少数派。

作为大规模国家建设进程的一部分，必须逐渐破除内在的"等级制度"，尤其是那些迫害"达利特"（受压迫阶级或所谓的"贱民"，约有1.6亿人）与"阿迪凡西斯"（原住民或所谓的"部落居民"，约有1亿人）的制度。同时，受压迫阶层与弱势群体的文化解放是迫切需要完成的任务。

仅管中国基尼系数比印度高，但在两国，除了中产阶级不断扩大之外，十亿美元级收入的人群和财富集中现象也在不断增长。

如果大多数人没有或只有很少的进入劳动市场的途径，和/或生活在所谓的贫困线以下，包容性与社会公平就难以实现。必须缩小不断扩大的收入差距；必须充分满足人民，尤其是年轻一代对印度新政府的承诺寄予的厚望；如若不然，人民期望的落空将会导致社会冲突增多。

印度社会迫切需要更多的生产性投资，如医疗和教育领域。

三、增强民主结构

除去1975—1977年的短暂时期，印度的民主发展从未间断。然而，2011—2012年发生的大量反腐败运动表明印度的民主存在显著不足。

体制性腐败、全国性的家族政治、权钱集中化和犯罪倾向等各种现象都在破坏印度民主的质量。印度各政党都缺乏真正的内部民主。这有可能增加对真正改革的压力，引发对真正改革的思考。

在地区或地方上，我们会发现反对派精英的兴起与存在。2011—2012年反腐败运动对当前政治阶层的存在提出了质疑。

数年间，我们会发现选民一方面通过投票罢免政府，另一方面通过重选来证明那些实现"良好治理"的人。要确保不仅仅是15%的发展基金投入目标群体,就像过去那样,而最好是全额投入("直接现金转移"),这一点非常重要。

社会主义党已经消失,而共产党正处于衰退晚期。然而,开明左派和社会民主活动在印度仍有活动空间。

多元主义偏好与"多数主义"倾向将成为多种民族和宗教团体实现社会融合的重要基础。

某种程度上,印度在政治上与中国形成了鲜明对比。但是,民主层面合法的后殖民执政阶层(Hartmut Elsenhans)是否能实现真正的革新,还有待观察。

四、经济重点

印度的国内生产总值仅为中国的五分之一。然而,印度经济的很大一部分是由所谓的"黑色经济"塑造的。

印度拥有巨大的国内市场。自1991年向世界经济开放以来,进入印度的国际资本越来越多。新政府试图通过高喊"印度制造"口号来吸引外商在多个经济领域(基础设施、保险、国防产品等)直接投资,并尤其希望壮大制造业。

在很大程度上,未使用的人力资源潜能巨大,一个相当重要的原因就是职业培训不足。为改善基础设施和能源产业,人力资源必须得到积极使用("双系统")。"清洁印度"(Swachh Bharat)运动旨在显著改变印度的卫生条件。

印度的现代化进程中需要一种策略,帮助印度从深陷困境的农业经济("农民自杀")过渡到工业经济。

五、印度与中国的差异

印度位于一个极其复杂的地区,南亚和西亚的几大风险中心都集中在这一地区。由此导致印度的军费开支居高不下,因为至少从理论上看,印度与中国和巴基斯坦的边疆战争的可能性不会排除。目前,印度是世界上最大的武器进口国。为了慢慢消耗印度,巴基斯坦对恐怖袭击实施"千刀万剐"策略。

印中之间大规模的双边贸易中,印度存在巨大的贸易逆差,从长期来看,这是印度无法承受的。

印度声称几十年后有可能超过中国成为世界上最大的经济体,或许这直到今天听起来还像乌托邦式的梦想。

六、展望

如果允许印度加入上海合作组织（SCO），这一决定必定很受欢迎。在距印中边界战争62年之后的今天，这些步骤和建立深度自信的措施以及民间社会接触的不断增强可能会对印度现有的信任缺失起到缓解作用。两国在阿富汗和中亚问题上进行过协商，同时也针对"布拉马普特拉河"（中文名称：雅鲁藏布江）的水位交流过相关数据。

中国开辟丝绸之路和海上丝绸之路就是源于对印度的浓厚兴趣。在接下来的五年中，中国准备向印度投资250亿美元——日本准备投资300亿美元，美国声称准备投资400亿美元——能加深印中两国之间进一步的交流。

印度和中国怎样才能以一种建设性的非对抗方式改善二者之间的关系呢？这样的提问应该成为金砖国家众多精英阶层建设性对话的一部分。印度前总理曼莫汉·辛格（Manmohan Singh）博士宣称，中国和印度在面临预防剧烈气候变化、核武器升级和恐怖主义的国际舞台上拥有同时和平崛起的充足空间。

金砖国家能否从西方国家的发展中汲取教训并奠定积极的社会政治和生态基调，为各自的社会创建另一种可持续发展模式呢？以各国社会愿景为基础的协调改革是一项根本要求。

因此，面对未来，无论国内还是国际，风险预防和危机管理都是金砖国家必须要做的工作。

种族隔离结束后南非的治理

[德] 阿诺德·威姆霍纳尔*

一、引言

此文献给金砖国家的治理现代化建设。文中记述了种族隔离制度结束后，南非在治理改进方面的成就和局限。鉴于金砖国家间互不干涉内政的原则，本文仅对南非在有关方面的进展进行描述，无意为其他国家树立榜样。然而，就治理问题交换彼此的看法也许能帮助其他国家更好地对他们自己的发展进行分析。在文章的第二部分，作者试图分析为什么在现有的政治体制内，这里指议会民主体制，治理方面错误的发展是能够得到纠正的。南非是怎样通过技术手段，如通过培训和控制，推进治理的现代化和进步的，在另一篇文章已进行论述。[1]

二、开端：种族隔离结束后的南非

南非共和国的宪法是世界上最现代、最自由的宪法之一。种族隔离结束后，这个国家经历了五次全国和地方选举，这些选举即使用最高的标准来衡量都是自由和公平的。司法机构依法独立裁决，媒体自由而且尖刻。该国的保民官办公处是一个独立的监督部门，其勇敢地对腐败进行揭露，直至最高领导人——总统。

南非执政的非洲人国民大会（非国大）的治理精英主要由曾经冒着生命危险为使自己的国家从种族隔离的桎梏下解放出来而战的党的干部组成，他们有着高度的道德节操。他们中的大多数人都是在流亡期间接受了高等教育，形成了世界主义的世界观。在纳尔逊·曼德拉的领导和指引下，他们找到了一条通向和平和解和非种族歧视的社会的道路。

鉴于其政治制度和其精英们的背景，南非有实现成功治理的理想的前

---

* 阿诺德·威姆霍纳尔（Arnold Wehmhoerner），欧洲进步基金会南非研究员。

提条件。该国需要成功的治理,是因为后种族隔离时代的政府面临着一项艰巨的任务,即帮助过去备受歧视的黑人人口中的大多数脱离贫困。对住房、教育和就业的需求十分巨大。显然这些困难需要超过一代人的努力才能解决。精英们面临的困境是要么保留大部分曾经的白人种族分离主义者继续进行管理,要么用一批新的缺乏经验的黑人同志换掉他们。对于新的黑人管理者和政治家的需求远远超过了人才的供应能力,因为除了国家政府以外,新成立的九个省级政府也需要有才干的男女工作人员参与管理。

三、成就与局限

政治上,非国大政府感到不得不对行政部门的种族构成进行改变,即使知道会带来相应的弊端。一个至少需要一个完整高等教育和培训周期才能完成的转变在短时期内就得到了推行。2013年11月,南非审计部长在一个新闻发布会上出示了2011—2012年的综合审计报告。报告显示只有5%的地方政府在审计中没有发现问题。尽管与以前的报告对比,出现了一些积极的迹象,但公共部门的违规支出仍然增加了33%。[2]南非合作治理部部长2014年10月说,令人遗憾的是在该国全部278位市政府财务总监中,有170位不合格。他补充说,有三分之一的市级政府不能正常运转。[3]非国大上台至今已有25年,上面援引的数字表明改革尚未完成,财务管理方面显然还须继续改进,这是有效治理的关键,是防止腐败的前提条件。

对于新政府在改善大部分黑人人口生活条件方面的表现,反对党和政府的评价截然相反。从全国几乎每天发生的、常常是带有暴力的对服务提供方面的抗议来看,政府所做的努力似乎不太成功。据估计,南非每年发生大约300次社区抗议事件。[4]过去10年中至少有43名抗议民众被警察杀害。[5]

表1提供了有关成就和失误的指标数据。可以发现,南非在大部分门类上都取得了进步,尤其在成人识字率、入学率和是否能获得清洁水源方面。社会福利支持目前已覆盖1500万人,这使南非每天生活费不足2美元的人口从2000年的18%下降到2011年的2.7%。令人忧虑的是出生时的预期寿命。艾滋感染者人数的增加在意料之中,因为新政府上台时疫情正好达到顶峰。持续高企的失业率反映出制造部门的萎缩,而不断走高的基尼系数显示该国经济增长的红利没有得到公平的分配。人类发展指数(HDI)排名的下降表明,与其他国家相比,南非的表现并不是非常好。

表 1　南非 1990—2012 年主要社会—经济表现指标[6]

	1990	1994	2000	2006	2009	2010	2011	2012	
出生时的预期寿命（岁）①	62	61	55	51	52				恶化 15.4%
（每千人）五岁前死亡率①	62.3‰	60.9‰	74.1‰	75.8‰	61.3‰		46.7‰		改善 25%
成人识字率①	76.2%		84.8%			89.3%			改善 13.1%
中学入学率（占总适龄人数百分比）	66.1%	79.7%	85.3%	95.0%	93.8%				改善 27.7%
是否能获得干净的水源*①	83%	83%	86%	90%	91%	91%			改善 8%
是否有改善了的厕卫设施**①	71%	72%	75%	77%	79%	79%			改善 8%
艾滋感染率①	0.5%	0.8%	14.8%	17.3%	17.2%	17.3%	17.3%		恶化 16.8%
人类发展指数排名（新兴市场国家）			107				123		下降 16 个名次
日均生活费不足 2 美元的人口②			18%	10.5%	6.3%	4.4%	2.7%		改善 15.3%
官方公布的失业率②		20%	26.7%	23.1%	23.6%		25.7%	24.9%	恶化 4.9%
基尼系数①			57.77%	67.4%	63.14%				恶化 6.6%

资料来源：①世界银行集团；②南非种族关系研究所。
* 包括自来水和抽水机抽来的水；
** 包括有遮掩的坑厕和抽水马桶。

南非种族关系研究所的弗兰斯·科隆尼（Frans Cronje）相信："我们所看到的成就与全国到处发生的抗议事件之间并不矛盾。这些抗议并不是服务方面的失误导致的，而是因为已经取得的成功提高了人们的期望值，这些期望值因为学校系统和就业市场方面的不足而难以满足。"[7]

所有南非人的物质条件已经得到改善，但针对服务提供问题的抗议将会持续，因为还有太多的人仍然生活在贫困之中，同时富人和穷人之间的鸿沟在全国各地都很明显。这些抗议活动的中心位于一些城镇和一些非正式定居地，并且还有更多的农村居民在持续不断地涌向这些地方。今年（2014），城镇居民人口比例已从1990年的52%上升至65%以上。[8]一个由黑人构成的中产阶层已经形成。但这个新产生的阶层严重依赖公共部门，而公共部门在1998年至2011年期间扩大了20%。[9]公共部门的增长又伴随着薪水的上涨。政府预算又因为需要向三分之一的南非人支付社会福利而备感压力。鉴于南非的经济增长率今年只有2%左右，这种政策显然难以维系。

四、腐败加剧

南非堕入腐败始于法国、英国和德国一些公司向南非新政府行贿，诱使该国与其达成协议，购买了尖端军用飞机、潜艇和护卫舰这些南非不需要的军火。执政党顶层明显的失职和违法不究似乎触发了政府各层面的腐败。尤其难以追责的是所谓的"官商勾结的招标商"（tenderpreneurs），即政要通过一个外人或家庭成员参与公司对政府合同的招标。在《黑人经济振兴法案》计划下，黑人拥有的公司在投标过程中享受优惠待遇。要求那些经选举上台的政客们①公布他们的商业联系的法定义务似乎起不到什么作用。南非在透明国际全球清廉指数的排名三年内骤降了18位。2010年，该国在178个国家里排名第54位，到了2013年，其在177个国家里排名第72位。②

南非总工会的秘书长瓦为（ZwelinzimaVavi）曾在多个场合公开批评政府打击腐败的决心不足。瓦为在2011年南非总工会中央委员会议的一份报告中表示，祖玛在2007年的非国大保罗瓜尼大会上当选党魁，随后我们便目睹了"一个势力庞大、贪污腐败且掠夺成性的领导人的崛起，而且他的施政纲领还是民粹主义"[10]尽管这一声明并没有得到所有成员公会的认可，但也强烈地显示了该问题的严重性。

五、内部整改管理

如果依宪法建立的机构如全国检察署或保民官办公处没有能力或被阻

---

① 议会成员道德准则与行为准则要求对金融或商业利益冲突做出声明。
② Http://www.transparency.org。

止对腐败进行有效的打击,那么人们就必须在议会民主制这个背景下看待政治层面的问题。不是选民们通过选举打败腐败政府,就是执政党自己从内部进行必要的改变。

今年(2014)5月的选举中非国大又丢失了一些选票,但与以前的选举一样丢的不算多。从2004年至2009年,该党丢掉了3.8%的选票,而在2009年至2014年期间,其又丢失了3.7%的选票。围绕该党的丑闻以及媒体连篇累牍的后续报道没有阻止非国大的支持者。因其解放了南非的黑人,人们与它的情感联系仍然强烈。在许多乡镇投票站,非国大获得了超过75%的支持率,甚至在今年发生过反非国大暴力抗议的拜克斯戴尔小镇,该党也获得了80%的支持率。一个评论员写道:"南非的乡镇宁愿放弃自己的公民权益支持非国大也不愿支持另一个党派,难以相信他们是用这种方式起诉腐败的。"[11] 在这种情况下,显然,现在的执政党不会害怕因为腐败或不起诉腐败官员而受到选民的惩罚。

非国大本身似乎没有能力对自己进行整改。在种族隔离时代,要加入当时被禁的非国大是冒着个人的风险的。这一点成了仅吸收有才干的、信仰坚定的党员的最佳天然过滤器。自2007年波罗瓦尼科大会以来,党员人数从62万多一点猛增到了120万。今天,许多人加入该党只是为了能在政府部门谋得一份工作。因把许多缺乏经验的干部推到高官位置导致了道德水准的下降——另外也由于平权运动,故而一些人重视经营利益关系网,而不是发挥自己在行政管理方面的能力。这种利益为上的策略已经改变了国大党的灵魂,侵蚀了该党的核心价值观。

在传统的社会——特别是在失业率较高的社会,个人以及他的家人的福祉依赖于一个更大家庭的支持,也就是他的宗族或部落。在这样的家长式社会里,支持家庭、宗族或部落的义务比遵守法律制度更重要。裙带关系在这种社会义务沉重的环境里常常不被认为是犯罪。在南非,传统的家长式行为模式在公共领域似乎正在加剧。

六、结论

南非政府在1994年首次不分种族的大选以后,面临着非常艰巨的任务。新的行政机构缺乏经验,但必须使大多数过去备受歧视的黑人人口的生活条件得到改善。不出所料,这导致了政府政策执行中的不足和控制的缺失,为腐败打开了机会之门。传统的家长式行为模式和对检察机关和监督机构的政治干预日益严重,使反腐败斗争变得愈加困难。如果这种情况持续下去,则唯有通过选举进行矫正。然而政治精英们目前并不担心会在选举中落败，因为选民们与他们的解放党——非国大依然有强烈的情感联系。

参考文献

［1］丹尼尔·普拉提杰斯：《促进南非治理现代化的相应和创新能力》，见本书，第193页。

［2］"Mail and Guardian", online, November 13, 2013.

［3］Siyabonga Mkhwanazi, " Fire Unqualified Municipal Finance Officers: Gordhan", *Daily News*, October, 7, 2014.

［4］Ebrahim Fakir, "Protests Are a Cry for Political Recognition", *Mail & Guardian*, mg. co. za, August, 29, 2014.

［5］Max du Preez, "Service delivery's ANC's Achilles Heel", *Pretoria News*, October 14, 2014.

［6］Richard Callend, "The Zuma Years", *Cape Town*, 2013, p. 14.

［7］South African Institute of Race Relations, *Press Release*, September 11, 2012.

［8］Max du Preez, "Service delivery's ANC's Achilles heel", *Pretoria News*, October 14, 2014.

［9］Richard Callend, "The Zuma Years", *Cape Town*, 2013, p. 416.

［10］COSATU Secretary-general, "Secretariat Report to the 5th COSATU Central Committee 2011", p. 10, in Richard Calland, *The Zuma Years*, Cape Town, 2013, p. 211.

［11］Vukani Mde, "Election Winners and Losers", *Sunday Independent*, November 5, 2014.

关于金砖国家对全球治理所做贡献的评估：
一个局外人的看法

[法] 爱丽丝·埃克曼*　　[法] 弗朗索瓦兹·尼古拉**

一、引言

  在过去十年左右的时间里，经济实力的变化非常迅速，美国等曾经处于主导地位的国家，现在正与几个新兴的（或重新复兴的）经济体进行竞争，而这些新兴经济体碰巧主要分布在亚洲（如中国和印度）。正如美国国家情报委员会一针见血地指出的那样，"从规模、速度、流动方向上看，现在的财富和经济权力大致是沿着从西向东的路径，在现代历史上是没有先例的。"（National Intelligence Council，2008）虽然经济实力的转移已经进行一段时间了，但2008年的全球金融危机（GFC）可以说是一个分水岭，因为此时，在那些曾经处于主导地位的国家，特别是美国，一些结构性弊端显现了出来，这进一步提升了新兴国家的势力和影响力。

  上面提到的经济实力分布的转移，一直伴随着新兴国家内部不断增长的、对于现有的"二战"结束后那段时期遗留下来的治理结构的不满情绪，他们认为这种治理结构不能代表新的经济实力对比现状。在这方面，2008年的全球金融危机又是一个关键的时刻，因为其清楚地暴露了国际金融治理机制的效率低下，进一步凸显了"二战"后形成的经济和政治治理框架的不足之处。这种不断高涨的不满情绪为呼吁更有力的改革铺平了道路。

  这些"正在崛起的国家"当中，有几个国家尤为突出，即金砖四国（巴西、俄罗斯、印度和中国）。这个称呼是高盛公司经济学家吉

---

 * 爱丽丝·埃克曼（Alice Ekman），法国国际关系学院研究员。
 ** 弗朗索瓦兹·尼古拉（Françoise Nicolas），法国国际关系学院亚洲研究中心主任。

姆·奥尼尔在2001年首创的。这四个国家有望在世界经济中成为重量级选手。

一开始,"金砖四国"仅仅被认为是一个朗朗上口的缩略词,并没有什么实质内容,也没有能够改变世界现有秩序的潜在能力。然而大约十年后,这个由外部观察者创造的缩略词确实具备了更多的实质性内容。金砖王国(现在又包括了南非)已经成为一个有相对完善结构的集团,在一些重要事务上有清晰的目标和议程。2008年的全球金融危机对于金砖国家来说也是一个分水岭,这个危机引发了对西方列强在全球治理中的领导地位的质疑。全球金融危机爆发后,金砖国家显然已经从一个经济存在变成了一个政治性国家群体。因此,金砖国家可能能推动全球治理基础结构的改革,而博桑-亨特(Beausang – Hunter, 2012)这样的研究人员几年前得出的金砖国家没有能力治理世界的结论可能是错误的。

本文旨在从一个局外人的角度对金砖国家在全球治理结构中潜在的作用做一个最新的分析。为此,本文将结合经济学家和政治学家的研究方法,以尽可能多地覆盖全球治理机制中的各个方面。本文要研究的一个重要问题是金砖国家是将挑战现有的治理结构,还是准备融入现有的治理结构中去。

本文的结构如下:第二部分提供一些关于金砖国家崛起的统计方面的背景资料;第三部分探讨金砖国家是如何在过去的几年中成功地影响了全球经济和政治治理结构,并对它们潜在的动机和目标进行评估;第四部分重点介绍它们在努力过程中将会面临的挑战。

二、金砖国家对全球治理的重要性

金砖国家之所以重要是因为它们是巨大而且(直到最近还)增长迅速的经济体。它们很重要还因为它们正逐渐尝试利用自己新近获得的经济影响力在全球治理机制中发挥更加积极的作用。

金砖国家的经济崛起已经是一个不争的事实。如表1所示,它们的经济权重以引人注目(和前所未有)的速度上升,而且这种趋势很可能将持续下去:根据国际货币基金组织最近的估计,截至2015年,世界经济增长中的61%将由金砖国家贡献。

其他指标,如外汇储备的分布也表明经济实力的新天平一直在向金砖国家倾斜,至少在向金砖国家中最大的国家,也就是中国倾斜,因为中国拥有庞大的外汇储备和国内储蓄。

表1 金砖国家2000年与2012年数据比较

	购买力平价GDP(10亿美元)	占世界GDP百分比	GDP(当期,10亿美元)	占世界GDP百分比	人口(百万)	占世界人口百分比	人均GDP(当期,美元)	占世界出口总量百分比
巴西	1379	3.2	645	2.0	174	2.9	3694	0.9
	2039	2.4	2252	3.1	199	2.8	11 339	1.3*
俄罗斯	1260	2.9	260	0.8	146	2.4	1775	1.6
	2178	2.5	2015	2.8	143	2.0	14 037	2.9*
印度	1818	4.2	477	1.4	1042	17.1	457	0.7
	4131	4.8	1842	2.5	1237	17.6	1489	1.7*
中国	3368	7.8	1198	3.6	1263	20.7	949	3.9
	10 748	15.5	8227	11.4	1351	19.2	6091	12.1*
南非	764	0.7	133	0,4	44	0.7	3019	0.5
	986	0.7	384	0,5	51	0.7	7507	0.7*
五国总计	8589	18.8	2713	8.2	2669	43.8		7.6
	20 082	25.9	14 720	20.3	2981	42.3		18.7*

资料来源:世界银行,世界发展指标。(每格中第一个值对应2000年,第二个值对应2012年)

*2013年数据。

关于后面这一点,问题在于,总体情况隐藏了一些截然不同的现实。举例来说,中国的外汇储备(近4万亿美元)比印度、俄罗斯和巴西的总和还大。总的来说,金砖国家间存在着实际上的不平等,金砖国家的崛起实际上主要是中国的崛起。中国在所有金砖国家里一枝独秀,而且这种优势无论是在人口方面还是在经济规模方面都将持续,尽管中国经济出现了相对的下滑。①

很自然,这些新的发展使联合国有关组织反映出来的"二战"后的权力分配越来越显得不足。比如,就像奥尼尔和特尔兹(O'Neill and Terzi, 2014)所阐述的那样:"如果全球货币体系根本上来说应该是全球贸易的反映,那么人民币的作用应该得到提升。"

但是金砖国家日益增长的重要性并不仅仅体现在经济领域。来自金砖

---

① 这一点将在第四部分进一步论述。

五国的联合国维和人员的数量是来自西方七国的五倍。这证明金砖国家对世界的和平、稳定、繁荣、发展和全球治理也发挥着很大的促进作用。

面对这些变化,工业化国家倾向采取一种矛盾的态度,一方面呼吁金砖国家"承担更多的责任",另一方面指责金砖国家破坏了现有的全球治理机制。

非常有趣的是,金砖国家已经意识到它们各自经济和政治份量的增加,需要它们联合起来,以提高它们作为一个集体的影响力。金砖国家是几个被认为可能会改变游戏规则的国家,但从2006年开始定期举办会议以来,它们也正日益成为一个现实的政治存在。后来他们决定每年召开峰会:首届峰会于2009年在叶卡捷琳堡召开,第二届在里约召开(2010年),第三届在三亚召开(2011年),第四届在新德里召开(2012),第五届在德班召开(2013),第六届在福塔莱萨召开(2014年)。随着时间的推移,"金砖国家"已经成为一个经济上的、同时在某种程度上也是一个政治上的现实存在。

三、金砖国家和全球治理结构:经济和政治方面的对比

因为它们影响力的提升,也因为它们勇于表达和捍卫自己未必与传统列强一致的利益,金砖国家无疑已经能够对全球治理结构施加影响。本节将探讨一些具体的案例,并尝试识别金砖国家的动力所在。

1. 金砖国家与全球经济治理:一个多管齐下的方法

在经济领域(金融和贸易),金砖国家针对全球治理的方法显然结合了维持现状的、渐进式的改良主义和更加激进的改革主义。本节就这种多层面的方法提供了证据。

在金融问题上,金砖国家采取的是两步走的方法。在很长的一段时间里,金砖国家大力倡导对全球治理结构逐步进行改革,尤其是推动国际货币基金组织配额制度的改革("重新分配份额和投票权"),以更好地反映金砖国家日益增长的影响力以及传统/工业化大国不断下降的影响力。

在金砖国家坚持不懈的压力之下,国际货币基金组织于2010年11月同意进行广泛的治理改革,以反映新兴市场国家与日俱增的重要性。尤其是通过了对配额制度的改革,这个制度能决定成员国的投票权。改革后,金砖国家的相对份额从总份额的10%提高到了14.8%。

这些最早的压力清楚地反映了改良主义者的方法,因为金砖国家当时寻求的是从内部改变全球治理结构,但并没有质疑这个机构的合法性。

然而随着时间的推移，因为工业化国家不愿意接受改良主义，出现了转向采取更加激进的改革主义方法的趋势。尽管 2010 年国际货币基金组织就正式通过了配额改革，却因未能获得美国国会的批准，一直未能实施。尽管代表着国际货币基金组织近 80% 票数的国家支持改革，但提案获通过所需越过的门槛是 85%①，而且美国因持有其 16.75% 的股份，因此拥有事实上的否决权。只要美国仍不愿意批准这项改革，修正案就无法通过。

鉴于其经济实力，金砖国家（特别是拥有庞大外汇储备的中国）现在有能力提出有关的备选机制。在福塔莱萨金砖国家峰会上（2014 年 7 月），金砖国家提议创建一个新的应急储备安排（CRA），涉及资金 1 千亿美元，目的是帮助金砖国家缓解与世界其他地区间的金融不平衡。这种机制显然是对国际货币基金组织的一种补充，甚至可能是一种取代方式。

同样，金砖国家也宣布建立了一个新的金砖国家开发银行［新开发银行（NDB）初始资金 1 千亿美元］，总部设在上海。新开发银行旨在为发展中国家的基础设施和发展项目提供资金，重点放在可持续发展上，强调创造更多的就业机会，减少贫困。这个举措是激进改革主义方法的又一个例证，因为这个新开发银行显然是总部位于华盛顿的世界银行的一个替代选择。

相比之下，在其他经济领域，金砖国家的作用不那么明显，但显然更倾向于维持现状。人们不应对这种不同的立场感到惊讶，因为举例来说，全球治理结构的逻辑在贸易领域与在金融领域观察到的是完全不同的。正如在关贸总协定下，世界贸易组织依据的是"一国一票"的原则。其结果是新兴国家并不觉得有对体制进行改革以发挥更大作用的迫切需求。

总的来说，金砖国家支持现有的贸易治理机制，尽管它们在制定规则的游戏中所起的推动作用有所不同。所有金砖国家都是世界贸易组织②成员国，因此都要求遵守公认的国际规则。然而，尽管在 2009 年首次峰会期间，各国都一致呼吁立即完成多哈回合贸易谈判，但他们最终走向了不同的方向，而印度常常被指阻挠有关的谈判。

在其他与贸易有关的领域里，金砖国家并不采取相似的立场。在印度因数次导致多哈发展回合谈判的破裂而广受指责的同时，中国却对贸易问题的多边治理显得特别支持。证明中国这种立场的一个有趣的例子是北京近期决定要求将其纳入服务贸易协定（TISA）的谈判。中国至今尚未加入该谈判的唯一原因是美国对此的反对。

---

① 份额的调整需要获得五分之三成员的 85% 投票权重支持。
② 中国于 2001 年加入世界贸易组织，俄罗斯于 2011 年加入。

值得强调的是，尽管所有金砖国家都加入了区域性贸易协定，而且可能因此被视为参与削弱世界贸易组织所体现的多边规则的制定机制，但它们在这个方面与其他大国是没有什么不同的。

简言之，在对待全球经济治理机制上，金砖国家的方式混合了从维持现状到激进改革的不同立场。有意思的是，中国可能被认为是风向的引领者。确实如此，中国是现有机制下最大的受益者，而金砖国家在与中国有关的领域倾向于采取更加合作的姿态（例如在多边贸易机制方面），而在其他可以显示自己强势的领域，或在有回旋余地的领域（比如在金融问题上），则更倾向于采取激进的改革主义的方法。

2. 金砖国家在全球政治治理议题上互相矛盾的立场

在外交政策和安全领域，金砖各国采取的也同样是维持现状、渐进的改良主义和更加激进的改革主义混合的方式，甚至比在全球经济治理领域还要严重。各国之间的分歧和不和仍然很多，这显然是采取共同举措的巨大障碍。

从严格意义上来说，在安全问题上，要金砖国家采取一致的方法在短期内似乎肯定是不可能的。这是国家层面上安全问题的性质所决定的。这还因为金砖各国在不同的地区所面临的安全问题非常不同：有些国家涉及紧张的海上和陆地领土争端（中国），一个国家在欧洲大陆直接卷入一场冲突（俄罗斯和乌克兰的争端），有关当事国并没有受到任何其他金砖国家直接或正式的支持。实际上，金砖国家之间，甚至任何两个金砖国家间都不存在安全方面的联盟。相反，某些金砖国家正与该集团以外的国家加强安全联系，如印度与美国和日本。即便是在中国和俄罗斯之间，尽管两国关系自 2014 年 5 月签订了 4 千亿美元的天然气供应协议以来似乎在走近，但在多个安全和外交政策领域，这两个国家之间还存在着相当紧张的关系。尤其是随着中国的"新丝绸之路"经济带这个在中亚地区宣布加强自己经济影响力的战略的推进（基础设施的开发、能源领域的投资等），两国可能会加紧争夺在该地区的影响力，而俄罗斯领导人正带着一定程度的猜疑关注事态的发展。①

在多个金砖国家之间，地理上的接近迄今并没有帮助取得一致的安全方略。相反，两个金砖国家如果地理上接近，比如中国和印度，它们之间现有的边境争端成为建立包容性安全共同体的严重障碍。除安全治理以

---

① 在中国领导人首次提出"新丝绸之路"这个概念一年多以后，在两国 2014 年 5 月签署天然气供应协议之后的一个联合声明里，俄罗斯才正式同意提及这个概念。

外，这些争端成为金砖国家建立更牢固的统一共同体的障碍。金砖国家中如果有两个国家发生现有安全争端升级事件，就可能对现有的经济合作产生负面影响，并严重削弱金砖集团的建设。例如，鉴于两国当前的领导层在边界问题的看法上仍然存在分歧，中印边境冲突升级的假设不能完全排除，甚至可能最终成为落实习近平2014年11月访印期间双方达成的重要经济合作项目的障碍（两国在德里签署了12项协议，其中一项宣布中国将在五年内投资200亿美元用于印度的基础设施建设）。

然而，金砖国家可以把它们之间现有的矛盾放到一边，在看起来比较容易解决的国际事务上发挥更重要的作用，特别是在涉及多国层面的问题上，如气候变化、武器扩散、网络安全等。然而，在上述大部分问题上因具体国情不同，同时因为某些涉及金砖国家的协议最初是在金砖国家集团外部形成的（如中美于2014年11月签署了一项有关气候变化的协议，宣布采取单方面措施，在2030年以前减少它们各自温室气体的排放），金砖国家的立场似乎相差甚远。

在更广泛意义上的外交政策和安全治理方面，金砖各国在决策过程中的影响力是不平等的。有些金砖国家，如中国和俄罗斯，是联合国安理会常任理事国。在是否有必要对安理会进行改革的问题上金砖国家间并没有共识。在这个特定问题上中国采取了一种保守的办法，支持现有的成员国结构。① 金砖国家间此类分歧使安理会的改革在短期、中期内都不太可能实现，尽管中国近几个月对其宣传策略进行了略微的调整（中国国家主席习近平在近期对印度的访问期间发表了一个印度期盼多年的声明——中国将支持印度在联合国安理会发挥更大的作用的愿望。②

在全球政治治理问题上，中国的措施也是在维持现状和积极改革间，甚至在是否创建或恢复某些机构的问题上摇摆，尤其是当其评估发现某项积极的改革在短期或中期不太可能带来对自己有利的明显变化的时候。例如，中国在创立或恢复新的安全/外交政策机构框架如亚洲相互协作与信任措施会议（CICA）方面正变得越来越主动。亚信会议有二十多个国家参加，包括金砖国家中的俄罗斯和印度。尽管这个机构仅仅关注本地区问题，而且因为本地区的主要大国（如美国和日本）并不是这个机构的成员，其应对突发冲突的能力还有限，但它强调中国在本地区及更广泛的范围内，在机构层面上的积极主动、有所作为。

---

① 中国和俄罗斯多年以来都不愿意增设联合国安理会常任理事国的席位。因为它们担心这可能会削弱它们拥有的否决权的独特性（Armijo, Leslie Elliott and Cynthia Roberts, 2014）。

② 中国是否会支持还有待确认。

四、主要挑战：中国在金砖国家问题上既务实又灵活的策略

中国在全球治理方面采取的是非常多样而灵活的策略。这使其他金砖国家很难在立场上跟得上中国的脚步。鉴于中国在金砖集团内，在经济和政治影响力上相对强大，中国可以成为整个集团的潮流引领者，带领金砖各国在一整套外交政策和安全议题上逐渐形成统一的立场。但实际上，形成统一的立场是很难的，因为金砖各国都倾向于把金砖集团这个组织当作达到本国外交政策目标的一个工具，而它们各自的外交政策目标又是大相径庭的。例如，中国目前侧重经济外交，尤其是基础设施的发展，这当然是其支持新成立的金砖国家开发银行以及金砖集团以外近期成立的其他金融机构，如亚洲基础设施投资银行（AIIB）的潜在的主要原因。中国于2013年提出倡议，2014年在其他亚洲国家的支持下成功创立了。总体而言，中国在金砖国家框架内所做的一切都是源于该国的国家外交政策目标和指导方针，而这种做法并不仅仅针对金砖国家。

近期，中国针对金砖国家的务实策略与俄罗斯对金砖国家的策略形成了鲜明的对照。在当前乌克兰危机的情况下，俄罗斯倾向于强调将金砖国家建设成更加野心勃勃的政治集团，与"西方"持有不同的立场。然而中国仍然主要把金砖国家看成是一个经济集团和促进其经济外交的工具，在反西方言论的使用上显得更加节制一些。

在意识形态层面，金砖国家奉行的当然不是同样的策略。它们中的大多数强调普世价值的存在，而中华人民共和国认为不同的文化决定不同的政治制度。这些国内政治环境的差异并没有妨碍金砖国家间加强经济合作，在前面提到的一些问题上采取共同的立场。但这些差异使某些非金砖国家有机会时不时用来离间金砖国家，至少会在言辞上进行离间。比如，日本已经在理论上把印度包括在其声称要建立的"亚太民主国家团结之弧"之中。

简单地说，在全球外交政策和安全治理问题上，金砖国家要较难推出共同举措。因为金砖国家面临着非常不同的自然和地区性安全挑战，它们在某些问题上针锋相对（如中国和印度之间的边境冲突、对乌克兰危机的不同立场等），而且与美国的关系也不尽相同。金砖国家间在外交政策导向及方法论上的差异是它们成为一个政治集团的重要障碍。鉴于其在全球经济和政治中的重要性，中国潜在地可以起到巩固金砖国家集团的领导作用，然而由于中国似乎仅把这个框架看成是一个可以用来达到其自己国家

的目标的一个机会，正如许多能为其所用的其他现有国际和地区框架一样，要其起到这样的领导作用似乎不太可能。从这个意义上来讲，中国对金砖国家务实的策略可以被视为一种"低调"，因为北京虽有这个能力，但并不像某些其他金砖国家那样怀有建立一个更加广泛的、拥有自己的目标或价值观的共同体的野心。

五、结论：金砖之路，任重而道远

金砖国家这个组织的存在，及其定期召开的峰会本身就是寓意重大的变化；然而，对于其所取得的实际效果仍然众说纷纭。金砖国家在一些问题上相对不明朗的立场表明它们还没有准备好像"二战"后的主导大国那样塑造世界的治理机制。另外，它们看起来也没有准备好或有意愿提出当前治理结构的替代解决方案。大部分情况下，单独的金砖国家实际上往往比作为一个整体的组织更加有影响力。

总体而言，根据我们的观察，金砖国家倾向于根据是否利益相关来调整它们在全球治理方面的策略：在有"相对优势"的问题上，或在它们感到比较有把握的问题上（如开发性融资或货币方面），金砖国家往往采取更加激进的改革主义的策略，但在保持现状对它们有利的问题上（如贸易，至少中国是这样），它们的立场则更加通融。

关于全球性议题（即最需要全球治理的气候变化、网络安全、武器扩散等问题），金砖国家间仍然存在主要的不均衡和立场上的差异。一个日益强大的金砖共同体正在建设中，但还没有形成提出替代旧的、正在衰落的全球治理机制的新的框架/解决方案的能力。金砖国家局限性的原因之一是中国，这个金砖国家中迄今最强大的国家，主要还是把金砖集团看成是部署其自己的外交政策目标的一个框架，而其他国际和地区性框架在中国眼中也起着同样的作用。

金砖国家间有着众多内部和外部的分歧。在具体全球治理改革问题上（如联合国安理会的改革问题），以及一系列尖锐和相对温和的国际问题上（从乌克兰危机到气候变化），意见分歧还相当严重，这可能潜在地会对正在进行的经济合作产生负面的影响。因此，对于金砖国家的一个主要的挑战是在足以使它们分道扬镳的强大压力下保持团结。

参考文献

[1] Armijo, Leslie Elliott and Cynthia Roberts, "The Emerging Powers and Global Governance: Why the BRICS Matter", in Robert Looney, *Handbook of Emerging Economies*, New York, Routledge, 2014 forthcoming.

[2] Beausang–Hunter, Francesca, *Globalization and the BRICS — Why the BRICS Will Not Rule the World for Long*, Basingstoke and New York: Palgrave Macmillan, 2012.

[3] Erthal Abdenur, Adriana, Paulo Esteves and Carlos Frederico Gama, "BRICS and Global Governance Reform: A Two-pronged Approach", 2013, http://www.dfa.gov.za/department/bricks_fifth_book2014.pdf.

[4] Hou Zhenbo, "The BRICS and Global Governance Reform — Can the BRICS Provide Leadership?", *Development*, 2013, 56 (56), pp. 356–362.

[5] National Intelligence Council, *Global Trends 2025, A Transformed World*, Washington, D.C.: Government Printing Office, 2008.

[6] Niu Haibin, "BRICS in Global Governance — 'A Progressive Force?'" Dialogue in Globalization, Fiedrich Ebert Stiftung, New York, 2012.

[7] Petropoulos, Sotiris, "The Emergence of the BRICS — Implications for Global Governance", *Journal of International and Global Studies*, 2013, May 2013, Vol. 4 Issue 2, p. 37.

从长远角度看大趋势、新兴技术以及治理面临的挑战

[美] 班宁·加雷特*

一、治理面临更大的挑战

为预测将来在国内和国际范围内进行治理要面对的环境，金砖国家，甚至世界上所有国家，必须考虑未来发展的大趋势和一些未知因素。我们不能预测未来发生的事情，但我们可以预测那些会改变未来世界的因素，以及预测未来世界将要面临的挑战和机遇。同时，我们也可以展望未来，看到每一个国家以及全世界的发展，其中有我们需要避免的未来，也有我们将要努力实现的未来。

其中比较确定的一点是，我们不能根据现在的世界去推断未来的世界是什么样。过去的许多历史事件可以说明许多趋势是相互影响的，其中的不确定因素和"黑天鹅事件"会产生破坏性的改变并出现某些断层现象。举几个历史事件的例子，我们经历了冷战之后，出现了苏联解体；美国"9·11"恐怖袭击事件之后，美国入侵伊拉克；2008年的金融危机导致后来的全球性经济大萧条。更进一步说，这些因素将会发生在科技高速变化的时代，科技的改变会使社会产生巨大的转变，甚至产生破坏性的影响。

然而，以下这一预测是有道理的：未来20年以及更长的时间内，无论是在国内还是国际范围内的治理都将比现在的难度更大，争议更多。随着全球人口数量增加了25亿，以及城市人口数量增长，共同的大趋势又产生了新的挑战，包括气候变化、资源使用限制，以及大规模城镇化。为实现国际合作并应对共同的挑战，一个国家的内部治理是否良好，将更多地影响到其他国家内部治理的情况。最能说明这一

---

* 班宁·加雷特（Banning Garrett），美国大西洋理事会原高级研究员，中美关系学者。

点的一个例子就是全球气候变暖。在地球上任何地方释放的碳分子在大气中聚集，它们将影响到整个地球。因此，世界上每一个国家尤其是碳排放大国中国和美国，其限制碳排放的政策，对全世界彻底解决气候变暖问题来说具有十分关键的作用。

即便全球的趋势和未知因素使世界面临许多令人畏惧的挑战，未来也并不是那么惨淡。全世界可能会面临来自以下方面的挑战：气候变化、食物、水、能源、城镇化、环境治理等。更进一步说，面临这些挑战的同时，我们也可以找到增强国家和国际安全繁荣的机遇。然而，治理对于处理这些挑战来说是至关重要的。政府（包括市级政府和省级政府）需要带头制定政策，建立公私合作项目来处理国内遇到的挑战。国家政府还需要在处理紧急冲突时，不忘明确优先处理事项，不计较自我利益，与其他国家一同制定协作政策并进行长期合作，包括发展并广泛传播新的科学技术来解决关键问题。这需要克服会破坏有效国际合作的民族主义和国家间竞争行为。在这点上，除非全世界共同面临巨大危机，否则不会出现明显加强合作的局面。这种危机，正如美国著名建国者本杰明·富兰克林的传世名句所言，将使所有国家"在一条船上"，"若不共生，皆将独死"。如果没有一个全世界共同面临的巨大危机，一个让所有国家"在同一条船上共存亡"的危机，需要每个国家"齐心协力，拧成一股绳，否则会分别被绳子吊死"，那么全世界也不会出现加强合作的局面。

二、未来治理面临的状况

目前全球许多方面的发展趋势都是积极的，比如：世界更加繁荣；世界贫困率大大降低；西方经济主导了长达两个世纪之后，全球经济再次大合流；先进科学技术的快速发展提高了人类各方面的生活质量；全球医疗卫生技术广泛提高，人类的预期寿命得到延长；因暴力事件死亡的人数大幅减少等。[1]

然而，未来的世界似乎将由聚合的大趋势和激增的不确定因素来决定。随着技术高速发展，城镇化速度前所未有，人口增长，全球中产阶级人口快速增长对食物、水、能源和其他资源需求增加，出现了许多单个国家无法控制的挑战，这些挑战会潜在影响所有国家的繁荣与安定，这些因素使得聚合和变化的速度越来越快。某个地区或功能区域产生的破坏性改变，可以迅速地传播到整个世界，比如2008年起源于美国的金融危机迅速传播到全世界，导致全球经济萧条，没有一个国家能够幸免，当然包括人口最多的金砖国家以及经济最强的美国。全世界共同面临的许多挑战，比如气候变化、食物和水资源短缺、资源匮乏,将会改变各个国家的政策环境,需要各国重新调整传统的国内政策,比如主权政策,强化国家领导人的作用,独立于其他国家之外来控制这个国家的命运。

三、相对确定的大趋势

"大趋势"在可预见的未来轨迹之内,是持续影响世界变化的主要驱动因素,比如人类对食物和水的持续需求。以下是一些将决定全球策略大环境的关键大趋势①:

- **人口**:某些地区的人口增长、其他地区的人口减少、全世界面临的人口老龄化问题,为国内和国际范围内的治理带来了新的挑战。最新的联合国报告预计,到2030年,全球的人口增长将超过10亿,从目前的72亿人口增长到83亿人口;到2050年,全球的人口增长将超过25亿,达到96亿人口的总数。几乎所有的人口增长都将发生在南方国家的城市和地区,特别是亚洲和非洲。同时,大多地区将面临人口老龄化,不再工作人口数量翻番,同时工作人口的数量将持续减少——这种状况已经在许多国家出现。将会有更多的人参与治理,但是可以工作、交税并且供养退休人口及儿童的人口数量将减少。几乎所有的世界人口增长、城市人口增长以及中产阶级人数的增长将出现在发展中国家。中国、巴西和印度最终将仍然是发展中国家,人口也不断老龄化。长期的人口增长是不太确定的,有些人预测到2100年,人口数量将达到120亿,另外有些人预计人口数量将在本世纪中叶达到极限——90亿,并且将有可能在本世纪末下降到60亿。有一个趋势是肯定的,那就是人口出生率将不断下降,在世界大部分地区新生人口不足以弥补死亡人口的数量,目前最不符合这一趋势的是非洲某些地区以及南亚地区。

- **全球中产阶级人数的增长**:全球中产阶级人数实现快速增长,有专家预计,到2030年,世界的中产阶级人数将由今天的20亿增长到50亿,这是人类社会的巨大成功。中国、巴西、印度的中产阶级人口数量增长十分快速,并且增长数量庞大,但是这一崛起的中产阶级人口又为治理带来了新的挑战。一方面,中产阶级的突出特点是能源和资源的消耗量比较

---

① 以下部分关于大趋势和不确定性的论述参见国家情报委员会四年一次的关于全球趋势的报道,信息来自最近的一篇《2030年的全球趋势:不一样的世界》,于2012年12月发表,http://www.dni.gov/index.php/about/organization/global-trends-2030。又见欧盟安全研究院2012年发表的《同时参见2030年的全球趋势:互联世界和多中心世界中的民众》,欧盟安全研究院,由欧洲政策分析系统支持(ESPAS),http://europa.eu/espas/pdf/espas_report_ii_01_en.pdf。

大，他们需要消耗更多的钢铁生产汽车，需要更多水泥建造房屋，需要更好的食物和更多的奢侈品，为了能够获得这些中产阶级生活的"必需品"，给政府带来了很大的负担。另一方面，中产阶级对政府的期待越来越高，从卫生医疗条件的提供，到教育、就业、环境等各个方面的要求——所有的政府为了满足这些方面的要求都在努力地改进。这些新崛起的中产阶级同时也是十分脆弱的，比如一个中产阶级家庭只要有一位成员生病，整个家庭就将陷入贫困。[2] 技术进步是全球经济增长和中产阶级富裕的关键因素，它同时也通过互联网和社交媒体建立了一个相互连接的世界，提高了个人和集体组织起来反对政府政策的能力，比如 2013 年春在巴西发生的事件就证明了这一点。当然政府也在利用网络进行监管和控制，无处不在的社交媒体使人们可以相互联络，这为促使市民参与政府治理带来了新机遇。

- **大规模城镇化**：到 2030 年，世界人口将增加 10 亿多，同样多甚至更多的人口数量将搬到城市生活（仅仅在中国也许就有 3 亿人口这样做）。到 2050 年，城市和城市边缘地区将会增加 25 亿人口，其中 90% 的增长将发生在亚洲和非洲。仅仅印度、中国和尼日利亚三个国家的城市人口增长就将占预计总人数的 37%。[3] 目前共有 10 亿人口生活在城市贫困地区和贫民窟中，这一数字到 2030 年将翻倍。城市是创新和经济增长的动力，600 个城市将产生 20% 的人口增长，这一人口数将产生 50% 的资源需求增长，这一数字在未来的几十年内还将继续增长。城市中有 10 亿贫困人口居住，如果目前的发展趋势持续，预计到 2030 年，这一数字将翻倍。最终，城市和城市边缘地区将会成为资源可持续利用的战场，同时也是应对气候变化、贫困问题等挑战的战场，这些地方的情况将决定人类在应对这些挑战的战役中是取得成功还是失败。

1800—2050 年人口大规模城市化进程

1800 年：10 亿人口中的 3% 或大约 3000 万人
1900 年：16 亿人口中的 14% 或大约 2.2 亿人
1950 年：25 亿人口中的 30% 或大约 7.5 亿人
2010 年：72 亿人口中的 50% 或大约 36 亿人
2030 年：83 亿人口中的 60% 或大约 50 亿人
2050 年：96 亿人口中的 70% 或大约 67 亿人

每年，城市人口增加 7000 万，到 2050 年我们将会有一百多个圣保罗吗？

● **对食物、能源、水的需求将持续上升**[①]：世界人口不断增长，中产阶级人数也不断增加，快速城镇化，将会大幅增加人类对食物、能源、水以及其他自然资源的需求量。到2030年，人类对食物的需求将增加35%，然而，食物产量提高又面临着各个方面的压力，由于城镇化、森林退化、沙漠化、作物种植单一化，以及水资源缺乏引起的可耕地面积的减小，加之气候变化，加剧了这一状况的恶化。到2030年，对水资源的需求将提高40%，然而洁净水资源的供应在不断减少。经济合作与发展组织估计，到2030年全世界将近一半的人口生活的地区将出现水资源缺乏的状况，气候变化影响天气状况，使冰川融化的速度加快。到2030年，全世界对能源的需求将增加40%－50%。虽然中期内，全世界对于能源的需求上涨，但是由于水压致裂、水平钻孔等新技术的开发使美国的石油和天然气的产量增加，全球油价下降，这一局面得到缓和。但是从长期的角度来看，这样的局面更加具有挑战性，随着需求上涨，页岩天然气和石油的产量在达到峰值之后就会下降，政府人员反对采用化石燃料系统，因为这可能会在接下来的20年内导致灾难性的气候变化问题。关于向可持续使用能源方面转变的问题，政府可能会面临巨大的压力，因为与此同时对于能源的需求正在持续迅速地上涨。这不仅可能会导致能源短缺，还会导致国内和国际的政治危机，因为它们要承受来自能源生产国家和想要保护自身权益的公司的压力。

● **权利传播和个性化赋权**：有能力影响国际事务的组织正在增多。国际系统现在更多地显现出分裂和分层的局面。中国、印度、巴西这些大国正在崛起，像土耳其、印度尼西亚、南非和墨西哥这样的中等国家也在世界舞台上扮演越来越重要的角色。同时，有更多的非国家组织、国际非政府组织比如科学与国家安全研究所和一些跨国企业，甚至包括一些极端暴力组织比如逊尼派极端组织基地组织，这些组织的出现使得国家主导国际事务的程度降低。另外，更好的教育、更富裕的生活、技术的进步，加大了个人影响国家治理和国际社会治理的程度。这些个人更加愿意参与到政治活动中，同时也会对政府提出更多的要求。他们也更有可能按照种族、信仰、文化、政治因素的不同或者是基于环境或者公共医疗条件来建立社区内不同的过渡身份。到2050年，会有几十亿的人口增加到影响治理的行列中。

● **全球共同面临的问题**：全球的环境问题将面临越来越多的压力和限制，这将影响到整个国际社会。环境和个人安全面临的挑战将会加剧，由于人口迅速增长、城镇化进程加快以及中产阶级的扩大，对食物、水、自

[①] 详情见《2030年的全球趋势》，第33—37页。

然资源的需求迅速增长。如果没有处理好这些问题，它们将会对所有的国家及国际系统造成长期的不利影响。当前，外太空被军事化和空间碎片不断堆集，针对商业和研究机构的网络攻击威胁着互联网的完整性和可用性，海洋面临着海军的竞争、海盗对资源的榨取以及环境的恶化。这些使有效的全球治理面临的挑战日益增加。这些全球共同面临的挑战需要加强国际合作和治理加以解决，保护全球共同的利益。

以上提到的各项大趋势说明，在未来的 10 年甚至更长远的时间内，对政府各个层面的要求将大大提高。更多的人对家园和其他地方的环境要求将越来越高，他们也会利用更多的工具比如社交媒体来组织活动，对政府施加压力，让政府提供更好的服务、更多的机会。新兴经济国家不断扩大的中产阶级将会对食物、水资源、可信赖的清洁能源提出更高的要求，他们会要求有更好的基础设施、更好的教育和医疗条件，以及更健康的环境。政府会发现满足这些要求比较困难，特别是对一些有限资源的需求持续扩大，因为这会导致价格升高，使得经济和社会更加不稳定。同时，一些贫困国家由于政府治理不善，将会由部落、种族和宗教的争端，以及经济和环境的压力导致出现冲突，甚至国家治理出现严重问题。因为环境和经济问题，从这些国家移民的人将会大量涌入邻国，这样的内部冲突将会导致区域的不稳定。

四、会产生不良影响的关键不确定因素

以上提到的各项大趋势说明了未来国家和个人将会遇到的可预见的挑战。但是，会在未来 20 年内影响全世界发展的不只是以上因素。其他一些关键性的不确定因素会和上述大趋势一起相互作用，影响发展。这些不确定性因素包括：

● **全球经济波动**：发达国家，特别是欧元区的发达国家，将会迎来长期的经济复苏。新兴经济体也会经历经济缓慢增长的过程。各个国家发展的步伐越来越不一致（不断恶化的基尼系数①），将会进一步增加面临的

---

① 世界银行将基尼系数定义为："（基尼系数）是衡量一个国家收入分配状况均衡程度的重要指标。洛伦兹曲线（Lorenz Curve），指在一个总体（国家、地区）内，'从最穷个人或家庭算起，用占总收入的累计百分率，除以占总人口的累计百分率'，所得收入百分比的点组成的曲线。基尼根据洛伦兹曲线提出了判断分配平等程度的指标。基尼系数最大等于 1，最小等于 0。前者表示居民之间的收入分配绝对不平均，即 100% 的收入被一个单位的人全部占有了；而后者则表示居民之间的收入分配绝对平均，即人与人之间收入完全平等，没有任何差异。"资料来源：http://data.worldbank.org/indicator/SI.POV.GINI。

挑战。虽然穷人和富人都会变得更加富裕，但是如果各个国家和地区保持目前的趋势，他们之间的差距就会继续不断扩大。贫富差距的不断扩大将会影响经济发展，影响政治稳定。同时，虽然经济迅速发展，发达国家和发展中国家的中产阶级将会受到更大的挤压，特别是当中产阶级和超级富豪阶层之间的差距扩大，缓慢的经济增长会导致许多脆弱的中产阶级陷入贫困。[4]世界上许多国家也在经历经济国家主义和贸易保护主义，由于中国重新将重点放在拉动消费内需方面，全世界产业的劳动力分布也在重新调整中，其他国家不再将中国当作低成本制造的平台，新的制造技术和更低的能源消耗会吸引更多的制造业撤回美国以及其他发达国家。另外，资源短缺的压力将会导致更多的经济危机。由于人们采用了不当的措施避免 2008 年的经济危机重演，可能会有新一轮的全球经济衰退。包括中国、印度、巴西和南非在内的发展中国家将有可能会陷入"中等收入陷阱"。2011 年，亚洲发展银行发布了一项报告：《2050 年的亚洲：实现亚洲的世纪》。① 报告指出，虽然最好的情况是亚洲经济的国内生产总值可能达到 148 万亿，占世界 GDP 的 51%，但是如果亚洲国家陷入中等收入陷阱，亚洲的 GDP 总和将会是 61 万亿，只占世界 GDP 的 32%。印度的 GDP 将会是 12 万亿，而不是 40 万亿；中国的 GDP 将会是 21 万亿，而不是 63 万亿。为了使亚洲国家不面临亚洲世纪的末日，亚洲发展银行提出的两大关键因素是内部治理的质量以及亚洲国家的合作能力。

- **全球气候变暖**：气候变化将会对本世纪内人类的生存造成最大的威胁。政府间气候变化专门委员会于 2014 年 11 月 1 日提出的《2014 年气候变化综合报告》[5]指出，科学家担心气候变化出现的时间将会比之前的报告提出的时间更早，造成的影响也将更大。② 气候变化加剧了水资源短缺和食物缺乏的局面，产生更大的移民和社会冲突；导致海洋酸化，威胁食物供给和生态系统；对全球卫生造成新的危机；造成更严重的极端气候；导致海洋平面上升，扩大暴风雨天气对沿海城市和基础设施造成的影响。气候变化对经济的影响已经可以被估算到，未来将会对经济造成更大的影响。气象科学家越来越担心，气候变暖的效应将会超过 2 度的限制，2 度

---

① http://www.adb.org/publications/asia-2050-realizing-asian-century.

② 政府间气候变化专门委员会《2014 年气候变化综合报告》总结道："持续排放温室气体将导致更进一步的气候变暖，并给气候体系带来永久变化，给人类和生态系统带来严重、不可逆转的危害的可能性将提高。限制气候变化带来的危害需要持久地大量减少温室气体排放。只有降低排放，并且做出适应性调整，才可以减轻气候变化带来的危害。"

是科学家们计算的气候变化将会带来的长期破坏的一个数值，比如气候变暖会导致格陵兰岛和南极洲西部地区冰川的融化，这会使海平面上升好几米。许多城市已经就应对气候变化采取了具体的措施，这些城市可以预见气候变化带来的危害，与世界上其他城市分享最佳措施，来降低碳排放量，更好地适应气候变化已经带来的影响。应对气候变化已经越来越成为许多城市需要优先解决的问题，也是许多城市与国家的治理和国际合作面临的考验。2014年11月，美国和中国降低温室气体排放的协议在北京发布，这是全世界两大经济体和两大碳排放国对于共同解决气候变化问题迈出的一个巨大的步伐。这个协议在美国国会仍然受到反对，但是它可以使得全世界更有可能在2015的巴黎会议上制定一个全球性的协议来取代之前的京都议定书。①

- **"黑天鹅事件"**：一些可能发生在任何时间的不可预计事件，比如自然灾害、极度恶劣的天气、流行病或者是恐怖分子使用核武器，可能改变国际政治的格局。目前西非国家面临的埃博拉疫情引发的危机说明，任何时间产生的传染性疾病都有可能在整个地区蔓延开来，破坏经济和国家的稳定。可以通过空气传播的H5N1病毒或其他类似病毒可以迅速成为全球性危机，使全球运输系统陷入瘫痪，导致数百万人死亡，对全球的经济、政治、安全造成破坏性的影响。一系列极端气候天气将会改变国际政治的方向，影响应对气候变化的措施，对全球的经济和地区、国家的政治稳定产生负面的影响，例如桑迪飓风对美国造成的影响。

- **冲突**：由于社会动乱、极端宗教主义、政府为大众提供服务能力的降低、区域和全球能力的转移、个人能力的提高等因素，未来将会出现更多、更严重的内部和区域性冲突。由于国家衰败、核武器扩散、恐怖分子极端行为的出现，世界的安全、稳定和繁荣将越来越脆弱不堪，特别是像中东和南亚地区这种不稳定地区。伊朗和叙利亚迅速崛起的逊尼派极端组织展现出非政府极端组织给国家和国际治理带来的挑战。中东地区的大动乱可能会引入外界的权力和石油供应的中断，导致全球经济不景气。如果不能良好地解决东亚和东南亚地区的领土争端，将会影响到这些地区的国家参与国际合作的能力，也会影响这些国家应对国际挑战的能力。乌克兰

---

① 此类中美合作是两国决策者和专家多年以来的关注焦点。例如，可参见2009年的一份报告，《中美就能源和气候变化合作路线图》，http://asiasociety.org/files/pdf/US_China_Roadmap_on_Climate_Change.pdf。该报告的合作者大部分在2009届奥巴马政府中充当重要决策人，中国的合作者也成为中国政府的主要建议提供者。

未解决的争端表明,即便是欧洲也没有能力对冲突和不稳定因素免疫,这些不稳定因素将有可能在未来 25 年内影响欧洲的和平和统一。气候变化将会改变一些条件,影响到社会稳定,造成社会冲突。

● **极端主义和国家分裂**:由于个人权利的扩大,或者部落、种族、宗教或其他身份的原因,又加上目前无处不在的社交媒体,极端主义和分裂主义的情况将更为严重。国家的权力和权威有可能越来越受到非国家组织者权力的限制,一些变得更加紧迫的国家间挑战也超出了国家的治理范围。国家在很多方面受到分离主义者和极端主义者的挑战,包括瓦济里斯坦和达吉斯坦的宗教激进组织、加泰罗尼亚和苏格兰的地方民族主义分子。新技术加上社交媒体,以及越来越容易获得的武器,帮助这些人更加容易影响无辜人群,在国家内制造不稳定因素,达到自己的目标。

● **国际合作差距加深**:随着国际化加深,各个国家之间的相互依赖也增强,国家政府更难独立处理新的挑战,但是一些国家间的组织处理问题也不合适,甚至无法面对 21 世纪面临的各项挑战。[1] 面对越来越多的挑战,由于现有的国际机制大部分是第二次世界大战后为了解决遗留问题而设立的,所以这些机制需要改革,或是建立新机制,这是很不容易的。在这些国际系统于 20 世纪 40 年代进行最后一次改革之后,全世界出现了 140 多个新的国家,这些国家也需要在国际机构的讨论会上有自己的位置,决定他们国家未来的命运。越来越普遍的民主意识让每一个国家都积极参与国际事务,同时也使得各国家平等出席代表会和有效决策之间取得平衡,变得越来越难。

五、指数技术和突然的改变

新兴的科技将会同潜在影响游戏规则的不确定因素和大趋势一起相互作用,产生更多的变化和不确定性。过去的 20 年,新技术对社会产生了巨大的影响。仅仅是互联网就已经改变了世界,改变了政府、商业和个人生活的运作方式。现在我们可以估计到,未来 20 年将出现更多改变我们生活、改变治理的新科技,比过去半个世纪出现的新科技都要多。技术领域和基于技术产生的创新领域的变化速度是指数增长的,而不是线性增长。

---

[1] 2010 年的报告《2025 年的全球管理:处于一个关键的转折点》列出了全球管理方面面临的许多挑战,由国家情报委员会和欧盟安全研究机构共同推出。http://fas.org/irp/nic/governance.pdf。

也就是说，就像摩尔定律所言，电脑芯片的容量在过去的 40 年内每 18 到 24 个月就会翻倍，其他的新技术翻倍的时间也是以常规的速度增长，而不是指数增长。① 为了更好地理解这一差异，假设你要走 30 步，每一步 1 码长，那么第 30 步走的距离同第 1 步一样都是 1 码长，这时候你发现自己离最开始的地方已经有 30 码的距离。如果你每迈出一步，就把距离增加一倍，尽管刚开始的几步不会距离太长，但是到第 30 步的时候，你迈开的距离将达到 10 亿码的长度，相当于地球周长的 **22 倍**。所以差别不仅仅是数量上的，两者带来的改变不是一个级别的。现在智能手机的计算效率比 1985 年的超级电脑更高，全世界数以亿计的人们把智能手机放在他们的包里和袋子里。② 手机的数据存储能力也大大提高了，价格却以指数效应递减。思考一下未来 20 年仅仅电子效率方面将带来的飞速改变。其他技术领域也开始产生巨大的指数级别的改变，包括智能机器人、生物技术、生物信息技术、能源和环境系统、药物、神经科学和纳米技术等领域。③

在基因学科领域，摩尔定律是发生在类固醇方面。人类基因组第一次排序花费了超过 10 亿美元。然而，今天就算对一个人的所有基因序列进行排序也只要花费 1000 美元，预计这一费用将很快降低到 200 美元。这一费用降低到原来的百万分之一，这不仅仅将帮助更多个人用于医学诊断，也将有助于通过大量数据分析某些疾病与基因的关系。④

---

① 雷·科兹威尔（Ray Kurzweill）认为，技术呈指数发展的趋势已经持续了几个世纪。见 Ray Kurzweill, *The Singularity Is Near*, New York: Penguin Books, 2005, Chapter 2。科兹威尔是奇点大学的成立者之一（http://singularityu.org/），该大学的使命是"教育、激发、培养领导人物，使用奇点技术解决人类面对的大型挑战"。关键指数技术的数据，请参见性能曲线数据库（http://pcdb.santafe.edu/）。需要注意的是，并不是所有的技术都得到指数发展。例如，在过去的一个世纪内，飞机和内燃机的性能发展并没有呈指数型。

② 麦肯锡公司指出，1975 年推出的最快的超级电脑花费了将近 500 万美元，现在的智能手机 iPhone 4 运算能力可以与它相提并论，然而 iPhone 4 只需要花费 400 美元。见 James Manyika, Michael Chui, Jacques Bughin, Richard Dobbs, Peter Bisson, and Alex Marrs, *Disruptive Technologies: Advances That Will Transform Life, Business and the Global Economy*, McKinsey Global Institute, May 2013, p.5, http://www.mckinsey.com/insights/business_technology/disruptive_technologies。

③ 关于 DNA 排序的成本下降速度的讨论，比摩尔定律更快，详见 Aaron Saenz, "Costs of DNA Sequencing Falling Fast — Look at These Graphs!" May 3, 2011, http://singularityhub.com/2011/03/05/costs-of-dna-sequencing-falling-fast-look-at-these-graphs/。

④ 以下表格由奇点大学凯伦·迈伦努克（Karen Myronuk）提供，2013 年 4 月 15 日。

12 项新兴技术

麦肯锡全球研究院 2013 年 5 月发布了一项报告:《将会改变生活、商业和全球经济的新兴技术》,这是最显著的一份预测新兴技术将对经济产生哪些影响的报告,麦肯锡观察到了 12 项将潜在地影响经济的技术①:

- 移动网络——越来越便宜,能够让移动设备连上互联网;
- 知识系统自动化——可以处理知识的智能软件系统,自动完成指令或者微妙地进行判断;
- 物联网——低价的感应器和制动器组成的网络,可以搜集数据、监测、完成决策,以及优化过程;
- 云技术——通过互联网来取代电脑硬件和软件的某些功能;
- 智能机器人——更加先进的机器人,有更强的感应器,更灵敏、更聪明,能够自动完成某些任务;
- 无人驾驶或准无人驾驶汽车——减少人类的参与,甚至无人就可以实现汽车的驾驶;
- 下一代基因组学——快速、低价的基因排序,先进的大数据分析,合成生物技术(DNA 写入);
- 能源存储,用于储存能源,包括电池的设备或系统;
- 3D 印刷——根据数字模型,将物品的各个表面打印出来,从而复制物品,是先进的制造技术;
- 超材料——在力度、重量、传导性方面有杰出特点的一些材料;
- 先进的石油、天然气开采和回收技术——让开采和回收非传统石油和天然气的方式更加经济;
- 可再生能源——在对环境的影响降低到最小的前提下,从可再生能源中获得电能。

麻省理工学院研究员埃里克·布林约尔松(Erik Brynjolfsson)和安德鲁·迈克菲(Andrew McAffee)认为,"我们正在进入第二次机器时代"[6],不仅仅单项技术在进行指数级别的改进,关键技术的整体也在经历转折点。两位研究员认为指数技术的发展将超过科幻小说的描写:"《星际迷航》电视剧中,名叫三录仪的设备可以扫描和记录三种数据:地理的、气象的和医学的。今天消费者使用的智能手机可以顺利完成这些任务;智能手机可以当作地震仪、天气预报仪、地图以及测试心率和呼吸的

---

① 参见第 237 页脚注②。

机器。最重要的是，它的使用领域没有任何限制。智能手机可以充当播放器、游戏中心、参考书、照相机和全球定位系统。《星际迷航》中，三录仪和人对人交流仪器是不同的装置，但是在今天的现实世界中，智能手机已经将他们的功能融合到一个设备上"[7]。

这些新兴技术也将对发展中国家产生重大影响。手机在促进经济和社会发展方面起到的作用是非常重要的，产生了巨大的生产力，促进了许多方面的创新。比如2007年，肯尼亚移动运营商萨法利电信公司（Safaricom）研发推出了M-Pesa的移动银行系统，可以完成转账和其他微金融服务。① 智能手机让发展中国家和地区的人们连入了宽带互联网，到2020年，这些人将会离不开互联网，这可以潜在地产生巨大的经济收入。3D印刷技术可以让依赖进口、自身缺乏足够制造能力的国家在缺乏先进的制造和供应链的时候，生产自己的产品。小企业可以使用当地的材料，为当地提供更多就业机会，鼓励更多人才创业。②

如今我们无法预计未来20年的技术快速发展将会带来什么样的改变。然而，我们可以通过今天的某些技术和发展趋势来预见到未来会有哪些潜在的技术发展，比如更快的电脑、3D和4D技术③更加广泛地得到应用、更多机器人、以人为核心的移动设备上网功能、利用生物技术得到的新的有机体。更难的是预测技术的二次甚至三次发展效应——社会的创新和这些创新对社会带来的改变。例如，即使专家们可以预测到互联网的广泛使用，但是像Facebook、Twitter这样由互联网的二次效应带来的新发明不能被预测，那么利用社交媒体进行社会运动和反抗，例如"阿拉伯之春"运动这样的三次效应就更不能被预计到，"阿拉伯之春"对该地区甚至全球产生的地缘政治效应是十分巨大的，这可以被认为是互联网产生的四次效应，而且这种影响还持续地影响着中东地区。

---

① M-Pesa是目前世界上最新研发的手机支付系统，用户使用身份证或护照就可以通过手机进行存钱、取钱、转账操作。Cecilia Kang, "For the Poor, Cellphones Can Offer Lifeline", *Washington Post*, September 8, 2010, http: //www.washingtonpost.com/wp-dyn/content/article/2010/09/07/AR2010090706625.html.

② 关于3D印刷技术的潜在影响之讨论，参见Thomas Campbell, Christopher Williams, Olga Ivanova and Banning Garrett, "Could 3D Printing Change the World?" http://www.atlanticcouncil.org/images/files/publication_pdfs/403/101711_ACUS_3DPrinting.PDF.

③ 关于4D印刷技术的讨论，参见Thomas A Campbell, Sklylar Tibbits and Banning Garrett, "The Programmable World", *Scientific American*; Thomas A Campbell, Sklylar Tibbits and Banning Garrett, *The Next Wave*: 4D Printing and Programming the Material World, http://www.atlanticcouncil.org/publications/reports/the-next-wave-4d-printing-and-programming-the-material-world.

专家可以在某种程度上自信地预测许多技术的发展轨迹。例如电脑会更快，更小，连接程度更高，将变得像手机一样便于随身携带，以及更加普遍使用。实体机器人和数字化的机器人将在人们的经济生活和个人生活中得到更加普遍的应用。个人和组织（包括公司和国家）都可以得到更多的数字权利。3D 印刷技术将使得个人可以把数字的东西打印成实物，可以自己设计并生产，可以创作，该技术将会改变制造业和其他产业。生物合成技术不仅会影响到医疗医药，也会影响到整个产业和环境。纳米技术将继续改变材料的制作，在分子层面上改变物质。

一般来说，技术收敛将会带来新的、不可预估的发展，新的科技发明将更进一步改变技术的未来。未来 10 到 20 年之内，其中最具有影响力的技术突破有可能是量子计算，它将会改变人类理解世界的能力，解决一些目前最快的电脑花几百年甚至几千年也不能解决的问题。① 量子计算机将终结我们所知道的加密技术，使整个网络系统陷入极大的风险，包括基础设施、电力和银行系统；还包括个人、商业和政府部门的运营和通讯。同时，量子计算机能够即时计算数万亿个方程式，在设计新材料或新药物方面产生突破，也能够为解决比如气候变化等复杂的环境问题提供更多解释。另一项非常重要的技术是核聚变技术，最近洛克希德·马丁公司表示在这方面取得了突破性进展。这一项突破在未来 10 到 20 年内，将有可能使可负担和可计算的核聚变发动机成为现实，从而能够长期提供无碳能源，让化石燃料系统成为过去式，同时也在未来面对气候变暖挑战时做出更实际的努力。②

简而言之，目前已经出现许多的技术发展，虽然我们目前并不知道这些技术在未来是否会作为重大发明被推广，即便有这个可能，我们也不知道什么时候可以被推广。更难的是如何预测社会将会如何使用这些技术以及它的二次、三次、四次效应。这些新技术足够处理全球面临的诸多挑战，例如气候变化、能源转变、对食物和水与日俱增的需求吗？

---

① 量子计算机不仅速度更快，而且将从根本上改变解决问题的方法。例如传统的计算机是通过逐一输入数字组合进行解密，需要十亿甚至数万亿次的尝试，但是量子计算机可以瞬间就输入所有可能的密码组合，从而迅速得到答案。由微软公司设计的虚拟模型计算出，传统计算机需要 31 000 年才能解决一个因子分解的问题，使用量子计算机只需要几秒钟或者几个小时就能解决。当量子计算机普及之后，网络上所有的密码都可以被瞬间解密。量子计算机也标志着解决难题的新时代已经到来。量子计算机可以即时探索上万种新材料或新药物可能的分子组合，结构，从而找到最合适的分子组合，从而可以解决一些挑战，例如，可以制造出室温超导体，或者精准地模拟气候变化。虽然初级阶段的量子计算机会比较大，但是最终它会变得很小，为网络以及个人带来巨大的新能量。参见网址：http://www.lockheedmartin.com/us/products/compact-fusion.html。

② Http://www.lockheedmartin.com/us/products/compact-fusion.html。

新技术会带来更多就业机会，还是减少机会？它们将会带来更多财富，还是更进一步加大社会不平等？它们会不会被个人、团体、政府利用来达到一些会产生破坏的目的，比如生物恐怖主义、网络战争以及机器人袭击等事件？它们促进民主还是加强专制？它们将会增强国际繁荣，促进国际合作，还是会导致新的冲突，造成更多零和竞争？以上是未来的一些问题，是关于新技术对社会带来的不确定影响以及治理面临的诸多挑战。

政府需要保护网络

请你设想一下我们今天的生活离开了网络会怎么样。我们不难想象到，经济将会崩溃，社会出现无序状态，政治叛乱，军队被严重削弱，以及其他的冲突。现代生活如果没有网络将陷入瘫痪，大多数交通系统、物流系统和食物供给系统将无法运行，银行和金融系统的交易终止，通讯系统不能工作，提供水和电的基础设施也将崩溃。简而言之，现代社会将会陷入未曾经历的文明危机。世界将不会变成20年前没有因特网的时代，也许会陷入工业时代前的状态。

因特网的突然消失造成的影响可能不像我们估计的那么大。大规模的太阳磁暴将每隔100年左右的时间出现一次，最近的一次太阳磁暴发生在1895年，那时候世界上还没有互联网。太阳磁暴会破坏卫星、电力网络以及许多敏感的电子装置。美国国家情报委员会的报告《2030年的全球趋势：另一个新世界》指出："除非我们能够找到应对的措施，否则，太阳磁暴会对世界上的社会和经济系统造成大范围的威胁。"[8] 2012年7月，地球侥幸没有碰上大规模的太阳磁暴，据专家分析，未来的10年内地球碰上太阳磁暴的几率是12%。[9]

当我们考虑到技术对社会造成的负面影响并且抱怨时——我们抱怨数字化连接的世界之脆弱，抱怨数字化带来的失业和数字化方面的安全威胁——我们也不能忽视了社会对科技的依赖程度。终止目前的科技发展是不可能的，试图解散今天的技术化社会将会是自杀性行为。人类自从发现火可以用来烤熟食物，就一直迈着科技进步的步伐。人类如果要避免文明产生巨大灾难的话，必须继续科学技术的发展历程，同时也要解决面临的重要挑战，例如气候变化这种由于技术发展而产生的问题。

六、真正决策性的挑战和机遇到底是什么？

指数发展型技术将会转变社会，带来新机遇并且对治理产生新的危险因素。政府需要顶着巨大的压力，处理潜在的人为或自然产生的危机风暴，许多方面都要提出前所未有的要求。由于不同社区存在的利益和意识方面的冲突，国家内部的治理以及利用无处不在的联络方式对各个层级进行组织将会变得越来越困难。我们无法选择保持现状，因为没有所谓的现状供我们选择，而是突然出现的改变引起了迅速增加的需求和压力。主要的挑战将会是如何搭建具有弹性和适应性的治理。

金砖国家以及其他大国，包括美国、日本和欧洲各国，需要从长远发展的角度考虑：为了确保我们的繁荣和安全，我们面临哪些真正的战略性挑战？金砖国家在谋求更大的发展，提高人民生活水平时，面临的最大威胁是不是西方国家建立的国际组织系统、法律和规范？有没有必要建立另一个平行的国际系统？或者说，是不是西方的组织系统已经成为其他国家在应对国际社会中严重、具有潜在威胁问题时的根基？其他国家是不是能够利用西方的组织系统更好地抓住新科技带来的机遇，更好地迎接全球面临的挑战，增强世界各民族的安定和繁荣？

我的观点是，从长远看来，全世界各国面临的常见战略性挑战比起目前不同国家之间的分歧更加具有威胁性，虽然这些分歧导致国家间彼此不信任，导致这些国家希望建立竞争机制，把对方国家看成是潜在的敌人而建立军事力量。常见的挑战包括：减缓气候变化，适应其带来的影响；随着需求的增加和可耕地面积的减少，保持充足的食物供给；即便需求增加，可使用水的供给减少，仍然加强洁净水的供给；即便对能源的需求不断大量增加，仍要加快从使用化石燃料到使用可再生能源的转变；需要建立可持续发展的基础设施，特别是在城镇地区，这些地区将决定环境和经济的可持续发展是否能够实现。

尽管未来预示着许多共同的危险和挑战，似乎大多数国家只是从零和游戏的角度考虑，越来越关注短期内和本国的狭隘利益。这种与时代脱轨的思考方式将会给这些国家和国际社会带来不良结果。

如果关注的是不正确的策略和问题，那么将会造成资源的极大浪费，也会错过很多宝贵的机会。其中有一个例子可以说明，那就是美国在2003年对伊拉克发起的战争。国家的差异和怀疑绝对不能成为国际合作不可逾越的障碍，因为国际合作对于保护国家安全和确保国家繁荣是非常必要的。我的观点是，进一步促成世界分裂将严重影响到所有国家的安定和繁荣，而建立竞争性的国际机构以及设立国际规范、规矩对此产生的影响却小得多。

虽然没有人能够非常自信地预言未来的世界将会如何演变，但是我们可以相信，所有国家各个层面上的决策者面临的挑战和选择将会由相互作用的大趋势所决定，这些大趋势就是我们说的不确定性，不可预知的"黑天鹅事件"，以及政府和非政府成员做出的决定。等待世界如何演变是可能的，但不是我们想要的。等待的本质实际上是什么也不做却希望最好的事情可以发生。我们必须做出努力，而不是等待，努力让事件的发生减少更多的不确定性，避免或弱化不利的发展曲线，增强得到双赢结果的可能性。而且，我们要抓住新兴科技带来的机遇，让目前面临的重大挑战有更多的解决方案，改变挑战的发展轨迹，创造一个更加繁荣、安定的未来，实现经济和环境的可持续发展。这样的努力包括：加强国际科学合作，建立公有私有合作关系，开发和应用创新科技模型，迎接国际重大挑战。

这次会议可能是倡导建立一个由金砖国家、美国和欧洲联合评估"二轨"项目的一个步骤，如果该项目可改变长期的全球趋势，改变世界的不确定性，对新兴科技进行整体评估，那么这次会议就是成功的。建立这样一个共同评估的过程将帮助我们超越目前的怀疑和争端，能够关注长期共同面临的挑战和机遇。由此我们可以得到一个结论，那就是每个国家确保安全和繁荣的最重要的一点就是需要与世界其他国家合作，共同解决面临的挑战，同时也要小心谨慎地处理不同国家之间的差异和争端，因为这些差异和争端会妨碍国际合作。①

参考文献

[1] See Simon Kuper, "Peace in Our Time", *Financial Times*, 17 January, 2014 http://www.ft.com/intl/cms/s/2/2177ebce-7e44-11e3-b409-00144feabdc0.html # axzz2r2KpzOlU; and Ian Morris, *What! What Is It Good For*? New York: Farrar, Straus and Giroux, 2014.

[2] Shawn Donnan, Ben Bland and John Burn‐Murdoch, "Fragile Middle: 2.8 bn People on the Brink", *Financial Times*, 13 April 2014, http://www.ft.com/intl/cms/s/2/

---

① 参见大西洋委员会中国国际研究所 2013 年的报告，《中美合作：世界未来的关键》，http://www.atlanticcouncil.org/images/publications/China-US_Cooperation_Key_to_the_Global_Future_WEB.pdf。该报告由中美专家合作写成，号召中国和美国在制定长期战略政策时保持合作，例如共同应对气候变化，面对能源、食物、水资源危机以及其他挑战时，将合作列为中美关系的战略框架。

e8f40868-c093-11e3-a74d-00144feabdc0. html#axzz2ymyjCfJ9.

［3］ "World Urbanization Prospects", 2014 Revision, *Highlights*, UN Department of Economic and Social Affairs, p. 5, http: //esa. un. org/unpd/wup/Highlights/WUP2014-Highlights. pdf.

［4］ See "Fragile Middle: 2.8 bn People on the Brink", *Financial Times*, 13 April, 2014, http: //www. ft. com/intl/cms/s/2/e8f40868-c093-11e3-a74d-00144feabdc0. html # axzz2ymyjCfJ9; and Branco Milanovic, "How We Can Strengthen the World's Fragile Middle Class", *Financial Times*, 28 April, 2014, http: //www. ft. com/intl/cms/s/0/78ca82c4-c584-11e3-97e4-00144feabdc0. html? siteedition = intl#axzz30GyhkVEd.

［5］ *Climate Change 2014 Synthesis Report: Approved Summary for Policymakers*, 1 November 2014, http: //www. ipcc. ch/report/ar5/wg2/.

［6］ Erik Brynjolfsson and Andrew McAffee, *The Second Machine Age: Work, Progress, and Prosperity in a Time of Brilliant Technologies*, New York: W. W. Norton, 2014, Chapter 1.

［7］ Ibid, Chapter 2.

［8］ National Intelligence Council, *Global Trends* 2030: *Alternative Worlds*, December 2012, p. 52, http: //www. dni. gov/index. php/about/organization/global-trends-2030.

［9］ "Near Miss: The Solar Superstorm of July 2012", *NASA Science News*, 23 July 2014, http: //science. nasa. gov/science-news/science-at-nasa/2014/23jul_superstorm/.

金砖国家间的合作对全球治理意味着什么?

[美] 拉尔夫·科萨*

一、引言

建立新的多极世界秩序已经成为当代国家政治论述中的老生常谈了。"金砖国家"(BRICS)这个词来源于一个英文缩略语,首次出现在高盛集团2001年的一篇论文之中,代表的是由巴西、俄罗斯、印度、中国和南非这几个新兴经济体构成的一个国家群体。对很多人来说,金砖国家的出现最好地宣示了世界史上一个新纪元的到来,因为这些国家日益提高的经济地位使它们要求更多地参与世界事务。有些人认为,随着这些正在崛起的大国争取在全球治理中发挥更大的作用并具备更好的代表性,它们注定将挑战西方主导的国际体系。另一些人可能会认为,它们的主要贡献应该是改革而不是替代现有的国际组织。只有时间才能告诉我们哪一种预测是正确的。

2014年7月在巴西福塔莱萨召开的金砖国家首脑会议引发了对该国家集团的未来及其国际影响的争论。引发争论的主要原因是含有72点共识的《福塔莱萨宣言》,其中包括同意成立金砖国家新开发银行(NDB),为金砖国家和其他发展中国家的基础设施和开发项目提供资金,以及关于建立一个应急储备安排的备忘录,以"帮助各国防范短期资金流动压力,促进金砖国家间的进一步合作,强化全球金融安全网,**并对现有国际安排提供补充**"[1]。成立替代性金融机构的可能性本身对于现有全球经济秩序就是一个具有挑战性的概念。关于这些机构将如何运作的条文又对有关争论起到了推波助澜的作用,因为这些条文对现有金融机构,如国际货币基金组织和世界银行等的运行提出了明确的批评。金砖国家福塔莱萨首脑峰会结束后,巴西财政部长曼特加(Guido Manteig)指出:"在世界银行,美国

---

* 拉尔夫·科萨(Ralph A. Cossa),美国战略与国际问题研究中心太平洋论坛主席。

拥有一票否决权，而在金砖国家新开发银行，所有股东都是平等的。"他继续说道："新开发银行的行长职位不会限于由来自特定洲的人选担任，而将是五年轮换一次，由来自金砖各国的人选轮流担任。"[2]

本论文将从金砖国家在国际治理议题方面的合作这个角度，对这个国家集团进行分析，既不想对金砖国家无故拍砖，也不会滥用溢美之词。我们承认自己有双重怀疑：既对金砖国家持有怀疑态度，也对美国/西方对金砖国家及其他所谓的"竞争对手"经济集团所采取的对策感到怀疑。本文将严格超越对集团差异的批评，而是将把重点放在金砖国家作为一个政治集团是否有能力对全球治理结构进行有意义的改革上。本文还将提出金砖国家间合作的几个主要障碍，包括最重要的障碍——中国与另外几个国家在结构和经济上的不均衡。我们希望读者们会发现这些批评、建议和意见是建设性的，因为这就是我们的意图所在。

二、金砖国家：不仅仅是世界上几个国家的简单代名词？

尽管"金砖国家"这个词和国际政治论述中的许多其他概念一样是西方人发明的，这个集团的创立在很大程度上却是源于对现有西方主导的全球经济和政治秩序的不信任和不满。高盛集团的吉姆·奥尼尔在2001年撰写他的论文《打造更好的全球经济金砖》时创造了"金砖四国"（BRIC）这个词（南非直到2011年才被纳入该集团）。这些国家在他看来具有巨大的经济增长潜力，将不可避免地重塑世界经济秩序。

表面上看，金砖五国之间不同的特点似乎多于共同点。然而，它们之间也有一些不可忽视的将它们联合在一起的因素。当前，巴西、俄罗斯、印度、中国，一定程度上也包括南非，是增长最快的和规模最大的新兴市场经济体。金砖国家最早的四个成员国占全球国内生产总值（GDP）的约四分之一，带上南非，全球增长的一半以上由金砖五国贡献。此外，据预测，到2050年，它们将取代目前七大经济体（G7）中的大多数，如果按购买力平价（PPP）计算，将占全球经济的三分之一。[3]在过去的20年里，金砖国家的人均GDP增长速度已经超过了全球趋势。它们的经济规模决定了全球投资的流向，对贸易的模式和走势有着深远的影响。

除了经济表现以外，其他一些特点也似乎将它们聚集在一起。首先，人口方面，它们是30亿人，即世界近一半人口的祖国，有着充满活力的、新兴的中产阶级，他们日益增加的收入使他们有更强的消费能力，进而推动了新的需求增长。尽管有证据表明金砖国家的人口增长正在减速或已陷入停滞——分别指中国和俄罗斯——但它们工作年龄人口的减少预计要比发达国家慢一些。[4]

第二，同样，在经济领域分享了成功的同时，这些国家在福利和教育等领域也有着相似的焦虑和挑战，包括国内变化、体制稳定、社会不平等和服务提供等。

最后，它们往往持有广泛共同的世界观，都非常重视主权原则。它们常常认为全球化有损它们的主权，是（西方）大国实施新殖民主义、对其进行剥削的工具。然而，让金砖各国走得更近、为它们打开了进一步制度化合作机遇之窗的恰恰是全球经济衰退。

国际环境中似乎有一个各种因素的汇合点为金砖国家的合作提供了共同的基础，强化了它们对全球治理领域共同目标的认识。首先，国际金融动荡的根源很大程度上来自美国的金融体系危机，使美国在国际舞台上被视为"不负责任的利益相关者"。其次，更重要的是，传统的、西方主导的金融治理中心被认为没有能力有效管理危机，带领世界走向复苏，这带来了国际金融体系合法性的危机。第三，一个新的动向是非西方地区性权力中心的崛起，以及它们对于让发展中国家在国际决策中更多参与的倡导。

金砖国家迅速抓住机遇，集中对全球治理架构进行了批判，同时提出了它们自己深化参与全球治理事务的意图。它们主要的批评涉及重要的多边机构，如世界银行、国际货币基金组织以及联合国，指出新兴经济体在这些组织的管理机构内没有被充分地代表。金砖国家早就要求这些组织对其内部机构进行改革，使权力分配更加公平，更好地反映它们日益上升的经济实力。仔细观察国际货币基金组织的投票权结构就能正确理解这些主张。国际货币基金组织内的投票权大小是由对这个组织的出资多少决定的。而出资多少取决于名义 GDP 等变量。如果 GDP 以被一些人认为能更好地反映一个国家的经济规模的购买力平价（PPP）计算，那么许多国家的投票权份额将会发生巨大的变化[5]。例如，如果进行改革，现在持有比巴西多出 50% 的投票权的比利时，其投票权将比巴西少三分之一。[6]

早在分别于 2006 年和 2008 年召开的第六十一届和第六十三届联合国大会的会议间隙，金砖国家对共同目标的意识就初见端倪。金砖国家聚集在一起，就合作领域以及在即将举行的国际论坛上将要研究的议题上采取联合步骤进行商讨。[7]金砖国家首次正式会议于 2009 年 6 月在俄罗斯叶卡捷琳堡举行。它们的联合声明呼吁"改革国际金融机构，以反映世界经济中发生的变化"：

应提高新兴市场和发展中国家在国际金融机构中的发言权和代表性。国际金融机构负责人和高级领导层选举应遵循公开、透明、择优原则。我们致力于推动多边外交，支持联合国在应对全球性威胁和挑战方面发挥中心作用。为此，我们重申，需要对联合国进行全面改革，使其更具效率，更有效地应对当今全球性挑战。我们重申，重视印度和巴西在国际事务中的地位，理解并支持它们希望在联合国发挥更大作用的愿望。[8]

从那时起，该集团就定期举行首脑会议，同时举行诸如"金砖国家治理体系与治理能力建设国际研讨会"以及后续的"金砖国家智库理事会会议"等两个会议，还举办同行学习活动。

三、金砖国家间在全球治理方面的合作

金砖国家的一个共同特点是对于现有全球治理结构的不满。它们似乎认为"二战"后一段时期内形成的世界秩序是一种过时的结构，不能满足新的、正在生机勃勃地崛起的地区性权力中心的要求。新的全球性威胁，如全球金融动荡、恐怖主义或气候变化不能仅仅在西方决策规则基础上加以解决。因此，金砖国家渴望从"规则接受者过渡到规则的制定者"[9]，从而影响全球决策，使之更能反映它们自己的需求（据称也包括发展中国家的需求）。下面这个部分将审视金砖各国有着紧密联系的共同诉求，以及已经开展合作的主要全球治理领域。

四、金砖国家与国际安全治理：人道主义干预的规范及联合国安全理事会

金砖国家已经在两个主要方面在联合国框架内进行了合作，以对国际安全领域的结果施加影响，对其结构进行改造。第一个方面涉及联合国安理会的改革，第二个方面侧重国际人道主义行动。

金砖国家在联合国结构内是否需要进行改革方面似乎持相似的观点。它们普遍认为联合国安理会已经落后于时代。联合国安理会包括五个有一票否决权的常任理事国——是美国、俄罗斯、中国、英国和法国，以及来自联合国地区性集团的、轮换担任的十个非常任理事国。随着印度和巴西加入对维和部队贡献最大的国家之列，同时它们也在准备增加自己缴纳的联合国会费，这两个国家正在游说，以期获得常任理事国席位。[10] 由于非洲国家在联合国内是第三大集团，它们毫无意外地提出了两个安理会席位

的要求，其中一个席位很可能是专门为南非预留的。金砖国家一直在集体呼吁扩大其在联合国安理会中的代表性。它们似乎结成了统一战线，支持该集团内的成员国为成为常任理事国所做的努力。在2011年发布的《三亚首脑会议宣言》中金砖国家称：

> 我们致力于推动多边外交，支持联合国在应对全球性挑战与威胁方面发挥中心作用。为此，我们重申，需要对联合国包括安理会进行全面改革，使其更有效，更有代表性，以更成功地应对当今全球性挑战。中国、俄罗斯重申重视印度、巴西和南非在国际事务中的地位，理解并支持其希在联合国发挥更大作用的愿望。[11]

这个声明在此后几年的宣言中被反复重申。[12]然而，尽管在言辞上支持扩大安理会，如果此项改革真的被认真考虑的话，俄罗斯和中国不大可能支持，因为这将稀释它们在安理会中的影响力。尽管如此，如果不是金砖国家作为一个政治集团的出现，这种支持性声明根本不可能发出。这使一些人相信，随着金砖国家间合作的加深，俄罗斯和中国未来可能会重新考虑它们的立场。

然而，即使在金砖国家内部，也有分歧。印度一直支持日本也拥有安理会常任理事国的席位，而东京也一直比中国更支持德里的努力，同时北京是强烈反对日本的有关努力的。所以，关于联合国安理会的"改革"的具体定义是什么并没有广泛的共识。

在人道主义行动方面，金砖国家曾多次反对根据"国家保护责任"（R2P）准则进行的人道主义干涉，因为它们认为这是对各国国家主权的侵犯。它们的集体反对传达了它们有能力在多边组织中集体表达自己共同观点这一讯息，同时也使人们对它们未来在此类行动的开展中将起的阻碍作用以及对全球治理准则的总体影响产生疑问。[13][14]

这从它们在利比亚和叙利亚危机问题上的表现可见一斑。2011年，利比亚内战爆发时，所有金砖国家成员在联合国安理会都占有席位（中国和俄罗斯为常任理事国，印度、巴西和南非为轮职非常任理事国）。内战的加剧以及卡扎非政权对其国内人民的暴行促使联合国安理会采取行动，通过了1973号决议，同意使用武力保护平民。除南非以外（其投了赞成票），其他金砖国家都投了弃权票。虽然弃权并不是公开的反对，但它们接下来对该人道主义行动的批评表明了金砖国家的集体立场。金砖国家单独地和集体地对该决议进行了谴责，称其将根本就未经同意的干涉措施强加于人。它们批评北约滥用了新兴大国对其的信任，超越联合国的授权，不是保护平民，而是推动政权更迭。[15]在2011年4月在中国三亚召开的金砖国家第三次首脑会议上，它们发表联合声明，对联军使用武力进行了谴责。

在利比亚危机上的经历似乎成了叙利亚事件的前例。[16]同年10月，法国带头草拟一项决议，谴责叙利亚政府镇压抗议者。决议称如果叙利亚政府不遵守该决议的规定，将考虑采取进一步的行动。俄罗斯和中国投票否决了该决议，同时南非、印度和巴西投了弃权票。尽管人道主义危机在叙利亚还在持续，由于西方国家和金砖国家在意见分歧，联合国还是没能在采取适当的反应上达成一致。尽管俄罗斯和中国在针对阿萨德政权的措施上有着坚定的立场，其他金砖国家的立场则相对更加中立。但它们都强烈反对任何利比亚式的军事干预。俄罗斯和中国的反对则更加激烈一些。5月，两国都投票否决了联合国安理会要求国际刑事法庭就在叙利亚发生的战争罪行进行调查的决议。包括中俄两国，共有15个国家投票反对该决议。这使有关的谈判变得更加复杂化，使危机的解决陷入了僵局。

许多人可能会认为在利比亚和叙利亚事件上，金砖国家间表现出了分歧而不是团结，尽管有时候它们所投的票是相同的。不同的金砖国家虽然同样投弃权票，并不是因为它们有共同的观点，而是出于各自的利益考虑。另外，有批评家说，在叙利亚问题上，所有投票的国家都支持决议的大部分，即对阿萨德的谴责。分歧点在于是否采取军事干预。

金砖国家中的两个成员，中国和俄罗斯，传统上一直扮演着朝鲜的保护者的角色。近期，联合国大会谴责了朝鲜的反人道罪行。中国和俄罗斯投票反对有关把平壤送上国际刑事法庭的建议。金砖国家的其他成员国似乎不那么倾向于保护平壤：南非和印度投了弃权票，而巴西则投票赞成该决议草案。5月，联大人权委员会重新讨论了这个议题，俄罗斯和中国又投了反对票，南非弃权，巴西投了赞成票，而印度不是该委员会的成员。鉴于其历史经历，南非在人权如此被践踏的情况面前保持沉默，尤其让人感到失望。

值得注意的是，金砖国家成员国有时也违背它们自己的不干涉和领土完整的原则，当危及到它们自己的利益时，则会打着人道主义的幌子，对其他国家进行军事干涉。印度和俄罗斯就有这样的例子。1971年，巴基斯坦在当时的东巴基斯坦对当地的民众进行军事镇压，印度对此表示了人道主义关注，并派遣军队前往当地。类似的是俄罗斯对格鲁吉亚的干涉及其近期对克里米亚的吞并，这些都是打着"国家保护责任"原则的幌子进行的。然而这些事件并没有妨碍它们对与曾被当作自己行为的借口完全一样的原则集体表示反对。

以上事实说明,"国家保护责任"原则无论是其未来的可行性还是其实施的方式,目的都是定义全球治理的国际准则。金砖国家无论是单独的国家还是作为一个集体对于这个准则的立场,即它们是否容忍、实施、强化甚至操纵"国家保护责任"这个原则,将决定全球治理在国际安全领域的方向及基于规则的国际秩序的未来,因为将来联合国安理会扩容之后将会包含更多的金砖国家成员国。巴沙尔·阿萨德寻求金砖国家帮助其"为了正义与邪恶斗争"[17]并不是偶然的。不说别的,这至少显示了金砖国家在国际安全舞台上不断提高的重要性,以及它们潜在的对于国际安全准则的日益增加的影响。然而很少有人会认为它的作用是积极的。

五、可能的替代选择:重塑全球经济治理(金砖国家的角色)

最让金砖各国如俱乐部一般凝聚在一起的是它们对在全球经济舞台上有更大的代表性和发挥更大领导力的渴望。尽管是一个协商性而非决策性组织,二十国集团是仅由工业化国家构成的七国集团和八国集团的升级版。二十国集团形成于全球金融危机期间,既包括工业化国家也包括新兴市场国家。它的成立向新兴经济体和地区性平衡因素很好地显示了发达经济体为加强国际合作、更有效地应对当代全球金融挑战所起的更大的作用。类似的发展以及金砖国家自己在全球水平上实现的经济权重的增长为国际经济体系带来了新的活力。

多年以来,金砖国家一直在表达对西方工业化国家垄断重要的国际金融机构,即世界银行和国际货币基金组织的领导位置的不满。传统上,世界银行行长的位置一直由美国人担任,而国际货币基金组织总裁的位置一直由欧洲人担任。金砖国家集体表达对这些机构的领导位置的渴求开始于2011年4月,当时的世界银行行长罗伯特·佐利克(Robert Zoellick)宣布有任。一个月后,国际货币基金组织总裁多米尼克·斯特劳斯卡恩(Dominique Struss-Kahn)也被迫辞职。金砖国家努力争取在国际货币基金组织和世界银行推行更加开放、更有竞争性和更唯才是用的领导选择机制。[18]这些努力部分取得了成功,也赢得了广泛的赞同。尽管国际货币基金组织最终还是任命了一位欧洲人,法国人克里斯蒂娜·拉加德(Christine Lagarde)做总裁,但世界银行行长的职位给了韩裔美国人金墉。

金砖各国还紧密合作,争取改变这些金融机构的投票权结构。在这个方面,全球金融危机也起着催化剂作用。为了更有效地应对全球金融危机及其副产品——欧元危机,这些金融机构急需更多的资金。因此,它们严重依赖来自新兴经济体，主要是中国和巴西的资金贡献，因为发达国家的经济陷入停滞，无法提供多余的资金流。[19]作为交换，金砖国家提出对这些机构的配额进行改革。配额代表着认缴资本及其相应的投票权，与各国的经济实力和其他权力资源成正比。

长期以来，金砖国家一直主张对配额进行有利于它们的调整，因为它们的经济权重近几年获得显著的提高。它们日益增加的出资为它们进行讨价还价提供了有利的基础。2010年的谈判达成了配额重新分配协议，包括世界银行向发展中国家分配3.3%的配额，国际货币基金组织向发展中国家分配6%的配额，主要受益者是金砖各国。[20]

在这里，说实在的，我们必须指出迄今为止美国政策上的一个重大的缺陷，或者说是失败。奥巴马政府支持金砖国家改革的努力，但因在协议后续实施上的迟滞而受到广泛的批评。[21]国际货币基金组织的改革在美国国会被搁置，而2014年11月进行的国会选举使在这方面取得进展变得更加无望。西方，尤其是美国总是虚伪地要求中国和其他金砖国家积极地发挥更加建设性的作用——记住，是要求它们成为"负责任的利益相关方"，但当这些国家为此努力的时候又不提供支持。对于金砖国家的倡议，华盛顿不应总是这样消极（见下文对金砖国家银行的讨论），对类似由中国提出倡议，如亚洲基础设施投资银行，不应该一概采取阻挠的态度。（美国有权就此类银行的目的、贷款标准，以及它们与现有的类似机构的关系/互补性提出尖锐的问题，但必须是建设性的，而不是一味地进行阻挠。美国目前的立场被认为主要是对其盟友施加压力，阻止它们加入。这进一步强化了美国正试图遏制中国的看法，对美国的外交政策目标起着适得其反的效果。）

最后，另一些倡议引发了关于金砖国家间不仅是更加巩固的合作关系，而且是对现有全球金融体系构成公然的制度性挑战的讨论。过去，金砖国家曾表示过希望脱离美元，开始用本地货币在金砖国家间开展贸易，甚至采用类似国际货币基金组织特别提款权的形式作为一种"全球性货币"。近期在巴西福塔莱萨召开的第六次金砖国家首脑会议上，它们重申了此前表达过的成立前文提到过的新开发银行的愿望，同时，他们还宣布设立一项"应急储备安排"（CRA），初期资本分别为500亿美元和1000亿美元。[22]新成立的机构旨在加强金砖国家间的合作，将资金引导至金砖国家认为需优先发展的领域，即较不发达国家的发展项目上去。他们还同意，各成员国对该银行的出资额应该相等，同时享有平等的投票权，这与现有的金融机构有着明显的不同。为了强化这一立场，金砖各国还通过了更加平等的"劳动分工"。中国上海将成为该银行总部的所在地,印度将提供该行的第一任行长,该行的第一任理事会主席将由一位俄罗斯人担任。

六、庞然大物——中国

尽管有前文所述的各种合作,金砖国家之间的分歧似乎和共同点一样多。例如,有人对它们的相对增长率和它们在经济和政治体制上的差异进行了分析,怀疑它们是否能持续保持经济强国地位,因而强烈质疑该集团到底能坚持多久。

过去两年里出现的经济减速的迹象使学者们对金砖国家"奇迹"产生了怀疑,引发了关于"普通金砖国家的崛起将顺从于个别金砖国家的崛起"的讨论。[23]中国两位数的增长率于2013年跌至8%以下,而其他新兴经济体的平均增长率下跌了4%,只有2.5%。[24]这不禁引发了一些人的疑问:"这是金砖国家的崛起,还是只是中国的崛起?"

在金砖集团内部,南非与其他国家相比经济规模非常小。另一方面,中国自从坐上世界第二大经济大国宝座以来,其经济体量又使其他成员国相形见绌。印度的人均GDP仅为1325美元,而巴西和俄罗斯则超过12 000美元(2011年的数据)。[25]与印度和巴西相比,中国和俄罗斯的经济相对开放。[26]巴西、印度和南非为富有活力的民主国家,中国是一个一党制国家,而俄罗斯是高度中央集权的体制。

然而,决定该集团是否可持续的主要并不是这些差异,而是中国这个庞然大物的存在。正如国王学院教授哈什·V. 潘特(Harsh V. Pant)指出的那样:"中国和金砖集团其他国家间在结构上的差异将是导致金砖集团功能紊乱的最重要因素。"[27]

不管怎样,中国是金砖国家间的纽带。其经济规模为该集团提供了动力。中国经济比所有其他金砖国家的经济总和还要大。[28]中国还是俄罗斯、巴西和南非最大的贸易伙伴,是印度的第二大贸易伙伴。同时,其他任何一个金砖国家对于中国来说在贸易额上都没有特别的重要性。它们之间的贸易量也不是特别大。值得注意的是,这五个国家之间似乎没有试图建立一个金砖国家自贸区,或对它们之间的贸易安排进行制度化。它们对此类经济融合似乎没有热情,尽管它们声称它们的经济规模加起来有能力重塑世界经济秩序。

毋庸置疑,金砖各国与西方的经济联系比它们彼此间的联系还要紧密。至于它们的外交政策联系,金砖国家位于世界不同的地区,大多数情况下只在多边场合才会碰面。作为它们彼此联系的纽带，中国在集团中，以及对该集团的态度将对有关合作起着推动或阻碍的作用。

中国经济在金砖国家中压倒性的优势已经引起了其他成员国对其在集团中主导地位的担忧，他们担心金砖国家会成为中国利益的工具。新开发银行就是一个有象征意义的例子。（在印度和俄罗斯的坚持下）各国同意对该行平等出资。它们还同意，所有成员具有平等的投票权。然而，平等并不一定意味着良好的合作。在这种多边机构中，领导力是很重要的。中国的经济规模和其与其他成员国的关系将可能使其有优势在该机构中扮演"协调者"的角色。[29][30]中国已经提出向凑足初始认缴资金有困难的巴西和南非提供补贴，如果这样，将提高中国在该银行的影响力。另一方面，中国对应急储备安排这个新基金的出资额是1000亿美元中的410亿，这个数字使所有其他成员国的出资额相形见绌。而这又为这些新机构中未来的权力分配埋下了猜忌的伏笔。尽管只是传闻，据说已经有批评者把将新银行的总部设在上海这个最大的成员国的城市与西方主导的金融机构的例子进行类比（如那些总部位于美国的机构）。[31]

来自印度这个最喜欢与中国对抗的伙伴的批评尤为激烈。2013年发表在《印度斯坦时报》上的一篇社论在谈论新开发银行时写道："中国太有钱，人们担心这家银行会成为北京的多边银行，这种担心已经使该银行先天不足。"社论继续写道："新德里虽然是该银行的倡议者，现在却踟蹰不前，生怕会用印度纳税人的钱为中国软实力的提升添砖加瓦。"[32]印度财政官员曾经指出，新开发银行将能使中国货币在海外的使用合法化。[33]尽管这些说法并不能代表官方的立场，它们还是反映了中国在该集团内占据压倒性优势带来的普遍的不信任，以及关于该银行作用的潜在的不同立场。

例如，中国的开发性金融活动可能会成为与其他金砖国家间不和的源泉。中国对基础设施"附带条件的援助"，对中国公司——大多数情况下是对国有公司——有利，同时其贷款大多与是否能帮助其获得自然资源密切相关。除经济原因外，中国还利用援助实现其外交政策目的，提升其在重要地缘政治地区的影响力。当国家借钱支持基础设施项目时（新开发银行的主要作用就是为发展中国家的基础设施项目提供资金），它们基本上就是获取外汇货币，作为项目进口所需的重要物资。鉴于中国在这些材料生产方面产能过剩，同时具备大量的工程技术和知识技能，参与这类项目相当于刺激国内经济，同时能提升其货币的国际化水平和其海外影响力。[34]

金砖国家会发现要协调资金和业务重点很困难，比如向谁提供资金以及通过什么途径提供援助等。这种不协调不仅与道德或不同的世界观有关，也源于利益方面的冲突。

中国太大，太有影响力，其观点不可能被忽视。传统上，对于自己不能高度控制的组织或安排，一般避免涉及。因此，项目资金来源的选择不仅会暴露金砖国家间的分歧，还将揭示谁最后会在最终决定时占得上风。金砖国家已经同意，新开发银行初期将为金砖国家自己的基础设施需求提供资金。但中国自己几乎不可能需要该银行的钱支持其发展项目。其他穷一些的金砖国家才可能需要这些资金。而这将强化集团内的不平衡。

中国对金砖国家的介入也是出于其全球战略利益的考虑。对中国来说，其经济的崛起是付出了代价的。由于其认为的美国的遏制和包围，外部环境发生了恶化。[35][36]然而，如果不把经济实力转变为综合国力，中国就不可能公开挑战美国的领先地位。因此，金砖国家对于中国建立自己的网络和合作伙伴关系以抗衡西方的霸主地位的努力似乎起着至关重要的作用。来自上海国际问题研究所的赵干城曾指出："（中国的）目标是通过合作强化其在国际体系中的地位，但同时，并不想以对抗的方式挑战美国。"[37]

尽管如此，无论中国何时和是否成功登上超级大国的位置，它似乎不可能一直如此看重金砖国家的重要性并推动"公平的"世界秩序。

比如，尽管多次发表了相互支持的声明，中国仍一直积极反对巴西和印度成为联合国安理会常任理事国的努力。[38][39]一方面，中国不愿意弱化其在联合国安理会中的制度性特权，俄罗斯也不愿意。另一方面，地缘政治方面的考虑似乎决定了中国对于联合国安理会改革的态度。中国和印度是地区性竞争对手，都寻求在相关邻近地区获得领导性地位。中印之间有未解决的边境争端，同时也对对方介入自己的势力范围保持警惕。印度对中国与其宿敌——巴基斯坦的紧密关系十分担心，而中国又因为印度"向东看"，即寻求深化印度与东亚国家合作的政策感觉受到了威胁。印度对日本支持其"入常"的态度投桃报李，也支持日本成为联合国安理会常任理事国，这又使问题进一步加剧。

前面提到的这些揭示了金砖国家间，尤其是相邻国家间要超越大国权力政治，寻求所谓的共同目标，中间还有很多困难。作为"主权鹰派"——这是学者们根据一些特征进行的归类[40]，一些人固执于对国家利益的狭隘理解，这使他们将地缘政治利益凌驾于任何多边合作之上。与中印关系相似的是，一种可怕的暗中竞争可能会破坏中俄两国合作的基础，而且可能会使金砖各国间相互猜疑。中国向中亚及俄罗斯远东地区的推进以及中国快速发展的经济和军事力量使俄罗斯警觉，它看到自己在自家后院的影响正在减弱。尽管莫斯科可能认为自己是中国平等的伙伴，但这个关系正日益变得不平等，这在未来会导致摩擦。

中国与其他两个金砖国家——巴西和南非的关系也并非没有任何问题。随着它们之间关系的发展，越来越多的分歧也浮出水面。中国对其货币的操纵已经给巴西和南非的制造领域带来明显的问题。2011年，巴西67%与中国产品构成竞争的出口业务失去了其国外市场份额。[41]巴西认为来自中国的竞争不公平，因为中国采取倾销政策。该国已开始对从中国进口的工业产品征收关税。[42]中国对南非经济不断增加的参与被认为威胁到了巴西对其周边市场的出口。[43]

南非的制造业也挣扎着与中国日益强大的经济影响力竞争。大量涌入的中国商品，已经导致明显的贸易不平衡，使南非越来越对中国保持警惕。[44]

七、合作中的障碍

即便中国接受"平等的"或者（更可能是）"平等关系中的老大"的角色，金砖国家间的合作还存在其他一些障碍。有些障碍已经在前文提到了，如传统的竞争关系（中印、中俄，等等）。当然，在社会和政治制度、民主原则和世界观方面也有明显的分歧。把该集团中的几个国家联合在一起的"共同价值观"少之又少。在国际论坛上合作时，它们通常不是阻挠、妨碍，就是非难，而不是提出积极的建议。在东盟地区论坛（ARF）上，中国和印度在这方面的表现尤为不好。该论坛有关超越信任建设措施、采取预防性外交政策（见《东盟地区论坛愿景宣言》）的努力遭到中国和印度的反对和阻挠。

正如前面提到的，除了日益加重的对与中国的双边贸易的依赖以外，各金砖国家对与外部国家的经济关系的依赖要大于它们互相之间的依赖。金砖国家之间的贸易和它们与美国、欧盟及一般意义上的西方的贸易额比起来不足挂齿。五个国家并没采取任何努力加强相互间的经济依赖或融合。印度甚至拒绝了中国对其参加在北京召开的2014年亚太经合组织（APEC）会议的邀请。在这次会议上，中国竭力推动亚洲太平洋地区进一步的经济一体化和合作。

金砖各国也都面临着重大的国内挑战，通常最突出的是腐败问题，但各国应对这些问题的方式和重点有所不同。政治团结方面也面临着挑战。面对俄罗斯粗暴干涉其邻国乌克兰的内部事务，金砖国家会继续保持沉默吗？中国持续在中亚扩大其影响力，这将带来什么后果？我们认为这个地区将最终上演 21 世纪版的"大博弈"，中国继续与巴基斯坦保持"特殊的伙伴关系"。如果印度和巴基斯坦这两个南亚邻国再度出现关系紧张（这几乎是不可避免的），会给中印合作带来什么样的影响？

即使是在原则上已经达成共识的领域，我们也没有看到付诸行动的具体建议。所有金砖成员国（和其他文明国家一样）都对"伊斯兰国"（ISIS）的反人类罪行表达了愤慨，认为宗教极端运动正带来日益严重的威胁。但他们对抗这种威胁的联合行动建议又在哪里？所有金砖国家都对大规模杀伤性武器的扩散感到忧虑，但都没有制定相关的行动路线图——实际上，其中有一个成员国至今还不是《核不扩散条约》的缔约国（把另一个金砖国家的核计划当作为自己的核武器计划的合法性辩护的主要借口之一）。

在本届"金砖国家治理体系与治理能力现代化建设国际研讨会"上，许多人都谈到金砖国家共同关注的问题，但很少有人提出具体解决这些问题的建议。确实，关于中国在十八届四中全会以后承诺改进自己本身的治理能力，大家谈了很多，很认真，很有见地，也很真诚，但对金砖集团如何推动更好的全球治理，中国有什么愿景，大家却没怎么提及。需要做的事情很多，可以从金砖智库委员会倡导的"二轨"机制出发，不仅制定共同的长期愿景和目标，还要制定实现这些愿景和目标的共同的战略和战术。正如其成员国明确指出的那样，金砖集团还是一个"成形中"的组织，至今还没有对这个组织进行过综合客观的分析。正如班宁·加雷特（Banning Garrett）建议的那样，需要从内部和外部对金砖集团进行深入的研究，金砖各国以及美国和欧盟也要共同对其进行研究。

八、结论

毫无疑问，"金砖国家"早已不只是投资论文中的一个术语，而已经成为一个现实的存在。它不仅充满活力，能对全球治理的常态产生影响，也似乎愿意朝这个方向共同努力。第一届首脑峰会召开至今才六年时间，金砖国家已经显示出它们积极参与全球治理议题的潜力，同时在多边机构中维护其共同的立场。签署成立新的金融机构是其发展中重要的一步，可能会挑战现有的全球安排，或对其起到补充的作用。

尽管如此，与其说它是一个国际性组织，不如说只是一个结构松散的国家群体，没有一个能起指导作用的共同的愿景。与欧盟，甚至与东盟不同，几乎不可能出现一个建立在共同的价值观或利益上的"金砖共同体"。迄今为止，把它们聚集在一起的与其说是共同追求的目标，不如说是因为它们都共同反对某种东西。它们之间的合作是因为有某些共同关切的一时便利之举，还是因为其他什么原因，还有待观察。

参考文献

［1］"BRICS Summit Issues Fortaleza Declaration：The New Development Bank and Contingent Reserve Arrangement Are Born"，*Larouche Pace*，July 15，2014，http：//larouchepac. com/node/31319.

［2］"BRICS Launch New Bank and Monetary Fund"，*Deutsche Welle*，July 16，2014，http：//www. dw. de/brics-launch-new-bank-and-monetary-fund/a-17789608.

［3］Mathur, S. , Dasgupta, M. and Sirohi, P. , *BRICS：Trade Policies，Institutions and Areas for Deepening Cooperation*，Indian Institute of Foreign Trade，Center for WTO Studies，New Delhi，2013，p. 4.

［4］Wilson, D. and Purushothaman, R. ，"Dreaming with BRICS：The Path to 2050"，*Goldman Sachs*，Global Economic Paper，Paper No. 99，p. 5.

［5］Vreeland J. R. ，"Governance at the International Monetary Fund"，*Georgetown University*，2009，pp. 6 – 7.

［6］Vreeland J. R. ，"Governance at the International Monetary Fund"，*Georgetown University*，2009，pp. 6 – 7.

［7］Stuenkel, O, "The Financial Crisis, Contested Legitimacy, and the Genesis of Intra-BRICS Cooperation"，*Global Governance*，19，2013，p. 615.

［8］"First Summit：Joint Statement of the BRIC Countries Leaders June 16，2009，Yekaerinburg, Russia"，http：//www. brics5. co. za/about-brics/summit-declaration/first-summit/.

［9］Roberts, S. , "Polity Forum：Challengers or Stakeholders? BRICS and the Liberal World Order：Intoduction"，*Polity*，Vol 42，No. 1，2010.

［10］Armijo, L. E and Roberts, C. , "The Emerging Powers and Global Governance：Why the BRICS Matter"，in Looney, R. (ed.)，*Handbook of Emerging Economies*，New York：Routledge，2014 forthcoming，pp. 1 – 27.

［11］"Sanya Declaration"，BRICS Information Centre，University of Toronto，April 14，2011 http：//www. brics. utoronto. ca/docs/110414-leaders. html.

［12］"The 6th BRICS Summit: Fortaleza Declaration", Information Centre, University of Toronto, July 15, 2014 http://www.brics.utoronto.ca/docs/.

［13］Keeler, C., "The End of Responsibility to Protect?" *Foreign Policy Journal*, October 12, 2011, http://www.foreignpolicyjournal.com/2011/10/12/the-end-of-the-responsibility-to-protect/.

［14］Bosco, L., "Abstention Games on the Security Council", *Foreign Policy*, March 17, 2011, http://bosco.foreignpolicy.com/posts/2011/03/17/abstention_ games_ on_ the_ security_ council.

［15］Stuenkel, O., "The BRICS and the Future of R2P: Was Syria or Libya the Exception", *Global Responsibility to Protect*, Vol. 6, Issue 1, 2014, p. 13.

［16］The Ministry of Foreign Affairs of the Russian Federation, "Statement in Explanation of Vote by Vitaly Churkin, Permanent Representative of the Russian Federation to the UN, on the Draft Resolution on the Situation in Syria", New York, October 4, 2011, http://www.mid.ru/bdomp/brp_ 4.nsf/e78a48070f128a7b43256999005bcbb3/9fd3c42bc7cfdddac3257 920004214bd%21OpenDocument.

［17］Gladstone, R. and Droubi, H., "Assad Sends Letters to Emerging Powers Seeking Help to End Syria War", *The New York Times*, March 27, 2013, http://www.nytimes.com/2013/03/28/world/middleeast/syrias-developments.html?_ r=1&.

［18］Armijo, L. E. and Roberts, C., "The Emerging Powers and Global Governance: Why the BRICS Matter", in Looney, R. (ed.), *Handbook of Emerging Economies*, New York: Routledge, 2014 forthcoming, p. 18.

［19］Gros et al., "The Case for IMF Quota Reform", *Council on Foreign Relations*, October 11, 2012, http://www.cfr.org/international-organizations-and-alliances/case-imf-quota-reform/p29248.

［20］Armijo, L. E and Roberts, C., "The Emerging Powers and Global Governance: Why the BRICS Matter", in Looney, R. (ed.), *Handbook of Emerging Economies*, New York: Routledge, 2014 forthcoming, p. 21.

［21］Rediker, D., "Losing at the IMF", *Foreign Policy*, October 10, 2012, http://www.foreignpolicy.com/articles/2012/10/10/losing_ at_ the_ imf.

［22］"The 6th BRICS Summit: Fortaleza Declaration", Information Centre, University of Toronto, July 15, 2014 http://www.brics.utoronto.ca/docs/.

［23］The Economist, "The BRIC Economies: Is the Fastest Period of Emerging-market Growth behind Us?" *Economist Debates*, August 20, 2013, http://www.economist.com/debate/days/view/1001.

［24］The Economist, "Global Economic Outlook 2015 — Key Findings", *The Conference Board*, November 2014, http://www.conference-board.org/data/globaloutlook/.

［25］Anon, "Chapter 1: Economic and Social Indicators: Comparison of BRICS Countries", *BRICS Joint Statistical Publication* 2012, 2012, p. 2 http://mospi.nic.in/mospi_

new/upload/bricks_ 2012_ 24aug12/htm/CHAPTER1. pdf.

[26] Toh, Ch. H. J, "Brazil, Russia, India and China (BRIC): Reshaping the World Order in the 21st Century", *US Naval War College* (no date), p. 3, https://www. usnwc. edu/Lucent/OpenPdf. aspx? id = 93.

[27] Pant, H. V., "The BRICS Fallacy", *The Washington Quarterly*, Vol. 36, No 3, 2013, p. 97.

[28] Pant, H. V., "The BRICS Fallacy", *The Washington Quarterly*, Vol. 36, No 3, 2013, p. 98.

[29] Krishnan, A., "China Shows Economic Clout with Push for New Banks", *The Hindu Business Line*, July 16, 2014, http://www. thehindubusinessline. com/economy/policy/china-shows-economic-clout-with-push-for-new-banks/article6217962. ece.

[30] Chowdhury, J., "Big BRICS for Small Nations: How Unconditional the NDB Conditions Be?" *Russia Today*, July 25, 2014, http://rt. com/op-edge/175512-brics-china-new-development-bank/.

[31] Sharma, M. S., "BRICS Bank: Worthless at Best, a Disaster at Worst", *Business Standard*, 2014, http://www. business-standard. com/article/economy-policy/brics-bank-worthless-at-best-a-disaster-at-worst-114071600571_ 1. html.

[32] "The Foundation Is a Bit Shaky", *The Hindustan Times*, March 28, 2013, http://www. hindustantimes. com/comment/editorials/the-foundation-is-a-bit-shaky/article1-1033876. aspx.

[33] Bagchi, I., "BRICS Summit: Member Nations Criticize the West for Financial Mismanagement", *The Times of India*, March 30, 2012, http://timesofindia. indiatimes. com/india/BRICS-summit-Member-nations-criticizes-the-West-for-financial-mismanagement/articleshow/12462502. cms.

[34] Weeks, J., "The New BRICS Bank — Force for Progress or Cause for Concern?" *Policy Research in Macroeconomics*, 2014, http://www. primeeconomics. org/? p = 3152.

[35] Glosny, M. A., "China and the BRICS: A Real (but limited) Partnership in a Multipolar World", *Polity*, Vol. 42, No. 1, 2010, p. 112.

[36] Sun, Y., "BRICS and China's Aspiration for the New 'International Order' ", *Brookings*, 2013, http://www. brookings. edu/blogs/up-front/posts/2013/03/25-xi-jinping-china-brics-sun.

[37] Glosny, M. A., "China and the BRICS: A Real (but limited) Partnership in a Multipolar World", *Polity*, Vol. 42, No. 1, 2010, p. 138.

[38] Tellis, A. and Mirski, S., "Crux of Asia: China, India and the Emerging Global Order", *Carnegie Endowment for International Peace*, 2013, http://carnegieendowment. org/files/crux_ of_ asia. pdf.

[39] [20] Armijo, L. E and Roberts, C., "The Emerging Powers and Global Governance: Why the BRICS Matter", in Looney, R. (ed.), *Handbook of Emerging Economies*, New

York: Routledge, 2014 forthcoming, p. 14.

［40］Roberts, S. , "Polity Forum: Challengers or Stakeholders? BRICS and the Liberal World Order: Intoduction", *Polity*, Vol. 42, No. 1, 2010, pp. 1 – 13.

［41］Anguilar, C. G. , "China-Brazil Relations: Disputes with Regional Implications", *Americas Program*, 2011, http://www.cipamericas.org/archives/5525.

［42］Pant, H. V. , "The BRICS Fallacy", *The Washington Quarterly*, Vol. 36, No. 3, 2013.

［43］Pereira, C. and De Castor Neves, J. A. , "Brazil and China: South-South Partnership or North South Competition?" *Brookings*, Policy Paper, No. 26, 2011, p. 6, http://www.brookings.edu/~/media/research/files/papers/2011/4/03%20brazil%20china%20pereira/03_brazil_china_pereira.pdf.

［44］Pant, H. V. , "The BRICS Fallacy", *The Washington Quarterly*, Vol. 36, No 3, 2013, p. 99.

德国经验与金砖国家治理*

[德] 卡斯腾·科伯尔**

女士们、先生们：

对于德国来说，今年这个11月份有着特殊的意义，因为这个月发生了两件历史性事件。

第一件事：就在几天前，也就是11月9日，我们举行了柏林墙倒塌25周年庆祝活动。我们沿柏林墙设立了8000个白色发光气球，长度绵延15公里。在上百万人的欢呼声中，这道发光的气球墙上升到柏林市的夜空中。

第二件事：几天后，我们将会实现我们期待已久的零赤字。德国联邦议院将迎来自1969年以来的首次预算平衡，45年以来首次无任何新债务产生！

通过这两个重大事件，我想同大家谈谈以下三件事情：

首先，东德解体和德国统一的原因；

其次，我们应从中得出的与我们目前的预算和财政政策有关的结论；

以及第三，金砖国家在这种形势下必然会面临的挑战。

一、东德解体和德国统一的原因

乍一看，柏林墙的倒塌和零赤字之间没有任何联系。但是，这两者对德国未来的意义不容忽视。这两件事情都很重要，且其重要意义不仅限于德国。我经常会听到外国友人和合作伙伴提及这两件事情，可见它们的重要性已超越了国界。这就是为什么今天我想和大家谈谈这两件事情。

1989年，冷战仍在继续。德国与欧洲出现分歧。很多人长期以来屈服

---

* 本文为作者在研讨会上的讲稿，标题为编者所加。

** 卡斯腾·科伯尔（Carsten Körber），德国联邦议会议员。

于现状,没有任何变化。然而,1989年的秋天,在短短几个星期内,情况发生转变。成千上万人突然走上街头为争取自由权而抗议。我出生在东德,那时我还是一个11岁的小学生。

东德领导层——政治、道义和经济上行将灭亡的阶层——无力应对这些示威活动。11月9日,当柏林墙被破坏时,东德的命运也就此无力回转了。

是什么导致了东德的解体呢?在我看来,有两个因素发挥了重要的作用:指令型经济体制和对个体的压迫。

即使在今天,国家也会经常参与到业务活动中,例如基本服务(如水、电、气)的提供。但是,单凭参与业务活动并不能构成指令型经济体制。在东德,国家会对商业、工业和贸易活动进行严格的监管。朝鲜和古巴如今仍是如此,但是即使是在这些国家,人们也会抱有改革的愿望。

东德的国家控制经济体制及其刚性五年规划无法满足人们的经济需求。40年以来,人们一直受中央计划经济体制的监管,从而导致了"短缺经济"。家庭通常要等上五年才能买得起一套公寓,十年后才能安装电话,十五年后,才能买得起特拉贝特(东德制造的一款汽车)。

与此同时,自20世纪70年代末以来,东德人民一直过着一种入不敷出的生活,其实以前也是如此。东德即将面临崩溃,要是没有两德统一,它早在1990年就已经崩溃了。这就是东德灭亡的经济原因。

东德灭亡的人文和社会原因在于这样一个事实,即人们深刻地认识到自己的不自由。重压之下,国家必然会灭亡。我给大家举两个例子:根据人口规模统计数据,1989年,斯塔西(Stasi,东德国家安全部门)可谓是人类历史上最大的情报机构,每180个居民中就有一名全职员工。互不信任使一切事物变得虚伪。此外,东德人被禁止出国,这一规定更加恶化了这一情形。在政党和国家眼中,只有那些享有特权的人才可以访问社会主义兄弟国家。按照规定,只有退休人员才能访问西德(德意志联邦共和国)。

正是这两个因素——经济制约和被囚禁感——的综合作用才导致了东德的灭亡。然而,1989年距现在已经有25年了,如今一切都变了。这就是为什么当看到这么多人在街头庆祝,我会感到很高兴。在德国联邦议院,听到德国总理默克尔在仪式上讲话,很多同事都感动得热泪盈眶。

直至今日,这个日子仍会使德国人为之动容。这个日子告诉我们,自由不是理所应当的事。在这一点上,朝鲜也给我们敲响了警钟。这一点是值得一提的,因为我经常会感到许多德国人认为日常中的自由是理所应当的。我们现在生活富裕，以至于我们都忘了我们现在所享受的自由和繁荣都不是自然而来或不言而喻的。

在柏林墙倒塌25周年纪念日之际，我们应该思考一下德国的未来。为打造美好的未来，我们必须记住过去，并从前车之览中吸取教训。

其中一个教训是，从长远来看，如果一个国家想要成功并延续下去，其经济表现必须与消费相匹配。

二、德国目前的使命

鉴于这样一个历史背景，德国目前这一代政治家肩负着特殊的使命。为了实现当前和未来的美好生活，我们应该从东德的灭亡中吸取什么经验教训呢？

德国（联邦、州和地方当局）现有债务总额约为2.5万亿美元。约占德国国内生产总值的75%，即人均31 000美元，这是一个事实。欧元区国家（如意大利和法国）甚至可能会面临更沉重的债务。但事实是，德国的债务现在已经达到了一个需要予以响应的规模。

我们已经意识到，在过去几十年中，德国人的生活明显入不敷出。因此，前联邦政府和各州政府采取了相应的行动。例如，"债务刹车"政策的采用，实际上就是禁止新债务的产生，这是一项正确的决策。我们目前正在编制2015年的预算——1969年以来的首次零赤字预算。这是一个没有任何新债务的预算。我们的目标是，截至2017年，将我们的债务占国内生产总值的比例减少至60%。

作为联邦议院预算委员会的一员，当然，我很高兴我们能实现零赤字预算。但我也知道，零赤字应该是一种规范。每年都应实现零赤字。

德意志联邦共和国面临着巨大的挑战。其社会市场经济亦是如此，尽管其自1950年以来有力地推动了经济的增长和繁荣。幸运的是，这一体制很成功，因此我们能成功地将末期疲弱的经济（如东德经济）整合进这一体制中。

这一模式依赖于正在不断向各人群阶层蔓延的繁荣情景。因为只有实现繁荣，经济和社会发展才能称得上成功。此外，这是一条久经验证的正确道路，财富的重新分配不会使推动生产力发展的因素承受繁重的负担。否则会对整体经济状况造成损害。

如果认真听，就会听到越来越多的德国人说，事情不能一如既往永远发展下去，我们需要新的控制措施，我们在经济管理方面要更加理性和富有远见，我们必须认识到我们很难维持长期繁荣。我们不能忽视这些警告。

社会主义所青睐的指令型经济体制已经过时了,越来越多的征兆表明,"不惜一切代价发展"的资本主义信条才是最终的出路。我们需要实现可持续发展。我们必须充分利用我们的自然资源并重视环境保护。

世界正在迅速变化。这种变化每天都在发生。金砖国家的崛起就是一个有力的证明。而且金砖国家发展状况良好。它们一直在赶超我们。

金砖国家致力于实现我们所拥有的一切,但又不会盲目照搬,它们成功地避免了我们曾经犯过的一些失误。5亿欧洲人,近9%的世界人口,GDP却能占世界GDP的25%。我们支付的社会保障福利占世界社会保障福利的50%以上。其中,大部分由德国支付。我们能承担得起这笔开支,这点很好,但是如果承担不起,最终结果只会是毁灭。

我是社会保障的坚定拥护者——强者始终都应该照顾弱者。但是,如果德国选择将一半以上的金钱用于资助社会保障福利(养老金、医疗保险和失业保险),而投资资金却不到这一总数的10%,在我看来,这种做法不是很明智。

目前,大约有157种与家庭相关的福利。这些福利每年要花费数十亿欧元。然而,我们却无法制定一种足以维持现有交通基础设施的投资方案。

结果会怎样呢?目前没有证据表明,任何家庭会因为这157种方案而多生一个孩子。但交通运输部证实,在德国现有的39000个公路桥梁中,15%亟待维修,而在26000个铁路桥梁中,三分之一处于危急状态。

我们目前是世界上领先的工业国家之一。然而,德国原材料缺乏。我们的人口正在萎缩。那么,如何才能维持这种领先优势呢?方法还是有的,也就是所谓的"通过创新实现增长"。因此,我们必须坚定不移地沿着我们选择的道路走下去。无论是今天、明天,还是后天。

世界不会停下前进的步伐来等我们。它正在迅速改变。如今,我也看到了中国的迅速变化。许多国家把我们当作榜样来效仿。他们从我们这里吸取经验教训,从而超越我们。

三、金砖国家面临的挑战

赶超和经济增长对金砖国家意味着什么?

● 会更加繁荣。更加繁荣就会意味着少生孩子。从长远来看,少生孩子就会导致人口问题。而一个国家的社会保障制度越广泛,其预算问题就会越糟糕。德国就是如此。

- 一个人越富裕,就会越自信,其参与政治和社会事务的愿望就会越强烈。这是我们从过去吸取的经验。历史还告诉我们,一种制度要想成功,其所依附的社会就必须创建参与所需的结构。
- 自"二战"以来,德意志联邦共和国的发展史正好说明了这一点。事实上,值得注意的是,其他国家也渴望拥有我们这种经济体制,但他们更渴望的是我们的开放和自由的社会,以及我们的生活方式。

德国如今是怎样的一种状况呢?新债务禁令("债务刹车")是近代最重要的政治决定之一。这对公共财政的可行性来说至关重要。在德国,人口结构的变化并不是一种新现象。老龄化人口越来越多,新生婴儿越来越少。我们必须证明我们的公共财政足以应付这种变化。

人口结构的变化将成为近几年,乃至近几十年来的一个重要的社会挑战。尤其是在当前的背景下,如果一个国家想要长期运行下去,健全的公共财政是一个基本前提。

工作人员的数量越来越少,资源和收入也在逐渐减少,而社会保障支出却在不断增加。越来越少的年轻人需要供养越来越多的老年人。即使是在今天,我们仍然可以预见,我们社会的年龄分布变化将会对我们的公共预算产生极大的影响。为了能在恰当的时机选择正确的道路,我们现在就要密切关注潜在的风险。而且,我们还必须坚持实现零赤字。

四、结论

预算管制并不是结束。只有实行稳健的财政管理政策的国家才算是一个正常运作中的国家。在经济低谷时期或在紧急情况下,健康的公共财政制度可以创造回旋的余地。零赤字预算可以激发人们对未来的信心。这种信心反过来还会有助于实现可持续增长。健全的公共财政是经济成功的基础。

德国从欧洲债务危机中吸取了有用的经验教训。我们将继续坚定不移地走可持续预算和财政政策这条道路。

在结束之前,我想对你们说,希望你们不要照搬我们在足球场上的经验,因为我们还想再次在2018年俄罗斯世界杯中夺冠!

然而,如果你们打算效仿我们现在的预算和财政政策,我们会很高兴见到。

BRICS: Not Glittering?

Papers from "The International Seminar on the Modernization of Governance Systems and Capacity of the BRICS Countries"

金砖在失色？ | "金砖国家治理体系和治理能力现代化建设国际研讨会"论文集

Deepening BRICS Cooperation with the Society Governed by Law

Guo Yezhou*

Distinguished guests, ladies and gentlemen:

First of all, please allow me to offer my warm congratulations on the successful opening of the "International Symposium on Building Modernized Governance Systems and Capabilities of BRICS Countries" and on the arrival of all the distinguished friends from BRICS countries, the United States, Europe and other countries and regions on behalf of the International Department of the Central Committee of CPC and China Center for Contemporary World Studies. Here, I would like to express my gratitude to concerned units and individuals from China and foreign countries for their devotion and contribution to this meeting. Among them, I would like to mention Konrad-Adenauer Foundation. Although it is not a member of BRICS cooperation mechanism, it is making its best endeavor to conduct a dialogue among friends of BRICS countries to discuss issues of common interest. I would like to take this opportunity to show my appreciation to Konrad-Adenauer Foundation.

The term "BRICS" emerged almost at the same with the birth of the new century. It was put forward by Goldman Sachs economist O'Neill in 2001. In the past 13 years, BRICS countries not only leaped into the front ranks of the world in economic growth, but also made significant progress in social development and poverty eradication, having made outstanding contribution to the implementation of the UN Millennium

---

* Guo Yezhou is Deputy Minister of the International Department of the Central Committee of CPC.

Development Goals. After the outbreak of the global financial crisis in 2008, BRICS countries have made even more extraordinary contribution to global economic and trade growth and become an ignorable figure in world economic development. Of course, we also note that during the past two years, BRICS countries faced significant downward pressure in terms of development. They are facing many challenges in social governance and many negative voices are merging among the international community, such as "BRICS is falling down ", "falling BRICS". We can interpret these views from two perspectives. On the one hand, someone hopes to bring BRICS down with these views, since like economic issues, 50% political issues are associated with psychology. On the other hand, these views remind us of a fact that in building national governance system and fostering national governance capacities, BRICS countries (including China) are indeed facing many challenges and new opportunities. For this reason, the Communist Party of China made a decision to deepen reform on the Third Plenary Session of the 18th Central Committee of the CPC in 2013 and to build a country governed by law on the Fourth Plenary Session of the 18th Central Committee in 2014. The two decisions serve a common goal, that is to promote the modernization of national governance system and governance capabilities to realize "two century goals" and the "China Dream", i.e. the great revival of the Chinese nation. I would like to give a brief review on relevant contents of the Fourth Plenary Session of the 18th Central Committee to you.

Foreign friends often ask me about two questions: firstly, is it feasible to govern a country by law and how to make it in conformity and compatible with China's current political system, in particular with the party system; secondly, how to realize the coordination between the process of promoting a country governed by law and the traditional culture and civilization. For the first question, my answer is yes and we must say yes, because a country governed by law is the only correct path proved by positive and negative lessons during the process of realizing modernization in many countries and also a correct path proved over the past 60 years' development experience and lessons. China must take the path of building a country governed by law to promote the modernization of national government system and governance capacities. As with how to make it in conformity and compatible with the traditional culture and political system, the Fourth Plenary Session of the 18th Central Committee gives us the following answers:

Firstly, realize the governance of the country by constitution. The Constitution is the fundamental law of China and the basis for all legal activities. In China, ruling a country by law means ruling it by the Constitution, and law-based administration refers to constitution-based administration. With regards to this, a lot of specific measures were proposed in the Fourth Plenary Session of the 18th Central Committee. For example, in order to improve the social and universal understanding of the Constitution and the consciousness of abiding by the Constitution, we designated December 4 as the National Constitution Day and officials nominated at the National People's Congress and its Standing Committee shall make a vow to the Constitution.

Secondly, make the government ruled by law. The government must act according to the law, specify responsibilities and duties and draw a clear line between the administration of law and the government by law. We are developing these two lists, in which we will specify what and how the government should perform.

Thirdly, realize judicial justice and judicial independence. Judging from the text alone, China's current legal system is sound and complete. Of course, we will bring some policies and experience to the legal level timely in accordance with the needs of reform and development and make adjustments and amendments to the existing law as needed. However, what's more important is how to implement the existing law in a fair and transparent manner. For this purpose, the Fourth Plenary Session of the 18th Central Committee brings forth several specific measures. For example, intensify the efforts for the cultivation of judges and lawyers; ensure the independence of human, finance and object through a variety of mechanisms of courts at all levels to avoid the influence of the interests of local government on the judicial process; record and disclose the judicial intervention of all government officials or party cadres and make a claim for lifelong responsibilities for serious consequences; judges shall adopt lifelong responsibility system for their judgments and so on.

Fourthly, build a society ruled by law. Let more people learn legal knowledge and enhance their consciousness of law abidance, law protection and law enforcement. Since farming civilization had been long dominated in China, our understanding of the law is not the same with other countries. My father told me that in the village where he grew up, most people think that the law mainly refers to the criminal law, and traffic law, tax law and environmental protection law are not the law in the true sense. A person will feel ashamed if he violates the criminal law and would not mention about such a thing, but one who violates the traffic law would not think so and sometimes would show off in his circle of friends. The building of a society governed by law is to make Chinese citizens to cherish the law government spirit and produce the awareness of abiding the law and safeguarding the dignity of the law. The task of cultivation of judges and formulating laws is tough. By contrast, the task of cultivating the society governed by law is even tougher.

Fifthly, combine the rule of law and the rule of virtue. We all know the benefits of the rule of law. However, China is such a vast country with distinct diversity that we cannot legalize all social life, which means high social governance costs. China is a country with 5000 years of civilization. In the course of 5000 years of development, many unwritten moral standards have formed and engraved in people's minds, which restrict people's moral behaviors and are the basic reference for us to manage this society. We want to bring them into full play in the process of building a country governed by the law. "Rule of virtue" is a typical saying with Chinese characteristics. In fact, it is adopted in the management practices in many countries. I have discussed the rule of virtue with my family and my father gave me a simple answer. He said that when you drive along the road when the green light is on according to the traffic law, it is driving by law, but when you stop the car in case someone is standing in the middle of the road, it is driving by virtue. I think this is a common sense in all countries. The rule of virtue is particularly important for China given its vastness and diversity. Therefore, we must play the role of moral code accumulated during the 5000 years' civilization in China's future governance process.

The Fourth Plenary Session of the 18th Central Committee proposed over 185 reform initiatives. I would not introduce them one by one, but I hope you can learn more about the contents of relevant documents and materials. After a careful reading, you will grasp the basic outline and direction of the future development of China, which is the basic reference to promote mutual knowledge. Mutual knowledge is the basis of mutual understanding, and mutual understanding is the prerequisite for mutual cooperation.

The structured cooperation has been implemented among BRICS countries for some time. In line with the open, inclusive, cooperative and win-win spirit, BRICS countries have made great progress through mutual cooperation. **Firstly, the cooperation content is deepened.** Starting from economic and trading issues, New Development Bank (NDB) and Contingency Reserve Arrangement were launched at the BRICS Summit in Fortaleza in 2014, marking the significant progress of BRICS cooperation. **Secondly, the cooperation scope is broadened.** We not only included South Africa in BRICS cooperation mechanism in 2010, and broadened the cooperation scope from economic and trading fields to political, security, environmental protection, human rights and some other fields. Trading and economic contents account for one third of the content of *Fortaleza Declaration,* which is a good proof. **Thirdly, mutual support and mutual coordination of multilateral institutions and multilateral occasion continue to strengthen.** Within the G20 and UN framework, BRICS countries are demonstrating their common position actively. I remember that in the Nuclear Security Summit held in March 2014 in the Netherlands, ministers of the five countries reached consensus on international issues. All these have demonstrated the positive results achieved by BRICS with the implementation of structured cooperation, as well as the joyous development momentum of cooperation.

BTTC plays a very important role in BRICS cooperation process. Think tanks are known as the "idea factory" and "policy base". BTTC has set up a council to give ideas and thoughts for the structured cooperation for BRICS countries. After BTTC's discussion, many ideas and thoughts have been included into the highest political level in BRICS cooperation mechanism. We are particularly pleased about it. Today, the holding of "International Symposium on Building Modernized Governance Systems and Capabilities of BRICS Countries" is another important event during the cooperation process of BTTC. I hope everyone would exchange views frankly in the discussion process, and say all things without reserve. Everything we discussed here are likely to be reflected in the governance practices of all countries in different forms. I also want to make a significant contribution in promoting BRICS countries to participate in global governance and realizing the modernization of governance systems and capabilities of BRICS countries during the process of two days' discussion.

At last, I wish the conference a great success. Thank you!

Cooperation among BRICS in Order to Influence Global Governance

Renato Baumann[*]

1. An Increasing Concern: Risk of Losing Focus

The set of countries known as BRICS was formally created in 2009, in a Summit that took place in Ekaterimburg, Russia. The Declaration divulged after the Summit contains 16 articles, and is essentially focused on the perception that the (then) four economies, are big and strong enough so as to be entitled to have a more significant saying in the global governance. It establishes the periodical meeting of Heads of State, Ministers of Foreign Affairs and Finance, as well as cooperation in security and agriculture. It also establishes mechanisms for an active participation of the civil society, via the business forum and an annual meeting of think tanks.

That position regarding their objective to influence global governance was a reflection of the significantly higher rates of GDP growth that the emerging economies presented in comparison to the industrialized economies: between 2005 and 2009 (when the first Summit took place), the average yearly GDP growth rates were as follows: Brazil 3.6%; Russia 4.1%; India 8.1% and China 11.4%. In this same period, the set of high income countries grew at an average yearly rate of 0.9% and the world as a whole at 2.1%.

The sixth Summit took place in 2014, in Fortaleza, Brazil. The

---

[*] Renato Baumann is the Director of International Division, Instituto de Pesquisa Economica Aplicada (IPEA), Professor of the Department of Economics of Universidade de Brasilia and Instituto Rio Branco, the Brazilian Diplomatic Academy.

Declaration issued after that meeting has no less than 72 articles (followed by a Plan of Action with 23 items and a list of other five "new areas for cooperation to be considered"). Needless to say, the types of subjects covered by these Articles are quite diversified.

Most analyses of the Fortaleza Summit tend to focus almost exclusively on the official creation of the BRICS Development Bank and the Contingent Reserve Agreement, and tend to ignore other decisions that are also very important.

For instance, the Fortaleza Declaration brings explicit references to the Post-2015 Development Agenda for the United Nations, to the adoption of common methodologies for social indicators, to the cooperation among the export credit agencies of the five countries, to a possible cooperation among the agencies of the five countries providing insurance and reinsurance, to a demand for a revision of quotas in the World Bank, to the adoption of a code of conduct for activities in the outer space, to cooperation in the fight against cybercrimes and corruption, among other subjects.

Two other dimensions are worth stressing. First, since the Durban Summit, the Declarations have mentioned the concern by the BRICS with regard to other countries that are not part of the group. In the Durban Declaration, 7 countries are explicitly mentioned, whereas the Fortaleza Declaration refers to no less than 12① countries. This is clearly a new, unprecedented position by the group with regard to the international scenario.

A second important aspect is that following the Durban Summit, the Heads of State of the BRICS countries have met their counterparts from Africa. It was understood that the formal participation of South Africa in the BRICS was less due to its economic potential than to its relative importance in regional terms. But several analysts were surprised to learn that following the Fortaleza Summit, the BRICS Heads of State have met a number of Latin American Heads of States. This brings into the group a regional dimension that was absent until now, and one that

---

① If the reference to the "arab-israeli" conflict is considered as one item in that statistic.

might have significant implications.

These sets of information suggest two types of interpretation. First, as illustrated by the number of articles in the six Summits, the number of issues dealt with by the BRICS has been increasing quite significantly. Second, and directly linked to the former, the formation of the group started with a cautious approximation, on the basis of the dissatisfaction by the four original countries with regard to their role in influencing global governance. Over time what was essentially an exercise based on an economic dimension has gained new dimensions and evolved towards totally new areas.

The official justification for this diversification of agenda is that because the mutual knowledge among these countries is limited, to the extent that there is an increase in the areas of common interest the higher the chance to identify the margin for joint action.

It goes without saying that the risk implicit in this strategy is for the group to lose focus on what is it that maintains their cohesion and homogeneous positions.

2. Margin for Hope: The Potential for Complementarity

The debates on the BRICS often stress four characteristics.

First, it is already well-known that the acronym was created by an economist from the financial market, who wanted an expression that could facilitate the reference to a few economies with good business opportunities.

Second, there are frequent manifestations of skepticism with regard to the future of the group, given that the five countries have quite diversified historical trajectories, with apparently different interests and different productive structures.

Third, emphasis is given to the basic features that have led to the very formation of the group. They are associated with a number of indicators. For instance, Brazil, Russia, India and China are (together with the US) the only countries that present simultaneously three conditions:(1) large geographic dimensions (over 2 million square kilometers); (2) a nominal

GDP over 600 billion US $; and (3) big population, over 100 million inhabitants. Furthermore, these countries concentrate half of the world poor population. The BRICS account for 42% of the total world population, 14% of world GDP and approximately 3/4 of total foreign currency reserves.①

All the BRICS belong to the financial G20, the most important existing forum as far as the global governance is concerned. According to some of the participants in those meetings, before the G20 meetings there have been systematic negotiations among the BRICS, far more intensely than by each BRICS with its neighbors. This seems to indicate that the five give a more significant weight to their joint position than to acting as representatives of specific regions.

One element that might contribute to consolidate the cohesion among the five countries is trade. But the actual weight of bilateral trade differs among BRICS. The "BRIC-Dependency" is more intense for Brazil than for any other of the five countries. Furthermore, the intensity of trade among the five is varied: whereas for Brazil it surpasses 20%, for China it does not reach 8%. It follows that joint interests should be looked for elsewhere.

The five countries present less fiscal problems than most rich economies and all of them are lenders to the US, via their stocks of US Treasury bonds. Since they contribute with over 80 billion US $ to the multilateral financial institutions, it is to be expected that the BRICS will over time keep pressing for reforms in the decision process in these organizations.

Furthermore, all the BRICS are now classified as "investment grade", and this status is bound to remain unaltered in the short run. Even if some of them, like Brazil and Russia, remain far too dependent upon the exports of commodities, hence more vulnerable to price fluctuations.

It is often forecasted that the BRICS (China in particular) will soon surpass the US economy. This makes the five economies not only economic powers but inevitably also active agents in the process of

---

① China alone accounts for almost 3/4 of the BRICS 4 trillion US $ worth of reserves, an indication of the difficulties met in identifying the procedures to help economies with liquidity shortage.

defining global policies.

Another skeptical view, less explored, puts emphasis on the fact that the five countries have different historical records of conflicts with their neighbors. More recently there has been open armed conflict between Russia and Ukraine and potential problems in the China Sea. India also has recurrent problems with its neighborhood.

This can impose a diplomatic challenge to the BRICS. A good deal of the justifications for the creation of the group has been associated with the joint will to influence more explicitly the global governance. This implicitly questions the existing order. It is not to say that the BRICS have an anti-Western speech, but clearly their decisions have to do with the search for an alternative international order. The capacity to influence the existing order has to do with the degree of cohesion among the BRICS. It is a basic condition for them to act jointly and in the same direction.

To the extent that the regional conflicts lead to the adoption of sanctions by the Western economies, this leads to a sensitive situation in that the required group cohesion will call for the support by the other BRICS. This will be no easy task if the other BRICS adopt a more pro-Western position in relation to each specific conflict.

In summary, there are elements that justify both overly optimist forecasts with regard to the BRICS as well as arguments to question that possibility.

3. Influencing Global Governance

What have been the major changes since the first BRICS Summit?

As shown before, one clear change has been the widening of the agenda. This broadens the potential for joint interest and mutual knowledge, at the same time that imposes the risk of losing focus in the definition of the actual objectives of the group.

Another difference has been the reduction in the differential of yearly rates of GDP growth between the set of emerging economies and the rich countries. Closer rates of growth weakens the "negotiating" position of the former, since the amount of time needed for catching up becomes much longer than before. What seemed to be a pressing reality justifying a high-speed change in global governance has become a little more than a desirable adjustment.

One often mentioned victory by the BRICS is the official approval of changes in the IMF quotas. Yet resistance from the US Congress (as well as from the European countries) has led to a situation of a non-materialized gain, since those changes have not taken place as yet.

At the World Trade Organization, the original initiatives that could have led to the take-off of the Doha Round of Multilateral Negotiations have been killed by an intra-BRICS disagreement that led to Indian resistance in relation to agricultural policies.

These points should be complemented by two basic characteristics: (1) intra-trade among BRICS still presents a number of barriers and low perspective of overcoming them: the efforts made to map the products with comparative advantages by each BRICS that faced barriers imposed by other BRICS has only been submitted to the Ministers of Trade in Fortaleza, with no concrete action afterwards; (2) bilateral investment flows remain predominantly resource-based.

In recent years the relative weakening of the WTO has had as a parallel movement the negotiation of an increasing number of bilateral and plurilateral preferential agreements. Some of these negotiations[①] take place among the biggest economies and comprise disciplines that go well beyond what have ever been negotiated within the WTO. This poses a challenge, in that some of the BRICS do not participate in any of these initiatives. Given the dimensions involved and the degree of ambition of the negotiating agendas, it is easy to fear that there might be significant impact over most trade flows.

Taken together, these features call for a cautious appraisal of the potential of the BRICS to influence global governance. Things have changed since the Ekaterimbug Summit. This is not to dismiss the

---

① The Transatlantic Trade Partnership (TTP), the US-European Union Free Trade Agreement (TTIP), the Regional Economic Partnership among Asian countries (RCEP), the Agreement on Services (TISA), just to name the most significant.

potential for BRICS countries to influence global governance. It may be that the intensity of gains might not be as big as originally expected, but a good deal of negotiating power remains in the hands of the five countries.

One dimension that the BRICS have to keep in mind is that they are not a new Bretton Woods. This means that all the negotiations have to take place in accordance to the existing rules and within the existing institutional apparatus.

Take, for instance, the BRICS Development Bank. A skeptical view would stress the small capital originally approved, much smaller than, say, the World Bank, not to mention some domestic Development Bank in the BRICS themselves, like the Chinese and the Brazilian development banks. This perception disregards the facts that (1) it is wiser to start a bank as a small player and gradually gain confidence by the financial market and (2) once formally created, the instrument can always be used to broaden its capital as well as to diversify its lines of action.

In view of these new features, what are some actual possibilities for the BRICS to influence global governance? One might suggest a few lines for action.

An important — rather inevitable — point of departure is to realize that the higher the degree of cohesion among the BRICS, the stronger their capacity to influence the international scenario.

The first set of initiatives has to do, therefore, with the promotion of convergence among the five economies. These initiatives comprise: (1) cooperation via the reduction in trade barriers in intra-BRICS trade; (2) cooperation in the exchange of technologies; (3) cooperation in the food and energy sectors; (4) more investment in infrastructure; (5) cooperation in fighting corruption and fiscal evasion; (6) accepting suggestions from the business and the think-tank councils, in order to identify new areas of action and/or new approaches.

Second, since the Fortaleza Summit, the BRICS have at their disposal a policy tool with a significant potential. The Development Bank is the first international institution since Bretton Woods that is not regional, but comprises partners from different regions. It must operate in accordance to the good practices of the financial markets, but at the same time it can be used in ways that make it independent and different from other multilateral institutions. An efficient operation by the Bank can become an important economic and political tool. From the moment of its formal creation, the BRICS Development Bank can become even more instrumental if the country members increase its capital. The analyses of the Bank should not forget that the most important aspect of it is the very fact of its existence as a mechanism that can be improved.

Third, the BRICS countries can and should try to influence the overall trade scenario. Russia is the most recent member of the WTO. But all the others have over time manifested their inconformity with the way the developing economies have achieved gains from the negotiations, as well as with the permanence of policies adopted by rich countries that negatively affect the economies of the less wealthy countries, such as export subsidies and a varied range of non-tariff barriers.

Recovering the capacity of the WTO to host multilateral negotiations, apart from its disciplinary role, is a must. This has to be done, however, in accordance with the new features of trade. The BRICS countries should join efforts to try and influence the adoption of some criteria that is harming or is bound to harm them in the near future.

At least two dimensions are to be worried about with regard to trade.

The BRICS should try to make joint efforts so as to develop a coordinated action in order to face the likely effects of the mega-agreements now being negotiated. Several BRICS do not participate in these negotiations, but all of them are subject to suffer the consequences of the new features being negotiated.

Another increasing concern has to do with the need of a concerted action in order to foster technical cooperation and harmonization of norms, so as to be able to cope with the so-called "private standards", based on which firms in the rich, importing countries determine the minimum standards to be adopted by certain products and deny the imports in case of non-compliance. Because this is not a governmental action, there is no ground for any formal complaint. Yet the consequences can be drastic for the exports from developing economies.

Fourth, there is a whole agenda of actions to be undertaken in the financial area. The BRICS countries should intensify their coordinated action within the G20, by identifying common interests and acting accordingly. The G20 is meant to be the main decision forum, and the BRICS should not miss the opportunity to "use" it in the pursuit of their objectives.

The BRICS have pressed and should continue to press for the concrete, effective change in the IMF quotas, as formally agreed. There have been some initiatives within the G20 to enforce the required changes, but they have not materialized so far. This must continue to be a common flag.

By the same token, and in accordance with the Fortaleza Declaration, actions should be taken in order to promote changes in the governance of the World Bank as well. Part of these changes has to do with breaking the tradition of always having a European citizen as the head of the IMF and a US citizen as President of the World Bank. It is, of course, not simply a matter of changing nationalities. Being able to nominate a chair from an emerging economy should imply his/her commitment with an agenda that is suitable for the set of developing countries.

Last but not least, a good deal of the (still limited) reforms that we have witnessed in the internationally adopted rules imposed to the financial markets, following the several crises that have taken place since the mid-1990s, has been decided at forums where the participation of developing economies is clearly either minority or non-existing. This explains, for instance, the difficulties imposed on several countries when they try to adapt their domestic financial regulation to, say, the Basel III agreement. The recommendation that follows for the BRICS is, hence, to have a more active voice in these forums. This requires a good deal of well-trained technical staff, as well as the identification, once again, of the adequate procedures and the desired adjustments.

4. Final Words

The BRICS is still very much "work in progress". There have been some remarkable achievements, but it still remains to identify a clear profile of the group as a whole. What was originally intended to become a tool that could help to re-shape the global governance has evolved into a broad set of good intentions.

The point emphasized in this article is that the group should not lose sight of its original purposes. The whole lot of joint initiatives to deepen bilateral relationship should be designed by keeping in mind the basic aspect that we are essentially consolidating an important tool to be able to influence the global governance, be it via new standards for the operation of multilateral organizations, by influencing trade disciplines or even via the operation of alternative sources of funding for infrastructure projects.

This article tried to show that there is margin for the BRICS to act in that direction. It is up to the member countries to figure out how they will coordinate their international policies.

BRICS Cooperation from the Global Governance Perspective

Liu Jinsong*

Your Excellency Deputy Director-General Guo Yezhou, Dear Colleagues, Ladies and Gentlemen,

It is my great honor to attend this international symposium. I would like to extend, on behalf of the Department of International Economic Affairs, Ministry of Foreign Affairs of PRC,my warm congratulations on the successful opening of the "International Symposium on Building Modernized Governance Systems and Capabilities of BRICS Countries"!

Governance, in English, means a kind of top-down administration, but it has rich connotations in Chinese. About 2300 years ago, Xunzi proposed the word "governance" for the first time to clarify everyone's responsibilities and the order of priority, so as to make everyone feel fair. I feel this is an interpretation with historic meaning.

On November 15, BRICS leaders held an informal meeting in Brisbane, Australia. This meeting is very successful, since it reflects a new global governance structure and philosophy. All parties reiterated that BRICS would act on the open, inclusive, cooperative and win-win spirit to further strengthen an all-round cooperation, promote the building of New Development Bank (NDB) and Contingency Reserve Arrangement, urge to implement IMF reform commitments, strengthen coordination on important issues of G20 and give support to the international community to respond to the Ebola outbreak. I noticed that BRICS leaders have

---

* Liu Jinsong is Deputy Director-General of Department of International Economic Affairs, Ministry of Foreign Affairs of the People's Republic of China.

reached some prominent consensus: firstly, BRICS cooperation mechanism should be driven in political and economic aspects. It should not only be the engine of world economic growth, but also be the shield of international peace. Secondly, the BRICS countries should accelerate cooperation projects, especially to achieve greater progress in financial cooperation. New Development Bank and Contingency Reserve Arrangement should be put in place and the domestic approval process should be accelerated. Thirdly, actively promote economic governance and urge developed countries to take responsible monetary policies to prevent negative spillover effects. Increase investment, particularly in infrastructure investment, to find driving force for sustainable growth.

Currently, the mass character is witnessed in emerging countries and developing countries; their international status is rising continuously and their role in international affairs continues to improve. These have become the prominent features of international relations in the 21st century. It is in this grand context that the BRICS countries develop rapidly in terms of cooperation and grow into an important force in promoting world economic recovery, influencing the evolution of international relations and the interaction of relations between major powers, as well as improving global governance. Since BRICS leaders met with each other for the first time in 2009, BRICS countries undergo large-scale development at the time of unfolding and gradual deepening of global governance reform following the international financial crisis. With the theme of Building Modernized Governance Systems and Capabilities of BRICS Countries, Today's meeting seizes the historic trend of the democratization of international relations and diversification of global governance and has a positive and practical significance. Now, I would like to express my views on BRICS cooperation briefly.

Firstly, BRICS is an indispensable participant in global governance. BRICS has vast territory, large population and broad market. According to the statistics released in 2013, the BRICS population represented 42.6% of the world population, the land area accounted for 29.3%, GDP took up 21.3% and total trade volume contributed 16.4%. Its socio-economic development achievements have attracted worldwide attention.

However, the international community has many doubts about the prospects of the BRICS countries, and it does face some fluctuations and difficulties. In fact, the economic and financial situation of BRICS is certainly better than some developed countries. BRICS is still the world's economic growth engine. Its overall debt ratio is far below the average level of developed countries. It has broad economic policy space, abundant means, and the potential of labor force, innovative development and domestic market is far from being released completely. BRICS is an important member of major international organizations and mechanisms, such as the United Nations, the World Bank, the International Monetary Fund, G20, and Financial Stability Board. It is constantly moving towards the center of the world stage. The important agenda of world peace and security, economy, finance, trade and development are inseparable from the participation of the BRICS countries.

Secondly, the BRICS countries have a common goal of global governance. As the first session of the second round meeting of BRICS leaders, the Fortaleza Summit held in July of 2014 is faced with an important mission of inheriting past traditions and breaking new grounds for the future. The "open, inclusive, cooperative, win-win" spirit was first proposed in the Summit, which not only represents the valuable experience in the course of BRICS cooperation, but embodies the common vision of BRICS countries for global governance. Fortaleza Declaration made it clear that "the global governance architecture based on the international power structure in the past has gradually lost its legitimacy and effectiveness", "BRICS is an important force for progressive change in the existing mechanisms, which is contributive to achieve more representative and fairer global governance, promote more inclusive global growth and build a peaceful, stable and prosperous world."

To my understanding, this progressive and non-confrontational reform includes three goals: the first is to promote the democratization of international relations to discuss issues together and push the international system to be fairer and more rational. The second is to reform the World Bank, IMF and other international financial institutions and to increase the representation and voice of emerging markets and developing countries. The third is to improve the influence on global issues, such as climate change, energy, and to provide more public goods, which is the common goal of BRICS in participating in global governance.

Thirdly, the capability of developing global governance agenda of the BRICS countries is growing. In recent years, with the continuous improvement of BRICS cooperation mechanism, a multilateral cooperation framework has been formed which is led by the leadership summit and supported by Meeting of BRICS National Security Advisors, Meeting of Foreign Ministers, Consultation of Resident Envoy of Multilateral Institutions and pragmatic cooperation in various fields. A political and economic "two-wheel driven" model has been formed with the gradual expansion of cooperation fields, which covers more than twenty areas, such as diplomacy, trade, think tank, finance, science and technology, agriculture, statistics, health, taxation and customs. As the BRICS countries have more and more common interests, common positions and proposals, it has become a reality in today's global governance to improve BRICS voice in international affairs, propose BRICS programs and contribute BRICS wisdom. In addition, BRICS pays much attention to exchanges and cooperation with developing countries in various regions. In 2013, the BRICS Leaders – Africa Dialogue Forum was held in Durban. This year, the BRICS Leaders – Latin America Dialogue Forum will be held in Brasilia. These new dialogues are contributive to reflect the common aspirations of emerging markets and developing countries from a wider range, and further expand their influence on international affairs.

Ladies and gentlemen, China has been a staunch supporter and constructive participant and facilitator of BRICS cooperation. Strengthening the cooperation with BRICS countries is an important diplomatic direction of China. China has always maintained that the BRICS cooperation is in line with the historical trend of multilateralism and democratization of international relations. While strengthening partnership, it may also serve as an important bridge to enhance North-South dialogue and South – South cooperation. We uphold the spirit of benefiting all the people and aims to bring benefits to people in the world through BRICS cooperation. We hope that the BRICS countries would move towards the direction of integrated large market, financial flows, infrastructure interconnection and cultural exchanges to deepen the pragmatic cooperation in various fields, especially in the launch of the New Development Bank, Contingency Reserve Arrangement and other major projects to achieve a new leap in participating in global governance.

Of course, you cannot deny that BRICS is not perfect and is still in its infancy. Internationally, there are some doubts on how far can BRICS go. However, BRICS has huge potential and bright future. As an old Chinese saying goes, "a gentlemen is not lured by fame and not afraid of slander." President Xi Jinping has said, the BRICS countries should not only manage their own affairs, but also properly handle its partnership with the rest of the world, so as to build a favorable BRICS cooperation mechanism. As long as we maintain confidence in the development path of BRICS countries, do not fear risks and do not be confused by any interference, the cause of the BRICS countries is to be prosperous without any doubt.

Ladies and gentlemen, Think tank cooperation is an important part of the BRICS cooperation and also one field with the longest cooperation time and the richest cooperation experience, especially in playing a unique role in making plans for BRICS cooperation and providing intellectual support. BTTC is like an exploration team that explores new resources and develops new incentives for BRICS future cooperation.

To realize the modernization of BRICS governance systems and governance capacities, the key is to strengthen planning, straighten the relationship between global governance and domestic agenda to achieve comprehensive and coordinated political, economic and social development. In this regard, the BRICS leaders place high hope on think tank cooperation. I noticed that at the BTTC Meeting held in Brazil in March, 2014, BTTC will spare joint efforts in preparing "BRICS Long-Term Strategy", and will take "promoting economic growth and development cooperation, peace and security, social justice, sustainable development and living quality, political and economic governance, making progress through the sharing of knowledge and innovation" as the five pillars of this file. Each BRICS country is responsible for one pillar. This is a work of great significance.

At the informal meeting held on the 15th day of this month, BRICS leaders considered that in addition to promoting the comprehensive growth strategy centered on structural reform developed at the Brisbane Summit, there is a need to strengthen their own reforms, promote economic cooperation roadmap and play a leading role in building infrastructure, responding to climate change and facilitating trade and investment and so on.

What I can tell you is that we are negotiating on the development of "BRICS Economic Partnership Strategy" through BRICS coordinators. Many contents of this file coincide with those of BTTC, which fully shows that the intergovernmental cooperation of BRICS countries and non-governmental cooperation of BTTC are moving towards the same goal. In fact, in order to create the BRICS government-industry-academia joint cooperation mechanism, we urgently need think tanks to participate in BRICS cooperation at all levels and fields. I wish that experts and scholars give suggestions on BRICS cooperation and seek common development of the BRICS countries and make plan for BRICS cooperation.

At last, let's go back to the word "governance". It is a medical term in Chinese which not only means to identify the cause of disease, but also to take the right medicine; it refers to disembowel and sew up a patient and make rectifications till he recovers to health. Today, we advocate promoting international governance reform and responding to hot issues. It is not a task of simply opening the patient's stomach and then leaving it alone. Such a terrible case is common. We should act as a general practitioner and stick to the Hippocratic Oath, i.e., always put human welfare in the first place.

I sincerely hope that experts will make more progress in promoting the development of "BRICS Long-Term Strategy" and outline a better tomorrow for the BRICS countries through full discussion and exchange. Wish the symposium a great success and you will have a good time in Beijing! Thank you.

Challenges for Innovation and Governance in a Slow Growth Economy

Anna Jaguaribe[*]

1. Summary

This note proposes a reflection on the challenges facing the BRICS countries in the current scenario of a slow growth global economy. It will look at some of the mainstream assumptions regarding the potential role of the BRICS countries in the global economy and how they fare in the present context of slow growth and increased competition for value added. It will argue that the international conditions for advancing further in the economic and social achievements of the last decade have changed and that a new understanding of development and of growth models is required. Policies fostering innovation have now gained center stage as well as new policy making capacities. The mindset, institutional framework and capacities required to advance in the present context differ from previous modernization and catching up efforts.

The BRICS have a unique opportunity to cooperate in developing innovation solutions and alternatives for the global challenges of a more sustainable growth model. The development of a collaborative framework on science and technology policy formulation and foresight should be a priority task and institutional endeavor.

2. Introduction

The rise of the BRICS has been associated with the pattern of globalization

---

[*] Anna Jaguaribe is the Director of Institute for Brazil – China Studies.

of the 1990s. The expansion of trade and investments, the rise in global manufacturing chains and the fragmentation of frontier industries such as electronics have all contributed to create new opportunities for growth and insertion in the global economy.

The explosive growth rates of China and its transformation into a global hub of manufacturing in electro-electronics is a testimony to these trends. One of the corollaries of the globalization wave of the 1990s is the change in terms of trade for manufactures and commodities. Increased demand for commodities and lower manufacture prices have helped to dismiss long held economic assumptions regarding the unequal terms of trade between manufactures and commodities.

The BRICS have been beneficiaries of this growth scenario. Increase in investment and demands for commodities confirmed the economic potential of emerging economies reverting the direction of growth from the Atlantic to the Pacific and from old to more recently industrialized countries.

The BRICS now account to 25% of global value creation. Almost half of the world's population lives in the BRICS countries and most of the future megacities will emerge in BRICS countries.

The economic dynamism of the BRICS endured the financial crisis of 2008 lending credit to the assumption that a turning point has been achieved in global development. Emerging economies in particular the BRICS by virtue of the expansion of their internal market and by successfully tapping the opportunities in the global market were deemed to have achieved self sustaining growth drives. Central elements contributing to the BRICS growth drive are: the nature and weight of their internal markets, repressed and growing demands coming from internal mobility, underdeveloped service sectors which still need reform and new production and service demands which stem from the internal characteristics of each country.

Moreover, the large scale diffusion of across the board innovations in production and communication eased productivity bottlenecks, accelerated changes in communications incorporating large sectors of lower income groups into the market.

The global affirmation of BRICS is a consequence of these economic facts. Likewise, the BRICS political agenda gains cohesiveness by advancing global governance rules which safeguard the prospects of a sustainable cycle of growth.

Notwithstanding their economic endurance throughout the crisis, it is also clear that the current scenario of slow economic growth in the global economy raises new national as well as global challenges for the BRICS which now face one crisis and two transitions. The effects of the financial crisis which challenges national economies in maintaining the gains of the past decade and the transitions to a new geopolitics of asymmetric multipolarity and an economic cycle of slower growth.

Slow international growth, diminished trade and productive investments put additional pressures on national economies to engage in policies of redistribution. It also curtails capacity to reform and expands the social services demanded by large emerging middle classes. There are increasing difficulties in competing for a growth edge in the global economy while at the same time catching up with new technology frontiers. The Figure bellow indicates some of the challenges facing the BRICS.

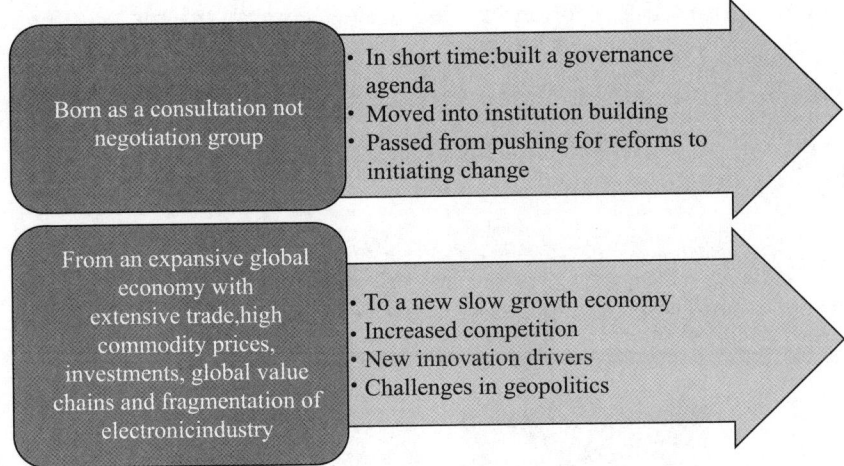

Figure 1 Some of the Challenges Facing the BRICS

For analysts of globalization the slow growth economy is not simply a reaction and adaptation to the crisis of 2008 but the result of global rites of passage from manufacturing to a service and innovation economy. A trend which tends in many respects to widen existing competition gaps amongst economies. In complex markets, the costs and risks associated with large scale innovation increase but also the struggle to gain shares and advantages through incremental product innovation. As pointed out by Breznitz, incremental innovation is like the running of the red queen in *Alice in Wonderland*, much effort has to be employed to stay in the race.

Slow growth also tends to lower commodity prices, diminish new productive investments and contract demand for the kind of manufacturing trade which characterized the last decade. For the BRICS countries a slow international economy and increased competition for value added brings to the fore the spectrum of the middle income or more appropriately middle technology trap.

That is: the possibility that having arrived at a middle income status. Few countries will be able to master the conditions to move in scale towards an innovation economy. A prognosis particularly awesome for countries which still have large efforts of catching up and reforms of national institutions to accomplish.

Furthermore, the economic slowdown comes in the context of technological uncertainties. While the need for change in models of growth highly dependent on non-renewable energies is evident. The shift in paradigm has not been accompanied with prospects of new cycles of technology driven of growth.

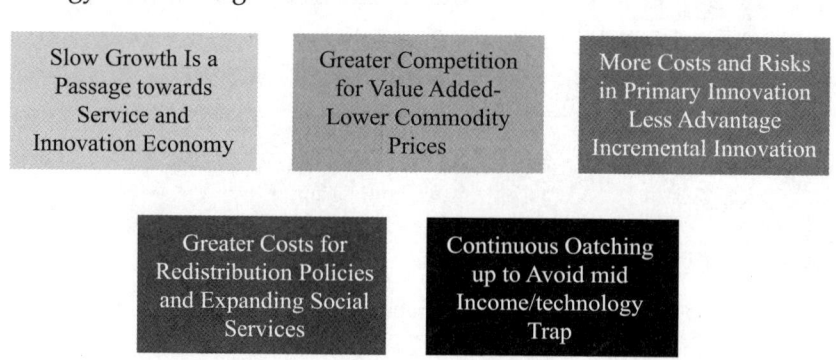

Figure 2 Characters of Economy Development in the Last Decade

In contrast to previous crisis and in particular what Piori and Sabel referred as the great divide in industrial production of the 1970s, the present moment does not seem to outline clear technological exits. The technologies which had underlined the alternatives in production patterns in the 1970s[①] are still unfolding and the energy challenges which will condition the long term options for technology and production in the near future have numerous outcomes.

The fact that technological innovations appear as unfolding potential transformations, more than clear cut options, fuels a debate on the role of innovation in economic growth and the nature of public policy in sustaining the innovation drive.

3. Slow Growth and Innovation

In a slow growth global economy with increased competition for value added, innovation gains a crucial space in the debate about the future. There are many indications that the great global expansion that started in the 1990s has completed a cycle.

The growth propelling force of industrial transformation and catching up diminishes when a certain level of development is reached. The transformations in the service sectors towards a more quality and technologically driven service sector are slower and less intense.

BRICS countries have sizeable imbalances in social and economic development, gaps which require constant investments so as to preserve a pattern of growth. Catching up, in this sense is a continuous process of increasing national potential in the search for value added.

Current academic discussion regarding innovation frontiers points to the continuous transformative capacity of information and telecommunication technologies and the disruptive potential of new knowledge platforms in biology, mechanics and physics. To these tendencies should be added the pervasive necessity for a sustainable new growth paradigm. A search, which is not reduced to changes in energy matrixes but also encompasses

---

① The essence of the great divide.

the production of food, uses of water and the organization of sustainable cities.

Sustainable development is not a clear cut economic or technological equation.

Zysman points out that the information revolution happened quickly because the semiconductor industry was already developed as a new industrial sector. The US government had financed a great part of the research and development associated with the industry. Furthermore, production by great firms such as Cisco and Intel were a consequence of the antitrust laws that prevented activities by ATT.

Today, energy matrixes are set and functioning and often recycling fossil options. Systemic changes will not be brought about by market pressures or the opportunities of superior technology or the rationality of costs. It will require clear vision, a change in policy mind set and long term planning. It will also depend on the potential role of the State acting not as a countervailing power to market failure but as a facilitator of systemic change.

4. Global Changes and National Governance Challenges

An international context of slow growth and increased competition increases the need for effective governance and institutional capabilities to formulate and implement policies geared towards change. Rodrick and Haussman point out that there are no great models or correct paths to ensure economic success or a virtuous integration into the global economy. The timing of policies, historical opportunities are sometimes more important than factor endowment. The manner in which each country embarks upon internal reforms and gains insertion in the global economy will be defined by their institutional context.

The globalization of the 1990s was a composite of national histories and all BRICS countries differ in their development stories. However, in spite of significant differences, there are important elements which the BRICS share in common.

In most BRICS countries, growth has brought about significant changes in social stratification, opening up economic and educational opportunities which alter established expectations regarding the future. This pattern of social mobility engendered by changes in economic opportunity and in rural life has led to profound transformation in savings and consumption transforming national markets and societies. Moreover, pressures for greater social opportunities persist and gaps in productivity, deficiencies in education, infrastructure and health strain the governance system.

In diverse ways the BRICS economies share the challenges of devising responses to complex national and international demands. Meeting the rising expectations of their large citizenship for better opportunities, competing for value added in the global market and promoting policies and institutions at the national level conducive to an innovation economy. Slow global growth puts a strain in all these tasks but makes special demands on national policies innovation.

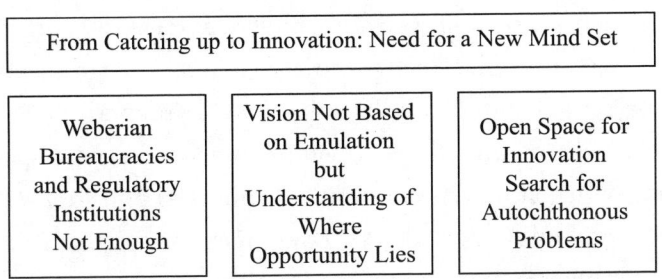

Figure 3 Global Changes and National Governance Challenges

During the past decade most BRICS countries have made special efforts to reform and update their national systems of innovation in order to effectively generate knowledge based economy.

There are significant differences in the national innovation systems of the BRICS countries. Over and above differences in expenditures, nature and scope of R&D, BRICS countries also vary significantly in their institutional profile, education endowments and history of cultural and scientific achievements .

Differences are particularly evident in education. Countries will vary in the quality of their primary and secondary educational system with Brazil, India, South Africa but also China showing very different gaps from Russia. Differences in numbers and quality of graduates from engineering schools are very large amongst the BRICS with China leading the group by a wide margin.

The contrast is also interesting in what concerns sources of funding and location of R&D. Brazil and China have been increasing steadily their investments in R&D but while in Brazil the bulk of financing is public and goes for basic research, in China, given the emphasis on incremental innovation R&D is development oriented and carried out at the firm level.

Polices are country specific because economic agents and processes are embedded in specific economic, social and political environment. It follows that theory and policy recommendation are highly individualized and generalizations regarding capacity building and institutional reform should be made with caution.

But, it is also clear that certain challenges remain common to the BRICS countries and what seems more relevant, certain strategies have proven to be more conducive to results. OECD innovation surveys have consistently pointed out that constant macroeconomic policies and convergence between macroeconomic, commercial and industrial policies will benefit the innovation drive. Long term investment in S&T has proven a fundamental asset in the development of information technologies. A guaranteed ground for experimentation and trial and error of technology options seems imperative for channeling innovations into commercial ventures. Tapping into global knowledge, using FDI efficiently and stimulating competition within national markets is a successful path towards secondary innovation. The successful experience of China and Korea in this regard is a case in point.

Each of these policy strategies has been embedded in institutional arrangements which have either facilitated or delayed the implementation of agreed goals. Economies of innovation require flexible institutions and constant state policies. "Weberian bureaucracies" and regulatory institutions are fundamental necessities but not sufficient responses to governance challenges.

By nature science and technology require what may seem contradictory policies: guaranteed long term investment and institutional continuity to guarantee research but also flexible policy mechanisms and quick responses to stimulate the passage of experimentation to commercial activity.

In a study regarding governance in the BRICS countries, the Bertelsmann Institute has developed a management index which associates capacities with accountabilities. The chart bellow regroups some of the variables relating to capability developed by the Bertelsmann study to look at the direction of interaction between policy goals and policy implementation.

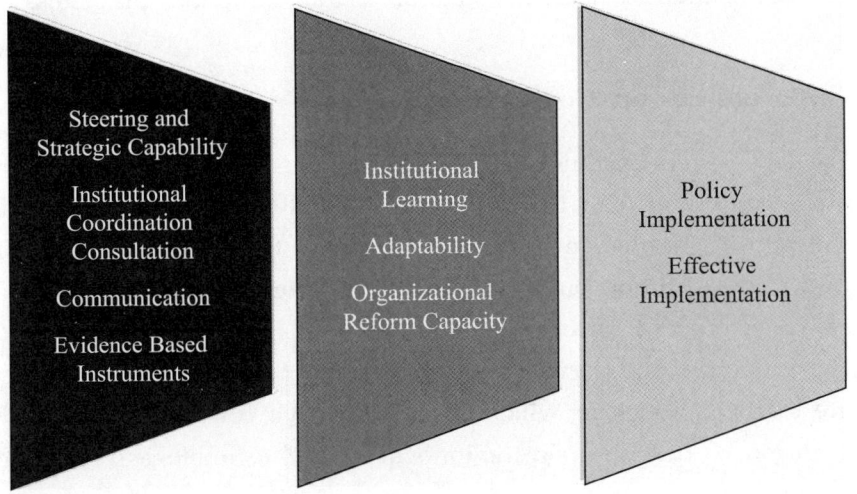

Figure 4 Variables Relating to Capability Developed by the Bertelsmann Institute

In the chart above, all variables are inter-related. While it is clear that steering and strategic capability, institutional learning, adaptability and reform capacity tare all required for efficient results and directly influence policy implementation. It is also the case that institutional learning depends on policy implementation and knowledge which comes from failure and that reform capacity will be influenced by consultation, communication and evidence based instruments.

It is evident that there is a systemic relation between capacities. Coordination and steering capacity are not just characteristics and (or) qualities of a particular bureaucratic set up, but the result of constant institutional learning and adaptability.

Because efficient institutional systems are highly interrelated, they are put to stress when growth and technological challenges have to be confronted.

The passage of a catching up to an innovation economy is such a situation. It requires a new mindset for public policy and new strategies in the relationship between public and private spheres of production. It demands an efficient and meritocratic institutional framework but also a long term vision which is not based on emulation. An understanding of where opportunities may lie which enables the creation of open space for innovation geared towards the solution of autochthonous problems.

5. Opportunities for Cooperation

The BRICS were born not as a negotiating but as a consultation forum. In a relatively short time, they have consolidated a common understanding of the reforms needed in the present system of global governance and moved into institution building. In so doing they have transcended the dilemma of pushing for change vs initiating change themselves.

The economic and social challenges facing the BRICS today directly relate to the manner in which they will strive towards a sustainable growth model and act upon the innovation and technological challenges associated with it.

The BRICS have many areas of compatibility in their national innovation systems and many development challenges in common. There are great opportunities to develop a framework for cooperating in global and common development challenges and being involved in design and framing of research questions about shared challenges.[1]

Science and scientific research are more widespread today than in the 1980s and scientific protocols are largely shared, still quality centers remains concentrated on centers and universities, largely outside of the BRICS. While the National Innovation Systems are increasingly more open and interconnected and R&D centers are increasingly globalized,

---

[1] Final report-knowledye, networks and Nations, 2011, The Royal Society, https://royalsociety.org/topics-policy/phjects/knowledyc-networks-notiuns/hport/.

BRICS countries still perform a large part of their R&D efforts nationally.

In the next decades the innovation challenge will be to associate scientific breakthroughs with disruptive technologies which will address social and economic issues. These challenges will in large part deal with questions which relate to global and social "commons" and most of the populations affected or benefitting from the correct policy making regarding these social "commons" are in the BRICS countries.

BRICS countries are well positioned to cooperate in the innovative drive in biology and pharmaceutics, alternative energy, food production and mobility and in the design of sustainable cities. All of the new large and mega cities to emerge in the next decades will be created in emerging economies. The urbanization models for these new cities will have to be rethought to accommodate the requirements of a more sustainable growth model and a more inclusive urban life and culture.

The BRICS should now engage in developing a framework for action in these new future innovation challenges. In fact, the political capital of the BRICS and the objectives, mission and scope of their new institutions should not be limited to the governance challenges of the present or to compensate deficiencies in global institutions which are not inclusive but also engage in the common challenges of the future.

An effort should be made to create a collaborative framework, a working agenda and program for: exchanging and evaluating S&T experiences, engaging in foresight concerning the innovation challenges and developing institutional arrangements to foster the collaboration of national centers and public laboratories on project specific endeavors.

References

[1] Bertelsmann Stifung (ed.), "Change Ahead Sustainable Governance in the BRICS", 2013.

[2] Dan Breznitz, *The Run of the Red Queen*, Yale University Press, 2011.

[3] J. Cassiolato, *Brics and Development Alternatives*, Anthem Press, 2011.

[4] Carl Dahlman, "Innovation Strategies China, India and Brazil", Oxford Papers, SLPMD number 023.

[5] "China Innovation Survey", OECD, 2007.

[6] Piori and Sabel, "The Second Industrial Divide", *Basic Books*, 1984.

[7] D. Rodrick and R. Haussman, *Economic Development as Self Discovery*, Harvard University Press, 2003.

[8] J. Zysman, "Brie Policy Papers", 2007.

[9] "Royal Society Knowledge Networks and Nations Report", 2011.

State Capacities and Innovation Policies: Lessons from and for the BRICS

Ana Célia Castro[*]

According to Celina Souza, "In a simplified form one can define state capacity as the set of tools and institutions that the State disposes of to establish goals, transforming them in policies and implementing them." Or, according to Peter Evans[1], it concerns the State's capacity **for action**. Due to the concept's breadth, disaggregating its components could help guide its empirical application. The political component concerns the "rules of the game" that regulate political, social, and economic behavior. In this sense, it is worth analyzing formal and informal institutions that condition the party system and executive-legislative relations, as well as the channels of mediation of interests and conflict resolution.

The **public policy** component concerns the **institutions and strategies** that influence **policy decisions**, their formulation, and execution. In this sense, this component could incorporate (1) the identification of the main characteristics of systems that govern specific policies; (2) analyses of the trajectories of specific policies; (3) **mapping the mechanisms of intra-governmental coordination or executive coordination**; (4) building of bureaucratic capacity and the degree of professionalization in the bureaucracy to investigate the conditions in which policies are formulated and executed and (5) the tax system, that is, revenues and expenditures, to investigate the state's capacity to collect taxes to finance policies, deliver public goods, and redistribute income among the different

---

[*] Ana Célia Castro is professor at Federal University of Rio de Janeiro.

social groups.[2]

As for state capacity, specifically policy capacity, in other words, capacity for implementing policies, the following definition is helpful:

> Policy capacity emerges from three interlinked policy choices: nature and sources of technical change and innovation; on the ways of **financing** economic growth, in particular technical change; mature of public management to deliver and implement both previous sets of policy choices. It is not a continuum of abilities but rather a **variety of modes** of making policy.[3]

The state capacity to formulate, manager, and implement (and in some cases to evaluate) science, technology, and innovation policy is the goal of this project. The purpose is to compare state and policy capacity based on an analysis of the national innovation systems of Brazil, China, and Argentina, to the extent these shed light on the facets discussed above- institutions and strategies, mechanisms for the coordination, financing, and implementation of innovation policy. As Peter Evans observes in "The State of Innovation"[4], comparisons are, in this case, relevant "for looking at how innovation is actually organized and **how it might be organized better**" (emphasis added).

The most recent literature on innovation and public institutional arrangements for science and technology emphasizes the role of the entrepreneurial states and their fundamental contribution to development policies in middle-income countries (but also in developed countries as United States). These positions share a consensus about the role of innovation in catching-up and leap-frogging processes.[5][6][7] This literature, of great analytical power, contributes to building a consensus on the role of innovation in catching-up and leapfrogging processes in these countries, despite their vulnerability to the possibility of being captured by technological traps, common to countries in rapid process of productive transformation. Industrial policy (and with it, innovation policy) has been considered crucial to overcoming the so-called threshold of development.

> The number of non-Western countries which have become developed is less

than ten — even stretching the categories of "non-western", "countries" and "developed". The list plausibly includes countries and religions like Japan, Russia, Taiwan of China, South Korea, Hong Kong of China, Singapore, and Israel. Such a low total suggests that the vast "development industry" created since the Second World War can hardly be counted a success. The non-western success cases had or have two conditions in common: first, external state enemies capable of conquering the territory; second, **a much more active and directive state** than is consistent with prevailing neoclassical development strategies.[8] (Hong Kong of China is a partial exception to the second condition.)

In this process, innovation, which is part of developmentalist industrial policy, seems to be the key to success, and perhaps the key to the door that separates blocks of development and developing countries. The countries that crossed the threshold were able to arrive to the technological frontier of the most important sectors of their economies, and moreover, these countries are, in the majority of cases, countries that effectively define the technological frontier in these sectors.

Coriat and Wallerstein (2006) contributed to this analysis from a different view point and called the attention to the increasing importance of what they have called a technical paradigm strongly based on science ("science based 2").[9] In these sectors — where the technical frontier seems to be located, as in biotech and information technologies — two dimensions are crucial: finance (capital markets) and intellectual property (the relevance of patents and the intellectual property system). These two dimensions are interwoven and are embedded in this new scientific paradigm.

The same could be said about the concept of secondary innovation, proposed or developed by Wu, Ma, and Chu, which places capacity-building at the center of the debate①.[10] There are at least three

---

① I would add the following: if a specific country over cross the frontier or it is located at the frontier, after a process of secondary innovation; if this process takes into account a particular trajectory and a successful one; if this trajectory reflects its own endowment of resources and capabilities-then this country tends to be able to define the physical and social technologies of this frontier. For the concept of social technologies see R. Nelson, and B. Sampat, "What Enables Rapid Economic Progress: What Are the Needed Institutions?" *Research Policy*, 37 (2008), pp. 1-11.

considerations about middle-income countries' technological traps. First, the position of sectors/companies as suppliers ("subcontractors") in global value chains.[11] In this case the trap merges from the difficult in creating technological capacity, or even from the obstacles resulting from its place in the value chain. Even catching-up seems difficult to achieve, even if it becomes the main goal. Working in its favor are the paths already known and trailed by leading countries. On the opposite pole are sectors/companies with the capacity to equip and leap-frog countries already on the frontier. This was and could be the situation of a few countries that already were able to cross the technological development threshold. And an intermediate position exists, where Brazil and China seem to be, some sectors are at the frontier (low-emissions tropical agriculture, deep water oil exploration, small and medium aircraft manufacturing, in the case of Brazil), while other sectors are not competitive. In these cases, the co-existence of trajectories deemed to be of "secondary innovation" is possible.

When the technological trajectory is not entirely defined in a given sector, the authors say, countries can advance through different paths or alternative trajectories, but tend to come upon limits relating to their technological capacity, a situation characterized as a crisis in the development process. When these limits are overcome, the national trajectory, which takes into account the existence of particular factors, becomes established and gives the country a competitive advantage with which it to move forward. Innovation, and the national innovation system in which it is found, seems to be the ace in the hole that will allow the country to reach the technological frontier in the sectors in which it could have comparative institutional advantages. This is another element that the comparative analysis in the Brazilian, Chinese, and Argentinian cases sought to highlight.

This ace in the hole seems probable when **a structuring of consensus** is plausible — on which sectors the entrepreneurial state[1] should promote

---

① The structuring of a consensus about which sectors will be prioritized and supported by innovation policy is not the only possible strategy but seems necessary or more effective in the case of middle-income countries. In countries such as the United States, as Block points out, the consensus is to support countries on the technological frontier, where it is located.

and incentivize, on where the frontier is located, and whether these countries find themselves, can reach it, or define the innovation frontier.[12] The process of structuring consensus depends on: the existence of a rearguard of institutions capable of undertaking prospective (and retrospective) studies that are effectively considered in the decision-making process; the continuous exercise of foresight or technological foresight, subject to processes of periodic revision; the capacity to take account of conflicts of interest, but equally to neutralize them when building structured consensus; and finally to count on a well-established but effective financial innovation system. What is at issue is not, per Kattel, a continuous set of abilities or expertise ("continuum of abilities"), but a variety of decision-making processes on long-term strategy and coordination in the development and implementation of political technologies.

Before pointing out the main indicators from case studies, it is necessary to highlight that the comparison of Brazil, China, and Argentina emerges in the framework of middle-income countries, whose analysis has the power to cross-pollinate, or in other words, of generating knowledge that could be relevant, not only in strategic decision-making processes, but equally for the governance of knowledge[13] in the case of innovation policy. More than the examples to follow①, what is important to analyze is the degree to which case studies highlight challenges, or represent impasses, to greater use of Brazilian institutional advantages in the formulation and implementation of innovation policy.[14]

Comparing the institutional architectures of the science, technology, and innovation systems of the three countries, it could be suggested that Brazil posses an institutional framework that, as a whole, is more complex and articulated than in the case of Argentina, without a doubt, and of China. In the Argentina case, it could be said that its constituitive parts pear to similar to the Brazilian system, while being in an earlier stage of development, but in the same direction when considering the near future. When one considers the case of China, it emphasizes that

---

① The benchmark notion is in contradiction with different possibilities, path dependences and varieties of capitalism. Institutional monocropping is vicious and normally conducts to bad results.

the institutional design or architecture does not reveal its decision-making capacity and much less the process of **structuring of consesus** around the innovation strategy adopted, as we will see below.

The configuration of the Brazilian innovation system seeks to integrate the teaching, research, and innovation financing systems, mainly through BNDES (Brazilian Bank for Economic and Social Development), FINEP (Financier for Projects and Studies), and the Sectorial Funds. In the Chinese case, the financing does not appear in the national innovation system organizational charts, but occurs directly through the banking system. The proximity of agencies with companies, on the national, sectorial, regional, and especially, local level, guarantees financing, once companies, independently from the structure of capital, but preferentially for state-owned enterprises, have been positively evaluated in their capacity to effectively contribute to the technological and industrial development of China. This is, without a doubt, a difference to be emphasized. Financing innovation is, by contrast, as a drawback of the Argentine system.

In the Brazilian context, there is a solid legal framework built as a result of a long maturation process that started as early as 1950. The same can be said about the institutions for financing science and technology, now incorporating the concept of innovation. The available resources, financing policy, and its instruments, have been the constant preoccupation of successive governments. However, the necessary flexibility to serve companies did not emerge as a trait of the system, much less the intervention into supply and defend by funds for innovation. There are many requirements, legal frameworks, and controls, especially on the part of courts of auditing (*Tribunal de Contas*); there is a lack of new companies willing to use the system and capable of delivering what they promise.

In the Chinese case, the coordinating role of MOST (Ministry of Science and Technology) through CASTED (Chines Academy of Science and Technology for Development) and CASS (Chinese Academy of Sciences), which act as think thanks, responds to the not obvious task of integrating the activity of technological foresight under one single strategic long-term vision, which materializes in the decision on which sectors and technologies to bet on. The building of consensuses, or of structured consensuses, depends on this integration among the exercises of foresight and strategic choices. This process is what Angang terms "collective presidency"[15].

In the Brazilian case, the role of government agencies such as CGEE and ABDI, to cite possible institutional counterparts, is exercised, among other fronts, through commissioning systemic and relevant studies, mainly retrospective, on the characteristics and challenges that the Brazilian innovation system faces or faced. However, and saving for a better analysis, there does not seem to be the same synergy between the studies developed, the building of consensuses and the strategic choice of sectors.①

In sum, the conclusions seem to point to the following comparative institutional advantages in the Chinese case, which at the same time are warnings, but could point to paths in the Brazilian case as well as in the Argentinian case.

1. The Chinese Innovation System inverts, or better yet, subverts that mode of operations that characterizes the Brazilian and Argentine systems. **The technological innovation that emerges from the actual economic system is at the top of the innovation system, and not at its base.** Private and public research is not the finish line, but the starting line.

2. The second layer of the system is the advisory apparatus for strategic decisions, exercised by the research institutes, think tanks, universities, and so forth.

3. Foresight exercises, permanent and subject to period review, are fundamentally taken into account when structuring consensus about the sectors that will be chosen in conceiving of long-term strategies.

4. Innovation financing appears to be widespread and not restricted to certain sectors or types of company according to capital structure, is not subject to many controls, and is carried out by the banking system. This last trait, which is not rooted in the institutional arrangement of the

---

① It was not possible to evaluate the Argentine case in this aspect because the interviews were carried out before the fieldwork in China, when this hypothesis was developed.

innovation system, should not be considered a comparative institutional advantage and instead a peculiar characteristic of the Chinese system.

5. The strategic choices seem to emerge in the building of consensuses, of a collective process of generating this structural consensus. It was not possible to observe the need for a coalition of interests, a characteristic of Western representative democracies, and present in the Brazilian and Argentinean decision-making processes.

In the Brazilian case, the conclusions seem to point to the following comparative institutional advantages, and suggest that the warnings, challenges, and possible obstacles that the Chinese experiences indicate should be kept in mind.

1. The Brazilian Innovation System possesses a mature institutional architecture, which is complex, evolved over decades, and seems adequate for decision-making, taking into account the interests of its different stakeholders, represented in the various institutional arrangements that constitute SNCTI (National Science, Technology and Innovation System).

2. Despite being relatively far from the nucleus of decision-making, Universities and Research Institutes, mainly the most connected to the ministries relevant to innovation, have contributed to elevate the production of science, technology, and innovation, which can be seen by evaluating Brazil's scientific output.[1]

3. The Brazilian System's financing is rooted in its very institutional architecture, which is in theory adequate to the system's functioning. The existence of excessive controls, however, could be disassembling the institutional advantage resulting from the financing system for Brazilian innovation. Complaints from institutions such as BNDES and FINEP about the scarcity of innovative companies that seek financing for

---

[1] Not only its output of scientific articles puts Brazil in a prominent position, but its successive National Innovation Conferences, such as the Fourth held in 2010, reveal Brazil's leading position in many fields of knowledge. "Brazil, by virtue of the historical moment it is in, its regional and cultural diversity, the size of its population, and the scientific level it has achieved, has a unique opportunity to build a new model of sustainable development, that respects nature and human beings. A model that must necessarily be based on high-quality science, technology, and education for all Brazilians." (Luiz Davidovich, CGEE, *Blue Book of the Fourth Conference on Science, Technology, and Innovation for Sustainable Development*, www.cgee.org.br/publicacoes/livroazul.php)

technology change is recurrent.

4. Evaluations suggest that the Brazilian legal framework is adequate to the needs of the innovation system. However, its specifications and application are still the source of doubts and regressions that impede that this competitive institutional advantage be considered as such.

5. The governance of the system foresees the representation and representativeness of the various interested parties in the innovation process. However, the decisions seem to be taken in circumscribed and limited spheres, which do not necessarily take into account the interests at stake, which should apparently be represented.

In terms of the Chinese experience, the most serious Brazilian disadvantages seem to be the following:

1. Despite the existence, complexity, and, above all, its recognized excellence in terms of scientific output, "the second layer of the system — or in other words, the advisory apparatus for strategic decision-making, such as research institutes, think thanks, universities, and so forth," does not necessarily participate in strategic choices in the development of Brazilian innovation policy.

2. The exercises in technological foresight, when they occur, are done in *ad hoc* manner and not systematically as in the Chinese case, this being one of the main recommendations for a joint cooperation platform.

3. The process of structuring of consensuses on the priorities of innovation policy, which sectors to choose, support, and even protect, could come to be the Achilles' heel of science, technology, and innovation policy in the Brazilian case.[①] Shared beliefs and strategic choices made in developing innovation policy reveal themselves to be essential in other historical examples of countries that were capable of crossing the threshold of development.

[①] The Argentine case did not have sufficient research material that would allow development of analogous conclusions, having contributed, such, as a counterpoint to the conclusions developed above.

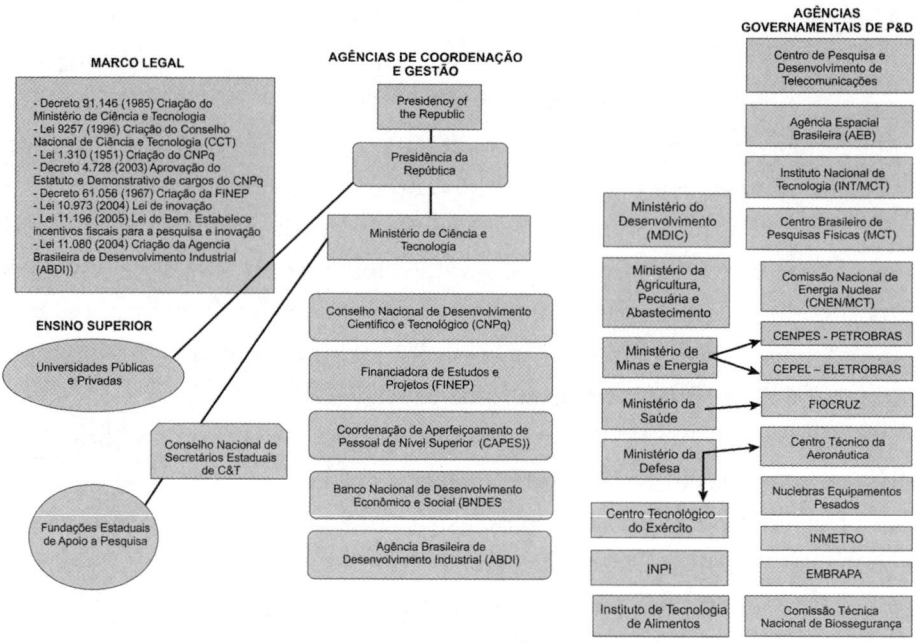

Figure 1 Brazilian National System of Science, Technology and Innovation

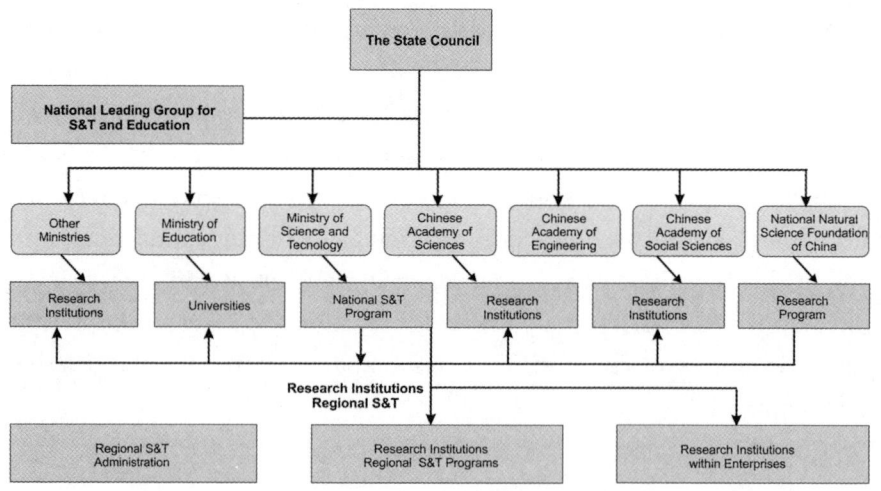

Figure 2 Governance Structure of China's Science and Technology System

Data Source: Rong Ping Mu, "Development of Science and Technology Policy in china", 2004, http://: www. nistep. go. jp/IC/ic040913/pdf/30 - 04ftx. pdf。

References

[1] Peter B. Evans, "O Estado como problema e solução", *Lua Nova Revista de Cultura e Política,* n. 28 /29, 1993, pp. 107 - 156.

[2] Celina Souza, "Comparative State Capacitiy", research report to IPEA (Institute of Economics and Applied Research), emphasis added, text for discussion, 2015.

[3] E. Karo and R. Kattel, "Public Management, Policy Capacity, Innovation and Development", *Brazilian Journal of Political Economy,* Vol. 34, No. 1 (134), January-March, 2014, pp. 80 - 102.

[4] F. Block and M. R. Keller, "State of Innovation", *The U.S. Government's Role in Technology Development,* Paradigm Publisher, Boulder, London, 2011.

[5] L. Weiss, *America Inc.? Innovation and Enterprise in the National Security State* , Cornell University Press, Ithaca and London, 2014.

[6] M. Mazzucato, "The Entrepreneurial State: Debunking Public vs. Private Sector Myths", Anthem Press, London, UK, 2013.

[7] F. Block and M. R. Keller, ob. Cit. , A. Primi, " Promoting Innovation in Latin America — What Countries Have Learned (and What they have not)", in *Designing and Implementing Innovation and Intellectual Property Policies,* University of Maastricht, 2014.

[8] R. Wade,"Doing Industrial Policy Better, Not Less", unpublished manuscript, August 2014. Thanks to Professor Robert Wade to allow me this citation. The importance of external enemies and exceptional political conditions in the eve of catching up processes was pointed out before by A. Abramovith, " Catching-up, Forging Ahead and Falling behind", *The Journal of Economic History,* 46 (2), pp. 385 - 406.

[9] B. Coriat and O. Wenstein, "Science-based Innovation Regimes and Institutional Arrangements: from Science-based '1' to Science-based '2' Regimes", *Towards a New Science-based Regime? Industrial and Innovation* See the seminal article by K. Pavitt, " The Innovation Process", in J. Fagerberg, D. Mowery, and R. Nelson (eds.), *The Oxford Handbook of Innovation* , Oxford University Press, Oxford, 2005, inclusive and sustainable, to add two important nowadays dimensions.

[10] Wu, X. , Ma, R. , and Chu, G. , "Secondary Innovation: The Experience of Chinese Enterprises in Learning, Innovation and Capability Building", *National System for Innovation Management* , in D. Teece, *Dynamic Capabilities & Strategic Management* , Oxford, 2009, Chapter 1.

[11] R. WADE, "States, Firms and Regional Production Hierarchies in East and Southeast Asia: Converging towards the Anglo-American Free Market Model, or Caught in a Medium Technology Trap?" in *International Seminar — Institutions and*

Economic Development: A Comparative Perspective on State Reforms, Rio de Janeiro, Anais, Rio de Janeiro: UFRRJ, 1997.

[12] F. Block and M. R.Keller, "State of Innovation", *The U S.Government's Role in Technology Development,*Paradigm Publisher, Boulder, London, 2011.

[13] L. Burlamaqui, A.C. Castro and R. Kattel, *Knowledge Governance: Reasserting the Public Interest,* Anthem Other Canon, 2012.

[14] Peter B. Evans, "O Estado como problema e solução", *Lua Nova Revista de Cultura e Política* , n. 28/29, 1993, pp. 107 - 156.

[15] H. Angang, "Collective Presidency in China", Institute for Contemporary China Studies, Tsinghua University, June 2003.

BRICS Role in Safeguarding Global Peace and Security

Georgy Toloraya[*]

The current world order has become chaotic and, as Henri Kissenger puts it, "there are no universally accepted rules." There are Western, Islamic, Chinese and Russian views...[①]

On the one hand, there is a clear tendency of globalization of the world economy, increasing influence of the transnational corporations, growing inter-dependence of the postindustrial states (mostly US, Western Europe countries and Japan) — which make military solutions of international disputes unprofitable. On the other — the end of bipolarity and absence of the global governance have led to a new division of spheres of influence. Social, economic and technological gap between various regions and countries is widening, while the rivalry between regional "centers of force" is aggravating.

The result is a fragmentation of the global security — some issues are regulated by international law, others — by sheer power politics. "Coalitions of the willing" is a clear example of attempts to find solutions favorable to a separate group of international actors while ignoring the internationally recognized mechanisms based on international law. Double standards in approaching similar issues (Kosovo – Crimea) has become a "norm", while new political technologies (human rights as a pretext for intervention, externally-sponsored "color revolutions" as a tool to undermine hostile states) as well as "information warfare" are

---

[*] Georgy Toloraya is Executive Director of Russian National Committee (NCR) on BRICS studies.
[①] http://www.spiegel.de/international/world/interview-with-henry-kissinger-on-state-of-global-politics-a-1002073.html.

used against hostile or unfriendly states.

At the same time traditional "hard" warfare is becoming an option as a result of attempts to break existing strategic balance by introducing new weapon technologies. In spite of all the efforts made by the international community, it has not succeeded in elaborating an adequate strategy to oppose local and regional threats in the post-bipolar stage, solving ethnic and political conflicts, especially those of trans-border nature (Afghanistan, Iraq, Libya and Syria). The global economic life is also becoming fragmented by creation (often by political motives) of isolated economic groupings and FTA's.

BRICS, which started as a grouping of economies, soon found out that the primary economic interests of the countries comprising BRICS make it necessary to change the basic rules of global governance. BRICS *Raison d'être* is becoming a "union of reformers" of the current financial and economic architecture. However, the latter is protected by an existing post-World War II political and military system, dominated by Western powers. Nobody wants a World War III to change it drastically (although, ironically, we are nearer to it than quarter of century ago). So the agenda of BRICS discourse in the new turbulent era of growing geopolitical contradictions between major powers, civilizational clashes, local conflicts have to necessarily include — in a increasing degree — the international security issues.

We should bear in mind existence of multiple **military threats for BRICS**: external, internal and trans-border (the latter are mostly associated with terrorism). Color revolutions may also lead to trans-border threats because the internal instability could lead to armed conflicts pulling in foreign forces.

At the same time the level of direct military threats for BRICS is relatively low, although a situation near some of BRICS countries is fraught with large-scale armed conflicts. For example, as Asian security experts note, " While only a decade ago direct military conflict between major powers seemed a remote prospect, the risks of inadvertent conflict and escalation are rising, especially in Northeast Asia."[1] Therefore, although we all should strive for provision of BRICS security using only political and diplomatic measures, other options should also be available as a last resort if vital allied interests of the BRICS countries are endangered.

Also, BRICS countries being important players in the global weapons' market might create a network to coordinate their policies and maybe enter into direct cooperation in weapon development, production and circulation.

In general, BRICS states are committed to **sustaining stable, safe and fair world order** through peaceful diplomacy and multilateralism, including fostering equal partnership between both developed and developing countries. This is a world order with a loose structure, with many centers of power of different capabilities, where power is diffused and responsibilities are appropriately shared. Such system is more like a world-wide democracy, or "nationacracy", where nation-states occupy different niches but have equal rights but different responsibilities. Not like a global monarchy or at best aristocracy system, suggested by the USA and its allies in the framework of a unipolar world, where NATO and US – Asia powers' alliances took the responsibility for security maintenance.

BRICS member states share a view that multilateral network diplomacy and rules-based global governance architecture are the best guarantor of stability and provides an effective framework for asserting common values and interests whilst upholding the principle of the sovereignty of nations. BRICS is therefore committed to the primacy of **international law**, insomuch as insufficient it might be.

However it is obvious the "supremacy" of international law today is at its lowest ebb ever. Unlike national legislation, international law has no single rule-maker, doesn't have common enforcement mechanism and is based on the sovereign equality of states and their voluntary will to use it. Strong powers tend to bend it into their favor and their motivations are often based on their national legal and public mentality.

Additionally, there are several basic contradictions in the existing international law system. The most hard to solve include the contradiction between the principle of territorial integrity on the one hand, and principles of self-determination, on the other (as Kosovo, Abkhazia, Crimea — and lately even Scotland and Catalonia examples have shown)[2]. Also there is a dilemma — individual rights and freedoms versus sovereignty and supreme interests of state as a representative of all the people's interests (which it is supposed to be-and there are no independent "judges" or mechanisms to determine it). Western approach to this problem, when "human rights know no borders"[3], corresponds neither to objective reality, nor to the interests of representatives of other civilizational legal systems.

Existing legal norms and systems are founded on a specific national soil and often reflect different national mentality. Therefore agreement of different sides on existence of a problem doesn't guarantee agreement on choice of methods and means of its solution. While some countries are ready to work on the elaboration of the norm to offer long-term legal solution of the problem, others attempt to look at it through the prism of short-term interests, accommodating legal norm in accordance with those. Thus it is vital to give priority to providing for cooperation between global actors demonstrating respect for the international law. The BRICS role here could be central.

The attempts for extraterritorial use of national legislation should be resolutely rejected — it looks like a war-time adventures, when citizens of one state are kidnapped at the territory of other states to be presented at a national court.

There exists a basic contradiction between normativism, having its roots in the Continental legal system, and precedent-based law system, typical to Anglo-Saxon legal tradition.[4] Approach to the international law on the precedent basis, characteristic of Anglo-Saxon law system with the philosophy of achievement of the desired outcome at any prices leads to temptation of creation of the virtual "judge" represented by one powerful state, and thus, to substitution of the international law by internal law and institutionalization of the unipolar world. It seems that US "preemptive action" doctrine and "humanitarian interventions", unilateral revision of the treaties on strategic stability, multiple breaches of the *Vienna Convention on Diplomatic Relations* of 1961 are to be regarded not as a result of certain "exceptional circumstances", but Washington's persistent efforts to transfer international law into a law on a "precedent basis". This in turn would only legitimize critical situation of the "right to use force" in the international relations, leading us back not as much into 19th – 20th centuries but even further to medieval times.

European countries (where tradition of continental law exists) due to a number of political circumstances are not able to provide real alternative to gradual erosion of normative content and functionality of the international law. However, BRICS which unifies five main (out of Huntington's eight) civilizations of the planet, can undertake such a mission. Three of the BRICS — Brazil, Russia and China — belong to the tradition of the continental legal system, while the other two — India and South Africa — inheriting the common law system but do not look at it as an absolute.[①] It is vital for BRICS countries — jointly and separately — pursue a policy of supporting multilateral international order, rule of international law and strengthening the UN role in sustaining global peace and security. Role of institutions rather than ad-hoc coalitions is also essential and should be strengthened.

BRICS countries in critical situation can demonstrate some unity, for example, during the voting in UNGA on Crimean issue in spring 2014, when the rest four of the BRICS refused to join into the Western-initiated resolution to condemn Russia. Use of this or that international law principles should be determined not by ideological dogma or considerations of political moment, but rather by clear international legal regulation of each specific case.

Normativism, characteristic for all of the BRICS countries legal doctrines would allow for a number of breakthroughs in that direction.

• Elaboration of legally consistent definition for the terrorism (which hampers elaboration of clear legal approach to participants of a range of internal conflicts creating conditions for their protraction, such as Syrian or Ukranian cases) and global Convention on the fight against terrorism

---

[①] http://en.wikipedia.org/wiki/Tort_law_in_India.

under the UN auspices;

• The issue of "national identity" and its status with regard to other basic values in international legal system

• The issue of legitimacy of sanctions levied unilaterally without authorization by the United Nations Organization.

• The issues of humanitarian limitations to economic and other sanctions, levied by international community;

• Clearer definition of "indirect aggression" and hostile activities to include propaganda and ICT issues.

Besides the international law, another crucial area for BRICS cooperation is **strengthening UN role** and status of regional organizations in preserving peace and security as well as strengthening the role of institutions. UN is seen by BRICS countries as a main institution responsible for international peace and security, and some of them urge its reform in accordance with current geopolitical realities giving them more say in preserving global peace and order.

The problem of expansion of the UNSC is very topical, althoug it raises contreversies within BRICS.① The lack of progress on this issue clearly hampers all further steps to bring the UN in line with the existing challenges, which in turn plays into the hands of those, favoring the "right of force".

It might make sense for BRICS countries to distance themselves from the format of the G4 (Brazil, India, Germany, Japan) as principal aspirants to become permanent UNSC members and move such efforts into the format of BRICS. This would help promote the idea of more adequate representation in the UNSC of the biggest regions of the developing world. At the same time the issue of veto right could become question of further negotiations. One can consider an idea of possibility of the newly adopted permanent members to voluntarily abstain from using veto right within the next 15 years.

In order to counter discredeting the international law, BRICS could

---

① http://debatewise.org/debates/2757-un-security-council-expansion-of/.

also use network approach and rely on wider unions with the use of their economic, political, civilizational and cultural influence: EurAsEC, SCO, MERCOSUR, CELAC, SAARC, SADC etc.

BRICS should also present a coherent **theoretical model of national development and international life**, aiming at elaboration of common system of values and priorities in the world economy, politics and law. A new concept should be based more on communality philosophical and ethical values, characteristic for most of BRICS civilizational value systems, to prevent excessive egoism and consumerism, and concentrate on sustainable development. Such a conceptual approach, eventually aimed at creating a new socio-economic model of development replacing liberal capitalism, would also contribute to promotion of BRICS global initiatives.

Practically the following steps might be taken:

• Establishing of the specialized BRICS Commission on International Law for regular consultation on most urgent international issues. Exchange and popularization of theoretical and historical heritage of BRICS countries philosophers and lawyers.

• Creating a "wisemen club", comprising a hundred of most noted social scholars and opinion-makers from BRICS countries to develop ideas on the future development paths of the mankind.

• Providing a platform for regular exchange on the institutional and individual basis of legal experts and political scientists from the BRICS countries.

• Providing a foundation of the permanent practice of joint BRICS initiatives in the area of codification and development of the international law in relevant committees, commissions and other structures of the UN and other international organizations.

The increase in current geopolitical confrontation also makes it urgent for BRICS as an organizstion as well as its member countries to play more proactive role in **conflict prevention and crisis mangement.** In the post-bipolar period the leverages that Warsaw Pact and North Atlantic Treaty Organization used to contain individual government and non-government actors rivalry during the Cold War have weakened, and that gave a free hand to the extremist forces, which are trying to achieve power and wealth by using national and religious factors and inflaming ethnic violence, aggressive nationalism and separatism, propagating various ideas of confrontation. It sharply aggravates the situation in those previously stable regions like Ukraine.

Analysis of the main trends in the field of military conflicts shows that since 1990s after the bipolar world order had crashed, the number of conflicts in the world has been steadily increasing and the zone of instability has been widening. During the Cold War, that zone lied mostly in Middle East. Nowadays it starts at Western Sahara and extends across the Heartland to Eastern Europe, Transcaucasia, Southeast, Central Asia and further on to East China Sea, where there are disputes about some islands. The threat of a global nuclear and conventional war has been reduced, but the threat of local military conflicts and hybrid wars has substantially increased.

The most acute disputes are as a rule those concerning basic national interests of the warring parties. These interests include state sovereignty, territorial integrity, social, political and strategic stability in the system of world community, state Constitutional order, free access to the vital economic and strategic zones and communications etc.

BRICS must evolve as a platform for creating contextualised discourse, and by mutual consultations develop viable and credible mechanisms to respond to local, regional and international political and social turbulence such as the events in Middle East, North Africa, Asia or Ukraine. These mechanisms must include structures providing coordination of diplomatic, political, military, information and other activities at all stages of the conflict management and adequately empowered to do that.

BRICS countries can declare a set of the following basic principles for conflict prevention:

- Commitment to the international law and UN role.
- Neutrality in case of the conflicts with participation of BRICS country.
- Uniform BRICS policy on local conflicts (via consultations).
- Non-violence and impartiality.

There are some practical steps BRICS can undertake for creating a system for conflict prevention and management (some of them have already started):

- Permanent consultation mechanism of foreign policy/security officials.
- Coordination of position on conflicts in international organization.
- Common policies on national identity and human rights protection.
- Network security cooperation with regional organizations and outreach countries
- Suggesting global treaties in new areas of security (non-weaponization of outer space, new types of weapons, etc.).
- Joint declaration or treaty on peaceful coexistence in BRICS area.
- Joint peacekeeping force — might be possible in the future?

Another important area of cooperation is **new types of offensive weapons** which pose dangers to global stability; they are normally not covered by any particular treaty, disrupt for established balance of power and in specific cases, and their usage could lead to a conflict. Since the side, which starts operating innovative types of weapons, gets an advantage, new kinds of weapons could also trigger an arms race.

For example, Unmanned Aerial Vehicles (UAV) are now among the most widely used types of military equipment. However, UAVs were not present during the last big wave of arms control agreements in the early 1990s and are not regulated by any particular international norm.[5] BRICS countries should jointly address this issue and offer a system of international regulations.

Traditional area for joint BRICS efforts is **non-proliferation and disarmament**.

Although India is not a member of NPT, BRICS support the existing non-proliferation regime and should take measures to strengthen it.

BRICS countries should establish a working group on the **Outer Space** with the participation of respective space agencies of the member states. The group will be given the task to come up with a consensus document on the peaceful cooperation in Outer Space. *Russian – Chinese draft Treaty on the Prevention of the Placement of Weapons in Outer Space and of the Threat or Use of Force against Outer Space Objects* could be taken as a basis.[6]

There are a number of areas of non-conventional threats and challenges BRICS countries canadress together. They include:
- **Countering international terrorism**

possible areas of cooperation include elaboration of the universal definition of terrorism and promotion of adoption of the UN *Comprehensive Convention on International Terrorism* ; deepening cooperation in exchange of information on terrorist groups financing; strengthening cooperation between relevant law enforcement agencies; signing an agreement on joint investigation of terrorist activities; joint counter-terrorism exercises.

- **Countering drug trafficking and international organized crime**

possible areas of cooperation include exchange of best practices by relevant anti-drug agencies of BRICS countries; development of recommendations aimed at improvement of the national legislations; signing agreement on exchange of relevant information and assistance in investigation of illicit drug trafficking; common educational programs to promote drug-free society at schools, universities, community centers with special target on youth; joint work of relevant health, anti-drug, youth and other agencies and ministries should result in development of social inclusion programs and health procurement in order to prevent further expansion of drug use nationally.

- **Information security and cyber security**

possible areas of cooperation include consensus-based vision of the new global internet governance architecture; countering roots and reasons behind the massive governmental surveillance in the internet; preparing an agreements on CBMs in cybersecurity area; creating joint IT-infrastructure and internet-sector projects.

- **Maritime security**

possible areas of cooperation include modernization and improvement of national legal systems and international criminal law in the maritime areas; creation of the joint or shuttle system of commercial fleet convoy; joint exercises of BRICS countries navies to counter piracy threat; agreements on protection of the coastline of BRICS countries and inland sea spaces in the case of hostilities launched.

- **Illegal migration**

possible areas of cooperation include cooperation in fighting human trafficking and illegal migration; exchange of best practices.

Overall the security agenda should be more and more diversified and increasingly be present in BRICS framework.

References

[1] "Advancing Cooperative Security in Asia Pacific:Ingredients of a 21st Century Security Order", Prepared by Paul Evans and Chen Dongxiao, concept paper for the third meeting of the Canada – China project on "Cooperative Security 2.0" to be held in Shanghai, 6 - 7, December 2014.

[2] Edita Gzoyan and Lilit Bandurya, "Territorial Integrity and Self-determination: Contradiction or Equality?" Http://www.noravank.am/upload/pdf/07.edita%20gzoyan%20lilit%20banduryan_21_century_02 - 2011.pdf.

[3] Salil Shetty, "Human Rights Know No Borders", http://www.amnesty.org/en/annual-report/2013/essay.

[4] Thomas Fleiner, "Common Law and Continental Law: Two Legal Systems", http://www.thomasfleiner.ch/files/documents/legalsystems_fulltext_final.pdf.

[5] Eugene Miasnikov, "Threat of Terrorism Using Unmanned Aerial Vehicles", http://www.armscontrol.ru/UAV/UAV-report.pdf; http://www.micropilot.com/pdf/uav-export-controls.pdf.

[6] Treaty on the Prevention of the Placement of Weapons in Outer Space/PROPOSED PAROS TREATY/Inventory of International Nonproliferation Organizations and Regimes © Center for Nonproliferation Studies, http://cns.miis.edu/inventory/pdfs/paros.pdf.

BRICS Cooperation to Promote Effective Global Governance and Fair World Order

Victoria V. Panova[*]

1. BRICS as Driving Force for Change

First full cycle of BRICS meetings is already a history and this year we have witnessed start of the new round, which was successfully launched with the BRICS Fortaleza Summit. Even though there's pronounced desire on the part of the BRICS themselves to continue working together, we once again see surge of discussions around viability of BRICS. Early this year there were multiple statements that this grouping had reached its "mid age". Nevertheless this is at least an overstatement, and objective observer would find both objective and subjective reasons for that grouping to continue existing. Among reasons to prove BRICS live and kicking one would site the following:

Progress on issues of convergence and understanding that alone none of the BRICS, even its strongest member — China — can pressure the "Northern club" for concessions and fair world order arrangements (trade and investments, finance and development, food security and cyber security, etc.). It is true, that China remains a game-changer, if it pleases, but at the same time only cumulative voice of the five countries could have a sound impact, and only in this case, the G7 or the USA would realize that they are not only in theory, but in practice no longer ruling the world. The most vivid example of that could be the issue of IMF quota reform. We know, that the fate of 2010 decided reform is

---

[*] Victoria V. Panova is Chief Strategy Planning Advisor, NCR BRICS, Russia.

being stalled by the USA Congress refusal to ratify the agreement. Recent threat from the BRICS to renew NAB for 3 months instead of 6 months and to consider further actions by the end of this year showed to the wealthy club that they have to start moving or things will spin out of their control.

Concept of desirability of peaceful and mutually beneficial co-existence and co-enrichment of diverse cultures and different civilizations opposing to the homogenized western-style world order is a very unique BRICS concept which lies in opposition to westernization and putting all nations and civilizations all over the world under the single press of only appropriate for the advanced economies model. We are now discussing suggesting to our BRICS partners the idea of the right of each nation and each of the world citizens for the social cultural identity. We believe this could be a game changer in the whole concept of globalized development.

Complementarity of economies and wide space for market integration, industrial and economic cooperation etc. are all BRICS Strenyth. Recently signed 400 billion gas deal between China and Russia certainly manifest that countries of BRICS have huge potential for further economic integration. It was also acknowledged at the last BTTC meeting that BRICS "may consider further cooperation in trade and investment that promotes further sustainable economic growth and development" and thus should aim at closer market integration of their respective economies. To these ends, it was agreed that BTTC would propose to further "investigate the institutional, administrative and socio-cultural obstacles and challenges that hinder business investment and development across borders".

Latest developments, namely the crisis in Ukraine and in this context joint reaction of BRICS to Australia's statements, manifested eagerness of all five countries to support each other even in situations were no full understanding of partner's position could be claimed. It is even more valuable for Russia since it understands that most of BRICS countries experience internal problems of their own that makes it extremely difficult for them to claim their position in outright support of Russia in the current situation. Among other outcomes firm position of BRICS forced once bullish Australian (as the G20 current chair) position to be softened and officially recalled.

It should be also stated that while Russia (also as one of the initiators of the BRICS gatherings) valued this format highly from the start, there seems to be growing understanding that this is the best format for the fact that even though countries may have divergent opinions on different matters, unlike in other structures, BRICS are ready to listen to each other and none seems to believe its view is the ultimate truth. While opposite tendencies are seen in the other grouping of the G7. Once they saw that BRICS is here to stay and that its members are ready to defend their proper national interests, they became much more aggressive in furthering their view of the world. Here I should give example of the recent G7 pre-summit conference I was attending. Such gatherings are usually organized to include not only (and actually to a lesser extent) academics, but also politicians and experts working on the matters within the scope of the Summit. This event was held in the Egmont Palace, which is the Foreign Ministry building and official events are often held there. What was most discouraging at the conference is that it wasn't eventually focused on positive achievements the G7 could strive at, but rather had dominating dividing tone, first of all focused on Ukrainian crisis, but what surprised me even more, had very negative tone against China, primarily due to situation in the East China Sea, but also developments around South China Sea and then stand-off with Vietnam. A number of speakers or those asking questions would talk about how the G7 should counter as they termed it "aggressive behavior of Russia and China". At the same time dominating tone was to welcome Russia back under certain circumstances. Nevertheless a lot has changed since 1990s — Russia is no longer feeling bound to submit to the G7 and concede its interests in order to be part of the elite club. While there might be issues important for cooperation, it is firmly believed that BRICS is probably even more elite now, since it's about emerging powers as opposed to geriatric powers of the West.

Thus, in contradiction to all actions taken by BRICS with their reformative (and not revolutionary) approach, the G7 has started considering more seriously how to preserve their dominant position not incorporating BRICS, but trying to leave them on the outskirts of world development. This is an extremely unwise approach especially taken that China and India are #2 and 3 economies (by PPP), and Russia and Brazil accordingly #6 and 7 economies in the world. Meanwhile we saw weaker prospects and even negative scenario for our economies in the coming future, it is vital that we firmly stand together to oppose tendencies or rather soften adverse consequences. Thus we should continue working on two levels — pressure within the established institutions and creating our duplicating institutions. BDB and reserve pool are a really good start. While we should consider: national payment systems (with Russian initiative of having its own with level of integration or possibility of mutually substituting character with the Chinese system + other Asian payment systems), rating agency, network universities (league), involving all stakeholders of our societies into the intra-BRICS cooperation, reaching out to developing countries (beyond Africa) and offering them cooperation deals, offering mutually beneficial cooperation schemes in our respective regions etc.

2. Framework for BRICS Multilateral Cooperation

Taken in general most of BRICS countries, with certain exception of Brazil, follow the line of non-acceptance of infringements in national sovereignty and their own autonomy, which is determined by the fact that none of them (including Brazil in this case) is ready to put limitations imposed by the established Western countries to their national agendas and policy decisions. Thus BRICS come out as "sovereignty hawks" pursuing policy of **protection of sovereignty and non-interference in internal affairs**, that are fixed explicitly in *Charter of the United Nations*, countering Western policies of intervention and economic and financial liberalization. Also Russia is interested in demonstrating with the BRICS benefits of the "network diplomacy", which would avoid "domestic political disincentives imposed by conditionality requirements typical of most Western institutions".[1]

Here one should also note that counter to general lines of thought in Western political science schools, Russian scholars see world arrangements through *Charter of the United Nations* lenses, attributing vital importance to democratic arrangements in the global governance scheme, where all countries are seen as equal and having a voice, rather than world society made up only of countries accepted as democracies by the established West. This is also reflected in official position of Russian Federation towards functioning of international institutions and relations between the countries.

The other common position, shared by all BRICS states is their support for **multilateral world** as opposed to unilateralism. As already exemplified by above statements, Russia first time explicitly came up with this idea promoting triangle of China – India – Russia and multivector diplomacy in the mid-1990s. This is also confirmed in official Russian documents. With the first half of the 1990s, with the Russian foreign policy initially concentrated in theory and practice on attempts of full integration with the Western countries and Western-dominated institutions, considerable change towards diversification was already noted in 1997 Presidential Address to Federal Assembly. Among the aims of foreign policy most important were:

• to protect national interests of Russia without going into confrontation, but rather based on strengthening stability and cooperation in international relations.

• to form the system of international relations that is based on the fact that "**our world in multipolar, and there should be no domination of one center of power**".

• Taken that "**the world in the 21st century should rely less on military power but rather on the power of law**".[2]

First practical manifestation on the part of Russia to foster multipolar world is seen by some experts in the series of visits in 1997 of the then Foreign Minister E. Primakov to Latin American countries with the signing of a number of agreements on "strategic partnership" with the leading states of the continent.[1]

---

① More on that see B. Martynov, Mnogopoliarny ili mnogotsivizationny mir? International Trends, http://www.intertrends.ru/twenty-first/014.htm.

Later on, the new Concept of Foreign Policy of Russia, adopted under the new President Putin in June 2000, stated that Russia would put efforts into "**formation of the multipolar system of international relations**" that reflect the reality of diverse world with the differences of its interests and based on "**mechanisms of collective decision-making**", priority of international law and "**democratization of international relations**".[3] In the next Foreign Policy Concept of 2008 Russia further stresses the fact that strengthened economic potential of the "**new centers of global growth, among others connected to more equal distribution of development resources**" resulting from liberalization of world markets. Thus economic power in those countries and regions is bound to lead to bigger political influence with further tendencies to polycentric world order.

Also the Concept of 2008 elaborates further with the notion of the fact that "**traditional cumbersome military-political alliances cannot fulfill the task of reaction to a full specter of modern threats and challenges, having trans-boundary character**", instead there's suggestion to base national activities on "**network diplomacy**" and flexible forms of multilateralism.

There's acknowledgement in the official vision of the world development that "**global competition for the first time in newest history acquires civilizational dimension, which presupposes competition between different values and models of development within universal framework of principles of democracy and market economy**". In the same document Russia also scolds the West for "**reacting to the prospects of loss by historic West its monopoly to globalization process**" including with inertia of "**containment of Russia**". And according to the document "**strategy of unilateral actions destabilize international situation, provokes tensions and arms race, deepens inter-state contradictions, instigate national and religious hatred, creates security threat for other countries, and leads to escalation of tensions in inter-civilizational relations**". All throughout the official discourse and documents there's also explicit statement on the **central role of the UN**, which along with the multipolarity, sovereignty, and rule of law principles are unequivocally shared by all the BRICS countries.[4]

As mentioned earlier, with the time BRICS matured, Russian

government came with bigger appreciation for the group. Actually, with the fact that Putin as a President in 2006 promoted the idea, it was with the Medvedev presidency, that this club came into being on the leaders' level. Today there's no way to underestimate importance attached to BRICS by Russian elite.

One of the articles of the incoming President Putin read that Russia "**would continue attaching priority to cooperation with the BRICS partners. This unique structure, created in 2006, most vividly symbolizes transformation from unipolarity to fairer world order**".[5] And then this view is reinforced by Russian foreign minister Lavrov's statement that BRICS creation proved to be "**one of the most significant geopolitical events since the beginning of the new century**"[6].

This mechanism is seen as a new model of global relations over the old barriers that divide East and West and North and South, and thus is bound to transform gradually into "**multilateral strategic partnership on a wide array of world economic and political issues**". Also Russia is quite ambitious in terms of the future for BRICS, believing the idea of a "bridge" between North and South or it being only active within the scope of the South would essentially limit its capabilities as an independent actor on the international arena.[7]

With this in mind it is possible to outline main directions where Russia sees a role for BRICS:

• International economic cooperation and establishment of a more democratic and fair financial and economic system;

• Promoting polycentric world and methods of network diplomacy, including through establishment of integration mechanisms on their respective continents, having complementary character (which is the way to put forward and reconcile attempts of creation of Eurasian Union by Russia);

• Strengthening cooperation within the United Nations and its Security Council, promoting role of the UN as a primary body for global governance;

• Fostering cooperation of BRICS within universal and regional organizations in order to preserve international peace and security;

- Coordinating positions on questions of global and regional stability and regional security, non-proliferation, regional conflict management;
- Promoting central role for the UN in combatting terrorism, and implementation of the UN Global counter-terrorism strategy;
- Putting joint efforts in coordination of fight against drug-trafficking within the UN and relevant regional institutions;
- Cooperating on international information security, joint fight against cyber-terrorism and cyber-crime;
- Cooperating with BRICS partners in the area of fighting marine piracy, undertaking joint efforts to create international mechanism on legal trial and punishment for pirates;
- Creating and strengthening external links of BRICS with leading developing countries (Argentina, Indonesia, Venezuela etc.) and international organizations (UN, SCO, AU, ASEAN,EvrAzES, UNASUR et al.);
- Cooperating on the basis of equality, complementarity and mutual benefit in economic, scientific and technological areas, having in mind BRICS countries' large resource base, biggest labor resources, large internal markets, aims of economic modernization and high tech, food and energy security, ameliorating quality of life of citizens.

3. BRICS Coordination within International Governance Structures

The initial idea behind BRICS meetings on leaders' level grew from the fact of the necessity to coordinate BRICS countries positions within the G20 grouping, emanating in response to the global financial and economic crisis. As mentioned earlier the first special foreign ministers' meeting of BRICS happened in 2008 in Yekaterinburg, to be followed by leaders' encounter next year at the same place. Today it is acknowledged that as a result of BRICS cooperation within the G20 came out significant achievements in international financial institutions reform (with major negotiations going on between BRICS and financial G7), even though many problems persist and BRICS have to take extra measures in order to promote its vision. Issue of IFI quotas was subject to very acute discussion during the Pittsburg G20 Summit in 2009, and it was at that meeting that the then President Medvedev along with other emerging countries came out with a proposal to increase general quota shares for emerging economies by 7% at the expense of the advanced economies, and as a result the final document stated "not less than 5%" margin. Thus it was to a great extent because of the five countries joint position, that share of emerging and developing countries in the World Bank grew from 43.97% to 47.19% of the total, with IMF share also increasing from 39.5% to 42.29%, thus making four of the BRICS countries in the top ten share-holders of the IMF① [China taking the 3rd place, India, Russia (enjoying slight increase from 2.49% to 2.71%) and Brazil — 8th, 9th and 10th accordingly] and moving them very close to having a cumulative veto power of 85% in the Fund (14.18% + South Africa with 0.6%).②

It was speculated that due to protracted ratification process for this decision, BRICS countries came up with a number of decisions — including study of establishment of BRICS bank, to be reported for September IMF/WB side-lines meeting of BRICS finance ministers, as well as reserve on declaration of additional resource pull for the IMF for the second line of defense. Eventually this came out as a decision of BRICS leaders meeting before the start of the LosCabos G20 meeting this June, with China committing 43 billion USD, Brazil, India and Russia — 10 billion USD each, and South Africa — 2 billion USD, conditioned that these resources would only be accessed when there'll be no more funds left and that BRICS countries would be able to monitor directions and aims of spending. Thus, even if this delay in allocating extra resources was meant to push European and American countries to ratify IMF reform package (which no one admits though, meanwhile out of the promised 456 billion USD, Japan came up with 60 bln USD, Germany

---

① It is necessary to note that so far only 2008 IMF decision came into force, the BRICS promoted reform package decided upon in 2010 haven't been ratified by necessary amount of countries (number of countries and their weight), among those USA (with American Presidential elections making it not likely for this to happen as scheduled by the end of 2012) and a number of European countries.

② A thorough study on the issue of the course of the reform was made in D. Smyslov, "Reformirovanie Mezhdunarodnogo valyutnogo fonda: problemy I resheniya", Finansy I upravleniye, *Informatsionno-analiticheskiye materialy*, Dengi I kredit, #1/2012, pp. 36–43, #2/2012, pp. 33–44.

54.7, France 41.4 — compared to 75 bln USD coming from all BRICS combined), this didn't seem work this way: money were set aside notwithstanding no real breakthrough on the matter.

Importance on the part of Russia is attached to stronger cooperation between BRICS in the view of stabilization of the world economy in the areas of energy and aviation, peaceful use of space, improving quality of healthcare system through joint projects in telemedicine and pharmaceuticals, nano-and biophysics, agriculture etc.

BRICS countries also serve as an engine for elaborating and promoting ideas not just within the G20, but also other international organizations. The Moscow agricultural ministers' meeting of 2010 led to creation of the information base to provide analysis on the state of food security of BRIC countries. In the same year the G20 put global food security as one of the nine key pillars of the Seoul Summit Multi-Year Action Plan for Development. This in turn led to a study by FAO along with other relevant international organizations on the way to mitigate risks of food price volatility submitted for the G20 Cannes Summit in November 2011, where among the recommendations there was a call to establish Agricultural Market Information System (AMIS), approved by the G20 leaders. Later, in March 2012 at the BRICS Delhi Summit, five countries came up with the publication of *Action Plan 2012 –2016 for Agricultural Cooperation of BRICS Countries,* which underlined that this agricultural information exchange system of BRICS (coordinated by China) should be linked to the AMIS "in order not to duplicate", although detailing out all segments of exchange, it was stressed that "information submitted by all members shall only be shared among ministries of agriculture of the BRICS countries".[8] Also as part of the second paragraph of the Action Plan on development of a general strategy (coordinated by Brazil)①, decision was reached on "creation of a BRICS group in FAO, which would act also within the United Nations World Food Program in order to coordinate initiatives to promote food security, projects in the area of food security and school meals, as well as incentivizing mechanisms for

---

① While Russia is responsible for the sub-topic of trade and investment promotion of BRICS agricultural cooperation.

purchasing local food of family agriculture".[9]

Another, even though to a certain point more contested area would be coordination within the UN. Thus, presence of all five countries in the UN Security Council in 2011 strengthened the dialogue of the group members on international peace and security. This continues to be the case further on as well.

Political agenda is the only one where BRICS countries start having a way for negotiation, which was clearly demonstrated by Libya and Syria cases. Meanwhile a number of others while being similar on a declaratory level, in reality are inherently dividing and thus remain out of the scope of BRICS. Among those would be relevant to remember the UNSC reform and nuclear disarmament.

Two out of all BRICS countries are permanent members of the UNSC, while the other threestrive for a way to be represented in that body on a permanent basis (with India and Brazil being within the G4 coalition along with Germany and Japan). While there's general consensus on the need of reform per se, goals of the final outcome differ and thus allow only for a lowest common denominator within the BRICS club. That is why we read as little as confirmation of the "**need for a comprehensive reform of the UN, including its Security Council, with a view to making it more effective, efficient and representative so that it can deal with today's global challenges more successfully. China and Russia reiterate the importance they attach to the status of Brazil, India and South Africa in international affairs and support their aspiration to play a greater role in the UN**" in the New Delhi BRICS Declaration.[10] Meanwhile there doesn't seem to be an immediate headway to satisfy the other three countries with the course of the reform, which doesn't have dangerous implications for BRICS being, for stumble block for reform of the UNSC isn't limited by opposition to simple expansion by China or Russia or even both. Russian position on the matter sites among its main goals higher efficiency of that body and its more representative character in order to take into account changed realities of the world, but also "**to react promptly and properly to arising crises and problems**". Meanwhile taken the fact that not a single model of reform enjoys overwhelming support, Moscow believes it counterproductive to try to push those through, since it would "**inevitably polarize General Assembly**" and instead, continue "**diligent work on rapprochement of positions without introducing fake deadlines**". What remains out of negotiation scheme for Russia though, are the prerogatives of the UNSC, including the veto right.[11]

Somewhat similar situation appeared with the appointments of heads of IMF first, and especially graphic — of the World Bank, when Brazil and South Africa came out supporting competing candidates for the post thus failing with the single stand on the issue and issuing hollow statement on welcome of the candidates from developing world, that are to "**be selected through an open and merit-based process**"[12]. While WTO case could be cited as emerging economies success, since now we have Brazilian R. Azevedu at the helm of the institution.

Unlike UNSC reform, problem of nuclear disarmament is even more multilayer, having divide not only between "haves" and "have-nots", but showing difference of approaches between "official members of the nuclear club" and "illegal possessors", those having potential for assured destruction and those with little capacity, etc.

Since there are more questions than answers in the existing non-proliferation regime, and all BRICS have different approaches to the matter, Russia prefers to concentrate within the group or on bilateral level on smaller bits, but no less important issues, where there's a possibility of considerable convergence of interests. To name but a few — cooperation of all BRICS countries in the area of nuclear safety, initiation of talks on the Treaty on Prohibition of Production of Fissile Materials for Nuclear Weapons and Nuclear Explosives at Geneva conference or joint Russian – Chinese proposal on the treaty on non-deployment of weapons in space.[13] All BRICS countries cooperated intensively within the UN in order to promote this initiative, had unified stand on non-use of force towards space objects.[14]

While the only way for dealing with the problems of possible non-proliferation regime is breached (with Iran as a case in point), Russia in line with other BRICS countries insists on diplomatic ways of problem resolution.

Otherwise, existing contradictions are directed to the bilateral level and discussions, for the value each government attaches to its BRICS identity.

References

[1] Cynthia Roberts, "Polity Forum: Challengers or Stakeholders? BRICs and the Liberal World Order," *Polity*, Vol. 42, No. 1, January 2010, p.10.

[2] Presidential Address to the Federal Assembly of B.N.Yeltsin, "Poriadok vo vlasti-poriadok v strane", March 6, 1997, http://www.intelros.ru/2007/02/05/poslanie_prezidenta_rosii_borisa_elcina_federalnomu_sobraniju_rf_porjadok_vo_vlasti__porjadok_v_strane_1997_god.html.

[3] "Concept of the Foreign Policy of Russian Federation", Moscow, June 28, 2000, Nezavisimaya Gazeta, NG-Politika, http://www.ng.ru/world/2000 - 07 - 11/1_concept.html.

[4] "Concept of the Foreign Policy of Russian Federation", Moscow, July 15, 2008, http://kremlin.ru/acts/785.

[5] V.Putin, "Rossija i meniyuschiysia mir", *Moscow News*, February 27, 2012, http://mn.ru/politics/20120227/312306749.html.

[6] S.Lavrov, "BRICS: A New-generation Forum with a Global Reach", in *BRICS: The 2012 New Delhi Summit*, eds. by J.Kirton, M.Larionova, and Y. Alagh, Newsdesk Media, 2012.

[7] S.Lavrov, Ibid.

[8] *BRICS: Action Plan 2012 -2016 for Agricultural Cooperation of BRICS Countries*, March 2012, http://www.bricsindia.in/actionPlan.html.

[9] *BRICS: Action Plan 2012 -2016 for Agricultural Cooperation of BRICS Countries*, March 2012, http://www.bricsindia.in/actionPlan.html.

[10] *Fourth BRICS Summit — Delhi Declaration*, March 29, 2012, http://www.mea.gov.in/mystart.php? id =190019162.

[11] Opozitsii Rossii na 66 sessii Generalnoi Assamblei OON, Ministry of Foreign Affairs of Russia, 2011, http://www.mid.ru/bdomp/ns-dmo.nsf/66d11ad1c1bc0a7bc32576790039c04a/b1d0994f63c95f86c32578ce0039986b! Open Document.

[12] Fourth BRICS Summit — Delhi Declaration, March 29, 2012, http://www.mea.gov.in/mystart.php? id =190019162.

[13] M.Ulianov, "Dalneishee razoruzhenie vriad li vozmozhno v formate tolko

Rossii i SSHA", February 9, 2012, http://www.interfax.ru/txt.asp? id =230110.

[14] D.Medvedev, "Strany BRIC: obschie tseli-obschie deistviya", April 13, 2010, http://kremlin.ru/news/7443.

National Security and Sustainable Development of the State

Aleksei Chagrin[*]

At recent time, a new look at security in a wide range of objects and sense (personality, society, state, entire international community) is being generated. It is tied and consistent with problems and ideas of transition of human civilization towards sustainable development. In particular, this view is reflected in the new National Security Strategy of the Russian Federation to a certain extent and in respect of strengthening security through development.

Unfortunately, there has been developed ambiguous understanding of nature and content of military security concept and there are different interpretations of it. Ambiguity of these concepts derived from different approaches in consideration of "security" phenomenon in a broad sense. It is important to note that recently, a new way in ensuring security development (especially when it concerns national security) is being derivated. It is now considered through the prism of problems of transition to sustainable state development.

From the context of formal approach, security is defined as safety of interests (including national) from internal and external threats.

Public approach to the definition of national security focuses on preservation of integrity, sustainability, stability and normal functioning of the country (the state and its society as a social system) at times when destructive effect is applied to it.

In any case, the way of understanding and resolving of theoretical and

---

[*] Aleksei Chagrin, the Head of the Science Research Center of Military Academy of the General Staff of the Armed Forces of the Russian Federation (MAGS AFRF).

practical problems of security through denial of dangers, struggling actual threats and dangers, following safety paradigm is set in minds of many scientists and experts in the field of security.

The essence of safety paradigm is quite simple. It can be expressed as thesis: "I'm safe because I'm able to detect and prevent dangers timely." Necessary prerequisite in this case is definition of security threats and perception of surrounding world through the prism of threats and dangers.

It is necessary to analyze and evaluate hazards and threats, determining probability of their realization. Evaluation of number of threats and dangers to the national security of the state is advised to be based on risk theory.

Russia has significant potential for sustainable development. Prerequisite for economic and social renewal of the country on a path towards sustainable development are: enormous intellectual capability; fundamental and applied sciences; vast natural resources; creation of basis for market institutions; elements of industrial and communications infrastructure, etc. Today, the main objective is acceleration of economical and social renewal of the country, modernization of production structures, provision of Russia's access to the position of an active participant and leading country in global sustainable development process.

Focusing efforts and resources on specific priorities for sustainable development, as follows:

• improvement of quality of life of Russian citizens by guaranteeing personal safety, as well as high life standards;

• economical growth, primarily achieved through development of national innovation system and human capital investments;

• science, technology, education, health and culture, which are developed by strengthening the role of the state and improvement of public-private partnership;

• ecology of living systems and environmental management, maintenance of which shall be achieved through balanced consumption, development of advanced technologies and appropriate reproduction of natural-resource potential of the country;

- strategic stability and equitable strategic partnership, developed on the basis of Russia's active participation in the development of multipolar world order model.

Russian Federation recognizes the need and possible gradual transition to sustainable development, involving balanced solution of socio-economical challenges, thus preserving favorable environment and natural resource potential in order to meet the needs of present and future generations.

Transition to sustainable development is proposed to be carried out in three stages. At the first stage it is necessary to solve acute social and economical problems; at the second — to conduct environmentally oriented structural changes in economical and social sphere; at the third — to realize the idea of V. I. Vernadsky about harmonization of nature and society. The ultimate goal is to ensure sustainable development of ecological and environment comfort for people's life.

The new vision of security reflects current trend in combination of security problems and gradual development without any cataclysms and catastrophes. It is not about extensive economically-centered model of competitive development, which can't be considered stable. It is about sustainable and innovative-stable balanced development. In this way of development quantitative parameters are minimized but qualitative parameters, factors and sources of development are maximized. Emphasis is done on consensual co-evolutionary forms of human interaction with nature as well as within society. This widely corresponds with no spheric concept of humanity development by V. I. Vernadsky.

In this case we can talk about the concept of sustainable development — the "Sustainable security" concept. Use of this approach will allow movement towards a new civilizational paradigm, where security and sustainable development are not only interrelated but represent a single integrated system. Within the state, Russia in particular, transition to this paradigm is considered primarily in connection with ensuring national security.

Compliance with certain principles concerning risks of implementation and destructive processes and phenomenon in the main spheres of human activity is an important condition for implementation of the new civilizational paradigm, in which security and sustainable development represent a single system (functional unit).

Identification, analysis and risk assessment in various spheres of human activities, their classification due to different backgrounds, their ranging and other systematization is a separate, quite difficult but very important objective.

The result of performing this difficult objective is quantitive evaluation of challenges, dangers, and threats accompanying transition of the international community in general and Russia in particular, on the way towards realization of new civilizational paradigm of balanced innovative and sustainable development.

Russia and BRICS after the Ukrainian Crisis

Alexander Lukin[*]

1. BRICS as the Structure of a Post-bipolar World

The collapse of the Soviet Union in the early 1990s caused a fundamental change to the long-standing system of international relations that was based on the confrontation between two centres of power. Although back in the Soviet era, some researchers noted a trend toward a multi-polar world as the leading states in each region grew in power, the Soviet Union's sudden departure from the scene left something of a vacuum. Although many states, even outside the Western world, disliked the Soviet Union and even criticized it, its absence left many states, especially larger ones, wary of a certain threat. That threat stemmed, first, from the instability in the international situation resulting from the end of a bipolar system that had guaranteed a certain order; and second, from the possibility that the one remaining center of power — now freed from any external checks and balances, might encroach on the interests of others.

Thus, when the United States celebrated its victory in the Cold War and Francis Fukuyama declared the "end of history", China, India, Brazil and many other countries of Asia, Africa and South America viewed that development with some uneasiness. Had the U.S. shown restraint, subsequent events might have unfolded somewhat differently, but under Bill Clinton, and to a greater extent George W. Bush,

---

[*] Alexander Lukin, the Head of the Department of International Relations at the National Research University – Higher School of Economics and the Director of the Center for East Asian and Shanghai Cooperation Organization Studies at Moscow State Institute of International Relations.

Washington set out to secure that victory and achieve world dominance for the United States. Europe either could not or would not pursue an independent course and, as always, kept in line with Washington's policy.

Working together, Western states increasingly attempted to assume the function of an international arbiter, substituting their own decisions for international law. This was seen in the West's decision to ignore the UN Security Council whenever that body did not rule as desired, and in granting NATO and its individual member states the right to intervene in international conflicts without Security Council approval. Western actions in the conflicts in Iraq, Yugoslavia — especially the violent secession of Kosovo from Serbia — and later in Libya, where the West clearly overstepped the powers granted to it by the UN Security Council, and then in Syria, where, without any international sanction, it supports the overthrow of a legitimate government — have all destabilized the entire region and inevitably aroused deep concern among non-Western states.

Under such circumstances, the disgruntled states have begun building bridges between each other. That cooperation was not initially directed against the West because all of the participants in that process are largely tied to the Western system and value their collaboration with it. However, they looked for ways to coordinate their positions on those aspects of the new Western-dominated world that did not suit them. That desire led to the creation or strengthening of institutions and groups in which Western states did not participate: ASEAN and various formats of associated cooperative endeavors, SCO, CELAC and, of course, BRICS.

Of these groups, BRICS — not formally an organization — has attracted the most interest. There are several reasons for this. First, the group brings together the largest and most influential non-Western countries. Second, it is not a regional but a global group that claims to represent the entire "South", or more broadly, the entire non-Western world. Third, BRICS actively puts forward its own initiatives as an alternative to Western projects for organizing the global economic and political order.

It is interesting that the name BRICS (originally "BRIC") was originally coined by Goldman Sachs analyst Jim O'Neill but that the group evolved very differently than he had expected. It turned out that political reasons provided the foundation of the group members' association, and not similarities between their economies or level of economic development. This is demonstrated by the way BRICS came into existence, gradually evolving and bringing together states from different continents and regions where they were the natural leaders. Its origins can be traced to the rapprochement of Russia and China based on shared geopolitical interests. Without this rapprochement that developed over two decades, BRICS most likely would never have appeared. (Although RIC formally remains a separate group, it has remained virtually inactive as such following the formation of BRIC.) The final touch has been the accession of South Africa, transforming the group into BRICS.

BRICS gains geopolitical significance by offering its own views on the processes at work in the world. One of the main topics BRICS addresses is the need to reform the global economy. The BRICS member states strongly propose increasing the representation of non-Western countries in international financial institutions, but they meet with fierce resistance from the traditional masters of global finance. It was the disappointment that BRICS experienced in its attempt to reform the World Bank and IMF and put them on more equitable footing that led the group to create its own development bank and pool of currency reserves. And while these institutions might not offer a comprehensive alternative to existing international financial institutions, they should help correct their pro-Western bias and provide non-Western states with an alternative when choosing the source for their financial development and in the event of a serious economic crisis.

Russian Foreign Ministry chief BRICS expert Vadim Lukov holds that reform of the global financial system is the most important of the group's four strategic interests. He considers the other three as strengthening the central role of the UN Security Council in the international system, making maximum use of the complementary nature of the member states' economies in order to accelerative economic development and modernizing the social sphere and economic life of those countries.① As we can see, only some of those goals are purely economic in nature.

2. The Ukrainian Crisis and BRICS

It is difficult to overestimate the significance of the Ukrainian crisis for BRICS, and for the world as a whole. In general terms, it has shown that the West will continue — and with greater persistence than ever — to build a unipolar world model, pulling an ever greater number of satellites into its foreign policy orbit and demanding conformance in both their foreign and domestic policies, saddling them with what the West calls "international" and even "universal" standards. Many states in the non-Western world view this approach as a new wave of colonialism that substitutes the ideological slogan of "democracy" for "more advanced culture", but that retains the same methods and goals. Of course, such circumstances will only increase the desire of the non-Western world to increase its mutual coordination.

Of course, the BRICS states differ greatly between each other, and their disagreements with the West also have different historical and political roots. Representing South America with its strong leftist and socialist tendencies, Brazil tends to disagree with the West, and especially with the United States in the area of social policy. For a country where the names of almost all major political parties includes the word "socialism", the entire political spectrum in the United States is too "right-wing" for its tastes. Moreover, South America is especially sensitive to any dictatorial attitude from the north and anything resembling Monroe Doctrine-type thinking. The situation is somewhat similar in South Africa, where communists are part of the ruling coalition and the pro-Western political elite stand accused of aiding and

---

① Interv'yu Posla po osobym porucheniyam MID Rossii V. B. Lukova «RIA Novosti» (Interview of Ambassador at Large of the Russian Ministry of Foreign Affairs V. B. Lukov to "RIA Novosti"), April 14, 2014, http://www. mid. ru/brp_4. nsf/newsline/33A1D346558B4C3944257CBD0032BFDD.

abetting the apartheid regime. Meanwhile, in Russia and India, anti-Western sentiment is increasingly taking on not only geopolitical form, but also a values-based meaning. In those states that have recently experienced a revival of religion, the people reject not so much the policies of the West as much as it does the moral values it imposes. The political system of the West does not elicit any particular objections, although differences do exist. A more secular China is perhaps closer to the West in its moral outlook, but its political system is the exact opposite of Western standards. It is not the nature of those differences that serve as the basis for cooperation, but the fact that they exist and the strong desire to resist any dictatorial attitudes by the West.

It is important for BRICS that the united "North" has recently chosen one of the group's members as an object for confrontation. This will strengthen the solidarity among BRICS member states, a unity that has already found expression in its collective protest against the attempt by individual Western members of G20 to forbid Russia from participating in the summit in Brisbane in November 2014. In March 2014 the BRICS Foreign Minister announced, "The custodianship of the G20 belongs to all Member States equally and no one Member State can unilaterally determine the exclusion of another Member State from the Summit."[1] This consolidated position has become a manifestation of the role of BRICS states as the representatives of the non-Western world in G20, where it consistently puts forward initiatives that serve as alternatives to those proposed by the collective "North". The success of this demarche is seen by the fact that the position of the West is diminishing in the G20.

By the way, the decision by the West to halt activities of G8 as one of the sanctions against Russia has even further crystallized the opposing poles in the Group of 20. Whereas previously Russia, as a member of both the G8 and the G20, could mitigate that polarity to some extent, now two sharply opposing poles will exist in the G20: the purely

---

[1] Media Statement on the Meeting of the BRICS Foreign/International Relations Ministers held on 24 March 2014 in The Hague, Netherlands, http://www. brics. mid. ru/brics. nsf/WEBmitBric/ 63AFCD6DA75BDFA544257CA70052CA90.

Western G7 group and BRICS, representing the rest of the world.

In this way, the Ukrainian crisis will only further consolidate BRICS. It has shown that the group is moving in the right direction and should strengthen its efforts to coordinate its actions in order to provide a real alternative to Western efforts to impose a unipolar world structure. That activity by BRICS will go a long way toward creating a truly multi-polar world structure.

For its part, Russia has an even greater interest in cooperation within the BRICS framework. This is not only because Moscow is seeking support in its confrontation with the West, but also for the deeper reason that the complete breakdown of mutual trust with the West, the West's sanctions and its attempt to use economic leverage to apply political pressure as well as Russia's actions in response have given greater impetus to the process of Russia's turning towards the non-Western world that had already begun before the current crisis. Given that the sanctions are unlikely to be repealed in the foreseeable future, Asian and South American states will gradually replace Europe as the exporters of many goods, especially food and agricultural products. Russia's hydrocarbon exports are gradually moving in the direction of China and the Asia Pacific Region. Russian political elite are beginning to understand that they cannot achieve the strategic goal of developing Siberia and the Far East without cooperating with their neighbors in Asia. On the whole, Europe and the United States are beginning to be viewed as unreliable partners who are ready to sacrifice economic ties for the sake of political pressure at any moment. Thus, not only ideology, but also objective circumstances and economic interests compel Russia to shift its attention to other regions. What's more, developing deeper cooperation with political and economic leaders in those regions, such as the BRICS member states, will become the key focus of Russian foreign policy.

Forming of BRICS Joint Position on International Financial and Monetary Systems Reform

Mikhail Golovnin[*]

Global economic and financial crisis of 2007—2009 became first global shock during globalization period and it led to the realization of the necessity of reforms in financial sector, which had been responsible for crisis spillover to economy as a whole in national and international scopes. Among systemic drawbacks of financial sector complex of actors' incentives, too liberal regulations, excessive relative size of financial sector, development of new financial products, inter-jurisdictional arbitrage should be pointed out. Widespread crisis contagion through international spillovers made the reform of the whole international financial system essential.

All BRICS countries, which are a part of emerging and developing countries group, were recipients of global financial shocks during 2007 – 2008. That is why they are interested in minimizing the threat of similar shocks in the future. BRICS countries can participate in international financial reform on three levels: (1) through their own policies on national level; (2) through addressing the common position on global forums (e.g. G20); (3) through joint actions in financial sector.

BRICS countries' role in global economy has significantly risen, especially during last decade. Their share in global GDP in USD on current exchange rates has increased from 10.9% in 2005 to 22.9% in 2013. However, financial sector developments in these countries underperform the global level with some exceptions for China and South

---

[*] Mikhail Golovnin, deputy director of the Institute of Economics of the Russian Academy of Sciences, the head of the Center of problems of globalization of the Russian economy.

Africa. For example domestic bank credit to private sector to GDP ratio varied in 2013 among BRICS countries from 51% to 52% in India and Russia, 70% to 71% in Brazil and South Africa to 140% in China, while average world indicator was equal to 89.6% .① Domestic stock market turnover to GDP varied from 33% to 37% of GDP in Russia, India and Brazil, amounted for 71% in China and 81% in South Africa, while world average indicator reached 70% .②

Gap between BRICS countries' GDP positions and role of their currencies on global foreign exchange market is even more evident. Aggregate share of all BRICS currencies in global foreign exchange market turnover accounted for only 7% in 2013 (taking into account the sum of 200 per cent as two currencies are involved in any transaction).③ Though the role of BRICS countries in global foreign exchange reserves (mainly because of China's position) is quite significant. In the mid of 2014 BRICS countries held 43% of global foreign exchange reserves.④ Thus current state of international monetary system is dependent on monetary and fiscal policy decisions of individual BRICS countries, namely exchange rate regimes and different reserve funds accumulations.

Thus we can realize that actions on national level in BRICS countries may have only limited effect in global scope. These actions usually involve measures on implementation of international financial reforms agenda. They include mainly preparations for implementation of the Basel III, solving the problems of systemically important financial institutions, strengthening supervision on "shadow" banking system, regulations of over-the-counter derivatives market etc. Although some interesting special initiatives like Chinese "internationalization of yuan" should be mentioned.

What more important from our point of view is forming the joint position on international financial system reforms agenda. BRICS

---

① http://data.worldbank.org/indicator/FD.AST.PRVT.GD.ZS/.
② http://data.worldbank.org/indicator/CM.MKT.TRAD.GD.ZS.
③ "Global Foreign Exchange Market Turnover in 2013", *Triennial Central Bank Survey*, Bank for International Settlements, Monetary and Economic Department, February 2014.
④ Calculations based on http://elibrary-data.imf.org/.

countries may represent in this reform process not only their own position, but also more general view of emerging and developing economies.

First, the scope of reform should be identified. It seems for us that wrong diagnosis may mean wrong cure and continuing disease. Underlying problems of recent global economic and financial crisis, as we have mentioned earlier, lay in financial sector. They broadly correspond with current directions of international financial system reforms, but still there are some important problems that have not been fully addressed. From point of view of developed countries, this is the problem of creating incentives for unlimited development of financial activities. From point of view of emerging and developing economies, one of the most important problems is connected with transmission of different kinds of shocks (mainly financial ones) from developed countries. It is closely connected with the problem of international capital movement's regulation.

Second, for the success of the whole set of reforms, it is important to "reform the reformers". It means that reform of international financial architecture is needed. One of the most sensitive questions is the under-representation of emerging and developing economies in decision making processes within international financial institutions. Thus BRICS efforts should focus on increasing these countries positions in International Monetary Fund and World Bank, including completion of 14th IMF Quota Review and initiation of the next review. This aim is complicated by the need to switch from national interests of BRICS countries to interests of the whole group of emerging and developing countries.

Third, international financial reform at its current framework does not take into account specifics of emerging and developing countries, which is connected for example with underdevelopment of financial markets in these countries on the one hand and at the same time with risks of uprising of financial bubbles in certain segments (usually with high level of foreign capital involvement). That is why the specific features of emerging and developing markets should be taken into account within international financial reform programs. BRICS countries may act as the engine for redesigning the reforms program framework. In cases, when emerging and developing countries interests coincide with international financial reforms path, BRICS countries should focus on assistance in working out and promoting the reforms agenda.

Fourth, BRICS countries should take into account costs and benefits of reforms and avoid promoting too costly reforms for them. The most prominent example of such a reform is the proposition to change current state of international monetary system. Drawbacks in international monetary system had not caused the global turbulence, although of course the system was affected by it. Sharp changes in US dollar position in global economy may lead to new serious turbulences, in which emerging and developing countries are not interested. This thesis does not mean that current state of international monetary system should remain constant. Of course gradual changes are needed. One of these possible changes can be the extension of external use of BRICS national currencies. Another one is connected with the need for already mentioned regulation of speculative international capital flows. For example, the question of introduction of a kind of Tobin tax in global scale can be discussed among BRICS experts and officials.

Within these directions of international financial and monetary reforms, BRICS countries may develop their own measures on implementation of these reforms as significant actors in global economy. Two important measures have already been proclaimed and are now on implementation phase: formation of the New Development Bank and pool of foreign exchange reserves. The New Development Bank may close the gap between the need for development financing in emerging and developing countries and investments of their official foreign assets in few developed countries government bonds. The pool of exchange reserves aims at stabilizing exchange rates of BRICS countries, as costs of exchange rate volatility in emerging economies is higher than in developed countries. Next step can be connected with measures on facilitating the use of BRICS national currencies in mutual economic relations of countries and new issues of securities, denominated in these currencies, on international financial markets.

Concrete Cooperation among BRICS Countries in Global Governance

H. H. S. Viswanathan[*]

In today's globalised world, where the interdependence is intense and complex, Global Governance, or paucity of it, is a serious challenge before humanity. Discussions on how to deal with transnational issues — whether they are trade liberalisation or investment, pandemics or drug trafficking, climate change or environment, human rights or responsibility to protect — seriously affect the lives of billions of people.

With the world rendered virtually borderless because of high speed transfers of goods, capital, pathogens and environmental consequences, the lack of Global Governance has emerged as the single most daunting challenge to Globalisation.

In this scenario, the emergence of the group called BRICS is of great significance. This is a group which is ideally suited to address issues of Global Governance. There are various questions that arise in this context. What does BRICS want? Is BRICS capable of bringing about meaningful changes? Can BRICS convince the status-quo powers that some changes are in the interests of everyone? Can BRICS and other emerging powers speak with a common voice on the issue of global governance?

Even though the term "global governance" is relatively new, the concept, in a general way, has existed for a long time in history. Whenever two or more entities — call them societies, tribes or groups of people — had regular interactions, some kind of ground rules had to be

---

[*] H. H. S. Viswanathan, a Distinguished Fellow at the Observer Research Foundation.

laid out. There may not have been an implementing agency, but there was an understanding that such rules were beneficial for all. What we talk of global governance today stems from this fundamental concept. Sure, over the centuries, circumstances have changed. The creation of Westphalian states in the 17th century led to rather rigid entities which had to deal with each other. As each one of them fought and pushed for its self-interest, some common ground rules evolved which everyone, or more precisely, the more important players, agreed on as being good for all. These were in the areas of trade, shipping and health. It is said that what precipitated the Berlin Conference in 1885 (which led to the division of the African continent into colonial territories) was the increase in the number of confrontations between ships of rival powers in the Congo River. It is of course a truism to state that historically global rules have been set by the most powerful countries to take care of their interests.

The post-Second World War period saw global governance rules set by the victors. Even though the second half of the 20th century saw the emergence of a large number of independent nations in Asia and Africa, they hardly contributed to global governance. Obviously, they were neither politically nor economically powerful enough to influence or change the set patterns of global governance.

1. How Globalisation Changed the Ground Realities

What has changed since then? The magic word is "globalisation". This process has managed to interlink countries in ways unimagined in the past. James Rosenau has referred to this as "the crazy-quilt nature of modern interdependence". What globalisation has done is to create a virtually borderless world with high velocity of movements of goods, capital, technology, diseases, criminals, drugs and environmental disasters. Today no nation can honestly say that none of these affects it. Hence, global governance or lack of it has achieved great significance as the most important challenge before humankind.

The other major outcome of globalisation is the emergence of new economic players. Many refer to it as the shift of the economic fulcrum from the developed world to the developing one. This is a remarkable shift since the emerging economies managed to play the game of globalisation by the rules set by the developed world and yet achieve considerable success. But have they been able to gain commensurate influence in global governance? The answer is in the negative. Some even feel that the term "emerging powers" does not adequately reflect their geo-political significance.

In the early 1990s many economists predicted that with the success of Globalisation, geo-economics will replace geo-politics in the world. But, subsequent developments have shown that this has not happened. Geo-politics still remains strong and the architecture of the post-Second World War has not changed.

2. What Exactly Is Global Governance?

Let us try to understand what is really meant by global governance. There are many definitions but none gives the complete picture. James Rosenau defines global governance as "a system of rules at all levels of human activity from the family to the international organisation". By this definition, practically nothing is excluded. What is to be noted is that governance, in this context, should not be confused with government. It is precisely because there is no global government there is need for global governance. In some ways this works in the opposite direction as compared to what happens within Westphalian states. There, the institution of government precedes governance whereas on a global level — it is the other way around — the idea of governance precedes the formation of an institution. Another definition of global governance is "governing, without sovereign authority, relationships that transcend national frontiers". The simplest and the most practical definition is "management of transnational issues through voluntary international cooperation". It is about managing issues without a formal government and the cooperation is voluntary.

While talking of global governance, one has to be clear of the three specific aspects-values, norms and rules. Effective global governance which is fair and equitable should pay attention to all the three aspects in that order and have, if not global consensus, at least the agreement of an overwhelmingly large majority of nations. Only then will the fourth aspect of governance, namely implementation, be effective and just.

Many problems in global governance have arisen because of the lack of attention to the three stages namely values, norms and rules or the by-passing of some of them. We have to only look at the controversies concerning human rights, non-proliferation, responsibility to protect or the International Criminal Court to appreciate the importance of the correct sequencing of the three stages in global governance.

History also shows that Global Governance always lags behind developments in technology, trade, travel, pandemics and environmental problems. Countries wake up to these issues only when they reach crisis proportions. Therefore, global governance should be visualised as a dynamic concept with constant monitoring and modifications.

The other term that had obtained currency in today's age is "global commons" and this is closely associated with global governance. This is generally meant to cover universal assets like oceans, atmosphere and outer space. Even this concept is not new. As early as the 17th century, the Dutch jurist Hugo Grotius developed the argument that oceans were international space. In today's context, we may have to include Cyber Space. With the greater interdependence of the economies of so many countries, the question of managing the global commons in an equitable way has become an absolute necessity.

Another factor to be kept in mind is that in today's world, global governance is not only about the governments of sovereign states. There are important non-state players who contribute significantly. Three of them are the corporate sector, the civil societies and the non-government organisations. Any new initiative on global governance today cannot succeed without bringing on board these stakeholders.

3. How Are Global Norms Made Attractive to All?

What can we learn from the history of global governance? There have been many success stories like coordination of telegraph communications, maritime understandings and health issues like either containing or preventing communicable diseases. One ideal example of global coordination among the private sector is the agreement of all GSM operators throughout the world to use the number 112 for emergency services. The examples in the financial sector are SWIFT (Society for World Inter-Bank Financial Telecommunication) and IBAN (International Bank Account Number). On the government side, we have the example of Interpol which makes annually over 5000 arrests of criminals and fugitive law-breakers from member countries.

The above examples show that success in Global Governance is possible if the discourse on the subject is not restricted to subjective moralistic principles, but takes into account the incentives for all to cooperate — ie. a more practical approach. New initiatives are more likely to succeed if all stake-holders feel that there is something in them for everyone. In this approach, BRICS could be an effective interlocutor. It can turn the discourse and debate on Global Governance towards making the norms attractive for all.

4. The Question of Global Institutions

One aspect which is central to global governance is the question of institutions which oversee the implementation of the rules. That has become the most crucial issue of debate in today's world and for obvious reasons. A certain bias in favour of the colonial powers and the victors of the Second World War seems to have been hard-wired into the Global Institutions. It is only natural that the victors set the rules and implemented them to their advantage without much regard for the adverse effects on others. This worked well as long as the global situation remained static. The end of the Cold War and the age of globalisation brought in a new paradigm which exposed the weaknesses of many of the aspects of global governance in existence. The time had come to have a fresh look at trans-national issues.

While talking of global institutions, three of them stand out as being totally anachronistic — IMF, World Bank and UNSC. The quota allocations and the voting powers in IMF and World Bank have no relationship to the existing distribution of economic power in today's world. Add to that the unwritten convention that IMF will always be headed by a European and the World Bank by an American. How can one expect the institutions to run efficiently and address complex issues when there are such outdated rules? Today, of all the important international institutions, G20 seems to be the only one which correctly reflects the global reality — the 20 countries account for 85% of the global GDP.

The BRICS initiatives in this regard have been fairly effective. It was due to the pressure of BRICS and other emerging economies that G20 in its 2010 Summit decided on the reallocation of the voting rights in the Bretton Woods Institutions. A small beginning was made but further progress has been stalled by the US Congress. This is a fight which BRICS will have to continue.

The other major achievement of BRICS is the creation of the New Development Bank (NDB) and the Contingency Reserve Arrangement (CRA). They may not replace the World Bank and the IMF, but they are certainly wake-up calls for these Institutions to undertake radical reforms. Some have even commented that had these Institutions changed with changing times, there may not have been a need for the NDB and the CRA.

The UNSC is another institution which is clearly out of sync. with the times. For it to be effective, it has to represent the current global reality which it does not. Most people agree on the need to expand the UNSC, but the idea has not seen any progress in the last two decades. BRICS, as a voice of the global South, has a responsibility to realise this goal. A lack of consensus on this issue is cited by the critics of BRICS as one of the weaknesses of the group. The credibility of the group will be enhanced greatly if the five countries could be on the same page on the issue.

Multilateralism is the bedrock of good Global Governance and all the five countries are staunch supports of this approach. They would like to see a world run on the sound principle of active multilateral initiatives.

They are also averse to use or threat of force in international relations.

BRICS' interest in global governance is also not about "high-tables" which have been mentioned repeatedly in commentaries. While it is important for emerging powers to be members of the international decision making bodies, it is not an end in itself. Repeated references to "occupying the high tables", in a way, trivialises the issue. The question of what is debated and decided at the high tables is as important, if not more critical, than who sits there. The BRICS countries have a fairly clear vision of what direction they would take when they are invited to these tables.

Some critics have projected the demand of emerging countries to have a greater voice in global governance merely as the desire of the elite of those countries to achieve a certain level of recognition. Nothing could be more absurd. In today's globalised world, the decisions taken on global issues by the concerned international organisations affect the lives and development of millions of people. Look at the intensity of discussions on issues like climate change, Doha Round of trade liberalisation, food security, water issues, responsibility to protect and human rights. We come back to the questions of values, norms and rules in all these where the emerging and developing countries have a vital stake in the formulation of the concepts from the very beginning.

BRICS countries have also made it clear that their demand for changes in global governance is inclusive and non-confrontational. Unfortunately, when BRICS countries talk about changes in Global Governance, it is seen as an attack on the West. The whole question is reduced to "West vs the Rest." The reality of today, however, is that the West needs the Rest. Even if, for argument sake, one concedes that the global order created after the Second World War had some logic of that time, it is evident that the world has changed qualitatively and in a drastic manner. No amount of tinkering of the old systems can help; we need some creative ideas from all the stake holders. It needed a crisis like the 2008 global financial meltdown for activating G-20 to take some steps where BRICS and other emerging powers were included in the decision making process leading to some beneficial outcomes. Should the world wait for similar crisis in other sectors before initiating reforms or is it prudent to start reviewing the existing structures and methods with the involvement of all?

5. Options for BRICS

On the issue of the current norms of Global Governance, BRICS has four options:

(1) Conform, ie. adjust to the existing systems. Except in some specific areas, this is unlikely.

(2) Reform. BRICS will try and modify the existing norms and institutions without drastically changing them.

(3) Bypass. In areas where BRICS feel that the system is totally unfair, they would ignore it provided it does not violate accepted principles of International Law.

(4) Recreate. BRICS could create new norms and institutions. NDB and CRA are examples of this. More such initiatives could be expected in the future. It is worth noting that even though the NDB and CRA are economic institutions, there is a larger political message. This is the first time in over 300 years that a Global Institution has been created without the participation of the developed West.

BRICS could pursue any of the options depending upon the issue and the situation. However, the approach would, as mentioned earlier, be non-confrontational with the objective of taking everyone along. BRICS will take all efforts to propose initiatives that resonate with a vast majority of countries, particularly in the developing world.

6. New Areas that BRICS Should Explore

As the role of BRICS in Global Governance becomes more pronounced, the group should explore new areas. One grave problem facing the world today is Cyber Security. So far, no effective global mechanism has been put in place. BRICS countries seem to have similar views on the problem and hence could cooperate to come up with a BRICS proposal.

Two other areas of interest are Standardisation and Bench-marking. These are domains of Global Governance in the non-governmental space. With the growth of the economies and the technologies in the five countries, it is time that BRICS makes its mark in these fields. For eg., India, China and Brazil are major producers of pharmaceuticals and it is only fair that they must have their own standards. Similarly, BRICS must develop its own Bench-marks on a variety of activities. In due course, we could also think of a BRICS Credit Rating Agency.

To conclude: Global Governance in today's world is vital and critical for the lives of billions. Hence it has to involve everyone. Any governance to be effective has to be and seen to be fair and equitable. Since the old systems are not, it is time to review and reform them. A group of emerging powers like BRICS is ideally suited to bring fresh and creative ideas to the table. They have the experience of going through the development process, taking advantage of globalisation and registering impressive growth rates. Yet, many of their problems are very similar to other developing countries. Hence, they are in the unique position of understanding the issues in the right perspective while having the strength to take on more responsibilities in global governance.

Along with Intra-BRICS cooperation in various sectors, working towards reforms in Global Governance has been one of the objectives of the Group from its very inception. This commitment has been reflected in the establishment of the NDB and the CRA. Much more needs to be done. That is why "Global Political and Economic Governance" has been identified as one of the five pillars of the BRICS Long-term Vision Document being prepared by the BRICS Think-tank Council (BTTC). This Document would provide a road map for the five Governments to act on.

BRICS Cooperation in
the Global Governance of Energy

Arunabha Ghosh[*]

1. Introduction

Resource security matters for the BRICS countries and the global economy. This is demonstrated by the rise of new consumers of mineral resources (South – South resource trade is now larger than South – North trade), the continued concentration of large-scale mineral production in a few economies, a step-change in price volatility as compared to three decades ago, the rapid increase in outward foreign investment by BRICS countries in resource-rich economies, and a rising trend of international disputes related to trade in minerals. Against this background, environmental constraints against resource exploration, production, and consumption are also driving the demand for greater resource efficiency.

Global energy markets are constantly changing character thanks to technological improvements, environmental pressures, rising demand, pricing policies, conflicts, and supply shocks. For the first time since 1995, US domestic crude oil production exceeded imports by 2 million barrels per day by the end of 2013. Meanwhile, China has already become the world's largest oil importer. These developments have profound implications for global security, because they raise questions about protection of sea lanes, interventions in oil rich but politically fragile states, and the role of markets versus resource nationalism.

BRICS countries face the imperative of sustaining high economic

---

[*] Arunabha Ghosh, CEO of the Council on Energy, Environment and Water.

growth rates. Already, they account for 24% of global oil demand and 20% of the natural gas market. These shares are expected to rise to at least 29% of oil and 26% of gas demand in 2030. They are expected to account for half of the increase in world energy use until 2040. Energy importers like China and India are deeply concerned about energy security (they will be importing 92% and 84% of their oil demand, respectively, by 2035).

The quest for energy is not for BRICS countries alone. The success of their strategies to secure resources will be, in part, a function of how commodity markets operate and whether other large demanders find merit in cooperation as against resorting to resource nationalism. Global energy and food prices have become more volatile in recent years and have also risen to levels not seen since the early 1970s. Only in recent weeks have oil prices fallen significantly, but there are enough geopolitical stresses across the world, which suggest that prices could rise again as global economic growth picks up pace and energy demand rises consequently. Further, water stress and scarcity is a growing threat to industry, agriculture, and electricity generation with aquifers over-exploited in the North China Plain and north-western India. Climate change remains the most complex and intractable global challenge. And many of the BRICS countries share climate and water risks with their neighbours.

The nexus between energy, food, water and climate will complicate and constrain policy choices. Effective domestic policy is needed and international drivers — shifting dynamics in commodity markets, disputes over water resources, or climate emergencies — will frame the responses of emerging powers. How could BRICS countries cooperate over and shape the global governance of energy, both to meet their respective needs but also to increase confidence in global energy markets?

2. Three Tensions in Energy Governance

Energy importers want predictable and uninterrupted supplies and exporters want stable demand. But there are additional questions of economic competitiveness, access to technologies and access to raw materials, while also ensuring environmental sustainability. This array of demands imposed on a complex milieu of institutions and rules reveals at least three sets of tensions.

The first tension is between **multipolarity and existing regimes**. With shifts in energy demand, an increasingly multipolar world will also have to find appropriate forums for cooperation and coordination on energy trade and investment policy. In the energy sector, multipolarity does not automatically translate into multilateral governance arrangements. The World Trade Organization, for instance, is only one among several options. Regional institutions offer alternative logics for cooperation: proximity of energy source and demand (the *North American Free Trade Agreement*, NAFTA); focus on a comprehensive approach, including securing supply, protecting investments and facilitating energy transit (*Energy Charter Treaty*, or ECT); and broader regional interests, such as the Association of South East Asian Nations (ASEAN) and the Economic Community of West African States (ECOWAS).

Furthermore, plurilateral agreements among small groups of countries also exist among energy suppliers, namely the Organization of Petroleum Exporting Countries (OPEC). Major consumers in the Asia – Pacific region have formed the Asia – Pacific Economic Cooperation (APEC) Energy Working Group. There are calls for bringing together major suppliers and users under an Energy Stability Board to coordinate emergency actions and give voice to emerging economies. Although small groups have their benefits for efficient decision-making, they need to maintain open membership to gain legitimacy. This is particularly the case when existing regional or plurilateral regimes do not include new energy actors, in turn undermining their effectiveness. Moreover, it is unclear which forums countries will choose to resolve contradictions and disputes.

The second tension is between **markets and states**. The nature of energy markets has changed since the oil shocks of the 1970s. The "fungibility" of crude oil has increased. About 50% (or 40 million barrels per day) is now traded openly. Oil is now a physical commodity and a financial asset. Growth in Liquified Natural Gas is feeding the development of spot markets for gas. While transactions on such a scale increase the efficiency of the energy market, energy is also subjected to increased risks of volatility. Energy security is of paramount concern to governments. The decentralisation of energy markets combined with rising demand in emerging economies begs the question whether countries will rely on markets to secure access to energy sources or whether state agencies will assume greater control.

The third tension is between **energy and the environment**. Globally, some 1.6 billion persons live without electricity. Even in China and India, more than half the population relies on traditional biomass for cooking. Today's rich countries carry the burden of responsibility for the climate crisis (in 2010 the average American emitted 10 times more CO_2 than the average Indian). But non-OECD countries, among them the BRICS, will account for almost the entire increase in energy-related CO_2 emissions from now until 2030. Thus, on one hand, these economies have to balance their priorities on energy access and climate change, and on the other, there are questions about how trade rules would govern energy subsidies in rich and emerging economies.

3. Need for Global Energy Governance

A world with multiple poles of energy suppliers, energy demanders and emerging economies has direct implications for coherence between different international organisations. The existing arrangements to govern energy do not adequately address growing multipolarity. There have been few signs of cooperation between existing powers in the energy sector and emerging economies. China and India were invited to the International Energy Agency's "Committee Week" in 2007 but remain observers.

The IEA remains a subsidiary body of the OECD, a developed countries' club, making it difficult to bring emerging economies formally into its fold. Meanwhile, competing pressures of energy demand, climate change and trade barriers are discussed in different forums, at the IEA, the UN Framework Convention on Climate Change (UNFCCC) or in the WTO, thus creating what scholars have called a complex of partially overlapping but not hierarchically ordered regimes. If these contradictions remain unresolved, emerging economies will seek alternative venues to secure energy supplies.

The concern over securing predictable access to energy resources dates back at least to the early part of the 20th century. Now, despite the rhetoric of energy independence, the world's leading economies inhabit a complex world of energy flows and institutions that seek to govern them. The resulting multipolarity means that existing arrangements for energy trade and investment need not necessarily adapt to the demands of emerging powers. Meanwhile, global oil and gas markets have become increasingly decentralised, which means that no one player can fully control energy flows. Yet, some of the largest energy companies are state-owned, raising questions about the relative influence of markets and states.

Seen from the perspective of an individual country, any notion of "governing" energy could imply restraints on its freedom of manoeuvre in securing energy supplies. Seen from the perspective of the energy trading system, an ungoverned energy market would have serious ramifications. Energy security, in other words, has become less a notion that countries can pursue independently and more a function of the interaction of sovereign states, private firms, financial markets, and regional and global institutions. If this interaction works well, then there is the potential to reconcile competing demands on energy resources, environmental sustainability and maintaining free trade and investment. If not, it could destabilise bilateral relations between states and even have geopolitical consequences.

4. How Could BRICS Cooperate on Energy Governance?

The above analysis suggests that one of the most immediate global governance priorities for BRICS countries relates to energy. Emerging powers, especially BRICS countries, have to recognise their growing stature as "rule shapers" not simply "rule takers", which offers them the opportunity to design robust international regimes for resource security. A few suggestions are listed below.

1. **Jointly bid to lower acquisition costs**: There is no avoiding reliance on imports for a range of energy and mineral resource needs. BRICS nations, particularly China and India, will continue to compete for resources. That said, the two countries have also cooperated from time to time (such as in Sudan, Syria or Myanmar) and professed to work together on exploration, production, refining, marketing, R&D, conservation, trading in oil and joint bidding in third countries. The BRICS could gain mutually if they explored avenues for collaborating amidst resource competition. First, by pooling financial and technological resources, large state-owned oil and gas companies they could form a formidable group to address energy security issues. Secondly, this partnership could mitigate concerns that energy suppliers and demanders would play off one against the other, thereby driving up prices.

2. **Develop optimal supply infrastructure for energy**: The intersection between maritime and energy security is a potentially serious source of friction. Much of the world's trade (including energy resources) depends on maritime routes. It is imperative to build the infrastructure that will meet long-term resource import and transport needs. BRICS countries need to work together and with other countries in the Asian region, which also have rising energy demands for cooperative action in energy supply infrastructure. For instance, India's ONGC Videsh has a stake in the gas pipeline from Myanmar into southwestern China. At their first dialogue on Central Asia in August 2013, China and India discussed the challenges of implementing the Turkmenistan – Afghanistan – Pakistan – India (TAPI) pipeline. Investments in third countries could help companies from both countries develop experience in working together and gradually build trust. China and India could also envision a network of pipelines, which they could share to tap resources in Russia, Central Asia and West Asia.

3. **Explore swap arrangements in oil and gas**: Another idea is to use

each other's equity oil and gas stakes through swap arrangements. Some commentators have suggested that India's gas production in the Sakhalin fields in Russia could be used by China in exchange for India accessing the latter's supplies from the Middle East, thereby reducing energy transportation costs for both countries. The challenge is that there is very little public information, including for experts who have served on regulatory bodies in India, about whether such swaps have been attempted or been successful.

4. **Promote business models in decentralised energy:** There is a strong case for promoting distributed energy infrastructure, through a blend of different renewable energy sources and via smart microgrids. This will help to reduce the load on the main grid, offer energy access solutions to those without basic forms of modern energy, and create opportunities for productive uses of renewable energy (such as in small agricultural operations, remote telecom infrastructure, schools and hospitals, etc.). Further, distributed energy, if supported by strong R&D efforts (as is evident in other major economies), could lower the risks for critical infrastructure, should the grid collapse or come under attack of any form.

India already has at least 250 firms providing decentralised energy services, each experimenting with different business models: selling products like lanterns, installing home systems (solar panels, biogas plants), or developing micro-grids. Meanwhile, China also has some of the largest programmes for clean cookstoves. Along with Brazilian and South African innovators and entrepreneurs, decentralised energy firms from China and India could develop business models for distributed generation in South Asia, Southeast Asia, Africa and South America.

5. **Create a dialogue forum for coordinated action on energy:** BRICS countries should promote a multi-regional dialogue forum to discuss and coordinate action on energy. The first task of the forum would be to increase transparency in energy markets with regular information on oil and gas purchases, long-term contracts and spot market prices. Secondly, the forum would facilitate discussions on how each member country's strategic reserves could be used to instil confidence in energy markets to

mitigate short-term supply shocks. Thirdly, by offering an open membership platform, the forum would attract other second tier but rapidly growing energy demanders and collectively press for a reduction in premiums charged on energy supplies. Fourthly, it could discuss protection of key energy supply routes (via land and sea). Fifthly, in a more institutionalised form, it could arbitrate on energy-related disputes and protect overseas investments.

If the BRICS were to collaborate on bidding jointly for assets, investing in energy infrastructure, swap arrangements, promoting renewable energy (including decentralised energy), and developing an open forum to discuss energy governance, it would greatly soothe concerns about resource nationalism. It would also send signals to energy markets that the major emerging economies are keen on working through market mechanisms rather than primarily rely on equity investments in overseas energy sources. At the same time, it would emphasise that the global energy order would have to become more inclusive to accommodate the needs of emerging economies.

BRICS International Finance Crisis and the Challenges of Governance

Bandi Prasad*

As individual countries, some of the constituents of the BRICS might be facing fluctuating fortunes in terms of growth, but as a group, it is making rapid progress, expanding its sphere of influence in global economy and finance, regional and world economic policy and multilateral initiatives. BRICS countries were not an exception to hit by two major global economic and financial crises in the decade of the 2000s, but are progressing pretty fast by playing a proactive role and making initiatives that will place them in a strong pedestal in dealing with matters of global development and governance.

This paper discusses the trends in the BRICS economics and financial markets development following the International financial crisis of 2008 and how this group is coping with certain concerns and uncertainties still daunting the world. It also discusses initiatives and efforts being deployed by the group that could lead them to play a much larger role in evolving frameworks for policy and better standards in global governance.

Following the international financial crisis of 2008, a few important trends evident in the BRICS group are:

(1) Economic growth is uneven and wavering. Though immediately after the crisis, BRICS economies have recovered, growth concerns persist in a few countries. China shows highest growth and India is recovering.

(2) Financial markets growth has been very robust. Except in China

---

* Bandi Prasad, He is the Founder and CEO of Growth Markets Advisory Services, India.

and Russia, stock market indices in the rest of the countries rose very sharply. Foreign investor interest in the BRICS countries remains high.

(3) BRICS have established multi asset class markets with a wide range of instruments in spot and derivatives markets that have seen strong growth in market depth. BRICS financial systems including banks, and trading in market segments such as equities, commodities, currencies and bond trading figure in global league tables.

(4) Shocks from developments in the global financial markets have not gone away completely. For instance some countries such as Brazil, India and South Africa were adversely affected by the Taper announcement in May 2013.

(5) BRICS have been playing a much larger and bigger role in aspects such as global economic policy, governance standards, and financial stability

(6) The New Development Bank (BRICS Development Bank) will open new vistas for BRICS playing a much larger and bigger role in development financing policies and strategies.

(7) Growing internationalization of currencies of BRICS will further reinforce their hold on world economy and financial markets.

(8) Corporate Governance frameworks have vastly improved though a few shortcomings still persist in company performance.

(9) The scope of engagement of BRICS with other developing countries in terms of trade, economic relations, development financing has expanded significantly.

(10) BRICS should evolve an extensive framework of cooperation within themselves and outside with the developing and the developed world, on a wider range of areas, to sustain the pace of economic and financial markets development and their continued engagement with the global economy and governance.

1. International Financial Crisis and BRICS

The concept of "BRICS" which emerged as an important investment opportunity in 2001 sustained and further strengthened the momentum of its growth and pace of development to emerge a decade later, as a community of nations to assume a larger role and responsibility in the conduct and the governance of the global economics and finance.

The global economic and financial crisis of 2008 is the second one to happen in a decade with the early 2000s rocked by a deep recession caused by a series of failures, including the burst of the Internet bubble and shortcomings in the corporate conduct and performance in the developed world, more importantly the United States. The second half of the year 2003 set the beginning for a strong revival, which continued for five years till 2008 when the world was hit by another crisis on the back of the global financial markets meltdown and subsequent slowdown in the world economy.

An interesting feature of both these episodes of slow growth and setback in global economics and finance is that a few countries in BRICS such as China and India were showing relatively stronger economic growth despite the slowing down of the global economy in general. However, recovery in financial markets is found to be much sharper and faster across the BRICS.

The real GDP growth of China hovered around 7.5% to 8.0% through out the four years 2001 −2004. India showed a small recovery from 4.2% annual growth in GDP in 2001 to 5.6% in 2003 and 5.9% in 2004. Brazil was able to move up its annual economic growth from 1.4% in 2001 to 1.5% in 2003 and 3% in 2004. Russia showed a marginal rise from 5% to 6%. Thus much of the BRICS were able to show annual economic growth rates relatively higher than the 2.4% annual economic growth that the world posted in 2001 which subsequently moved up to 3.2% in 2003 and 4.1% in 2004.

The recovery of the stock markets however was much sharper and faster. In as many as 20 out of 25 major emerging economies, stock prices rose by over 25% in 2003, the second half of the year in which markets resumed their ascent, and in as many as eight countries the rise was more than 75%. Twenty of these countries also experienced appreciation of their respective currencies against the dollar. Emerging economies in Asia were particularly experiencing new found growth after six years of structural reforms following the Asian economic crisis in which China and India were leading the growth. Specific to BRIC countries, stock indices during the years 2002 and 2003 rose from -17.2% to 10.5% in China, 4% to 80.4% in India, -45% to 140.9% in Brazil, 24.3% to 42% in South Africa and 38% to 58.7% percent in Russia. The markets in emerging markets in general and BRICS in particular became quite ecstatic less than two years of one of the severest recession that the world economy has witnessed.

The global economic and financial crisis of 2008 was much severe in intensity and impact. Beginning with the filing of bankruptcy by Lehman Brothers on September 2014, the subprime crisis being the trigger for the economic meltdown, led to severe impact on the wall street finance, with leading financial institutions coming up under intense selling pressure. By March 2009, S&P 500 reached three digit levels and Dow Jones and other global indices faced severe erosion. At the height of the financial markets crisis, the number of S&P 500 scrips trading at less than US $10 rose ten fold and the New York Stock Exchange had temporarily suspended its $1 minimum share price requirements to prevent large scale delistings. The year 2009 saw one of the biggest and most coordinated efforts to restore global economic growth not seen since the Second World War. Total fiscal stimuli and financial support programmes were launched costing a massive 30% of the world GDP. The US unveiled a $700 billion Troubled Asset Recovery Program (TARP) with Euro zone countries and United Kingdom announcing extensive support measures to rescue/nationalize banks. The reports around that time mentioned that almost a trillion US dollars of government guaranteed bank debt was created to support and rescue banks.

IMF too launched special assistance programme to low income and distressed countries. Government had to buy stakes in the banks to restore viability of the banks. The share of the government in Citibank rose up to 34% in the US and the British Government shareholding in Royal Bank of Scotland and Llyods Banks grew up to 70% during this period.

Developed and developing countries launched massive programmes of fiscal stimuli and financial support. The size of the fiscal stimuli amounted to 5.5% of the GDP in the United States, 4.7% in Japan and 5.4% in Australia. In China it was 6.2%, Brazil 5.6%, South Africa 7.4%, 5.4% in Russia and 1.8% in India. There was massive reduction in the interest rates across. In tune with the developed countries, BRICS too reduced interest rates sharply excepting China and these included, 400 basis points by South Africa, 350 basis points by Brazil, 175 basis points by India and 100 basis points by Russia. Between September 30, 2008 and 2009, US Fed Funds rate was reduced from 2.00% to 0.15%, ECB Interest Rate from 4.25% to 1.00%, and Reserve Bank of India Repo rate from 9.00% to 4.75%.

Growth was impacted all across the developed and developing countries, the after affects of which appear to be continuing even now. Whereas the yearly economic growth of the advanced economies slipped from 0.1% in 2008 to −0.1% in 2010, but rose to 2.0% in 2010 to be again expected to slip back to 1.6% in 2014. US and Euro Area with annual economic growth rates of 3.7% and 2.6% respectively in 2009 have seen respective annual economic growth rates falling to less than one percent by 2010 and are likely to post negative growth rate of −0.2% for the year 2014.

Among the BRICS, China continued to maintain the momentum by showing annual growth of 9.6% in 2008, 9.2% in 2009, 10.4% in 2010, which is likely to be subdued to 7.4% in 2014. India which posted 8%−9% growth in 2008 and 2009 showed a further rise to 10.3% in 2010 but has slipped since then to reach a level of 5.6% by 2014. Annual economic growth of Brazil was anemic in 2009 with the exception of 5.2% in 2008 and 7.5% in 2010 but is now likely to slip to 0.3% in 2014. Russia that posted 5.2% annual growth rate in the economy in 2009 saw it falling to −7.8% in 2009 but quickly rose to 4.5% by 2010 but likely to be very small at 0.2% in 2014. Annual economic growth rate of South Africa in 2014 is expected to 1.4%, lower than the 3.1% that it showed in 2010.

The stock markets on the other hand showed smart recovery and speed. The lows that global stock markets reached in March 2009 were recovered with rapid pace when the markets climbed back by more than 50% in the next six months. A Deutsche Bank report at that time placed gains of this nature happening in less than 0.5 percent of the time and the record of such rally in the last six months was seen only during 1932 – 1933. Between march 9, 2009, and September 30, 2009, Dow Jones Index jumped from 6547 to 9712, FTSE from 3542 to 5133, S&P 500 from 677 to 1057, India's BSE Sensex from 8160 to 17 126, Shanghai from 2118 to 2779, Bovespa from 36 741 to 61 517 and RTS from 576 to 1254. The stock price rise gained further in most of the BRICS markets with the benchmark BSE Sensex crossing the 27 000 mark (October 30, 2014), Brazil to 52 411, South Africa to 48 202. Indices of China and Russia however did not change much during this period as by the end of the October 2014: China's index was at the level of 2435 and Russia at 1047.

2. Continuing Concerns

Though a greater amount of resilience in the economy and the markets was found in the BRICS management, excepting China, volatility of varying degrees is not uncommon in other BRICS economies in respect of the real economy and the financial markets. One of the major drivers of uncertainty in the emerging markets following the 2008 crisis was the reduction in fiscal stimuli, tapering of the bond purchases and possible tightening of the interest rates in the United States and the Euro region that became aspects of concern and volatility in the financial markets in emerging economies in general and BRICS in particular.

The intense pressure faced by the BRICS countries reacting to the possible reduction of Federal Reserve bond purchase programme in the US and tightening of interest rates came into display in the second half of 2013 where stock and currency markets experienced wild bouts of volatility which also compounded the problems at the growth front. Deceleration of domestic economic growth in some of the BRICS countries has further brought renewed pressures in the year 2013.

In the background of growth slippage and concerns on reversal of foreign flows into domestic markets, BRICS currencies faced steep erosion in value against the US dollar and other major international currencies. Between May 22, 2013, when the Fed Chairman made his first "taper" speech, and August 21, 2013, Brazilian real fell by 14.9%, Indian Rupee by 11.7%, South African Rand by 5.8%, Indonesian Rupiah by 6.9%, and Turkish Lira by 5.3%. However, most of the emerging economies including BRICS recovered values of the currency during September 2013. By early 2014, most of the emerging markets and in particular BRICS countries have managed to discount the effects of the Taper with not much volatility seen despite several pronouncements made by the Federal Reserve on the scope of reduction and actually beginning of the tapering. Post crisis the prospects of the emerging markets was uneven. While domestic economic growth has been wavering, financial markets have been relatively robust. Moreover, the concerns of the tapering effect in the US is now countered by a massive fiscal stimulus programme by Japan to which the markets have reacted in a very positive manner in the last week of October 2014.

Uneven growth still affects the prospects of the emerging markets including the BRICS. International Monetary Fund, in its annual World Economic Outlook (October 2014) summarized the growth prospects of different regions in which BRICS nations are located such as "**Steady Growth Ahead**" for Asia; "**Still Losing Speed**" for Latin America (Brazil), "**Coping with Geopolitical Uncertainties**" for CIS (Russia); and "**Maintaining Speed**" for Sub Saharan Africa (South Africa)

3. BRICS Financial Markets Land Scape: Growing in Size and Significance

Notwithstanding the fluctuations in the economy and the markets, the relatively expansive financial architecture that the BRICS nations have been able to build over a period of time now brought these countries to the fore of prominence in global financial markets. The impressive size and scale of financial markets that the BRICS countries have built over time could be seen from a number of financial indicators.

As per data available for September 2014[1], the market capitalization of BRICS was at about USD 9 trillion accounting for 13% of the world market capitalization. China, India and Brazil have market capitalization levels of USD trillion or more. Value of share trading is about USD 8 trillion accounting for nearly 19% of the global stock market value of share trading. China alone has USD 4.7 trillion of market capitalization and USD 6.6 trillion of value of share trading. BRICS also account for an impressive number of companies listed in the stock markets with the number nearing 9000 level, most of it coming from India. BRICS countries now have multi asset class segments and a well-developed spot and derivative markets. Index futures (China) Index futures and options (India, Brazil, Russia and South Africa), Single stock futures and options (India, Brazil, Russia, and South Africa), ETF Futures (South Africa), Currency Futures (India, Brazil Russia, and South Africa), Interest Rate Options (Brazil), Interest Rate Futures (China, India, Brazil, Russia, and South Africa), Commodities Futures (China, and India), Commodities Futures and Options (Brazil, Russia, and South Africa) are fairly developed in the BRICS that has become a magnet for global portfolio investments which continue to evince great interest in the BRICS financial markets. Exchanges of various multi asset classes including stock, commodity, currency, and interest rates in BRICS countries have assumed leadership and recognition in terms of market activity and volumes traded. Among the top 30 derivatives exchanges in the world, the representation from the BRICS countries is quite impressive with 12 exchanges.

On the new issuance markets too, BRICS have strong representation. Of the largest ever IPOs in the world, three are from China: Bank of China (USD 11.1 billion/2006), ICBC (USD 21.98 billion/2006), Agricultural Bank of China (USD 22.11 billion/2010) and the most recent Alibaba E commerce portal that places it among the worlds largest with an issue size of USD 25 billion.

BRICS countries hold prominent positions in several aspects of the

---

[1] World Federation of Exchanges, London.

global finance. Brazil (Bovespa) and China (Shanghai and Hong Kong) are in the Top 10 countries in Market Capitalization, China (Shanghai, Shenzhen) in the Top 10 in Value of Stocks traded, India in the Top 5 in Equity Derivatives. BRICS countries also hold top position in equity options. Russia and Johannesburg are in the Top 5 in Bond Trading, Brazil in the Top 5 in Interest Rate Derivatives, India in the top in Currency Futures (number of contracts traded), India among the Top 3 in commodity futures and China (HK)/South Africa is in the Top 5 exotic derivatives traded. USD-INR contract holds the top position for being largest number of contracts traded. Of the Top 20 metal futures contracts, eight are from India. BRICS accounted for nearly 50% of the new capital raised in global exchanges in 2011. China accounted for nearly 40% of the new capital raised globally in the last three years. The Share of BRICS during the ten years period of 2002 −2011 rose from 3% to 13% in regard to market capitalization; from 1% to 9% in value of share trading; from 9% to 21% in new capital issued. The number of Banks from BRICS in the World Top 1000 Banks rose to 216 in 2013. (China 111, India, 40, Russia 38, Brazil 27). In 2013, China took the top slot in the Top 1000 World Banks (The annual list published by The Banker, London) with ICBC topping the league tables on the basis of the Tier One Capital putting aside the long standing league heads such as Bank of America and JP Morgan. ICBC continued to hold the position of the world's top bank in The Banker Worlds Top 1000 Banks in ranking for the year 2014.

On banking, 21 of the world's top 100 banks are from the BRIC countries with three of the top 10 coming from China. Each of the BRIC nations has representation among the world's top 100 banks.

BRICS also have advanced significantly in trading of foreign exchange markets. According to the Triennial Central Bank Survey on Foreign Exchange Turnover (February 2014), average daily foreign exchange turnover in Russia was at USD 74 billion, China USD 55 billion, India USD 53 billion, South Africa USD 24 billion and Brazil USD 18 billion.

Trading in foreign exchange markets averaged USD 5.3 trillion per day in April 2013. This is up from USD 4.0 trillion in April 2010 and USD 3.3

trillion in April 2007. FX swaps were the most actively traded instruments in April 2013, at USD 2.2 trillion per day, followed by spot trading at USD 2.0 trillion. The US Dollars retained the top most position, the role of the Renmimbi in global FX trading surged, in line with increased efforts to internationalize the Chinese currency. Renminbi turnover soared to $120 billion with the currency emerging as the ninth most actively traded currency in 2013, with a share of 2.2% in global FX volumes, mostly driven by a significant expansion of offshore renminbi trading. During the period 2001 to 2013, the share of Renminbi in global average daily turnover rose from almost nothing to 2.2%, Ruble from 0.3% to 1.6%, Brazilian Real from 0.2% to 1.1%, Indian Rupee from 0.2% to 1% and the Zambian Rand from 0.9% to 1.1%.

Cooperation has expanded in BRICS financial markets. Index futures on bench mark indices of each of the BRICS countries are being cross listed. Cooperation in using local currencies in settling bilateral trade are also growing. The through link of Hong Kong Stock Exchange and Shanghai Stock Exchange, the work on which is currently in progress, is likely expand the scope for further collaboration of securities industry in Asia and among the BRICS.

BRICS countries have been active players pursuing international business opportunities and investing in overseas markets. Outward foreign direct investment from China rose from $1 billion in 2000 to $68 billion in 2010, from $3 billion to $51 billion in Russia, $2 billion to $11 billion in Brazil. Total FDI from these five countries rose from a level of $7 billion in 2000 to $146 billion in 2010. Total Outward FDI for all the five countries during this period amounted to USD 688 billion.

BRICS have established strong relationships with Less Developed Countries and Low Income Countries (LICs) in terms of bilateral trade as also providing development assistance. Exports of LICs to BRICS grew from USD 15 billion in 2000 to USD 61 billion in 2009. In 2010, China and India accounted for 90% of the import of agricultural products and raw materials from the LICs. More than 50% of exports of the manufactured goods from LICs went to China, followed by Brazil (14%), Russia, India and South Africa (10% each). The main component of exports from LICs are crops, minerals and other raw materials, especially fuels and metals. Africa's trade with the BRICS, for example, has grown faster than the continent's trade with any other region in the world, doubling since 2007 to USD 340 billion in 2012, and is projected to reach USD 500 billion by 2015.

BRICS countries are also relatively rated well by credit rating agencies with Moodys (2013) rating of Brazil at Baa2 (June 2011), Russia at Baa1 (March 2013), India at Baa3 (December 2011), with an indication of an upgrade made in October 2014, China at Aa3 (April 2013) and South Africa at Baa1 (July 2013).

BRICS have advanced significantly in internationalization of the local currencies. Chinese Yuan is now directly traded against nine currencies including USD, the euro, the Japanese yen, the British pound, the Aussie and New Zealand dollars, Russia's rouble, Malaysia's ringgit and the latest being added is the Singapore dollar. The use of the Yuan in cross-border trade settlements is set to grow by 50% to 6 trillion Yuan (USD 988 billion) in 2014, according to a Deutsche Bank estimate. This amounts to approximately 20% of China's global trade volume, compared with an estimated 17% in 2013, the bank said. Yuan is the second currency after the USD widely used in trade settlement. A large amount of the trade within the CIS countries is settled in the Russian currency. India too is embarking on bilateral arrangements to use local currency in the trade settlement.

4. The New Development Bank

The most recent initiative that is envisaged to further expand the realm of influence of is the New Development Bank that the BRICS decided to form in the sixth annual meeting held in Fortaleza, Brazil in July 2014. It was in the New Delhi summit in 2012 that the idea of a development bank came into being. From a concept a couple of years ago, to an important intervention that reflects the collective commitment, the NDB could be a key catalyst in pushing for more space for the BRICS community in the leadership of global economy and finance, now with a more powerful and potent instrument of development financing. From recipients of aid and assistance for quite long, which continues even now in some of the countries (such as India), the group will now turn to financing among themselves as also for other less developed economies.

An important challenge and opportunity for the NDB is how it will manage development financing. The templates of the current development financing particularly in the realm of conditionalities and clearances (in areas of environment and governance etc.) have been severely protested and contested by the recipients. Similarly the dominance of the decision making of the rich countries in regard to the business mandates of the development banks will now get reduced with the new bank. It would be interesting to watch how the new bank will deal with this aspect.

Notwithstanding the new bank, there would still be a lot the world needs in terms of development assistance. With a World Bank, and a development bank for every region — Asia (ADB), Africa (AfDB), Latin America (IADB) and Caribbean (CDB) and a host of specialized and domestic DFIs in almost every nation, there is still no access for 4 billion people to electricity, 0.9 billion to clean drinking water and 2.6 billion to sanitation. The proposed New Development Bank of the BRICS could add little more to the capacity.

What distinguishes NDB is it's positioning. NDB could be a departure from the earlier models, where the developed nations set up development banks to extend finance to developing countries as a part of the larger engagement with the world and to continue with the sphere of influence in shaping the global economic policy. For the BRICS Community, NDB could be an important instrument in the overall strategy to evolve as a countervailing block to the existing global power base. Going forward, NDB could complement the other major initiatives such as Contingency Reserve Fund ($100 billion) announced in Durban Summit (2013) to help BRICS nations, help each other in foreign exchange management, an alliance of exchanges that could challenge the might of the western countries in the world of financial markets and derivatives (cross listing of benchmark equity derivatives indices of the exchanges of the five countries) and of energy (establishing a fuel reserve bank and an energy policy institute) which together could emerge as a potent force to challenge and contest the current Washington Consensus that runs most of the global affairs. China and India will also be active partners in the USD 100 billion Asian Infrastructure Bank which is being planned.

5. The Challenge of Global Governance

A study by the European Union (European Parliament, 2012)[1] observed The role of Brazil, Russia, India, China and South Africa (BRICS) as emerging protagonists in international development cooperation is significantly and rapidly changing. Over the last decade, BRICS have increased their financial as well as technical assistance and established distinct ways and means of economic cooperation, especially through south – south cooperation with Low Income Countries (LIC). BRICS are striving for more political influence, thereby challenging traditional western donors such as the EU. BRICS impact on LICs through trade, foreign direct investment and development financing are significant and these south – south efforts need to be reflected in EU development strategies".

While the consensus continues to surge on the importance of the BRICS and their role in the global governance, critic of the very grouping is also not uncommon. A recent report[2] puts the contrarian view to the general perception on the BRICS. "They are for all intents and purposes, a "GDP Club". As resource rich economies, they have adopted a development paradigm based on intensive extraction of natural resources (e.g. fossil, bio fuels and mineral etc.), which drive most of their exports. They have pursued GDP growth with little or no investment in human development, thereby allowing the gap between the haves and have not to widen. In the few common initiatives developed so far, such as the proposal for the BRICS Development Bank, the focus has been on infrastructure investment for new forms of extractive practices, an approach to economic development that is increasingly volatile and unsustainable in a global context marked by extreme financial instability, costly and potentially catastrophic environmental pressures and rising inequality. In line with their focus on extractive development, Brazil, China, India and South Africa sank the world's hopes for a binding agreement on climate change in the Copenhagen negotiations of 2009. Yet, as some have argued "if the international community fails to confront its most serious challenges — for the need for a sound global economic architecture to addressing climate change — The BRICS countries are the ones that will pay the highest price".

The governance framework of the BRICS should be able to address to both the issues amply and adequately to evolve a perfect blend. There is growing recognition around the world about the important roles that the BRICS countries play in global governance, but at the same time critics argue that this community is exploitative in nature with little concerns about people, nature and environment which need to be banlanced. This emerges as an important chanllenge for the BRICS think tanks.

Given different positions in which BRICS are placed and prospects that they hold in regard to economic growth, share in global production as compared to the developed world, it is natural that the former appears to be differing with the later on a host of issues which is not something unusual. BRICS are growing in scope and significance, the key driver behind the grouping being the rapid economic growth and trade where as the developed markets are more concerned about sustaining what is achieved amidst slow growth. Such diversity is bound to produce major differences in regard to a wide range of issues in the realm of global governance as evidenced by wide differences that the developed world and the developing world had on several issues ranging from liberalization of trade to climate change to energy efficiency and environmental protection.

It is in this context that thinks tanks engaged in BRICS cooperative work should engage more in deliberating on evolving frameworks and strategies towards achieving a healthy blend of rapid growth which BRICS are known for, with care and concern for people and environment, which the developed world advocates. The diversity of the political and economic systems of the BRICS countries could make designing a common agenda other than mutually beneficial business, quite a challenge. Not withstanding it being a daunting task, scope exists for BRICS designing a governance framework that has more relevance for the developing world and at the same time addresses to the concerns of the developed world. Surely scope exists for evolving newer paradigms and templates in various aspects of growth and governance as relevant to the developing world that now has a larger stake in the world affairs. The view that the domestic conditions in developing could restrict the scope for designing global frameworks is contested in some circles.[3]

First, it does not seem that legal or cultural impediments to financial development are as serious as one might have concluded from recent literature. Somewhat facetiously, one does not have to have the good fortune of being colonized by the British to be able to have vibrant financial markets. However, the main impediment we identify — the political structure within the country — can be as difficult to overcome as more structural impediments. Nevertheless, our second main implication is that to the extent a country can be coaxed to be open, it makes it less easy for domestic incumbents to retard financial development.

BRICS now have an opportunity to play a proactive role in conceiving and designing innovative formats and frameworks for governance. Representation from BRICS is at the helm of certain international organisations such as World Trade Organization (Roberto Azevedo of Brazil), UNIDO (Li Yong as Director General), International Monetary Fund (Zhu Min of China as Deputy Managing Director), provide numerous opportunities to interact on a wide range of issues that are of global in nature to put forward interesting alternatives.

A few issues that could emerge in this context as significant for enhancing the scope of governance in the BRICS countries and in which working towards a consensus that will address to the domestic concerns and at the same time be consistent with the global templates could be aspired for, are discussed below.

a. **Economic Freedom and Inclusion**

Growing incidence of peoples' aspirations turning towards political and economic freedom is becoming more pronounced in the world, especially in the developing world. And this inspiration is driven mostly by the desire to be an integral part of the growth that is taking place. It cannot be denied that in many emerging markets, growth and development have enlarged the income inequalities among the rich and the poor and continuing trend of this nature could be a potential powder keg in many countries. It is important for the leadership to address this issue to redress the resentment growing out of income inequalities by evolving appropriate policies and instruments of inclusion. Financial system has an important role to reduce the inequalities by providing better access to credit and other economic opportunities. Financial Inclusion thus emerged as an important policy agenda in many countries. This challenge of growing income inequality happens to be very significant among the BRICS except Brazil.

b. The Role of Public Markets

BRICS represent faster economic growth for which the financial resources will flow from public and private markets, which have a complementary role in development financing in the modern economics. However, it is important to develop the public capital markets, to enhance the level of transparency and disclosure, which could be vital for the orderly conduct of the markets. Equally important would be expanding the asset classes and instruments for investment, trading, hedging and risk management with sufficient safety nets built in for investor protection. BRICS made good progress in developing the size of the public capital markets, but scope still exists for expanding the realm of activities and product base. A combination of public and private capital market should harness the potential of the enterprise and entrepreneurship among the BRICS and other developing countries. While expanding the role of the public capital markets BRICS could endeavor to emerge as a role model for other developing and transition countries in terms of trade, investment and bilateral assistance.

c. Corporate Governance

Of all the factors that are believed to have contributed to the global financial crisis, corporate governance is the most important and critical one. A report on the corporate governance by the UNCTAD[4] observed in this regard: "The impact of the global financial crisis on the world economy has served to underscore the interconnectedness of the health of large global enterprises and the livelihoods of ordinary people. To be sure, the causes of the crisis are complex and the remedies that have been proposed are multifaceted. Yet corporate governance features strongly." An interesting aspect in this regard is that the developed world has been nudging the developing world and the BRICS to adopt stronger framework of corporate governance but deficiencies that were found among the public and private sectors in some parts of the developed world were quite damaging that attracted huge amount of penalties and punitive action. Right from fixing the Libor rate to mis-selling structured products to a wide range of market malpractices came into light. Major banks in the United States since the crisis broke out agreed to pay USD 127 billion as fines to settle regulatory actions initiated against them with Bank of America alone paying to the tune of USD 74.58 billion since 2010. Some of the Euro area countries have faced near default immediately after the crisis as the conditions prevailing on the fiscal management were not disclosed in accordance with the extant agreements concerning the country reporting standards of the European Union.

BRICS countries, though have vastly revamped and refined the corporate governance systems, some surprises continued to spring out occasionally. Disclosures made by some Chinese companies during the listing in the US markets (reports brought out by Muddy Waters Research), deficiencies came up in some of the Indian companies post listing (DLF), an oil company involved in bribery scandal in Brazil that surfaced before the elections (Petrobas), questions about the conduct of corporate governance certain companies in Russia that came out in late 2013 (TNK-BP, OAO Pharmstandard, and OAO Uralkali) formed discussion points on the shortcomings of corporate governance among the BRICS in various platforms.

A study by the United Nations Center for Trade and Development, which analyzed the corporate governance practice of 188 companies from 22 emerging markets, including the BRICS in regard to 52 disclosure items in five categories namely financial transparency, board and management structure and process, ownership structure and exercise of control rights, corporate responsibility and compliance and auditing, finds that " (a) There are troubling gaps in the disclosure of audit related issues with some of the key UNCTAD ISAR (International Standards of Accounting and Reporting) benchmark disclosure items in this category largely missing both in regulation and in company practice. Given the importance of auditing disclosure in assessing the quality of a company's governance, regulators should consider new disclosure requirements in line with international best practices. (b) More disclosure is almost always welcomed by investors, but there are good arguments for avoiding excessive disclosure: reporting can be costly and not all information is useful information. Regulators should focus on a core set of mandatory disclosure items. (c) Companies do not always comply with mandatory disclosure rules. In most countries direct enforcement by government of disclosure rules is impractical: there are too many individual disclosure points to check. Policy makers should consider focusing on a smaller set of leading enterprises, or conducting random reviews. Periodic checks, combined with moderate fines, could send a signal that regulators take disclosure seriously. (d) Regulators cannot do everything; investors must play an active role as market participants and communicate with investee companies about disclosure gaps. Policy makers should promote responsible investment and active ownership by investors. Investors should be encouraged to engage in dialogue with companies to ensure they meet regulatory requirements and voluntary best practices. A policy challenge faced in many countries is how to make disclosure based regulation work. The findings of this report indicate a three-fold approach: increase the number of required items; increase the clarity of disclosure regulations; and ensure that the information reaches the general public".

d. Regulatory Reform

In the aftermath of the financial crisis, United States[1] has launched a series of reforms aimed at bringing reforms in five key areas that include: (a) promote robust supervision and regulation of financial firms; (b) establish comprehensive supervision and regulation of financial markets; (c) protect consumers and investors from financial abuse; (d) improve tools for managing financial crises; and (e) raise international regulatory standards and improve international cooperation. Though BRICS countries too have brought in similar reforms, scope exists for the enhancement and enforcement of such measures to make the financial system responsive, responsible and accountable to the people. Regulatory reforms and refinements have emerged as critical policy options in view of the surge of global investing in all the countries of the BRICS community, as also their growing participation in the affairs of the global economy and finance. While regulation has been settling down with managing older issues, new challenges continue to crop up. The G20 in 2014 will focus on four key areas of (a) building resilient financial institutions (b) end too-big-to fail (c) address risks from shadow banking (IMF's Global Financial Stability Report of October 2014 devoted a separate chapter on this subject) and (d) making derivatives market safer. Earlier at the Pittsburg Summit of the G20 held in 2009, a number of reforms in the financial markets regulation were initiated which among others include: (a) more and better quality capital, with a leverage ratio and perhaps countercyclical buffers, (b) better liquidity and risk measurement, (c) enhance disclosure of off-balance sheet exposures, (d) oversight of credit rating agencies, (e) better regulation of

---

[1] The Department of the Treasury of the United States on 17 June 2009 published a white paper on financial regulatory reform in the United States entitled "Financial Regulatory Reform — A New Foundation: Rebuilding Financial Supervision and Regulation" (United States Department of the Treasury, 2009). (a) Financial Services Oversight Council, whose function it would be to "identify emerging systemic risks and improve interagency cooperation" (which is similar in function to the European Systemic Risk Board, discussed below); (b) A Consumer Financial Protection Agency, tasked with protecting consumers in credit, savings, and payments markets and (c) A National Bank Supervisor, with responsibility for federally chartered depository institutions.

market practices and underwriting standards, (f) the use of centralized clearing and exchanges for more over the counter (OTC) derivatives, (g) better alignment of compensation with long-term value creation, (h) the use of supervisory colleges, legal frameworks and contingency planning for coordination of cross-border issues in a crisis and (i) improved resolution tools and frameworks.

As BRICS play an important role in the design and implementation of the G20 agenda, best practices in the regulatory reform could receive due attention in the domestic financial market policies of the constituent countries.

e. Emerging Currency Regimes

An important outcome of the rise of the BRICS, apart from these being emerging as key contributors for the global economic growth, some of the countries such as China and Russia are also emerging as new and emerging currency regimes, more importantly the former. An IMF report[5] on the subject of emerging currencies observed that "Key EM currencies with potential for internationalization are the Brazilian Real, Chinese Renminbi, Indian Rupee, Russian Ruble, and South African Rand. All these economies have significant regional importance and economic weight. Despite severe data limitations, there is evidence that the use of these EM currencies in international transactions has increased markedly in the past few years. For instance, use in foreign exchange derivatives increased by 50% for the real, doubled for the rupee and the ruble, and increased about twelve-fold for the renminbi. Offshore markets for EM currencies are growing, with sharp increase in recent years reflecting EM's increasing global economic clout. Development of offshore markets contributes to interest in the currency and facilitates its use internationally". More than 900 financial institutions in over 70 countries are already doing business in the Chinese RMB. A recent report of the Bank for International Settlements[6] brought out important aspects of the internationalization of Renmimbi which among others include: (a) Peoples Bank of China setting up bilateral local currency swap facilities with 20 overseas central banks and monetary authorities to the tune of RMB 1.6 trillion, (b) growth of Renminbi deposits and CDs in Hong Kong growing from about RMB 322 billion at the end 2010 to nearly 1 trillion RMB by end 2013, off shore Renminbi bonds outstanding reaching a level of nearly RMB 500 billion from RMB 100 billion in 2010 etc.

According to the latest BIS Triennial Survey, average daily turnover of CNY market surged from USD 0.6 billion in 2004 to USD 20.0 billion in 2013. A report of the Asian Development Bank[7] describes important features of the Chinese currency emerging as an important instrument in trade settlement, bond issuance, trading, investment and as reserve currency.

Since the mid 2000s, Russia has been making efforts to strengthen the status of Rouble into a currency for bilateral settlement as also progress towards international currency. Trade with Russia accounts for 44% of the trade between the CIS countries. Countries strongly oriented towards trade with Russia include the CIS countries, Mongolia, Finland and Turkey. Russia also trades intensively with the Baltic countries, Bulgaria, Syria and Poland. Settlement of border trade in national currencies between China and Russia which has begun as a pilot project in 2003 now accounts for 99% of all transactions settled in roubles. Border trade in national currencies as a proportion of total Russian – Chinese commodity turnover grew from 0.5% in 2003 to 7.3% in 2008. According the central banks data of the respective countries, payments for commodities traded between Russia and other EurAsEC countries exceeded $50.9 billion in 2008 of which over 50% of the payments were made in rubles with USD taking the second place and the share of Euro at just 13%.

India is preparing to lobby major trading partners including Japan, Iraq and Venezuela to accept rupee payments for some of their exports, one of a series of moves to stabilize the volatile currency and make it more globally acceptable. Restrictions on large transactions of rupees against foreign currencies are intended to protect India from sustained speculative assaults, but they also limit interest in the rupee and foreign investment flows. A panel set up in August 2013 to study currency swaps has now won support from the finance ministry, the commerce ministry and the central bank to target about 10 countries for such deals, focusing on oil exporting nations and others that run large trade surpluses with India. The Commerce Ministry[8] in December 2013 has finalized a list of 23 countries with which India can trade in local currencies to save precious foreign exchange and strengthen the rupee. The list includes oil-exporting nations such as Angola, Algeria, Nigeria, Oman, Iran, Iraq, Venezuela, Qatar, Yemen and Saudi Arabia. Other countries on the list include Russia, Japan, Singapore, Australia, Indonesia, South Korea, Malaysia, Mexico, South Africa and Thailand.

The use of domestic currency as an international currency brings a number of benefits and an opportunity to reduce transaction costs and exchange rate risk; payments could be made in domestic currency; improved competition and institutional competitiveness and performance will lead to reduce cost of funding. These developments will bring in enormous range of benefits to the domestic financial systems in terms of intensity of business, market depth and transactional density. Though it is important to manage risks associated with the endeavors of being an international currency that among others could include: reduced autonomy of setting domestic interest rates, scope for increasing volatility, pressures on financial stability that will be more acute for financial systems without adequate scale and depth.

To pursue further internationalization, it is important for the countries to evolve policy actions that involve macroeconomic stability, strengthening of monetary based framework, capital account reforms, liquidity strengthening initiatives, proper coordination of various reforms including sequencing and strengthening, and capacity building.

BRICS will stand to gain from collaborative and cooperative endeavors that will help each other to strengthen the respective currencies in the use of bilateral trade settlement.

In addition to the above, from strengthening the perspective of governance strengthening, BRICS need to give due focus and attention to other important aspects such as fair laws that promote competition, growth of the private sector, strengthening access to finance, empowering people with skills and expertise, ensuring gender balance while promoting growth, incentives for business integrity and ethics, corporate social responsibility, adoption of clean technology and efficient energy management processes, protection of environment and labour laws, support to climate management, strengthening regional cooperation etc.

Though the BRICS economies experienced uncertainty and turbulence in the domestic economic growth after the financial sector reforms, the pace of development in the financial markets has been quite impressive. BRICS have been successful to argue and articulate their point of view in the global forums regarding to the emerging needs and requirements of the developing world; and a commitment towards this could be seen from the formation of the New Development Bank which will begin to take shape soon. BRICS also have expanded their realm of engagement and influence in several international financial institutions and policy-making bodies that would be helpful in crafting strong and robust processes for further development.

While the energy of the BRICS in terms of demographic strength and dividend, lower cost of resources, easier access to markets etc, have enabled them to emerge as a strong and vibrant community that set new benchmarks in domestic economic growth and contribution to the world economy. For ensuring further strength and continued success, it is the scope, quality and extent of governance measures that will matter the most.

Table 1 Corporate Governance in the BRICS Countries

No.	List of disclosure items in the UNCTAC ISAR benchmark	Countries				
	Ownership Structure and Exercise of Control Rights	Brazil	India	China	Russia	South Africa
1	Ownership structure	9/10	10/10	8/10	8/10	10/10
2	Process for holding annual general meetings	6/10	6/10	8/10	10/10	3/10
3	Changes in shareholdings	7/10	8/10	7/10	6/10	7/10
4	Control structure	9/10	8/10	9/10	8/10	6/10
5	Control and corresponding equity stake	10/10	5/10	9/10	8/10	4/10

Table 1 (continued)

No.	List of disclosure items in the UNCTAC ISAR benchmark	Countries				
	Ownership Structure and Exercise of Control Rights	Brazil	India	China	Russia	South Africa
6	Availability and accessibility of meeting agenda	8/10	9/10	9/10	8/10	9/10
7	Control rights	7/10	6/10	8/10	10/10	6/10
8	Rules and procedures governing the acquisition of corporate control in capital markets	9/10	4/10	8/10	9/10	9/10
9	Anti-takeover measures	1/10	0/10	1/10	1/10	0/10
Financial Transparency						
10	Financial and operating results	10/10	10/10	10/10	10/10	10/10
11	Critical accounting estimates	8/10	9/10	9/10	9/10	8/10
12	Nature, type and elements of related-party transactions	9/10	10/10	9/10	9/10	10/10
13	Company objectives	10/10	10/10	10/10	10/10	10/10
14	Impact of alternative accounting decisions	5/10	5/10	7/10	8/10	9/10
15	The decision-making process for approving transactions with related parties	7/10	3/10	4/10	7/10	3/10
16	Rules and procedures governing extraordinary transactions	4/10	6/10	5/10	9/10	5/10
17	Board's responsibilities regarding financial communications	10/10	9/10	9/10	8/10	9/10
Auditing						
18	Process for interaction with internal auditors	9/10	10/10	7/10	8/10	10/10
19	Process for interaction with external auditors	7/10	9/10	7/10	8/10	9/10
20	Process for appointment of external auditors	8/10	10/10	8/10	9/10	7/10
21	Process for appointment of internal auditors/scope of work and responsibilities	4/10	6/10	2/10	6/10	6/10
22	Board confidence in independence and integrity of external auditors	8/10	10/10	8/10	9/10	7/10
23	Internal control syste	10/10	9/10	10/10	8/10	7/10

Table 1 (continued)

No.	List of disclosure items in the UNCTAC ISAR benchmark	Countries				
Auditing						
24	Duration of current auditors	3/10	9/10	5/10	3/10	1/10
25	Rotation of audit partners	2/10	0/10	0/10	0/10	2/10
26	Auditors' involvement in non-audit work and the fees paid to the auditors	3/10	9/10	7/10	4/10	4/10
Corporate Responsibility and Compliance						
27	Policy and performance in connection with environmental and social responsibility	10/10	7/10	8/10	10/10	9/10
28	Impact of environmental and social responsibility policies on the firm's sustainability	7/10	7/10	5/10	5/10	6/10
29	A code of ethics for the board and waivers to the ethics code	4/10	10/10	2/10	2/10	2/10
30	A code of ethics for all company employess	9/10	7/10	4/10	5/10	10/10
31	Policy on "whistle blower" protection for all employees	6/10	8/10	2/10	1/10	6/10
32	Mechanisms protecting the rights of other stakeholders in business	10/10	9/10	5/10	7/10	9/10
33	The role of employees in corporate governance	8/10	7/10	4/10	3/10	3/10
Board and Management Structure and Process						
34	Governance structures, such as committees and other mechanisms to prevent conflict of interest	10/10	10/10	9/10	9/10	10/10
35	"Checks and balances" mechanisms	10/10	8/10	9/10	6/10	9/10
36	Composition of board of directors (executives and non-executives)	10/10	10/10	10/10	10/10	10/10
37	Composition and function of governance committee structures	10/10	10/10	9/10	8/10	10/10
38	Role and functions of the board of directors	9/10	9/10	10/10	10/10	9/10
39	Risk management objectives, system and activities	10/10	9/10	10/10	8/10	10/10

Table 1 (continued)

No.	List of disclosure items in the UNCTAC ISAR benchmark	Countries				
Board and Management Structure and Process						
40	Qualifications and biographical information on board members	8/10	10/10	10/10	7/10	8/10
41	Types and duties of outside board and management positions	9/10	10/10	10/10	6/10	9/10
42	Material interests of members of the board and management	3/10	10/10	8/10	5/10	10/10
43	Existence of plan of succession	4/10	6/10	7/10	1/10	9/10
44	Duration of director's contracts	0/10	0/10	1/10	1/10	0/10
45	Compensation policy for senior executives departing the firm as a result of a merger or acquisition	3/10	10/10	10/10	7/10	10/10
46	Determination and composition of directors' remuneration	3/10	10/10	10/10	7/10	10/10
47	Independence of the board of directors	7/10	10/10	10/10	6/10	10/10
48	Number of outside board and management position directorships held by the directors	9/10	10/10	10/10	6/10	10/10
49	Existence of procedure(s) for addressing conflicts of interest among board members	4/10	9/10	4/10	5/10	4/10
50	Professional development and training activities	3/10	6/10	2/10	4/10	7/10
51	Availability and use of advisorship facility during reporting period	6/10	5/10	5/10	2/10	7/10
52	Performance evaluation process	3/10	9/10	9/10	2/10	10/10

Source: Corporate Governance Disclosure in Emerging Markets: Statistical Analysis of Legal Requirements and Company Practices, New York and Geneva: UNCTAD, 2011

Note: Each square shows: the number of enterprises disclosing each UNCTAD ISAR benchmark item/number of enterprises studied in the market.

References

[1] "The Role of BRICS in the Developing World", Policy Department, *Directorate*

General for External Policies, April, 2012.

[2] "On the BRICS of Collapse? Why Emerging Economies Need a Different Development Model", paper prepared by the Centre for the Study of Governance Innovation (GovInn) University of Pretoria (South Africa). The quote in the end of the paragraphs pertains to D. Rodrik, "What the World Needs from the BRICS", *Project Syndicate*, 10 April, 2013.

[3] A quote found in W. Bratton and J. McCahery, "Comparative Corporate Governance and the Theory of the Firm: The Case against Global Cross-Reference", *Columbia Journal of Transnational Law*, 38 (1999): 213 - 97.

[4] United Nations Conference on Trade and Development, "Corporate Governance in the Wake of the Financial Crisis: Selected International Views", New York and Geneva, United Nations, 2010.

[5] Samar Maziad, Pascal Farahmand, Shengzu Wang, Stephanie Segal, and Faisal Ahmed, directed by Udaibir Das and Isabelle Mateosy Lagoago, 2011, *Internationalization of Emerging Market Currencies: A Balance between Risks and Rewards*, SDN/11/17 Washington: International Monetary Fund, October 19, 2011.

[6] Chang Shu, Dong He, and Xiaoqiang Cheng, "One Currency, Two Markets: The Renminbi's Growing Influence in Asia – Pacific", BIS Working Papers, No 446, Monetary and Economic Department, Bank for International Settlement, April 2014.

[7] Il Houng Lee and Yung Chul Park, "Use of National Currencies for Trade Settlement in East Asia: A Proposal", *ADBI Working Paper Series*, No. 474, April 2014.

[8] *The Hindu Business Line*, December 24, 2013.

India Moves Ahead: Courtesy E-Governance

Rajnish Ahuja*

Development of BRICS countries is seen as a major development in global context. BRICS group brings together five great forces who account for a share nearly 21% of the world GDP. These countries face twin challenges of maintaining a sustained growth and good governance. Contribution of services sector to the GDP of BRICS has been increasing over the years. India's share in the services sector as percentage of GDP has increased from 54.5% in 2009 to 57% in 2013. This indicates the continued growth of India as a services export economy. India's prowess in Information technology and Information technology enabled services has been recognized worldwide.

E-Governance provides a transparent way monitoring, assessment and implementation of the services. The diffusion of E-Governance into the operating systems and procedures of any economy would do away with the bureaucratic bottlenecks. This could be measured with the help of a development index. The United Nations assesses the global e-development through an "E-Government Development Index" (EGDI). The index is composed of three important dimensions, namely, provision of online services, telecommunication connectivity and human capacity and ranges from 0 to 1. India and South Africa are under the Middle EGDI group (0.25 to 0.50); rest of the BRICS countries are amongst the High EGDI group (0.50 to 0.75).

Indian government came up with a National E-Governance Plan[1] (NeGP) on May 18, 2006, which takes a holistic view of E-Governance

---

* Rajnish Ahuja, Associate Fellow at Pahle India Foundation, New Delhi, India.

[1] Http://india.gov.in/e-governance/national-e-governance-plan.

initiatives across the country. The objective of NeGP is to bring public services closer home to citizens, as articulated in the Vision Statement of NeGP.

> Make all Government services accessible to the common man in his locality, through common service delivery outlets, and ensure efficiency, transparency, and reliability of such services at affordable costs to realize the basic needs of the common man.

National E-Governance Plan comprises of 31 Mission Mode Projects (MMPs)[1] out of which 12 are at central level, 13 at the state level and the rest at an integrated level. The MMPs at central level comprise of banking, insurance, income tax, pensions, passports etc.

Table 1 Mission Mode Project of National E-Governance Plan

Central MMPs	State MMPs	Integrated MMPs
Income Tax	Municipalities	National E-Governance Service Delivery Gateway (NSDG)
Central Excise	Education	India Portal
E-Office	Crime and Criminal Tracking Network & Systems	Electronic Data interchange (EDI) for e-Trade
Insurance	Agriculture	E-Courts
Immigration, Visa and Foreigner's Registration & Tracking (IVFRT)	Public Distribution System	E-Biz
MCA 21 (Ministry of Corporate Affairs)	Health	Common Service Centres
UID (Unique Identification Project)	Employment Exchange	
National Population Register	E-Panchayat	
Pensions	Treasuries	
Passport	Commercial Taxes	
Banking	E-District	
Posts	Road Transport	
	National Land Records Modernization Programme (NLRMP)	

---

[1] Http://india.gov.in/e-governance/mission-mode-projects.

Indian government has been working in direction of ensuring maximum governance. The Indian government has developed an Indian development gateway (http://www.indg.in/) which is a single window for access to information and services, mainly for the rural communities. The site has provisions like, registration with the concerned employment exchange for the rural poor, registration of "Village Level Entrepreneurs" for the purpose of sharing the experiences and success stories among each other and online citizen services which include everything a rural community needs it know, whether it be the daily agricultural commodities rate, selling the agricultural products online or online educational services. The site also provides information and services in sectors, like, rural energy, health and social welfare.

To reduce the absenteeism in government departments, Indian government launched a scheme in October 2014 to keep a check on the working of government offices in Delhi. The portal (http://attendance.gov.in/) provides statistics about the departments registered on the website and the registered employees.

To ease out burden of compliances, an increased transparency and development of a conducive environment for industrial development, Shram Suvidha Portal, has been launched by the Labour Ministry of India in October 2014. It acts as a single window for compliance of labour laws, and reduces the burden for small and medium enterprises. A transparency into labor inspections was long awaited by the industry and the same has been incorporated in the scheme. Four major features of Shram Suvidha Portal are:

• Unique Labour Identification Number (LIN) will be allotted to Units to facilitate online registration.

• Filing of self-certified and simplified Single Online Return by the industry. Now Units will only file a single consolidated return online instead of filing 16 separate returns.

• Mandatory uploading of inspection Reports within 72 hours by the Labour inspectors.

• Timely redressal of grievances will be ensured with the help of the portal.

Here are some of the best practices in E-Governance followed by states in India:

1. Gujarat

One of the Indian States, Gujarat has set some of the best examples in sphere of E-Governance. These are listed below:

• Gujarat State Wide Area Network (GSWAN)[①]— Gujarat State Wide Area Network is an advanced communication infrastructure used for exchange of Data, Voice and Video information between two or more locations, separated by significant geographical distances. The motivating factor for GSWAN is the modernization of intra-governmental communication setup that would improve administrative effectiveness and efficiency and bring reliability and accountability in overall system of Government-to-Government (G 2G) functioning. It connects 7 districts on 8 Mbps, 19 districts on 4 Mbps and 1 district with 2 Mbps to the state capital, Gandhinagar using leased circuits.

• State Wide Attention on Grievances through Application of Technology (SWAGAT) — This practice addresses the grievance redressal of the citizens in Gujarat through innovative E-Governance technology. It is hosted on 4th Thursday of every month in presence of the Chief Minister.

• The Integrated Workflow and Document Management System (IWDMS) project by Government of Gujarat (GoG) has been implemented to improve the accountability, transparency and effectiveness in government administration, all levels of the administrative hierarchy. GoG has given stress to Change Management and Top-down approach for successful implementation of IWDMS project.

Hospital Management Information System (HMIS) in Gujarat has provided efficient and quality health services to the citizens through Govt. Medical Colleges/District Civil Hospitals, and has improved delivery of quality health care services, especially to the poor people in the state. Assists the doctors and medical staff to improve health

---

① Http://www.gswan.gov.in/.

services with readily reference patient data, work flow enabled less-paper process and parameterized alarms and triggers during patient treatment cycle.

• Gujarat Land Acquisition Model — The model followed by Gujarat Industrial Development Corporation (GIDC) has been successful in reducing the complexities across all processes in getting the land. The options available to an entrepreneur while purchasing land in Gujarat are: Private Land, Land in Special Economic Zones or Industrial Park, Land in GIDC estate or government land. Tujaratcess of land acquisition needs to be fair in terms of compensation to the land owners in order to avoid any litigation in the future. Therefore, the price determination of the land is based on the market prices. A 10% of the differential amount of acquisition price and land price recovered by GIDC is paid to owners over and above. The GIDC land is classified as non-agricultural, thus removing the need for "No Objection Certificate". While acquiring the land, GIDC ensures of providing employment to one member of each family whose land is acquired.

The next step after acquisition of land is development of infrastructure like roads, power and water supply. The estate development is carried out on Public Private Partnership model (PPP) by GIDC where land is acquired by Industrial Associations. The up-gradation for infrastructure facilities is done by contribution from the Government up to an extent of 60%, by GIDC to an extent of 20% and the rest 20% by the private promoters. The final step after development of land is allotment of land. The information regarding the land is made available on an online portal with a mention of all the infrastructure facilities available at the site. For a better land management, land inventory is updated on live basis using a Geographic Information System based application. This helps investors to carry out their research regarding the land and saves a lot of time for them. In case of any grievances, GIDC has come up with GIDC MITRA which is an online grievance redressal and monitoring system.

• E-Dhara[1] was introduced to enable access and maintenance of

---

[1] Http://revenuedepartment.gujarat.gov.in/e-dhara-forms.

Village Land Records in an easy, transparent and secure manner by digitizing all land records in Gujarat. E-Dhara Kendras(E-DK) take up day to day activities of land records such as mutations (Mutation means transfer or change of title in the records of the local municipal body for the concerned property) and issue of Record of Rights (RoR). This has helped to create an E-Governance environment in rural areas where computerized copies of RoR available to farmers and landowners by paying a nominal fee. This has created a new source of revenue records and the biggest benefit has been the minimized tampering of land records and eases in administration of other land related department like acquisition, grant, etc.

2. Maharashtra

The state of Maharashtra introduced MAITRI (Maharashtra Industry Trade and Investment Facilitation Cell), a single window Government to Business System for clearances required to set up an industry. The online system provides consolidated information to the investors regarding the investment process for expansion of the existing infrastructure or setting up a new business. With each application, two major levels of hierarchy have been mapped which comprise of processing at the district level and approving authority. All the forms and supporting documents for set up of industry are readily available online. MAITRI provides for direct supervision of principal secretary, industry and the nodal officers from the related departments during the process. The service caters to the projects to the tune of INR 100 million or more. The system will issue 31 clearances and approvals required in the process of setting up an industry.

The clearance issue system is investor friendly as it provides visibility of applications to the stakeholders at each stage of processing as well as approval. MAITRI provides information regarding investment policies, citizen charter, government co-ordinates up to district level and circulars available on the portal. Such an online system removes hassles related to repeated visits to the departments. It also helps in removal of redundancies, as the information collection is through a single channel.

3. Rajasthan

The Government of Rajasthan has "Single Window Clearance System" for the investors, which used for grant of permissions and clearances within a specified period of time. The state of Rajasthan has made it mandatory for investors to apply through Single Window for industrial investments more than INR 10 million. The applicant is allowed to register with a username and password only after filling of requisite online Entrepreneur registration form. This has been done to avoid creation of dummy user ids. The status tracking of proposals is structured and does not bypass any department. The investor gets to alerts through e-mail for each step of application and therefore transparency is maintained through the whole process.

4. Andhra Pradesh

An example of public private partnership for provision of services to masses is setting up of E-Seva centres or community one stop shops to pay taxes, utility bills, birth and death registrations, application for passports, etc. There are around 400 service counters spread across the state.

The best practices stated above for some of the Indian states present the growth of e-governance. With an aim to reduce the bureaucracy and ensuring maximum governance, Indian government plans for "Digital India Campaign". The initiative aims for high speed internet in all the villages at affordable rates. The goal is increased digital literacy amongst the masses through increased broad band connectivity. To increase the area covered under broadband connectivity, the investment is to be shared by public administration and private companies, which make use of part of the infrastructure to provide broadband connectivity services to the private market. The targets should include: Interconnection of all public administration and bringing broadband investment to areas where it would not have been considered profitable by the incumbent or other telecom operators based on a pure market-driven perspective, contrasting the geographical digital divide as in the rural areas.

Judicial Modernization Reform in China's State Governance

Guo Feng[*]

China is undergoing an unprecedented modernization reform in its judicial system. At the Fourth Plenary Session of the 18th Central Committee of the Communist Party of China convened last month, what deliberately studied and discussed was how to advance rule of law in China in an all-round manner; what set were objectives of building a socialist system of rule of law with Chinese characteristics and building China into a socialist country of rule of law. The judicial modernization reform is aimed to further develop and improve socialist system with Chinese characteristics and advance modernization of state governance system and governing capabilities in order to realize the beautiful Chinese Dream. I will take this opportunity to introduce the following three matters to our friends from BRICS countries.

1. Why Does China Need Judicial Modernization Reform?

After more than 90 years of hard work by Chinese people from all ethnic groups under the leadership of Chinese Communist Party, the impoverished and backward old China has been transformed into an increasingly prosperous and strong new China. As China's overall national strength is substantially growing, the prospect for the great national rejuvenation becomes brighter. In addition to a staggering GDP of 47.3 trillion yuan in 2011, major breakthroughs were also made in

---

[*] Guo Feng, the Deputy Director General of the Research Office of the Supreme People's Court of the People's Republic of China.

manned space program, lunar probe program, super computer and high-speed rail.

As a developing country, however, China is still facing many issues. Among these are: a prominent lack of balance, coordination and sustainability in development; a big gap between urban and rural development and in income distribution; more issues popping up concerning people's vital interests, such as education, employment, social security, medical care, housing, ecological environment, drug and food safety, production safety, public security, law enforcement, justice, etc; some people confronted by difficulties in life; a lack of moral values and integrity in some areas; war on corruption confronted with severe difficulties with frequent occurrence of corruption cases in some areas.

There is a big gap between rapid economic growth and laggard development in rule of law. Among the problems in implementing rule of law are: a lack of law compliance, strict law enforcement and adequate punishment for breach of law; law enforcement by multiple departments, and selecting targets in law enforcement; a lack of compliance with laws and regulations, transparency, manners in law enforcement and judicial system; people's backlash against injustice and corruption in law enforcement and judicial system; a lack of respect for and faith in laws and a weak sense of compliance with and use of laws to protect their rights among some people; a weak sense of law compliance, beach of law, putting opinions and powers over laws and bending laws for personal gains among some civil servants and senior government leaders.

Now, China's political, academic, commercial communities and the civil society have reached a consensus, which is, to advance rule of law. As the basic way of governance, rule of law should play an important role in state governance and social administration. With everyone being equal in front of law, the law must be adhered to, law enforcement must be strict, and breach of law must be punished. Judicial reform will be deepened to perfect the existing judicial system and to ensure judicial independence. Chinese Communist Party, any organization or any individual must not act above the constitution and the law.

2. Objectives for China's Judicial Modernization Reform

(1) **Consolidate the socialist system with Chinese characteristics.** This system includes the socialist market economy system, the socialist democratic political system and the socialist legal system, all of which were formulated under the leadership of the CPC, in accordance with China's constitution and in line with China's national conditions. This system can better promote people's all-round development and common prosperity, so as to build a modern socialist country that is prosperous, strong, democratic, civilized and harmonious.

(2) **Uphold social fairness and justice.** It should be noted that fairness and justice is the fundamental feature of the socialism with Chinese characteristics. Putting in place should be a fair social security system featuring equal rights and interests, equal opportunities and fair rules, so that people can have equal rights to participation and development. Through judicial systerm's justice-upholding functions, infringed rights and interests can be protected and remedied, yet criminal acts sanctioned and punished.

(3) **Promote social harmony.** Social harmony represents the essential attribute of the socialism with Chinese characteristics. Efforts should be made to ensure and improve people's livelihood; innovate in social administration; strike a balance between reform, development and stability; maximize social harmony; invigorate social innovation, so that people can live and work in contentment in an orderly society and the country can enjoy lasting political stability.

(4) **Build a fair, efficient and authoritative judicial system.** Judicial authorities should play an important role in state politics and power execution, namely power checks. The constitutional status of courts must be upheld because they courts on the behalf of the state exercise judicial powers which are unchallenged final powers.

3. Major measures to promote China's judicial modernization reform

(1) **Eliminate senior officials' intervention in judicial process to defend the authority of justice.** In order for the accountability system to better

function, a register system should be established to put on record officials' intervention in judicial process. Disciplinary punishment will be given to those who have intervened; criminal prosecutions will be brought up to those who have caused cases involving unjust, false or wrong charges or other serious consequences. Efforts will be made to perfect laws and regulations on such criminal acts as interference with judicial functions, defiance of verdicts and rulings and contempt of court. A protection mechanism will be put in place to enable judicial personnel to better perform their duties, provided that they, especially judges and prosecutors, will not be transferred, dismissed or demoted for unlawful reasons or through unlawful procedures.

(2) **Eliminate regional protectionisms' intervention in judicial process to make it easier to file a legal case.** Supreme People's Court will set up circuit courts to try major administrative, civil and commercial cases involving different administrative regions. In order to truly solve difficulties in case filing, trial and execution, efforts will be made to explore the possibility of setting up special courts to try cross-region cases. A reform will be made to ensure all cases accepted by courts, and will be put on record. Courts are obligated to file and accept legitimate cases in order to defend litigants' rights of action.

(3) **Eliminate internal intervention in judicial process and put in place an accountability system for case handling.** Efforts will be made to make clear powers and rights of judicial personnel working on different levels so as to improve the internal monitoring and checking mechanisms. Within the judicial system, one shall not illegally intervene in others' ongoing cases. If someone accesses to a specific case, this will be put on record on a register system. In addition, efforts will be made to ameliorate the accountability system for cases jointly processed by a presiding judge and a collegiate bench.

(4) **Reform and transform the litigation system into one centered on court trial.** In this new system, the facts and evidence of an ongoing case must stand the test of the law. Since the evidence-based adjudication, regulations will be fully implemented; all evidence must be collected, kept, examined and used in strict accordance with the law. The system

of witnesses and appraisers testifying at court will be improved to ensure that court trial plays a decisive role in fact-finding, evidence-verifying, right of action protecting, fair and just ruling.

(5) **Reform the system of judge selection.** Efforts will be made to establish a judicial personnel management system that accommodates the features of this profession; to perfect the mechanism for judge selection featuring unified recruiting, orderly communication and all-level participation. Currently in China, being a judge doesn't require many professional qualifications, which is not in sync with the authoritative status of this profession. According to *Law on Judges,* anyone who, at or above the age of 23, holds a bachelor degree in law and has worked in this field for two years is deemed qualified to be a judge at a grass-roots court or intermediate court; other conditions remain the same, anyone who has worked in this field for three years is deemed qualified to be a judge at a provincial supreme court or even at Supreme People's Court. The recruiting for this profession should be, like other legal professions, open to lawyers, professors of law and government departments. In this way, talents who are financially sound, have abundant work experience in this field and some social reputation can join this community and bring it a level up as a whole. Put in place should be an incentive system for judges, which is in line with this profession's features.

(6) **Build an open, dynamic, transparent and people-centered judicial system.** By virtue of information technology, China is vigorously advancing "Sunny Justice", a program designed to open trial procedures, verdicts and relevant information to the public. This move is aimed to expose every link in judicial process to litigants' and public supervision. All courts in China have been built an information management system featuring complete hardware equipment, internet coverage, real-time data generation and resource sharing. A name list will be built to expose to the public those who are able to yet deliberately don't execute court rulings.

(7) **Strengthen judicial guarantees for human rights.** Legal principles should be upheld in judicial process. For instance, criminal charges should be finalized and sanctioned by law; presumption of innocence

should prevail in cases where there is an evidence shortage; illegally-gained evidence should be excluded. Efforts will be made to beef up judicial supervision on judicial measures and investigative means that restrict personal freedom, prevent extorting confessions by torture and illegal collection of evidence from the source, and perfect the mechanism of preventing cases involving unjust, false or wrong charges from happening and carrying out timely remedial measures. Accelerate the establishment of a legal system for monitoring, deterring and punishing those who are able to yet deliberately not execute court rulings. Measures will be taken to separate final ruling and conclusion of lawsuit, lawsuit and visit bypassing the immediate leadership to higher levels.

(8) **Reinforce supervision on judicial activities.** Contact between judicial personnel and litigants, lawyers, persons specially involved in the case or intermediate organizations should be in line with relevant regulations and standards. It's strictly forbidden for judicial personnel to contact litigants and lawyers in person, leak or seek details of a case, accept dinner invitations or take bribes, introduce business to lawyers, among other things. Tough measures will be taken to punish those who seek personal gains in judicial process in order to prevent interest tunneling.

"Urban Development Trap" — A Major Problem Concerning Local Governance in BRICS Countries

Yuan Baocheng[*]

Distinguished guests, ladies and gentlemen,

I'm honored to attend this conference. I come from Dongguan City, Guangdong Province in south China. Dongguan is labeled as the "city of modern manufacturing industry". Over the past three decades, Dongguan has benefited much from the reform and opening up. It has achieved rapid industrialization and urbanization through a strategy spearheaded by export-oriented economy. There are more than 600 000 market entities in the 2 460-square-kilometer city. It boasts a GDP of 550 billion RMB, ranking 20th among large and medium-sized cities in China, and a total import-export volume of 150 billion USD, ranking fifth in the country. In the meantime, like many other cities in the BRICS countries (Brazil, Russia, India, China, South Africa), Dongguan is also faced with quite a few problems concerning local governance. The most acute problem is the problem of "urban development trap", which is the very topic that I'd like to discuss with you today.

Inspired by the term of "middle income trap", I generalized the concept of "urban development trap". As is known, the "middle income trap" is put forward by the World Bank. It means that when the GDP per capita of a country or region reaches 4 000 USDs, contradictions brought by rapid development are likely to appear all together. Without effective transformation of the development pattern, the contradictions will lead to economic stagnation and social instability. As a result, it is impossible for

---

[*] Yuan Baocheng, the Deputy Secretary of Dongguan Municipal Party Committee and Mayor of Dongguan.

such a country or region to join the high income club. As for Dongguan, its GDP per capita is about 10 000 USDs, far more than 4 000 USDs. Nevertheless, economic transition and social transformation remain two serious challenges in this city. In fact, as the development of a city goes on, development dividend will gradually decrease and even disappear, and the city may thus fall into a trap. Consequently, its development may stop and even fall back. In short, there may appear a trap which may not have so much to do with the income of the city. Therefore, I came up with the concept of "urban development trap" based on the term of "middle income trap". And next, I'd like to share with you the measures Dongguan has taken and the experience it has gained when faced with an urban development trap.

1. The Problem of "Urban Development Trap" in the Local Governance of Dongguan and Its Responses

Rome was not built in a day. Like some cities in the BRICS countries, Dongguan faces an "urban development trap" which is not formed in a day; various problems accumulate in the course of economic and social development and if not resolved in time, they can lead to serious consequences.

Trap one — industries are turning low-end and hollowing out

Dongguan's response — making transformation and upgrading a new normality for development.

Most of the BRICS countries are developing countries. Cities in these countries are suffering a weak basis in early industrialization and lack of funds, technology and market access. They can only rely on large-scale introduction of foreign capital to achieve rapid industrialization. This no doubt will bring about rapid prosperity of the city, but may also from the outset sow a series of drawbacks to industrial development: on the one hand, most of the introduced enterprises are at the low end of the industrial chain and see low added value in their products; on the other hand, when the economic development of the city reaches a certain extent, profit-driven industrial capital will seek to move to lower-cost areas, industrial hollowing-out accompanying gradient transfer constitutes an alarming problem. To this end, Dongguan has taken targeted measures. **For the problem of industries turning low-end**, the main task is to promote enterprise to upgrade locally, expand from manufacturing to technology research and development (R&D), brand marketing and other links, and gradually occupy the high-end of the industrial chain. The municipal government of Dongguan has set up a special fund of 10 billion RMB for science and technology, whereby to guide and support enterprises in their technological transformation and R&D. The annual number of patent applications and grants has topped 20 000 in the recent three straight years, and technological innovation has become an important driving force for the city's development. Meanwhile, brand building having been vigorously promoted, 13% of the processing trade enterprises of the city have established their own brands, including the acquisition of more than 400 international brands. A clothing business in Dongguan, through improving production processes and creating high-end brands, has effectuated a top price of 120 000 RMB of a sweater article, and thus achieved an added value topping the profit of a mid-range car. In addition, the city has, via the integration of industrial chains, created competitive industrial clusters such as electronic information, footwear and clothing. The self-supply rate of a whole set of computer in Dongguan has reached 95%; one of ten pairs of athletic shoes around the world comes from Dongguan; one out of five people owns a sweater produced in Dongguan. **For the problem of industrial hollowing-out**, the main jobs are, alongside supporting the private economy and enhancing the endogenous development momentum, to continue to administer by law, optimize government services, and reduce the overall cost of doing business of enterprises; to retain high-quality companies with superior legal and international business environment and replace the old backward industries, thus completing and enhancing the development support after industrial gradient transfer, and materializing the policy of "emptying the cage and replacing the bird" and achieving the effect of "Nirvana". The past three years, the city has relieved its enterprises of tax for businesses and related costs totaling more than eight billion RMB. It has successively introduced 188 major projects, each with an investment of over 600 million RMB or 100 million USDs, and thus achieved a total investment of 317 billion RMB, which will, after going into operation, release a production value of more than one trillion RMB, equivalent to another Dongguan economy. Among these projects, the smart phones and other emerging industries have formed scale, popular products, such as Apple, Samsung, and the three domestic brands of Huawei, Coolpad, OPPO, all base their production in Dongguan, which contributes to about one eighth of global mobile phone shipments. Dongguan has proved that there is no end to upgrading, and that as long as unremitting efforts are made, the traps of low-endness and hollowness can be overcome.

Trap two — management of large number of new immigrants and service problems.

Dongguan's response — gradually promote the equalization of basic public services.

The rapid industrialization in the BRICS countries has formed large-scale centralized production. The original inhabitants of the city alone cannot meet the demand for labor, and it is necessary to import a large amount of labour. Dongguan, with only 1.8 million odd indigenous people, sees a total population exceeding 10 million, and is one of the cities with the largest number of new immigrants in China. The combination of such labor force and international capital, while having generated a surprising burst of economic vitality of the city, has also brought enormous pressure to urban services and management. In default of proper handling, such problems may easily rise as security chaos, group conflicts and slums. With a view to this, Dongguan has set up new special agencies for immigrant service management, whereby to promote the equalization of basic public services, and strive to provide residential treatment for the new immigrants while strengthening social management and safeguarding urban order. For example, in education, the city has adopted the points system to provide public school places for children of new immigrants. Coupled with places created by private schools, the city has absorbed 609 000 immigrant children apt for compulsory education, which accounts for 76.1% of the total number of students. In terms of social security, the city tries its best to integrate all new immigrants into such security systems as pension, medical, and work injury insurance. Paying only dozens of RMB per year, a new immigrant can enjoy an annual hospitalized medicare payment of up to 200 000 RMB and a reimbursement of up to 500 000 for serious illness medicare. Of course, due to the limit of governmental finance and other factors, we are currently unable to provide residential treatment for all new immigrants. But with the progress of equalization of public services, new immigrants in Dongguan are having an increasing sense of belongingness, and the huge human resource is gradually transforming into a talent resource increasingly favorable for urban development.

Trap three — development problems brought by rapid urbanization.

Dongguan's response — a new type of urbanization featuring networked, poly-centric form of concentration.

As for the BRICS countries, in most cases, rapid industrialization means rapid urbanization. Many cities in the BRICS countries have encountered such problems as population explosion, traffic jam, housing problems and environmental deterioration. In academic circles, it is believed that two forms of urbanization are worth being paid attention to. One is mono-centric, featuring centralized expansion; and the other is poly-centric, featuring localized expansion. And Dongguan has chosen a new type of urbanization similar to the second form. In Dongguan, based on a special administrative framework under which towns are directly governed by the municipal government, a poly-centric development pattern with the downtown as the great center and 28 towns as smaller centers has taken shape. Enough ecological isolation belts have been retained between these centers. Besides, urban and rural areas are closely linked with each other through an integrated network of roads and railways, gas, water and electricity. So a half-hour traffic circle is formed inside the city and high speed transportation is achieved. In such a poly-centric development pattern, the rural areas are laid emphasis on, and as a result, maladies brought by excessive agglomeration in a mono-centric city are effectively avoided. In addition, the urban spatial layout is more reasonable; production and transportation are more orderly; and the environment is also much better. At present, even with a population of over 10 million, Dongguan doesn't seem crowded compared with other cities of the same scale. There are 1.6 million cars running in the city, but there is little traffic jam. Besides, the housing price of Dongguan is merely a half or even a third of that of neighboring large cities. Therefore, in comparison with citizens of other cities, Dongguan citizens are suffering less work stress and living a more comfortable life.

Trap four — resource consumption and environmental destruction brought by industrialization.

Dongguan's response — giving great impetus to environmental remediation and ecological construction.

Across the world, most old industrial cities including those in the BRICS countries have experienced "treatment after pollution". Along with its rapid development, Dongguan is also faced with a series of problems such as ecological damage, environmental pollution and resource shortage. Recent years, we have thought much about the extensive development pattern which is at the cost of resource and environment. We have vigorously advocated ecological civilization and paid attention to a low-carbon economy so as to achieve green rise even though the environment has reached its capacity. To be specific, in order to pay off its environmental debts, the Dongguan municipal government has put more than 50 billion RMB into environmental remediation and ecological construction. A system of sewage and refusal disposal has been established, covering the downtown area and all the 28 towns. It has well facilitated pollution abatement and ecological restoration. As a result, the average PM 2.5 level of Dongguan is around 43 in 2013, and air quality of the city is above the average in the country. Besides, there is ecological preservation area, 16 forest parks and five natural conservation areas in Dongguan, altogether making up nearly a half of its area. Its forest coverage rate is 36.7% and greening rate of its built-up area is 44.3%, which make Dongguan outstanding among industrial cities in the BRICS countries. In fact, Dongguan has been put on the

International Garden City list by the United Nations Environment Programme (UNEP), and it's also on the Chinese Garden City list and the list of Model City for Environmental Protection. Now, the city of Dongguan seems like a big garden, boasting fine ecology with green hills, clear waters, massive trees and bright flowers. In a word, with persistence and great efforts, Dongguan has successfully explored a development road of its own. As the foundation of the development of Dongguan, the manufacturing industry is well integrated and complementary with the eco-development of the city.

2. Experience Ggained in Dealing with the Urban Developmental Trap

First, we should handle properly the relation between the industrial development and the urban development. Rapid industrialization and urbanization are the two typical features of the BRICS countries. The key to address the problem of urban development trap lies in the fusion of production and city. The counterpart of the English word "city" in Chinese is "Cheng Shi", which vividly shows that a city should not only have a "Cheng", the hardware platform, but also a "Shi", the industrial foundation. The industry promotes the city development, while the city contributes to the industrial upgrade. The BRICS countries can't unilaterally pursue the urbanization while not considering the industry because a blind expansion of a city in land area is just like building a castle on the sands. Neither can they just concentrate on the development of industry while ignoring the promotion of city construction. Otherwise it will cause the urbanization level to lag behind the process of industrialization, pose difficulty in supporting more high-level enterprises and talents that want to move in and constrain the improvement of the industrial level.

Second, we should handle properly the relation between the traditional industry and the emerging industry. The industrial gradient transfer and substitution are the normal law of economic development. However, the promotion of industrial transformation and upgrade doesn't mean we can simply eliminate the traditional industries or develop the emerging industries blindly. There is no outdated industry but obsolete technology. Similarly, there is no sunset industry but sunset products. Most products of the traditional industry are the necessities of life. There are always demands and markets for them. The key lies in how we transform and upgrade them, and improve their added value. The strategic emerging industries, represent the commanding heights of the future economy, but we can't develop them blindly and enter a homogeneity competition with other countries. We must base on the local industrial foundation and concentrate on developing some relatively competitive industries, thus gradually forming a new group of industries with their own distinctive features.

Third, we should handle properly the relation between the environment protection and the economic growth. Xi Jinping, the General Secretary of the CPC Central Committee, said, "While we want prosperity and wealth, we also want clear water and green hills, but we don't want the prosperity and wealth at the expense of clean water and green hills. In fact, only clear water and green hills can bring us prosperity and wealth." From an economics standpoint, the ecological environment is viewed as a resource that can be priced and exchanged. Therefore it is not only a natural wealth, but also a social and economic wealth critical to the growth of a local economy. The BRICS countries must insist on the ecological protection if they want to achieve better economic development. Meanwhile, they should use the financial resources and experience accumulated from the economic development to further establish a good ecological environment. Only by doing these, the BRICS countries can achieve the organic unity and mutual promotion of the economy and the ecology.

Fourth, we should handle properly the relation between the government guidance and the market push. Government and market are the two major driving forces that play a dominant role in the city development. In order to address the problem of urban development trap effectively, we must use the two hands of government and market in a proper way. On the one hand, the government should take a responsible attitude towards the further development of a city and steer the industrial development and city construction towards a right direction through strengthening the top-level design. On the other hand, the government should bring into full play the decisive role of the market in the allocation of resources and improve efficiency in the use of funds, technology, talents and other factors so as to stimulate the vitality of economic and social development.

The above-mentioned several points are some practices and experience regarding how Dongguan copes with the problem of the urban developmental trap. All of you present here are prominent experts and scholars and elites in the political and business circles from the BRICS countries. We cordially welcome you to come and visit Dongguan, feel the charm of this famous modern manufacturing city and plan together with us for the future development of the cities in the BRICS countries.

Thank you.

Promoting BRICS Bank Cooperation in a Pragmatic Way

Zou Lixing[*]

On July 15, 2014, the *Sixth BRICS Summit — Fortaleza Declaration and Action Plan* officially announced to establish the New Development Bank (known as the BRICS Bank), ushering in a new stage in the cooperation of BRICS countries. However, a slew of issues wait to be solved from the announcement to the actual operation of the bank, with its positioning, relation with various parties and operating mechanism being the most important ones. Properly handling those issues and promoting the development of the BRICS Bank in a pragmatic way is of great importance for global governance.

1. Rational Position of BRICS Bank

Composed of leading developing countries in today's world, the BRICS are major representatives of the "emerging forces" in the 21st century. The five member states — Brazil, China, India, Russia and South Africa — are major powers in Latin America, Asia, Eurasia and Africa respectively, which play a significant role in world politics, and they have become critical in world economy as well thanks to their sustained and high-speed economic growth in the past two decades. However, the BRICS countries will face an onerous construction cause for a very long time to come and still lag behind the developed countries. Due to various internal and external factors, especially the economic and social

---

[*] Zou Lixing, the Vice President of the Research Institute of China Development Bank and the Vice Chairman of China Social and Economic System Analysis Research Society.

transformation inside and the financial crisis outside, there are less advantages but more disadvantages for the BRICS countries to continue their high-speed economic growth, and what they enjoyed in the past 20-plus years will hardly be seen again. In the 21st century, the BRICS countries will constitute a major force to drive the balanced development of world economy, but they won't be able to completely change the current global governance landscape. The BRICS Bank is a builder of common interests for developing countries, and also a participant, supplement and cooperator in the global governance reform.

First, BRICS Bank is a participant in the adjustment of international financial structure. The international financial structure today that has taken shape over a long history displays serious imbalance in that most international financial institutions are dominated by developed countries, while developing countries have a very limited say, which is detrimental to the sound governance and balanced development of the world. The global financial governance needs to reflect the changes in market economy and the characteristics of emerging economies. Establishing the BRICS Bank is a significant part of the global financial system reform, because it caters to the needs of emerging and developing countries, takes an active part in international financial reform, and helps promote the balanced world development.

Second, BRICS Bank is a supplement to international financial institutions. It's impossible and unnecessary for the BRICS Bank to replace the World Bank. A diversified international market needs diversified international financial institutions. The World Bank has contributed and will continue to contribute to the global economic recovery and development after WWII, but it and other existing international financial institutions alone are unable to meet the demand of the BRICS countries and other developing countries for faster infrastructure construction. Primary studies show that developing countries need more than USD 1 trillion capital a year for infrastructure investment, and the infrastructure shortage is especially serious in Brazil, South Africa, Russia and India, but the around USD 150 billion loan that World Bank can provide every year is far from enough to meet their needs. Therefore, establishing the

BRICS Bank is an important supplement to existing international financial institutions.

Third, BRICS Bank is a cooperator in the international financial system. Countries and regions worldwide are seeing growing inherent consistency today, and BRICS countries and the global community are mutual markets and drivers for each other. A closer cooperation among the BRICS countries and their joint establishment of the BRICS Bank is not only a step to keep strengthening their own growing momentum, but also a process to deepen economic globalization and pursue win-win collaboration. While deepening their own reforms, the BRICS countries also play an active part in global governance, strengthen the coordination of macro policies in the international community, push the reform of international financial system, and drive economic globalization in the direction of universal benefit and win-win development.

Fourth, BRICS is a builder of common interests for developing countries. Developing countries are in a passive and disadvantaged position in the global governance layout. How to air the voice of the weak and defend the common interests of developing countries amid the global governance reform? First of all, we need to keep in mind that developing countries' common interests aren't something waiting for us to discover and defend, but need to be built through the interaction of international community. The common appeals and goals of developing countries exert a lasting and significant influence on international politics and economics as well as on the structure of each country itself. Second, developing countries need to establish their image and adopt new strategy under new circumstances, which is a lesson from historic experience and also a realistic choice. Third, as a representative institution of developing countries, the BRICS Bank will be a new participant in creating the international community, and will earnestly safeguard the common interests of developing countries by assuming special functions and creating a new working mechanism to accomplish specific tasks. Fourth, while insisting on creating a modern bank with BRICS characteristics, the BRICS countries also hold on to development through cooperation, and will always uphold the banner of cooperation and display the cooperative spirit no matter what difficulties and barriers they encounter. Adhering to cooperative planning and construction, they will seek common ground and shelve difference through cooperation with the ultimate goal of common development.

In sum, the BRICS Bank, as a new-type trans-regional development-oriented financial institution, will participate in, supplement, cooperate with and build the existing international financial system through market-based operations, and support the BRICS countries and other developing countries in infrastructure construction and sustainable development. A rational positioning of the BRICS Bank is helpful for properly dealing with all kinds of complicated relations and reducing international resistance during its establishment and development.

2. Properly Handle Four Relations

(1) **Relations among members of the BRICS Bank.** BRICS countries' insistence on the principle of "seeking common ground and shelving differences" and their earnest efforts on internal coordination and cooperation lay the foundation for promoting the BRICS Bank.

On the one hand, the BRICS countries shall hold on to their common interests and appeals, identify their dynamic common goals, and intensify their mutual recognition and complementarity. The biggest common point among BRICS countries is that they are all emerging market countries, their common appeal is economic development, and the field where they are most likely to reach a consensus is infrastructure construction. All BRICS countries are faced with such tasks as technological innovation, industrial upgrade, energy consumption reduction, pollution control, eco-protection and the improvement of people's livelihood. Therefore, the BRICS Bank will provide financing and intelligence services and rationally allocate the production factors of BRICS countries, so as to complement each other with respective strengths and push for the realization of their common goals.

On the other hand, differences among the BRICS countries shall be recognized. In spite of their common interests and appeals, they are by no means an absolute community of shared interests, and their differences shall be fully taken into account when carrying out businesses. Since the five BRICS countries are in the similar development stage, there is competition among them in the economic and trade fields, differences are obvious in their political system, religion, culture, history and tradition, and divergence exists in their development paths as well. Therefore, the BRICS members shall adopt a tolerant and rational perspective, try to show more coordination and understanding, seek common ground and shelve differences, and avoid falling into a zero-sum trap. That's the only way to ensure the smooth progress of the BRICS Bank.

(2) **Relations between BRICS Bank and other developing countries.** The BRICS Bank isn't exclusive to the BRICS countries, but is open to other developing countries as well. As an inclusive and open trans-regional development bank, the BRICS Bank can and should prioritize the interests of the BRICS countries in certain aspects, but in a more macroscopic sense, it should look beyond that scope to a broader horizon when it comes to the source and destination of capital. This is not only good for pooling together the forces of emerging economies, but can also provide a new platform for the cooperation among developing countries.

The BRICS Bank can also carry out institutional cooperation with developing countries on issues where they can reach consensus, and forge a "united front" to safeguard their common interests. The world economy has been centered in developed countries for a long time, whereas developing ones have stayed in a marginalized position, forming the fact of "the strong north and the weak south". As developed countries are dominant in international financial institutions, they don't give sufficient consideration for developing countries' interests. On the contrary, the BRICS Bank is committed to reflecting and defending the ideas and interests of developing countries, providing medium and long-term low-interest loans for its members and other developing countries to implement infrastructure projects, and avoiding any mandatory additional conditions to the loans. In this way it strives to truly realize "equality, mutual benefit and common development" for all developing countries.

(3) **Relations between BRICS Bank and international financial institutions.** The BRICS Bank may bring a shock to the existing international financial order, but the relations between it and existing international financial institutions are neither a "zero-sum game" nor a replacement, but complementary. The former is a healthy supplement to the international financial system. Compared with global financial institutions such as the World Bank and IMF, the BRICS Bank places more premium on infrastructure loans and investment to developing countries, and the Contingency Reserve Arrangement is aimed at helping the member states deal with short-term liquidity pressure and strengthening the global financial security net. As the BRICS Bank members are all emerging countries in similar development stage, they have a better understanding of the reality and national conditions in developing countries, and can adapt the Bank's services to their economic development needs by optimizing the mechanism. Besides, as regards loan approval, the BRICS Bank will only look at the financial status of the borrower without interfering in its internal affairs, which is very different from what the existing international financial institutions do.

Compared with sub-regional development banks such as the Asian Development Bank, African Development Bank and Inter-American Development Bank, the BRICS Bank has the same interest appeal, carries the same mission, serves similar customers and aims for the same regional goal. Such broad similarities serve as the foundation for their cooperation. However, unlike sub-regional development banks, the BRICS Bank is a trans-regional intercontinental bank that makes arrangements and optimizes resource allocation among different continents, so it is a supplement to sub-regional development banks from a macro perspective. Such a cooperative and complementary relation between those two types of banks is not only reflected in their consistent cooperation principles and the resonance of cooperative spirit, but also in the all-sided efforts made by BRICS Bank members to promote the development and cooperation in their respective region.

(4) **Relations between BRICS Bank and the UN.** The BRICS Bank is a

new engine to realize the UN Millennium Development Goals and propel south – south collaboration. Its appearance indicates in a way that emerging economy countries will have their own investment and financing channel and relatively independent economic backup and organizational structure. Although the BRICS Bank has only a small amount of capital in the beginning, it is a significant step in emerging economies' pursuit for economic rationality on the world level, and demonstrates the BRICS countries as a positive force in reforming the global economic governance.

The establishment of the BRICS Bank and the design of its operating mechanism represent a new paradigm for south – south collaboration. First, it's a democratic cooperation. The initial subscribed capital is evenly shared by all founding members, the Bank is headquartered in Shanghai, and the first President andfirst chairs of the Board of Governors and the Board of Directors are recommended by India, Russia and Brazil respectively. Such a systematic arrangement reflects the equality of the five BRICS countries without preference to anyone. What also reflects equality is the contribution to the Contingency Reserve Arrangement, whereby each member state decides its share according to its own economic status. Second, this is a substantive cooperation. The BRICS Bank is a new platform of financial cooperation that turns the collaboration among BRICS countries from abstract to concrete, from nominal to substantial, and from economic and trade fields to a wider range of areas including economy and finance. Third, this is an in-depth cooperation. The financial cooperation platform is good for deepening the ties and communication among the five BRICS member states.

The world today suffers from reduced potential of economic growth, sluggish investment and spreading trade protectionism, posing new challenges to the BRICS countries. Especially after the US began to taper its quantitative easing policy, some emerging economies have seen a raft of severe issues, such as capital fleeing, currency devaluation and economic slowdown. The establishment of the BRICS Bank will help set up a financial security net for BRICS countries themselves, reduce their reliance on developed economies and the impacts from the adjustment of international monetary policies, and facilitate stable, sustained and sound economic development. The Bank will also serve as an important bridge for south – north communication, intensify the dialogue and collaboration between developed and developing countries, in a bid to jointly steer the world toward greater balance and universal benefit.

3. Carefully Design Operating Mechanism

(1) **Rationally define the functions of BRICS Bank.** The fundamental and unchanging function of the BRICS Bank is to support developing countries' infrastructure construction and sustainable economic and social development with financing and intelligence services. However, its functions may be dynamic in the long term as the concept, purpose and means of construction and development change. The World Bank has provided referable experience in this regard. In the end of 1940s, the World Bank was focused on pushing the reconstruction in Europe, but it shifted its focus to economic issues in less developed countries in the 1950s and the early 1960s, when its priority was to help increase the GDP in poor countries. Today it has expanded its focus to income distribution, poverty alleviation, environmental protection and cultural development. The means of development have also changed from focusing on capital accumulation, foreign exchange and large industrial projects like transportation and power station construction to small-scale agriculture, reproduction and the provision of urban and rural social services. Such changes reflect the law of things and adapt to the needs of economic and social development. The newly founded BRICS Bank shall have such a strategic vision and pragmatic plan to deal with future changes.

The medium and long-term dynamism of BRICS Bank's functions doesn't affect its definite tasks in the next decade, which mainly include the following three.

The first task is consulting and planning. By studying the development strategy of BRICS countries and the world at large, it shall formulate a medium and long-term investment and financing plan for the BRICS countries, organize personnel exchange and training, and promote those countries to develop in a coordinated, sound and sustainable way.

The second task is loan and investment. The BRICS Bank shall set up an effective investment and financing mechanism to finance the following four areas. First, it shall finance infrastructure, help BRICS countries and other developing countries accelerate infrastructure construction, and improve the conditions for economic and social development. Second, it shall finance agriculture, small enterprises and environmental protection, help BRICS countries and other developing countries enhance their capability of ensuring grain security, facilitate the development of medium and small-sized enterprises, and protect the environment. Third, it shall finance human resource development, increase basic health and education services, and improve the basic skills and working competence of poverty-stricken people. Fourth, it shall finance reform, help BRICS countries and other developing countries develop their governance capability, and form a political environment and market mechanism conducive to long-term stability and development.

The third task is guarantee and risk control. By means of guarantee and guidance, the BRICS Bank shall help BRICS countries and other developing countries turn their natural resources into the driving force of development, and assist the BRICS countries in improving their productivity, production level and labor conditions. By coordinating with other international institutions in loan or guarantee, the BRICS Bank shall prioritize more urgent projects and promote the lasting and balanced growth of international trade. By setting up the risk pre-warning and prevention mechanism, it shall urge concerted efforts to cope with instabilities in the financial market and safeguard financial and economic security.

(2) **Actively explore the BRICS currency mechanism.** In reference to IMF's experience in special drawing rights, the BRICS Bank shall set up a BRICS currency system as the media to perform its functions. There are three options for consideration. The first is to set up a currency basket composed of the currencies of all five BRICS countries; the second is to set up a currency basket based on the BRICS currency but including the currencies of some other developing countries as well; and the third is to

set up a new currency basket with IMF's basket of special drawing rights as the basis with the addition of the BRICS currencies including RMB. In terms of progressive reform, the BRICS Bank can adopt a double-track system at first, meaning it continues to use the US dollar to perform its functions on the one hand, and establishes the currency swap mechanism among BRICS countries and speeds up the creation of the BRICS currency on the other. The first option of BRICS currency is more appropriate in the initial stage. The currencies of the five BRICS countries are selected to form a currency basket at a ratio commensurate with each country's economic scale, and it will perform the currency function in the Bank's financial activities and daily operation. Whatever choice the BRICS Bank makes, it will be a supplement and improvement of the existing international currency system.

In addition to the BRICS currency basket, an accounting unit, clearing, calculating and reserve system shall also be established in the BRICS currency system. They can be regarded as a new content to the international clearing system, or a BRICS clearing mechanism can be considered when conditions are right.

There is an essential difference between the BRICS currency system and the IMF special drawing rights. While the latter is a right of capital use allocated by IMF to its members, the former isn't a right but a media for the BRICS Bank to perform its key functions, and a cooperation framework aiming to promote the use of currencies of BRICS countries.

(3) **Energetically innovate the operating mechanism of BRICS Bank.** Mechanism is more important than institution and the vitality of BRICS Bank lies in mechanism innovation. First, the fundraising mechanism shall be innovated. China's experience shows that what developing countries lack isn't capital, but a mechanism to raise capital or to turn all kinds of resources into construction capital. We shall try all means to set up an effective fundraising mechanism to turn the resource advantages in BRICS countries and other developing countries into fundraising advantages. Second, the Bank governance shall be innovated. The BRICS Bank shall combine advanced theories and technologies with actual conditions in the BRICS countries, design a reasonable governance

structure that balances fairness with efficiency, and become a bond between the market and government activities. Third, the operating mechanism shall be innovated, and the principle of "strategic mutual trust, policy support, professional management, business model, risk sharing and common development" shall be upheld. Based on the strategic mutual trust among BRICS countries, they shall formulate and provide legal and policy guarantee, concentrate capital on cross-regional infrastructure construction and basic fields, give full play to technical professionals, form a reasonable business model, and set up a risk control system and mechanism. The purpose is to ensure the sound operation of the BRICS Bank, promote the healthy and fast development of BRICS countries and other developing countries, and contribute to the sound governance and balanced development of the world in general.

China Development Bank has made remarkable achievements in supporting China's development. It is willing to learn from the BRICS Bank and other international financial institutions and share its own experience and technologies, in a bid to contribute to the development of the BRICS Bank and the sustainable growth of global economy.

References

[1] Editors, H. H. S., "Viswanathan Nandan Unnikrishnan", in *Search of Stability, Security and Growth: BRICS and a New World Orders,* Observer Research Foundation, New Dalhi, 2012.

[2]黄华光、周余云主编:《调整 创新 合作——2012年金砖国家智库论坛论文集》,北京:党建读物出版社2013年版。

[3][美]玛莎·芬尼莫尔:《国际社会中的国家利益》,袁正清译,上海:上海世纪出版集团2012年版,第95—104页。

BRICS in the Global Economic Governance

Zhao Zhongxiu   Sun Jingying*

Informal Intergovernmental Organizations (IGOs) are defined as a group of associated states having explicitly shared expectations (rather than formalized treaties) that participate in regular meetings but have no independent secretariat, headquarters, or permanent staff. BRICS allows its member countries to pursue the shared goal of expanding their influence in formal IGOs. This has been effective in part because this arrangement allow flexibility for their various political, economic, and strategic goals.[1] BRICS as an informal IGO is playing a major role in global economic governance. In the meanwhile, reforms have occurred in many global governance institutions to increase the representation of the large emerging economies.

1. Current Global Economic Governance

The construction of the current global governance structure was lead by the US.[2] The Bretton Woods system established in New Hampshire in 1944 was embedded in economic multilateralism, such as the IMF, World Bank and the GATT (now WTO). These institutions set the post war order and serve as the "rules of the game" to ensure the global economic governance. Although few emerging markets participated in the Bretton Woods negotiations, the rise of these countries' economies would not be so without participating in the current economic system. Hence, BRICS has incentives to maintain the fundamentals of the current

---

* Zhao Zhongxiu, Vice President of the University of International Business and Economics. Sun Jingying, Post-doc. research fellow, Peking University.

system.

However, institutional arrangements and international agreements consolidated and created since 1945 for global economic governance are facing new challenges and opportunities in the light of the rise of newly industrialized and emerging economies, like BRICS.[3] New forms of cooperative relationships towards global economic governance will only evolve with better-aligned structures, objectives and norms to reflect the preferences of emerging powers within a multipolar world.

According to the BRICS Research Group, the five countries together account for 43% of the world's population, 30% of the earth's landmass, and 25% of the world's share of global gross domestic product (GDP).[4] BRICS have been credited with nearly 50% of the world's economic growth. Their share is expected to increase further, as members' growth rates surpass the average annual growth rate of the world economy.[5]

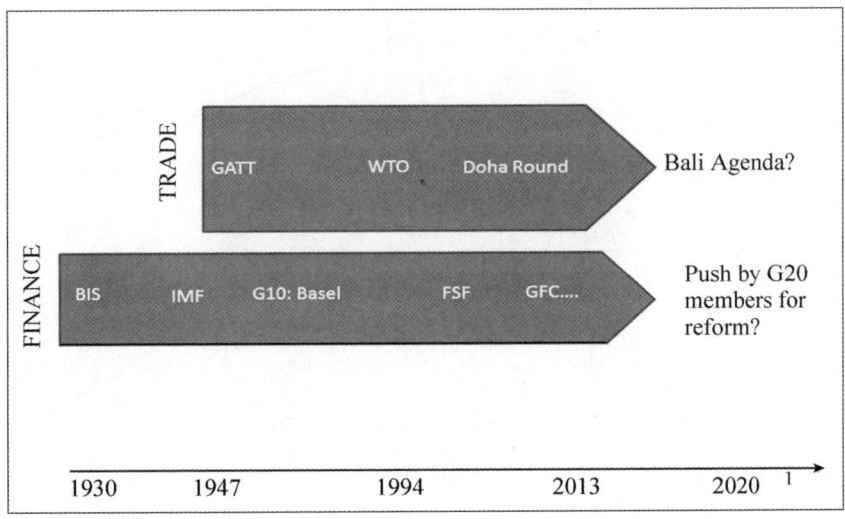

Figure 1 Progress in Negotiations for Global Economic Governance

Data Source: Zhenbo Hou, Jodie Keane and Dirk Willem te Velde, "Will the BRICS Provide the Global Public Goods the World Needs?" ODI Report, June 2014, http://www.odi.org/publications/8540-will-brics-provide-global-public-goods-world-needs. FSF (Financial Stability Forum), GFC (Global Finance Crisis).

The BRICS accounts for over 40% of the world's total foreign exchange reserves-amounting to approximately $ 4.4 trillion.① A report in *The Economist* suggests that if the BRICS countries were to set aside one-sixth of their reserves, they could create financial institution similar size as the International Monetary Fund. Further, in contrast to the budget deficits and soaring debts of the West, BRICS's public-debt levels are mostly modest and stable.[6] Trade among these five countries was valued at $230 billion in 2011 with an annual average growth rate of 28 per cent. It is expected to reach $500 billion by 2015.② The BRICS share of global trade has also doubled in this period and was estimated at 14 per cent in 2008.③ Foreign Direct Investment (FDI) from BRICS countries have increased from $10 billion in 2002 to $146 billion in 2010 — although China and Russia represent more than 75 per cent of the BRICS's total FDI, while Brazil and India account for around 10 per cent each.④

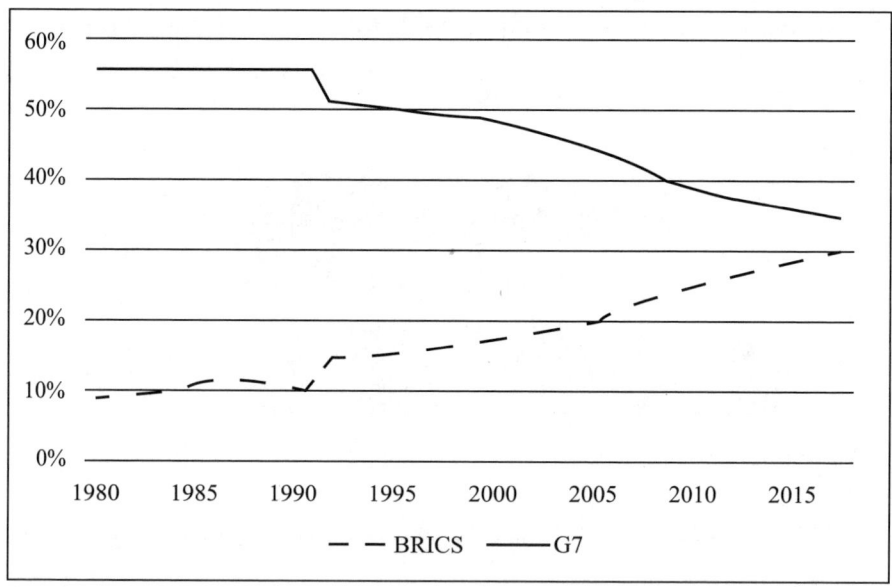

Figure 2 Share of World Gross Domestic Product (GDP) (PPP)
Data Source: IMF, 2013.

---

① http://www.bloomberg.com/news/2012 - 06 - 24/brics-biggest-currency-depreciation-since-1998-to-worsen.html.

② http://www.thehindubusinessline.com/industry-and-economy/article3254980.ece.

③ http://www.gfmag.com/archives/147-february-2012/11604-special-report-brics.html # axzz27VbP0CMR.

④ UNCTAD, 2011.

(1) IMF/World Bank-Quota Shares and Voting Power

Formal dominance of traditional powers in IMF and World Bank lies in the distribution of quotas — capital subscriptions and their associated voting rights — among countries. The basic patterns of quota allocations were determined at the 1944 conference in Bretton Woods. Quotas were roughly proportional to the economic and other power resources each founding member country controlled. As of 2008, and prior to the current recent rounds of quota renegotiations, the US held a 15% quota in the World Bank and a 17.41% quota at the IMF. In both institutions, a super-majority (ranging from 70% to 85%, depending on the type of issue) has been required for significant decisions, implying that the US plus one or two key allies has always had an effective veto.

As membership based organizations, the IMF and World Bank each represent a near-universal membership of 188 countries. The recently agreed governance reforms at the IMF and the World Bank are an important step to enhance the voice and representation of emerging market and developing countries in those institutions. This will more accurately reflect their changing weight in the world economy.

Although IMF is to oversee the international monetary system and monitor the economic and financial policies of its member countries, unlike the General Assembly of the United Nations, where each country has one vote, decision-making at the IMF was designed to reflect the position of each member country in the global economy. Each IMF member country is assigned a quota that determines its financial commitment to the IMF, as well as its voting power. Similarly, it lacks the rule making function of the trade regime and enforcement mechanism of the trade regime. Unlike WTO, its governance structure is relatively less democratic.

One underlying problem in both the World Bank and the IMF is that, their financial assets are relatively small to in a world of globalized capital. In order to retain their influence in shaping global economic models, then they must locate additional funds. The obvious sources for increases in capital subscriptions are the large emerging economies in the financial G20, and particularly the BRICS. The large emerging powers including the BRICS, has quickly bounced back from the financial crisis in 2009.[7] Even prior to the crisis the emerging powers were becoming more important in global finance. For example, in 2010, there were five Chinese, three Brazilian, and one Russian banks among the top 25 banks globally ranked by profits — and Chinese institutions held the two top slots.[8]

In November 2010, the IMF agreed on reform of its framework for making decisions to reflect the increasing importance of emerging markets and developing countries. The reforms will produce a shift of 6% of quota shares to dynamic emerging market and developing countries. This realignment will give more say to a group of countries including the BRICS. For the timeline of the reform, the Board of Governors, the IMF's highest decision-making body, must ratify the new agreement by an 85% majority before it comes into effect. The plan is for the reform to be implemented in 2012. Subsequent reforms of quotas and governance were agreed in 2010 but are not yet in effect.①

In Table 1, BRICS altogether accounts for only 11.03%, less than the U.S. share 16.75 per cent and G7 share 43.09%. This is a reflection that BRICS is not a dominant power in the international economic arena now.

Table 1　IMF Members' Quotas and Voting Power (2012)

	Quota		Votes	
	Millions of SDRs	% of Total*	Number**	% of Total*
BRICS	27 411.80	11.51	277 803	11.03
Brazil	4 250.5	1.79	43 242	1.72
Russia	5 945.4	2.50	60 191	2.39
India	5 821.5	2.44	58 952	2.34
China	9 525.9	4.00	95 996	3.81
South Africa	1 868.5	0.78	19 422	0.77
G7	108 044.90	45.37	1 085 608	43.09

---

① Http://www.imf.org/external/np/sec/memdir/eds.aspx.

Table 1 (continued)

	Quota		Votes	
	Millions of SDRs	% of Total*	Number**	% of Total*
US	42 122.4	17.69	421 961	16.75
UK	10 738.5	4.51	108 122	4.29
France	10 738.5	4.51	108 122	4.29
Germany	14 565.5	6.12	146 392	5.81
Italy	7 882.3	3.31	79 560	3.16
Canada	6 369.2	2.67	64 429	2.56
Japan	15 628.5	6.56	157 022	6.23

Data Source: IMF website, http://www.imf.org/external/np/sec/memdir/members.aspx#2.

* At the present time all 188 members are participants in the Special Drawing Rights Department.

** Voting power varies on certain matters pertaining to the General Department with use of the Fund's resources in that Department.

Though they have not yet achieved their aims of greater voting power in the international financial institutions, BRICS have demonstrated that they are a force to be reckoned with. In 2011, as the world's largest developing countries, the BRICS issued a statement declaring that the tradition of appointing a European as managing director undermined the legitimacy of the IMF and called for the appointment to be merit-based.[9] Traditionally, the managing director of the IMF has always been a European while the World Bank President has always been a US citizen nominated by the United States, the largest shareholder in the bank. The nominee is subject to confirmation by the board of executive directors, to serve for a five-year renewable term.

New quota negotiation rounds began in late 2008 in both the Bank and the Fund.[10] Quota redistribution — popularly known as the debate over "chairs and shares" — has been a longstanding demand of developing countries.[11] In the aftermath of the global financial crisis, BRICS have sought to make "reform" of the international financial institutions an issue that could work for them. The BRICS found seemingly easy agreement on the broad topic of linking increased contributions (capital subscriptions) to quota reform: developing and transitional countries deserve a larger say in how the Bank and the Fund are run.

As for the leader selection process in IMF and World Bank, BRICS have demonstrated their willingness to act as one voice. BRICS efforts have received positive feedbacks and reached reconcilement in the result. However, compared with the quota and voting share (Table 1 and 2), the new leader selection is more or less a symbolic trial than the fundamental change of the overall global economic governance.

Table 2　Major Global Economic Governance Institutions and Respective Decision-making Mechanisms

		Members	Decision-making System
Formal IGOs	IMF/ WB	Members: 188 Brazil: Jan.14, 1946 Russia: Jun.1/16, 1992 India: Dec. 27,1945 China: Dec. 27,1945 South Africa: Dec. 27, 1945	**IMF** (1) Board of Governors is the highest decision-making body, which has the right to approve quota increases, special drawing right (SDR) allocations, the admittance of new members, etc. (2) The Executive Board (the Board) is responsible for conducting the day-to-day business of the IMF. It is composed of 24 Directors, who are appointed or elected by member countries or by groups of countries, and the Managing Director, who serves as its Chairman. (3) The Managing Director, currently is the head of Staff and Serves as Chairman of the Executive Board.
			World Bank (1) The President of the Bank is the president of the entire World Bank Group. The president, is responsible for chairing the meetings of the Boards of Directors and for overall management of the Bank. (2) The Boards of Directors consist of the World Bank Group President and 25 Executive Directors. The President is the presiding officer, and ordinarily has no vote except a deciding vote in case of an equal division. The Executive Directors as individuals cannot exercise any power nor commit or represent the Bank unless specifically authorized by the Boards to do so. In both institutions, a super-majority (ranging from 70 to 85 percent, depending on the type of issue) has been required for significant decisions.

Table 2 (continued)

		Members	Decision-making System
Formal IGOs	WTO	Member: 160 Brazil: Jan.1, 1995 Russia: Aug. 22, 2012 India: Jan.1, 1995 China: Dec. 11, 2001 South Africa: Jan 1, 1995	(1) Decision-making up to member states through either a Ministerial Conference or through the General Council. WTO's rule-based system of governance is based on a system of one vote per member and all members must agree on all new agreements. (2) Director-General has little power over matters of policy; the role is primarily advisory and managerial.
Informal IGO	G20 / G8	Canada, France, Germany, Italy, Japan, Russia, UK, US, EU / Argentina, Australia, Brazil, China, India, Indonesia, Mexico, Republic of Korea, Saudi Arabia, South Africa, Turkey	The G20 operates without a permanent secretariat or staff. The group's chair rotates annually among the members and is selected from a different regional grouping of countries. The chair is part of a revolving three-member management group of past, present and future chairs, referred to as the "Troika". The incumbent chair establishes a temporary secretariat for the duration of its term, which coordinates the group's work and organizes its meetings. The role of the Troika is to ensure continuity in the G20's work and management across host years.

Data Source: Website of IMF, World Bank, WTO and G20.

(2) WTO

The rule-based system of governance adhered to by WTO members are based on a system of one vote per member and all members must agree on all new agreements. The system is therefore democratic in principle, although in practice negotiations may often boil down to a limited number of countries and stand-offs in positions. This has increasingly been the US and EU versus newly emerging economies.

The major difference between the GATT and WTO, and hence the creation of the Doha Round is that reciprocity between developed and developing countries came into conflict. By the time GATT was transformed into the WTO, intra-OECD trade in manufactures was virtually barrier free. Hence, back then trade agenda shifted between OECD and developing countries; developing country liberalization and the OECD; and intra-developing country liberalization.[12] The agenda also shifted so as to focus on liberalization and disciplines in sectors other than manufactures such as agriculture and services. Developing countries, particularly emerging economies, were expected to make concessions in their manufacturing sectors. Developed countries in turn, were also supposed to undertake liberalization in their agricultural sector. One major challenge to overcome is that during the Doha Round WTO members strived to combine a series of disparate accounts into one package-the "Single Undertaking" — that all members would sign up to.[13]

Table 3 Progress and Difficulties Encountered in Doha Round

Progress	What was agreed at the ninth Ministerial Conference includes ten texts which comprise the Bali Package Trade Facilitation; General Services; Public Stockholding for Food Security Purposes; Understanding on Tariff Rate Quota Administration; Export Competition; Cotton; Preferential Rules of Origin for Least Developed Countries; Operationalization of the waiver concerning preferential treatment to services and services suppliers of least developed countries; duty-free and quota-free market access for least developed countries; and a monitoring mechanism on special and differential treatment.
Current Difficulties	(1) Liberalization in the agricultural sector and food security issues. (2) No binding commitments on export subsidies in agriculture.
Divergence in Positions	No divergence in positions is apparent. (1) Like-minded countries are negotiating for an international services trade agreement (i.e. TiSA). (2) Still disagreement of treatment of US and EU subsidies and Indian safeguards. (3) Stagnation of Post-Bali Agenda.

Data Source: Author analysis.

(3) G20

The Group of Twenty (G20) is the key forum for its members' international economic cooperation and decision-making. Its membership comprises 19 countries plus the European Union. Each G20 president invites several guest countries each year. G20 has emerged as an informal grouping to resolve finance coordination issues and comprises finance ministers from the major developed countries and selected emerging economies. Currently, all BRICS countries are in G20.

The group of ten advanced economies (G10) has met regularly in Basel since 1962 to discuss monetary and financial matters.[14] In response to this, a group of 24 developing countries was established in the early 1970s as a Southern-based counterpart, although it has far less policy impact. In comparison, the G7 group of industrialized nations has met regularly since 1975. The group of G7 and G10 countries established a working group called the Basel Committee on Banking Supervision (BCBS) in 1975 to explore issues related to global finance. This group created the *Basel Capital Accord* in 1988: a framework to assess the capital position of cross border banks. In 1997 core principles for assessing the capital position of trans-border banks was also established. The G7 established the Financial Stability Forum (FSF, now known as the Financial Stability Board) in 1999 to facilitate information exchange and cooperation related to the supervision and surveillance of commercial financial institutions. However, the creation of three working groups has been amongst civil servants rather than at the ministerial level.[15]

The G20 serves a useful grouping that can increasingly be used for trust building (in areas such as financial governance). Major global financial, fiscal and monetary issues are being discussed at the G20. With this platform, G20 countries, through collective discussion, they have made lots of progress on fiscal and monetary coordination, as well as providing a context that might be better than the alternative. The G20 has also been used to promote the case of concluding the WTO Doha Round, but without less success. Besides, G20 had success in promoting global development by introducing new issues into the debate.

Besides, G20 has made suggestions on the IMF and World Bank reform and agenda in different summits. For example, one of the G20's early harvests in 2009 was an agreement to increase threefold the resources of the International Monetary Fund (IMF) to $750 billion to support new Special Drawing Rights at $250 billion, with a further $250 billion allocated towards trade finance, and $100 billion towards support for conditional lending by multilateral development banks. The

G20 countries committed to shifting 5% of the IMF quota share from over-represented countries to under-represented countries, and to increase the voting power of developing and transitioning countries in the World Bank by 3%. However, how their decisions are subsequently translated into actions and enforcement is rather more questionable.

Table 4   Membership Change since the G20 Called for Reform in 2008

Global Financial Regulatory Body	Previous Membership	Previous Developing Countries Member	Time of Expansion	Expansion to include Members From
International Organization of Securities Commissions Organization (IOSCO)	Australia, France, Germany, Hong Kong of China, Italy, Japan, Mexico, Netherlands, Canada, Spain, Switzerland, UK, USA	Mexico	February 2009	Brazil, India, China
Basel Committee on Banking Supervision (BCBS)	Belgium, Canada, France, Germany, Italy, Japan, Luxemburg, Netherlands, Spain, Switzerland, Sweden, UK, USA	None	March 2009	Australia, Brazil, China, India, Republic of Korea, Mexico, Russia
Financial Stability Board (FSF/B)	Australia, Canada, France, Germany, Hong Kong of China, Italy, Japan, Netherlands, Singapore, Switzerland, UK, USA	None	March 2009	Argentina, Brazil, China, India, Republic of Korea, Mexico, Russia, Saudi Arabia, Turkey, Spain, European Commission

Data Source: Adapted from Griffith-Jones and Young (2009) and Griffith-Jones (2009).

2. BRICS' Role in the Current Global Economic Governance

BRICS countries may not be of the equal economic or political importance on a global level, but they are leaders within their respective regions. To more or less the same extent, BRICS perceive themselves outside the current major global governance structure and have, on many occasions, confronted the representatives of the old power. BRICS past common experiences formulated a conceptual common ground among the BRICS members. What strengthened BRICS formation as an entity is to adjust global governance structure to reflect the new developments in the global political and economic scene based on multi-polarity principle.

The growing importance of BRICS in global economy does not automatically lead BRICS to have greater voice in the WTO, and other international economic governance structures. More often, BRICS has acted individually or in sub-group before they act collectively.

Table 5 BRICS Positions in the Current Global Economic Governance

	Trade Issues	Finance Issues
BRICS	Disparate Views. Expansion of developing countries' participation in the decisive "Green Room" (phases of trade negotiations)	(1) Brazil joins India, China, and South Africa who have already adopted the Basel III framework. Russia has postponed implementing the framework until January of 2014. (2) Pushing for reform process in the IMF or World Bank, to increase weight of EMDCs in the world economy, so as the 2010 reform by January 2015. (3) Look forward to initiating the next shareholding review at the World Bank, which is due by October 2015.
Brazil	Blocked DFQF (Duty Free Quota Free)	Implementing Basel III
Russia	Focused primarily on lifting trade restrictions that are harming domestic producers	Russia has postponed implementing the framework until January of 2014
India	Supportive of a "small package" focused on LDC issues	Implementing Basel III
China	Committed to the multilateralism at the WTO but also open for plurilateral negotiations.	Implementing Basel III
South Africa	Supports a small package that would give LDC suppliers preferential treatment in developed countries; Supports the sharing of information by customs agents to promote trade facilitation.	Implementing Basel III

Data Source: Author analysis.

(1) IMF/World Bank Reform

In 2009, BRICS made the initiative to push for the quota and voting share reform, which promoted to transfer quota and shares in IMF and World Bank to emerging economies and developing countries respectively 7% and 6%, as well as a new quota reform plan. In June 2014, BRICS leaders again pushed forward the reform in IMF to ensure the representation of the emerging economies and developing countries, and new share percentage review in World BankGroup by October 2015.[16] BRICS' policy positions on IMF and World Bank reform are clearly reflected in the Sixth BRICS Summit-Fortaleza Declaration. BRICS "remain disappointed and seriously concerned with the current non-implementation of the 2010 International Monetary Fund (IMF) reforms", strengthen the "modernization of its governance structure so as to better reflect the increasing weight of emerging markets and developing countries in the world economy". The Fund must remain a quota-based institution. BRICS call on the IMF to develop options to move ahead with its reform process, in case the 2010 reforms are not entered into force by the end of the year. Besides, BRICS insist that the reform be finished "by the postponed deadline of January 2015".①

BRICS welcome the goals set by the World Bank Group to help countries end extreme poverty and to promote shared prosperity. However, BRICS are promoting "the institution and its membership to effectively move towards more democratic governance structures". BRICS look forward to initiating the work on the next shareholding review at the World Bank as soon as possible in order to meet the agreed deadline of October 2015.

BRICS have been very active in improving the international financial architecture through our multilateral coordination and through our financial cooperation initiatives. Besides, BRICS view the New Development Bank as in a complementary manner to increase the diversity and availability of resources for promoting development and ensuring stability

---

① Sixth BRICS Summit — Fortaleza Declaration, http://www.chinadaily.com.cn/language_tips/trans/2014-07/17/content_17814819_2.htm.

in the global economy.①

(2) WTO

Not all the 20-25 leading traders in the WTO enjoy regular invitations to the high table of multilateral negotiations or other small-group meetings. The election of Mr. Roberto Azevedo as the new Director General of the institution enhances Brazil's role as a mediator between the North and the South. The indicator of the growing importance of the BRICS in the global trading system is the extent to which WTO decision-making processes have been adapted and reformed to accommodate them. The old Quad has been replaced by new groupings that have taken the shape of the "New Quad" ② or G4, the Five Interested Parties (FIPs), the G6 and the G7. These groupings represent the high tables of decision-making, where the first steps are taken towards building consensus, and Brazil and India (along with the EU and the US) are invited to all of them. At the July 2008 talks, the grouping was extended to seven, including China (besides the EU, US, Brazil, India, Australia and Japan). This inclusiveness is not just a form of tokenism. As the EU and the US have seen repeatedly since 2003 (when the first major deadlock of the Doha Development Agenda occurred at the Cancún ministerial), Brazil, India and China individually or in coalition, are not afraid of using their veto power.

For trade issues, BRICS reaffirms their support for an open, inclusive, non-discriminatory, transparent and rule-based multilateral trading system, and continue efforts towards the "successful conclusion of the Doha Round of the World Trade Organization (WTO), following the positive results of the Ninth Ministerial Conference (MC9), held in Bali, Indonesia, in December 2013".③

Also BRICS reaffirm "commitment to establish by the end of this year

---

① Sixth BRICS Summit — Fortaleza Declaration, http://www.chinadaily.com.cn/language_tips/trans/2014-07/17/content_17814819_2.htm.

② New QUAD refers to the most important four players in WTO negotiations. They are India, Brazil, United States and the EU.

③ Sixth BRICS Summit — Fortaleza Declaration, http://www.chinadaily.com.cn/language_tips/trans/2014-07/17/content_17814819_2.htm.

a post-Bali work program for concluding the Doha Round, based on the progress already made". The prioritized issues include: the Public Stock-Holding for Food Security Purposes and the Agreement on Trade Facilitation. BRICS strongly support the WTO dispute settlement system as a cornerstone of the security and predictability of the multilateral trading system. Besides the multilateral trade system, BRICS recognize the importance of Regional Trade Agreements, while try to keep them open, inclusive and transparent, as well as refraining from introducing exclusive and discriminatory clauses and standards.[①]

(3) G20

In rallying for more representation by developing countries on the global stage, the BRICS stated their strong support for the role of the G20 as "the premier forum for international economic coordination and cooperation of all its member states" and highlighted that "the G20 is broader, more inclusive, diverse, representative and effective." The increased representation of developing countries in international economic governance is envisioned to mitigate discriminating trade policies, sanctions, and coercion. In particular, the BRIC economies stressed that "sustainable development models and paths of developing countries should be fully respected and necessary policy space of developing countries should be guaranteed."[②]

(4) The New Development Bank By BRICS

The cooperation of BRICS has resulted in various progresses in the formation of new global economic governance, which has not only showed a potential paradigm for other developing countries, but also served as a good example for the developed countries to realize the shortcomings of the current global economic governance.

In the New Development Bank (NDB), there is a president (an Indian for the first six years), a Board of Governors Chair (a Russian), a Board

---

[①] Sixth BRICS Summit — Fortaleza Declaration, http://www.chinadaily.com.cn/language_tips/trans/2014-07/17/content_17814819_2.htm.

[②] Brazil, Russia, India and China, "II BRIC Summit — Joint Statement", 2010.

of Directors Chair (a Brazilian), and a headquarter (in Shanghai) and regional center in Johannesburg.① The NDB has been given $50 billion in initial capital. As with similar initiatives in other regions, the BRICS bank works on an equal-share voting basis, with each of the five signatories contributing $10 billion. The capital base is to be used to finance infrastructure and "sustainable development" projects in the BRICS countries initially, but other low-and middle-income countries will be able buy in and apply for funding.

Table 6   The New Development Bank of BRICS

Business Units	Capital Arrangement	Member Obligations	Decision-making Mechanism and Voting Shares
Bank Capital	Starting capital of $50 billion, with capital increased to $100 billion over time.	BRICS will initially contribute $10 billion each to bring the total to $50 billion.	The Decision-making system is supposed to be universal consensus. Each member cannot increase its share of capital without all other 4 members consent. The bank will allow new members to join but the BRICS capital share cannot fall below 55%.*
CRA	$100 billion.	41% by China, 18% by Brazil, India, and Russia, and 5% by South Africa.**	(1) The Governing Council shall take decisions by consensus and shall be responsible for high level and strategic decisions of the CRA. (2) The Standing Committee shall be responsible for the executive level and operational decisions of the CRA and shall comprise one Director and one Alternate Director appointed by each Party. (3) Decision-making is taken by weighted voting, the weight attributed to each Party's vote shall be determined as follows: (i) 5% of total voting power shall be equally distributed among the Parties; and (ii) the remainder shall be distributed among the Parties according to the relative size of individual commitments. So among BRICS, the voting share of BRICS will be respectively: 18.1%, 18.1%, 18.1%, 39.95% and 5.75%.***

* "BRICS Bank Ready for Launch-Russian Finance Minister", Russia & India Report, 10 July 2014, Retrieved 20 July, 2014, http://in.rbth.com/economics/2014/07/10/brics_bank_ready_for_launch_-_russian_finance_minister_36599.html.

** Treaty for the Establishment of a BRICS Contingent Reserve Arrangement.

*** Author calculations.

① Http://news.yahoo.com/cabinet-welcomes-brics-development-bank-115111670.html.

BRICS's NDB will supplement the insufficiency of current multilateral financial institutions. NDB complements the current and regional financial institutions, for better and more efficient utilization of global financial resources. Besides, the Contingency Reserve Arrangement (CRA) will provide additional USD 100 billion liquidity protection to member counties during balance of payments difficulties. The CRA — unlike the pool of contributed capital to the BRICS bank, which is equally shared — is being funded 41% by China, 18 percent from Brazil, India, and Russia, and 5% by South Africa. In the Contingent Reserve Arrangement, the voting share difference between China and Brazil, Russia and India is 2.2 times, less than the gap of 2.7 times between U.S. (the largest shareholders in IMF, with 16.75% voting share) and Japan (the second largest shareholders with 6.23%).[17] This arrangement as an important institutional achievement to alleviate the short-term liquidity difficulties will help member countries to prevent financial crisis, promote monetary cooperation among emerging economies and strengthen the global financial security network.

3. Outlook for Further Strengthening BRICS in Global Economic Governance

The BRICS's preferences, singly and jointly, for global governance turn on reform and evolution, not revolution. The basis of the BRICS rooted in the long-term common economic interests of the member states, which include reforming outdated global financial and economic architecture, strengthening the principles and standards of international law and supporting the complementarity of many sectors of their economies. BRICS partnership has diversified the growth of the world economy and become a driving force for the democratization of international economic relations.[18]

The coming together of BRICS is rooted in the outcomes of the global financial crisis and the aspiration of the member countries to have a stronger voice in the management of international financial systems. Analysts point out that this convening has provided the member countries with a stronger peer connect. Further, BRICS countries are able to accessat least 10 key regional bodies. (See table 7) If used effectively, their coming together allows them a strategic advantage across a range of global forums.

Table 7　BRICS and the 10 Key Regional Bodies

	BRICS's Participation in the 10 Key Regional Bodies
BRICS	The Commonwealth of Independent States (CIS) The Collective Security Treaty Organization (CSTO) The Eurasian Economic Community (EurAsEc) The Shanghai Cooperation Organization (SCO) The Asia – Pacific Economic Cooperation (APEC) forum The Union of South American Nations (UNASUR) The Mercado Comun del Sur (Mercosur) The African Union (AU) The South African Development Community (SADC) And the South Asian Association for Regional Cooperation (SAARC)

Source: Author collected.

BRICS policymakers could enhance their global influence by discovering common preferences that they can join forces to pursue. The BRICS's principal collective goal thus far has been the creation of greater ongoing global influence for themselves. It makes more sense to conceptualize BRICS as in the process of building capacity. It remains to be seen whether the BRICS in the future will coordinate to tackle important global issues, such as climate change and building effective domestic institutions that might be emulated in the developing world.

In keeping with the outcomes of the 2014 Summit (Fortaleza), member countries have taken steps to follow through on the commitment to deepen and expand trade cooperation between BRICS countries. This has been done primarily by way of adoptingbilateral and regional trade agreements, encouraging domestic companies to invest in BRICS countries, creating new mechanisms to enhance trade and investment cooperation, and initiating new development financial institutions and instruments.

References

[1] "The BRICS and the Future of 'Informal' IGOs", February 5, 2014, http://www.isn.ethz.ch/Digital-Library/Articles/Detail/? lng=en&id=176226.

[2] Barry Eichengreen, *Globalizing Capital — A History of International Monetary System*, Princeton University Press, 1996.

[3] J. Keane and D.W. te Velde, *The New Landscape of Economic Governance: Strengthening the Role of Emerging Economies*, EDC2020 Working Paper, 2012, http://www.edc2020.eu/121.0.html.

[4] Ella Kokotsis, "Advancing Accountability in BRICS Governance", BRICS New Delhi Summit, 2012.

[5] Mikhail Titarenko, "Potential to Boost Performance as an Engine of Global Growth", BRICS New Delhi Summit, 2012.

[6] Anon, "The Trillion-dollar Club", *The Economist*, 15 April, 2012.

[7] Carol Wise, Leslie Elliott Armijo and Saori Katada eds., *Unexpected Outcomes: How Emerging Markets Survived the Global Financial Crisis*, book manuscript, under review.

[8] Philip Alexander, "Top 1000 Banks 2011", *The Banker*, 30 June, 2011.

[9] Robin Harding, "BRICS Say European IMF Claim 'Obsolete' ", *Financial Times*, 24 May, 2011. Sebastian Mallaby, "Can the BRICs Take the IMF?", *Foreign Affairs*, 9 June, 2011.

[10] Martin A. Weiss, "Multilateral Development Banks: General Capital Increases", Washington, D.C.: Congressional Research Service, 27 January, 2012; Robert H. Wade, "Emerging World Order: From Multi-polarity to Multilateralism in the World Bank, IMF, and G20", *Politics & Society*, Vol. 39, No 3, 31 August, 2011.

[11] Kapur, "The Changing Anatomy of Governance", Edwin M. Truman ed., *Reforming the IMF for the 21st Century*, Washington, D.C.: Peterson Institute of International Economics, April 2006.

[12] P. Collier, "Why the WTO Is Deadlocked: And What Can Be Done about It", Mimeo, 2005, Available at: http://users.ox.ac.uk/~econpco/research/pdfs/WTO-deadlock.pdf.

[13] J. Rollo, "Global Europe: Old Mercantilist Wine in New Bottles?" Special Issue on the *EUs New Trade Policy in Aussenwirtschaft*, Edited by Simon Evenett, 2007.

[14] J.A. Scholte, "Governing Global Finance", CSGR Working Paper, 2002, No. 88,/02, http://wrap.warwick.ac.uk/2030/1/WRAP_Scholte_wp8802.pdf.

[15] S. Griffith-Jones and K. Young, "Reforming Governance of International Financial Regulation: Have the G20 Done Enough?" IPD and Hewlett Policy Brief, 2009, http://policydialogue.org/files/publications/Griffith-Jones_Young_Policy_

Brief.pdf; S. Griffith-Jones; "Perspectives on the Governance of Global Financial Regulation", paper prepared for the Commonwealth Finance Ministers Meeting, 2009, http://academiccommons.columbia.edu/catalog/ac:153941.

[16] Xu Xiujun, "BRICS and Global Economic Governance System Reform from the Emerging Economies Perspective", *Contemporary World*, August 2014.

[17] Jiang Xufeng, "The BRICS Change in Global Economic Governance Order", http://bank.hexun.com/2014 - 08 - 19/167661958.html.

[18] Zhang Yan, "BRICS Works for Shared Prosperity", *The Hindu*, 13 April, 2011.

Analysis on Modernization of State Governing Capacity of BRICS — From the Perspective of State-building

Chu Songyan* Jia Lunan**

Modern state-building is a historical process that promotes a reasonable development of the relationship between state and society as well as that between state and market. But this process varies in different countries. Tilly described sate-building as "a permanent system that offers professional personnel and control over territorial integrity through a centralized independent state that can practice monopolistic violence to a given population."[1] After patrimonialism (up until AD 1500), agent system (from AD 1400 to AD 1700), nationalization (from AD 1700 to AD 1850) and specialization (from AD 1850 on), European governments gradually attained direct control over military forces and taxations. Then armies, administrative bodies and other specialized institutions were established, which substantially expanded governments' capacities for surveillance and upholding political orders. In *Social Origins of Dictatorship and Democracy,* Moore compared France, Russia, China, Japan, India and Germany, and pointed out that differences between hierarchical relationships or alliance relationships in these countries led to different targets of violence use, which resulted in the births of democratic regime, fascism and communism.[2] In *States and Social Revolutions,* Skocpol pointed out, in her analysis of the Great French Revolution (1789), the Russian Revolution (1917) and the Chinese Revolution (1911–1949), a country's independent capacity for pursuing goals is determined by its capacity for organizing coercive forces and its

---

* Chu Songyan, professor and doctoral supervisor of Chinese Academy of Governance.
** Jia Lunan, doctoral student admitted by Chinese Academy of Governance in 2014.

relationships with other powerful interest groups both at home and abroad. She believed, though there were differences between these three countries' internal structures and historical circumstances, the revolutions all led to a centralized and bureaucratic nation state with an appeal to general public, where top-down bureaucratic management and top-down popular participation were all strengthened.[3]

Whether their research spanned a long history or singled out several comparable countries in a given historical period, the above mentioned scholars all attached much importance to the role that a country's capacity plays in maintaining social stability and advancing economic development. It's worth noting that, due to differences in development stages and natural endowments, different countries' state-building footprints vary. Newly independent countries after World War II, including China, were catching up on western modernizations when pursuing state-building, in which governments' political power centralization and capacity for control over economic and social development were also being strengthened. During this process, the developing countries, including China, all came to realize that modernization theories centered on the west, if excluding their histories and experiences, would be a flower-covered trap; modernization indeed delivers fruitful results only if the country in question sees a rise in its national strength by taking into full account its own historical traditions, natural endowments for development and role in the global stage. Against today's backdrop of reflecting on and reshaping modernization, the rise of BRICS and their coping with challenges in the modernization process begin to show that modernization and state-building are in sync with each other, which can be seen as a practical experience.

1. State Governing Capacity: Forerunners' and Catch-upers' Experience

State-building is a process, in which a given country adjusts state-market, state-society and society-market relationships through institutionalization to a point where they are conducive to its existence, continuance and strength. During this process, the country in question is a rational actor, but also serves as a comprehensive system. As such, the state-market and state-society relationships built by the country become external factors that shape and constraint its behaviors, while the state governing capacity reflected in the operation of its internal political parties and bureaucratic systems in turn influence the development of market and society. The relative independence of state behaviors not only provides order and system guarantees for economic and social development, but also can adjust the dynamic equilibrium between state, market and society. In this sense, the independence and orientation of state governance behaviors are indispensable to a country's overall development. Thus, state-building not only can serve as a perspective from which we review modernization process, but also helps us ponder China's political development. The Third Plenary Session of the 18th Central Committee of the Communist Party of China, by setting as general objectives "perfecting and developing China's socialist system with Chinese characteristics, advancing modernization of the system and capacity for state governance", aimed to highlight the significance of state-building at a new start point. It's worth noting, however, "modernization of the system and capacity for state governance" in Chinese context comes from the perspective of state-building, which lays more emphasis on national governance and management. "Less government, more governance" raised by the west, however, focuses on the management of public affairs. The common ground between the governance crisis confronted by developed countries and the national rejuvenation pushed forward by China, in theory, is how to revive the theory of state. In other words, in today's environment where risks in information technology, post-industrialization, people's mobility and trans-boundary issues compound one another, how to re-discover the role a state plays in this process? This is the key area where the modernization of state governance system surpasses the modernization in industrialization era. Then, what constitutes state governing capacity?

Different researchers in different times gave different answers. Max Weber, for example, believed that a rational country should be able to act independently, calculate cost-benefit and implement institutionalization.[4]

According to the report "Build State Capacity for Poverty Reduction" issued by UNRISD (United Nations Research Institute for Social Development, 2010), a country should be able to provide guarantees for the following five aspects, that is, helping access new technologies, mobilizing and moving resources to production sectors, executing standards and regulations, establishing social treaty, funding and supervising social service programs. In order to do so, a country must have the capabilities to form necessary alliance or find political solutions, provide resources for investment and social development, allocate resources to production sectors and sectors that promote social welfare.[5] No matter how researchers define a given country's state governing capacity during state-building, **it basically takes on two manifestations: the ability to advance economic development and the ability to mediate and resolve social disputes. The ability to promote economic growth is the fundamental decisive force for state-building while the ability to mediate and resolve social conflicts serves as an indicator for the reinforcement of state-building. Found expression in a given country's institutionalization or rule-of-law process, these capabilities rely on social members' proactiveness to advance economy and willingness to create harmony in life together. As such, during this process, the equality of social members as the principal role in society needs to be strengthened on one hand; and they need to be united around common interests on the other.** As China has been deeply engaged in globalization, during state-building and modernization, we not only need to focus on the current circumstances and future development direction, but also need to pay attention to the modernization of governance system in China from a global standpoint.

(1) Forerunners' Experience

Since developed countries in Europe and North America have completed modernization, their state governance systems, on which state governing capacity builds, have gone through a long institutionalization process. In Britain, for instance, the bourgeois revolution started in 1640 and the Glorious Revolution seemed to have ended in 1688, but actually it's not the case. The *Bill of Rights* was adopted in 1689 — the constitutional state determined the basic relationships between individuals, society and state through legislation. Thus abuse of state powers were constrained by institutional regulations and legal principles made legitimate. Although later political parties fighting for votes in order to form an administration became the widely accepted way of power generation, it didn't mark the maturity of Britain's governance system. It wasn't until 1928 that women in Britain were allowed to vote, which indicated a basic modernization of Britain's governance system. As the subject of its governance system expanded to all adult citizens, Britain saw a rise in its capabilities to advance economy and its tax base, which enhanced its national strength. In 1787, the draft US federal constitution was approved by representatives in Constitutional Convention; in 1789, the federal government started to function. But this didn't mark the establishment of America's state governance system. After mid-19th Century, Democrats and Republicans competing with each other gradually became the widely accepted way of administration formation; in 1920, women in America were allowed to vote; in 1964, *Civil Rights Act* was passed. It was then that colored races, including the black, were fully entitled to citizenship, which represents the basic completion of America's state-building. In addition, it wasn't until 1960s that aborigines in Canada and Australia were entitled to suffrage. In this sense, the modernization of state-building and governance system in developed countries basically completed in 1960s, a time when their economies were booming. "Modernity incubates stability, modernization breeds turmoil" raised by Huntington is a conclusion he drew from the historical fact that western developed economies were prospering and basically completed state-building process.[6] During the economic boom after World War II, every developed country in the west knitted all its citizens together with a social security network of welfare systems. As a result, states' capabilities to control society, individuals and market through administrative powers were effectively strengthened.

The institutionalization of state governance and the reinforcement of state governing capacity these developed countries have gone through can offer some experience in the following aspects. First, these nations maintained the integrity and independence of its national sovereignty;

second, the legitimacy of the sources of their state powers were recognized not only by their own people also by the world as a whole, which is a perfect reflection of Social Contract Theory; third, equal access to state governance systems by people of different sexes and races were ensured, and equality in the freedom of speech and voting rights among different social classes, all of which contributed to political absorption; fourth, the supervision and transparency of power execution were realized through check-and-balance systems and expansion of citizens' rights.

(2) Catch-upers' experience

As for countries that gained independence after World War II, strengthening of state governance was realized through institutionalization of political system during modernization. Many newly independent nations, however, such as South Korea, Indonesia, Thailand and Brazil, all tried to enhance their state governance capacities by imitating western democracy models at first. But instead, they got 15 years of social turmoil and conflicts as well as economic stagnation from liberating political systems and social mobility.[7] Then with military intervening in politics, authoritarian regime came into being. In such regimes, state governance system was highly concentrated, that is, political powers were highly concentrated yet not open. Though social conflicts were suppressed, market was open, thus rapid economic growth was gained. South Korean, Indonesia and other countries maintained economic growth for over 30 years, which changed the structure of social interests and popular mindset. A more open society made it possible that people's mentality for comparison became an advantage, thus new way of state governance started to appear. The experience these countries share is: first, they paid a price for copying western political systems and then started exploring their own development paths; second, authoritarian regimes, of their own choosing, fostered rapid economic growth, realized industrialization and brought about changes in social structures and values; third, it promoted coordination between power delegation and civil rights protection.

Deng Xiaoping said in his famous Address in South that, "it will probably take another 30 years before we can build a more mature and stable set of systems in all respects, under which policies and guidelines will be more stable."[8] Based on China's economic and social development and from the perspective of national strategic development, Mr. Deng, as the then national leader of China, made this argument. And China's development practices over the years prove that China is still in the midst of institutionalization. When western democratic theory scholars studied China's transformation, they were more focused on how China should realize political transformation under the guidance of western democracies and their democratic development paths. As a result, they tended to barely take into consideration China's state-building or state governing capacity at the time when making relevant timing predictions. The long-term objective for China's political development is to establish a super-size socialist democracy featuring a coordinated development in all fields. The modernization of China's state governance system and capacity constitutes a phase of the long-term objective. According to Mr. Deng's strategic vision, China will see the completion of state governance system modernization and a steep rise in its governing capacity by 2022. This will be reflected in two aspects. First, the ruling capacity of the ruling party should be enhanced to cater to social and economic changes, which is a matter of legitimacy. Second, the political managing ability of the government should be improved to mobilize and make the most of social resources to remedy defects and flaws in social governance. These two aspects combined together enhanced China's abilities to advance economy and to mediate and resolve social disputes. This process involves expanding general public's options and institutionalizing government responses to it.

2. Major Risks and Challenges Facing BRICS in the Modernization of state governing capacity

Quite a few scholars predict that BRICS will leave US far lagged behind in terms of contribution to the world economy in the next 20 years, which will make it comparable to G7 or other world-leading international organizations. BRICS are in a complicated development process, in which state-building and modernization are intertwined. In addition, these countries' modernization drives fundamentally rely on huge consumption of their own natural or social resources. But substantial wealth accumulations haven't led to a development pattern of sustainability, they are still facing many uncertainties ahead. In the context of a modernization full of challenges and opportunities, BRICS governments are also seeking response measures while conducting overall adjustments to their systems in all respects.

(1) Risks of Unsustainability in BRICS's Economic Growth Patterns

The economic policies adopted by Brazil after its independence not only fostered the primary blueprint for rapid completion of modernization, but also bred the crisis it was confronted with in later development. Brazil's economic growth was largely dependent on inflation strategies, which on some level boosted its national economy and allowed its government to accumulate a great deal of wealth in a short period of time through "Inflation Taxes", which is of significance in ensuring investment. But this long-term inflation was keeping Brazil in an imbalanced development pattern, which eventually went out of hand. Although the Brazilian government has been sparing no efforts in containing the negative repercussions of inflation, the root of inflation is still there and an even bigger crisis might break out. In addition, this imbalanced development strategy has caused structural contradictions in Brazil's economic development. As Brazil's industrialization was primarily built on agricultural export, a sluggish agricultural sector and a lack of industrial development in rural areas led to migration of a huge number of people to the city, causing serious social problems. This pattern didn't narrow the disparity between urban and rural development.[9] In addition, government investment in capital economy is way higher than that in public services, which also constitute a risk in Brazil's future development of modernization.

Russia has long been confronted with difficulties in transforming its economy under the leadership of its central government. The biggest barrier to Russia's economic development is the extensive growth pattern that it's inherited from Soviet Union, which has resulted in it having no core competitiveness in today's new economic environment. As its advantages in military technologies are fading away, the overdependence on an economic growth driven by resources export is actually the extension of the extensive growth pattern, whose negative effects are becoming increasingly prominent in Russia's building of a modern economic growth model. Being historical heritages, these risks cannot be defused any time soon.[10] Reasons for that are as follows: (a) As most major enterprises in Russia are resource-based and have intertwined interests with government departments, they don't have enough incentive for innovation; (b) Lured by vested interests when advancing the transformation from a resource-based economy to an innovation-driven one, it's realistic for Russia to enhance its national strength by taking advantage of its resources; (c) As its manufacturing is far lagged behind developed economies, it's very difficult to commercialize its natural resources; (d) Due to inadequate government input in innovation and high-tech industry, the international market doesn't have much confidence in Russia's economic development; (e) Since the senior leadership is not so interested in modernization and economic transformation, there is still a powerful force in the decision-making body trying to protect vested interests; (f) Russia' relations with the West are largely based on interavailability rather than mutually-beneficial cooperation, so there are still many uncertainties in its effort to boost modernization with support from developed countries.

India has made great achievements in outsourcing software and IT services, but its inadequate investment in manufacturing will result in a sluggish modernization development. Thus, realizing modernization by "being the world's back office" may well be India's beautiful wish. The reasons for that are fourfold. First, with a huge population, it's not enough for India to solely rely on the international market to meet its domestic demand for consumer goods. With underdeveloped infrastructure in service and manufacturing sectors and insufficient input in technological innovation, India hasn't developed a market for translating software R&D results into products, so it can only linger in the peripheries of developed countries by trading technology for products. Second, a sluggish manufacturing sector has led to a weak ability of modern industries to absorb rural labor force, compounded with a slow-progressing urbanization and rural development, the modernization lacks driving forces, like a tree without roots. Third, IT sector, the pillar industry, is over-dependent on international market, so it can only follow the trend and cannot establish a stable macro-economic structure. However, economic stability is one of the prerequisites for modernization. Fourth, though the group nurtured in IT sector only makes up a small proportion of the total population, an elite community, they enjoy a large part of social wealth while most people are marginalized in wealth distribution. Since a long-term imbalance in distribution can easily distort economic and social development, a modernization with such structure is not a comprehensive one.

The rich resources in energy, precious metal and gem mine gas laid a solid foundation for South Africa's modernization and given it an important role in global politics and world economy. As developed economies continue to pick up momentum and developing ones, especially BRICS, are back on track, there is a strong demand for South Africa's strategic resources in the international market. However, as mineral reserves are shrinking and exploration becomes more difficult and costly, mining industry's share of the national economy is declining. A long-term over-dependence on mining has caused South Africa a structural problem, which affects the exploration of new economic dimensions. Firstly, the low saving deposits of South African families and enterprises led to weak domestic investment and inadequate government investment in infrastructure; secondly, as it didn't take advantage of economic development trends during wealth accumulation, the failure to provide a favorable environment for high-tech talents led to over-supply of low-skilled workers and loss of high-skilled talents; thirdly, a slow progress in infrastructure in logistics and information service, a necessary condition for economic growth, becomes a bottleneck for core competitiveness enhancement.[11]

(2) BRICS's National Governance System Fails to Match Economic and Social Development Process

Brazilian scholar Pires believed that Brazil had not built up a political and economic system to revolutionize the country since the beginning of 1930s, but pursued the "conservative modernization" which only reflected the economic demands and would not affect the benefits distribution pattern under the pressure of the outside world, without considering the overall economic and social development, so today's modern engineering still faces huge development challenges. With a lack of state control over income distribution and a high Gini Coefficient, a huge income gap appears both from the micro level of enterprises and the macro level of the state. Faced with significantly uneven regional development, public input only cares for the better development of developed areas, while leaving backward areas being increasingly worse. For lack of management and services, city outskirts have become the dark side of the modern city.[12]

Russia holds a dominant position in aspect of markets. However, a mighty government does not equal to a strong governance capacity. Russia's economic structure seldom frees itself from the influence of state intervention in economy and control of all economic and social programs during the Soviet period. The state-owned economy accounts for a large proportion of the national economy. Large enterprises lack motive force for competition and innovation and SMEs are immature and their development prospects are dim due to high costs of entering the market. In response to the financial crisis in 2008, the intensity and scope of state intervention increased rather than decreased. Compared with other BRICS countries, the process of Russia's market economy is obviously slow. Besides, various systems for supporting of modern economic system are imperfect, including low marketization level, poor efficiency, poor government administration and services. Marketization results accumulated for many years are depleted along with the increasingly deepening corruption of Russian regime. The grim situation forces

Russia's leadership to think about the transformation of political system. Medvedev had noted the goal of Russian democracy is the unified construction of legal system, comprehensive national power, information technology and the credit society.[13]

Caste traditions and poor reconciliation of tradition and modernity in political life makes India's national governance system caught in a dilemma. On the one hand, political elites strive to maintain its widespread power to manipulate the government and parliament decisions and despise the spirit of democracy; on the other hand, they actively speak in defense of democratic system, wasting a lot of political and social resources available for modernization construction and thus weaken the ability of national governance.

(3) Social issues become more acute along with the deepening of modernization reform

Brazil's social problems are mainly reflected in the followingeight aspects: (a) Income disparity and poverty are worsening. After the economic reform in 1980s, a large number of state assets became privately possessed in the midst of Brazil's private sector boom, which resulted in a widening wealth gap. (b) More and more people are becoming unemployed and semi-unemployed. As Brazil's rapid industrialization after the war led to a weakened rural economy, many rural residents migrated to urban areas seeking opportunities. In addition, after the market economy-oriented reforms, the state sector's ability to absorb labor force sharply dropped and technological revolutions led to a higher standard for labor force's specialized skills. So, the unemployment in Brazil will not be any better any time soon. (c) Crime rate in urban areas is higher. If a country only pays attention to economic development and neglect social building, this is an inevitable result. (d) Rural land is concentrated in the hands of big land owners. With a great deal of premium land resources, they don't create any value while farmers live in long-term poverty with no land to tend. This will easily cause the two sides to come into violent clash. (e) Discrimination against women is still there. This makes social inequality worse.

(f) Racism is a long-standing problem. Brazil's development has been largely built on agricultural economy in colonial times, but people of color still cannot get a better position in social wealth distribution. (g) There exist serious flaws in the social security system. With a sharp increase in the Brazilian population and the gradual formation of an aging society, the pension system is facing serious challenges. Facing huge shortfall in funding high pensions, plus with a high inflation rate and uneven income distribution, the prospects for a sustainable society are grim. (h) Education is lagged behind economic development. With inadequate input in basic education and without favorable policies for national education, social investment is increasingly concentrated in industries of high profitability. High drop-out rate and illiteracy pose a threat to developing a reserve of labor force with higher educational level.

India is faced with many social governance problems, such as low quality, surplus labor, intensified social stratification based on the caste system, imbalanced urban and rural distribution, explosive growth of instability factors. What is more troublesome is that the rapid development of information technology gives a strong impetus to the relations between domestic terrorist forces, religious extremism and separatism. In the Internet age, subversive forces join forces to create troubles and spread dangerous speech, which makes people confused and brings tremendous risks for social modernization. Moreover, India faces serious religious risks, such as the exclusiveness of Sikh, Islam and Hindu sects, increasing the risk of social disintegration.

There are also many problems in China's economic, political and social fields. It now faces a double tension force. One is from outside, i.e. the increase of the likelihood of conflicts due to the increase of China's national strength and intensified competition in international space. The other is from inside: on one hand, the post-industrial and information technology upgrades lead to urbanization, aging and other issues, which greatly increases people's participation desire and demands for rights; while at the same time, the modernization of national governance system is reflected in the institutionalization of people's demands for rights and participation desire by the use of the system in a timely manner and release of relevant channels to give more options for people to choose relevant rights, while at present, this tension is more and more obvious.

3. Strengthening of BRICS's Governance Capacity and Key of China's National Governance

BRICS countries are fully aware of the important role of national governance on political order and economic and social development, and therefore have adopted relevant reform measures to improve governance capacity. China also proposed major initiatives on deepening the reform in an all-round way combined with its own development.

(1) Measures Taken by Other BRICS Countries to Strengthen National Governance Capacity

Amado Servo, a Brazilian scholar, points out, Brazil's economic growth model is shifting from unilateralism — being totally dependent on major capitalist countries to develop itself, to multilateralism — paying more attention to emerging markets and organizations in developing countries. After experiencing the two development modes lying on the two ends of economic strategy, one relies heavily upon export-based economy and the other is the self-reliant development of domestic market, Brazil's "relative independent strategy" is mature seeing from the selection of the modernization path. On one hand, Brazil focuses on adjusting the relationship between the government and the public, such as the practice of electronic members, which draws parliamentary representatives and voters closely with each other. On the other hand, through the readjustment of intergovernmental relations, Brazil balances the differences between regional development, improves the management capacity of the municipal government, optimizes the labor division and cooperation mechanism between central and municipal governments, and local governments actively guide the civil society and private sectors to reinvigorate social reform. Shown in the analysis of the innovation plan for data base advocated by Brazilian regional governments, 60% of the private sector and the civil society or entities have formed a partnership, the projects involved including: housing, community building, budget planning, development planning, environmental protection, public service outsourcing and debt risk sharing mechanism.

Based on the efforts made by Vladimir Putin and Medvedev during their alternate tenure, Russia transfers the existence basis of a country from the possession of resources by the ruling group to the support of the masses. The relaxation of policy-making limitation of parties and the resolution of governor's election enlarge the openness of political field, and the construction of a dialogue platform between the Government and the public and tolerance policy for opposition group also increase the credibility and support of the ruling party. With respect to anti-corruption, the higher level promotes the transparency of official property and establishes a property disclosure system through top-down reform measures, and dissolves redundant institutions by referring to the political reform experience of Western countries, realizing a streamlining government through function integration and curbing the rise of transnational corruption through cooperation with international communities. Seleznev observed that a few basic principles should be set out in Russia's national governance system. Firstly, Russia should take reform as the overall goal of leading the motivation mechanism to finally achieve modernization. Secondly, under the premise of taking centralized leadership as the country's primary political and cultural characteristics, stimulate social organizations to participate in policy system construction, so as to realize a two-way driving force. Thirdly, from the perspective of political ethics, pay attention to citizens' preferences of nationalism and egalitarianism. Fourthly, ensure strict monitoring of funds disbursement, and conduct a comprehensive struggle against corruption on the federal and regional levels. Fifthly, mobilize all social forces, especially the efforts of both government and enterprises to further improve the legal system, so as to ensure the legitimacy of each reform initiatives.[14]

India has made great efforts in bridging the social division. First of all, it safeguards the representation of ethnic minorities through legislation. *Act on Protection of Civil Rights* has set up the ratio of representation of people of different castes and from different tribes in the coalition government. Currently, the proportion of listed castes and tribes has reached 15% and 7.5% among all educational institutions and various organizations run by the central government and the federal government, with 27% seats reserved for underprivileged groups. Secondly, favorable policies have been strengthened for attracting investment in the north, highlighting the federal government's boost to transfer payment. India established the Northeast Management Committee to guide the management planning of backward regions, implement management in its *Five - Year National Development Plan 2007 - 2012*. By putting "Rural Development Fund" and other financial support into infrastructure construction, improvement of medical and health conditions and promotion of agricultural technology, it strives to narrow development disparity between regions. Thirdly, in order to protect the interests and rights of minority groups, it's stipulated in every *Five - Year Plan* that the funds earmarked for tribal minorities must take up 50% of the total budget. The central government has also adopted preferential policies on higher education for ethnic minorities, a move aimed to ensure minority students make up no less than 5% of the total enrolment. Finally, by legally absorbing the social members of different races and castes in decision-making processes through the democratic parliamentary system, it instills the concept of democracy in minority areas and resolves the gap between different cultures with modern philosophy, global civilization and other "soft power" to provide reasonable collision mechanism and cushion space for social conflicts.

(2) Emphasis of China's National Governance Capacity

In 2013, The Third Plenary Session of the 18th Central Committee of the CPC proposed the overall goal of deepening reform with national governance system and modern governance as the important contents. China's national governance system and governance modernization are different from those of the developed countries, and also differ from those adopted by the neighboring countries after World War II, such as Brazil, South Africa and Russia. Generally speaking, China's national governance capacity should be further strengthened on the basis of the modernization of national governance system. The core is an institutionalized issue, or rather a legal issue. As with today's China, the ability of economic development mainly relies on decentralization, as long as we proceed with government reform of administrative approval, take "no crime without a law" as the limiting boundaries of government power and strengthen regulation and implementation, Chinese government's ability of economic development will not be weakened. The emphasis of China's current national governance capacity is the ability to mediate and resolve social disputes, which need to be strengthened from two aspects. One is political integration and the other is political participation. Political integration mainly settles the elastic problem of political system, while political participation mainly solves the inclusive problem. The aim of political integration is to reach a consensus, for example, anti-corruption, the issue we are talking about now, is a social consensus. But how to do after reaching this consensus, is a question of political participation since interests compromise is based on consensus.

With respect to political integration, the primary issue is political party integration. It should be said that political absorbing channels of China's ruling party are open and the non-differentiation of party admission of all walks of life is achieved after the proposition of "Three Represents" and the amendment to political party constitution on the 16th National Congress of the CPC. After the withdrawal of totalitarian countries, the market is able to develop and grow, resulting in the production and blooming development of social organizations and community-based organizations in public field. It is worth noting that the ruling party is playing their role in market and social development and growth, resulting in the "replacement of politics by political party" phenomenon. For example, grassroots organizations should be established in the non-public economic and social organizations. But how to give the integration role of grassroots organizations into full play, the current situation of various regions is not the same. We are still exploring the way to make the political party to play their role in grassroots organizations, community-based organizations, social organizations and non-public economy.

After the implementation of the civil service system, compulsory examination system has been widely recognized. In recent years, the election of NPC deputies in both rural and urban areas has been implemented and the role of CPPCC members in absorbing elites is increasingly prominent. The current anti-corruption campaign, to some extent, also contributes to the political integration.

However, this political integration is subject to the impact of inadequate professional level and relies on the respond of government to public demands. It is worth noting that political integration is also subject to several issues. One lies in the elite consensus alliance within the national governance system, the communication mechanism of which is still in the formation process. What is an elite consensus alliance? Various circles should be included in the so-called alliance, such as political circle, academic circle, business circle, social circles, entertainment circle, and so on, to form a bottom consensus and intellectual circulation, so as to guide a wide range of social consensus. However, information sharing and human circulation mechanisms are not sufficient among elites of various sectors. In recent years, it is a common phenomenon for scholars to serve temporary positions in government agencies, and since 2013, civil servants working in government agencies can also deliver speeches in research centers, which is a very good signal. This alliance will speed up the process of institutionalization and bridge the internal gap within the elite group.

Another problem is that the social division mechanism for the realization of interests is not yet implemented. Why's that? Enterprises in the market are responsible for primary distribution task and the government for the redistribution task. However, the current mechanism for evaluating the success of distribution is still relatively simple, which is mainly based on money and power. Other issues must yield to money and power and ultimately subject to power. As a result, the relatively simple and centralized social evaluation mechanism is not conducive to the implementation and compliance of systems. As such, the diversification of professions should be stressed, such as the socialization of professional qualification certification, rather than be controlled by the government. If the social division mechanism is not formed, political integration efforts will decrease, which is not conducive to resolve social conflicts.

Political participation is another one. It includes the smoothness and activation of existing political participation channels, including the perfection of mechanisms related to public representatives, election of public representatives. Although the election of NPC deputies in both rural and urban areas has been implemented, technical operation is relatively rough from the generation of public representative candidates to the division of electoral distric. Currently, the liaison mechanism between the public preventatives and voters has not been built up in a large scale. Along with the elected representatives, non-elected representatives are required to express their views and adopt proposals. To be simple, they are opinion leaders or pushers of public opinions, and so they have huge influence on the setting of many social issues, especially in the agenda-setting of public affairs, which shows the transfer of the power of the Interne from the government to the community. It is necessary to carry out negotiation on agenda-setting of public affairs, which is why deliberative democracy is proposed in many regions, but the primary thing is the agenda setting.

Social infrastructure is needed for orderly political participation, which is still relatively weak for now. The autonomy of community and social organizations is also included. According to relevant research, party branch secretary and directors of community committees are often not residents of the community, so this will form a "mismatch" phenomenon, and will hinder the community to become a unified body. The last one concerns social organizations. The data of non-governmental organizations of Ministry of Civil Affairs shows that little more than 500 000 people have registered under the Ministry of Civil Affairs, but the number of grassroots organizations of people's organizations is over 6 million. These organizations fail to play their role as social basis. How to take advantage of these resources to ensure smooth popular participation? This is an urgent problem to be solved through institutional, standard and procedural governance capacity.

References

[1] Tilly, Charles, ed., *The Formation of National States in Western Europe*, Princeton NJ.: Princeton University Press,1975.

[2] Barrington Moore,Jr.,*Social Origins of Dictatorship and Democracy: Lord and Peasant in the Making of the Modern World*,Boston: Beacon Press,1966.

[3] Skocpol, Theda, *States and Social Revolution*,Cambridge: Cambridge University Press, 1979.

[4] [德]马克斯·韦伯:《经济与社会》,商务印书馆 1998 年版。英文版见 Max Weber, *Economy and Society*,California: University of California Press,1978.

[5] UNRISD, Building State Capacity for Poverty Reduction, 2010.

[6] [美]塞缪尔·亨廷顿:《变化生活中的政治秩序》,上海人民出版社 2008 年版。英文版见 Samuel Phillips Huntington, *Political Order in Changing Societies,* Yale Univeristy Press, 1968.

[7] 房宁等:《自由、威权、多元——东亚政治发展研究报告》,社会科学文献出版社 2011 年版。

[8]《邓小平文选》,第 3 卷,人民出版社 1993 年版。

[9] 张宝宇:《巴西经济发展与社会发展关系问题》,载《拉丁美洲研究》2005 年第 2 期。

[10] 陆南泉:《俄罗斯经济二十年(1992—2011)》,社会科学文献出版社 2013 年版;王树春:《俄罗斯经济现代化前景探析》,载《现代国际关系》2011 年第 11 期。

[11] 马燕坤:《南非软实力建设之理论实践》,载《河北北方学院学报》2012 年第 5 期。

[12] [巴西]马科斯·科尔代罗·皮雷斯:《经济增长、城市化和社会不平等:对保守现代化的思考》,载《国际社会科学杂志》2013 年第 4 期。

[13] 陆南泉:《俄罗斯经济二十年(1992—2011)》,社会科学文献出版社 2013 年版。

[14] [俄]谢列兹尼奥夫:《21 世纪俄罗斯的改革选择》,载《求是学刊》2013 年第 1 期。

Leadership of CPC and Rule of Law in State Governance Modernization

Zheng Changzhong*

In China's politics, the relationship between leadership of CPC and rule of law has attracted great attention of the general public. That is because their relationship concerns the healthy development of modern politics in China. As the Fourth Plenary Session of the 18th Central Committee of the Chinese Communist Party was held, which mainly focused on rule of law, the relationship between leadership of CPC and rule of law once again became a hot topic among the Chinese people. Since China's politics and the relationship between the leadership of CPC and rule of law are both developed in dealing with realistic public affairs which is part of state governance, we reasonably assume that the relationship between CPC's leadership and rule of law can be studied from views of state governance and modernization, attempting to provide theoretical thoughts and advices for appropriate handling of their relationship in the background of all-round reform.

1. Leadership of CPC and Rule of Law in State Governance

State governance is a formation process of orderly public society through effectively handling of public affairs by using public power. As a matter of fact, it is just another name of politics in scope of state community, but in concept, its difference from politics lies in that politics is defined on focus of public power, while state governance is defined on focus of effective handling of public affairs. The concept of state

---

* Zheng Changzhong, the Executive Vice Director of Center for Party Building and State Development Studies at Fudan University.

governance seems to lay more importance to practices and effectiveness. As such, the so-called state governance is more of an arrangement of power from views of effective handling of public affairs.

In modern background, political parties, state and society are the three major elements in state governance, of which state is the main body of public power, political party is a major force that connects society and constitutes and operates the public power, while society is a decisive force that promotes state development. According to Marxism, social elements fall in two parts namely market and narrow society. From views of state governance, the ideal effect can only be realized when good and cooperative relationship has been built between the three above-mentioned elements, public affairs are handled in an effective manner and orderly public life is achieved.

Therefore, the relationship between political parties, state and society has become a key issue in the state governance system in modern political context. In the current political context, one of the important conditions for full functioning of state elements is rule of law, simultaneously political party takes the leadership and society has a decisive role. Thus, the relationship between political party, state and society becomes the relationship of CPC's leadership, rule of law and people's feeling as masters.

Among them, CPC's leadership refers to the leading position of CPC in the state governance system within scope of political structure, which has a leading role on the construction and operation of public power and integrates and leads various social powers. Rule of law means that within the state structure, the operation of public power and handling of public affairs should follow the constitution, laws and regulations. People's mastering means that social will built on individual wills has the decisive role to political development, whether in political structure or in state structure. For this reason, the relationship between the three elements, especially between CPC's leadership and rule of law is actually defined by different operation logic of politics in different logic structures and does not contradict with one another. As such, the Communist Party of China proposed the idea of "organic unity of CPC's leadership, people's mastering and rule of law".

Modern state governance was formed in China as a result of modern political development logic and political development in China, and followed the fact that the People's Republic of China was founded by the Communist Party. The relationship between CPC and state is therefore stressed and becomes a key issue in the political development in China. As a result, the relationship between CPC's leadership and rule of law accompanies the entire process of political development in modern China.

2. All-round Deepening Reform and State Governance Modernization

In order to overcome the contradiction between demands for organization by modernization of China and the loose status in traditional Chinese society, after the People's Republic of China was founded, a planned economic system dominated by state power was established in China in macro sense, while in micro sense, numerous units centralized on basic CPC organizations were built up in Chinese society, which provided the organizational basis for modernization in China. As the organizational logic developed, there came the phenomena that CPC replaced government in many aspects and social will tended to draw behind.

In order to provide modernization with sustained power, the Communist Party of China decided to reform and open up to other countries. Through adjustment and reform for certain period, on the 14th National Congress of CPC, a decision was made to establish market economy system in China, and since them the gene of modern society began to grow in China. In order to adapt to the requirements of market economy for laws, the idea of rule of law was put up on the 15th National Congress of CPC, marking comprehensive commence of state construction. As the ideas of market economy and rule of law were put into practice, the ruling party also needed adjustments, and for this purpose, the idea of "Three Represents" was put forward on the 16th National Congress of CPC. As market economy goes further and with the formation of network society, on one hand the diversity comes to emerge in society; on the other hand a great number of social organizations come into being. As a result, the task of building a harmonious society was put forward on the 17th National Congress of CPC, which marked the formation of modern society in China. Till then, the main elements in modern state governance system have basically formed.

Although the main elements have formed, we also find two phenomena: firstly, the functions of various elements are not fully developed and their roles are not sufficiently played, and secondly, organic internal connections have not yet formed between elements on basis of the modern state governance system. For these reason, on the Third Session of 18th National Congress of CPC, the idea of top-level design and all-round deepening of reform is put up to boost the modernization of state governance system and capacity.

3. Legal Construction Lays a Foundation for State Governance Modernization

From the forgoing, to promote the further development of reform and to facilitate modern state governance, two key tasks are required: on one hand, the functions of main elements in state governance system need to be fully developed and played; one the other hand, the state governance system as a whole needs to be organically integrated. When analyzed from general principles of political development or viewed from the formation process of modern state governance in China, driving forces and inherent development are required from the CPC and state elements. However, there is difference in the functions and content of innovation between political party and state elements. As for a state, it emphasizes on rule of law, while for a party, it means the innovation of the leadership and way of ruling.

After state is founded, politics has been always focused on state power, therefore, state elements always take a fundamental position in state governance. In modern political conditions, state act is regulated by constitution and laws, and rule by law is one of the important symbols of modern states. At the same time, to promote further development of reform, one of the issues to be solved is the relationship between government and market, while market is cultivated by government. The key to the transformation of their relationship lies in the government reform. Market economy, by nature requires rule by law. Similarly, from views of human history of modern politics, rule by law is also an important measure to regulate government act. Therefore, state governance by law is the fundamental key to the modernization of both state elements and the state governance system. This means that in the modernization process of state governance, rule by law will provide the foundation for modernization of a state and the modernization of state governance systems.

We come to the conclusion from the analysis as given above, governance by law should be promoted in at least the following aspects, to realize modern state governance. Firstly, the authority of constitution must be enhanced to improve the effectiveness of functions of various state elements. Secondly, the roles of rule by law should be strengthened in reform and construction, in order to concretize the spirits of rule by law in China's reform. Thirdly, the regulation of government by law should be enhanced, to realize self-adjustment of state elements on basis of the requirements of modern state governance. Fourthly, the achievements in China's reform should be concretized in all aspects and become a part of the legal construction, to promote the realization of modern state governance.

4. Rule by Law Promotes Innovation in Leadership of CPC and Way of Ruling

As a modern party, the Communist Party of China has two functions: the leading function and the ruling function. The leading function refers to the roles of CPC in political structure and the ruling function refers to the roles of CPC in stare structure. However, regardless of the structure, all changes to state elements as a result of enhanced governance by law require innovation and development on terms of the way of interaction with the political party.

For the phenomena that party and government were not independent from each other and that the political party took the place of governments in many aspects, after the reform and opening up of China, the CPC launched the political system reform featured by separation of party from government. Through several rounds of reform, the political reform were basically completed both in terms of organization and functions, which marked that the way of leadership and ruling of CPC has been adapted to requirements of modern state governance.

However, we can also see that with the further development of reform and the ideas of modern state governance, in the background of enhancing governance by law, the task of political reform has changed from separation of ruling party from governance to the regulation of relationship between the ruling party and governments. This means in the background of enhancing governance by law and modern state governance, the relationship between ruling party and state has entered a new stage, which also means that the innovation in CPC's leadership and way of ruling has come to a new stage of adaption to the construction of a state ruled by law.

Specifically, we believe that the reform should focus on innovation in the way of leadership and the way of ruling. The innovation in CPC's leadership aims to lead the society development to serve the effective governance of CPC on one hand, and to promote efficient development of the modern state on the other hand. The innovation in CPC's way of ruling aims to observe the principles of rule by law, to regulate the relationship between ruling party and state authorities and to effectively convert people's will to state will.

China's Modernization of Governance Capabilities: Advantages, Problems and Measures

Bao Chuanjian[*]

1. Introduction

In the wake of the Third and Fourth Plenary Session of the 18th Central Committee in November 2013 and October 2014, respectively, governance and rule of law had taken on added salience in both the policy arena and the academic community (He, 2014; Yu, 2014). The modernization of state governance capabilities was dubbed as the Fifth Modernization after the Four Modernizations set forth by Zhou Enlai in 1963 and enacted by Deng Xiaoping in 1978 (Li, 2014). We take modernization as a dynamic process, and this essay aims to tease out the connotations of the modernization of governance capabilities based on the evolution of the concepts of governance and good governance in China. The difference between rule of law and rule by law reflects the bureaucratic transition from state-machine-based regulation to joint governance by various social organizations.

The thought of governance can be dated back to ancient times in both China and the western world. In China, the famous legend of Great Yu Controls the Water, which happened in 4 000 or so years ago, reflects the modest idea of governance. The Chinese philosopher Lao-tzu, the author of *Tao Te Ching*, was well-known for his metaphor that "govern a great nation as you would cook a small fish". This analogy was quoted by President Xi twice in 2013 and 2014 respectively. Nevertheless, the

---

[*] Bao Chuanjian, assistant researcher, Central Compilation & Translation Bureau.

western countries took the lead to the theoretical study of governance, with Oliver E. Williamson pioneered the expansion of governance study in social sciences by his groundbreaking paper *Transaction cost Economics: the Governance of Contractual Relations* published in 1979. With the rise the new institutionalism, governance entered into the mainstream study of sociology and political science (Offe, 2009).

Chinese scholars formally embraced the idea of governance in the beginning of the 21st century. In the last century there even was no generally agreed-upon translation of the English word governance. It was in 2000 that the counterpart of governance in Chinese had been fixed at *zhili* (Burns, 2010). Meanwhile, the concept of governance and its Chinese translation, *shanzhi*, raised thematic discussion in China's academia (He, 2000; Yu, 2000). It is noteworthy that in many European languages as well as Hebrew, there is still no agreed-upon translation of governance (Levi-Faur, 2012; Torfing and Sorensen, 2014).

More governance, less government has characterized the political reforms in many countries (Yu, 2014). What is governance and good governance? Even today, there were still many scholars asking such question (Fukuyama, 2013; Lynn, 2012; Norris, 2011). The World Bank defines the governance as

> Governance consists of the traditions and institutions by which authority in a country is exercised. This includes the process by which governments are selected, monitored and replaced; the capacity of the government to effectively formulate and implement sound policies; and the respect of citizens and the state for the institutions that govern economic and social interactions among them (Kaufmann, Kraay and Mastruzzi, 2011).

With regard to good governance, World Bank's *Worldwide Governance Indicator* includes six dimensions, which are, voice and accountability, political stability and absent of violence, governance effectiveness, regulation quality, rule of law and anti-corruption. Rothstein (2012) argues that rule of law, administrative efficiency and representative democracy etc., would not appropriately define governance, rather, governance should be thought as impartiality. This kind of definition pays much more attention to the role of institutions. We think, both rule of law and impartiality play decisive role in the development of promoting social welfare.

Some development economists argue that good governance will lead to economic development and vice versa (Baland, Moene and Robinson, 2010). However, this kind of casual relationship between governance and development did not impress other scholars in the field. The study on ending Africa's poverty find that many African countries have relatively good indicators of governance based on their per capita income, but stuck in the poverty trap for many years (Sachs et al., 2004).

In light of China, the sustained economic growth of more than 35 years has transformed, to some extent, the Washington census to Beijing census. And there is also a China Model. However, in terms of several popular indicators of governance, China scores less even very low compared to its giant economic size. Some observers boil this sharp contrast down to a China Paradox (Rothstein, 2014). The lack of a Weberian state in China has been the central topic in some recent literature (Zhou and Lian, 2012; Zhou, 2013).

China promoting the concept of modernization of state governance capabilities is a fresh attempt to deliver governance dividend and seek sustainable development, and on the other hand echoes theoretically to the aforementioned paradox. What is the *raison d'être* of governance in China? What are the advantages, problems facing China's fifth modernization? How to implement the reforms of governance? We discuss these issues in the following.

Advantages for Fulfilling Governance Modernization

President Xi pointed out that generally China's governance system and governance capabilities have unique advantages and are able to meet the requirements of the condition of our country. Concretely, we specify three unique advantaged as follows.

First, the successful economic transformation. The gradual transformation adopted by China outperformed the radical transformation by many

Eastern Europe countries. The reform and opening-up policy initiated in early 1980s and the strategy of "crossing the river by feeling the stones" contributed to the economic growth of China. With the advent of the reform policy, we have witnessed great changes in areas such law-based governance, citizen participation, democratic policy-making, social governance, public service, government accountability, political transparency, administrative efficiency, decentralization and development of social organization. China's success in economic development and social transformation, or in other words, China being able to maintain long-term economic development with social stability, primarily benefited from the success of the reform of governance in the last decades (Yu, 2014).

Second, the effective top-level design. Strong statehood generates shadow of hierarchy, which provides incentives for various social participants to cooperate (Borzel and Risse, 2010). China's political regime produces a strong background of shadow of hierarchy, which leads to higher social efficiency than that under what is called limited statehood. Both the reform of governance and the building of socialism law system have to take the basic conditions of the country into consideration. Under the direction of top-level design, we have seen progress in a bevy of reforms, including rural reform, state owned enterprises reform, reform of *hukou* system, financial reform, fiscal decentralization, anti-monopoly, anti-corruption and internationalization of Reminbi.

Third, self-instructed institutional innovation. Since the opening up and reform in the 1980s, Chinese government and a plethora of social organizations (civil society) took part in the practice of governance and good governance. This kind of cooperation and exploration has important implications on the building of a harmonious society. The government has been well aware of the significance and impacts of the institutional dividend, and has taken a panoply of measures to encourage and support institutional innovation and build institutional confidence. The driving force for reforming state governance system was considered to be economic development, political progress, citizens' demand and globalization shock, but the direct impetus comes from pressure, incentive and institution. And the institution is the long-term propulsion (Yu, 2014). In the process of building socialism law system, we will continue to learn from abroad, let alone the lessons we had drawn from the West. As a result, some of the nowadays common practices, including hearing system, one-stop service, government accountability, lawyer system, new spokesman and participatory governance, are directly or indirectly related to their western counterparts. Ruttan (2006) argued that resources endowments, cultural endowments and technological progress can result in institutional innovation.

Problems Facing China's Governance Modernization

China will have to make more efforts in the following areas to improve governance. In other words, only have these problems been well harnessed would China fulfill the goal of governance capabilities modernization.

First, the problem of social inequality. China has suffered from one of the most severe problems in the world, as the Gini Coefficient had reached 0.5 in recent years. Social inequality can lead to social instability, and both have the potential to undermine the legitimacy of the ruling Party. China's income disparity has gradually increased, including disparity between coastal and inland areas, between rural and urban areas, as well as that within provinces. The wealthy upper class increasingly transferred their wealth abroad and sought permanent residency or even immigration. Since the 3rd Plenary Session, the government has made lashings of efforts to cope with the challenges, including unifying rural and urban pension insurance and reforming health insurance plans.

Second, the problem of officialdom worship. With regard to the current condition of the country, the perception and phenomenon of officialdom worship have generated negative impacts on the quality of governance participants. Yu (2013) stated that the Official Rank Standard (guanben zhuyi) represents a power-based form of political culture and socio-politics, in which power is the most important relation among all social relations. Again, democracy and the rule of law are the only way to deal with the issue of the Official Rank Standard and to promote a shift away from traditional political civilization toward the modern political civilization. The 3rd Plenary Session has taken "getting rid of the perception of the officialdom worship" as an important task of the governance reform.

Third, the problem of corruption. China's corruption problem appears to be startling in terms of its scope and scale. Beyond its economic loss in terms of productivity and tax income, the political outcome of corruption has been well understood. The new government's anti-corruption battle has been encouraging so far, and time will tell the extent to which governing corruption and "placing power in the cage of law" is successful.

Fourth, the problem of environmental pollutions. China's environmental quality was challenged by the reduction of water resources, air pollution, desertification, deforestation, climate change and unbridled resource waste. Environmental problems have direct impact on the health of the residents, and on economic growth and global warming. These problems could also be a factor potentially impacting political stability. Since the 3rd and 4th Plenum, an overabundance of regulation has been taken to deal with environmental degradation. It's an encouraging step, but the key point lies in the implementation.

Fifth, the problem of mismatch of great economic power and soft power. As a rising power, China's modernization of governance capabilities should gain a foothold both domestically and abroad. China has a rich tradition of emphasizing the role of cultural communication and soft power. Nevertheless, according to 2013 Pew Global Attitudes survey, the international image of China was not particularly positive or negative. Comparatively, the image of the United States was generally better than China. China has to pay much more attention on this issue to reduce its soft power deficit.

Measures to Be Taken for Governance Capabilities Modernization

The key of the modernization of state governance system lies in the reform and innovation of the institutions, or the braking and rebuilding of innovations. Governance modernization is a dynamic process, we have to enhance good governance and good enough governance and reduce bad governance and rule of man. Fulfilling governance capabilities modernization entails institutional innovations through the lens of the combination of politics, economy, culture and technology.

First, promote law-based governance of the country and carry forward deliberative democracy. The coexistence of regular governance and movement governance characterized the governance practice in China's history. Although regular governance has a unique regime logic, movement governance or national movement was basically a kind of rule of man, as the Great Leap Forward and Cultural Revolution reflected (Feng, 2011; Zhou, 2012). Building socialism law system and the transformation from rule of man to rule of law are important handholds for promoting the modernization of state governance system and governance capabilities. In the process of deepening the reform, Official Rank Standard should be gotten rid of, and elaborate the advantages of deliberative democracy. The clientelism and patrimonialism in the political cycle should be constrained via effective institution designs, and constitution-based governance and constitution-based government should be promoted.

Second, innovate governance logic and elaborate multi-level governance. China has its own political organizational structure and incentive mechanism, which is different from typical Weberian state. Multi-governance has become one of the directions of the development of modern governance. Multi-governance involves the dynamic cooperation of government, non-governmental organizations and civil society.

Third, build service-oriented government and foster professionalized governance, President Xi pointed out that China's state governance system and governance capabilities have to be improved partly through the enhancement of the quality of government officials. The modernization of state governance capabilities requires the executive possess qualified skills and expertise, which arguably are in short supply. The best way to provide qualified practitioners is education and on-the-job training. Some current failures in the field of governance are due to the poor quality of public service. According to a survey conducted by the United Nations, China has got comparatively high scores in the E-Government Development Index (EGDI). Nevertheless, China lags far behind South Korea, France, Japan and US in the ranking (United Nations Department of Economic and Social Affairs, 2014). China may draw lessons from developed countries in providing more efficient public services.

Fourth, innovate public diplomacy and enhance soft power. To become a responsible stakeholder in the world stage, China needs to strike a balance between public diplomacy and soft power, as the former is mainly from government while the latter from society. Only correctly understand what the soft power is and its difference from public diplomacy can China build more positive international image(Shambaugh, 2014).

Fifth, set up concrete indicators of governance to meet incentive expectation. The modernization of governance capabilities has got its goals at the macro levels. However, currently there is no criteria to judge the extent to which the governance is modernized. In other words, in practice there should be some measurable indicators to fill the knowledge gap of what modernization signifies at the micro level. The measurement of governance has been a hot research topic, yet there is no generally agree-upon indicators (Norris, 2011). The Worldwide Governance Indicators (WGI) developed by World Bank and Corruption Perceptions Index (CPI) proposed by Transparency International are among the popular indicators used to assess governance quality around the world, but these composite indexes deriving from a passel of dataset cannot be replicate publicly since the underlying data are not publicly available. Hence, these indicators can be controversial regarding their methodology and then credibility. We argue that governance modernization should be built on the base of a scientific measurement system which is absent in China. A sound measurement system of governance performance may give rise to consistent incentive expectation which is of vital importance in guiding the practice of local governance and multi-level governance.

Concluding Remarks

Promoting modernization of state governance capabilities and rule of law are the steps towards good governance and prosperity in China. Governance modernization provide a theoretical solution to the sustainable development, that is, governance dividend. Modernization of state governance system and governance capabilities responds to the question on how China will build socialism law system and sustain economic growth in post-2015 agenda. The Modernization may provide a new form of institutional dividend, i.e., governance dividend for the development of a variety of participants, including grass-roots and civil society, under the leadership of the Party. Given the problems facing governance reform, the key to the modernization is the breaking and building of institutions. We may also expect that China's exploration in the modernization of governance capabilities can be useful for other developing and emerging economies.

References

[1]何增科:《理解国家治理及其现代化》,载《马克思主义与现实》,2014 年第 1 期,第 11—15 页。

[2]俞可平:《推进国家治理体系和治理能力现代化》,载《前线》,2014 年第 1 期,第 5—8 页。

[3]李景鹏:《关于推进国家治理体系和治理能力现代化——"四个现代化"之后的第五个"现代化"》,载《天津社会科学》,2014 年第 2 期,第 57—62 页。

[4]刘海年:《依法治国:中国社会主义法制建设新的里程碑》,载《法学研究》,1996 年第 3 期,第 50—56 页。

[5]Guillermo A. O'Donnell, "Why the rule of law matters", *Journal of Democracy*, 15 (4), 2004, pp32 - 46.

[6]Mayling Birney, "Decentralization and Veiled Corruption under China's 'Rule of Mandates'", *World Development*, 53, 2014, pp55 - 67.

[7] Volker Schneider and Dirk Hyner, "Security in Cyberspace: Governance by Transnational Policy Networks", in *New Modes of Governance in the Global System:*

Exploring Publicness, Delegation and Inclusiveness, edited by Mathias Koenig-Archibugi and Michael Zurn, pp.154 - 176. New York: Palgrave Macmillan, 2006.

[8] Claus Offe, "Governance: An 'Empty Signifier'?" *Constellations*, 16 (4), 2009, pp.550 - 562.

[9] John P. Burns, "Western Models and Administrative Reform in China: Pragmatism and the Search for Modernity", in *Comparative Administrative Change and Reform: Lessons Learned*, edited by Jon Pierre and Patricia W. Ingraham, pp.182 - 106, Montreal: McGill-Queen's University Press, 2010.

[10] 何增科:《中国转型期的腐败、治理与善治》,载《中国社会科学季刊》(香港),2000 年秋季号。

[11] 俞可平主编:《治理和善治》,北京:社会科学文献出版社 2000 年版。

[12] Laurence E. Lynn, Jr., "The Many Faces of Governance: Adaptation? Transformation? Both? Neither?" in *The Oxford Handbook of Governance*, edited by David Levi-Faur, pp.49 - 64, New York: Oxford University Press, 2012.

[13] Jacob Torfing and Eva Sørensen, "The European Debate on Governance Networks: Towards a New and Viable Paradigm?" *Policy and Society*, forthcoming.

[14] Francis Fukuyama, "What is Governance?" *Governance*, 26 (3), 2013, pp.347 - 368.

[15] Pippa Norris, "Measuring Governance", in *The SAGE Handbook of Governance*, edited by Mark Bevir, pp.179 - 200, New Delhi: SAGE Publications India Pvt Ltd., 2011.

[16] Daniel Kaufmann, Aart Kraay and Massimo Mastruzzi, "The Worldwide Governance Indicators: Methodology and Analytical Issues", *Hague Journal on the Rule of Law*, 3 (02), 2011, pp.220 - 246.

[17] Bo Rothstein, "Good Governance", in *The Oxford Handbook of Governance*, edited by David Levi-Faur, pp.143 - 154, New York: Oxford University Press, 2012.

[18] Bo Rothstein, "The Chinese Paradox of High Growth and Low Quality of Government: The Cadre Organization Meets Max Weber", *Governance,* forthcoming.

[19] 周雪光、练宏:《中国政府的治理模式:一个"控制权"理论》,载《社会学研究》,2012 年第 5 期,第 69—93 页。

[20] 周雪光:《国家治理逻辑与中国官僚体制:一个韦伯理论视角》,载《开放时代》,2013 年第 3 期,第 5—28 页。

[21] Tanja A. Börzel and Thomas Risse, "Governance without a State: Can It Work?" *Regulation & Governance*, 4 (2), 2010, pp.113 - 134.

[22] Vernon W. Ruttan, "Social Science Knowledge and Induced Institutional Innovation: An Institutional Design Perspective", *Journal of Institutional Economics*, 2 (03), 2006, pp.249 - 272.

[23] 冯仕政:《中国国家运动的形成与变异:基于政体的整体性解释》,载《开放时代》,

2011 年第 1 期,第 73—97 页。

[24]周雪光:《运动型治理机制:中国国家治理的制度逻辑再思考》,载《开放时代》,2012 年第 9 期,第 105—125 页。

[25]Shambaugh David, "China at the Crossroads: Ten Reform Challenges", edited by Brookings, 2014, http://www. brookings. edu/~/media/research/files/papers/2014/10/01% 20china% 20crossroads% 20reform% 20challenges% 20shambaugh% 20b.pdf.

[26] Jeffrey Sachs, John W. McArthur, Guido Schmidt-Traub, Margaret Kruk, Chandrika Bahadur, Michael Faye and Gordon McCord, "Ending Africa's Poverty Trap", *Brookings Papers on Economic Activity*, 1, 2004, pp.117 - 216.

Brazil's Approaches to Strengthen the Building of Its National Governance Capacity in the New Century and the Inspirations

Chen Xiaoling[*]

1. Background of Strengthening Building of Governance Capacity

(1) **National economic and social development caught in bottleneck.** From the 1950s to the 1980s, Brazil shifted its development model from exporting of primary products to importing substitution industrialization (ISI) and its steps of industrialization, urbanization and modernization accelerated. GDP growth reached an annual average of 9%, particularly from 1964 to 1973 when the growth rate soared to 11.3%. Brazil became the eighth largest economy in the world and one of the middle-income countries and the achievement is referred as the "Economic Miracle of Brazil". However, as the fast economic growth was built on the reliance on borrowing from international financial institutions, its foreign debt soared along with the fast economic growth. Due to the impact of the world oil crisis in the 1970s and the increase of credit rates, Brazil's inflation rocketed and it became heavily in debt. It was stuck in stagnation for the entire 1980s. In the 1990s, Brazil abandoned the ISI model and pushed neoliberal reform which enabled the country's shift from an import-led development model to an export-led one and the shift from a state-dominated economy to a market economy. While bringing about macroeconomic stability and the ease of debt burden, the reform increased external dependence and vulnerability of the country's

---

[*] Chen Xiaoling, the Director of Latin American Affairs Bureau of International Department of the CPC Central Committee.

economy and resulted in financial crises in 1999 and 2002 and an economic downturn. Meanwhile, as the military government and the civilian government that advocated neo-liberalism put undue emphasis on economic development and overlooked social justice, imbalance in economic and social development worsened and there was serious injustice in social distribution. There was increasing number of marginalized groups and different kinds of social conflicts showed signs of exacerbation. The Gini Coefficient remained above 0.6 for dozens of years.

(2) **Governance stuck in predicament.** In 1985, Brazil ended the authoritarian regime and began its political democratization process. In 1988, it formulated the Constitution and established the multiparty, presidential and federal governmental system, forming a political pattern of multiparty competition and coalition administration. However the governance performances of the traditional parties were less than satisfactory and they lacked the ability and the means to solve the political, economical and social challenges of the country. First of all, the decision-making and execution powers of the government were weakened due to excessive amplification of the functions of general elections by the party politics, as a result the government is unable to push forward in-depth systemic and institutional changes due to its inability to resolve political conflicts and to promote sustained and coordinated economic and social development; second, the government seemed inadequate in response to the diversity of interests and lacked ability to actualize social integration; third, some party and political leaders saw laws as trifling matters. They often ignore the laws and are lax in law enforcement. Embezzlement and bribe-taking were rampant and the government lacked effective means to curb corruption. The public's trust in political parties declined and disappointment in politics rose. The representative democracy fell into crisis and the national governance got stuck in predicament.

2. Main Approaches of the Center-left Government to Strengthen Building of Governance Capacity

(1) **Improving democratic consultation, increasing civil rights, administrating according to the law and promoting the democratization and the rule of law in national governance.** The first was to bring together the most extensive powers. Prior to forming the government, President Lula increased dialogue and consultation with the different parties of the election coalition and with all sectors of the society. He called to put aside partisan differences and form a coalition government that is composed of traditional left-wing parties, center-right parties and other political elements. After taking office, he paid more emphasis on coordinating the interests of different parties and even broke the convention and attended several important activities of the Congress and contacted the opposition leaders. He made personal efforts to win the support from the representatives of different parties. The second was creating a social and economic development council to open up further channel for airing of opinions. The council is composed of 82 representatives from the government, congress, businesses, trade unions, religious groups and the education sector. Their main task is to reflect public opinion and offer suggestions and ideas. The third was coordinating the relations between the federal and the local governments to win local supports and enhance administration efficiency. Within three months after he took office, he had had direct conversations with all the state governors and 1 900 mayors from across Brazil. The fourth was encouraging public participation in politics and setting up grass-root organizations. The fifth was vigorously promoting the rule of law in national governance. President Rousseff attached great importance to the rule of law in governance and clarified the accountability system and the guidelines for decision-making. She proposed to create a "clean and efficient government" and was resolute in handling corruption problems within the government. In the first two years of her administration, she removed seven ministers on suspicion of corruption and promoted the amendment of the relevant articles in the anti-corruption law.

(2) **Strengthening macro-regulation, optimizing market mechanism and promoting stable economic growth.** After taking office, Lula emphasized the positive role of market in the allocation of resources. He did not take radical economic reform policies and insisted to have the primary budget surplus target, the floating exchange rates and control of inflation control as his main economic policies. In the meantime, he strengthened the overall macro-control of the government and approved the public-private partnership program in a bid to solve the financing difficulties. He increased government's investment in the production sector and enhanced productivity. His government intensified the construction of highways, communication facilities and other infrastructures, strengthened logistics support for economic development, lowered taxes on production activities and promoted development of industries. Foreign exchange reserve increased and foreign debts were rearranged, and the financial risk-resisting capacity was strengthened. The government encouraged enterprises to enhance their technological innovation capacities and increase the added value of export products. In order to promote the comprehensive economic growth and to counter the international financial crisis, his government launched economic growth-boosting programs respectively in 2007 and 2010 to stimulate economic growth by controlling public spending and increasing investment in construction of infrastructures. Since Rousseff took office, she has decisively adjusted macroeconomic policies in accordance with the changes both at home and abroad in order to ensure stable economic growth. She has adopted a flexible currency policy and a prudent budget policy. She has strengthened financial regulation, increased financial transaction taxes, expanded the scope of collection and contained the appreciation of BRL, Brazil's domestic currency. She has given support for industrial development and has launched the "Bigger Brazil", "SME Preferential Loan", "Logistics Investment" and other plans. She has strengthened trade protection measures to protect domestic industry and market and steadily promote tax reforms such as unifying the commodity circulation service tax of all the states, expanding the scope of industrial product taxes and reducing and exempting payroll taxes, etc.

(3) **Improving income distribution, increasing domestic demand and easing social conflicts.** Lula stressed "social justice, employment and welfare" in his presidential campaign in 2002. After he took office, he formulated a development strategy that calls to build a "Brazil for All People", which put social inclusion as the priority goal of his social policies and put the solving of poverty issues and improvement of people's livelihood as focuses of his administration: First of all, setting up a "Social Development and Anti-Hunger Ministry" to promote the "Zero Hunger" and the "Bolsa Familia" programs which are aimed to alleviate poverty and fight against hunger in the entire population. Second, great increase of investment in education. Lula's government launched a literacy program, which provided scholarships to native Indian and black students based on their proportions in the population. There were massive construction of federal technical schools, universities and university towns and a program to ensure everyone can go to university and a higher education student financial aid program were implemented. Third, increase of investment and technical support for agriculture. Lula's government increased subsidy for family farms by eight times and strengthened assistance for the landless farmer families to settle down. It provides small agricultural loans to families with annual income lower than BRL 2 000 and agricultural insurance for farmer suffering natural disasters. After President Rousseff took office, she continued to focus on people's livelihood in her administration: she launched a "no-abject poverty in Brazil" program which allocates BRL 20 billion (or about USD 10 billion) every year to provide relief money to destitute population and provide training on production skills. She also launched the "My home, my life" affordable housing program to provide cheap affordable housing for medium and low income families. Through the "National Technical Education and Employment" and the "Occupational Training" systems, the Brazilian government provides youngsters skill improvement training courses to help them become more employable. The "Science without Borders" project helps Brazilian students to study in world's top universities. It is expected that by 2014, about 100 000 students will have benefited from the project.

(4) **Strengthening biological protection and increasing capability of sustainable development.** First of all, including biological protection in the national development strategy. In 2008, the country released its "National Program to Combat Climate Change" which proposed to reduce its rate of deforestation by 49% in 2017 on the basis of the average rate of the years from 2006 to 2009. The Program became a law after being reviewed and approved by the Congress and the government set up a dedicated administration committee to supervise the implementation of the Program. Second, the country introduced on its own a voluntary emission reduction plan. In 2009, it announced its voluntary greenhouse gas emission reduction plan which promised to further reduce its greenhouse gas emission by 36.1% – 38.9% in 2020 on the basis of the expected volume through control of deforestation, increasing the use of biomass fuels, transforming industrial production methods, promoting the supply of clean electricity and enhancing the efficiency of agricultural and animal husbandry production. Third, it increased investments in biological protection and set up the Amazon Fund and the National Fund to Combat Climate Change, etc. Fourth, it released decrees and administrative measures on building and expanding national forest parks and biological parks and on protection of the sanitation and health of the native Indians. Fifth, it has strengthened development and utilization of bio-energy, which has effectively made up for the shortage of the supply of the traditional energy. Brazil has been one of the world's leaders in the research and utilization of clean energy, particularly in terms of bio-energy. At the end of 2009, the Lula government released a decree to make it compulsory to add 5% biodiesel into the diesel and 25% ethanol into the gasoline that are sold in the market. In the meantime, the government intensified assessment and control of the impact of bio-energy on the environment. In 2007, the country introduced the "biological certificate" mechanism on bio-fuels. Bio-fuel producing enterprises found to have conducted illegal deforestation or misuse of land will not be granted biological certificate or business license.

(5) **Promoting big power diplomatic strategy to maintain development space.** While continuing to consolidate the traditional relationship with

the US and Europe, the Lula administration were more active in promoting relations with other big powers and in participating in international affairs in order that Brazil as a regional big power, plays a more important role and has a greater influence in the restructuring of international political and economic relations to create a benign external environment for the country's economic development, win more external resources and accumulate more advantages. First of all, it has committed itself to consolidate the strategic partnership with Argentina, strengthen construction of the South Common Market and strive to promote the integration of South America. Second, it has enhanced Brazil's international influence through extensive participation of international affairs. It has carried out active diplomatic offensives, promoted the reform of UN and strived to become a permanent member of the UN Security Council. It has taken an active part in multilateral mechanisms such as BRICS, G20, etc. in a bid to take a leading role in global trade negotiations. Third, it has deepened cooperation with the developing countries in many fields, strengthened and developed strategic alliances with large developing powers and promoted the establishment of a new international political and economic order. Fourth, it has adopted pragmatic principles in handling relations with the developed countries and has been resolute in safeguarding its national interest and its independence in decision-making to seek to establish "close, constructive and balanced relations with the US and Europe". Since Rousseff took office, she has put more emphasis on positioning Brazil as a "big power". While carrying forward the multilateral diplomatic policy, she was more steadfast in safeguarding sovereign security and in developing a "global diplomatic" strategy.

3. Preliminary Results of Strengthening the Building of Governance Capacity

(1) **The ruling position of the left-wing has been constantly consolidated.** First of all, the Workers' Party has won presidential elections for three times in a row and has successfully realized handover of power between

the old and new generations of leaders. It has become the longest ruling party since the Brazilian military government returned the power to the people. Second, the seats of the ruling coalition in the Congress have been increasing rapidly and are now taking up 65% and 68% respectively in the upper and lower houses. The Workers' Party has become the second largest party in the upper house and the largest party in the lower house. The Rousseff administration has become the strongest government since the re-democratization of Brazil. Third, the ruling power of the center-left coalition has been strengthening in the states and cities throughout Brazil. In 2010, it won the election in 16 of the 27 states across the country. It achieved overwhelming victory in the municipal elections in 2012 when the Workers' Party won 635 mayoralties, up 14% compared with the municipal elections in 2008. Fourth, Lula and Rousseff are the presidents that enjoy the highest public approval ratings in Brazil's history, among whom Rousseff has made a historic record of 77%.

(2) **Steady economic growth**. From 2003 to 2012, Brazil's economy maintained an average annual growth rate of 4%. Its total imports and exports rose from USD 106.9 billion in 2002 to USD 465.7 billion in 2012. The country risk index fell from 1 460 points to 180 points; the public debt-to-GDP ratio fell from 60.6% to 40.3%. Its foreign exchange reserve rose from USD 378 billion to USD 379 billion and its inflation rate dropped from 12.5% to 5.84%. The unemployment rate fell from 11.7% to 5.5% and the global ranking of its economic aggregate rose from 13th in 2003 to 6th in 2011.

(3) **Continuous improvement of people's livelihood**. From 2003 to 2011, the poverty population of Brazil reduced by 50.64% and the destitute population dropped by 47%, indicating that Brazil has achieved United Nations Millennium Development Goals ahead of time. It has created 2420 jobs, increased the middle class population by 40 million. So far, the middle class accounts for 52% of the country's total population. The social structure is gradually changing from pyramid-shaped to olive-shaped and the Gini Coefficient has dropped from 0.594 to 0.519, the lowest since 1960.

(4) **The ecological environment has kept turning for the better**. The deforestation of the Amazon rainforest has been declining year by year since 2005, and the level fell to the lowest point in 2012. During the years between 2006 and 2010, Brazil reduced carbon emission by about 1 billion tons. In the meantime, the proportion of bio-energy in the total energy consumption structure has risen to 24%, far ahead of the international average of 13.6%.

(5) **Rising international influence**. Brazil's diplomatic efforts to become a permanent member of the UN Security Council have been recognized by the international community to some extent. It is now "no longer regarded as just a participant in the Western Hemisphere, but has become a real global player". In the Doha Round talks and in negotiations on the reform of the international financial system, Brazil has become the voice for the developing countries. In addition, Brazil is playing a significant role in important international issues such as world poverty reduction, energy and food crises, global climate, the UN peacekeeping operations, human rights, etc. Because of its rising influence, Brazil succeeded in its bids to host the 2014 World Cup and the 2016 Olympics, which has greatly inspired the national pride of the Brazilian people.

4. Some Inspirations

(1) **People must be the purpose of the efforts of strengthening social management.** During process of Brazil's economic and social transformation, the unbalance, unharmonious and unsustainable problems aggravated and the social structure experienced profound adjustment. The interest parties became increasingly diversified and there were increasingly different demands. Social conflicts had intensified. Brazil's center-left government cares about people's concerns and wishes and follows closely public opinions. It has established extensive, multilayered and institutionalized deliberative democracy mechanism and has kept up with the trend of social thoughts, which has inspired the creative vitality in the society and has to some extent promoted social harmony. Its

experience shows that strengthening social management must have people as their purpose and the government must adhere to the service-first philosophy and turn it into a service-oriented government.

(2) **Proper handling of the relationship between the market and the government is key to strengthening economic governance.** Brazil started promoting neo-liberal market-oriented reform after 20 years of military dictatorship. The drawbacks of the highly centralized governance and of the laissez-faire free market development models have been all too apparent. After the center-left coalition came to power, while insisting to allow market to be the decisive part in resource allocation, the government has also been active in playing the regulating role, focusing on solving the problems such as imperfect market system, undue government interference and inadequate supervision, etc. It has been relatively effective in maintaining the macroeconomic stability and has promoted market competition, maintained market order and has made remedies where market failed. Their experience shows again that the healthy development of the market economy must be the combination of the spontaneous adjustment of the market and the macro-regulation of the government.

(3) **Maximum reflection of fairness and justice is the foothold of strengthening the governance capacity.** Brazil's center – left government believes that unfair distribution is the greatest cause of social instability, therefore it gives priority to social policies, increases social investments, and strives to make the distribution system reflect the social fairness and justice to allow economic development and the growth of wealth to benefit the majority of the people, in order to win public support and the recognition of the international community to consolidate its power base. Their experience shows once again that the starting point and the foothold of strengthening governance capacity must be based on the promotion of social equity and justice, and on improving people's well-being. It is necessary to promote fairness in opportunities, rules, rights and distributions in political, economic, social and cultural fields, strive to guarantee and improve people's livelihood and try its best to enable a good life for the people.

ANC's Challenges in Governance
—Reflected in the 2014 Election

Shu Chang*

On 7th of May, South Africa held its fifth national elections since the end of apartheid. The ruling African People's Congress (ANC) won the elections once again, securing 62.15% of the votes and 249 seats out of the 400 seats in parliament. The Democratic Alliance (DA), the official opposition, maintained its position as the biggest opposition in the country by garnering 22.23% of the votes and 89 seats in parliament. The Economic Freedom Fighters (EFF), led by former leader of ANC youth league Julius Malema, emerged as a new force, winning 6.35% of the votes. This makes the EFF the third largest party in parliament. In provincial elections, the ANC won in eight of the provinces, while the DA took office in Western Cape.

This election took place as the ANC celebrated its 20th anniversary as the ruling party since the end of apartheid. This is South Africa's first election in the Post-Mandela Era. This is also the first time the young generation born after the establishment of Democratic South Africa took part in the voting. Therefore, this election has drawn widespread attention and was regarded a weather vane for South Africa's future political development.

The results of the election have shown that the DA has made steady progress and the EFF has emerged as a black horse. However, the ANC managed to keep its leading position by getting 62.15% of the votes and won in all provinces except Western Cape. This is a manifestation of the

---

* Shu Chang, a Staff of African Affairs Bureau of International Department of the CPC Central Committee.

solid support the ANC enjoyed. DA, the official opposition, won 22.23% of the votes, a big increase from 16.66% in the last election. But this result is lower than the 30% goal and only slightly higher than 22% in the 2011 local government elections. The DA is still mainly supported by the white and the colored. The room for future development is limited if the image of the DA as a "White Party" remain unchanged. The EFF emerged as a black horse and became the third largest party in Parliament. In the context of high unemployment rate and acute social contradictions, the EFF put forward some populist and radical policy proposals, such as the use of land for free and nationalization of mines and banks. These proposals are attractive to some of the young people and the most disadvantaged population, but it is very difficult to turn these proposals to reality. Although the EFF took away some of ANC's former supporters, it would not be able to pose any real threat to the ANC due to its small number of grassroot organizations. As most of the people who voted for the EFF used to support other opposition parties, the rise of the EFF only made other opposition further marginalized. Therefore, although the major opposition parties got more votes than before, they were not strong enough to challenge the ANC due to their race composition and policy orientation. The ANC remains the dominant party in South Africa and will continue its dominance in the short and mid term. However, the ANC faced its toughest test of the past two decades in this election due to the death of Nelson Mandela, the COSATU's intention to break away, the "Nkandla House" scandal, and the rise of EFF. The election reflected the difficulties and challenges facing the ANC despite its success in the election.

1. Lower Enthusiasm from the Electorate

The turnout of the electorate has decreased and the ANC's supporter base has narrowed. Young voters were not enthusiastic in politics. This election has witnessed a lower turnout. According to statistics, about 25.39 million eligible voters registered for election and about 18.66 million, or 73.47% of the registered voters finally participated in the voting. Compared with 89.28% in 1999, 76.73% in 2004 and 77.30% in 2009, the turnout has gone down. It is worth particular attention that the young voters who have got the election right for the first time were not very enthusiastic in voting. About 7 million young people born after 1994 were eligible voters, accounting for about 30% of the total. But only 33.3% of them registered, accounting for 2.5% of the registered voters. At the same time, the ANC got less of the votes compared with the supporting rate of 69.69% in 2004 and 65.90% in 2009. In provinces like Eastern Cape, Free State, Limpopo, Mpumalanga and Western Cape, where the ANC used to get around 80% of the votes, the ANC's supporter base has also narrowed. The ANC has got less than 70% of the votes in Eastern Cape, Free State and Western Cape. In the meantime, the DA's supporter base has widened.

Currently, the official unemployment rate in South Africa is as high as 25% and 70% of the young people aged between 18 and 34 are not employed. The gap between the rich and the poor is wide, with the Gini Coefficient reaching 0.69. Affected by the global financial crisis in 2008, South Africa's economic development has been slow. Its GDP growth rate in 2014 was only 1.9%. 85% of the black are part of the low income group. Since 1994, the ownership of only 6% of the land were transferred to the black, far lower than the 30% goal. Unemployment, poverty and inequality remained the prominent problems in South Africa. The masses were very eager to redress the historical injustice and improve their wellbeing. Their wishes remained unsatisfied. In this context, what the masses care are jobs and life, instead of politics and election. As their practical needs were not met, some of the traditional supporters of the ANC chose to stop supporting the ANC. Some even chose to support other political parties. The young voters born after 1994 never experienced the bitterness of apartheid. This made them less grateful to the ANC. As predicted, the ANC's biggest enemy was not the opposition, but the lessening of voter enthusiasm. The ANC's glory in overthrowing the apartheid regime has become part of the past. Only by addressing realistic issues people, especially the young, care most, like poverty and employment and improving people's wellbeing can the ANC stimulate people's enthusiasm in politics, reverse the trend of narrowing supporter base and consolidate its ruling status.

2. For ANC Solid Support in Rural Area, but a Shrinking One in Cities

The election result has shown that the ANC enjoys far more support in the rural areas than in the more developed areas. The number of voters in the cities supporting the ANC has even been decreasing. The ANC enjoys solid support in relatively backward provinces like Mpumalanga and Limpopo, getting almost 80% of the votes. In the most developed provinces of Gauteng and Western Cape, the percentage of voters supporting the ANC is lower than its national average. The ANC even lost the election in Western Cape. Gauteng is the most developed province in South Africa. Its GDP accounts for 33% of the national total. It is not only the most industrialized and urbanized city, but also where the ANC headquarter sits. However, the percentage of voters supporting the ANC has been decreasing, from 68.4% in 2004 to 64.04% in 2009. Before this election, the ANC redemarcated the provincial border, bringing part of the Northwest Province to Gauteng. This didn't stop the ANC's supporting rate in Gauteng from dropping to 54.92%, securing only slightly more than half of the votes. In the biggest city of Johannesburg and administrative capital of Tswane, the ANC's supporting rate is only less than 10 percentage points higher than that of the DA. If the ANC doesn't act properly or promptly, the ANC might lose these two cities in the 2016 local elections. Western Cape has the largest white population. Its capital Cape Town is one of the most developed cities in the country. The ANC lost Cape Town in the 2009 general election and got 34% of the votes this time, same as last time. The DA got 57.26% of the votes, further consolidating its position in Western Cape.

Generally speaking, voters in the rural areas are less influenced by the outside world and more cognitive of the ANC's historical contribution. They are more loyal to the ANC. For example, Limpopo is the cradle of ANC's armed struggle and Eastern Cape is the home town of many anti-apartheid leaders including Nelson Mandela. The ANC is blessed with mass support in these provinces. However, voters in the urban areas pay more attention to realistic issues. They are more diverse in ideas and influenced by the multi-party democracy of the West. They prefer rotation of ruling parties. Statistics have shown that urban voters accounted for 43% of the total in this election. The majority of the urban voters were black middle class. The black middle class, though beneficiaries of the ANC policies, were no longer loyal to the ANC due to the change of economic status and influence of the Western democratic values. The decline of former national liberation movements in Zambia and Zimbabwe both started from the shrinking of urban support base. The ruling Zimbabwe African People's Congress — Patriotic Front was almost reduced to a "rural party" and forced to form a government of national unity in 2009. Although its support base is still relatively solid, the ANC must remain highly vigilant to the trend of shrinking support in the urban areas.

3. Problems Inside the ANC Lead to Decreased Appeal

Since it took power in 1994, the ANC has been transforming from a national liberation movement to a governing party. The focus of its work is shifted to government affairs. With an increasing number of experienced cadres entering various government departments, the ANC for a time neglected its own party-building and problems emerged among its members. **First, the party is plagued by continuous infighting.** For a long time, the left and right forces in the ANC and the Tripartite Alliance have been fighting over policy lines. In the 52nd Congress at the end of 2007, Jacob Zuma was elected president of the ANC with the support of its left allies, mainly the SACP and the ANC Youth League, defeating President Thabo Mbeki who followed neo-liberal policies. But due to constant pressure exerted by the Capital at home and abroad, Zuma has basically inherited the policy line of Mbeki after he took office, which caused dissatisfaction of some radical forces and widened the differences over policy lines inside the party and the Alliance. Some believe the ANC has betrayed its political program, and it is sliding to a middle way with fading left color. The internal struggles broke out again in the 53rd Congress. The ANC is divided into camp "Pro-Zuma" and camp "Anti-Zuma". The former rallied around the left-wing in the party and put an all-out effort to support Zuma's reelection, while the latter launched "ABZ campaign" (Anyone But Zuma) and eventually nominated Kgalema Motlanthe, the ANC Vice-present as the candidate. Although Zuma ultimately won with 75% of the votes and managed to sweep out all the major characters of the Anti-Zuma camp, the election was considered as one of the most intensely contested competition in the party's history. The infighting is more serious than ever before. **Second, the party's organizational development is lagging behind.** The ANC membership has grown from 600 thousand in 2007 to 1.25 million at present, but quality of the membership fails to keep up with the speed of quantitative growth. Irregularity in recruitment of members, inactivity and falsification of membership are common occurrence in grassroots organizations. According to South African media, some provincial leading organs of the ANC, such Limpopo Provincial Executive Committee once became paralyzed as a result of factionalism, violence and murder broke out in some grassroots and local organizations as members scramble for power. The ANC urgently needs to transform from quantity-oriented to quality-oriented development. **Third, the ANC has serious corruption problems.** With their ideal fading and conviction weakened, some ANC members began to show corruption tendencies such as abuse of power for personal gains or power-for-money deal. Senior ANC officials even President Zuma is often caught in all kinds of corruption scandals. Last year the South African Minister of Justice Jeff Radebe said in the past four years President Zuma had cost 8.8 million Rand in court on cases including "Arms deal" "Spy Tapes" "Gupta-gate". This year, Zuma found himself again trapped by "Nkandla House" scandal weeks before the general election. Relevant report revealed that Zuma allegedly used public money in the name of security upgrade to build a swimming pool, an amphitheater, and cattle pen for its family homestead in Nkandla, KwaZulu-Natal. The cost shoot up after Zuma assumed presidency from a 27 million budget to 246 million actual expenditure, making a record high among all South African presidents and totaling eight times of how much Former President Mandela spent on refurbishing two of his private houses. The controversy was exposed just six weeks before the election and became the most negative factor affecting ANC's election prospect. The event was amplified and hyped by opposition parties and media which lost no time to attack Zuma and the ANC. Some South Africans believe the ANC has given up many values Mandela represents and corruption is the biggest irony for the South African liberation. ANC must take stronger measures against corruption to win people's trust back and increase its moral appeal in the post-Mandela era. Failure to deal with the above-mentioned problems may lead to a split in the Alliance or loss of important supporters, which will undermine ANC's ruling foundation.

4. The Triparitite Alliance is Beset with Difficultics Internally and Externally

South African left-wing forces such as the South African Communist Party (SACP) and the Congress of the South African Trade Union (COSATU) have been long-time ally with the ANC. They provided strong and critical support to the ANC in their struggle to end apartheid and in every election. Over the years, dissatisfaction about ANC's free-market economic policies has been growing in the SACP and the COSATU. COSATU in particular has shown its disagreement with the ANC on many issues including corruption and misconduct of senior officials, Gauteng toll road fees, labor legislation and youth employment subsidy plan, with Zwelinzima Vavi, the Congress General Secretary openly criticizing President Zuma and his government. Before the election, the COSATU split into two groups with one vehemently criticizing the ANC and the other remaining supportive. The biggest affiliate of the COSATU — National Union of Metalworkers of South Africa (NUMSA) threatened to walk out and establish a new workers' movement or party. With over 300 thousand members, NUMSA's run-away would be a heavy blow to the Alliance. At the same time, independent and more radical trade unions emerged to compete with dominant ones. The 2012 Marikana

Miner's Strike which resulted in the death of over 40 people was a result of conflicts between trade unions. The Marikana Mine area was dominated by the long-existing National Union of Mineworkers (NUM), but its presence has been encroached by an emerging union — Association of Mineworkers and Construction Union (AMCU) in recent years. Strife over workers' representation at the mine broke out from time to time. In August, 2012, AMCU started striking at Marikana Mine without consent of NUM and some of its workers assaulted staff in NUM's office. The confrontation soon escalated to violent conflicts leading to the death of 9 people. South African police opened fire when they tried to disperse the striking workers, killing 34 and injuring 78. The incident, described as "the darkest moment since the end of apartheid" by South African media, not only damaged unity of trade unions' movement, but also swerved the unconditional support of mineworkers to the ANC. In election this year, the ANC witnessed conspicuous decline in its popularity in the mining province — Northwestern Province as votes decreased to 67.69% from 72.89% in 2009 and 80.71% in 2004, while the EFF won 12.53% in its first run. In addition, the Alliance is facing external pressure. With gap between the people's expectation and reality keeps widening, some ultra-left forces have become people's new favorite. Take the EFF for example, the party is founded less than one year before the election by Julius Malema, who used to be President of the ANC Youth League and Zuma's henchman — "the future leader of ANC" is what Zuma called him — but later expelled from the ANC for his attempt to block Zuma's reelection and destroy unity of the Party. With radical left slogans such as acceleration of land reform and mining nationalization, Malema — a populist and demagogue was able to win the support from youth and disadvantaged group, successfully making EFF the 2nd largest opposition after the election. The Tripartite Alliance for the first time faced challenge from both ends of political spectrum — the right DA and the left EFF. It is expected that under continuous internal and external pressure and double envelopment from both left and right, the ANC-led Tripartite Alliance is going to trudge forward, but how to deal with these challenges would be a serious test to its governing capacity.

The Role of BRICS in Global Reform: What Is Our Vision?

Narnia Bohler－Muller[*]

1. Introduction

The grouping of the "rising powers" called BRICS — Brazil, Russia, India, China and South Africa — has established itself in a very short period of time as a global player to be taken seriously.[①] Broadly speaking, the BRICS agenda is revisionist, with a focus on the rebalancing of global power relations and the reform of international institutions of economic and political governance such as the United Nations Security Council (UNSC); the International Monetary Fund (IMF); the World Bank (WB) and the World Trade Organisation (WTO).

After sketching a brief background, this paper looks at the kinds of reforms being called for by BRICS. The main enquiry is whether adequate progress has been made in attaining the vision of BRICS in this regard. Although there is more clarity around the common aspirations of the five member states, articulated through the efforts of the BRICS Think Tank Council (BTTC) established in 2013 in South Africa, progress in the area of reforms of existing global institutions of governance has been slow. Despite this, BRICS is continuing to use its soft power and its focus on multilateralism to good effect. It is possible that this ever expanding influence may speed up the reform processes in future.

---

[*] Narnia Bohler－Muller, member of the HSRC BRICS Think Tank Secretariat.
[①] See in general Kornegay and Bohler-Muller *Laying the BRICS of a New Global Order: From Yekaterinburg 2009 to eThekwini 2013*, AISA Press, 2013.

2. Background

The Delhi Summit Declaration and Delhi Action Plan of 2012 called for a general academic evaluation and development of a future long-term vision and strategy for BRICS.[①] As a result, in preparation for the 2013 Leadership Summit in Durban (eThekwini), South Africa mandated the Human Sciences Research Council (HSRC) to serve as the think tank for the country, joining the already established think tanks in the other four countries, namely:

- Institute for Applied Economic Research (IPEA), Brazil;
- National Committee for BRICS Research (NRC/BRICS), Russia;
- Observer Research Foundation (ORF), India; and
- China Centre for Contemporary World Studies (CCCWS), China.

These five national think tanks met on the side-lines of the leaders'Summit hosted by South Africa in 2013 entitled "BRICS and Africa: Partnership for Development, Integration and Industrialisation". Under the leadership of the HSRC, they signed a Declaration of establishment, subsequently adopted by the BRICS leaders, which formally established the BRICS Think Tanks Council.[②] The purpose of this Council is to organise and to coordinate academic input from the BRICS Academic Forum and to make policy recommendations and offer guidance for consideration by the BRICS leaders at the annual Summits. The BTTC's role is also to mobilise, facilitate and stimulate research and to exchange research-based analysis and recommendations on the formulation and reformulation of BRICS-related public policies and development programmes. These functions render the BTTC a Track II diplomacy institution. As part of the initial work of the BTTC, the Council was mandated to develop a long-term vision and strategy for BRICS, which is in line with the provisions of the Delhi Action Plan as articulated above.

[①] For a full text for the Fourth Summit Declaration and Action Plan, see http://www.brics5.co.za/about-brics/summit-declaration/fourth-summit/ (accessed on 7 January 2015).

[②] For details of the key functions of the BTTC, see http://www.hsrc.ac.za/en/departments/sabtt/bttc (accessed on 7 January 2015).

The BTTC's BRICS long-term vision document, which was adopted by leaders in 2014 at the Fortaleza Summit, Brazil, focuses on five Pillars:

(1) Promoting cooperation for economic growth and development;

(2) Maintaining peace and security;

(3) Promoting social justice, sustainable development and quality of life;

(4) Reforming the global political and economic governance architecture;

(5) Attaining progress through knowledge and innovation sharing.

In line with the theme of this conference in Beijing[①], the reform of global political and economic governance is one of the priority themes, which also falls under Pillar four of the BRICS vision document. As mentioned in all the Summit Declarations of BRIC(S) since its inception in Yekaterinburg in 2009[②], member states aim to use multilateral diplomacy to leverage and exert pressure for significant reforms and balanced representation within international organisations responsible for political and economic governance, including: the United Nations Security Council; the International Monetary Fund; the World Bank; and the World Trade Organisation.

This trend towards polycentricity and commitment to multilateralism has seen BRICS emerge — and rise — as a powerful player on the global stage. Thus it can be argued that the international "playing field" is being levelled by groupings such as BRICS.

Arguments that emphasize the differences among and between the BRICS, and the perceived and real difficulties of its members to come up with common positions, are lagging behind the evolution of diplomacy and miss two important points:

(1) BRICS is **already** a political reality; and

(2) BRICS displays a solid political unity in favour of reforms in the rules and structures of the existing international order.[③]

Within this context, BRICS member states are committed to assuming an increasingly significant role in international relations concomitant

---

① International Symposium on Building Governance Systems and Capabilities of BRICS Countries, Beijing, 19 – 20 November, 2014.

② South Africa joined BRIC on 24 December, 2010, creating BRICS.

③ Discussed below.

with their growing global and regional economic and political significance. In order to continue to facilitate real change, there is a need for BRICS to strengthen its agenda around common interests. Some recommendations follow, although it is certainly not an exhaustive list:

• Share experiences on good governance and transparency;

• Comprehensive reform of the UN, World Bank, and IMF to be inclusive, more effective and more efficient; and

• Promote reforms to encourage productive investment as opposed to speculation fuelled by financial gains and unregulated credit.

The paragraphs below focus on the reform process, and its strengths and weaknesses, starting with the reform of the UNSC.

3. Reform of the United Nations and Its Security Council

Despite rumblings of the establishment of an "alternative world order", BRICS has consistently expressed a commitment to the centrality of the United Nations and respect for the rule of international law. However, there have been calls since 2009 for the reform of the UN and especially the UN Security Council. The call for reform is mainly focused on the need for the UNSC to be more democratic, representative, efficient, effective and responsive. This was emphasised again in the Fortaleza Leadership Declaration, which stated — albeit vaguely — that:

> China and Russia reiterate the importance they attach to Brazil, India and South Africa's status and role in international affairs and support their aspiration to play a greater role in the UN. (Fortaleza Declaration 2014)

The UN celebrates its seventieth anniversary in 2015. Since transition from the League of Nations in 1945, membership of the UN General Assembly (UNGA) has grown from 51 members to 193 member states in 2013.[1] But the decision-making Security Council composed of 15

---

[1] For details of membership of UNGA see http://en.wikipedia.org/wiki/Member_states_of_the_United_Nations (accessed on 7 February 2015).

member-states, of which 10 are non-permanent while 5 are permanent, remains largely unchanged. The United States (US), China, Russia, France, and Britain (the Permanent Five or P5) wield veto power, and therefore hold sway over the UN's work of maintaining international peace and security.

Thus, proposals for reform — including from BRICS — continue to emerge because the UNSC still represents an outdated global order, unchanged since 1945, and excludes the say and input of, for instance, Brazil, India and (South) Africa. It is no secret that the latter member states of BRICS each seeks a permanent seat on the UNSC. For instance, after the Fortaleza Leadership Summit, South Africa renewed its call for reform of the UNSC that includes at least two permanent seats for Africa. This is in line with Pretoria's "African Agenda", which places the continent firmly at the center of South Africa's foreign policy initiatives.[①]

In 2013 President Zuma addressed the 68th Session of UNGA by proposing a target for a reformed, more inclusive, democratic and representative UNSC by 2015, the year in which the world body will be celebrating its 70th anniversary. South Africa's effort to have Africa represented in the UNSC is consistent with the *Ezulwini Consensus* which represents the continent's common position on reform of the UNSC.[②]

This Consensus seeks to push for two African states, to be nominated by the African Union (AU), as permanent members of the UNSC with veto power, and five non-permanent African seats. Although admittedly a big ask, this makes sense as a result of the fact that the majority of UNSC resolutions relate to the continent. Brazil and India (alongside Germany and Japan, collectively known as the G4) have endorsed the

---

① For details of the White paper on South African foreign policy — *Building a Better World: The Diplomacy of Ubuntu* (Department of International Relations and Cooperation), see http://www.safpi.org/publications/white-paper-south-african-foreign-policy-building-better-world-diplomacy-ubuntu (accessed on 7 January 2015).

② African views on the reform of the United Nations Security Council, see http://www.safpi.org/news/article/2013/african-views-reform-unsc-ezulwini-consensus-and-sirte-declaration (accessed on 7 January 2014).

Ezulwini Consensus by making recommendations for an African permanent seat①, although South Africa has not been expressly mentioned. Russia and China have also called for reform of the UNSC, but wish to maintain their veto votes and do not support the veto being extended to other members, including their BRICS partners. For instance, China does not support the inclusion of India as a permanent member of the UNSC. Russia has endorsed democratic reform of the UNSC, but maintains its stance that new members should not be allowed to veto decisions for at least the first fifteen years.②

The question is whether Russia and China (members of the UNSC P5) will ever freely and openly endorse The India - Bruzil - South Africa Dialogue Forum (IBSA) bid for permanent seats with veto power privilege.③ However, this question must be considered in the context of the current state of affairs, including BRICS solidarity demonstrated by the launch of the New Development Bank (NDB) and Contingency Reserve Arrangement (CAR) in July 2014. With this growing consensus, it has been suggested that Moscow and Beijing will soon be endorsing South Africa's and other BRICS partners' bids for UNSC permanent seats, but without necessarily giving away — or granting — veto power. Thus Brazil, India and South Africa will probably have to settle for **limited reform** of the UNSC, comprising of an expansion without alteration or abolition of veto power.④

Based on the above mentioned dynamics, it is important for BRICS to agree to the *nature* of reform of the UNSC, because if this agreement cannot be reached, reforms — even limited ones — will not happen in the foreseeable future.

---

① See page 519 footnote ②.
② Personal conversation with a Russian diplomat.
③ Tshepho Mokwele, "South Africa's Call for UN Security Council Reform: An Explicit BRIC Countries' Backing Forthcoming?" at http://thedailyjournalist.com/the-strategist/south-africas-call-for-un-security-council-reform-an-explicit-bric-countries-backing-forthcoming/ (Accessed on 19 October 2014).
④ Mokwele above.

4. Reform of the International Monetary Fund and World Bank

At the top of the agenda, in order to ensure effective international economic and financial governance, the BRICS member states aim to play a leading role in formulating positions on international monetary and financial system reforms on behalf of member states and other emerging markets and developing countries (EMDCs). One of the priorities in this regard is to ensure strengthened cooperation within the framework of international organisations to collectively promote mutual interests in the area of international finance and trade.

As a clear sign of progress, BRICS launched its New Development Bank in July 2014. The bank, to be headquartered in Beijing, is "aimed at funding infrastructure projects in developing nations···with $100 billion currency reserves pool to help countries (including member-states) forestall short-term liquidity pressures" (Fortaleza Declaration 2014). This bank would also provide the Global South countries with, for example, unconditional loans and aid in stark contrast to "one-size-fits-all" (also known as "cookie cutter") conditions imposed by the Bretton Woods Institutions (the IMF and the WB) that has left developing countries with massive debts.

To illustrate the revisionist agenda of BRICS, pressure continues for the reform of the IMF and WB so as to be more democratic, representative and effective.

In the Fortaleza Declaration (2014) BRICS articulated its criticism of lack of IMF reforms very strongly in para. 18:

> We remain disappointed and seriously concerned with the current non-implementation of the 2010 International Monetary Fund (IMF) reforms, which negatively impacts on the IMF's legitimacy, credibility and effectiveness...We call on the membership of the IMF to find ways to implement the 14th General Review of Quotas without further delay. We reiterate our call on the IMF to develop options to move ahead with its reform process, with a view to ensuring increased voice and representation of EMDCs, in case the 2010 reforms are not entered into force by the end of the year. We also call on the membership of the IMF to reach a final agreement on a new quota formula together with the 15th

General Review of Quotas so as not to further jeopardize the postponed deadline of January 2015.

Para. 19 of the 2012 Declaration was dedicated to the reform of the WB, which was less strongly articulated:

> We welcome the goals set by the World Bank Group to help countries end extreme poverty and to promote shared prosperity. We recognize the potential of this new strategy in support of the fulfillment of these ambitious goals by the international community. This potential will only be realized, however, if the institution and its membership effectively move towards more democratic governance structures, strengthen the Bank's financial capacity and explore innovative ways to enhance development financing and knowledge sharing while pursuing a strong client orientation that **recognizes each country's development needs** ... (own emphasis)

Furthermore, BRICS has made it clear that the NDB and CRA will not replace the IMF and WB, but will operate alongside these existing global finance institutions, as illustrated in para. 19 of the Fortaleza Declaration:

> We have been very active in improving the international financial architecture through our multilateral coordination and through our financial cooperation initiatives, which will, in a **complementary manner**, increase the diversity and availability of resources for promoting development and ensuring stability in the global economy (own emphasis).

The IMF and the World Bank were created at an international conference convened in Bretton Woods, New Hampshire, United States in July 1944 (the Bretton Woods Institutions). The goal of the conference was to establish a framework for economic cooperation and development that would lead to a more stable and prosperous global economy after the end of the World War II.[①] While this goal remains central to both institutions, their mandate is constantly evolving in response to new

---

① For an outline of the history of the Bretton Woods Institutions, see http://www.brettonwoodsproject.org/2005/08/art-320747/ (accessed on 7 January 2015).

economic developments and challenges, for instance the 2008 global financial crisis.

The IMF's mandate is to promote international monetary cooperation and to provide policy advice and technical assistance to help countries build and maintain strong economies.[①] The Fund also provides loans and helps countries design policy programmes to solve balance of payment problems when sufficient financing on affordable terms cannot be obtained to meet net international payments. As per current IMF norms, each member country is assigned a quota based on its relative position in the world economy. A member's quota determines its maximum financial commitment to the IMF and its voting power, and has a bearing on its access to IMF financing.

On the other hand, the World Bank promotes long-term economic development and poverty reduction by providing technical and financial support to help countries reform particular sectors or implement specific projects and policies — for example, building schools and health centers, providing water and electricity, fighting disease, and protecting the environment.[②]

In attaining its vision, it is incumbent upon BRICS to be more assertive in assuming a leadership role in global political and economic governance and to seek greater equity for the developing world in general and Global South in particular. As mentioned, BRICS has consistently emphasised that the reform of Bretton Woods Institutions is central to this objective and member states have voiced their concerns around the **status quo** via global platforms such as the G20 and also at the six annual BRICS — Leadership Summits.

In addition, at the October 2014 meetings of the IMF and WB, BRICS — from the side-lines — called for faster reforms of these institutions. In addition, IMF managing director Christine Lagarde stated that:

---

① For the mandates of the IMF and WB, see http://www.imf.org/external/np/exr/facts/imfwb.htm (accessed on 7 January 2015).

② For the mandates of the IMF and WB, see http://www.imf.org/external/np/exr/facts/imfwb.htm (accessed on 7 January 2015).

> To be effective in the 21st century, we (IMF) need to be adequately resourced and adequately reflect the dynamic nature of our global membership… To that end, the vast majority of our members have approved an IMF governance measure: the 2010 Quota reform. We now await approval by our largest shareholder the United States which we hope will happen soon. (October 2014)

The US has been delaying implementation of the quota reform, agreed to by IMF member countries in 2010, for a major realignment in the ranking of quota shares so that the Fund better reflects global realities. Despite support from President Barack Obama, the US Congress is yet to give its approval for the reforms. The Congress approval would have paved the way for emerging economies to receive a greater share in the IMF. Currently, the US has 16.75% out of total votes and 17.69% of the total quota in IMF. Since important IMF decisions need 85% approval, this cannot happen without US approval.①

Although reforms have been delayed, there has been some progress: the common position of BRICS has allowed augmentation of a total share of emerging and developing countries in the World Bank from 43.97% to 47.19%; and in the IMF, from 39.5% to 42.29%. Four of the BRICS countries (excluding South Africa) are within the top ten of IMF shareholders. The total voting power of BRICS would rise from around 11% to 14.68% if reform is finalised.②

In sum, with regard to reform of the IMF and WB, the aim of BRICS is to attain equity and fairness, which is an overriding imperative for all five member states. There is clear agreement that there is a need for greater voting quota distribution for emerging powers and developing countries in the Bretton Woods Institutions. As mentioned, reforming the IMF quota system has been long overdue, but is resisted by the US. However, BRICS missed a chance to show that they have a joint strategy

---

① An explanation of the IMF quota system can be found at http://www.imf.org/external/np/exr/facts/quotas.htm (accessed on 7 January 2015).

② Victoria Panova, "BRICS's New Institutions and Their Impact on International Political Economy", 2014, at http://www.e-ir.info/2014/09/27/bricss-new-institutions-and-their-impact-on-international-political-economy/ (Accessed on 19 October 2014).

to achieve the much needed reforms when they failed to agree on a non-European candidate to occupy the post of Managing Director of the IMF when Strauss-Kahn resigned in 2011.①

5. Reform of the WTO

The World Trade Organization — operationalised on 1 January 1995 — is a "rules-based" organisation that provides a negotiating forum for trade liberalisation through multilateral agreements and trade dispute settlement.② The WTO has grown from its 128 original members to 160 members as of September 2014, with an additional 24 countries that have applied to accede to the WTO. Of the BRICS countries, Russia was the last to join in 2012.

Past WTO Rounds have displayed fundamental asymmetries in the negotiation position of developed and developing countries. The fact that developed countries account for a large share of world trade (for instance just the US and EU account for 38% of imports and 23% of exports) gives them considerable bargaining power.③ Apart from having similar levels of per capita income, these countries also often exhibit a tendency for collective bargaining in international negotiations. In contrast, emerging and developing country groupings tend to be fragmented and un-coordinated. BRICS would do well to rally emerging and developing economies together for effective collective bargaining power. As stated in para. 21 of the Fortaleza Declaration:

> We believe all countries should enjoy due rights, equal opportunities and fair participation in global economic, financial and trade affairs, recognizing that countries have different capacities and are at different levels of development.

---

① Oliver Struenkel "Failure to Counter Lagarde's IMF Bid Shows that BRICS Are far from United", 2011, at http://www.postwesternworld.com/2011/05/29/incapacity-to-counter-lagardes-imf-bid-shows-that-brics-are-far-from-united/ (accessed on 7 January 2015).

② For the mandate of the WTO, see http://www.wto.org/english/thewto_e/coher_e/coher_e.htm (accessed on 7 January 2015).

③ See comprehensive trade profiles on the WTO website database at http://stat.wto.org/CountryProfile/WSDBCountryPFView.aspx?Language=E&Country=CO (accessed on 7 January 2015).

> We strive for an open world economy with efficient allocation of resources, free flow of goods, and fair and orderly competition to the benefit of all. In reaffirming our support for an open, inclusive, non-discriminatory, transparent and rule-based multilateral trading system, we will continue our efforts towards the successful conclusion of the Doha Round of the World Trade Organization (WTO) ⋯ We strongly support the WTO dispute settlement system as a cornerstone of the security and predictability of the multilateral trading system and we will enhance our ongoing dialogue on substantive and practical matters relating to it, including in the ongoing negotiations on WTO Dispute Settlement Understanding reform ...

6. Closing Remarks

It is clear that BRICS wants to see the international balance of power change, and will therefore as "new" or "rising" powers seek to alter the **status quo** in ways that favour their interests and those of the developing world in general.

The incremental but important changes (mentioned above) that are taking place serve to reflect the way in which BRICS chooses to "do things differently", as expressed by Victoria Panova, one of the members of the BTTC:

> ... in the form and method of decision-taking and suggested new model of cooperation, which does not tolerate dictatorship or pressure, and is founded on mutual respect and support.①

It is clear that all member states agree that reform is needed, sooner rather than later. There are however many obstacles and questions that remain: what does this reform look like, and when will it happen? This is where the role of the BTTC becomes important as the vision and long term strategy for BRICS is developed in a spirit of compromise. Furthermore, in strengthening its soft power, BRICS should empower international and national civil society and NGOs to supplement the calls from various stakeholders for accelerated reforms within the

---

① See poge 524 footnote ②.

Bretton Woods Institutions. There is a clear need for consistent public scrutiny of the reform process, and this scrutiny may very well serve to speed up the reform process as more players become involved in the game of global change.

The Impact of Financial Liquidity and Capital Flows on South Africa

Seeraj Mohamed*

1. Introduction

The focus of this paper will be on the South Africa economy. It fits into the sub-topic "BRICS countries' challenges in governance under the international financial crisis" and the impact of continued poor regulation of global finance and capital flows on the South African economy. It will consider the policy choices in South Africa and how these affect outcomes within a context of inadequate global financial system governance.

This paper considers the impact on the South African Economy of the interaction of the macroeconomic and financial policies of the post-apartheid government with increasing integration of global capital markets and large but volatile capital movements. It shows that the economic policy choices during this period of increasing global integration and volatility had a negative impact on the South African economy. The economy is sensitive to changes in global liquidity and has been seriously affected by contagion during periods of financial crises, including the Asian financial crises and the most recent global financial crisis. I argue that the important influence of deregulated financial markets and flows on the South African economy during the period of global financial volatility has been to influence the South African economic growth path. Investment and growth in capital stock in the

---

* Seeraj Mohamed, Director of the Corporate Strategy and Industrial Development Research Programme (CSID) in the School of Economic and Business Sciences at the University of the Witwatersrand, Johannesburg (Wits University).

period before the global financial crisis went to sectors of the economy that benefited from increases in private sector credit that led to increased debt-driven consumption and financial speculation. At the same time productive sectors of the economy in manufacturing and services had very little or even negative increases in capital stock.

This paper does not argue that South Africa is a simply a victim of the poor regulation of global financial markets. The large growth in the financial sector since the end of apartheid, the relatively high rate of economic growth before the global financial crisis and the shape of the South African economic growth path show that certain sectors and parts of society have benefited, if only for a short period, from the volatility in global financial markets. However, South Africa as a whole has not benefited and the goals of the post-apartheid government to address high levels of unemployment, poverty and inequality have been constrained by the economic growth path of the country and their economic policy choices.

Therefore, South Africa is not a simply a victim of poor regulation of global financial markets, instead the macroeconomic and financial policy choices taken by the South African Government since the end of apartheid has increased the influence of volatility and crises on the South African economy. Better governance of global finance that reduces volatility, crises and contagion would benefit the South African economy, but the ability to address the key economic problems will depend on the economic policies and their implementation in South Africa.

2. Background on Global Governance

The problem of financial volatility and crises is a global problem. Since the breakdown of the Bretton Woods arrangements during the 1970s, there was widespread and competitive deregulation of financial markets (Helleiner, 1994). The Bretton Woods arrangements were implemented to maintain stability in the global financial system after World War II. The aims were to allow countries to recover from the war, to promote growth and development of economies, to maintain full employment in countries and to rebuild the global trading system.

The lesson of the Great Depression (1928 – 1933) for the authors of the Bretton Woods agreement was that there was a need to maintain global financial stability and to support countries that would face balance of payments and financial problems. Countries were allowed to impose capital controls to limit the potential destabilising impact of foreign capital inflows and outflows on their economies. The erosion of the Bretton Woods arrangements created space for increased global financial activity and opportunities for avoiding capital controls. As a result, the formation of the Eurodollar market after World War II and other possibilities for offshore financial activities spurred on deregulation of financial activities in many countries. Instead of working to maintain financial stability in their national economies, countries embarked on a competition of drawing in foreign capital from other countries by deregulating their financial systems.

The deregulation of financial markets, which included liberalisation of cross-border capital flows, allowed greater financial integration across the globe. It also allowed increased cross-border financial activities and increased speculative financial activities around the globe. It became clear very early on with the International Debt Crisis that started in Latin America in 1982 that deregulation of and increased integration of global financial markets led to growth in capital flows across borders that could create conditions not only of macroeconomic instability within a single country, but could lead to contagion that affected many other countries.

The problems were not confined to developing countries. During the 1980s and 1990s, there were several banking crisis in smaller developed economies (such as Spain, Sweden, Finland and Norway). The larger financial centres also suffered from increased liquidity, bubbles and crashes after increased financial deregulation, including the US (for example the 1987 global stock market crash also called Black Monday, the savings and loans crisis, 1989 – 1991) and the collapse of Japan's asset price bubble in 1990. According to Grabel (2001), there were 12 financial crises in developing economies, including the Mexican crash of

1994 and the Asian financial crisis that started in 1997.

The widespread deregulation of financial markets during the 1980s and 1990s led to a massive growth in global financial markets and extraordinary increases in global liquidity. For example, Palma (2009) showed that "the four components of the stock of global financial assets (equity, public and private bonds and bank deposits) increased 9-fold in real-terms between 1980 and 2007 — from USD 26.6 trillion to USD 241 trillion. The deregulation of the financial sector meant that financial institutions could increase liquidity through increasing leverage. There was increasing use of derivatives and securitized debt and rapid growth in new financial institutions such as hedge and private equity funds. These financial instruments and financial institutions were inadequately regulated.

According to Helleiner (1994), the end of the Bretton Woods era caused a change in the governance of global and national financial markets. The role of state and global institutions changed from preventing financial crises to cleaning up after crises. The change also meant that institutions such as the International Monetary Fund (IMF) and Bank for International Settlements (BIS) played a larger role than before, as they helped countries to recover from crises provided they followed certain types of macroeconomic policy reforms. However, the new systems of governance have not served to stabilise the global financial system. In a sense a lot of the initiatives to stabilise the global financial system have occurred in a very different paradigm from the one which influenced the Bretton Woods arrangements.

Miguel d'Escoto Brockmann, President of the 63rd Session of the United Nations General Assembly, in his foreword to the "Report of the Commission of Experts of the President of the United Nations General Assembly on Reforms of the International Monetary and Financial System" (21 Sept 2009), says:

> As the Commission stresses with considerable frequency, the present crisis demonstrates failure at many levels — of theory and philosophy, of institutions, policies and practices, and, less overtly, of ethics and accountability. The essential insight of the report is that our multiple crises are not the result of a

failure or failures of the system. Rather, the system itself — its organization and principles, and its distorted and flawed institutional mechanisms — is the cause of many these failures. (United Nations, 2009, p.8)

The Group of experts that authored the report came from every region of the world and the commission was chaired by Economics Nobel laureate Joseph Stiglitz. They were clear that the problem was with free market economics perspectives that advocated limited state involvement in financial markets, because they believed that financial markets operated efficiently and correctly reflected the risks and costs associated with financial transactions. In this view, markets left to themselves would correctly value financial assets, and crises were caused not by endogenous problems in financial markets but exogenous factors such as political interference and regulation.

In his foreword to the UN report, d' Escoto Brockmann also says:

> The financial crisis that erupted in the United States in September 2009 is the latest and most impactful of several concurrent crises — of food, of water, of energy, and of sustainability — that are tightly interrelated, connected in important ways by an imperious economic perspective that has been implemented, often under duress, across the globe during the last 35 years. In this perspective, market logic solves nearly all social, economic and political problems. (ibid).

He carries on to voice his disappointment with the lack of accountability and corrective action for the Global Financial Crisis and points to a problem in global economic governance. He says that a solution to the crisis should involve broad democratic participation of countries:

> An alternative, complementary explanation is that there is a deep flaw in our system of global economic governance. According to democratic principles, those who are deeply affected by a policy should have a say in their formulation, and those who are responsible for massive failures and injury should be held accountable. Our present system of global economic governance does not meet either of these fundamental tests of democratic governance. (ibid., p.9)

An important response to the crisis after the collapse of Lehman Brothers in 2009 was to set up the process considering financial regulation and governance using the G20 countries as a more inclusive forum. This paper cannot discuss the successes and failures of the G20, except to say it is a praiseworthy initiative that has not been able to assert adequate influence over the largest economies and their financial institutions. Stiglitz (2009) has publicly criticised the G20 for not dealing with the problem that too many financial institutions are too big to fail. My view is that his criticism points to a larger problem where countries such as the US have bailed out the largest financial institutions and see much of their future economic activity linked to the continued global role these institutions will play. They therefore, will discuss regulation and governance of the global economy as long as it does not have significantly negative impacts on their large financial institutions. However, this comment is not to argue that the G20 is ineffective, it is to show that global financial governance is a difficult task with different perspectives and economic interests playing out. It is not a process that should be abolished but possibly expanded to more countries.

The rest of this paper discusses the difficulties South Africa has faced with a global financial architecture with inadequate regulation of financial activities and institutions. As mentioned in the introduction, the argument is not that South Africa is a victim to the unregulated global financial environment. It shows that South Africa has chosen to follow the same type of policies that led to inadequate regulation of global financial markets and, therefore, has become more sensitive to global volatility and crises. It also argues that these policy choices at a time of increased global financial volatility have had a negative impact on the South African economy.

3. South Africa and Global Finance

The apartheid Government, influenced by global deregulation trends, deregulated the South African financial system during the 1980s. The next section considers the impact on the South African banking system.

The section that follows discusses the impact of deregulated cross-border capital movements on South Africa.

4. The South African Banks

The current structure of the South African banking system, characterised by high levels of concentration, was shaped by the particular colonial and apartheid economy. There was continuity in the approach to regulation and liberalisation from the 1980s apartheid government through to 2007 and the financial crisis. The role of non-banking financial institutions, including formal and informal lenders has grown as the role of other institutional investors, such as hedge funds, venture funds, and private equity funds. Using the Financial Services Board's definition, the size of the shadow banking system has grown significantly in South Africa during the post-apartheid period. Foreign banks were allowed to play a much larger role in the South African economy as well after 1994.

The banks retained their ethnic identities through most of the 1900s until the adoption of the DeKock Commission's recommendations, which were adopted in the Financial Institutions Amendment Act, No.106, of 1985. The deregulation of the banks included removal of activity constraints of the banks and the demutualisation of building societies. This deregulation, combined with disinvestments for political reasons during the 1980s, led to restructuring and consolidation in the formation of new banking groups, but the market remained concentrated. The deregulation led to the South African banking market resembling that of the US with its multi-function "supermarket banks" by 1994.

Reform during the post-apartheid period conformed to the adequacy requirements required by Basel. After the global financial crisis there was announcement of a policy shift towards a "twin peaks" approach, separating regulation of capital adequacy and bank behaviour with regard to their clients. The twin peaks approach may help deal with the high level of fragmentation in the South African regulatory environment. This approach, however, does not address the legacy of historical inequality and need for a more direct developmental role for banks in

South Africa. As a result, the focus of the banks and other financial institutions in South Africa is still to serve the same business, and predominantly the white groups they served in the past. At the same time, they play an important role in the financialisation[1] of the South African economy. The banks will continue to be regulated largely by the Reserve Bank while non-bank lenders will register with the National Credit Regulator.

Therefore, the large South African banking groups, other than involvement in relatively small projects to increase services to previously unbanked people, seem to behave similarly to those in the US and Britain where the moves away from intermediation to securitisation, investment services and trading in exotic financial instruments and financialisation, in general, and have advanced most.

South African banks have also become too big to fail[2], concentrated the domestic economy and further internationalised their activities. In fact, the largest South African banks are now not only actively pursuing expansion into other countries, but have become part of or closely aligned to larger global banking groups, such as Barclays and the Industrial and Commercial Bank of China. The change in their business, their internationalisation and financialisation raises many questions about South African banks and what role they can play in addressing the backlog of the large group of unbanked people and more generally how

---

[1] Financialisation is the growing role and influence of finance in all aspects of society. With regard to non-financial corporations, financialisation refers to their greater involvement and a greater share of their profits and revenues being earned from financial subsidiaries and speculation in financial assets. Households are also seen to be affected by financialisation with the state's withdrawal from-and increased privatisation of welfare and basic services. Households have increasingly invested in financial assets and consumed financial services to build pension funds and acquire risk mitigation and insurance services. Overall, neo-liberal policies to reduce the role of the state in the economy and to liberalise trade and financial markets are seen responsible for creating the conditions for the growth of finance and financialisation. See Epstein (2005) for discussion of financialisation and definitions.

[2] The view that South Africa's banks are too big to fail is shared by analysts in the financial sector. For example, an article by Bloomberg titled "Is Standard Bank Too Big to Fail", *Bloomberg*, 13 August, 2010, http://www.moneyweb.co.za/moneyweb-financial/standard-bank-is-too-big-to-fail) quotes Tracy Brodziak, a banking analyst at Old Mutual as saying that Standard Bank is "definitely a systemically important bank in South Africa".

they can contribute to the development of the South African economy?

The Government says that the South African banks are safe and that their resilience during the financial crisis shows that they are safe. I believe that they are asking the wrong questions. Their definitions of safe are those that have emerged in a context where the business of banking has shifted towards increasingly risky activities where they are inadequately regulated and many have become too big to fail. The South African banks may have weathered the storm, but they have become more risky and too big to fail. They weathered the crisis during 2008 because the remaining capital controls at that time had limited their exposure to US toxic debt. However, the increased financial systemic risk has occurred, because deregulation of finance and banking during the 1980s and 1990s allowed the South African banks to emulate the US banks in terms of their changing functions and behaviour.

5. Global Capital Flows

The apartheid Government, influenced by global deregulation trends, deregulated the South African financial system during the 1980s. Their attempts to deregulate capital movements led to a banking crisis and the apartheid Government had to declare a unilateral moratorium on debt repayments in 1985.

The post-apartheid government continued with financial liberalisation and allowed more freedom of movements of capital into and out of the country. Movements of capital by non-residents were relatively unregulated while residents have been allowed increasing freedom of capital movements out of the country over the past two decades. The path to liberalisation of cross-border movements was slower for South African residents, but there were regular increases in the amounts South Africans could move abroad from 1994.

The South Africa National Treasury of the Government celebrated its macroeconomic success when the South African economy's economic growth rate headed towards 5% from 2004, and by 2005 was over 5%, and stayed at that level until 2007.

However, these claims of success have to be questioned. The reason for declining inflation was increased imports from countries like China, which meant that South Africa was importing deflation. The reason for high economic growth rates from 2004 to 2007 were similar to the US and other countries where debt driven consumption grew and there were bubbles in real estate and stock markets leading up to the global financial crisis. The high growth rates were due to debt driven consumption and real estate and financial market speculation. The factors that caused the short period of high growth from 2003 to 2007 were damaging for the economy and society.

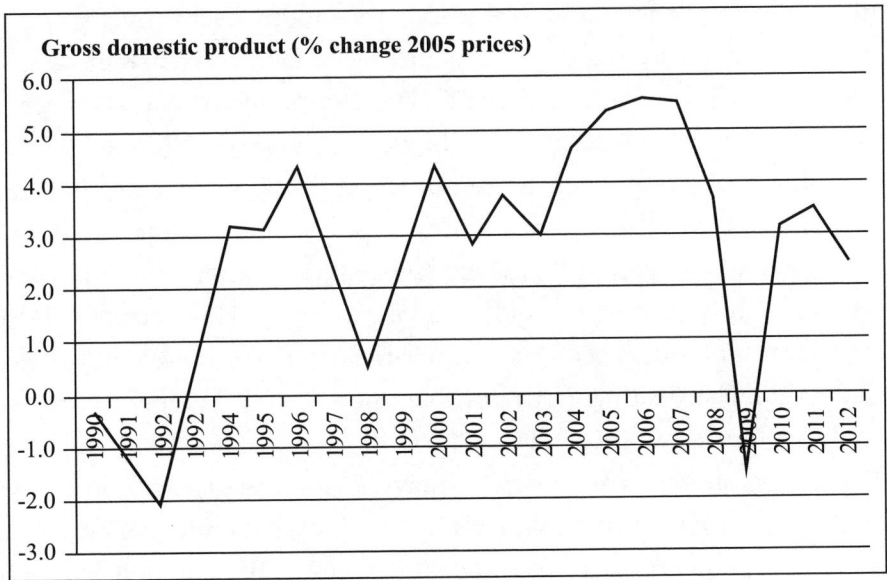

Figure 1: South African GDP (percentage change 2005 prices)

Data Source: SARB.

The increased short-term inflows into the South African economy from 1994, caused immense problems for the economy. As mentioned above, surges of short-term speculative capital flows create macroeconomic fragility and vulnerability to financial crisis and contagion. The volatility in short-term net portfolio flows created a highly volatile exchange rate for the Rand. Investors and importers and exporters all faced tougher and more uncertain business conditions.

Together with a regime of low inflation due to increased imports and inflation targeting, the uncontrolled capital flows into the country created a situation where macroeconomic policy was procyclical and caused exaggerated upturns and downturns that were associated with inflows and outflows of short-term capital. On one hand, surges of short-term inflows were associated with increased access to credit, strengthening of the Rand, cheaper imports and lower inflation that led to lowering of interest rates by the SARB. The lower interest rates would drive further borrowing for debt driven consumption and speculation in asset markets.

On the other hand, large outflows of short-term capital were associated with weakening of the Rand, fewer imports and increasing inflation that led to a rise of interest rates and tightening of credit. After the collapse of portfolio inflows during 2000 and 2001, South Africa had a currency crisis where the Rand dropped at its weakest point by 35% to the US dollar. The SARB responded to inflation due to the weaker currency by raising interest rates four times during a period of one year. The SARB were more constrained with raising interest rates after the collapse in portfolio inflows during the global financial crisis. However, the SARB kept the level of inflation as one of their main concerns and South Africa maintained higher real interest rates than the US, most European countries and their other trading partners.

The rise in short-term net capital flows was associated with increased liquidity in domestic financial markets. Credit extension to private sector increased by about 23% from 2000 to 2008, but private business investment increased by only 4%. The increased liquidity associated with surges in net short-term portfolio flows was not used for productive investment but created a situation where credit was misallocated towards debt driven consumption and real estate and financial speculation.

The open capital markets were an important component of the financialisation of the South African economy. The role of institutional investors within the economy had grown, because the liberalisation of financial markets meant that the private sector played a more important role in the provision of services. The private sector played a larger role in allocation of provisioning for retirement, insurance and medical aid schemes as well as in provision of education and healthcare. There was also growth in financial institutions that serviced the wealthy and other financial institutions such as hedge funds and private equity funds. There was acceleration in the growth of derivatives and securitised debt markets from 2003 (Mohamed, 2010). These institutional investors and financial institutions used the increased credit available to directly participate in driving up real estate and equity prices and supplied households with loans to drive up these asset prices. They also indirectly caused asset price inflation by their support for increasing household debt levels. They used derivatives and securitised debt to promote even greater liquidity and higher levels of debt.

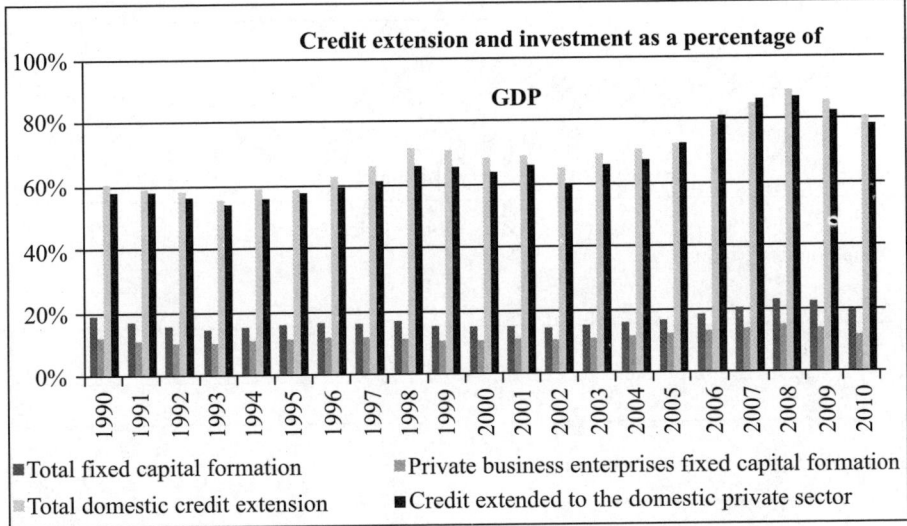

Figure 2: Credit Extension and Investment as Percentages of GDP

Data Source: SARB.

Figure 3 shows the growth in South African house prices and Figure 4 shows the share price indices. South African house prices increased more than any other country in the world. The increased liquidity created increased demand for houses and commercial space that drove up house prices and increased new housing and commercial property developments. The rise in prices created a sense of increased wealth that drove higher prices and spurred huge levels of speculation in real estate markets and speculative property development. The share prices also climbed and the bubble popped only once the global financial crisis started. The result was massive misallocation of capital towards speculation and lower levels of investment.

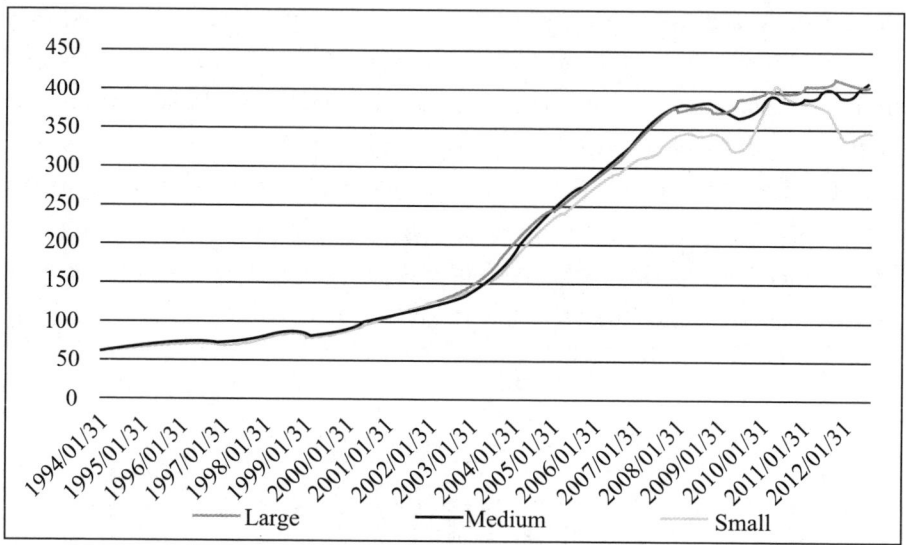

Figure 3: ABSA House Price Index
Data Source: Quantec.

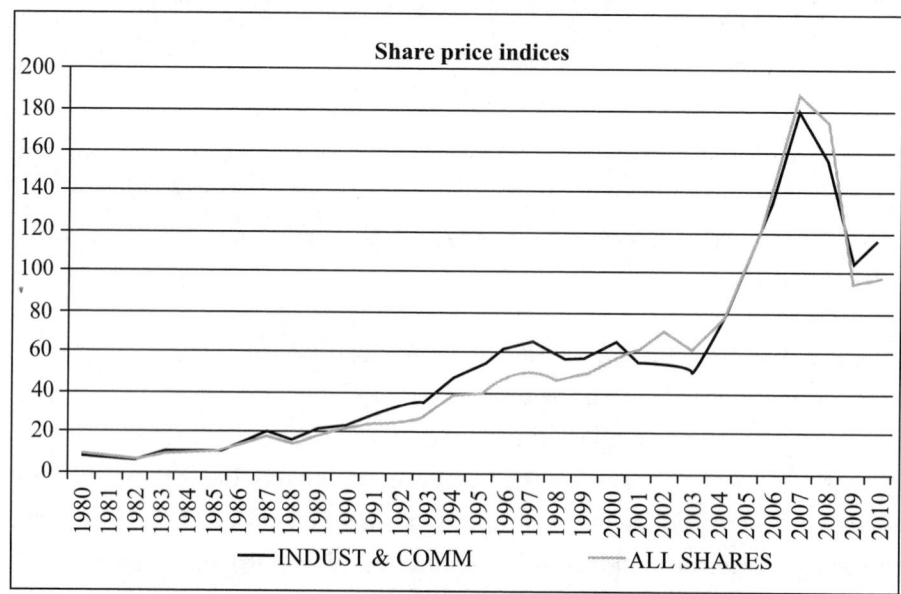

Figure 4: Johannesburg Securities Exchange Share Price Indices
Data Source: Quantec.

South African non-financial corporations had become financialised. This was a process that started in the largest corporations that listed offshore, particularly in London and New York, during the late 1990s. These corporations were forced to comply with the demands of the shareholder value movement which had grown in power during the 1990s.

Ernst and Young (2002) in a review of South African mergers and acquisitions for 2001 states:

> Shareholder activism has been slow to take off in South Africa, but like all global trends it is one, which is catching up with us very quickly. The prominent South African companies that have listed offshore over the last two or three years have already been exposed to the higher level of transparency demanded in global markets. South African companies with a more domestic orientation are under pressure to emulate their global peers. (p.27)

By the early 2000s, as mentioned in the quote above, the shareholder value movement's influence over South African firms had grown. The shareholder value movement demanded focus on core business, simpler corporate structures and higher short-term rates of return on their investments. Listed South African corporations, even giants such as the Anglo American Corporation, were forced to restructure and unbundle non-core businesses and to simplify their convoluted corporate structure. As with many of their US counterparts, these large corporations appeased the shareholder value movement's demands for higher returns by getting involved in increasing financial activities and speculation in financial markets.

Figure 5 shows that by the early 2000s financial assets as a percentage of fixed capital stock for non-financial corporations in South Africa had grown to 250%. The rapid growth in this ratio which approximately doubled during the 1980s was associated with labour reforms, increasing political unrest and heightened international isolation, as well as the high interest rates that followed adoption of neo-liberal macroeconomic policies. The growth of this ratio by another 50% during the 1990s may be associated with business's response to the democratic changes, further reform of labour legislation, liberalisation of trade and financialisation of the non-financial corporations.

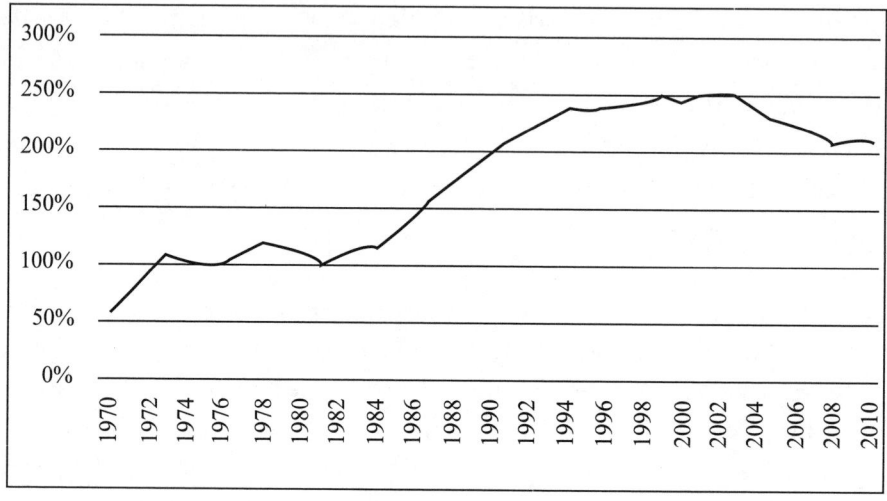

Figure 5: Financial Assets as a Percentage of Fixed Capital Stock for Non-financial Corporations in South Africa: 1970 – 2010

Data Source: Ashman, Mohamed and Newman (2013).

The increasing reliance on finance for income and profits by non-financial corporations and the influence of the shareholder value movement on their behaviour and structure have however further financialised these corporations. The consequence of financialisation has been that the huge growth in acquisition of financial assets relative to fixed assets that started during the 1980s has not only been maintained but has grown more. It has meant that retained profits and growing debt of South African non-financial corporations have been allocated over a long period away from productive investment towards speculative and short-term investments.

The South African financial sector grew in size after the deregulation that started during the 1980s. The growth in demand for financial assets and the emergence of new types of financial institutions and instruments led to growth in size and depth of the financial institutions. The largest banks' business has shifted from intermediation to expansion of credit and increased dealing in financial assets. The policy choices of the post-apartheid government have meant that government was unable to direct current and future savings of households and enterprises away from financial activities towards productive activities.

The financial sector attracted short-term and speculative rather than long-term productive capital from abroad. The short-term capital inflows not only financed a large current account deficit, but these inflows may have actually contributed to the growing trade deficit. The short-term inflows are associated with a growing capital account, because the large portfolio inflows have led to a situation where net factor income transfers within current account have been more than 2% of GDP on average over the last decade. The short-term flows may have helped with the balance of payments but at the expense of productive investment and employment creation. Further, the view that is often heard from government that South Africans do not save enough and that low savings is the cause of poor levels of investment in the economy, has to be challenged. The increase in gross savings was driven by capital inflows from the rest of the world because of South Africa's high interest rates and high returns in capital markets. As I show above, these surges in short-term inflows have increased access to credit and may be the reason that gross domestic savings has stagnated since 2002. Further, it is worth keeping in mind that for most South Africans, low domestic savings is due to poverty and inequality.

Conclusion

The democratic South African Government has continued with the apartheid Government's agenda of adopting neo-liberal macroeconomic and finance policies, including deregulating domestic financial markets and cross-border capital movements. The result has been increased concentration in the South African financial markets, particularly banking, and an economy that has grown increasingly sensitive not only to cross-border capital flows but also the sentiment of developed economy financiers and credit ratings agencies. The financialisation of the economy has not been confined to financial markets and their growing influence over economic policy, but has affected every aspect of South African society through the services and risk management and abatement strategies of households and firms. The largest South African corporations have become financialised through their increasing dependence on capital markets, the role of the shareholder value movement and the increased alignment of executive management with the wishes of the shareholder value movement. The result has been increasing focus on short-term returns, more dependence on financial activities and speculation in financial markets for their profit levels, and in general, a shorter-term perspective on productive investment and labour and skills development.

The period leading up to the crisis showed the influence of increased global financial liquidity and increased speculative foreign capital on the economy. The economic growth rate grew well but in an environment where investment stagnated and unemployment grew. Capital was allocated towards sectors of the economy that benefited from increased debt-driven consumption and financial speculation. The economic growth path of the country has been influenced by the financialisation of the economy and the increased role and influence of finance. The major impact is that the economy has not shifted onto a new growth path where industrialisation has increased and more jobs are available. Instead, the economy has lost capital stock and capacity to further industrialise and has become more dependent on mining and extractive activities. The financial crisis has shown that this economic path is not sustainable.

The macro-economic and financial policy choices of government have made the economy more sensitive to foreign capital flows and the views of the people dominating global financial markets and credit ratings agencies. The economy has become more reliant on short-term capital flows to balance trade deficits. The continued problems of governance in global financial markets and the continued importance of hot money flows around the world means that South Africa will remain vulnerable to the negative impacts associated with deregulated financial markets.

There is a need for the South African government to reassess its macroeconomic and finance policy choices. A shift in their policy would lead to many of the developed country financiers and credit ratings agencies spreading concern about the credibility of South African economic policies and credit ratings downgrades that could push up the costs of capital for South Africa. The new BRICS development Bank, the contingent reserve arrangement and in more general terms increased business with BRICS partners could help with a transition towards a more efficient macroeconomic and financial policy framework in South Africa. The BRICS institutions and partnership could reduce the cost of a shift in South Africa's economic policies that supports the goals of government in addressing the economic legacy of apartheid.

If the South African Government chooses not to changes its macroeconomic and financial policies, the BRICS arrangements and partnerships will be important for helping South Africa cope with increasing volatility in financial markets and the associated macroeconomic risks and fragility of its continued financial openness. However, the prospects of realigning investment and employment creation away from consumption and speculation towards building and deepening the industrial base will be lower. Big business, including the large South African banks and financial institutions, have become financialized and look towards speculation in domestic and global financial markets for increasing their returns.

References

[1] S. Ashman, S. Mohamed and S. Newman, "The financialization of the South African Economy and Its Impact on Economic Growth and Employment", a working paper produced for UNDESA, 2013.

[2] Bloomberg, "Is Standard Bank Too Big to Fail", by Tracy Broziak, August 13, 2010, http://www.moneyweb.co.za/moneyweb-financial/standard-bank-is-too-big-to-fail (downloaded on August 15, 2010).

[3] Gerald Epstein, "Introduction: Financialization and the World Economy", in Gerald Epstein (ed.), *Financialization and the World Economy*, Edward Elgar, Cheltenham and Northampton, 2005.

[4] Ernst and Young, "Mergers and Acquisitions: A Review of Activity for the Year 2001", 2002, available online at http://www.ey.com/ZA/en/Home.

[5] I. Grabel, "Averting crisis? Assessing Measures to Manage Financial Integration in Emerging Economies", presented at the conference on "Financialization of the Global Economy" held by the Political Economy Research Institute (PERI) at the University of Massachusetts, Amherst, December 7 - 8, 2001.

[6] E. Helleiner, *States and the Resurgence of Global Finance: From Bretton Wooods to the 1990s*, Cornell University Press, 1994.

[7] Seeraj Mohamed, "The State of the South African Economy", in R. Southall, D. Pillay, P. Naidoo and J. Daniel (eds.), *New South African Review 1: Development or Decline*, Wits University Press, Johannesburg, 2010.

[8] G. Palma, "The Revenge of the Market on the Rentiers — Why Neo-liberal Reports of the End of History Turned Out to Be Premature", *Cambridge Journal of Economics*, 33(4), 2009, p.829.

[9] United Nations, "Report of the Commission of Experts of the President of the United Nations General Assembly on Reforms of the International Monetary and Financial System", UN Printers, New York, NY., 2009.

Responsive and Innovative Capacity to Promote Governance Modernization in South Africa

Daniel Plaatjies[*]

1. Introduction

The 1994 constitutional democratic state in South Africa not only had to undo the decades of economic, political and social segregation and inequality, but also the complex residues of structural and functional deficiencies in governance and government from the apartheid state. It can be argued that the co-operative governance nature of the constitution was also based on a post-conflict political reconciliation between the races, ethnicities and spatial geography.

The constitutional state and government were consequently tasked with the obligation that brings about structural and functional integration of various provinces (state and municipal governments), including addressing the structural deficiencies of the economy. This paper focuses on the interventions and mechanisms that contributed to effective ways that promotes governance modernisation within the South African state.

The constitutional state established a governance and government system of constitutional law and legislation. These form the foundation of a regulatory and rule-bound system. The constitutional state comprises three autonomous and independent spheres of government — an Executive, Parliament and Judiciary — all deriving power from the constitutional law. In addition, the constitution also establishes a multilayer constitutional state with national (central), provincial and

---

[*] Daniel Plaatjies, the Executive Director at the Human Science Research Council (HSRC).

local governments. These multilayer governments functions essentially in a co-operative "intergovernmental" governance system with multilayer constitutional and legislative administrations of state.

2. Rationale for Governance Modernization

The obligation to respond to constitutional requirements of a social contract between three spheres of government, business and capital interests, civil society organisations and citizens in the government and governance of country. This obligation pushed the government, central government, in particular, to find effective ways to produce social and economic integration and cohesion of citizens that militates against structural inequalities and poverty. The government was also aware that to be effective it needed to respond to social and economic infrastructure led growth and development, including attracting an increase in domestic and foreign direct investments in these infrastructures.

South Africa, in post-apartheid, didn't have the luxury to first establish governance system and thereafter find effective ways promote governance modernization. Both had to be done simultaneously in order to build political and social reconciliation and stability, and to ensure economic continuity. As such further incentives and rationale for effective governance are based on:

• Comprehensive and consolidated response to structural barriers to sustainable development through new institutional and organisational frameworks, structures and systems.

• Improving government and governance that enables improvements in public goods and service delivery through various mechanisms.

• Establishment of new institutions and reorientation of apartheid-oriented institutions to respond to new constitutional order and regime.

• Increasing recognition to respond to polarised nation and differing economic and social needs and demands on the state resources.

• Need to find a durable mix of potential solutions to structural problems in South African society and between the economic elites and the citizens.

- Improving participatory system and structures in the governance of the country for citizens given disenfranchised past in the share of government.
- Increasing ownership and control over global influences over the domestic government and governance and its role into international and world affairs.
- Enhancing and solidifying rule-bound system and structures with predictable outputs and outcomes in policies and legislation, economic governance (especially financial and fiscal management) and improvements in accountability.
- Increasing recognition of an increasing multipolar world order in the interests of citizens and the protection of the sovereignty of country.
- Deliberate and conscious embracement of new knowledge and innovations to improve overall government and governance performance.
- Including, being able to manage the influences and characteristics of economic, political and social performance and governance.

3. Steering Capacity of Central Government

The steering capacity of the central government over the last 20 years driven by different political executive administrations, though the same political party in government, produced a number of innovations and responsive shifts in education, social welfare and protection, and economic policies driven by the narrative of policy changes from the RDP, GEAR, ASGISA, New Growth Path, and the recent National Development Plan. These shifts in institutional and organisational arrangements responded to growing demands on the state post 2009 to create a longer economic, social and political vision and plan for the country. The steering capacity of the 2009 government included changes in the configuration of the central state through the establishment in the Presidency of a National Planning Commission; a Department of Economic Development (economic macro and micro planning) function shifted from National Treasury; and a Department of Performance Monitoring and Evaluation.

In essence these strategic administration changes in the political government and government improved innovations in planning and performance monitoring, including building new systems for effective governance, leadership and management within the central government. Moreover, it delivered:

• New Impact-oriented planning for government through an Outcome-based Priorities (OBPs) System.

• 12 OBPs covering all sectors from social services to national security — an innovative shift from management by objectives (MBOs).

• New strategic plan format for government that's driven by the OBPs System within multi-level planning and governance linked to macroeconomic framework.

• National Development Plan 2030 with a Diagnostic Report (overwhelmingly evidence-based in most instances) that influences and in many ways conditions planning, programming and projects.

• Macroeconomic framework envelopes a multi-years Medium-Term Strategic Framework (MTSF), Medium-Term Expenditure Framework (MTEF), OBPs and Strategic Plans, Medium-Term Budget Policy Statement (MTBPS), National Budget Review, Intergovernmental Fiscal Framework (Division of Revenue).

• All these frameworks contribute to economic and social policy stability within the business of government and governance.

• Performance monitoring and evaluation system exists based on the 12 OBPs in the main, creates a conditions for regulatory impact assessments by the Department of Performance Monitoring and Evaluation (since 2014 the Department of Planning and Performance Monitoring).

4. Vertical and Horizontal Coordination

Policy governance, leadership and management coordination in the business of government, is critical to ensure confidence and an investment in the policy programmes of the government, including enhancing the ability to monitor the collateral impact of various policies and legislation on each other. The South African central government executive policy and programming coordination and management of governance matters by the political Executive (Cabinet) are supported by a Cabinet Clusters System: Social; Economic; Investment and Employment; International Relations and Peace and Security; Justice and Crime Prevention; and Governance and Administration. These clusters operate at national level comprising of appropriate national executive authorities (ministers). In order to strengthen governance and government between the central and provincial governments, a Presidential Coordinating Council, comprising the President and nine Premiers (Governors) of subnational governments (provinces) exits. The Presidential Coordinating Council is also directly supported through other political executive policy coordination of various ministerial councils in the constitutional shared functions between central and subnational governments. These ministerial councils on a central-provincial shared function comprises of national Minister and Member of Executive Councils at provincial governments. The most senior executive administrators in central government departments and the administrative heads of provinces, together form a Forum for Director-Generals referred to as FOSAD.

5. Broader Participation in Governance

Government established the social actors forum of consultation on economic and social development policies, National Economic Development and Labour Council (NEDLAC). There are also open sub-regional and broad-based community forums/meetings between government and citizens (imbizos) convened by the central government executive.

6. Financial Governance and Administration

The constitution establishes the South African Reserve Bank through an Act of Parliament for the Reserve Bank and has the "mandate to achieve and maintain price in the interest of balanced and sustainable economic growth in South Africa". The Reserve Bank has "considerable degree of autonomy in the executive of its duties".

Innovations and modernisation of the fiscal and financial governance of public purse is derived from responsive and increased capacity established through a legislative and regulatory system (rule-bound system). The distribution of funds is annually determined through a national Appropriation Act and a Division of Revenue Act. On the division of revenue and intergovernmental fiscal mandates, the Financial and Fiscal Commission have both constitutional and legislative influence through its advisory role over the approximation of allocations to provincial and local governments.

At various levels of government, that is central, provincial and local government administrations have different financial legislation. Local government legislation includes Municipal Property Rates Act (2004), Municipal Systems Act (2000), Municipal Structures Act (1998), and the Municipal Finance Management Act.

On the other hand, central and provincial government administrations are regulated through Chapter 10 section 195 (values and principles of the Public Service), Public Service Act (1996), Public Finance Management Act (1996), and the Intergovernmental Relations Framework Act (2005).

7. Integrity in Executive and Administrative Governance

Integrity in the constitutional law driven system is critical for effective ways promoting and establishing mechanisms for governance modernisation. In order to ensure executive and administrative accountability, a Ministerial Handbook for the Executive is regularly reviewed to ensure responsive and rule-bound governance of obligations, benefits and incentives for the political executives. This Ministerial Handbook contribution to good governance is enhanced by a Register of Members Interests (members of Parliament), Code of Ethics and Parliamentary Oversight Committees on the Executive and Administration. The overall system of constitutional law governance and government is further enhanced by state, institutions supporting constitutional democracy such as the Auditor-General, Public Protector and SA Human Rights Commission.

8. Outcome Based System

In South Africa, the Outcomes system was introduced in 2009 as a specific innovative orientation to building and establishing a results-oriented approach in government. The purpose, according to the Department of Monitoring and Evaluation (DPME) "was to ensure an outcomes (rather than simply outputs or activities) orientation within government, to focus on a limited number of key strategic priorities of government, and to promote a coordinated whole-of-government approach to achieve these outcomes, going beyond the silos".

In order to assist systems thinking, outcomes model of any type is conceptualized within outcomes theory as a visualized outcomes structure, and presented as a vertical visual hierarchy. (see Figure 1) At the bottom of the hierarchy are the lowest-level actions undertaken by players (inputs or interventions), these then lead up through a set of steps, activities generating outputs, which are linked by causal links to outcomes, and to the highest-level outcomes at the top (impact) of the visual model. It is these highest-level outcomes in the outside world that it is hoped a program or intervention will improve.

The above hierarchy of performance indicators has been well articulated in the DPME in the Guide to the Outcomes Approach (see Version 27, May, 2010). It is stated that outcome planning means planning backwards from the outcome to be achieved, to improve the lives of the people, to work out how best to achieve it, i.e. the outputs that should be produced and the range of activities to achieve the outputs, and what resources will be required to carry out the activities. Planning for outcomes and impact also require identification of the different departments that will carry out specific activities in the results chain (ibid).

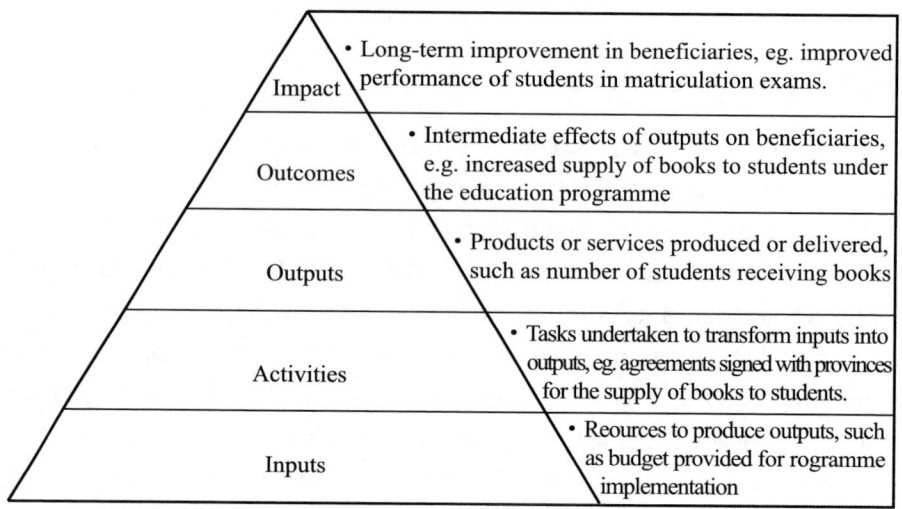

Figure 1: Hierarchy of Performance Indicators and the Results Chain

Source: Based on DPME, "National Evaluation Policy Framework", *The Presidency*, No. 23, 2001, Figure 2, p. 9.

As elaborated in the literature, outcomes system refers to any system which attempts to deal with specifying, prioritizing, justifying, measuring, attributing and/or holding parties to account for changes in outcomes of any type and the steps which lead up to those outcomes. Varieties of outcomes systems include: results management systems, strategic planning systems, performance management systems, performance measurement systems, program evaluation, evidence-based practice systems, investment strategies, value-for-money exercises, benchmarking exercises, contracting for outcomes systems, paying for performance systems, etc. Thus, outcomes theory provides space for conceptualizing the principles which determine the adequacy of such systems, whether or not such systems are well constructed, and allows for making specific recommendations that should improve existing systems in future designs.[1]

In developing the outcomes system in South Africa, the planning system first embarked upon problem analysis to ensure that there was a clear understanding of the problem (from the point of view of the needs and concerns of the intended beneficiaries) and that the plan is relevant and focused on root causes. This was followed by a formulation of a "theory of change", based on the best available knowledge about causes and effects, in order to facilitate the use of evidence from monitoring and evaluation to test the veracity of posited relationships through experience, and to build reliable knowledge based on what works under what conditions. The chain logic in the outcomes system is designed to enable programme management to track progress and test whether the outputs are actually a necessary and sufficient condition to achieve the outcome. Finally, the planning system ensured that at each level of the results chain, clear measurable indicators, baseline and targets were set to facilitate effective progress monitoring and evaluation of results (DPME, December, 2010).

Perhaps a vital but hidden element in the Outcomes system approach is that it is a form human rights based approach (HRBA) to development programming. At the centre of programming, research and analysis in HRBA is the recognition that the need for action should be placed at the provincial, municipality and local government, as well as national levels, if sustainable solutions to development challenges are to be found. If followed in a participatory manner, the exercise should enable communities to build their own capacity, in relation both to themselves and the structures of local government immediately above them. It should enable them to overcome key capacity constraints, leading to effective implementation of programmes. It should also enable local and international development partners to support the government's basic strategy of economic development, social mobilization and community empowerment, thereby creating an effective partnership in pursuit of development.[2]

References

[1] P. Duignan, "What Are Outcomes Systems?" *Outcomes Theory Knowledge Base*, Article No. 216, 2009, http://outcomestheory.wordpress.com/article/what-are-outcomes-systems-2m7zd68aaz774 - 15/.

[2] Urban Jonsson, "Human Rights Approach to Development Programming", UNICEF, 2009.

The EU and the BRICS

Fraser Cameron*

1. Introduction

One of the strangest groupings to enter the world stage in recent years has been the BRICS — the acronym coined in 2001 by Jim O'Neill, Goldman Sachs chief economist, to describe the world's four largest developing economies — Brazil, Russia, India and China (South Africa joined the BRICS in 2010). He suggested that the BRICS were going to shape globalization in the next 50 years, when he predicted they would come to dominate the world economy. He argued that even then (2001) the global economy could no longer be assessed simply with reference to the large advanced economies. Nor could global policy issues, such as currencies, trade imbalances or climate change, continue to be discussed solely by the G7/G8 — the US, Japan, Germany, the UK, France, Italy, Canada (and Russia).

Initially, the four countries chosen by O'Neill had different reactions to the designation. There was delight in Russia, bafflement in China, cynicism in Brazil and indifference in India. South Africa lobbied hard to become the sole representative from the African continent. Now, the countries are using the idea to forge tentative links. There are annual summits, ministerial meetings and a small growth industry in publications about the BRICS.

The BRICS all agree that the US/EU should not be so dominant in the world economy. The cohesive factor is a common interest in promoting

---

* Fraser Cameron, the Director of the EU – Asia Centre in Brussels.

changes in the global landscape. They object to Western unilateral action in political/security affairs — but are quiet when one of their own members annexes a neighbour (Russia/Crimea). They seek greater influence in the IMF and other bodies. The BRICS grouping thus creates a space that promotes the relevance of each of its members, but it is not a cohesive grouping in major political, security, economic or trade issues.

The EU has strategic partnerships with all BRICS countries. It has not so far recognized the BRICS as a group and there is no pressure to do. Brussels does not consider the BRICS capable of acting together on any major global issue. This paper examines the rise of the BRICS, assesses similarities and differences between the BRICS, especially on governance, and considers how the EU reacts to the BRICS individually and collectively.

2. The Rise (and Fall?) of the BRICS

The rise of the BRICS is linked to their dramatic growth rates in recent years. Their share of world output has doubled in the past decade, from 7.5% to 15%. Their shares of global population (42%) and territory are even higher. China and India are by far the world's two most populous countries, with 1.39 bn and 1.27 bn inhabitants respectively. Compared with the Asian giants, Brazil, with 202 m, Russia, with 142 m, and South Africa, with 53 m, are minnows. (the EU has 500m and the US 322 m)

China is by far the dominant BRICS in terms of the economy. Its share in world output at purchasing power parity raised from 8% in 1980 to 16.5% in 2013. China's share of BRICS output was around 53% in 2013, up from 42% in 1990. Neither Brazil nor Russia achieved a significant rise in their share of world GDP over the past two decades. Even India's rise was modest-up from 4% in 1990 to 6% in 2009. The story, then, has been of the rise of the two Asian giants and especially of China. Yet the notion of the BRICS does capture the reality of a shift in economic power away from the old developed countries, particularly Western Europe and Japan, to "emerging countries". The recent financial crisis has accelerated this change.

Compared to the EU and US, China and India have survived the financial crisis almost unscathed. In the past five years China's economy grew by 8.5% annually and India's by 6.6%. But Brazil, Russia and South Africa have experienced much more modest growth. The slowdown is continuing in all the BRICS in 2014.

Can the BRICS impart dynamism to the world as a whole? The answer is not clear. In 2013 the GDP of the BRICS was over 30% of global GDP, but most growth comes from China. The BRICS are not playing the "locomotive" role that other countries have played in the past. Most growth comes inside the BRICS. The net stimulus to demand imparted to the rest of the world depends on a decline in their trade surpluses or rise in their deficits.

China is now the "workshop of the world" — a high-investment, high-growth behemoth, with a powerful competitive position in manufacturing. The country's economy is also far more open than that of India: in 2013, the ratio of merchandise trade to China's gross domestic product was 67%, compared with 32% for India. India is relatively stronger in skill-intensive services: the ratio of trade in services to GDP was 15%, against 7% for China. Brazil has a far more closed economy than either of the Asian giants, with a ratio of merchandise exports to GDP of a mere 22% in 2013 and a ratio of service exports to GDP of 5%. Half of its exports were of food and raw materials. In 2013, manufactures made up less than a fifth of Russia's exports. It is an exporter of fuels and minerals.

But trends are not inevitable and governance problems could well mean that these remarkable growth rates falter. The problems facing China and Russia today are potentially the most troubling for the rest of the world. In China's case it is the risk that an economic slowdown could turn into something more damaging. With Russia, it's the possible economic fallout from the conflict in Ukraine. The sanctions imposed by the west, and the anxiety among investors that there might be more, have aggravated a slowdown that was coming anyway. Some $85 billion has been pulled out of Russia this year.

Like Russia, Brazil is an economy where commodities exports have played an important role in the successes of the 2000s. In Russia it was oil and gas. Brazil has iron ore and agricultural commodities such as soya, coffee and sugar. While all the Brics have slowed this decade, the weakest performers now are Brazil and Russia. Their average growth rates have been below the Asian Brics all along and this year they slowed even further. For 2014 as a whole, the IMF has projected only very little growth for those two — 0.3% for Brazil and 0.2% for Russia.

It is also worth putting these figures into context. For example, the UK exports more to Belgium than the BRICS. The US invests more in Benelux than BRICS. The EU exports more to Switzerland than BRICS. The transatlantic economic, trade and investment relationship is still the most important in the world.

3. Governance

The BRICS are plagued by corruption, poor governance and lack of agreed regulatory rules. They all face massive internal problems, especially huge inequalities and poverty. Some BRICS leaders, e.g. Xi and Modi, recognize the problem and have made it political priority, but some Putin, Zuma, Rousseff have been less keen to highlight the problem of corruption. In the 2013 Transparency International Corruption Index all the BRICS rank very high (SA 72/177, Brazil 74, China 80, India 94, Russia 127). In the latest Legatum Governance Index the BRICS also fare badly (SA 54/150, India 56, Brazil 63, China 66, Russia 113).

Apart from massive corruption, the BRICS also face many other governance problems ranging from the quality of thebureaucracy, lack of infrastructure, absence of rule of law, independent media, regulatory oversight, competition, quality of education, skilled workers, etc. Where is the BRICS Google/Apple/Facebook? Too much of the economy in all of the BRICS is controlled by the state with adverse consequences for markets and the environment. The World Bank estimates that China loses half its growth due to the appalling environmental damage caused to the country.

4. How Cohesive Are the BRICS?

The centre of gravity of the world may be tilting from the US and Europe to Asia, accelerated by the financial crisis, but the new global order is unlikely to pivot around the BRICS. Three democracies, a democracy with authoritarian leanings and an outright authoritarian state cannot rally around the "shared values" that such gatherings like to espouse.

India and China are strategic competitors as much as allies. India is nervous of China's military rise and what some in New Delhi regard as Beijing's ambitions to encircle India with a string of strategically placed ports. Russia is a big resource exporter, China an insatiable importer. That could be complementary. Yet Russia watches with alarm as China steals a march on grabbing African resources, and jealously guards its influence in central Asia. Brazil is in less fierce competition with the other three. But it is also on the wrong side of the world. South Africa is simply too small to make a difference.

Yet it would be wrong to be cynical. Other groups, too, are riddled with contradictions and competing objectives. The global financial crisis does provide an opportunity to challenge a world order too long dominated by rich countries often serving their own interests. The BRICS are right to demand a greater say in bodies where Europe is over-represented, such as the UN and IMF. They are right, too, to contemplate alternatives to the world's overdependence on the dollar.

5. Differences

It is debatable whether the BRICS have anything more in common than their size and economic potential. The structures of the five economies are very different, with Brazil specializing in agriculture, Russia and South Africa in commodities, India in services and China in manufacturing. Their experience of the global recession has been equally variable. It is a very diverse grouping. Its unifying criteria are high economic growth, a certain economic backwardness and large size.

In economic development, Russia is superior to the other BRICS. In 2013, Russian GDP per capita was $14 612, still more than twice that of China (6 807). Goldman Sachs forecasts that Russia will be the only BRICS country to approach European per capita income levels by 2050. Russia's higher income level is also evident in superior social indicators. In most regards, Russia is slightly more advanced than Brazil but head and shoulders above China and India. Most impressively, more than 2/3 of Russians of university age are enrolled in university, compared with less than 1/5 of the Chinese. In terms of education, Russia matches the West. The differences with the BRICS in consumption are also great. There are 7 times more cars in stock per capita in Russia than in China in 2013 (233 per 1000 people compared to 34 in China).

Until the Ukraine crisis, one could argue that in many ways Russia was already converging with the West. It is more in line with the EU than other BRICS on issues such as support for the UN and climate change. And it has about half of its reserves in Euros.

Nor is there a single model of economic management that the BRICS espouse and want to propagate. Indeed, there are wide and growing contrasts between, say, the moves towards a social democratic market economy in Brazil, buttressed by fiscal orthodoxy, and the increasingly authoritarian politicised intervention in Russia. In the Doha Round of WTO global trade talks, where India and Brazil have been in a core negotiating group, they have battled to put together a comprehensive negotiating position. Brazil's interests as a highly competitive agricultural exporter have clashed with India's wish to protect its small farmers

Yet aside from the long-running debate about giving developing countries more votes in the IMF, it has proved hard to hammer out a substantive set of subjects on which the disparate BRICS countries have the same interests. They have already had to drop the subject of exchange rates. The differences in India's and China's approaches to industry and the wider culture gap between the neighbours could hardly be greater. China has a single-minded focus on productivity and economic growth that India may never match, while India has a democratic, civil and legal culture that its neighbour is unlikely to grasp.

But it is the tensions between the BRICS countries, which are usually swept under the carpet, that are likely to prevent substantive agreements. Trade disputes have been common among the five. Brazil has had disputes over market access with both Russia and China, and its strategy of seeking full liberalisation of agricultural trade in the Doha trade talks has come up against India's insistence on protection for its rice farmers. Indian and China covet Russia's natural resources, particularly its oil and gas. As an old friend of Moscow, New Delhi has had some limited success in accessing Russian energy reserves, but China has greater spending power.

Politics, too, separates the BRICS as much as it unites them. India, China and Russia are all in the same neighbourhood and are all nuclear powers while Brazil and South Africa, neither nuclear powers, are on another continent and have almost no trade with Russia and little with India. Meanwhile, much of the highly militarised border between China and India is still disputed and the two sides have fought a number of wars over this territory. China and Russia have fought a couple of border wars as recently as the late 1960s and have struggled for decades to get along.

Chinese academics and policymakers, as well as the general public, believe China has far outstripped the other members of this artificial country bloc. Goldman Sachs reckons that China may well become the world's largest economy before 2030. Collectively, the BRICS economies could well surpass output in the G7 countries which have dominated the management of the global economy by 2032. The BRICS already have a bigger share of world trade than the US. China, the world's biggest goods exporter in 2008, has been supplemented by India's software and back-office exports, Russia's oil and gas and the domination of a number of agricultural commodity markets by Brazil's super-competitive farmers.

So as the world emerges from recession, is this a transformational moment when the centre of gravity in the global economy and its governance decisively shifts? Is this a pivot point such as the second world war, where the confident, innovative US muscled aside the weakened, debt-laden economies of Europe and remade the global financial architecture? And, most immediately, are BRICS consumers up to the task of rebalancing the world economy by supplanting their acquisitive American counterparts?

The most likely answer is: not yet. Not only are the BRICS such a disparate group that almost any generalisation is problematic, but China, the dominant member of the quartet, still seems wedded to an economic model dependent on demand elsewhere. The BRICS might almost have been chosen for their disparate abilities rather than their similarities. China's size and openness to trade give it as much economic clout as the rest put together. India, similar in population but poorer and economically more insular, is chiefly notable to investors and trading partners for its software and business services. Brazil, despite a sprinkling of manufacturers, remains one of the world's most efficient agro-exporters; Russia, after feebler attempts to diversify, essentially just sells oil and gas. South Africa, with its high levels of unemployment and inequality and others issues linked to them such as crime, damage investment and growth.

A Chinese growth model based on heavy investment and exports has accompanied vast current-account surpluses across East Asia, matched by a current-account deficit in the US. And despite doing its bit to keep economic growth going during the crisis, it is far from clear that the middle kingdom has effected a shift towards consumer demand that a true engine of world growth would achieve. With a great flourish, Beijing announced a huge stimulus package during the financial crisis and loosened bank credit. But its ability to create self-sustaining growth was suspect. Rather than handing out cash to consumers to get them spending — a move that might also have encouraged imports — a large chunk of the stimulus went into the old favourite, fixed investment.

Despite pockets of profligacy, if anything, China's has become less rather than more of a consumer economy in the past decade. Its overall savings rate grew over the decade. Although much of this rise reflected corporate savings, household savings rose, too, and a greater share of national income went to companies rather than consumers in the first place. The lack of a social safety net is one of the main reasons that

Chinese households save: for educational needs, security in case of illness and caring for parents. Changing deep-seated structural factors such as this will not be quick. Nor will it be achieved simply by letting the renminbi rise.

As for the other BRICS, whose trend growth rate is slower than China's, they are unlikely to have a noticeable effect on global demand for some time. Although growth in Brazil and India held up well during the crisis, the former is a relatively mature economy with less scope for rapid growth; the latter, an underperformer with a chronic public finance problem and a household savings rate even higher than China's. Meanwhile, Russia, whose economy contracted sharply during the global recession, still depends on oil prices and South Africa whose economy is fragile, struggles to avoid recession.

6. EU Attitudes

A decade of rapid growth is not enough for the BRICS to seize the baton of global economic leadership from the US and Western Europe. The grouping, or some of them, may have astonished the world with their progress over the past 10 years. But it will require a qualitative improvement as well as more growth to consolidate that shift of power.

The EU sees no reason to deal with the BRICS as a grouping, and this is unlikely to change in the foreseeable future. The EU is negotiating major new agreements with three of the BRICS — Russia, China and India, although all negotiations with Russia are suspended because of Ukraine. The EU has agreements with Brazil and South Africa. With China there are disputes on the economic, trade and political fronts. There are differences of opinion on whether China has lived up to its WTO commitments in areas such as intellectual property rights and on whether there is a level playing field for European investors. The talks on a new investment agreement will be an important bellwether of Chinese attitudes. The negotiations with India have stalled on the trade front over issues, such as market access for services and environmental and social standards.

7. Conclusion

The BRICS are a very loose grouping which enjoy banding together to demonstrate the rise of the emerging powers vis-à-vis the US and Europe. There has been a steady increase in the number of meetings at all levels with a mix of emphasis on political-security and economic issues. But their many disparities and policy differences mean that there is little prospect of the BRICS developing into a coherent body in terms of political, security or economic issues. The two most noteworthy developments have been agreement on a New Development Bank and on the Contingent Reserve Arrangement. But these developments are at an early stage and it will some time to assess their impact.

The BRICS have not sought formal relations with any outside body, and given the above differences, it would be a meaningless effort if they did. As for the EU, it has not regarded the BRICS as a grouping with which it can engage in any worthwhile policy issue. This is unlikely to change in the future. At the same time, it needs to pay attention to the BRICS and seek to deepen relations with the individual members. Ensuring that each BRICS member views the EU as an important strategic partner is the best way to counter any BRICS developments that could be harmful to EU interests.

Crisis Management and Risk Prevention in BRICS Countries' Modernization Process
— Observations about India

Klaus Voll[*]

I will concentrate to a large extent on the "case-study India", but also permit myself some references to the bilateral relationship between India and China.

In my opinion, it is important to develop a clear understanding of the respective power-systems and their inner dynamics in the various BRICS countries. It would be desirable, if this conference could approach this task to a certain extent on the basis of the existing country-specific expertise and perhaps develop a kind of theoretical approach for the different proto-types of governmental systems in the five countries.

The organizers speak of "modernization processes", yet without saying more precisely, what they exactly mean by that. I prefer the premises of a "critical theory of modernization", which has been developed by the Bolivian political scientist H. C. Felipe Mansilla. It combines modernization with elements of critical and emancipative country-specific approaches, based on insights of social sciences. Only in a historical and reconstructive manner, the various evolutionary stages of a country can be adequately presented and afterwards different scenarios about developmental processes assessed.

It is naturally not possible to analyze the risk-prevention and crisis-management with regard to often uncoordinated modernization processes. Who are the real actors, who steers these processes with

---

* Klaus Voll, the Advisor on Asia to the Foundation for European Progressive Studies (FEPS) in Brussels.

corresponding objectives? Is this only the state or do private economic actors, as well as civil society groups, play an essential role?

1. Some Relevant Data of the Mega-society (societies) of the Indian Union

Population in 2014: About 1.27 billion. people, compared to China with currently 1.37 billion. India will overtake China in 2028 with 1.45 billion. as the most populous nation in the world. For 2050 a population of 1.6 bn. for India and 1.3 billion. for China are forecast. In India, the population will have increased by nearly five times within a hundred years since independence in 1947, with repercussions for the ecological balance.

Yet, population control by the state is in India politically not possible. Therefore, the demographic advantage could turn into a "demographic curse", given the huge amounts of unemployable youth.

Each year, about 12 million people are entering the Indian labor-market, which is already characterized by mass unemployment. How can this demand be met under widely prevailing conditions of "jobless growth"?

Secessionist groups within the Indian Union are existing in Jammu & Kashmir as well as in India's Northeast. They use force and terrorist means. Autonomy-seeking groups within the parameters of the Indian Union operate by and large peaceful. The Indian state succeeded in its history to fight militarily secessionist movements, to co-opt them into the ruling class or respectively to grant them autonomy.

In various parts of the country, armed groups are operating under the leadership of the Communist Party of India (Maoist).

2. Social Trends

The Indian caste system is reducing its impact gradually ("silent revolution"), nevertheless one can still observe a dominance of the traditional upper castes, who represent a minority of the population of about 17% to 18%. These traditional caste-hierarchies can even be traced within religious minorities.

In built "structural force", particularly against "Dalits" — "oppressed" or so-called "untouchables", numbering about 160 millions — and "Adivasis" — "original inhabitants" or so-called "tribals" — (a term unthinkable in independent Africa) — numbering about 100 millions, has gradually to be eliminated as part of a tremendous nation-building process. At the same time, cultural emancipation of the oppressed and disadvantaged sections is an urgent task.

Although the Gini Index for China is higher than in India, there are in both countries a growing number of people owning incomes as $-billionaires and a concentration of wealth, besides the growing numbers of middle classes.

Inclusiveness and social equity are difficult to achieve, if large parts of the population have no or only an insufficient access to the labor market and/or are living below the so-called poverty-line. The widening income-gaps and the high expectations with regard to the promises of India's new government, particularly amongst the youth, have to be adequately met, otherwise frustrations could lead to increasing social conflicts.

India definitely requires more productive investments in society, like health and education.

3. Strengthening of Democratic Structures

India looks back, except for a short period between 1975 to 1977, to an uninterrupted democratic development. Yet, the massive anti-corruption movement in 2011/12 demonstrated the remarkable deficits of India's democracy.

Phenomena like systemic corruption, country-wide political dynasties as well as plutocratic and even criminal tendencies in the political class undermine the quality of Indian democracy. A lack of real internal democracy can be observed across parties. This could lead to increased pressure and thinking about true reforms.

Regionally and locally one can observe the emergence and existence of counter-elites. The anti-corruption movement in 2011/12 questioned the very existence and legitimacy of the political class.

Since years one can observe, that the electorate votes out governments, but confirms on the other hand through re-election those who deliver "good governance". It is important to ensure, that not only 15% of the development funds reach the target-groups, like in the past, but ideally the full amount ("direct cash transfers").

The socialist parties have disappeared and the Communists are in terminal decline. Yet, there is an unoccupied space for an enlightened left and social-democratic movement inIndia.

The preference for pluralism versus the temptation of "majoritarianism" will be an essential corner-stone for the social integration of various sub-nationalisms, ethnic and religious groups.

To a certain extent, India represents politically an anti-thesis to China. But it has to be seen, if a renewal from within the democratically legitimized post-colonial State Class (Hartmut Elsenhans) is really possible in India.

4. Economic Priorities

China's Gross Domestic Product is nearly five times the size of India's. Yet, a large part of the Indian economy is molded by the so-called "black economy".

India possesses a huge internal market. With the opening towards the world economy in 1991, international capital entered increasingly the country. The new government is trying to attract with the slogan "Make in India" foreign direct investment in several sectors of the economy (infrastructure, insurance, defense production etc.) and wants especially to expand the manufacturing sector.

It's immense and to a large degree unused human resources, not the least because of insufficient vocational training, have to be constructively used ("dual system"), in order to improve above all infrastructure and the energy sector. The *Swachh Bharat* ("Clean India") campaign is intended to change dramatically the hygienic conditions.

The modernization process requires a strategy to transit from an agrarian economy, with wide-spread symptoms of agrarian distress ("farmer suicides"), to employment generation.

5. Differences between India and China

India is located in a highly complicated region with several crisis centers in South and West Asia. This leads to very high military expenditures, since, at least theoretically, a two frontier war with China and Pakistan cannot be fully ruled out. Currently India is worldwide the biggest importer of weapons. Pakistan follows a strategy of "a thousand cuts" with terrorist inroads, in order to bleed India.

The big bilateral trade between India and China suffers from a huge and in the long-term not sustainable Indian trade-deficit.

As utopian as it might sound still today, India has allegedly the potential, to outflank China and become after several decades the largest economy in the world.

6. Perspectives

The alleged admission of India as a full member into the Shanghai Cooperation Organization (SCO) would be certainly welcome. Such steps and further confidence-building measures as well as increasing civil societal contacts could, 62 years after the India-China border war, reduce the still existing caution and trust deficit in India vis-à-vis China. There are consultations between both countries with regard to Afghanistan and Central Asia as well as an exchange of data with regard to the water levels of the Brahmaputra (Chinese: Yalu Zangbu Jiang or in Tibetan Tsangpo).

China's silk-route and maritime silk-route initiatives are followed with great interest in India. The intention of China to invest $ 25 billion. during the next five years in India — Japan intends $ 30 billion. and the US allegedly $ 40 billion — can only improve the further engagement between both economies.

How can India and China improve their relationship in a constructive and non-antagonistic manner? Such questions should form a part of constructive bilateral dialogues as well as between various sections of the elites from BRICS countries. The former Indian Prime Minister Dr. Manmohan Singh claimed, that there is sufficient space for the simultaneous and peaceful rise of China and India at the international stage with its challenges to prevent dramatic climate change, nuclear proliferation and terrorism.

Can the BRICS states create an alternative and sustainable development model for their societies, which learns from the mistakes of Western development and set positive socio-political and ecological accents? Based on visions for their societies, concerted reforms are an essential requirement, definitely in India but certainly also in all the other BRICS countries.

Risk prevention and crisis management are therefore a sine qua non both internally and internationally between the BRICS countries in the years to come.

Governance in South Africa after Apartheid

Arnold Wehmhoerner*

1. Introduction

This article is a contribution to governance modernization in BRICS countries. It describes the achievements and constrains for good governance in South Africa after the end of apartheid. Considering the principle of non-interference in internal matters among BRICS countries, it serves as a description of developments in South Africa and does not intend to serve as an example for other countries. The exchange of views on governance, however, might help other countries to better analyze their own developments. The author in the second part of the article tries to analyze how unwanted governance developments could be corrected within an existing political system, in this case a parliamentary democracy. Governance modernization and improvement in South Africa through technical means like for example training and control is dealt with in another article.[1]

2. The Outset: South Africa after Apartheid

The Republic of South Africa has one of the most modern and liberal constitutions in the world. After apartheid the country went through five national and provincial elections which were all even by the highest standards free and fair. The judiciary rules independently according to the laws and the media is free and very critical. With the office of the Public Protector, the country has an independent watchdog which

---

* Arnold Wehmhoerner, Correspondent for Southern Africa of the Foundation for European Progressive Studies (FEPS).

fearlessly uncovers corruption up to the highest office, the Presidency.

South Africa's governing elite of the ruling African National Congress (ANC) consists mainly of party cadres who under threat to their lives fought for the liberation of their country from apartheid what required a high degree of moral integrity. Most of them were in exile where they received tertiary education and developed a cosmopolitan view of the world. With Nelson Mandela they had a leader who showed the way to peaceful reconciliation and to a non-racist society.

Considering the political system and the background of its elite, South Africa has ideal pre-conditions for successful governance. The country needs this because the post-apartheid government faced a tremendous uphill task namely to lift the majority of the former discriminated black population out of poverty. The demands for housing, education and jobs were overwhelming and obviously would need efforts that would last longer than one generation. The dilemma the elite faced was either to keep most of the former white apartheid administration or to replace them with new but often inexperienced black comrades. The demand for new black administrators and politicians by far outstretched the available capacities because beside the national government also the newly created nine provincial administrations needed to be filled with capable women and men.

3. Achievements and Constrains

The ANC government felt politically compelled to transform the racial composition of the administration even if shortcomings were to be expected. A change that would need at least one circle of tertiary education and training to achieve was pushed through within a short period. In November 2013 the Auditor General at a press conference presented his consolidated 2011/12 report and stated that only 5% of local governments received a clean audit. Despite some positive pattern in comparison to the previous report irregular expenditure increased by 33% for public entities.[2] The Co-operative Governance Minister said in October 2014 that regrettably out of 278 chief financial officers in all municipalities 170 of them were not qualified. He added that 1/3 of the municipalities are dysfunctional.[3] 25 years after the ANC government took over the above quoted figures indicate that the transformation has not been completed and that there is obviously a strong need for continuous improvements in financial management, the key to good governance and a precondition to avoid corruption.

The performance of the new administration regarding the improvement of the living conditions of the majority of the black population is evaluated contrarily depending on whether such verdict is given by the opposition or by the government. Judging from the nearly daily often violent service delivery protests all over the country, the efforts of the government seem to have not been very successful. It is estimated that there are roughly 300 incidents of community protests a year in South Africa[4] and at least 43 protesters were killed by the police in the last 10 years.[5]

Table 1 gives some indication of the achievements and failures. In most categories improvements can be noted, especially with adult literacy, school enrolment, access to water and sanitation. Social welfare support now reaches 15 million people and this is responsible for the fact that the proportion of South Africans living on less than $2 per day has declined from 18% in 2000 to just 2.7% in 2011. Worrying is the worsening life expectancy at birth. The increase in HIV prevalence was to be expected because the new government took over just as the epidemic reached its peak. The continuously high unemployment rate reflects the shrinking of the manufacturing sector while the rising Gini Index points to the fact that the economic gains of the country are not distributed fairly. The fall in the Human Development Index (HDI) ranking could be interpreted that in comparison to other countries South Africa did not fare that well.

Frans Cronje from the Institute of Race Relations believes that, "There is no contradiction between the successes we identify and the protests that are commonplace around the country. These protests are not a function of the failure of delivery but rather in that this success has raised expectations that cannot be met because of shortcomings in the school system and the labour market."[7]

Table 1: Performance of Key Socio – economic Indicators in South Africa (1990 – 2012)[6]

	1990	1994	2000	2006	2009	2010	2011	2012	
Life expectancy at birth (years)①	62	61	55	51	52				15.4% points worse
Under five mortality rate (per 1000)①	62.3‰	60.9‰	74.1‰	75.8‰	61.3‰		46.7‰		25% points better
Adult literacy①	76.2%		84.8%			89.3%			13.1% points better
School enrolment, secondary (% gross)①	66.1%	79.7%	85.3%	95.0%	93.8%				27.7% points better
Access to improved water source* ①	83%	83%	86%	90%	91%	91%			8% points better
Access to improved sanitation** ①	71%	72%	75%	77%	79%	79%			8% points better
HIV prevalence①	0.5%	0.8%	14.8%	17.3%	17.2%	17.3%	17.3%		16.8% points worse
HDI rank (emerging markets)			107				123		16 places worse
People living on less than 2 $/day②			18%	10.5%	6.3%	4.4%	2.7%		15.3% points better
Unemployment rate, official②			20%	26.7%	23.1%	23.6%	25.7%	24.9%	4.9% points worse
Gini Index①				57.77%	67.4%	63.14%			6.6% points worse

Data Source: ① World Bank Group; ② South African Institute of Race Relations.
* Tap or pump
** Protected pit latrines or flush toilets

The material conditions of all South Africans have improved but the service delivery protests will continue, because too many people are still living in poverty and the huge gap between the rich and the poor is obvious everywhere in the country. The centres of the protests are the townships and informal settlements to which people from rural areas continuously move to. The proportion of the urban population increased from 52% in 1990 to over 65% in 2014.[8] A black middle class has formed. But that new class is heavily relying on the public sector which has been increased by 20% between 1998 and 2011.[9] This increase in the public sector went along with rising salaries. The government budget is further stressed by social welfare payments to every third South African. Considering South Africa's low economic growth rates of around 2% in recent years, it is obvious that this policy cannot be continued.

4. Increase of Corruption

South Africa's fall into corruption started with the arms deal when French, British and German companies bribed the new government into buying sophisticated war planes, submarines and frigates which the country does not need. The perceived failures and impunity at the top of the governing party seem to have triggered corruption at all levels of government. Especially difficult to track are the so called "tenderpreneurs", politicians who through straw men or family members are involved in companies which tender for government contracts. Under the "Black Economic Empowerment" scheme, black owned companies get preferences in tender processes. The legal obligation of elected politicians① to make public their business interests does not seem to make a difference. On the Corruption Perceptions Index of Transparency International, South Africa dropped within 3 years 18 places. In 2010 the country was ranked 54th out of 178 countries, and in 2013, 72nd out of 177 countries.②

The Secretary General Zwelinzima Vavi of South Africa's largest trade union federation, COSATU, criticised on several occasions publicly the

---

① Executive Code of Ethics and Code of Conduct for Assembly Members which require statements on conflicts of financial or business interests.

② www. transparency. org.

government's lack of determination to fight corruption. In a report to the June 2011, COSATU central committee meeting Vavi states that after the Polokwane congress of the ANC 2007 when Zuma was elected party president, we have seen "the emergence of a powerful, corrupt, predatory elite, combined with a conservative populist agenda"[10]. Although this statement is not shared by all member unions of the federation, it is still a strong indication for the seriousness of the problem.

5. Internal Corrective Control

If constitutional institutions like the National Prosecution Authority or the Office of the Public Protector are not able or are prevented from fighting corruption efficiently, one has to look at the political dimension in a parliamentary democracy. Either the electorate through elections could defeat a corrupt government or the governing party itself could bring about the necessary changes from inside.

At this year's May elections, the ANC continued to lose votes, but moderately as in past elections: 3.8% from 2004 to 2009 and 3.7% from 2009 to 2014. The scandals surrounding the party and their continuous reflection in the press did not deter ANC supporters. The emotional link to the liberation party is still strong. In many township voting stations, the ANC achieved more than 75% and even in the township Bekkersdal where this year violent anti-ANC protests took place, the party won 80%. One commentator writes: "It is an incredible indictment that South Africa's townships would ratherdisenfranchise themselves than support alternatives to the ANC."[11] Under these circumstances, it is obvious that the governing elite at present do not have to fear punishment by the electorate for corruption or non-prosecution of corruptive officials.

The ANC itself seems to be incapable of asserting a corrective influence. To become a member of the ANC during apartheid when the party was banned was connected with personal risks. This was a natural positive filter for the caliber and convictions of party members. Since the Polokwane Congress in 2007, the membership of the party grew from slightly more than 620 000 to more than 1.2 million. Today many join the party in order to have access to jobs in public institutions. The moral decline was facilitated by the deployment of many inexperienced cadres into high government positions also as a result of affirmative action who then worked on patronage networks instead of exerting the necessary administrative skills and controls. This patronage policy has changed the soul of the ANC and has eroded the party's core values.

In traditional societies especially with high unemployment, the individual's wellbeing and that of his family depends on the support of the extended family, his clan or his tribe. In such paternalistic societies, the obligation towards the supporting family, clan or tribe is more important than the adherence to the legal system. Nepotism in such surroundings of strong social obligations is often not seen to be a crime. It seems that in South Africa traditional patterns of paternalistic behavior are on the advance in the public sector.

6. Conclusion

The South African government faced a very difficult task after the first non-racial elections in 1994. The living conditions of the majority of the former discriminated black population had to be lifted with a new and inexperienced administration. Not unexpectedly this led to short comings in the implementation of government policies and to a lack of control which opened opportunities for corruption. The fight against corruption is made difficult by the increase of traditional patterns of paternalistic behavior and by political interference with prosecution and watch-dog institutions. If this continues, the only correction could come through elections, but the political elite at present do not have to fear defeat at elections, because the emotional link of the electorate to the ANC — the party of liberation — is still strong.

References

[1] Daniel Plaatjies: "Responsive and Innovative Capacity to Promote Governance Modernization in South Africa", see p. 539 in this book.

[2]"Mail and Guardian", online, November 13, 2013.

[3]Siyabonga Mkhwanazi, "Fire Unqualified Municipal Finance Officers: Gordhan", *Daily News*, October, 7, 2014.

[4]Ebrahim Fakir, "Protests Are a Cry for Political Recognition", *Mail & Guardian*, mg.co.za, August, 29, 2014.

[5] Max du Preez,"Service delivery's ANC's Achilles Heel", *Pretoria News*, October 14, 2014.

[6] Richard Callend,"The Zuma Years", *Cape Town*, 2013, p.14.

[7]South African Institute of Race Relations, *Press Release*, September 11,2012.

[8] Max du Preez, "Service delivery's ANC's Achilles heel", *Pretoria News*, October 14, 2014.

[9] Richard Callend, "The Zuma Years", *Cape Town*, 2013, p. 416.

[10] COSATU Secretary-general, "Secretariat Report to the 5th COSATU Central Committee 2011", p. 10, in Richard Calland, *The Zuma Years*, Cape Town, 2013, p211.

[11] Vukani Mde,"Election Winners and Losers", *Sunday Independent*, November, 5, 2014.

Assessing BRICS's Contribution to Global Governance: An Outsider's Perspective

Alice Ekman[*]   Françoise Nicolas[**]

1. Introduction

Over the past decade or so, economic power has been shifting very rapidly, and once dominant powers such as the United States are now in competition with a number of newly emerging (or re-emerging) economies which happen to be primarily located in Asia (China and India). As aptly put by the US National Intelligence Council, "In terms of size, speed and directional flow, the transfer of wealth and economic power now under way — roughly from West to East — is without precedent in modern history." (National Intelligence Council, 2008) While the shift of economic power has been under way for some time already, the 2008 global financial crisis (GFC) was arguably a watershed moment when a number of structural weaknesses in once dominant powers, especially the United States, came to the fore, thus further enhancing the clout and influence of the newly emerging countries.

The aforementioned shift in economic power distribution has been accompanied in the emerging countries by a growing sense of dissatisfaction with the existing governance structures inherited from the post WWII period and deemed unrepresentative of the new economic balance of power. Here again, the 2008 GFC was a key moment because it clearly exposed the inefficiency of international financial governance mechanisms, highlighting further the inadequacy of the post WWII

---

[*] Alice Ekman, Research Fellow of French Institute of International Relations (Ifri).
[**] Françoise Nicolas, the Head of Centre for Asian Studies of Ifri.

economic and political governance framework. This rising discontent paved the way for more forceful calls for reform.

Among the "rising powers", a small group sticks out: These are the so-called BRIC (Brazil, Russia, India and China) after an expression coined for the first time in 2001 by Jim O'Neill, an economist with Goldman Sachs. These four large countries were expected to become heavy weight players in the world economy.

At first, the BRIC were thought to be merely a catchy acronym with little substance and little potential to change the prevailing world order. Some ten years later, however, there is definitely more substance behind the acronym coined by an outside observer, and the BRICS (now including South Africa) have emerged as a relatively well-structured group with a clear vision and agenda on a number of important issues. The 2008 GFC was again a watershed moment for the BRICS which started questioning the primacy of the Western powers in global governance structures. In the wake of the GFC, the BRICS have apparently shifted from being an economic reality to a political grouping. As a result, the BRICS are likely to contribute to the overhaul of the global governance infrastructures and the conclusion reached a couple of years ago by researchers such as Beausang – Hunter (2012) as to the BRICS's inability to rule the world may no longer be valid.

The aim of the paper is to offer an updated analysis, from an outsider's perspective, of the potential role of the BRICS in global governance structures. To that end, the paper will combine the approaches of an economist and of a political scientist so as to cover as many facets as possible of global governance mechanisms. A major issue to be examined is whether the BRICS will challenge the existing governance structures or get integrated into them.

The paper is organized as follows: the second section provides some background facts based on a statistical overview of the rise of the BRICS; the third section examines how the BRICS have managed to influence global economic and political governance structures over the past few years and assesses their potential motivations and objectives; the fourth section highlights the challenges they will be facing in this endeavor.

2. Why BRICS Matter for Global Governance

The BRICS matter because they are large and (until recently) fast-rising economies. But they also matter because they have gradually tried to take advantage of their newly gained economic clout to play a more active role in global governance mechanisms.

The economic rise of the BRICS is now a well-established fact. As shown in Table 1, their economic weight has risen at a dramatic (and unprecedented) pace and the trend is likely to continue: according to recent estimates by the IMF, by 2015, the BRICS are expected to account for 61 per cent of world economic growth.

Table 1 BRICS in 2000 and 2012

	GDP in PPP (USD bn)	Share in world GDP (%)	GDP (current, USD bn)	Share in world GDP (%)	Population (millions)	Share in world population	GDP per capita (current USD)	Share in world exports (%)
Brazil	1379	3.2	645	2.0	174	2.9	3694	0.9
	2039	2.4	2252	3.1	199	2.8	11 339	1.3*
Russia	1260	2.9	260	0.8	146	2.4	1775	1.6
	2178	2.5	2015	2.8	143	2.0	14 037	2.9*
India	1818	4.2	477	1.4	1042	17.1	457	0.7
	4131	4.8	1842	2.5	1237	17.6	1489	1.7*
China	3368	7.8	1198	3.6	1263	20.7	949	3.9
	10748	15.5	8227	11.4	1351	19.2	6091	12.1*
South Africa	764	0.7	133	0.4	44	0.7	3019	0.5
	986	0.7	384	0.5	51	0.7	7507	0.7*
Total BRICS	8589	18.8	2713	8.2	2669	43.8		7.6
	20 082	25.9	14 720	20.3	2981	42.3		18.7*

Data Source: World Bank, World Development Indicators. (the first value corresponds to 2000 and the second to 2012)

* 2013.

Other signs, such as the distribution of foreign exchange reserves, also suggest that the emerging balance of economic power has been tilting in favor of the BRICS, at least in favor of the largest of the BRICS countries, namely China which holds vast quantities of foreign exchange reserves and huge amounts of domestic savings.

On the latter point, the snag is that the overall picture hides contrasted and differentiated realities. By way of illustration, China's stock of foreign exchange reserves (standing at almost USD 4 trillion) is greater than those of India, Russia, and Brazil combined. Overall, some BRICS appear to be more equal than others and the rise of the BRICS is actually primarily the rise of China. China outshines all the others and this dominance is here to stay, in spite of China's relative economic decline, both demographically and in terms of economic size.[1]

Quite logically, as a result of these new developments the post WWII distribution of power, as reflected in the UN-related international organizations, is deemed to be increasingly inadequate. As explained by O'Neill and Terzi (2014) for instance, "If the global monetary system is at all supposed to be reflective of global trade, then the role of the RMB needs to increase."

But the rising weight of the BRICS is not exclusively apparent in the economic sphere. The UN peacekeepers from the BRICS are five times as many as those from the Western seven countries. This proves that the BRICS are also contributing much to world peace and stability, prosperity and development and global governance.

In face of these changes, industrial countries tend to take an ambivalent stance, on the one hand calling for more "responsibility" on the part of the BRICS, and on the other accusing them of undermining existing global governance mechanisms.

Interestingly enough, the BRICS have realized that the rise in their individual economic and political weight may be pooled so as to make them collectively more influential. The BRICS are a group of countries identified as potential game-changers, but they are also increasingly a political reality ever since they started meeting on regular basis in 2006.

---

[1] This point is elaborated further upon in section 4.

They later on decided to hold annual summit meetings: the first Summit took place in Yekaterinburg in 2009, the second in Rio (2010), the third in Sanya (2011), the fourth in New Delhi (2012), the fifth in Durban (2013) and the sixth in Fortaleza (2014). Over time, the BRICS has become an economic, and perhaps to a lesser extent a political, reality.

3. BRICS and Global Governance Structures: Economics and Politics

Because of their rising weight but also because of their readiness to express and defend their own interests which may not be in line with those of traditionally dominant countries, the BRICS are no doubt in a position to influence global governance structures. This section examines a number of concrete cases and tries to identify the motivations of the BRICS.

(1) BRICS and global economic governance: a multi-pronged approach

In the economic sphere (finance and trade), BRICS's approach to global governance apparently combines status quo preservation, progressive reformism and more radical revisionism. This section provides evidence of this multifaceted approach.

On financial issues, the BRICS have taken a two-step approach. For a long time, the BRICS have been strong advocates of a gradual reform of global governance structures, pushing in particular for a reform of the IMF quota system ("redistributing shares and chairs") so as to better reflect the growing weight of the BRICS and the declining weight of the traditional/industrial powers.

Under the BRICS's insistent pressure, in November 2010, the IMF agreed wide-ranging governance reforms to reflect the increasing importance of emerging market countries. In particular a reform of the quota system, which also determines the voting rights of the member states, was adopted. Following the reform, the relative share of the BRICS is planned to rise from 10% to 14.8% of the total.

These first pressures clearly reflect a reformist approach, because the BRICS sought at the time to change global governance structures from within but did not question the legitimacy of the institution.

Over time, however, there has been a shift towards a more revisionist approach, as a result of industrial countries' reluctance to accept reformism. Although officially adopted in 2010, the IMF quota reform is still to be implemented because of the US Congress failure to ratify it. While countries representing nearly 80% of IMF votes have approved the reforms, the required threshold is 85% [1], and the US has a de facto veto with its 16.75% shareholding. With the United States still unwilling to approve the reform, the amendment cannot go through.

Thanks to their financial capabilities, the BRICS (in particular China with its huge foreign exchange reserves) are in a position to propose alternative mechanisms. At the BRICS Summit in Fortaleza (July 2014), the BRICS have proposed to create a new contingent reserve arrangement (CRA) totaling USD 100 billion, the objective of which is to help them smooth over financial imbalances with the rest of the world. This mechanism is clearly a way of supplementing, and possibly supplanting, the IMF.

Similarly, the BRICS have also announced the creation of a new BRICS Development Bank [New Development Bank (NDB) with an initial capital of USD 100 billion] headquartered in Shanghai. The NDB is poised to finance infrastructure and development projects across the developing world with a focus on sustainable development, where the emphasis will be more on job creation and poverty alleviation. Again, this move is indicative of a revisionist approach, since the NDB is a clear alternative to the Washington-based World Bank.

In other economic areas in contrast, the role of the BRICS is less clear but apparently more favorable to the preservation of the status quo. This different position should not come as a surprise because the logic of global governance structures in the trade area for instance is very different from that observed in finance. As was the case with the GATT, the WTO for instance is based on the "one country, one vote" principle. As a result, emerging powers do not perceive a strong need to reform the system in order to gain a larger role.

Overall, the BRICS are supporting the existing trade governance

---

[1] The realignment of the quota shares requires acceptance by three-fifths of the members having 85% of the total voting power.

mechanisms, although they do not all contribute in the same way to the rule-setting game. All BRICS are now members of the WTO[①] and all are thus expected to abide by internationally agreed rules. However, while they jointly called for a prompt conclusion of the Doha Round of Trade Negotiations during their first Summit in 2009, they eventually went in different directions and India is usually blamed for blocking the negotiations.

In other trade-related areas, the BRICS do not take a similar stance. While India is widely held responsible for the breakdown of the recent Doha Development Round, China, in contrast, appears to be particularly supportive of the multilateral governance of trade issues. An interesting illustration of this position is the recent decision by Beijing to ask for its integration into the negotiations on the Trade in Services Agreement (TISA). The only reason why China is not yet participating in the negotiations is because the US is opposing it.

It is worth stressing that although all BRICS are engaged in regional trading agreements and may thus be seen as contributing to undermine the multilateral rules-setting system embodied by the WTO, they do not differ in this respect from the other large powers.

In a nutshell, vis-à-vis global economic governance institutions, the BRICS's approach blends different stances spanning from status quo preservation to radical reform. Interestingly enough China may be thought to set the trend. Indeed, the BRICS tend to adopt a more accommodative stance in areas where China has been a major beneficiary of the existing system (as in the case of the multilateral trading system) while they tend to lean towards revisionism in areas where it has more muscle and more leeway (as on financial issues).

(2) BRICS' ambivalent stance on global political governance issues

In the foreign policy and security sphere, BRICS' approach to global governance also combines status quo preservation, progressive reformism and more radical revisionism, but even more than in the field of global economic governance, divergences and divisions among countries remain

---

[①] China joined the WTO in 2001 and Russia in 2011.

numerous and appear as significant obstacles to the building of a common approach.

On security issues in a strict sense, BRICS certainly do not appear to be able to build a common approach anytime soon. This is due to the nature of security considerations at the national level. This is also due to the fact that BRICS are facing very different security issues in very different locations: some are involved in tense maritime and territorial disputes (China); one is directly involved in a conflict on the European continent (Russia, with Ukraine) with no direct or formal support of any other BRICS, etc. As a matter of fact, there is no security alliance among the BRICS or even between any pair of BRICS countries. On the contrary, some BRICS countries are reinforcing security ties with countries outside the BRICS group, such as India with the US and Japan. Even between China and Russia, which are often seen as getting closer following the $400 billion gas deal signed in May 2014, tensions remain significant on a number of security and foreign policy issues. In particular, reinforced competition for influence may emerge between the two countries in Central Asia in the context of the development of China's new "silk road economic belt", a concept announcing the reinforcement of China's economic presence in the region (infrastructure developments, investments in the energy sector, etc.), and which the Russian leadership is following with some degree of suspicion.[①]

Geographical proximity did not help so far in building common security approach among several BRICS countries. On the contrary, when two BRICS countries are geographically closer, as it is the case of China and India for instance, the existing border disputes between them represent significant obstacles to the building of an inclusive security community. Beyond security governance, these disputes represent obstacles to the building of a stronger BRICS community as a whole. An escalation of tensions regarding existing security issues between two BRICS countries would likely impact existing economic cooperation negatively and significantly weaken the building of the BRICS block. For

---

[①] It is only in the joint statement issued in May 2014 following the signing of the gas deal, more than one year after the Chinese leadership first mentioned it, that Russia formally agreed to mention the concept.

instance, the hypothesis of anescalation of tensions on China – India border disputes cannot be fully dismissed considering the divergences of views existing between the two current leadership on the issue, and may ultimately represents obstacles to the implementation of the significant economic cooperation projects agreed during Xi's visit to India in November 2014 (both countries signed 12 agreements in Delhi, one of which announcing China investing USD 20 billion in India's infrastructure over five years).

Still, the BRICS could put on the side their existing points of tensions and play a significant role in international issues which may appear easier to deal with, and particularly relevant to address at the multinational level, such as climate change, arms proliferation, cybersecurity, among other issues. However, on most of these issues the BRICS tend to position themselves differently given the specificities of their national context, and some agreements involving BRICS members are made first outside of the BRICS grouping: China and the US signed an agreement on climate change in November 2014, announcing unilateral measures to reduce their greenhouse gas emissions by 2030.

On foreign policy and security governance in broader terms, the BRICS are unequal as far as their weight in the decision-making process is concerned. Some, such as China and Russia, are permanent members of the UN Security Council (UNSC), and there is no consensus among the BRICS on the need to reform the UNSC. In this specific case, China is following a conservative approach, supporting the existing membership structure.[1] Such divergences among BRICS countries make the reform of the UNSC unlikely in the short and medium, even if China has been slightly adjusting its communication strategy on the topic in the last few months (during his recent visit to India, Chinese President Xi Jinping made a statement — expected for many years by India — that his country will support India's aspiration to play a greater role at the

---

[1] China and Russia were for many years reluctant to expand the permanent membership of the UNSC, as they fear it would dilute the uniqueness of their own access to the veto. (Armijo, Leslie Elliott and Cynthia Roberts, 2014)

United Nations).①

On global political governance issues, China's approach is also hovering between status quo preservation, progressive reformism and even creation or revival of institutions when it assesses that progressive reformism is unlikely to lead to significant readjustment to its advantage in the short or medium term. For instance, China is becoming more proactive in building or reviving new security/foreign policy institutional framework, such as the Conference on Interaction and Confidence-building Measures in Asia (CICA), which includes more than 20 participants, and several BRICS countries (Russia, India). Although this institution focuses exclusively on the regional context, and although its ability to face flashpoints may remain limited given that key regional players (such as the US or Japan) are not part of it, it underlines China's new proactive behavior at the institutional level both in the region and beyond.

4. Major Challenge: China's Pragmatic and Flexible Approach to BRICS

The fact that China's approach to global governance is very diverse and flexible makes it difficult for other BRICS countries to follow China's position with the same degree of flexibility. Given China's stronger comparative economic and political weight in the BRICS grouping, China could act as a trendsetter for the entire grouping, leading progressively to a common position on a set of foreign policy and security issues. In practical terms, however, common positions are hard to come by, as BRICS countries tend to consider the BRICS grouping as a tool to enhance their own national foreign policy objectives, which greatly differ from one country to another. For instance, China's current focus on economic diplomacy, and in particular on infrastructure development, is certainly the main factor underlying its support of the newly created BRICS Development Bank, as much as of other recent financing institutions

---

① China's support would need to be confirmed.

outside the BRICS, such as the Asian Infrastructure Investment Bank (AIIB), which China initiated in 2013 and managed to create with the support of other Asian countries in 2014. In general terms, all the moves made by China in the framework of the BRICS grouping are derived from its national foreign policy objectives and guidelines, and as such are not specific to the BRICS.

Recently, China's pragmatic approach to the BRICS highly contrasts with Russia's. In the present context of the Ukraine crisis, Russia tends to emphasize the building of a more ambitious political grouping among the BRICS, which would differ from the "West" in its positions, whereas China continues to see the BRICS primarily as an economic grouping and as a tool to enhance its economic diplomacy, and appears more moderate in its use of anti-western rhetoric.

At an ideological level, BRICS countries certainly do not follow a common approach. The majority of them emphasize the existence of universal values, while the People's Republic of China, argued that political systems are culturally specific. These differences in the domestic political context do not prevent the BRICS countries from reinforcing economic cooperation and adopting common positions on a number issues as mentioned earlier, but they represent dividing lines which non-BRICS countries can underline and even instrumentalize from time to time, at least rhetorically. For instance, Japan theoretically includes India when it talks about the building of an arc of solidarity among democratic countries in the Asia – pacific.

In a nutshell, regarding global foreign policy and security governance issues, it is hard to see a common BRICS's approach emerging. The BRICS countries are facing very different security challenges in nature and locations, they are opposing each other on specific issues (border disputes between China and India, various positioning towards the Ukraine crisis, etc.), but also positioning themselves differently vis-à-vis the US. Divergences in foreign policy orientations but also methodology among BRICS countries represent significant obstacles to the building of a political grouping. Given its global economic and political weight, China could potentially act as a leader for the consolidation of the BRICS grouping, but this is unlikely to happen as China seems to consider this framework as an opportunity to enhance its own national objectives among many other existing international or regional frameworks at its disposal. In this sense, China's pragmatic approach to BRICS can be viewed as "low-key", as Beijing has the power but does not have the ambition to build a more comprehensive community of objectives or values, contrary to some other BRICS members.

5. Conclusion: Still a Long Way to Go for the BRICS

The mere existence of the group and its regular summit meetings are potentially important changes; however, the jury is still out on their concrete achievements, and their relatively unclear stance on a number of issues suggests that they are not yet in a position to shape the world governance mechanisms in the way then dominant powers did in the wake of the WWII. Moreover, they appear neither ready nor willing to propose alternative solutions outside the existing governance structures. Also, more often than not, individual BRICS are actually more influential than the group as a whole.

Overall, our observations suggest that BRICS tend to adjust their approaches to global governance according to the issue at stake: more revisionism was found to prevail on issues where the BRICS have a "comparative advantage" or feel more comfortable (such as development financing or currency for instance), but a more accommodating stance is adopted on issues where BRICS have an interest in preserving the status quo (trade for instance, at least as far as China is concerned).

On global issues (for which global governance mechanisms are most needed — climate change, cybersecurity, arm proliferation, etc.), major asymmetries and diverging position remain among the BRICS. An increasingly strong BRICS community is under construction, but not yet able to provide an alternative framework to the old and failing global governance mechanisms. One of the reasons underlying this limitation is that China, the most powerful BRICS country to date, is mostly considering the BRICS as a framework to deploy its own foreign policy objectives, and equally considers other international and regional frameworks to do so.

Internal and external factors of divisions among BRICS country are numerous. Divergences of views remain strong on specific global governance reform (such as the reform of the UNSC), as much as on a set of hard and soft international issues (from Ukraine to climate change), which can potentially undermine on-going economic cooperation projects. In this context, a major challenge for the BRICS countries is to remain united while pressures are strong to actually keep them apart.

References

[1] Armijo, Leslie Elliott and Cynthia Roberts, "The Emerging Powers and Global Governance: Why the BRICS Matter", in Robert Looney, *Handbook of Emerging Economies*, New York, Routledge, 2014 forthcoming.

[2] Beausang-Hunter, Francesca, *Globalization and the BRICS — Why the BRICS Will Not Rule the World for Long*, Basingstoke and New York: Palgrave Macmillan, 2012.

[3] Erthal Abdenur, Adriana, Paulo Esteves and Carlos Frederico Gama, "BRICS and Global Governance Reform: A Two-pronged Approach", 2013, http://www.dfa.gov.za/department/bricks__fifth_book2014.pdf.

[4] Hou Zhenbo, "The BRICS and Global Governance Reform — Can the BRICS Provide Leadership?" Development, 2013, 56(56), pp. 356-362.

[5] National Intelligence Council, *Global Trends 2025, A Transformed World*, Washington, D.C.: Government Printing Office, 2008.

[6] Niu Haibin, "BRICS in Global Governance — 'A Progressive Force?'" Dialogue in Globalization, Fiedrich Ebert Stiftung, New York, 2012.

[7] Petropoulos, Sotiris, "The Emergence of the BRICS — Implications for Global Governance", *Journal of International and Global Studies*, 2013, May 2013, Vol. 4 Issue 2, p37.

Taking the Long View: Megatrends, Emerging Technologies, and Challenges to Governance

Banning Garrett[*]

1. Governance Faces Increasing Challenges

BRICS Nations — indeed all nations — need to consider long-term megatrends and uncertainties to foresee the changing context in which they will have to manage national and international governance. While we cannot predict the future, we can foresee many of these factors that will shape the world forward and the challenges and opportunities the world will face. We can also envisage different possible futures for both individual nations and the global community, including those we want to avoid as well as those we would like to strive to realize.

One relative certainty is that the world of the future will not be a simple extrapolation of the world of the present. The many interacting megatrends, uncertainties and possible "Black Swans" will produce disruptive change and discontinuities, as we have seen in the past such as the end of the Cold War and collapse of the Soviet Union, the 9/11 terrorist attack on the United States and subsequent US invasion of Iraq, and the 2008 financial meltdown and near global depression, to mention a few. Moreover, these factors will be taking place in an era of accelerating technological change that will also be a major source of transformative and disruptive impacts on society.

One prediction is probably justified, however. Governance — whether

---

[*] Banning Garrett, former senior reseacher at the Atlantic Council.

within nations or among nations — will become more difficult and contentious on over the next two decades and beyond as another 2.5 billion people are added to the global population and to the population of cities, while at the same time, many of the megatrends pose growing challenges, from climate change to resource constraints to massive urbanization. The stake of each nation in every other nation's internal governance will increase along with the need for international cooperation to meet common challenges. This mutual vulnerability is demonstrated most starkly by global warming. Carbon molecules emitted anywhere on earth affect the entire planet as they accumulate in the atmosphere. Thus the policies of every state — especially those of the biggest emitters, China and the United States — are of critical importance to the entire global community.

While global trends and uncertainties pose daunting challenges to the world, the future need not be grim. The global community potentially can meet the challenges of climate change, food, water, energy, urbanization, environmental remediation, etc. Moreover, meeting these challenges will offer opportunities to enhance national and international security and prosperity. Governance will be critical to meeting the challenges, however. Governments — including city and provincial governments — will often need to take the lead in setting policies and creating public – private partnerships to cope with internal challenges. National governments will also have to set priorities beyond immediate disputes and narrow self-interest to cooperate with other nations to coordinate policies and to engage in long-term collaboration, including in the development and wide dissemination of new technologies and innovations to address critical problems. This will require overcoming crippling nationalism and national rivalries that inhibit effective international collaboration. At this point, however, significantly enhanced international cooperation may be unlikely to occur without a major global crisis that demonstrates that all nations are indeed in the "same boat" and need to "hang together or they will hang separately", in the immortal words of one of America's most famous founding fathers, Benjamin Franklin.

2. The Future Context for Governance

There are many recent global trends that have been positive, including greater prosperity, decline in the global poverty rate, and the trend toward global economic re-convergence after two centuries of Western economic preponderance; improved quality of life in a myriad of spheres driven by rapid scientific and technological advances; widespread improvement in global health and life expectancy; and a huge overall reduction in death through violent conflict.[1]

Nevertheless, the global future is likely to be shaped increasingly by converging megatrends and proliferating uncertainties. The rate of convergence and change is increasing, driven by the accelerating pace of technological development, unprecedented urbanization, population growth, and rapid expansion of the global middle class and demands for food, water, energy and other resources, and a wide range of challenges beyond the control of any one country yet potentially affecting the prosperity and security of all countries. Disruptive change in one geographic or functional area can spread quickly to the entire world, as was demonstrated by the 2008 financial crisis originating in the United States that quickly threatened a global depression. No country, and certainly not those with the largest populations and largest economies like the BRICS and the United States, will be immune. Global challenges like climate change, food and water shortages, and resource scarcities, will shape the strategic context for all nations and require reconsideration of traditional national concerns such as sovereignty and maximizing the ability of national leaders to control their country's destiny independent of the rest of the world.

3. Relatively Certain Megatrends

"Megatrends" are major drivers of global change that are relatively certain to continue on a foreseeable trajectory, such as increasing demand for food and water. Some of the key megatrends that will shape the global strategic context include[①]:

- **Demographics**: Population growth in some areas, population shrinkage in others, and aging almost everywhere — will pose new challenges for governance domestically and internationally. The most recent UN report forecasts global population will increase by more than one billion from the current 7.2 billion to 8.3 billion in 2030 and by more than 2.5 billion to 9.6 billion by 2050. Virtually all of that net population growth will be in urban areas in the Global South, especially Africa and Asia. At the same time, most societies will be aging, often with a doubling of the percentage of the population that is no longer in the work force while the total of the working age population declines — a situation that is already beginning to affect most countries. There will be more people to govern but fewer people to work and support retirees and children — and pay taxes. Nearly all of the growth in the global population, urban dwellers, and the middle class will occur in developing countries. China and eventually Brazil and India will be still developing countries with aging populations. Population growth over the longer term is highly uncertain, however, with some projections as high as 12 billion by 2100 and others suggesting that population could peak by mid century at 9 billion and even decline to 6 billion at the end of the century. One trend is clear, however, and that is declining fertility rates to below replacement in most of the world, with some parts of Africa and South Asia the most prominent exceptions at the moment.
- **Rising global middle class**: The rapidly expanding global middle class — projected by some experts to grow from about two billion people today to five billion in 2030 — is a major success for humanity. The rapid and massive growth of the middle class in China, Brazil and India has been especially remarkable. But this rising middle class also puts new strains on governance. On the one hand, "middle class" is characterized mostly

---

[①] Some of the megatrends and uncertainties described below are explored in the National Intelligence Council's quadrennial unclassified global trends reports, most recently *Global Trends* 2030: *Alternative Worlds*, released in December 2012, http://www.dni.gov/index.php/about/organization/global-trends-2030. See also *Global Trends* 2030: *Citizens in an Interconnected and Polycentric World*, European Union Institute for Security Studies, Sponsored by the European Strategy and Policy Analysis System (ESPAS), 2012, http://europa.eu/espas/pdf/espas_report_ii_01_en.pdf.

by consumption of energy and resources, from steel for cars and concrete for housing to better food and luxury goods, putting growing strains on governments to obtain the "necessities" of middle class life. On the other hand, the middle class tends to have rising expectations of government, from provision of health care and education to jobs and the environment — expectations that nearly all governments struggle to fulfill. This emerging middle class is also often fragile, just one crisis such as an illness pushing the family back into poverty.[2] While technology has been the critical factor in the growth of the global economy and the prosperity of the middle class, it has also created an interconnected world through the Internet and social media that provides an unprecedented ability of individuals and groups to organize themselves to oppose government policies, as was dramatically demonstrated in Brazil in the spring of 2013. While governments are also using these tools for surveillance and control, the growing ubiquity of connectedness and social media offers new opportunities for engaging citizens in the governance process.

• **Massive urbanization is transforming societies and straining government capacities:** More than one billion people will be added to the global population by 2030 and an equal or greater number will move to cities (possibly some 300 million in China alone). A total of about 2.5 billion people will be added to urban and peri-urban regions by 2050, with 90% of the increase concentrated in Asia and Africa. Just three countries — India, China and Nigeria — together are expected to account for 37% of that projected growth in urban population.[3] There are also currently about 1 billion people living in urban poverty and slums and this could double by 2030. Cities are the engines of innovation and economic growth with 600 cities with 20% of global population producing 50% of global growth — a percentage contribution that is expected to increase in coming decades. Cities are also home to 1 billion people living in poverty, a number that is projected to double by 2030 if the current course is maintained. Ultimately, urban and peri-urban areas are where the war for sustainability — including the challenge of climate change — and for prosperity, will be won or lost.

> **Massive Urbanization (1800 – 2050)**
>
> 1800: 3% of 1 billion or about 30 million
> 1900: 14% of 1.6 billion or about 220 million
> 1950: 30% of 2.5 billion or about 750 million
> 2010: 50% of 7.2 billion or about 3.6 billion
> 2030: 60% of 8.3 billion or about 5 billion
> 2050: 70% of 9.6 billion or about 6.7 billion
>
> 70 million people added to cities each year
> 100 more Sao Paulos by 2050?

- **Massive growth in demand for food, energy, and water**[①]: The growing world population, the rapidly expanding global middle class, and rapid urbanization, are expected to spur a significant increase in demand for food, energy, water, and nearly all other natural resources. Demand for food is expected to rise by 35% by 2030, for example, while significantly increasing food production faces strong headwinds with shrinking arable land resulting from urbanization, deforestation, and desertification as well as monocrop failures and water shortages, all exacerbated by climate change. Demand for water is projected to increase by 40% by 2030 while supplies of clean fresh water are shrinking. The OECD estimates that by 2030, nearly half of the world's population will live in areas of severe water stress, aggravated by the impact of climate change on weather patterns and glacier melt. The demand for energy is projected to increase by 45% – 50% by 2030. The medium term energy picture has brightened with the rapid development of hydraulic fracturing and horizontal drilling leading a large increase in oil and gas production in the United States and the sharp decline in the global price of oil. The long-term picture is likely to be more challenging, however, as demand grows, shale gas and oil production likely peaks and declines, and fossil fuel energy systems face increasing political opposition as a result of possible catastrophic climate change — induced events in the

---

① See *Global Trends 2030*, pp. 31 – 37, for more detail on this set of issues.

next two decades. Governments could be under intense pressure to make a rapid transition to renewable energy at the same time that demand for energy is increasing sharply. This would produce not only possible energy shortages but domestic and international political challenges from energy producing countries and companies seeking to protect their interests.

- **Diffusion of Power and Individual Empowerment**: The number of players with actual or nascent capacity to influence international affairs is increasing. The international system evinces increasing signs of fragmentation and stratification. In addition to the rise of China, India, and Brazil as major powers, middle powers such as Turkey, Indonesia, South Africa, and Mexico are playing an ever more important role in the international arena. Growing numbers and types of non-state actors, from international NGOs and multinational enterprises to violent extremists organizations like ISIS and Al Qaeda, have reduced the ability of states to dominate international affairs. Moreover, individual empowerment, fueled by education, rising prosperity, and a host of technologies, has become an increasingly important factor affecting governance both within states and internationally. These empowered individuals are more willing to engage in political activities as well as to make more demands on government. They are also more likely to build activist communities subnational or transnational identities based on ethnicity, religion, culture, political concerns, and shared causes such as the environment and public health. Several billion people will be added to this pool of empowered individuals and groups potentially challenging governance by 2050.

- **Global Commons**: There will be increasing stresses and strains on the environmental global commons that will affect the international community. Many challenges to the environment and human security will be intensified by rapidly increased demand for food, water, and natural resources due to growing population, urbanization, and rapid expansion of the middle class. If not managed well, these challenges could have a significant and long-term adverse impact on all nations and the global system. There are also increasing challenges to effective management of the global commons, including militarization of outer space and accumulation of space debris; cyberspace, which has become a sphere of military, commercial and intelligence hacking that threatens the integrity and viability of the Internet; and oceans as areas of naval contention, piracy, resource extraction as well as environmental degradation. Such threats to the global commons require increased global cooperation and governance to protect shared interests.

These megatrends indicate that over the next decade and beyond, demands on governments at all levels likely will increase significantly. More people with rising expectations and greater awareness of conditions at home and elsewhere will have more tools, especially social media, to organize and put pressure on governments to provide more services and opportunities. The rising middle class in the emerging economies likely will expect and demand more and better quality food and water, more reliable supplies of cleaner energy, improved infrastructure, better education and health care, and healthier environments. Governments could find it difficult to meet these rising expectations, however, especially growing demand for increasingly limited resources, which will push prices upward and exacerbate economic and social instability. At the same time, some of the poorest countries with ineffective governments may be pushed into internal conflict and state failure by tribal, ethnic, and religious strife as well as economic and environmental stresses. These internal conflicts could lead to regional instability as environmental and economic migrants spill into neighboring states.

4. Key Uncertainties with High Potential Impact

The megatrends summarized above constitute a relatively foreseeable set of challenges facing individuals and nations. But they are not the only foreseeable factors that will influence developments in the next two decades. The megatrends will interact with a number of critical uncertainties. Some of those uncertainties include:

• **Global economy volatility**: Developed countries, especially in the Eurozone, may face a prolonged period of recovery, while emerging economies are also experiencing slowing growth. Increasing inequality in almost all countries (worsening Gini Coefficients①) could further compound the challenges. Although the rich and the poor alike may become richer, the absolute gaps between them have been widening and will likely to continue to do so, both within and among countries and regions if the current course is maintained. This growing inequality could undermine both economic growth and political stability. Moreover, the middle class may continue to be squeezed not only in developed countries but also in developing countries despite more rapid economic growth, especially as the gap widens between the middle class and the super rich and slowing economic growth results in many people in the "fragile middle class" falling back into poverty.[4] The world also could experience growing economic nationalism and trade protectionism as well as an accelerating adjustment of the international industrial division of labor. As China refocuses on domestic consumption-led growth, other nations increasingly displace China as the low-cost manufacturing platform, and new manufacturing technologies and lower energy costs encourage the return of manufacturing to the United States and other developed countries. In addition, major economic crises could result from the increasing pressure on resource availability. And, of course, there could be another global financial meltdown as it seems that inadequate measures have been put in place to prevent a repeat of the 2008 crisis. Moreover, developing countries, including China, India, Brazil and South Africa, face the possibility of falling into the "middle income trap." The Asia Development Bank in 2011 released a report, *Asia 2050: Realizing the Asian Century* ② that warned that although the best case scenario

---

① The Gini Coefficient (or Gini index) is defined by the World Bank thusly: "(the index) measures the extent to which the distribution of income or consumption expenditure among individuals or households within an economy deviates from a perfectly equal distribution. A Lorenz Curve plots the cumulative percentages of total income received against the cumulative number of recipients, starting with the poorest individual or household. The Gini Index measures the area between the Lorenz curve and a hypothetical line of absolute equality, expressed as a percentage of the maximum area under the line. Thus a Gini Index of 0 represents perfect equality, while an index of 100 implies perfect inequality." Source: http://data.worldbank.org/indicator/SI.POV.GINI.

② http://www.adb.org/publications/asia-2050-realizing-asian-century.

could lead an Asian economy of $148 trillion GDP that was 51% of global GDP, if Asia succumbed to the Middle Income Trap, its total GDP would be only $61 trillion and 32% of a much smaller global GDP. India's GDP could be only $12 trillion instead of $40 trillion and China's could be only $21 trillion instead of $63 trillion. Two of the key factors cited by the ADB as determining whether Asia experiences Doomsday of the Asian Century are the quality of internal governance and the ability of Asian nations to cooperate.

- **Global Warming**: Climate change may pose the greatest existential threat to humanity in this century. The *Climate Change 2014 Synthesis Report* of the Intergovernmental Panel on Climate Change (IPCC) released November 1, 2014[5] reflected increased concern of scientists that climate change is happening faster and with greater impact than was concluded by earlier reports.① Climate change is exacerbating water shortages and food production challenges; sparking greater migration and social conflict; acidifying the oceans, threatening food supplies and the global ecosystem; creating new threats to global health; contributing to more extreme weather events; and raising sea-level, magnifying the impact of storm surges threatening coastal cities and infrastructure. Climate change is already having a measurable impact on economies and is likely to take a far greater economic toll in the future. Climate scientists are increasingly concerned that global warming will exceed the 2 centigrade limit thought to preclude passing a tipping point of massive, disruptive and long-term climate change, such as the melting of the Greenland and West Antarctica ice sheets that could lead to sea level rise of many meters. The focus of most of the practical responses to climate change have taken place in cities, which often foresee imminent threats and share best practices with other cities around the world also seeking to mitigate carbon emissions and adapt to climate change impacts already

---

① The IPCC 2014 Synthesis Report concludes that, "continued emission of greenhouse gases will cause further warming and long-lasting changes in all components of the climate system, increasing the likelihood of severe, pervasive and irreversible impacts for people and ecosystems. Limiting climate change would require substantial and sustained reductions in greenhouse gas emissions which, together with adaptation, can limit climate change risks."

underway. Responding to climate change is likely to be an increasingly important priority and test of cities, national governance, and international cooperation in the future. The US – China agreement to cut greenhouse gas emissions announced in Beijing November 12, 2014, was a step toward greater climate change cooperation of the two largest economies and carbon emitters. The agreement, which faces stiff opposition in the US Congress, could nevertheless enhance chances for a global agreement in Paris in 2015 to replace the Kyoto accord.[①]

● **"Black Swans"**: Unpredictable events that could happen at any time, such as natural disasters, extreme weather events, pandemics, or nuclear weapon use by terrorists, could be game-changers in international politics. The current Ebola crisis in West Africa demonstrates the possibility of a pandemic emerging at any time and spreading throughout a region, devastating economics and even destabilizing countries. An airborne H5N1 or similar pandemic could rapidly become a global crisis, shutting down global transportation and killing tens of millions of people with a devastating impact on the global economy, politics, and security. A series of extreme weather events, foreshadowed by Hurricane Sandy's impact on the United States, could change the trajectories of global political efforts to deal with the consequences of climate change as well as negatively affect the global economy and the political stability of nations and regions.

● **Conflict**: Internal and regional conflicts could become more common and more intense as a result of social unrest, religious extremism, declining ability of governments to provide public goods, shifts in regional and global power, and individual empowerment. The world's security, stability and prosperity may become increasingly fragile as a result of state failure, nuclear proliferation, or dramatic acts of terrorism, especially in unstable regions like the Middle East and South Asia. The

---

① Such US – China cooperation has been the focus of many key policymakers and experts in both China and the United States for many years. See, for example, the 2009 report, *A Roadmap for U. S. -China Cooperation on Energy and Climate Change*, http://asiasociety. org/files/pdf/US_China_Roadmap_on_Climate_Change. pdf. Many of the collaborators on the report became key policymakers in the administration of President Obama in 2009 and many of the Chinese collaborators are key advisers to the Chinese government.

sudden rise of ISIS in Iraq and Syria demonstrates the challenge of extremist non-state actors to national and international governance. A major conflict in the Middle East could draw in outside powers, disrupt oil supplies, and send the global economy into recession. Failure to resolve or indefinitely shelve territorial disputes in East and Southeast Asia could limit the ability of regional states to cooperate in global as well as regional efforts to cope with global challenges. The unresolved conflict in Ukraine shows that even Europe is not immune to conflict and instability that could undermine the last 25 years of European peace and integration. And climate change could exacerbate nearly all of the conditions that affect social stability and conflict.

- **Extremism and fracturing of the nation-state**: Extremism and separatism are likely to be fueled by individual empowerment and tribal, ethnic, religious, and other identities, strengthened by ubiquitous social media. The power and authority of the nation-state is likely to be increasingly circumscribed by the rising power of non-state actors and the growing importance of transnational challenges beyond the state's control. The state is being challenged in many cases by separatist and extremist forces, including religious fundamentalists in Waziristan and Dagestan and regional nationalists in Catalonia and Scotland. New technology, from social media to more accessible weapons, have increased the ability of disaffected groups to create domestic instability in pursuit of their objectives.

- **Global cooperation gap widening**: Increasing globalization and interdependence could make it more difficult for national governments to manage new challenges on their own, but transnational institutions may be increasingly ill-suited or even incapable of meeting twenty-first century challenges.[①] To meet the growing challenges, existing global mechanisms, most of which are legacy institutions from the post-World War II era designed to solve problems from the inter-war period, must be reformed or replaced. That will not be easy. There are 140 more countries today than there were when the global system was last reformed in the 1940s and all feel entitled to a seat at the table when

---

① Many of the challenges for global governance are outlined in the 2010 report, *Global Governance 2025: At a Critical Juncture*, jointly produced by the National Intelligence Council and the European Union Institute for Security Studies, http://fas.org/irp/nic/governance.pdf.

decisions are made that will affect their own destinies. This widely shared ethos of democratic participation of all nations makes it difficult to strike a balance between equity of representation and efficacy of decision-making.

5. Exponential Technologies and Disruptive Change

Emerging technologies will interact with these potentially game-changing uncertainties and megatrends to produce even more change and uncertainty. New technology has had an enormous impact on society in the last twenty years. The Internet alone has transformed the world, including the operations of government, business, and personal lives. Now consider that it is likely there will be far more technological change affecting our lives — and the challenges of governance — in the next twenty years than in the past half century. The pace of change in many areas of technology and the innovations based on those technologies is exponential rather than linear. That is, like "Moore's Law" of computer chip power doubling every eighteen to twenty-four months that has proven accurate for four decades of the computer revolution, the capability of many other new technologies is also doubling at a regular pace rather than increasing incrementally.[①] To visualize the difference, if you take thirty one-yard-long steps, the thirtieth step is also one yard long like the first step and you will find yourself thirty yards from where you started. If you doubled the length of each step, while your first few steps will not be very long, your thirtieth step would be about 1 billion yards, or more than **twenty-two times** the circumference of the earth. The difference is thus more than

---

① Ray Kurzweill, *The Singularity Is Near*, New York: Penguin Books, 2005. Kurzweill argues that technology has been on an exponential path of development for centuries. See chapter 2, "A Theory of Technology Evolution: The Law of Accelerating Returns". Kurzweill is the cofounder of Singularity University (http://singularityu.org/), which states that its mission is to "educate, inspire and empower leaders to apply exponential technologies to address humanity's grand challenges". See the Performance Curve Database (http://pcdb.santafe.edu/) for data on some key exponential technologies. It should be noted that not all technologies have developed exponentially. The performance of the airplane and the internal cumbustion engine, for example, has not improved exponentially over the last century.

just quantitative. It is a different world of change. Today's smartphone has more computing power than the most powerful supercomputer in 1985, and there are hundreds of millions of people carrying around that computing power in their pockets and purses.① The capacity of digital storage has similarly increased and the cost has decreased at an exponential pace. Think about that pace of change continuing for another twenty years just in computing power. Significant exponential change is taking place in many other areas of technology, including artificial intelligence and robotics, biotechnology and bioinformatics, energy and environmental systems, medicine and neuroscience, and nano-technology.②

In genomics, Moore's Law has been on steroids. The first sequencing of a human genome cost more than $1 billion. Today, the cost is about $1000 for total personal genome sequencing and the cost is expected to soon drop further to $200. This million-fold drop in price will not only help with individual medical diagnosis but also with big data analysis to discover genetic links to specific diseases and disorders by analyzing millions of genomes and crowdsourcing analysis. ③

Not only are individual technologies on an exponential curve of improvement, but the combination of key digital technologies is at an "inflection point", according to MIT researchers Erik Brynjolfsson and Andrew McAffee, who maintain that "we are entering a second machine age"[6]. Brynjolfsson and McAffee note the convergence of exponential technologies can surpass the expectations of science fiction: "On the *Star Trek* television series, devices called tricorders were used to scan and record three kinds of data: geological, meteorological, and medical.

---

① McKinsey Global Institute points out that the fastest supercomputer in 1975 cost $5 million compared with $400 for its computing power equal, the iPhone 4. James Manyika, Michael Chui, Jacques Bughin, Richard Dobbs, Peter Bisson, and Alex Marrs, *Disruptive Technologies: Advances That Will Transform Life, Business and the Global Economy*, McKinsey Global Institute, May 2013, p. 5, http://www.mckinsey.com/insights/business_technology/disruptive_technologies.

② This list was presented by Karen Myronuk, Singularity University, on April 15, 2013.

③ For a discussion of the cost curve on DNA sequencing falling faster than Moore's Law, see Aaron Saenz, "Costs of DNA Sequencing Falling Fast—Look at These Graphs!" May 3, 2011, http://singularityhub.com/2011/03/05/costs-of-dna-sequencing-falling-fast-look-at-these-graphs/.

> **Twelve Disruptive Technologies**
>
> There have been efforts to forecast the economic impact of disruptive technologies, most notably by the McKinsey Global Institute (MGI). In a May 2013 report, Disruptive Technologies: Advances that Will Transform Life, Business and the Global Economy, MGI examined twelve "potentially economically disruptive technologies"①:
> - **Mobile Internet** — increasingly inexpensive and capable mobile computing devices and Internet connectivity
> - **Automation of knowledge work** — intelligent software systems that can perform knowledge work tasks involving unstructured commands and subtle judgments
> - **The Internet of Things** — networks of low-cost sensors and actuators for data collection, monitoring, decision-making, and process optimization
> - **Cloud technology** — use of computer hardware and software resources delivered over a network or the Internet, often as a service
> - **Advanced robotics** — increasingly capable robots with enhanced senses, dexterity, and intelligence used to automate tasks or augment humans
> - **Autonomous and near-autonomous vehicles** — vehicles that can navigate and operate with reduced or no human intervention
> - **Next-generation genomics** — fast, low-cost gene sequencing, advanced big data analytics, and synthetic biology ("writing" DNA)
> - **Energy storage** — devices or systems that store energy for later use, including batteries
> - **3D printing** — additive manufacturing techniques to create objects by printing layers of material based on digital models
> - **Advanced materials** — materials designed to have superior characteristics (e.g., strength, weight, conductivity) or functionality
> - **Advanced oil and gas exploration and recovery** — exploration and recovery techniques that make extraction of unconventional oil and gas economical
> - **Renewable energy** — generation of electricity from renewable sources with reduced harmful climate impact

Today's consumer smartphones serve all these purposes; they can be put to work as seismographs, real-time weather radar maps, and heart-and breathing-rate monitors. And, of course, they're not limited to these domains. They also work as media players, game platforms, reference works, cameras, and global positioning system (GPS) devices. On *Star Trek*, tricorders and person-to-person communicators were separate devices, but in the real world the two have merged in the smartphone"[7].

---

① James Manyika et al., p. 4.

These emerging technologies could also have a game-changing impact on the developing world. Cell phones have already played a critical role in boosting economic and social development in the developing world with, in many cases, huge productivity gains and innovations such as the M‑PESA mobile phone money transfer and microfinance system, developed in Kenya and launched by Safaricom in 2007.① Smartphones are now bringing broadband Internet access to hundreds of millions of people in the developing world, which could be virtually "wired up" by 2020, potentially producing huge additional economic and social gains. 3D printing could enable countries with little manufacturing capability currently relying on imports to produce many of their own goods without need for advanced infrastructures and supply chains. Small local businesses could use local materials while providing employment and unleashing the entrepreneurial talents of the local population.②

It is impossible to predict what the accelerating pace of change in technology will lead to in the next twenty years. However, one can already foresee some potential technological developments that are likely by building on current technologies and trends, such as faster computers, wider and more advanced use of 3D and 4D printing③, more ubiquitous robots, enhanced mobile computing with the individual at the center, and creation of new designer organisms with biological building blocks. Far more difficult is to predict second-and third-order effects of technology—social innovations and the implication of those innovations for society. For example, even after experts could foresee the vast expansion of the interactive Internet, second order effects such as the

---

① M‑Pesa, currently the most developed mobile payment system in the world, allows users with a national ID card or passport to deposit, withdraw, and transfer money easily with a mobile device. Cecilia Kang, "For the Poor, Cellphones Can Offer Lifeline", *Washington Post*, September 8, 2010, http://www.washingtonpost.com/wp-dyn/content/article/2010/09/07/AR2010090706625.html.

② For a discussion of the potential impact of 3D printing, see Thomas Campbell, Christopher Williams, Olga Ivanova, and Banning Garrett, "Could 3D Printing Change the World?" http://www.atlanticcouncil.org/images/files/publication_pdfs/403/101711_ACUS_3DPrinting.PDF.

③ For a discussion of 4D printing, see Thomas A Campbell, Sklylar Tibbits and Banning Garrett, "The Programmable World", *Scientific American*, November 2014; and see Thomas A Campbell, Sklylar Tibbits and Banning Garrett, *The Next Wave: 4D Printing and Programming the Material World*, http://www.atlanticcouncil.org/publications/reports/the-next-wave-4d-printing-and-programming-the-material-world.

innovations of Facebook and Twitter were not anticipated, nor were third-order effects like the use of those innovations for social movements and upheavals like the "Arab Spring," which has had dramatic fourth-order impacts on regional and global geopolitics that continue to convulse the Middle East.

Experts can foresee trajectories of development of many technologies with a certain level of confidence. Computers will become faster, smaller, more connected, more wearable as well as mobile, and more ubiquitous. Robots, of both the physical and digital varieties, will be increasingly ubiquitous in people's economic and personal lives. Both the individual and the organization (whether business or the state) will have access to more digital power. 3D printing will empower the individual to become a digital-to-material, design to product, creator, and the same technology will transform manufacturing and many other industries. Synthetic biology will not only impact health care and medicine but also industry and the environment. Nanotechnology will continue to improve the ability to manipulate matter at the molecular level across almost all areas of material invention.

More generally, technological convergence will spur new, unexpected developments while new scientific discoveries will likely further transform our technological future. One of the most consequential disruptive technological breakthroughs in the next 10 – 20 years is likely to be quantum computing, which will transform people's ability to understand the world and solve problems currently insoluble by even the fastest conventional computers crunching numbers for hundreds or even thousands of years.①

---

① Quantum computers will not just be faster but will approach problem solving in a fundamentally different way. Instead of searching for a solution sequentially, such as decryption, where billions or trillions of possible combinations need to tested one after another, a quantum computer could try all combinations simultaneously to find the key. One simulation by Microsoft indicated that a factoring problem that would take 31 000 years to solve on a conventional computer could be resolved in a matter of seconds or hours on a quantum computer. When quantum computers become available, much if not most current encryption, including on the Internet, will be subject to nearly instantaneous decryption. Quantum computers could also mark a new age in solving intractable problems. A quantum computer could simultaneously explore thousands of possible molecular combinations for a new material or drug to find the best combination in short order. These could include such challenges as a creating a room temperature superconductor or accurately and in detail modeling climate change. Although the the first quantum computers will be very large, they could eventually be very small and provide immense new power to individuals and the Internet of Things.

Quantum computers will end encryption as we know it, putting at risk the entire system of Internet security, which includes infrastructure, power and banking systems as well as personal, business and government operations and communications. At the same time, quantum computers, by their ability to solve trillions of equations simultaneously, could make breakthroughs in designing new materials or drugs while also providing far more understanding of complex environmental phenomena like climate change. Another possible game-changing technology is fusion power, which was brought forward by the surprising recent announcement by Lockheed Martin of a fusion power breakthrough. The announcement raised the possibility of affordable and scalable fusion power generators within the next 10 – 20 years that would provide carbon-free long-term energy that could quickly obsolesce and disrupt the global fossil fuel energy system while making more realistic future efforts to combat global warming.[①]

In short, the outlines of a huge array of technological developments can already be identified, although we cannot predict with certainty whether these will come to fruition as major innovations and, if so, when that would occur. It is even more difficult to foresee how societies will use new technology and its second-, third- and fourth-order effects. Will new technology be harnessed to meet global challenges such as climate change and energy transition and growing demands for food and water? Will new technology be a source of more jobs than it destroys? Will it lead to more wealth for all or further exacerbate growing inequality? Will it be used by individuals, groups, or governments for destructive purposes, including bioterrorism, cyber warfare, and robotic attacks? Will it advance democracy or authoritarianism? Will it enhance prospects for global prosperity and cooperation or lead to new conflict and zero-sum competition? These are just some of the questions about the future that demonstrate the great uncertainties about the impact of technology on society and the challenges of governance.

---

① Http://www.lockheedmartin.com/us/products/compact-fusion.html.

> **Governments Need to Protect the Internet**
>
> Envision the disappearance of the Internet from life today. It is not difficult to paint a picture of economic collapse, social disarray, political upheaval, military paralysis, and extensive conflict. The disappearance of the Internet would cripple modern life, including most transportation systems, logistics and food provision, banking and financial transactions, all communications systems, and the infrastructure controlling provision of water and electricity. In short, modern societies would collapse into a previously not experienced civilizational crisis. The world would not return to the pre-Internet era of twenty years ago but perhaps to a pre-industrial age.
>
> The possibility of the Internet's sudden disappearance is not as far-fetched as it may seem. Massive solar geomagnetic storms occur in less than one hundred-year intervals, the most recent hitting the earth was in 1859, before the world was wired up. Such a storm could knock out satellites, the electric grid, and many sensitive electronic devices. "Until cures are implemented," the US National Intelligence Council's report, *Global Trends 2030: Alternative Worlds*, warns, "solar super-storms will pose a large-scale threat to the world's social and economic fabric."[8] In July 2012, earth experienced a near-miss of such a massive solar storm, and according experts there is a 12% chance of a direct hit in the next ten years.[9]
>
> So as one considers the impact of technology on society and lament its downsides — from vulnerabilities of the digitally connected world to digital unemployment and new technologically-enable security threats — it is important not to lose sight of society's deep dependence on this technology. To stop the science and technology train is not possible and to try to dismantle today's technological society would be suicidal. Humans have always been a technological species since they harnessed fire and cooked food. Mankind must continue the advancement of science and technology while addressing critical challenges such as climate change that technology has helped create if a civilizational catastrophe is to be averted.

6. What Are the Real Strategic Challenges and Opportunities?

Exponential technologies will transform societies, presenting new opportunities as well as dangers for governance. Governments will be under extraordinary stress from potentialcrises, many produced by the convergence of megatrends and uncertainties, making unprecedented demands on governance in multiple dimensions, including domestically and internationally. Maintaining the status quo will not be an option because there will be no status quo — rather increasing demands and stresses punctuated by sudden, disruptive change. Building resilience and adaptive governance will be primary challenges.

The BRICS and other major nations, including the United States, Japan and Europe, need to take the long view and ask what are the real strategic challenges we face in ensuring the security and prosperity of our people? Is the Western-established world system of international organizations, laws and norms really the threat that faces BRICS nations as they seek to develop and improve the lives of their citizens? Is there a need to create an alternative, parallel international system? Or have the Western institutions become the foundation — however flawed — that all nations need to build on and transform to better respond to the serious and even potentially existential threats facing the international community as well as to better seize the opportunities presented by new technology and innovations to meet global challenges and enhance the security and prosperity of all nations and peoples?

In my view, the common strategic challenges facing all nations are far more threatening in the long run than current differences and disputes among major nations that are fueling distrust and the desire to establish rival institutions and build up military forces based on perceptions of each other as potential enemies. These common challenges include: mitigation of climate change and adaptation to is effects; maintaining adequate food supplies in the face of rapidly increasing demand and declining arable land; enhancing the supply of usable fresh water in the face of vastly increasing demand and declining supply; the need to rapidly transition from fossil fuels to renewables amid huge increases in energy demand; and the need to build sustainable infrastructure, especially in urban regions, where the war for environmental and economic sustainability will be won or lost.

While the future portends of more common dangers and challenges, it seems that most nations are increasingly focused on near-term and narrow national interests, often from a zero-sum perspective. This disconnect could result in bad outcomes for these nations as well as for the global community.

Focusing on the wrong strategic threats and priorities can prove extremely costly in both resources wasted and opportunities forgone. An example of such a high-cost strategic blunder, in my view, was the US invasion of Iraq in 2003. National differences and suspicions must not become insurmountable obstacles to the international cooperation that is necessary to protect the national security and prosperity of each nation. In my view, efforts to further divide the world — much less create competing global institutions, norms and orders — could put at risk the security and prosperity of all nations.

Although no one can predict with confidence how events will play out in the years ahead, we can be confident that the challenges and choices facing decision-makers at all levels and in all countries will be shaped by the interplay of megatrends, known uncertainties, unexpected "black swan" events, and the decisions of governments and nongovernmental actors. Waiting to see how events unfold is a possible but undesirable choice. Waiting is, in effect, a decision to do nothing and hope for the best. We can and must do better than that by working to shape events in ways that reduce uncertainty, avoid or ameliorate undesirable trajectories, and increase the likelihood of win-win outcomes. Moreover, we can seize opportunities provided by new and emerging technologies to "scale up" solutions to the major challenges and change their trajectories to produce a more prosperous and secure future that is economically and environmentally sustainable. This effort could include enhancing global scientific cooperation and public-private partnerships to develop and deploy technologies and innovative models to meet the global grand challenges.

A step that this conference could champion would be to establish a Track II project for joint assessment by the BRICS with the United States and Europe, of long-term global trends, game-changing uncertainties, and emerging technologies. Such a joint assessment process would look beyond current suspicions and disputes to focus on long-term common challenges and opportunities. This could lead to a conclusion that the security and prosperity of each country requires placing top priority collaboration with the rest of the world to address common challenges while carefully managing differences and disputes to prevent them from precluding such international cooperation.①

References

[1] See Simon Kuper, "Peace in Our Time", *Financial Times,* 17 January, 2014 http://www. ft. com/intl/cms/s/2/2177ebce-7e44-11e3-b409-00144feabdc0. html # axzz2r2KpzOlU; and Ian Morris, *What! What Is It Good For?* New York: Farrar, Straus and Giroux, 2014.

[2] Shawn Donnan, Ben Bland and John Burn – Murdoch, "Fragile Middle: 2.8 bn People on the Brink", *Financial Times,* 13 April 2014, http://www.ft.com/intl/cms/s/2/e8f40868-c093-11e3-a74d-00144feabdc0.html#axzz2ymyjCfJ9.

[3] "World Urbanization Prospects", 2014 Revision, *Highlights,* UN Department of Economic and Social Affairs, p. 5, http://esa. un. org/unpd/wup/Highlights/WUP2014-Highlights.pdf.

[4] See "Fragile Middle: 2.8 bn People on the Brink", *Financial Times*, 13 April, 2014, http://www. ft. com/intl/cms/s/2/e8f40868-c093-11e3-a74d-00144feabdc0. html#axzz2ymyjCfJ9; and Branco Milanovic, "How We Can Strengthen the World's Fragile Middle Class", *Financial Times*, 28 April, 2014, http://www.ft.com/intl/cms/s/0/78ca82c4-c584-11e3-97e4-00144feabdc0.html? siteedition = intl#axzz30Gyh kVEd.

[5] *Climate Change 2014 Synthesis Report: Approved Summary for Policymakers*, 1 November 2014, http://www.ipcc.ch/report/ar5/wg2/.

[6] Erik Brynjolfsson and Andrew McAffee, *The Second Machine Age: Work, Progress, and Prosperity in a Time of Brilliant Technologies*, New York: W.W. Norton, 2014, Chapter 1.

[7] Ibid, Chapter 2.

[8] National Intelligence Council, *Global Trends 2030: Alternative Worlds*, December 2012, p.52, http://www.dni.gov/index.php/about/organization/global-

---

① See the Atlantic Council – China Institute of International Studies 2013 report, *China – US Cooperation : Key to the Global Future* , http://www. atlanticcouncil. org/images/publications/China-US_Cooperation_Key_to_the_Global_Future_WEB. pdf. This report was the work of a joint US – China working group of experts. The report called for the US and China to place cooperation on long-term strategic challenges, including climate change, energy, food, water, and other common threats, as the strategic framework for the US – China relationship.

trends-2030.

[9]"Near Miss: The Solar Superstorm of July 2012", *NASA Science News*,23 July 2014, http://science.nasa.gov/science-news/science-at-nasa/2014/23jul_superstorm/.

Cooperation among BRICS:
What Implications for Global Governance?

Ralph A. Cossa*

1. Introduction

The making of a new multi-polar world order has become a cliché in contemporary international political discourse. The BRICS term, an acronym which made its first appearance in a 2001 Goldman Sachs paper, stands for the grouping of the emerging economies of Brazil, Russia, India, China and South Africa. The BRICS is for many the greatest manifestation of the start of a new era in world history as these countries' increasing economic weight is reflected in demands for greater political participation in world affairs. These rising powers are seen by some as destined to challenge the western-dominated international system as they strive for a greater role and better representation in global governance. Others may argue that their major contribution could be in reforming, not replacing existing international organizations. Only time will tell which, if either prediction, is correct.

The recent BRICS summit in Fortaleza, Brazil, in July 2014 stirred debate about the future of the group and its international impact. The main reason has been the 72-point Fortaleza Declaration which, among other elements, includes an agreement on the establishment of a BRICS New Development Bank (NDB) to fund infrastructure and development programs in the BRICS and other developing countries and a memorandum for the establishment of a Contingent Reserve Arrangement, which aims

---

* Ralph A. Cossa, the President of the Pacific Forum of Center for Strategic and International Studies, Washington, DC.

to "help countries forestall short-term liquidity pressures, promote further BRICS cooperation, strengthen the global financial safety net, and **complement existing international arrangements**"[1]. The prospect of establishing alternative financial institutions is by itself a rival idea to the existing global economic order. Provisions on how these institutions will run add more fuel to the fire as they explicitly criticize the operation of the existing financial institutions such as the IMF and the World Bank. In the aftermath of the BRICS Summit in Fortaleza, Brazil's finance minister Guido Manteiga noted that, "at the World Bank, the US has a veto. In the BRICS's New Development Bank, all shareholders are equal." He continued, "presidency of the NDB will not be the prerogative of a particular continent; instead, it will change every five years, rotating among the BRICS countries."[2]

This paper examines the BRICS grouping in the light of their cooperation in global governance issues. The aim is not to throw bricks at BRICS, but we won't be throwing bouquets either. We admit to being dual skeptics: skeptical about BRICS but also skeptical about US/Western approaches to BRICS and other so-called "rival" economic groupings. The paper goes beyond criticisms of group diversity in absolute terms and instead focuses on the ability of the BRICS as a political grouping to meaningfully introduce reforms into the global governance structure. It also raises the issue of the major impediments for cooperation, including most importantly, the structural and economic imbalance between China and the rest of the group. We hope the readers will find the criticisms and suggestions and observations to be constructive, since this is their intent.

2. BRICS: More than an Acronym in the International Alphabet Soup?

While the term BRICS, like many other concepts in international politics discourse, is a western construction, the genesis of the grouping was instigated to a large degree by distrust and discontent with the existing western-led global economic and political order. What Jim O'Neil of Goldman Sachs saw when he coined the term in his 2001 paper

"Building Better Global Economic BRICs" (South Africa was included in the grouping in 2011) was a tremendous potential for economic growth in these countries which would inevitably reshape the world economic order.

On the surface, there appear to be more characteristics that separate BRICS countries from one another than there are characteristics that all five have in common. Nonetheless, there are some not insignificant unifying factors. Currently, Brazil, Russia, India, and China and to a lesser extent South Africa constitute the fastest growing and largest emerging market economies. The four original BRIC countries account for about a quarter of the global Gross Domestic Product (GDP) and along with South Africa more than half of global growth. Furthermore, it has been projected that by 2050 they will have displaced most of the top seven economies (G7) and account for a third of the global economy, if measured in purchasing power parity (PPP) terms.[3] Over the past two decades, the rate of growth of per capita GDP in the BRICS has outpaced the global trend. Their economic size shape global investment flows and has profound impact on trading patterns and trends.

Beyond their economic performance, other characteristics also seem to group them together. First, demographically, they constitute the homelands of three billion people or just below half of the world's population with a dynamically emerging middle-class which fuels new demand growth as higher spending power derives from rising incomes. Despite evidence of deceleration or stagnation in their population growth rate — the case of China and Russia respectively — their working-age population decline is projected to be slower than in the developed economies.[4]

Second, in the same fashion that these countries share their triumph in the economic sphere they also share similar anxieties and challenges including domestic changes, institutional stability, social inequality, and service delivery issues in sectors such as welfare and education.

Last, they tend to share common broader worldviews. They all attach great importance to the principle of sovereignty. They often view globalization as detrimental to their sovereignty and as a vehicle for their exploitation from other (western) powers in what they perceive as neo-colonialism. What brought the BRICS closer, however, opening a window of opportunity for more institutionalized cooperation was the global economic recession.

There was a confluence of factors in the international environment that seems to have provided a common ground for cooperation and strengthened the BRICS perception of a common goal in the global governance sphere. First, the origins of international financial instability, largely founded in the United States' financial system crisis, which caused the US be seen as an "irresponsible stakeholder" in the international arena. Second, and more importantly, the perceived inability of the traditional Western-led financial governance centers to effectively manage the crisis and lead to recovery, which created a legitimacy crisis of the international financial system. Third, a new dynamic, was the rise of non-Western regional power centers and their advocacy for greater participation of the developing world in international decision-making.

The BRICS were fast to grasp the opportunity to focus their coordinated criticism on the global governance architecture while outlining their intentions for deeper engagement in global governance affairs. Their main criticisms involve key multilateral institutions such as the World Bank, the International Monetary Fund (IMF), and the United Nations, pointing out the underrepresentation of the new emerging economies within the governing bodies of these institutions. The BRICS have long demanded reform within these bodies and more fair distribution of power that would reflect their rising economic weight. Looking into the IMF's voting structure these claims are put in perspective. Voting power in the IMF is determined by contributions to the institution. However, contributions are determined by variables such as the GDP in nominal terms. If the GDP was measured in PPP terms which some argue better reflects a country's economic size, there would be a dramatic change in the voting shares of many countries.[5] For instance, Belgium, which currently holds 50% more votes than Brazil, would have 1/3 less than Brazil after reform.[6]

Early glimpses of consciousness of their common goals appeared in meetings on the sidelines of the Sixty-first and Sixty-third UN General Assembly, in 2006 and 2008 respectively. The BRICS gathered to identify areas of cooperation and possible joint steps on issues examined in the context of the upcoming international forums.[7] The BRICS' first official meeting was held in Yekaterinburg, Russia, in June, 2009. Their joint communiqué called for "the reform of international financial institutions, so as to reflect changes in the world economy":

> The emerging and developing economies must have greater voice and representation in international financial institutions, and their heads and senior leadership should be appointed through an open, transparent, and merit-based selection process. We express our strong commitment to multilateral diplomacy with the United Nations playing the central role in dealing with global challenges and threats. In this respect, we reaffirm the need for a comprehensive reform of the UN with a view to making it more efficient so that it can deal with today's global challenges more effectively and the importance we attach to the status of India and Brazil in international affairs, and understand and support their aspirations to play a greater role in the United Nations.[8]

Since then the group holds regular summits, track two meetings such as the International Symposium on Building Governance Systems and Capabilities of BRICS Countries and the follow-on BRICS Think Tank Council Meeting, and peer learning activities.

3. Cooperation amongst the BRICS in Global Governance

As mentioned, a common characteristic that all the BRICS share is their grievance with the existing global governance structure. They appear to argue that the world order of the post-World War II era is an antiquated structure that fails to meet the demands of the new and dynamically rising regional power centers. New global threats such as global financial instability, terrorism, or climate change cannot be solely addressed based on western decision-making formulas. Therefore, the BRICS desire their transition from "rule-takers to rule-makers"[9] and thus shape global decision making in a way that is more inclusive of their own needs (and allegedly of the developing world as well). The section that follows examines the main global governance areas where their common vision has been bundled and cooperation has taken place.

4. BRICS and International Security Governance: Humanitarian Intervention Norm and the United Nations Security Council

There are two main areas where the BRICS have cooperated within the United Nations (UN) in an effort to shape outcomes and change structures in the international security realm. The first regards the reform of the United Nations Security Council (UNSC) and the second focuses on international humanitarian action.

The BRICS seem to hold similar views on the need for reforms within the UN structure. It is widely believed that the UNSC remains anachronistic. It is composed of five permanent members with a veto power — US, Russia, China, Britain, and France — and ten rotating members from the UN regional groups. With India and Brazil being among the largest contributors of peacekeeping forces as well as in the process of increasing their UN payments the two countries are pitching for a permanent membership.[10] Since the African group is the third largest group within the UN, it comes as no surprise that it has raised demands for two permanent seats, one of them probably to be reserved for South Africa. The BRICS have collectively advocated broadening representation in the UN Security Council and there seems to be a common front in backing their co-members' efforts for permanent membership. In 2011 in their Sanya Summit Declaration the BRICS stated:

> We express our strong commitment to multilateral diplomacy with the United Nations playing the central role in dealing with global challenges and threats. In this respect, we reaffirm the need for a comprehensive reform of the UN, including its Security Council, with a view to making it more effective, efficient and representative, so that it can deal with contemporary global challenges more successfully. China and Russia reiterate the importance they

attach to the status of India, Brazil and South Africa in international affairs, and understand and support their aspiration to play a greater role in the UN.[11]

This statement has been repeated in the declarations in subsequent years.[12] Yet, despite rhetorical support for Security Council expansion, Russia and China are unlikely to support such a reform if it was under serious consideration because it would dilute their influence on the Council. Nevertheless, the fact that such supportive statements would not have taken place if the BRICS had not emerged as a political group make some believe that deeper cooperation among them in the future might make Russia and China reconsider their position.

Even here, however, there are disagreements. India has been supportive of Japan also having a permanent seat, just as Tokyo has supported Delhi's bid much more strongly than does China, which also strongly opposes Japan's bid. So there is no common definition of what UNSC "reform" would look like.

In regards to humanitarian action, in many instances the BRICS have opposed humanitarian intervention, expressed by the responsibility to protect (R2P) norm, since they deem it as an encroachment to the national sovereignty of individual states. Their collective opposition not only sends a message about their ability to collectively express their common views in multilateral organizations but also generates questions about their future role and ability to obstruct the development of such actions and overall impact on global governance norms.[13][14]

The cases of the Libyan and Syrian crises are indicative. In 2011, when the Libyan civil war erupted, all BRICS members held a seat in the United Nations Security Council (China and Russia as permanent members and India, Brazil and South Africa in rotating seats). The intensification of the internal clashes and the Gaddafi regime's atrocities against its own people prompted action by the UN Security Council which approved the use of force to protect civilians, wrapped in resolution 1973. With the exception of South Africa (which voted for), the rest of the BRICS members abstained. Abstention was not open opposition but the criticisms that followed the humanitarian action are indicative of the BRICS collective stance. The BRICS individually and collectively condemned the resolution as imposing far-reaching measures that were not agreed in the first place. They criticized NATO for abusing emerging powers good faith by exceeding UN mandate and instead of the protection of civilians it was pushing for regime change.[15] In their third summit in Sanya, China, in April 2011, their joint declaration denounced the use of force by the allied forces.

The Libyan experience seems to have worked as a precedent for the Syrian case.[16] In October the same year, France took the initiative to draft a resolution in which the Syrian regime's crackdown on protesters was condemned. The text considered further action if the Syrian regime failed to comply with the resolution's provisions. Russia and China vetoed the draft while South Africa, India and Brazil abstained. Despite the ongoing humanitarian crisis in Syria the UN has failed to reach agreement on appropriate responses mainly because of the dichotomy of opinions between the western powers and the BRICS. Although, Russia and China hold a firm stance towards measures against the Assad regime, the rest of the BRICS hold a more neutral position. Nevertheless, they all strongly object to any Libya-style military intervention. Russian and Chinese objections go much further, however. In May both vetoed a U.N. Security Council resolution that would have asked the International Criminal Court (ICC) to investigate war crimes in Syria. They were the only two of 15 countries to vote against the resolution. This has complicated negotiations and has created an impasse to resolve the crisis.

Many would argue that the Libyan and Syrian cases represent disaccord within the BRICS rather than unity, even in cases where their votes were in harmony with one another. Each BRICS abstained not because of common views with the group but because of their very own individual interests. Additionally, critics say that in the Syrian case, all voted for most of the resolutions that condemn Assad; the disagreement was on the military intervention.

Two BRICS members, China and Russia, have also served as traditional protectors of North Korea, recently condemned by the UN General

Assembly for crimes against humanity. China and Russia voted against the measure, which recommends that Pyongyang be taken to the ICC. The other members seem much less inclined to protect Pyongyang, with South Africa and India abstaining and Brazil voting in favor of the draft resolution. When the UNGA Human Rights Commission reviewed the issue last May, Russia and China also voted against, South Africa abstained, and Brazil voted in favor; India is not currently a member of the commission. Given its history, it is especially disappointing to see South Africa remain silent in the face of such human rights abuses.

It is noteworthy that the BRICS members have at times breached their own principle of non-interference and territorial integrity and have militarily intervened in other states under the banner of humanitarian reasons when their own interests were at stake. Indicative are the cases of India and Russia. In 1971, due to Pakistani military's crackdown on people in what was then East-Pakistan, India expressed humanitarian concerns and moved its military there. Similarly, Russia's intervention in Georgia and its recent annexation of Crimea took place under the banner of the R2P principle. Nevertheless, these events have not obstructed them from collectively opposing the same exact principle that they used as a pretext for their own activities.

The above are revealing of the fact that both the future viability of the R2P norm and the way it will be implemented are meant to shape the international standards of global governance. The BRICS's individual as well as collective stance towards such norms — their willingness or unwillingness to tolerate, implement, strengthen or even manipulate R2P — backed by a future expanded UN Security Council to include more BRICS members could determine the direction of global governance in the international security realm and the future of a rule-based international order. It is not by chance that Bashar al-Assad has sought for the BRICS's help in his "fight of good against the evil."[17] If nothing else this move signifies the growing important role that the BRICS play in the international security arena and their potential increasing impact on the international security norms. Few, however, would brand this as a positive role.

5. A Possible Alternative: Reshaping Global Economic Governance (The Role of the BRICS)

The BRICS club's strongest area of convergence is their desire for greater representation and leadership on the global economic stage. Although deliberative rather than decisional, the G20 group is an elevated form of the G7 and G8 which consisted only of the industrial countries. The formation of the G20 amidst the global financial crisis, which includes both the industrial and emerging-market countries, has been a significant manifestation of the greater role that the developed economies attest to both the emerging economies and the regional balance in an effort to strengthen international cooperation and effectively tackle the contemporary global financial challenges. Such developments as well as the BRICS's own realization of their economic weight on a global level, have brought new dynamics in the international economic regimes.

For years the BRICS countries have expressed their discontent with the leadership monopoly of the western industrial countries within the key international financial institutions, namely the World Bank and the IMF. Traditionally the World Bank's presidency goes to an American while the IMF managing director is European. The opportunity to collectively express their desire for leadership roles within these institutions rose in April 2011 when the then World Bank President Robert Zoellick announced his desire to step down. A month later the IMF Managing Director Dominique Strauss – Kahn resigned. The BRICS pushed for a more open, competitive and meritocratic leadership selection process in the IMF and the World Bank[18], with some success and broader sympathy, even though the IMF ultimately appointed another European Director, the French Christine Lagarde, and in the World Bank went to a Korean-American, Jim Yong Kim.

The BRICS have also closely cooperated in changing the voting power structures of the financial institutions. Here again the global financial crisis was a catalyst event. In order to effectively respond to the global financial crisis and its sub-product, the Eurocrisis, the financial institutions had been in dire need for additional capital. Therefore, they relied heavily on contributions from emerging economies, predominantly China and Brazil, since the advanced countries' economic stagnation could not facilitate extra capital flows.[19] In exchange the BRICS demanded quota reforms within the institutions. Quotas represent capital subscriptions and associated voting rights, and are proportional to the economic and other power resources of the countries.

For long the BRICS have been advocating quota readjustment in their favor since their economic weight has been extensively more significant in recent years. Their expanded financial contributions provided a good base for bargain and in 2010 negotiations resulted in quota reallocation deals that included 3.3% quota allocation toward the developing countries in the World Bank and 6 percent in the IMF with the major beneficiaries being the BRICS.[20]

It is here that, in fairness, we must point out a major shortcoming, indeed failure, in US policy to date. The Obama administration backed the BRICS effort for reform but has been widely criticized for the inertia in implementation of the deals that followed.[21] IMF reform has been held up in the US Congress and the November 2014 Congressional elections make progress even less likely than before. It is hypocritical of the West in general and US in particular to challenge China and the other BRICS members to step up and play a more constructive role — remember the "responsible stakeholder" challenge — and then not be supportive when such efforts take place. Washington needs to be less negative toward BRICS initiatives (see BRICS Bank discussion below) and stop being outright obstructionist regarding similar Chinese initiatives such as the Asian Infrastructure Investment Bank. (The US is right to ask tough questions regarding the objectives and lending standards of such banks and how they relate to/complement existing organizations and one another, but this should be done in a constructive rather than obstructionist manner. The current US position, largely perceived as pressuring its allies not to join, reinforce the view that the US is trying to contain China, which is counterproductive to US foreign policy objectives.)

Last, other initiatives have stirred discussions about not only a more strengthened cooperation amongst the BRICS but also an overt institutional challenge to the existing global financial architecture. In the past the BRICS expressed their desire to move away from the dollar and start conducting intra-BRICS trade in local currencies and even to use an IMF-style Special Drawing Rights as a "global currency". Recently, in their Sixth Summit, in Fortleza, Brasil, they reiterated their previous desire to establish the aforementioned New Development Bank while they also announced the creation of a Contingency Reserve Arrangement (CRA) with initial capital of US $50 billion and US $100 billion respectively.[22] The new institutions aim at strengthening BRICS cooperation and channel funds in areas that the BRICS consider priorities, i. e. development projects in economically less advanced countries. It has been also agreed that member states will contribute equally to the bank's capital and share equal voting rights, an apparent difference with the existing financial institutions. To strengthen this position, the BRICS have also agreed to a more equal "division of labor". China will host the bank's headquarters in Shanghai, India will appoint the first President of the bank, and the first chair of the board of governors will be from Russia.

6. The China Dimension

Despite the aforementioned instances of cooperation, the BRICS seem to be as much divided as united. For instance, the durability of the group has been vividly questioned based on their continuity as economic powerhouses, a focus on comparative growth rates, their divergent economies and political systems.

Signs of economic deceleration in the past two years have made scholars skeptical about the BRICS "miracle", prompting discussions "that the rise of the 'rest' (BRICS) will yield to the rise of the select"[23]. China's double digit growth has fallen to lower than 8% in 2013 while average growth rate in the other emerging economies fell by 4% to just

2.5%[24], causing some to ask "Is it the rise of BRICS, or just the rise of China?"

Within the BRICS, South Africa is deemed tiny in economic size in comparison to the rest of the group. China on the other hand economically dwarfs the rest since it has climbed second among the biggest economies in the world. India's per capital GDP is only USD 1 325 while Brazil and Russia surpass USD 12 000 (data from 2011).[25] China and Russia are relatively open economies in contrast to India and Brazil.[26] Brazil, India and South Africa are vibrant democracies, China is a one-party state, while Russia's system is highly centralized.

Nevertheless, it is not so much this diversity that will determine the sustainability of the group as it is China's overwhelming presence. As King's College Professor Harsh V. Pant puts it, "the structural disparity between China and the rest is the most important contributor to the dysfunction of the BRICS idea."[27]

For better or worse, China is the link that connects the BRICS. Its economic weight is the one that has given momentum to the group. The Chinese economy is larger than all the other BRICS's economies combined.[28] China is also the largest trading partner of Russia, Brazil, and South Africa and the second largest of India. At the same time, none of the other BRICS is particularly important to China's trade in terms of value or has significant trade volumes with the others. Of note, there appears to be no effort to establish a BRICS Free Trade Area or to otherwise institutionalize trade arrangements among the five. There appears to be no willingness for any type of economic integration, despite the claim that their collective economic weight has the potential of reshaping the world economic order.

Needless to say, the BRICS countries have stronger economic ties with the West than they have with each other. In regards to their foreign policy relations, the other BRICS are so regional that their encounters take place mostly in multilateral settings. Being the connecting link among them, China's attitude within and towards the group will play a significant role in promoting or hampering cooperation.

China's economic preponderance within the BRICS already raises other members' concerns over its dominance in the group and over the BRICS becoming a vehicle for Chinese interests. The NDB is an indicative case. Contributions to the bank have been agreed on an equal basis (after the insistence of India and Russia). It has been agreed also that every member will have equal voting rights. Equality, though, does not necessarily mean good coordination. In such multilateral institutions leadership is important. China's economic weight and relations with the other members will probably provide it with the advantage of taking the role of the "coordinator."[29][30] China has already proposed to subsidize the entry of Brazil and South Africa who struggle to ensure the adequate funds and, if that happens, it will expand China's leverage within the bank. On the other hand, China's contribution to the new fund, the CRA, is USD 41 billion of the initial USD 100 billion, dwarfing the contribution of all the other members. This harbors suspicions over the future distribution of power within the new institutions. Although quite anecdotal, critics have drawn parallels between headquarters of the new bank being based in Shanghai, a city of the largest member, and the Western-led institutions' cases (institutions being based in the US).[31]

Voices from India especially, China's most antagonistic partner have been particularly critical. An editorial from 2013 in *The Hindustan Times* wrote on the issue of the NDB, "The BRICS Bank is already crippled by concerns it will become the multilateral bank of Beijing because of China's deeper pockets", and continues, "New Delhi, having proposed the idea now drags its heels for fear it will be subsidizing Chinese soft power with India's taxpayers money."[32] Indian finance officials in the past expressed the view that the NDB will legitimize the use of Chinese currency overseas.[33] Although, by no means these statements represent official positions, they illustrate, nevertheless, the general mistrust towards China's preponderance in the group, as well potential different positions on the function of the bank.

For example, China's development finance practices could become a source of discord within the BRICS. China's "tied aid" for infrastructure favors the Chinese, mostly state-owned, companies while its loans often are closely tied with access to natural resources. Apart from economic reasons, China uses its aid for foreign policy objectives, to advance its influence in geopolitically important regions. When countries borrow money to fund infrastructure projects (NDB's main role is to fund infrastructure projects in the developing world) they are basically obtaining foreign currency to import the substantial materials for the project. Given the fact that China has a production overcapacity in such materials and engineering technology and expertise, its involvement in such projects functions as a domestic stimulus, while it enhances internationalization of its currency and its overseas influence.[34]

BRICS could find it difficult to coordinate on funding and operational priorities, such as who to fund and the way through which they provide aid. This disaccord will not only be based on morals or different worldviews but also stem from conflicting interests.

China is too big and influential for its views to be discarded and traditionally does not get involved in organizations or arrangements that it cannot control to the highest possible degree. Therefore, the upstream selection of project funding will not only reveal disagreement among the BRICS but also who will eventually have the upper hand in final decisions. The BRICS have agreed that initially the bank will fund the infrastructure needs of the BRICS themselves. But China is highly unlikely to need the banks' money to fund development ventures. It is the other poorer BRICS members that might need it. This will reinforce the imbalances within the group.

China's involvement in the BRICS stems also from global strategic interests. For China its economic rise has come with a price; the deterioration of its external environment due to what it perceives as containment and encirclement by the US.[36][37] However, not being able to translate its economic power into comprehensive national power, China cannot openly challenge US primacy. Therefore, the BRICS group seems to be vital for China in its effort to build networks and partnerships that will help it counterbalance western supremacy. Zhao Gancheng, of the Shanghai Institute of International Studies, has indicatively stated, "(China's) objective is through cooperation to strengthen its position in the international system, but at the same time, not try to challenge the

US in a confrontational mode."[38]

Nevertheless, when and if China manages to assert itself to superpower status, it seems highly unlikely that it will continue to ascribe the same importance to the BRICS and promote an "equitable" world order.

Despite solidarity declarations, for example, China has actively opposed Brazil's and India's bid for permanent membership in the UNSC.[39][40] On one hand, China is not willing to yield its institutional privileges within the UNSC. Nor does Russia. On the other hand, geopolitical considerations seem to determine China's stance toward UNSC reform. China and India are regional rivals who seek to play a leadership role in their common neighborhood. China and India have unresolved border disputes, while they are wary of its others' intrusion within their spheres of influence. India is concerned about China's close partnership with its perennial enemy Pakistan, while China feels threatened by India's "Look East" policy, one that seeks for deeper involvement of India in East Asia. India's *quid pro quo* support for a Japanese permanent UNSC seat further compounds the problem.

The aforementioned reveal the difficulties, especially for the neighboring BRICS to transcend great power-politics in favor of allegedly common goals. Being "sovereignty hawks" — a characteristic that scholars use to group them together[41] — and entrenched behind a narrow interpretation of national interest will make them prioritize their geopolitical interests higher than any multilateral cooperation. Similarly to the Sino – India relation, a creeping competition might undermine the foundations of the Sino – Russia cooperation and spillover suspicion against each other within the BRICS. China's advancement into Central Asia and the Russian Far East as well as China's fast economic and military development alerts Russia, which sees its influence in its backyard waning. Although Moscow may think that it is an equal partner to China, the relationship becomes increasingly unequal, which will fuel future frictions.

China's relations with the other two BRICS — Brazil and South Africa — are not frictionless, too. The more their ties grow, the more their differences surface. China's manipulation of its currency has caused significant problems for the manufacturing sectors in Brazil and South

Africa. In 2011 almost 67% of the Brazilian export business competing with Chinese have lost foreign market share.[42] Brazil regards Chinese competition unfair because of China's dumping policies and has started imposing tariffs on Chinese industrial goods imports.[43] China's growing economic engagement in South America is deemed threatening for Brazilian exports in neighboring markets.[44]

South Africa's manufacturing is also struggling to compete with China's growing economic clout. The influx of Chinese goods in South Africa has created significant trade imbalances turning South Africa increasing wary of China.[45]

7. Roadblocks to Cooperation

Even if Cshina accepts an "equal" or (more likely) "first among equals" role, there are other roadblocks to cooperation. Some, like traditional rivalries (China – India, China – Russia, etc.) have already been mentioned. There are, of course, also significant differences regarding social and political systems, democratic principles, and world views. There are few "common values" binding the group together. When they cooperate in international forums, it is usually to block, impede, or criticize, rather than make positive recommendations. China and India have been particularly bad in this regard when it comes to the ASEAN Regional Forum (ARF), where its efforts to proceed beyond confidence building measures to preventive diplomacy (as called for in the ARF Vision Statement) have met with Chinese and Indian objectives and obstruction.

As mentioned previously, all are also more dependent in their economic relations with others than they are with one another, beyond their growing reliance on bilateral trade with China. Trade among BRICS members is dwarfed each member's rate with the US, EU, and West in general. No efforts are being made to create greater economic interdependence or integration among the five. Indian even turned down China's invitation to come to the 2014 Asia Pacific Economic Cooperation (APEC) Leaders Meeting in Beijing, where China promoted greater economic integration and cooperation within the Asia Pacific region.

All also face significant internal challenges, high among them in many instances being corruption, but have different approaches and priorities in dealing with them. Political solidarity is also challenging. Can all continue to remain silent as Russia violently interferes in the internal affairs of its Ukrainian neighbor? How about as China continues expanding its influence in Central Asia, an area we have argued could eventually host a 21st Century version of the Great Game (see PacNet #73 — The great game in Central Asia, Sep 30, 2014). How will China's continuing "special relationship" with Pakistan impact Sino-Indian cooperation the next time tensions between the two South Asian neighbors rise (as they inevitably will).

Even in areas where they agree in principle, we are yet to see concrete proposals for action. All BRICS members (as has the rest of the civilized world) have expressed outrage over ISIS' crimes against humanity and see the growing threat posed by radical Islamic movements. But what are their proposals for joint action to counter this threat. All worry about proliferation of weapons of mass destruction but have charted no paths forward — in fact, one member remains outside the NPT Regime (and sees the nuclear program of one of its BRICS colleagues as one of the main justifications for its own nuclear weapons program).

At this "International Symposium on Building Governance Systems and Capabilities of BRICS Countries", many spoke about common concerns but few provided concrete recommendations on how to address these concerns. Indeed, a lot has been said, very seriously and with great insight and sincerity, about China's commitment to improve its own governance capabilities in the wake of the 4th Plenum, but little has been said about China's vision for how BRICS can promote good global governance. Much more needs to be done, starting with track two efforts driven by the BRICS Think Tank Council, to develop not just a common long-term vision and objectives, but also to develop the common strategies and tactics required to get there. BRICS is still a "work in progress", as its members clearly point out. It is yet to be subjected to comprehensive objective analysis. Deeper examination is needed both within and outside BRICS and, as Banning Garrett suggested, among the BRICS, US, and EU jointly as well.

8. Conclusion

It is indisputable that the BRICS have gone beyond being an investment paper term into a real formation that not only has the dynamic to influence global governance norms but seems willing to work as a group toward this direction. Only six years after their first meeting, the BRICS nations have already demonstrated their potential to actively engage in global governance issues, and advocate common positions in multilateral institutions. The agreement on the establishment of new financial institutions is a crucial development that could challenge or complement the existing global arrangements.

Nevertheless, it remains not so much an international organization as a semi-structured grouping without a common vision under which it can be guided. Unlike the EU, or even ASEAN, there is unlikely to be a BRICS community built on common values or interests. Thus far, what they are against still appears to be a greater unifying factor than what they are for. It is still to be seen whether their cooperation stems from something more than temporary convenience on issues of common concern.

References

[1] "BRICS Summit Issues Fortaleza Declaration: The New Development Bank and Contingent Reserve Arrangement Are Born", *Larouche Pace,* July 15, 2014, http://larouchepac.com/node/31319.

[2] "BRICS Launch New Bank and Monetary Fund", *Deutsche Welle,* July 16, 2014, http://www.dw.de/brics-launch-new-bank-and-monetary-fund/a-17789608.

[3] Mathur, S., Dasgupta, M. and Sirohi, P., *BRICS: Trade Policies, Institutions and Areas for Deepening Cooperation*, Indian Institute of Foreign Trade, Center for WTO Studies, New Delhi, 2013, p.4.

[4] Wilson, D. and Purushothaman, R., "Dreaming with BRICS: The Path to 2050",

Goldman Sachs, Global Economic Paper, Paper No.99, p.5.

[5] Vreeland J.R., "Governance at the International Monetary Fund", *Georgetown University*, 2009, pp.6 - 7.

[6] Vreeland J.R., "Governance at the International Monetary Fund", *Georgetown University*, 2009, pp.6 - 7.

[7] Stuenkel, O, "The Financial Crisis, Contested Legitimacy, and the Genesis of Intra-BRICS Cooperation", *Global Governance*, 19, 2013, p. 615.

[8] "First Summit: Joint Statement of the BRIC Countries Leaders June 16, 2009, Yekaerinburg, Russia", http://www.brics5.co.za/about-brics/summit-declaration/first-summit/.

[9] Roberts, S., "Polity Forum: Challengers or Stakeholders? BRICS and the Liberal World Order: Intoduction", *Polity*, Vol 42, No.1, 2010.

[10] Armijo, L.E and Roberts, C., "The Emerging Powers and Global Governance: Why the BRICS Matter", in Looney, R. (ed.), *Handbook of Emerging Economies*, New York: Routledge, 2014 forthcoming, pp. 1 - 27.

[11] "Sanya Declaration", BRICS Information Centre, University of Toronto, April 14, 2011 http://www.brics.utoronto.ca/docs/110414-leaders.html.

[12] "The 6th BRICS Summit: Fortaleza Declaration", Information Centre, University of Toronto, July 15, 2014 http://www.brics.utoronto.ca/docs/.

[13] Keeler, C., "The End of Responsibility to Protect?" *Foreign Policy Journal*, October 12, 2011, http://www.foreignpolicyjournal.com/2011/10/12/the-end-of-the-responsibility-to-protect/.

[14] Bosco, L., "Abstention Games on the Security Council", *Foreign Policy,* March 17, 2011, http://bosco.foreignpolicy.com/posts/2011/03/17/abstention_games_on_the_security_council.

[15] Stuenkel, O., "The BRICS and the Future of R2P: Was Syria or Libya the Exception", *Global Responsibility to Protect*, Vol. 6, Issue 1, 2014, p.13.

[16] The Ministry of Foreign Affairs of the Russian Federation, "Statement in Explanation of Vote by Vitaly Churkin, Permanent Representative of the Russian Federation to the UN, on the Draft Resolution on the Situation in Syria", New York, October 4, 2011, http://www.mid.ru/bdomp/brp_4.nsf/e78a48070f128a7b432569990 05bcbb3/9fd3c42bc7cfdddac3257920004214bd%21OpenDocument.

[17] Gladstone, R. and Droubi, H., "Assad Sends Letters to Emerging Powers Seeking Help to End Syria War", *The New York Times*, March 27, 2013, http://www.nytimes.com/2013/03/28/world/middleeast/syrias-developments.html?_r=1&.

[18] Armijo, L.E. and Roberts, C., "The Emerging Powers and Global Governance: Why the BRICS Matter", in Looney, R. (ed.), *Handbook of Emerging Economies*, New

York: Routledge, 2014 forthcoming, p.18.

[19] Gros et al., "The Case for IMF Quota Reform", *Council on Foreign Relations,* October 11, 2012, http://www. cfr. org/international-organizations-and-alliances/case-imf-quota-reform/p29248.

[20] Armijo, L.E and Roberts, C., "The Emerging Powers and Global Governance: Why the BRICS Matter", in Looney, R. (ed.), *Handbook of Emerging Economies* , New York: Routledge, 2014 forthcoming, p.21.

[21] Rediker, D., "Losing at the IMF", *Foreign Policy,* October 10, 2012, http://www.foreignpolicy.com/articles/2012/10/10/losing_at_the_imf.

[22] "The 6th BRICS Summit: Fortaleza Declaration", Information Centre , University of Toronto, July 15, 2014 http://www.brics.utoronto.ca/docs/.

[23] The Economist, "The BRIC Economies: Is the Fastest Period of Emerging-market Growth behind Us?" *Economist Debates,* August 20, 2013, http://www.economist.com/debate/days/view/1001.

[24] The Economist, "Global Economic Outlook 2015 — Key Findings", *The Conference Board,* November 2014, http://www. conference-board. org/data/globaloutlook/.

[25] Anon, "Chapter 1: Economic and Social Indicators: Comparison of BRICS Countries", *BRICS Joint Statistical Publication 2012,*2012﹐ p.2 http://mospi.nic.in/mospi_new/upload/bricks_2012_24aug12/htm/CHAPTER1.pdf.

[26] Toh, Ch.H.J, "Brazil, Russia, India and China (BRIC): Reshaping the World Order in the 21st Century", *US Naval War College* (no date), p.3, https://www.usnwc.edu/Lucent/OpenPdf.aspx? id =93.

[27] Pant, H.V., "The BRICS Fallacy", *The Washington Quarterly,* Vol. 36, No 3, 2013, p.97.

[28] Pant, H.V., "The BRICS Fallacy", *The Washington Quarterly,* Vol. 36, No 3, 2013, p.98.

[29] Krishnan, A., "China Shows Economic Clout with Push for New Banks", *The Hindu Business Line* , July 16, 2014, http://www. thehindubusinessline. com/economy/policy/china-shows-economic-clout-with-push-for-new-banks/article6217962.ece.

[30] Chowdhury, J., "Big BRICS for Small Nations: How Unconditional the NDB Conditions Be?" *Russia Today* , July 25, 2014, http://rt.com/op-edge/175512-brics-china-new-development-bank/.

[31] Sharma, M.S., "BRICS Bank: Worthless at Best, a Disaster at Worst", *Business Standard* , 2014, http://www. business-standard. com/article/economy-policy/brics-bank-worthless-at-best-a-disaster-at-worst-114071600571_1.html.

[32] "The Foundation Is a Bit Shaky", *The Hindustan Times* , March 28, 2013,

http://www.hindustantimes.com/comment/editorials/the-foundation-is-a-bit-shaky/article1-1033876.aspx.

[33] Bagchi, I., "BRICS Summit: Member Nations Criticize the West for Financial Mismanagement", *The Times of India*, March 30, 2012, http://timesofindia.indiatimes.com/india/BRICS-summit-Member-nations-criticizes-the-West-for-financial-mismanagement/articleshow/12462502.cms.

[34] Weeks, J., "The New BRICS Bank — Force for Progress or Cause for Concern?" *Policy Research in Macroeconomics*, 2014, http://www.primeeconomics.org/? p =3152.

[35] Glosny, M. A., "China and the BRICS: A Real (but limited) Partnership in a Multipolar World", *Polity,* Vol.42, No.1, 2010, p.112.

[36] Sun, Y., "BRICS and China's Aspiration for the New 'International Order'", *Brookings*, 2013, http://www.brookings.edu/blogs/up-front/posts/2013/03/25-xi-jinping-china-brics-sun.

[37] Glosny, M. A., "China and the BRICS: A Real (but limited) Partnership in a Multipolar World", *Polity,* Vol.42, No.1, 2010, p.138.

[38] Tellis, A. and Mirski, S., "Crux of Asia: China, India and the Emerging Global Order", *Carnegie Endowment for International Peace*, 2013, http://carnegieendowment.org/files/crux_of_asia.pdf.

[39] [20] Armijo, L. E and Roberts, C., "The Emerging Powers and Global Governance: Why the BRICS Matter", in Looney, R. (ed.), *Handbook of Emerging Economies*, New York: Routledge, 2014 forthcoming, p.14.

[40] Roberts, S., "Polity Forum: Challengers or Stakeholders? BRICS and the Liberal World Order: Intoduction", *Polity*, Vol. 42, No.1, 2010, pp. 1 - 13.

[41] Anguilar, C. G., "China-Brazil Relations: Disputes with Regional Implications", *Americas Program*, 2011, http://www.cipamericas.org/archives/5525.

[42] Pant, H.V., "The BRICS Fallacy", *The Washington Quarterly,* Vol.36, No.3, 2013.

[43] Pereira, C. and De Castor Neves, J. A., "Brazil and China: South-South Partnership or North South Competition?" *Brookings,* Policy Paper, No. 26, 2011, p.6, http://www.brookings.edu/~/media/research/files/papers/2011/4/03%20brazil%20china%20pereira/03_brazil_china_pereira.pdf.

[44] Pant, H.V., "The BRICS Fallacy", *The Washington Quarterly,* Vol. 36, No.3, 2013, p.99.

German Experience and Governance in BRICS*

Carsten Körber**

Ladies and gentlemen,

This is a very special November for Germany. Two historic dates fall this month.

First: A few days ago, on November 9, we celebrated the 25th anniversary of the fall of the Berlin Wall. 8000 illuminated white balloons marked the course of the Wall along a 15 km stretch. To the cheers of more than one million people, this wall of light then rose into the night sky over the city.

Second: In a few days time, we will have our long-awaited "black zero", our zero deficit. The German Bundestag will adopt the first balanced budget since 1969. The first budget without any new debt for 45 years!

I would like to draw on these two momentous occasions to talk to you about three things:

Firstly, the reasons for the collapse of the German Democratic Republic (GDR) and the resulting reunification of Germany;

Secondly, the conclusions that should be drawn from this for our current budgetary and financial policies; and

Thirdly, the challenges that the BRICS countries are bound to face in this context.

---

* This is the author's speech in the Symposium and the title was added by the editor.
** Carsten Körber, member of the German Bundestag.

1. The Reasons for the Collapse of the GDR and the Resulting Reunification of Germany

At first glance there is little to link the collapse of the Wall with our "black zero". But both occasions have a significance for Germany's future that should not be underestimated. They are important, and not just for us. As I have heard repeatedly from many of our foreign friends and partners, they have an impact far beyond Germany's borders. That is why I want to talk to you about both of them today.

1989. The Cold War continues. Germany and Europe are divided. Many people have long since come to terms with the status quo. No change is in sight. But then in the autumn of 1989, within a few short weeks, the pace picks up. Hundreds of thousands of people were suddenly prepared to take to the streets and protest for their right to freedom. I myself come from East Germany and was an eleven-year schoolchild at the time.

The GDR leadership — politically, morally and economically moribund — had nothing with which to counter these demonstrations. The fate of the GDR was sealed when the Wall was breached on November 9.

What was it that led to collapse of the GDR? In my opinion, there are two factors that played an especially large role: the command economy and the oppression of the individual.

Even today, the state is often involved in business, for example with regard to the provision of basic services such as water, electricity and gas. But that alone does not constitute a command economy. In the GDR, the actions of business, industry and trade were minutely regulated by the state. The only countries where that is still the case today are North Korea and Cuba, and even there, there is a desire for reform.

The GDR's state-controlled economy with its rigid five year plans was unable to meet the economic needs of the people. The "economy of shortages" was the result of 40 years of central economic planning. Families normally had to wait five years for a flat, ten years for a telephone, and fifteen years for their *Trabant,* a GDR-produced car.

At the same time, the GDR had lived far beyond its means since the late 1970s, if not before. The GDR was bankrupt. Without reunification it would have been totally insolvent in 1990. That was the economic reason for the country's demise.

The human, social reason for its demise lay in the fact that the people were profoundly aware of their lack of freedom. A heavy weight bore down on the country. Let me give you two examples. Measured by population size, the *Stasi,* the GDR's security service, was in 1989 the biggest intelligence agency in the history of mankind, with one full-time employee per 180 inhabitants. Mutual distrust coloured everything. And, to compound this, the people of the GDR were banned from travelling abroad. Only those who had, in the eyes of the Party and the State, earned special privileges were allowed to travel to socialist brother states. As a rule, it was only old-age pensioners who were granted permission to travel to the West, to the Federal Republic of Germany.

It was the combination of these two factors — the economic constraints and the feeling of being imprisoned — that led to the end of the GDR. But 1989, the year of change, already lies a quarter of a century behind us. That is why I was so glad to see so many people celebrating together in the streets this year. At the ceremony in the Bundestag with Chancellor Merkel, many of my fellow parliamentarians were moved to tears.

It was good to see how much this day still moves us Germans. This day shows that freedom cannot be taken for granted. North Korea reminds us too. This point is worth making, as I frequently have the impression that many people in Germany take freedom for granted in their everyday lives. We are so well off we have forgotten that neither our freedom nor our prosperity are normal or self-evident.

The 25th anniversary of the fall of the Wall is, however, also a suitable juncture to ponder the future of Germany. To shape the future, one must remember the past and draw the right lessons from it.

One lesson is that in the long run, performance must match consumption if a state is to succeed and endure.

2. A Special Responsibility of the Current generation of German Politicians

The current generation of German politicians bears a special responsibility in the light of our history. What lessons can be drawn from the downfall of the GDR for our today and tomorrow?

It's a fact that the German state as a whole (Federation, *Länder* and local authorities) now has debts amounting to around 2.5 trillion dollars. That is 75% of our GDP, or 31 000 US dollars per capita. There are perhaps states in the eurozone, such as Italy or France, which are even deeper in debt. But it's a fact that the German debts have now reached proportions that demand a response.

We have realised that we Germans have lived markedly beyond our means in the past decades. The previous Federal Government and the *Länder* Governments therefore took action. The adoption of the "debt brake", a *de facto* ban on new debt, was and remains a step in the right direction. We are about to adopt the budget for 2015 — the first zero deficit budget since 1969. The "black zero" is on its way. A budget without new debt. It is our goal to reduce our debt stock to under 60% of GDP by 2017.

I myself am a member of the Bundestag's Budget Committee. Of course I am delighted that we will have this "black zero". But I also know that a zero should be the norm. Every year.

The Federal Republic of Germany faces tremendous challenges. And so does its social market economy, which has endowed the country with widespread growth and prosperity ever since 1950. Fortunately, this system was so successful that we were able to integrate a terminally ailing economy like the GDR's into it successfully.

This model depended on prosperity being spread as widely as possible across population strata. For only then could economic and social development be described as successful. On the other hand, and this is the fine line that always has to be trod, this redistribution of wealth must not impose such onerous burdens on those driving growth that their productivity suffers too much. That would be harmful to the entire economy.

If you listen carefully, you will hear ever more people in Germany saying that things cannot continue as they are forever, that we need new restraint, that we need more reason and far-sightedness in our economic management, that we have to realise it will be difficult to maintain our prosperity in the long term. We cannot afford to ignore such warnings.

Just as the command economy favoured by Socialism is obsolete, the omens increasingly suggest that capitalism's blind credo of "growth at all costs" is itself on the way out. We need sustainable growth. We have to take care of our natural resources and take environmental protection seriously.

The world is changing rapidly. Every day. This has been proven dramatically by the rise of what we know as the BRICS countries. And they are good. They are catching up with us all the time.

And by aspiring to what we have, but not blindly copying us, they have been able to avoid some of our mistakes. 500 million Europeans, almost 9% of the world population, generate a quarter of the world GDP. We pay for more than 50% of all social security benefits in the world. A good proportion of these are paid out in Germany. It's nice to be able to afford it. But if you can't, it is ultimately the path to ruin.

I am a firm champion of social security — the strong must always take care of the weak. But if we inGermany choose to spend more than half our money on financing social security benefits-above all pensions, health insurance and unemployment insurance — whilst investing less than 10% of the total, we are, it seems to me, heading in the wrong direction.

There are currently some 157 financial family-related benefits. These cost billions of euros each year. But at the same time we are unable to produce aprogramme of investment sufficient to maintain our existing transport infrastructure.

And the outcome? There is no evidence of any statistical effect to show that a single additional child has been born as a result of these 157 programmes. But the Transport Ministry has just ascertained that 15 per cent of the 39 000 road bridges in Germany are in urgent need of repair. A third of the 26 000 railway bridges are in a critical condition.

We are currently one of the world's leading industrial nations. But Germany has no raw materials. Our population is shrinking. So how can we retain our lead? There is a way. It is called "growth through innovation". That must remain our chosen path. Today, tomorrow and in the future.

The world won't wait for us. It is changing fast. Today, too, I have seen this in China. Many of the world's nations look at us as a role model. They take their lead from us.

3. The Challenges that the BRIKS Countries Are Bound to Face

What does this process of catching up and economic growth mean for you, the BRICS countries?

- You are generating more prosperity. More prosperity means fewer children. In the long run, fewer children mean demographic problems. And the bigger a state's social security system, the worse the budgetary problems will be. Just look at Germany.

- The greater the individual's prosperity, the greater their self-confidence, and the greater their desire for political and social participation. This is what history has shown us. It has also shown us that for a system to endure with success, the society in which it is placed must create the structures needed for such participation.

- The history of the Federal Republic of Germany since World War II can be viewed as illustrative of this. And indeed it is noticeable that others aspire to our economic system, but above all to our open and free society, to our way of life as a whole.

Where is Germany today? Deciding to introduce the ban on new debt, the "debt brake", was one of the most important political decisions of recent times. It is of key importance for the viability of our public finances. Demographic change is not a new phenomenon in Germany. People are getting older and older. Fewer and fewer children are being born. We have to proof our public finances against this demographic change.

Demographic change will be one of the central social challenges of the years and decades to come. Especially against this backdrop, sound public finances are a basic prerequisite if the state is to retain its ability to function in the longer term.

The number of people in work is decreasing. Resources and revenue are diminishing. Expenditure on social security is increasing. Ever fewer earners have to provide for proportionally more people in their old age. Even today it is foreseeable that especially the changes to the age distribution in our society will have a significant impact on our public budgets. To be able to set the right course in good time, it is vital for us to keep a close eye on potential risks even now. We will have to hold on to this black zero in the future, too.

4. Conclusion

Budgetary discipline is not an end in itself. Only a state exercising sound financial management is a functioning state. Healthy public finances create room for manoeuvre during the low points of the economic cycle or in emergencies. Zero deficit budgets inspire confidence in the future. This confidence is in turn the basis for sustainable growth. Sound public finances are the foundation for a successful future for any economy.

Germany has drawn the right lessons from the European debt crisis. We will continue to pursue this path of sustainable budgetary and financial policy.

Before you go, I'd like to ask you not to copy us on the football field. We want to win the World Cup again in Russia in 2018!

But we would be delighted if you were to take a leaf from our book when it comes to our present budgetary and financial policy.